# Work and Wellbeing

Wellbeing: A Complete Reference Guide, Volume III

# Wellbeing: A Complete Reference Guide

**Volume I: Wellbeing in Children and Families**
*Edited by Susan H. Landry and Cary L. Cooper*

**Volume II: Wellbeing and the Environment**
*Edited by Rachel Cooper, Elizabeth Burton, and Cary L. Cooper*

**Volume III: Work and Wellbeing**
*Edited by Peter Y. Chen and Cary L. Cooper*

**Volume IV: Wellbeing in Later Life**
*Edited by Thomas B. L. Kirkwood and Cary L. Cooper*

**Volume V: The Economics of Wellbeing**
*Edited by David McDaid and Cary L. Cooper*

**Volume VI: Interventions and Policies to Enhance Wellbeing**
*Edited by Felicia A. Huppert and Cary L. Cooper*

# Work and Wellbeing

## Wellbeing: A Complete Reference Guide, Volume III

*Edited by Peter Y. Chen*
*and Cary L. Cooper*

**WILEY** Blackwell

*Registered Office*
John Wiley & Sons Ltd, The Atrium, Southern Gate, Chichester, West Sussex, PO19 8SQ,
UK

*Editorial Offices*
350 Main Street, Malden, MA 02148-5020, USA
9600 Garsington Road, Oxford, OX4 2DQ, UK
The Atrium, Southern Gate, Chichester, West Sussex, PO19 8SQ, UK

For details of our global editorial offices, for customer services, and for information about
how to apply for permission to reuse the copyright material in this book please see our
website at www.wiley.com/wiley-blackwell.

The right of Peter Y. Chen and Cary L. Cooper to be identified as the authors of the editorial
material in this work has been asserted in accordance with the UK Copyright, Designs and
Patents Act 1988.

*Library of Congress Cataloging-in-Publication Data*

Work and wellbeing / volume editor, Peter Y. Chen; editor-in-chief, Cary L. Cooper.
      pages cm. – (Wellbeing : a complete reference guide; volume III)
   Includes bibliographical references and index.
   ISBN 978-1-118-60836-4 (cloth : alk. paper)
1. Industrial hygiene.   2. Work environment.   3. Quality of work life.   4. Well-being.
I. Chen, Peter Y.
   HD7261.W65 2014
   650.1–dc23                                                    2013030507

A catalogue record for this book is available from the British Library.

Cover image: © Ekely / Getty
Cover design by cyandesign.co.uk

Set in 10.5/14pt Galliard by Laserwords Private Limited, Chennai, India
Printed and bound in Singapore by Markono Print Media Pte Ltd

1   2014

# Contents of this Volume

About the Editors ix

Contributors xi

Full Contents of *Wellbeing: A Complete Reference Guide* xiii

Introduction to *Wellbeing: A Complete Reference Guide* xxvii

**Part 1   Introduction** 1

1   Introduction: From Stress to Happiness 3
    *Peter Y. Chen and Cary L. Cooper*

2   Conceptualizing and Measuring Wellbeing at Work 9
    *Cynthia D. Fisher*

**Part 2   Resources, Coping, and Control** 35

3   Job DemandswResources Theory 37
    *Arnold B. Bakker and Evangelia Demerouti*

4   Positive Psychology and Coping: Towards a Better
    Understanding of the Relationship 65
    *Philip Dewe*

5   The Role of Workplace Control in Positive Health
    and Wellbeing 91
    *Erin M. Eatough and Paul E. Spector*

**Part 3   Happy Workers and Happy Organizations** 111

6   The Happy Worker: Revisiting the "Happy–Productive
    Worker" Thesis 113
    *Peter Hosie and Nada ElRakhawy*

7   Organizational Characteristics of Happy Organizations 139
    *Bret L. Simmons*

Contents of this Volume

**Part 4   Character and Wellbeing**                                157

  8   Character and Wellbeing                                        159
      *Thomas A. Wright and Tyler Lauer*

  9   Stress, Health, and Wellbeing in Practice: Workplace
      Leadership and Leveraging Stress for Positive
      Outcomes                                                      175
      *James Campbell Quick, Joel Bennett, and*
      *M. Blake Hargrove*


**Part 5   Organizational Strategies to Promote Wellbeing**         205

 10   Cancer, Work, and the Quality of Working Life: A Narrative
      Review                                                        207
      *Tom Cox, Sara MacLennan, and James N'Dow*

 11   Lead Well, Be Well: Leadership Behaviors Influence Employee
      Wellbeing                                                     235
      *Jennifer Robertson and Julian Barling*

 12   Organizational Coping Strategies and Wellbeing                253
      *Gordon Tinline and Matthew Smeed*

 13   Workplace Mistreatment: Recent Developments in Theory,
      Research, and Interventions                                   263
      *Michael Hanrahan and Michael P. Leiter*

 14   The Sustainable Workforce: Organizational Strategies for
      Promoting Work–Life Balance and Wellbeing                     295
      *Ellen Ernst Kossek, Monique Valcour, and Pamela Lirio*

 15   Development of a Theoretically Grounded Model
      of Sexual Harassment Awareness Training Effectiveness         319
      *Lisa M. Kath and Vicki J. Magley*

 16   The Working Wounded: Stigma and Return to Work                339
      *Lori Francis, James E. Cameron, E. Kevin Kelloway,*
      *Victor M. Catano, Arla L. Day, and C. Gail Hepburn*

 17   Job Stress in University Academics: Evidence from an
      Australian National Study                                     357
      *Anthony H. Winefield*

Contents of this Volume

**Part 6  From Research to National Policy**                    379

18  Longitudinal Research in Occupational Stress: A Review of
    Methodological Issues                                        381
    *Robert C. Brusso, Konstantin P. Cigularov, and*
    *Rachel C. Callan*

19  Measuring Wellbeing in Modern Societies                     409
    *Paul Allin*

    Index                                                       465

# About the Editors

**Peter Y. Chen** is Professor of Management at the University of South Australia Business School and former Professor of Psychology at Colorado State University. He is Fellow of the Society for Industrial and Organizational Psychology and on the Board of Directors for Mates in Construction SA Ltd. He served as Associate Editor of the *Journal of Occupational Health Psychology* (2005–2010) and as President of the Society for Occupational Health Psychology (2006–2007). Professor Chen was ranked 29th (2000–2004) based on ISI citation impact in 30 management journals. He is the coauthor of *Correlation: Parametric and nonparametric measures* (2002), and has written or cowritten over 90 journal articles, book chapters, and encyclopedia entries.

**Cary L. Cooper**, CBE, is Distinguished Professor of Organizational Psychology and Health at Lancaster University Management School, U.K. He is the author/editor of over 150 books, has written over 400 scholarly articles for academic journals, and is a frequent contributor to national newspapers, TV, and radio. He is the Chair of the Academy of Social Sciences (comprised of 46 learned societies in the social sciences, with nearly 90,000 social scientists), President of RELATE, President of the Institute of Welfare, and immediate past President of the British Association of Counselling and Psychotherapy. He was the Founding President of the British Academy of Management, Founding Editor of the *Journal of Organizational Behavior*, and is currently Editor-in-Chief of the international scholarly journal *Stress & Health*. He has received honorary doctorates from a number of universities (e.g., University of Sheffield, Aston University, and Heriot-Watt University). He has been awarded honorary fellowships by the Royal College of Physicians, Royal College of Physicians of Ireland, British Psychological Society, European Academy of Occupational Health Psychology, and Institute of Occupational Safety and Health. In 2010 Professor Cooper was awarded the Lord Dearing Lifetime Achievement Award at the *The Times Higher Education* Awards for his distinguished contribution to higher education. He was lead scientist on the U.K. Government's Foresight program on Mental Capital and Wellbeing, which had a major impact in the United Kingdom and Europe. Professor Cooper was Chair of the Global Agenda Council on Chronic Diseases in the World Economic Forum in 2009–2010. In 2012, *HR* magazine voted him the Fourth Most Influential HR Thinker. In 2001, he was awarded a CBE by the Queen for his contribution to occupational health.

# Contributors

**Paul Allin**, Imperial College London, U.K.

**Arnold B. Bakker**, Erasmus University Rotterdam, The Netherlands and Lingnan University, Hong Kong

**Julian Barling**, Queen's University, Australia

**Joel Bennett**, Organizational Wellness and Learning Systems, U.S.A.

**Robert C. Brusso**, Old Dominion University, U.S.A. and ICF International

**Rachel C. Callan**, Old Dominion University, U.S.A.

**James E. Cameron**, Saint Mary's University, Canada

**Victor M. Catano**, Saint Mary's University, Canada

**Peter Y. Chen**, University of South Australia, Australia

**Konstantin P. Cigularov**, Old Dominion University, U.S.A.

**Cary L. Cooper**, Lancaster University, U.K.

**Tom Cox**, Birkbeck, University of London, U.K.

**Arla L. Day**, Saint Mary's University, Canada

**Evangelia Demerouti**, Eindhoven University of Technology, The Netherlands

**Philip Dewe**, Birkbeck, University of London, U.K.

**Erin M. Eatough**, University of South Florida, U.S.A.

**Nada ElRakhawy**, Al Garhoud Private Hospital, United Arab Emirates

**Cynthia D. Fisher**, Bond University, Australia

**Lori Francis**, Saint Mary's University, Canada

**Michael Hanrahan**, Acadia University, Canada

**M. Blake Hargrove**, Shippensburg University, U.S.A.

**C. Gail Hepburn**, University of Lethbridge, Canada

**Peter Hosie**, Curtin University, Australia

**Lisa M. Kath**, San Diego State University, U.S.A.

**E. Kevin Kelloway**, Saint Mary's University, Canada

**Ellen Ernst Kossek**, Purdue University Krannert School of Management, U.S.A.

**Tyler Lauer**, Manhattan, Kansas, U.S.A.

**Michael P. Leiter**, Acadia University, Canada

**Pamela Lirio**, EDHEC Business School, France

**Sara MacLennan**, University of Aberdeen, U.K.

**Vicki J. Magley**, University of Connecticut, U.S.A.

**James N'Dow**, University of Aberdeen, U.K.

**James Campbell Quick**, The University of Texas at Arlington, U.S.A. and Lancaster University Management School, U.K.

**Jennifer Robertson**, Western University, Australia

**Bret L. Simmons**, University of Nevada, U.S.A.

**Matthew Smeed**, Robertson Cooper, U.K.

**Paul E. Spector**, University of South Florida, U.S.A.

**Gordon Tinline**, Robertson Cooper, U.K.

**Monique Valcour**, EDHEC Business School, France

**Anthony H. Winefield**, University of South Australia, Australia

**Thomas A. Wright**, Fordham University, U.S.A.

# Full Contents of *Wellbeing: A Complete Reference Guide*

**Volume I     Wellbeing in Children and Families**
*Edited by Susan H. Landry and Cary L. Cooper*

| | |
|---|---|
| About the Editors | ix |
| Contributors | xi |
| Full Contents of *Wellbeing: A Complete Reference Guide* | xiii |
| Introduction to *Wellbeing: A Complete Reference Guide* | xxvii |

1   Introduction                                                                                          1
    *Susan H. Landry*

**Part 1     The Development of Early Social and Cognitive Skills**
            **Important for Child Wellbeing**                                          **5**

2   Children's Self-Regulation and Executive Control: Critical for
    Later Years                                                                                          7
    *Caron A. C. Clark, Miriam M. Martinez, Jennifer Mize Nelson,*
    *Sandra A. Wiebe, and Kimberly Andrews Espy*

3   Children's Emotion Regulation in Classroom Settings                          37
    *C. Cybele Raver*

4   Early Math and Literacy Skills: Key Predictors of Later School
    Success                                                                                               55
    *Greg J. Duncan, Chantelle Dowsett, and Joshua F. Lawrence*

5   Children's Intrinsic Motivation to Learn: Does It Decline over
    Time and, If So, Why?                                                                         73
    *Verena Freiberger and Birgit Spinath*

**Part 2   Parenting and Children's Development**                         **89**

 6   Parents' Role in Infants' Language Development and
     Emergent Literacy                                                      91
     *Catherine S. Tamis-LeMonda, Rufan Luo, and Lulu Song*

 7   Can Parents Be Supported to Use a Responsive Interaction
     Style with Young Children?                                            111
     *Susan H. Landry*

 8   Parenting and Executive Function: Positive and Negative
     Influences                                                            131
     *Claire Hughes, Gabriela Roman, and Rosie Ensor*

 9   The Nature of Effective Parenting: Some Current
     Perspectives                                                          157
     *Joan E. Grusec, Dilek Saritaş, and Ella Daniel*

10   Parenting and Early Intervention: The Impact on Children's
     Social and Emotional Skill Development                                179
     *Catherine C. Ayoub, Jessical Dym Bartlett, and*
     *Mallary I. Swartz*


**Part 3   School and Child Care: Settings that Impact Child
            and Family Wellbeing**                                        **211**

11   High-Risk Home and Child-Care Environments and Children's
     Social-Emotional Outcomes                                            213
     *Lisa S. Badanes and Sarah Enos Watamura*

12   Classroom Peer Relations as a Context for Social
     and Scholastic Development                                           243
     *Gary W. Ladd, Becky Kochenderfer-Ladd, and*
     *Casey M. Sechler*

13   The Importance of Quality Prekindergarten Programs for
     Promoting School Readiness Skills                                    271
     *Andrew J. Mashburn*

14   Consistent Environmental Stimulation from Birth to
     Elementary School: The Combined Contribution of Different
     Settings on School Achievement                                       297
     *Robert C. Pianta*

**Part 4   Stress and Family and Child Wellbeing**                    **321**

15   Poverty, Public Policy, and Children's Wellbeing                 323
     *Aletha C. Huston*

16   Early Life Stress and Neurobehavioral Development                345
     *Sarah Stellern and Megan R. Gunnar*

17   Neighborhood Effects and Young Children's Outcomes               361
     *Dafna Kohen and Leanne Findlay*

18   The Family Check-Up: A Tailored Approach to Intervention
     with High-Risk Families                                          385
     *Anne M. Gill, Thomas J. Dishion, and Daniel S. Shaw*

Index                                                                 407

**Volume II   Wellbeing and the Environment**
*Edited by Rachel Cooper, Elizabeth Burton, and
Cary L. Cooper*

About the Editors                                                     ix
Contributors                                                          xi
Full Contents of *Wellbeing: A Complete Reference Guide*              xiii
Introduction to *Wellbeing: A Complete Reference Guide*               xxvii

 1   Wellbeing and the Environment: An Overview                       1
     *Rachel Cooper*

**Part 1   Wellbeing and the Neighborhood**                          **21**

 2   Urban Neighborhoods and Mental Health across the Life
     Course                                                           23
     *Erin Gilbert and Sandro Galea*

 3   The Impact of the Local Social and Physical Local
     Environment on Wellbeing                                         51
     *Anne Ellaway*

 4   Density and Mental Wellbeing                                     69
     *Christopher T. Boyko and Rachel Cooper*

5   Neighborhoods and Social Interaction                          91
    *Scott C. Brown and Joanna Lombard*

6   Living in the City: Mixed Use and Quality of Life            119
    *Graeme Evans*

7   "We Live Here Too"... What Makes a Child-Friendly
    Neighborhood?                                                147
    *Karen E. Martin and Lisa J. Wood*

8   A Step Too Far? Designing Dementia-Friendly Neighborhoods   185
    *Lynne Mitchell*

9   Walkable Neighborhoods: Principles, Measures, and Health
    Impacts                                                      219
    *Tim G. Townshend*

10  Quality of Urban Spaces and Wellbeing                        249
    *Mags Adams*


**Part 2   Wellbeing and Buildings**                             **271**

11  Children and the Physical Environment                        273
    *Lorraine E. Maxwell and Gary W. Evans*

12  Wellbeing and the School Environment                         301
    *Andy Jones and Flo Harrison*

13  The Built Housing Environment, Wellbeing, and
    Older People                                                 335
    *Rachael Dutton*

14  Workplace and Wellbeing                                      373
    *Jeremy Myerson*

15  Linking the Physical Design of Health-Care Environments to
    Wellbeing Indicators                                         391
    *Sarah Payne, Rachel Potter, and Rebecca Cain*


**Part 3   Wellbeing and Green Spaces**                          **419**

16  Wellbeing and Green Spaces in Cities                         421
    *William Sullivan*

17  Environmental Interaction and Engagement: Supporting
    Wellbeing                                                          445
    *Richard Coles*

**Part 4  Wellbeing and the Environment: Other Factors
         and the Future**                                             **499**

18  Crime and the Urban Environment: The Implications for
    Wellbeing                                                          501
    *Caroline L. Davey and Andrew B. Wootton*

19  Transport and Wellbeing                                            535
    *Nick Tyler*

20  Air Quality and Wellbeing                                          569
    *Ben Croxford*

21  Implications of Low-Carbon Design of Housing for Health
    and Wellbeing: A U.K. Case Study                                   579
    *Michael Davies, Ian Hamilton, Anna Mavrogianni,
    Rokia Raslan, and Paul Wilkinson*

22  Cobenefits of Insulating Houses: Research Evidence and Policy
    Implications                                                       607
    *Philippa Howden-Chapman and Nicholas Preval*

23  The Multiple Pathways between Environment and Health               627
    *Marketta Kyttä and Anna Broberg*

24  Summary: Wellbeing and the Environmental Implications for
    Design                                                             653
    *Rachel Cooper and Elizabeth Burton*

Index                                                                  669

# Volume III  Work and Wellbeing
*Edited by Peter Y. Chen and Cary L. Cooper*

About the Editors                                                      ix
Contributors                                                           xi
Full Contents of *Wellbeing: A Complete Reference Guide*               xiii
Introduction to *Wellbeing: A Complete Reference Guide*                xxvii

# Full Contents

**Part 1    Introduction**                                                     1

1    Introduction: From Stress to Happiness                            3
     *Peter Y. Chen and Cary L. Cooper*

2    Conceptualizing and Measuring Wellbeing at Work                   9
     *Cynthia D. Fisher*


**Part 2    Resources, Coping, and Control**                              35

3    Job Demands–Resources Theory                                     37
     *Arnold B. Bakker and Evangelia Demerouti*

4    Positive Psychology and Coping: Towards a Better
     Understanding of the Relationship                                65
     *Philip Dewe*

5    The Role of Workplace Control in Positive Health
     and Wellbeing                                                    91
     *Erin M. Eatough and Paul E. Spector*


**Part 3    Happy Workers and Happy Organizations**                      111

6    The Happy Worker: Revisiting the "Happy–Productive
     Worker" Thesis                                                  113
     *Peter Hosie and Nada ElRakhawy*

7    Organizational Characteristics of Happy Organizations           139
     *Bret L. Simmons*


**Part 4    Character and Wellbeing**                                     157

8    Character and Wellbeing                                         159
     *Thomas A. Wright and Tyler Lauer*

9    Stress, Health, and Wellbeing in Practice: Workplace
     Leadership and Leveraging Stress for Positive
     Outcomes                                                        175
     *James Campbell Quick, Joel Bennett, and
     M. Blake Hargrove*

**Part 5   Organizational Strategies to Promote Wellbeing      205**

10   Cancer, Work, and the Quality of Working Life: A Narrative
     Review                                                      207
     *Tom Cox, Sara MacLennan, and James N'Dow*

11   Lead Well, Be Well: Leadership Behaviors Influence Employee
     Wellbeing                                                   235
     *Jennifer Robertson and Julian Barling*

12   Organizational Coping Strategies and Wellbeing              253
     *Gordon Tinline and Matthew Smeed*

13   Workplace Mistreatment: Recent Developments in Theory,
     Research, and Interventions                                 263
     *Michael Hanrahan and Michael P. Leiter*

14   The Sustainable Workforce: Organizational Strategies for
     Promoting Work–Life Balance and Wellbeing                   295
     *Ellen Ernst Kossek, Monique Valcour, and Pamela Lirio*

15   Development of a Theoretically Grounded Model
     of Sexual Harassment Awareness Training Effectiveness       319
     *Lisa M. Kath and Vicki J. Magley*

16   The Working Wounded: Stigma and Return to Work              339
     *Lori Francis, James E. Cameron, E. Kevin Kelloway,*
     *Victor M. Catano, Arla L. Day, and C. Gail Hepburn*

17   Job Stress in University Academics: Evidence from an
     Australian National Study                                   357
     *Anthony H. Winefield*


**Part 6   From Research to National Policy                      379**

18   Longitudinal Research in Occupational Stress: A Review of
     Methodological Issues                                       381
     *Robert C. Brusso, Konstantin P. Cigularov, and*
     *Rachel C. Callan*

19   Measuring Wellbeing in Modern Societies                     409
     *Paul Allin*

Index                                                            465

## Volume IV   Wellbeing in Later Life
*Edited by Thomas B. L. Kirkwood and*
*Cary L. Cooper*

About the Editors                                                          vii

Contributors                                                                ix

Full Contents of *Wellbeing: A Complete Reference Guide*         xi

Introduction to *Wellbeing: A Complete Reference Guide*         xxv

1   Introduction: Wellbeing in Later Life                             1
    *Cary L. Cooper and Thomas B. L. Kirkwood*

**Part 1   Longevity and Wellbeing**                                  7

2   The Changing Demographic Context of Aging                        9
    *Roland Rau and James W. Vaupel*

3   Biological Determinants and Malleability of Aging              31
    *Thomas B. L. Kirkwood*

4   Wellbeing as Experienced by the Very Old                       53
    *Carol Jagger and Katie Brittain*

**Part 2   Factors Influencing Wellbeing**                           67

5   Psychological Wellbeing in Later Life                           69
    *Kate M. Bennett and Laura K. Soulsby*

6   Nutrition and Lifelong Wellbeing                                91
    *C. Alexandra Munro and John C. Mathers*

7   Physical Activity, Exercise, and Aging                        105
    *Grainne S. Gorman, Josh Wood, and*
    *Michael I. Trenell*

8   Capability and Independency in Later Life                     125
    *John Bond*

9   Combating Isolation Through Technology in Older
    People                                                        145
    *Peter Gore*

10  Wellbeing and Vitality in Later Life: The Role of the Consumer
    Industry                                                          165
    *Michael Catt and Frans J. G. van der Ouderaa*

11  Education and its Role in Wellbeing                               181
    *Jim Soulsby*


**Part 3   Wellbeing at the End of Life**                            **197**

12  The Threat to Wellbeing from Cognitive Decline                   199
    *Louise Robinson and Lynne Corner*

13  When Vitality Meets Longevity: New Strategies for Health in
    Later Life                                                       219
    *Rudi G. J. Westendorp, Bert Mulder, A. J. Willem van der Does,*
    *and Frans J. G. van der Ouderaa*

14  Maintaining Wellbeing Through the End of Life                    235
    *Julian C. Hughes*


**Part 4   Comparative Perspectives on Wellbeing**                   **253**

15  Cultures, Aging, and Wellbeing                                   255
    *Ngaire Kerse, Mere Kēpa, Ruth Teh, and Lorna Dyall*

16  Wellbeing in the Oldest Old and Centenarians
    in Japan                                                         275
    *Yasuyuki Gondo, Yasumichi Arai, and Nobuyoshi*
    *Hirose*

17  Wellbeing in Later Life in Eighteenth-Century England            287
    *Helen Yallop*


**Appendix**

    Foresight Mental Capital and Wellbeing Project: Mental
    Capital Through Life: Future Challenges                          299
    *Thomas B. L. Kirkwood, John Bond, Carl May, Ian McKeith,*
    *and Min-Min Teh*

Index                                                                389

# Volume V   The Economics of Wellbeing
### *Edited by David McDaid and Cary L. Cooper*

About the Editors                                                            vii

Contributors                                                                  ix

Full Contents of *Wellbeing: A Complete Reference Guide*                      xi

Introduction to *Wellbeing: A Complete Reference Guide*                      xxv

1   Introduction                                                               1
    *David McDaid and Cary L. Cooper*

**Part 1   Perspectives on the Economics of Wellbeing**                       **11**

2   A Short History of Wellbeing Research                                     13
    *Laura Stoll*

3   Income and Wellbeing: A Selective Review                                  33
    *Brendan Kennelly*

4   Does Money Buy Me Love? Testing Alternative Measures of
    National Wellbeing                                                        49
    *Arthur Grimes, Les Oxley, and Nicholas Tarrant*

5   The Impact of the Great Recession on Economic Wellbeing:
    How Different Are OECD Nations and Why?                                   83
    *Lars Osberg and Andrew Sharpe*

6   Was the Economic Crisis of 2008 Good for Icelanders? Impact
    on Health Behaviours                                                     111
    *Tinna Laufey Ásgeirsdóttir, Hope Corman, Kelly Noonan,*
    *Þórhildur Ólafsdóttir, and Nancy E. Reichman*

7   Mental Health: A New Frontier for Labor Economics                        157
    *Richard Layard*

**Part 2   Promoting Wellbeing: The Economic Case**
       **for Action**                                                        **179**

8   Investing in the Wellbeing of Young People: Making the
    Economic Case                                                            181
    *David McDaid, A-La Park, Candice Currie, and*
    *Cara Zanotti*

9   Investing in Wellbeing in the Workplace: More Than Just a
    Business Case                                                    215
    *David McDaid and A-La Park*

10  Promoting the Health and Wellbeing of Older People: Making
    an Economic Case                                                 239
    *A-La Park, David McDaid, Anna K. Forsman, and
    Kristian Wahlbeck*

11  Promoting and Protecting Mental Wellbeing during Times of
    Economic Change                                                  261
    *David McDaid and Kristian Wahlbeck*

12  Making Use of Evidence from Wellbeing Research in Policy
    and Practice                                                     285
    *David McDaid*

Index                                                                299

## Volume VI   Interventions and Policies to Enhance Wellbeing

*Edited by Felicia A. Huppert and Cary L. Cooper*

About the Editors                                                    ix
Contributors                                                         xi
Full Contents of *Wellbeing: A Complete Reference Guide*             xiii
Introduction to *Wellbeing: A Complete Reference Guide*              xxvii
Introduction to this Volume                                          xxxv

1   The State of Wellbeing Science: Concepts, Measures,
    Interventions, and Policies                                      1
    *Felicia A. Huppert*

Part 1   Individual and Group Interventions across the Life
         Course                                                      51

2   Parenting Interventions to Promote Wellbeing and Prevent
    Mental Disorder                                                  53
    *Sarah Stewart-Brown*

3 Promoting Mental Health and Wellbeing in Schools          93
   *Katherine Weare and Melanie Nind*

4 An Exploration of the Effects of Mindfulness Training
   and Practice in Association with Enhanced Wellbeing
   for Children and Adolescents: Theory, Research, and Practice   141
   *Christine Burke*

5 MindMatters: Implementing Mental Health Promotion in
   Secondary Schools in Australia                         185
   *Louise Rowling and Trevor Hazell*

6 A Systematic Review of Mental Health Promotion in the
   Workplace                                              221
   *Czesław Czabała and Katarzyna Charzyńska*

7 Wellbeing Begins with "We": The Physical and
   Mental Health Benefits of Interventions that Increase Social
   Closeness                                              277
   *Bethany E. Kok and Barbara L. Fredrickson*

8 The Experience Corps®: Intergenerational Interventions to
   Enhance Wellbeing Among Retired People                 307
   *George W. Rebok, Michelle C. Carlson, Kevin D. Frick,
   Katherine D. Giuriceo, Tara L. Gruenewald, Sylvia McGill,
   Jeanine M. Parisi, William A. Romani, Teresa E. Seeman,
   Elizabeth K. Tanner, and Linda P. Fried*

9 Enhancing Mental Health and Mental Wellbeing in Older
   People: Important Concepts and Effective Psychosocial
   Interventions                                          331
   *Anna K. Forsman, Eija Stengård, and Kristian Wahlbeck*

**Part 2   Interventions to Create Positive Organizations
           and Communities**                             **355**

10 Wellbeing as a Business Priority: Experience from the
   Corporate World                                        357
   *Catherine Kilfedder and Paul Litchfield*

11 The Power of Philanthropy and Volunteering             387
   *Sara Konrath*

12 Community Change: The Complex Nature of Interventions to
Promote Positive Connections                                                   427
   *Sue Roffey and Jacqueline Barnes*

13 The Health and Wellbeing Effects of Active Labor Market
Programs                                                                       465
   *Adam P. Coutts, David Stuckler, and David J. Cann*


**Part 3   The Policy Perspective**                                            **483**

14 Creating Good Lives Through Computer Games                                   485
   *Daniel Johnson, Peta Wyeth, and Penny Sweetser*

15 Retooling for Wellbeing: Media and the Public's Mental Health   511
   *Marten W. deVries*

16 Policy and Wellbeing: The U.K. Government Perspective           541
   *David Halpern*

17 Measuring what Matters                                                      561
   *Juliet Michaelson, Charles Seaford, Saamah Abdallah, and
   Nic Marks*

18 Mental Health and Wellbeing at the Top of the Global Agenda    599
   *Eva Jané-Llopis, Peter Anderson, and Helen Herrman*

19 How can Subjective Wellbeing be Improved?                                   611
   *John F. Helliwell*

Index                                                                          633

# Introduction to *Wellbeing: A Complete Reference Guide*

## Cary L. Cooper

### Lancaster University, U.K.

This series of six volumes explores one of the most important social issues of our times, that of how to enhance the mental wellbeing of people, whether in the developed, developing, or underdeveloped world, and across the life course from birth to old age. We know that 1 in 4–6 people in most countries in the world suffer from a common mental disorder of anxiety, depression, or stress. We also know that mental ill health costs countries billions of dollars per annum. In the United Kingdom, for example, mental health-care costs have amounted to over £77 billion per annum, the bill for sickness absence and presenteeism (people turning up to work ill or not delivering due to job stress) in the workplace is another £26 billion, and the costs of dementia will rise from £20 billion to an estimated £50 billion in 25 years' time (Cooper, Field, Goswami, Jenkins, & Sahakian, 2009). In Germany, the leading cause of early retirement from work in 1989 was musculoskeletal disease but by 2004 it was stress and mental ill health, now representing 40% of all early retirements (German Federal Health Monitoring, 2007). In many European countries (e.g., Finland, Holland, Norway, and Switzerland) the cost of lost productive value due to lack of mental wellbeing is a significant proportion of gross domestic product (McDaid, Knapp, Medeiros, & MHEEN Group, 2008). Indeed, the costs of depression alone in the European Union were shown to be €41 billion, with €77 billion in terms of lost productivity to all the economies (Sobocki, Jonsson, Angst, & Rehnberg, 2006).

The issue of wellbeing has been around for sometime but has been brought to the fore more recently because of the global recession and economic downturn, which have made the situation worse (Antoniou & Cooper, 2013). But it was as early as 1968 that politicians began to talk about the inadequacy of gross national product as a measure of a society's success. In a powerful speech by Bobby Kennedy at the University of Kansas, when he was on the campaign trail for the Democratic Party nomination for U.S. President, he reflected:

> But even if we act to erase material poverty, there is another greater task, it is to confront the poverty of satisfaction—purpose and dignity—that afflicts us all. Too much and for too long, we seemed to have surrendered personal excellence and community values in the mere accumulation of material things. Our gross national product, now, is over $800 billion a year, but that gross national product—if we judge the United States of America by that—that gross national product counts air pollution and cigarette advertising, and ambulances to clear our highways of carnage. It counts special locks for our doors and the jails for the people who break them. It counts the destruction of the redwood and the loss of our natural wonder in the chaotic sprawl. It counts napalm and counts nuclear warheads and armoured cars for the police to fight the riots in our cities. . . . Yet the GNP does not allow for the health of our children, the quality of their education or the joy of their play. It does not include the beauty of our poetry or the strength of our marriages, the intelligence of our public debate or the integrity of our public officials. It measures neither our wit nor our courage, neither our wisdom nor our learning, neither our compassion nor our devotion to our country, it measures everything in short, except that which makes life worthwhile.
>
> University of Kansas, March 18, 1968,<br>http://www.americanswhotellthetruth.org/portraits/robert-f-kennedy

Since that time there have been numerous studies to show that the wealth of a country is not related to its happiness (Cooper & Robertson, 2013); indeed, as you earn far beyond your means you may become less happy or content. More recently, we have had politicians like former President Sarkozy of France, Prime Minister Cameron of the United Kingdom, and the King of Bhutan extoll the virtue of gross national wellbeing; that is, that the goal of a nation's politicians should be to enhance wellbeing among its citizens, with gross national product being only one indicator of a country's success. Indeed, Prime Minister Cameron has instituted an annual assessment of this through the U.K. Office of National Statistics which measures wellbeing among a large sample of the U.K. population, publishing the results, highlighting concerns, and ultimately considering policies to deal with them. The World Economic Forum of leading global companies, nongovernmental organizations, international bodies, and global charities now has one of its Global Agenda Councils on "mental health and wellbeing." Happiness and wellbeing indices abound (e.g., The Happy Planet), and many countries are being compared and assessed on a range of quality-of-life metrics. Indeed, in April 2012, 79 countries in the General Assembly of the United Nations signed the Bhutan Agreement, supporting the view that an overarching goal of a country should be to enhance the wellbeing and happiness of its people.

The biggest study of its kind undertaken by any government was the 2 year U.K. Government's Foresight project on mental capital and wellbeing, the aim of which was "to produce a challenging and long-term vision for optimising mental capital and wellbeing in the United Kingdom in the 21st century—both for the benefit of society and for the individual" (Cooper et al., 2009). Mental capital was defined as the metaphorical "bank account of the mind," which gets enhanced or depleted throughout the life course (see figure). Mental wellbeing was defined as "a dynamic state that refers to individuals' ability to develop their potential, work productively and creatively, build strong and positive relationships with others and contribute to their community" (Beddington et al., 2008).

Over 85 international science reviews were commissioned to assess the factors that influence an individual's mental capital and wellbeing throughout life, from early childhood to school years to working life to old age. There were numerous findings in this report, which were costed and developed as potential government policy and/or interventions. An example of some of the findings were: (a) if society does not catch learning difficulties in children early enough, there will be increased personal and economic costs downstream, leading to depleted mental wellbeing in terms of increased antisocial behavior as well as significant health costs; (b) if society does not identify the common mental disorders (CMDs) of anxiety, depression, and stress early enough, and provide appropriate treatment and support, society won't be able to tackle the 1 in 4–6 people suffering from depression and other CMDs; (c) with the workplace being more insecure, people working longer hours, and being more overloaded, occupational stress in many countries is now the leading cause of sickness absence and presenteeism, which has implications for the viability of businesses and their productivity; and, finally, (d) with the doubling of over-65-year-olds and the tripling of over-80-year-olds over the next 30 years, society needs to deal with the consequences of dementia now with preventative strategies, better early diagnosis, and more successful and evidence-based treatment regimes. The Foresight project developed many recommendations to enhance mental capital and wellbeing not only in the United Kingdom but also for other countries (Cooper et al., 2009), and its legacy has provided a roadmap for how other countries should think about this in the future, in terms of both policies and interventions for wellbeing.

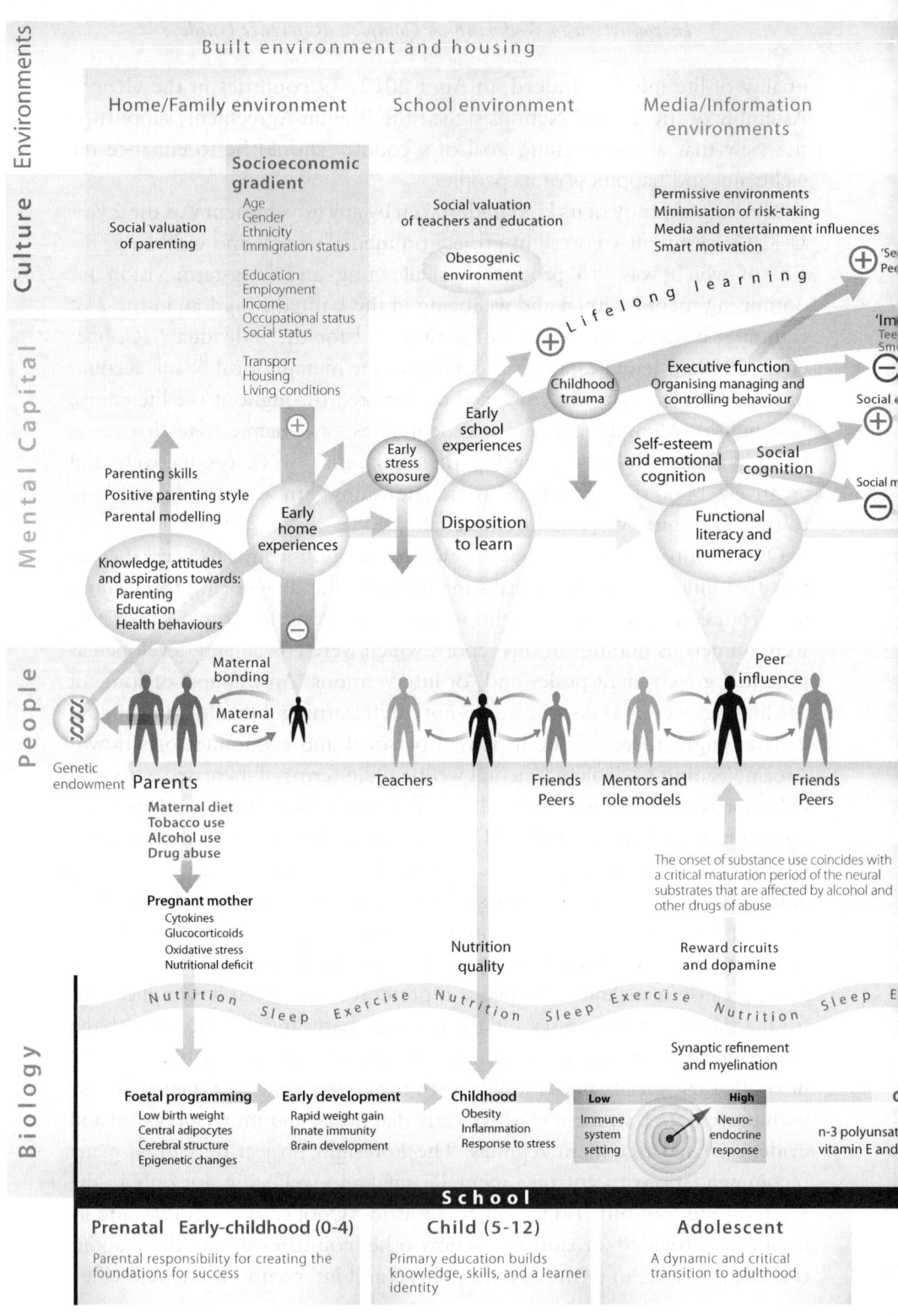

**Figure.** Synthetic View of the Mental Capital Trajectory.

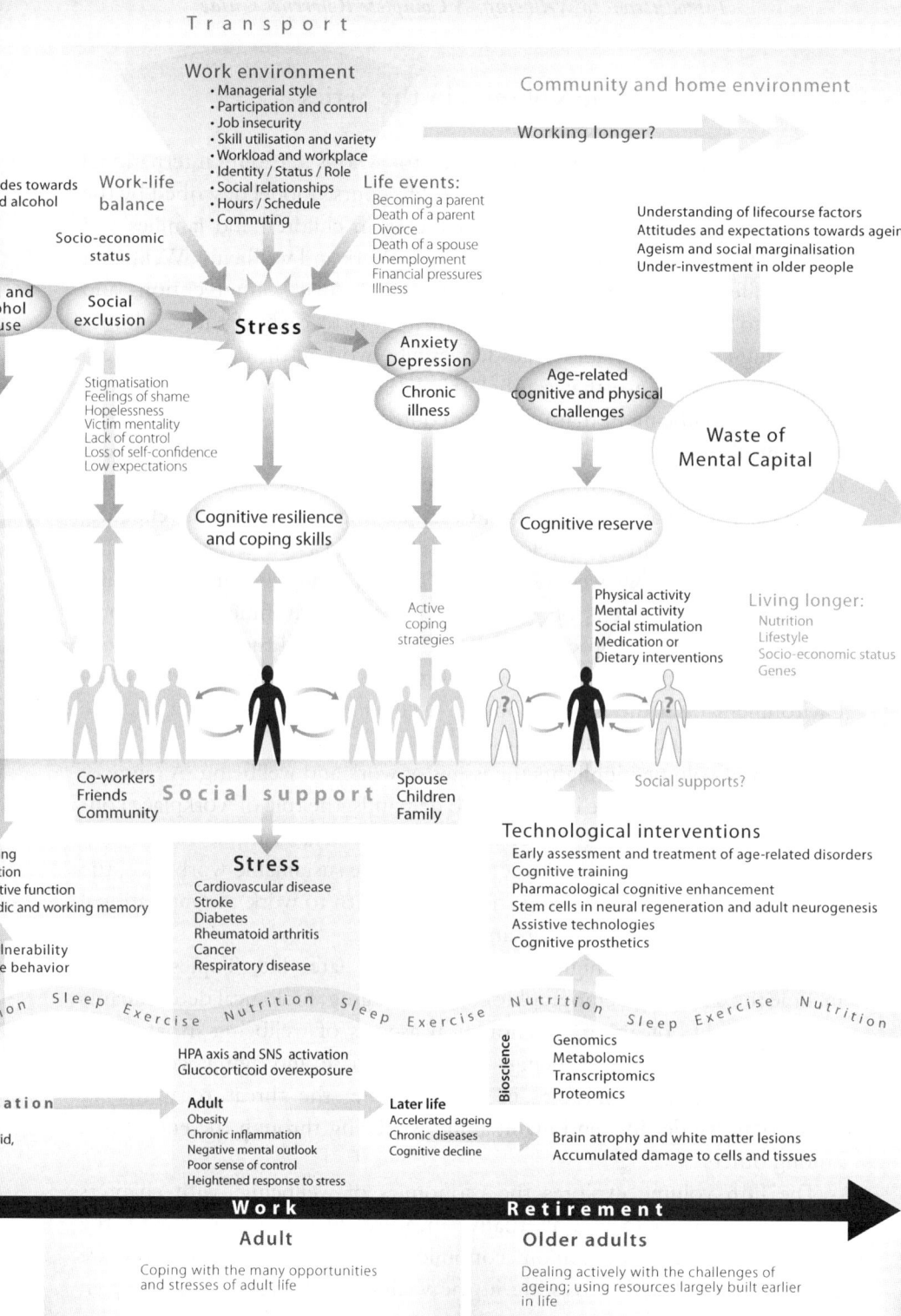

Transport

Work environment
• Managerial style
• Participation and control
• Job insecurity
• Skill utilisation and variety
• Workload and workplace
• Identity / Status / Role
• Social relationships
• Hours / Schedule
• Commuting

Community and home environment

Working longer?

Work-life balance

Socio-economic status

...des towards
...d alcohol

Life events:
Becoming a parent
Death of a parent
Divorce
Death of a spouse
Unemployment
Financial pressures
Illness

Understanding of lifecourse factors
Attitudes and expectations towards ageing
Ageism and social marginalisation
Under-investment in older people

...g and
...ohol
...use

Social exclusion

Stress

Anxiety
Depression

Chronic illness

Age-related
cognitive and physical
challenges

Waste of
Mental Capital

Stigmatisation
Feelings of shame
Hopelessness
Victim mentality
Lack of control
Loss of self-confidence
Low expectations

Cognitive resilience
and coping skills

Cognitive reserve

Active
coping
strategies

Physical activity
Mental activity
Social stimulation
Medication or
Dietary interventions

Living longer:
Nutrition
Lifestyle
Socio-economic status
Genes

Co-workers
Friends
Community

Social support

Spouse
Children
Family

Social supports?

...ning
...ntion
...utive function
...odic and working memory

...ulnerability
...ve behavior

Stress
Cardiovascular disease
Stroke
Diabetes
Rheumatoid arthritis
Cancer
Respiratory disease

Technological interventions
Early assessment and treatment of age-related disorders
Cognitive training
Pharmacological cognitive enhancement
Stem cells in neural regeneration and adult neurogenesis
Assistive technologies
Cognitive prosthetics

...tion  Sleep  Exercise  Nutrition  Sleep  Exercise  Nutrition  Sleep  Exercise  Nutrition

HPA axis and SNS activation
Glucocorticoid overexposure

Bioscience

Genomics
Metabolomics
Transcriptomics
Proteomics

...mation

...cid,

Adult
Obesity
Chronic inflammation
Negative mental outlook
Poor sense of control
Heightened response to stress

Later life
Accelerated ageing
Chronic diseases
Cognitive decline

Brain atrophy and white matter lesions
Accumulated damage to cells and tissues

Work                    Retirement

Adult                   Older adults

Coping with the many opportunities
and stresses of adult life

Dealing actively with the challenges of
ageing; using resources largely built earlier
in life

Maintenance            Decline

## The Volumes in the Series

Each volume in the series has a senior editor who is a leading international scholar in a particular field, following the life-course model described by the Foresight program. We start with Wellbeing in children and families and progress to Wellbeing and the environment, Work and wellbeing, Wellbeing in later life, The economics of wellbeing, and, finally, Interventions and policies to enhance wellbeing. The contributors to each of these volumes are distinguished international academics who work in the domain covered, reviewing the evidence that can help to develop policies and interventions to enhance wellbeing in that particular context.

In the first volume on children and families we explore four different themes, with a number of chapters under each of these: the development of the early social and cognitive skills that are important in child wellbeing, parenting and children's development, school and child care-settings that impact child and family wellbeing, and stress and family and child wellbeing.

The second volume is on wellbeing and the environment. This comprises sections, with chapters in each, on wellbeing and the neighborhood, wellbeing and buildings, wellbeing and green spaces, crime and the urban environment (and the implications for wellbeing), and wellbeing and the environmental implications for design.

The third volume highlights the issues of work and wellbeing. A range of topics is covered here: the impact of job demands, the role of workplace control, the organizational characteristics of "happy organizations," leadership behaviors that influence employee wellbeing, the sustainable workforce, the "working wounded" (including stigma and return to work), organizational coping strategies and wellbeing, and many more.

The fourth volume highlights wellbeing in later life. Topics covered include the changing demographic context of aging, biological determinants and malleability of aging, psychological aspects of wellbeing in later life, nutrition and lifelong wellbeing, physical exercise and aging, combating isolation through technology in older people, the threat to wellbeing from cognitive decline, and maintaining wellbeing through the end of life, among others.

The fifth volume explores the economics of wellbeing, with chapters on income and wellbeing, alternative measures of national wellbeing, the impact of the great recession on economic wellbeing, whether recessions are good for one's health, investing in the wellbeing of children, investing in wellbeing in the workplace, promoting health and wellbeing of older people and protecting population mental health, wellbeing during an economic crisis, and many others.

Finally, the sixth volume highlights interventions and policies that can enhance wellbeing throughout the life course. There are three sections, with chapters on the state of wellbeing science, individual/group interventions on childhood and adolescence, promoting mental health and wellbeing in schools, mindfulness training for children and adolescents, interventions in working years and post retirement, mental health promotion in the workplace, intergenerational interventions to enhance wellbeing among retired people, interventions to create positive organizations and communities with wellbeing as a business priority, the power of philanthropy and volunteering, and creating community connections. Finally, policies are discussed, such as mental health and wellbeing at the top of the global agenda, how subjective wellbeing can influence policy, media and the public's mental health, and promoting wellbeing through new technology.

These volumes contain the leading-edge research, practice, and policies to help government, businesses, local authorities, and global institutions consider how we can action some of what Bobby Kennedy suggested were an important set of outcomes for a successful society. Our institutions need to change, and we as individuals need to do so as well, if we are to achieve personal wellbeing, or as Abraham Lincoln wrote during the American Civil War, "it is not the years in your life which are important, but the life in your years." Winston Churchill reflected on this as well, when he wrote in an essay on how he dealt with the excessive pressures of life and found solace: "many remedies are suggested for the avoidance of worry and mental overstrain by persons who, over prolonged periods, have to bear exceptional responsibilities and discharge duties upon a very large scale. Some advise exercise, and others, repose. Some counsel travel, and others, retreat. . . no doubt all of these may play their part according to individual temperament. But the element which is constant and common in all of them is Change. . . a man can wear out a particular part of his mind by continually using it and tiring it, just in the same way as he can wear out the elbows of his coats. . . but the tired parts of the mind can be rested and strengthened, not merely by rest, but by using other parts. . . it is only when new cells are called into activity, when new stars become the lords of the ascendant, that relief, repose, refreshment are afforded."

I hope that these volumes will provide you with the science, practice, and tools to enhance the mental wellbeing of people in your own work.

# References

Antoniou, A., & Cooper, C. L. (Eds.) (2013). *The psychology of the recession on the workplace*. Cheltenham: Edward Elgar Publishing.

Beddington, J., Cooper, C. L., Field, J., Goswami, U., Huppert, F., Jenkins, R., . . . Thomas, S. (2008). The mental wealth of nations. *Nature, 455*(23), 1057–1060.

Cooper, C. L., Field, J., Goswami, U., Jenkins, R., & Sahakian, B. (Eds.) (2009). *Mental capital and wellbeing*. Oxford: Wiley Blackwell.

Cooper, C. L., & Robertson, I. (Eds.) (2013). *Management and happiness*. Cheltenham: Edward Elgar Publishing.

German Federal Health Monitoring (2007). *Trends in causes of early retirement*. http://www.gber.bund.de.

McDaid, D., Knapp, M., Medeiros, H., & MHEEN Group (2008). *Employment and mental health*. Brussels: European Commission.

Sobocki, P., Jonsson, B., Angst, J., & Rehnberg, C. (2006). Cost of depression in Europe. *Journal of Mental Health Policy and Economics, 9*(2), 87–98.

# Part 1
# Introduction

# 1

# Introduction

## *From Stress to Happiness*

### Peter Y. Chen

University of South Australia, Australia

### Cary L. Cooper

Lancaster University, U.K.

Prior to the collapse of the dot-com bubble in the United States, a company the first author worked for had a bigger plan to grow. In a fall afternoon of 1999, one of his colleagues, called John, sent a message to say that he would be late for an appointment because of a meeting request from the VP. After he came back from the meeting, John revealed that his position had just been terminated after more than 20 years of service. Understandably, his disbelief, anger, and worry were evident—and about 30 minutes later he experienced a bad stomachache (Chen, 2007).

Occupational stressors and job strains experienced by workers, such as what John went through, are not foreign to us. We have witnessed workers who have suffered from depression and humiliation while being abused or harassed (Barling, Dupre, & Kelloway, 2009; Leiter, Laschinger, Day, & Gilin-Oore, 2011), some who have lost their lives at work (Gittleman et al., 2010) or who have developed cardiovascular illness in demanding jobs without much personal control (De Lange, Taris, Kompier, Houtman, & Bongers, 2003).

The grim reality we face today, as described above, is not new, and the focus on workers' wellbeing has not improved significantly in recent decades (Ilgen, 1990). Wellbeing at work has been a major concern since the turn

*Work and Wellbeing: Wellbeing: A Complete Reference Guide*, Volume III.
Edited by Peter Y. Chen and Cary L. Cooper.
© 2014 John Wiley & Sons, Ltd. Published 2014 by John Wiley & Sons, Inc.
DOI: 10.1002/9781118539415.wbwell01

of the last century. Hugo Münsterberg, 1898 President of the American Psychological Association, researched accident prevention and safety promotion and published his work in *Psychology and industrial efficiency* (1913). The author of the first textbook on the subject of industrial and organizational psychology (Viteles, 1932) spent almost half of the book covering topics such as industrial accidents, fatigue, and safety. Ilgen (1990) voiced a similar concern, and reminded organizational researchers that occupational health is a timeless concern for humanitarian and utilitarian reasons, as well as obvious economic reasons.

There are numerous job stressors at work, with different levels of severity and frequency. Some of them are inherent in the job, and some of them may not easily be eliminated or isolated. Although we are not immune from exposure to these psychosocial hazards, there are venues for governments, societies, organizations, management, as well as individual workers to build and sustain healthy workplaces in which workers utilize their talents to achieve high performance as well as pursue happiness (Quick, 1999).

Over the past decade, positive psychology (Seligman & Csikszentmihalyi, 2000) has stimulated our thinking to consider taking a balanced approach in job stress research and practice. There is considerable evidence suggesting the benefit of focusing on positive aspects of work contexts and activities, and beliefs and attitudes to build a healthy workplace, as well as to improve workers' wellbeing. Following the World Health Organization's (1948) definition of health, we believe that a lack of negative aspects in a workplace does not constitute a sufficient condition of having a happy and healthy workplace. To follow this line of thinking, we have planned this volume by inviting world-renowned scholars and rising stars to explore ways of addressing workplace stress from the perspectives of positive psychology.

In Chapter 2, Fisher provides an in-depth and thorough review of a family of wellbeing constructs and operationalizations, and recommends ways of reaching a consensus of defining and conceptualizing wellbeing at work. Then, in Chapter 3, Bakker and Demerouti present a refined job demands–resources theory that integrates past job design and job stress theories. This refined theory undoubtedly advances research in job demand and resources, and clearly offers actionable approaches to reduce job demands and increase job and personal resources.

In Chapter 4, Dewe leads us to consider how the positive psychology movement affects research in work-related coping, and how coping through positive emotion and appraisals leads to success and positive outcomes. Eatough and Spector (Chapter 5) articulate how job control contributes to positive health and wellbeing by providing an insightful synthesis pertaining to the nature of job control from both subjective and objective perspectives.

Hosie and ElRakhawy (Chapter 6) and Simmons (Chapter 7) explore characteristics of happy workers and happy organizations, respectively. They also review the factors that facilitate being happy workers and organizations, and provide convincing arguments why these characteristics would provide competitive advantages for organizations to succeed and be sustainable in the current fast-moving environment.

In the next two chapters, attention is turned to the role of person characters and experience to counter work stress, and pathways of pursuing happiness. Wright and Lauer (Chapter 8) eloquently articulate how characters are conceptualized, what are important characters in different work occupations, and how characters serve the foundation of wellbeing at work. In Chapter 9, Quick, Bennett, and Hargrove offer insights into how one can build strong leadership and promote a healthy workplace via five positive pathways: strength of character, self-awareness, socialized power motivation, requisite self-reliance, and diverse professional supports.

The focus of the next eight chapters is on organizational strategies that promote wellbeing at work. Cox, MacLennan, and N'Dow (Chapter 10) present a very timely topic faced in workplaces that has not been adequately addressed in the management and applied psychology literature. They introduce approaches that organizations can use to assist workers with cancer to maintain quality of working life and wellbeing. Simple things to most people's minds, such as toilet facilities and access, could make huge differences in improving workers' wellbeing at work. Robertson and Barling (Chapter 11) review the leadership literature and discuss the distinctions between poor and positive leadership, and how positive leadership behaviors can enhance workers' wellbeing. Tinline and Smeed (Chapter 12) suggest practical strategies at both organizational and individual level that can not only assist workers to cope with job stressors, but also increase workers' wellbeing and health, motivation, as well as productivity. Hanrahan and Leiter (Chapter 13) provide a review about workplace incivility, which is considered to be a common psychosocial hazard routinely faced by workers around the globe. They summarize recent theoretical developments, and suggest ways of reducing incivility based on their recent work on incivility intervention.

Kossek, Valcour, and Lirio (Chapter 14) discuss the connections among sustainable workforce, work–life balance, and wellbeing, and propose three human resources strategies to develop sustainable workforces by strengthening work–life balance and wellbeing. In Chapter 15, Kath and Magley review the literature of sexual harassment awareness training, which has been understudied in the sexual harassment literature. They further propose a comprehensive sexual harassment awareness training model that captures key factors to be considered by organizations, including design issues, individual factors such as attitude and motivation, organizational factors such as workgroups' cynicism about organizational change and training transfer climate, as well as proximal and distal training outcomes. Francis, Cameron, Kelloway, Catano, Day, and Hepburn (Chapter 16) bring our attention to challenges faced by injured workers after they return to work. Adverse consequences of stigmatization on injured workers after they return to work have profound impacts on workers, organizations, and societies. The authors provide insightful recommendations to organizations about how management can alleviate and counter the stressful stigmatization faced by injured workers. Winefield in Chapter 17 documents the rising stress experienced by academic staff members over the past three decades. He provides ways of reducing stress and improving wellbeing based on his research in Australian tertiary institutions.

To improve wellbeing in the workplace with sound evidence cannot be achieved without adequate methodology. Brusso, Cigularov, and Callan (Chapter 18) discuss and recommend approaches of investigating causal processes of occupational stress and wellbeing. Finally, to reflect and extend Fisher's essay in Chapter 2 of this volume, Allin (Chapter 19) highlights the role of governments in promoting the happiness of citizens, sharing with us his unique insight into the U.K. Government's policy and measurement program of wellbeing. He points out that knowing the level of national wellbeing and its impacts not only informs policy makers about what really matters to the citizens they work for, but also offers directions and actions to address barriers to improved wellbeing.

In contrast to focusing on the dark side of job stress in past stress research, this volume provides an array of essays that outline how governments, organizations, as well as individual workers are striving for wellbeing and happiness, as well as building and sustaining healthy workplaces by taking positive and proactive approaches with solid evidence. It is our belief that absence of job stress is not sufficient for pursuing wellbeing and happiness.

# References

Barling, J., Dupre, K. E., & Kelloway, E. K. (2009). Predicting workplace aggression and violence. *Annual Review of Psychology, 60,* 671–692.

Chen, P. Y. (2007). The meaning of occupational health psychology: Personal reflection. *Society for Occupational Health Psychology Newsletter, 1,* 1. http://sohp.psy.uconn.edu/Downloads/SOHPNewsletterV1.pdf.

De Lange, A. H., Taris, T. W., Kompier, M. A. J., Houtman, I. L. D., & Bongers, P. M. (2003). "The *very* best of the millennium": Longitudinal research and the Demand-Control-(Support) model. *Journal of Occupational Health Psychology, 8,* 282–305.

Gittleman, J., Gardner, P., Haile, E., Sampson, J., Cigularov, K. P., Ermann, E. D., Stafford, P., & Chen, P. Y. (2010). City center and cosmopolitan construction projects, Las Vegas, Nevada: Lessons learned from the use of multiple sources and mixed methods in a safety needs assessment. *Journal of Safety Research, 41,* 263–291.

Ilgen, D. R. (1990). Health issues at work: Opportunity for industrial/organizational psychology. *American Psychologist, 45,* 273–283.

Leiter, M. P., Laschinger, H. K. S., Day, A., & Gilin-Oore, D. (2011). The impact of civility interventions on employee social behavior, distress, and attitudes. *Journal of Applied Psychology, 96,* 1258–1274.

Münsterberg, H. (1913). *Psychology and industrial efficiency.* Boston: Houghton Mifflin.

Quick, J. C. (1999). Occupational health psychology: Historical roots and future directions. *Health Psychology, 18,* 82–99.

Seligman, M. E. P., & Csikszentmihalyi, M. (2000). Positive psychology: An introduction. *American Psychologist, 55,* 5–14.

Viteles, M. S. (1932). *Industrial psychology.* New York: W. W. Norton.

World Health Organization (1948, April 7). *WHO definition of health.* http://www.who.int/about/definition/en/print.html.

# 2

# Conceptualizing and Measuring Wellbeing at Work

## Cynthia D. Fisher

### Bond University, Australia

Happiness and wellbeing are important to people both in general and in the workplace, and have implications for mental and physical health (Diener, 2000; Lyubomirsky, King, & Diener, 2005). Rath and Harter (2010) identify five domains comprising overall wellbeing, and conclude that career wellbeing is probably the most important of the five for most people. Organizational scholars have long been interested in job satisfaction and related positive attitudes and experiences involving work, jobs, and employers. This interest has intensified following the rise of positive psychology (Seligman & Csikszentmihalyi, 2000), which directs attention toward flourishing and vibrant mental health rather than merely the absence of stress, mental illness, and suffering. Organizational scholars have followed this lead with streams of research called positive organizational scholarship (Cameron, Dutton, & Quinn, 2003; Cameron & Spreitzer, 2011) and positive organizational behavior (Luthans, 2002; Nelson & Cooper, 2007), as well as a great deal of research on engagement and on positive moods and emotions at work. Our understanding of the antecedents and consequences of happiness and wellbeing in the workplace is growing rapidly (Fisher, 2010).

The purpose of this chapter is to consider what might be meant by wellbeing at work. Many constructs and measures potentially fall under this umbrella, and wellbeing at work has been operationalized in a wide variety of ways. I will describe some existing conceptualizations and definitions, discuss a variety of approaches to measuring these phenomena, and then

*Work and Wellbeing: Wellbeing: A Complete Reference Guide*, Volume III.
Edited by Peter Y. Chen and Cary L. Cooper.
© 2014 John Wiley & Sons, Ltd. Published 2014 by John Wiley & Sons, Inc.
DOI: 10.1002/9781118539415.wbwell02

recommend means of both broadening and deepening the conceptualization and assessment of wellbeing in the workplace. I begin with the general psychology literature on the meaning of wellbeing, and then apply insights from that literature to the more specific domain of workplace wellbeing.

# Wellbeing in Life

Philosophers and researchers have defined happiness and wellbeing in a variety of ways (Kesebir & Diener, 2008). There are a great many conceptual and operational definitions of these terms, and the same terms have been used inconsistently by different authors. Some conceptualizations and operationalizations are well established, while others are much newer and less consensually held. The major division is between *hedonic* views of wellbeing as pleasant feelings and evaluations, versus *eudaimonic* views which suggest that wellbeing involves engaging in behavior that is self-actualizing, meaningful, and growth producing (Ryan & Deci, 2001; Ryff & Singer, 2008).

## Hedonic Wellbeing

Much of the research on wellbeing has focused on the hedonic aspect of experiencing a pleasant life. "Subjective wellbeing" (SWB) is a well-established and frequently studied construct in this tradition. SWB is widely agreed to contain three aspects (Diener, 1984): the frequent experience of positive affect, the infrequent experience of negative affect, and positive cognitive evaluations of life satisfaction. Affective wellbeing is often measured with Bradburn's (1969) Affect Balance Scale. Diener et al. (2010) have recently developed the 12-item Scale of Positive and Negative Experiences (SPANE). This scale uses both broad affect (e.g., good, unpleasant) and specific emotion (afraid, joyful) terms, rated on frequency of occurrence over the preceding 4 weeks. The instrument is designed to be scored for positive affect and negative affect, and if desired, for affect balance by subtracting the negative affect score from the positive affect score.

There has been considerable debate as to whether or not positive and negative affect are opposite ends of the same bipolar continuum, or are separable unipolar dimensions that are less than perfectly correlated. The latter opinion holds the upper hand at present (Schimmack, 2007). Positive and negative affect add uniquely to the prediction of some outcomes, and their ratio or relative frequency has important implications (Diener, Sandvik,

& Pavot, 1991; Fredrickson & Losada, 2005). Therefore, both affects should be included in definitions and measures of subjective wellbeing. However, this does not resolve the problem of how best to conceptualize and measure positive and negative feelings. The affective component of wellbeing is sometimes conceptualized largely as hedonic tone, pleasant versus unpleasant moods and emotions. The affect circumplex adds a second dimension of high to low arousal (Russell, 1980). Another conceptualization rotates these two axes 45 degrees to define a dimension of positive affect running from high arousal pleasant feelings (e.g., enthusiastic, active, strong) to low arousal unpleasant feelings (e.g., dull, sluggish), and a second dimension of negative affect running from high arousal negative feelings (e.g., distressed, nervous, hostile) to low arousal positive feelings (e.g., placid, relaxed) (Watson & Tellegen, 1985). The 20 adjectives in the Positive and Negative Affect Scales (PANAS; Watson, Clark, & Tellegen, 1988) are commonly used to assess these constructs. Thompson (2007) provides a shortened and internationally validated version of the PANAS. An alternate approach is found in the Subjective Happiness Scale, which ignores arousal and the unipolar versus bipolar issue and assesses general happiness with four items such as "Compared to most of my peers, I consider myself: 1 = less happy, 7 = more happy" (Lyubomirsky & Lepper, 1999).

The other component of subjective wellbeing is a judgment of life satisfaction. This is sometimes measured by a single item, or alternatively by the 5-item Satisfaction with Life Scale (Diener, Emmons, Larsen, & Griffin, 1985). Sample items in this instrument include, "In most ways, my life is close to my ideal" and "So far I have gotten the important things I want in life."

## Eudaimonic Wellbeing

Philosophers believe that eudaimonic wellbeing is also important. This involves living a good life, not just a pleasant one. Eudaimonic approaches are linked to the satisfaction of basic human needs for competence, autonomy, relatedness, and self-acceptance. The focus is on growth, purpose in life, meaning, pursuing self-concordant goals, self-actualization, and virtue (Sheldon & Elliot, 1999; Warr, 2007). This approach has roots in Greek philosophy, but a much newer and less-developed base in measurement and empirical research than subjective wellbeing (Waterman, 2008). The eudaimonic tradition concentrates on positive psychological functioning, called flourishing by Keyes (2002, 2005), rather than feelings of personal pleasure. Kashdan, Biswas-Diener, and King (2008) note that

11

any aspect of wellbeing that is not explicitly affective seems to be considered eudaimonic. Ryff and her colleagues (Ryff, 1989; Ryff & Singer, 2008) suggest six dimensions of psychological wellbeing, none of which refer directly to the experience of pleasure. These are self-acceptance, purpose in life, environmental mastery, positive relationships, personal growth, and autonomy. Ryff (1989) has developed scales for measuring these factors.

Research based on the "strengths" view suggests that eudaimonic wellbeing involves using one's personal strengths often in daily life (Buckingham & Clifton, 2001; Seligman, Steen, Park, & Peterson, 2005). Another concept related to eudaimonic wellbeing is the experience of purpose or meaning in life (e.g., The Meaning in Life Questionnaire; Steger, Frazier, Oishi, & Kaler, 2006). Sometimes measures of energy/vitality are also considered eudaimonic, though one could also argue that these are high arousal positive emotions that instead comprise one of the three aspects of subjective wellbeing (Kashdan et al., 2008).

There is currently a debate in the literature as to whether hedonic and eudaimonic dimensions of wellbeing are conceptually and empirically separable (e.g., Kashdan et al., 2008; Raibley, 2012; Waterman, 2008). In practice, they are highly correlated. There is considerable evidence that behaving in eudaimonic ways is predictive of hedonic pleasure (Kashdan et al., 2008; Sheldon, Ryan, & Reis, 1996; Steyer, Kashdan, & Oishi, 2008; Waterman, 2008). Waterman explains that this is expected, because it is pleasant and satisfying to be self-actualizing. He also points out that eudaimonic wellbeing is sufficient but not necessary for hedonic happiness, and that measures of hedonic and eudaimonic wellbeing have somewhat different causes and different predictive relationships with outcomes. He suggests that both types of wellbeing are important and should be measured. King, Hicks, Krull, and Del Gaiso (2006) have confirmed a strong relationship between positive affect and the eudaimonic experience of meaning in life, but interestingly have shown that positive affect can be a cause as well as an effect of the short-term experience of meaning.

## Social Wellbeing

There also may be a third distinct aspect of wellbeing to complement the hedonic aspect of inner pleasure and the eudaimonic aspect of inner growth, autonomy, and self-realization. It is the more outer-directed aspect of social wellbeing (Keyes, 1998). This is consistent with basic need theories which all acknowledge the importance of social relationships. A major review by

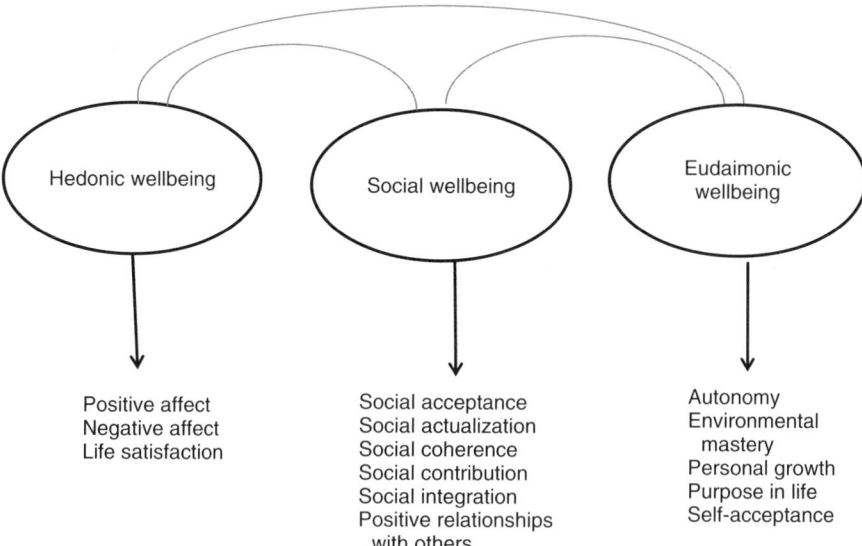

**Figure 2.1.** Model of Overall Wellbeing in Life. Adapted from Gallagher, Lopez, & Preacher (2009).

Baumeister and Leary (1995) demonstrates the pervasive importance of social relationships for human wellbeing. They conclude that individuals need frequent interactions in stable relationships with others that involve giving and receiving care. Gallagher, Lopez, and Preacher (2009) proposed and found empirical support for a hierarchical structure of wellbeing as shown in Figure 2.1. The three second-order factors (hedonic, eudaimonic, and social wellbeing) have unique indicators but are quite highly correlated and combine to indicate overall wellbeing. Gallagher et al. make the case that each dimension should be assessed separately.

## Other Multidimensional Models of Wellbeing

Recent European research by Huppert and So (2013) suggests a three-dimensional model of wellbeing/flourishing. The dimensions are positive appraisal (life satisfaction), positive functioning (engagement, competence, meaning, and positive relationships), and positive personal characteristics (emotional stability, vitality, optimism, resilience, positive emotion, and self-esteem).

Two additional models of the dimensions of wellbeing appear in Martin Seligman's work. His original model of "authentic happiness" contained three elements thought to be essential for overall happiness and life satisfaction: positive emotions, engagement (defined as experiencing states of deeply engaged interest called flow; see Csikszentmihalyi, 1990), and meaning or purpose in life (Seligman, 2002). His more recent thinking expands beyond life satisfaction or happiness to what he simply calls "wellbeing theory." This five-element construct combines hedonic, eudaimonic, and social components by adding two elements to the earlier authentic happiness model. These are accomplishment (success/winning/mastery) and positive relationships with others (Seligman, 2011). When all elements are in place, individuals are expected to flourish. Fredrickson and Losada (2005, p. 678) define flourishing as living "within an optimal range of human functioning, one that connotes goodness, generativity, growth, and resilience." Keyes (2002) and Huppert and So (2013) provide specific diagnostic criteria for flourishing. We will now turn to a discussion of wellbeing in the workplace, and consider how ideas from the general wellbeing literature might inform our understanding of wellbeing at work.

## Wellbeing at Work

Organizational scholars have been measuring aspects of satisfaction, happiness, or wellbeing at work for nearly a century. A great number of concepts might be construed as belonging to the family of wellbeing constructs, including job satisfaction, job involvement, affective organizational commitment, work engagement, positive and negative emotions and moods at work, flow states, intrinsic motivation, thriving, and vigor (Fisher, 2010). Although I focus here on indicators of high wellbeing, constructs involving very low wellbeing, such as burnout, could also be included on the list. In parallel with the research on general wellbeing shown in Figure 2.1, the separate aspects of wellbeing at work might fit together to comprise overall wellbeing in the workplace as shown in Figure 2.2. Happiness, the inner circle, is the experience of pleasant moods and emotions while working. It is one of three components of subjective wellbeing at work. The second circle includes negative moods and emotions at work and cognitive judgments of work satisfaction and similar attitudes. The higher level construct of overall wellbeing at work adds eudaimonic and social wellbeing components. Figure 2.2 will guide the following discussion of the ways in which organizational scholars have and should conceptualize and measure wellbeing in the workplace.

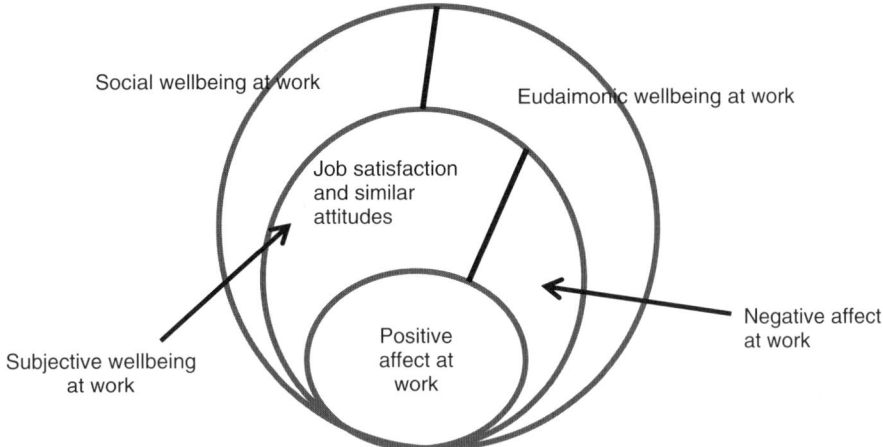

**Figure 2.2.** Components of Overall Wellbeing at Work.

It is very clear that wellbeing at work is multidimensional (e.g., Grant, Christianson, & Price, 2007; Page & Vella-Brodrick, 2009; Warr, 2013). Many concepts and measures used in organizational behavior appear to straddle these different dimensions of wellbeing, often combining cognitive judgments with affect, hedonic happiness with eudaimonic wellbeing, or eudaimonic with social wellbeing. Furthermore, some aspects are commonly measured, and measured very well, while other important components of overall wellbeing at work have been largely ignored. This suggests considerable scope to broaden the ways we think about and assess wellbeing at work.

### Subjective Wellbeing at Work

Subjective wellbeing includes positive attitudinal judgments as well as the experience of positive and negative affect. Workplace approaches to each of these will be discussed in turn.

*Satisfaction and related attitudes.*
Organizational researchers have been interested in *job satisfaction* since the 1920s, and it is the most commonly researched phenomenon in all of organizational behavior (Weiss & Brief, 2001; Wright, 2006). We are good at measuring it, with many well-validated measures of both overall job satisfaction and facet satisfactions (e.g., supervisor, pay, work itself) being available. Collections of job attitude measures can be found in Cook, Hepworth, Wall, and Warr (1981) and in Fields (2002).

While job satisfaction was famously described by Locke as "a pleasurable or positive emotional state resulting from an appraisal of one's job or job experiences" (1976, p. 1300), several scholars have pointed out that most commonly used measures of job satisfaction do a much better job of capturing cognitive judgments than hot emotional reactions (Brief, 1998; Brief & Weiss, 2002; Organ & Near, 1985; Weiss, 2002). Facet satisfaction scales are especially cognitively laden (Fisher, 2000). Faces scales (Kunin, 1955), which ask respondents to choose among faces displaying happy to unhappy expressions about their job, appear to elicit both cognitive judgments and affect related to work (Brief & Roberson, 1989; Fisher, 2000). Job satisfaction might be considered the workplace analog of life satisfaction—an important component of subjective wellbeing, but by no means the whole story.

*Organizational commitment* is also a commonly assessed job attitude. Commitment based on personally identifying with the organization's goals and values (normative commitment), and/or feeling part of the organizational family (affective commitment), seem to represent affectively tinged judgments that may be important components of wellbeing at work. Common measures of commitment are the Organizational Commitment Questionnaire (Mowday, Steers, & Porter, 1979) and the three-dimensional measure by Meyer, Allen, and Smith (1993). One might argue that normative and affective commitment also tap elements of eudaimonic and/or social wellbeing in the form of identifying with the important goals of a larger collective and therefore experiencing added meaning or purpose to one's work activities.

*Affect at work.*
Since the mid-1990s, there has been an explosion of interest in positive and negative affect at work, defined as typical or transient moods or emotions experienced while working. There are a number of measures of affect at work, many based on the affect circumplex idea that affect has two major dimensions: hedonic tone and arousal. The Positive and Negative Affect Scales (PANAS; Watson et al., 1988) are popular and have been adapted with "at work" instructions. The PANAS have been criticized, however, for including only high arousal terms. Other measures based on the affect circumplex include the Job-Related Affective Well-Being Scale (Van Katwyk, Fox, Spector, & Kelloway, 2000), the Job Affect Scale (Brief, Burke, George, Robinson, & Webster, 1988; Burke, Brief, George, Roberson, & Webster, 1989), Warr's (1990) two-dimensional measure of anxiety–contentment and depression–enthusiasm, and

16

Daniels' (2000) measures of affective wellbeing featuring five first-order factors (anxiety–comfort, depression-pleasure, bored–enthusiastic, tiredness–vigor, and angry–placid) and two second-order factors (positive and negative affect). Fisher's (1997) Job Emotions Scales assess eight positive and eight negative specific emotions that occur commonly at work, without regard for arousal level. In experience-sampling research, where questionnaires must be shorter, organizational researchers often create their own affect scales by choosing four or five positive and negative mood items. Gee, Ballard, Yeo, and Neal (2012) have validated a brief measure of tense and energetic arousal suitable for use in experience-sampling studies.

Shirom's (2003, 2011) concept of *vigor* at work is defined as a positive affective experience involving feelings of physical strength, emotional energy, and cognitive liveliness. Shirom's vigor measure includes items such as "I feel full of pep" (physical strength), "I feel able to show warmth to others" (emotional energy), and "I feel mentally alert" (cognitive liveliness) while at work. One might argue that feeling lively and strong belong to the high positive affect dimension of subjective wellbeing, and that emotional energy for others is a component of social wellbeing.

Bakker and Oerlemans (2011) have mapped five commonly used indicators of high and low hedonic wellbeing at work on to the affect circumplex. Specifically, they suggest that engagement belongs in the high pleasantness high arousal quadrant, job satisfaction in the high pleasantness low arousal quadrant, workaholism in the low pleasantness high arousal quadrant, and burnout in the low pleasantness low arousal quadrant. Finally, happiness as an emotion is considered to be high pleasantness and moderate arousal.

On the whole, there would seem to be many acceptable choices for measuring satisfaction, affect, mood, and emotions in the workplace. Together, a global work attitude measure plus an affect at work measure may provide fairly thorough coverage of the workplace equivalent of subjective wellbeing. Eudaimonic wellbeing at work has historically attracted less attention, though there are measures that address eudaimonic aspects of the work experience. Interest in this component of overall wellbeing at work seems to be increasing and will be discussed below.

## Eudaimonic Wellbeing at Work

A number of constructs in organizational behavior display at least partial overlap with eudaimonic wellbeing. These include job involvement, work engagement, thriving, flow and intrinsic motivation, meaning in work, and calling at work.

*Job involvement* is an older construct that consists of identifying closely with one's work and basing identity and self-esteem on one's work role (Lodahl & Kejner, 1965). As the opposite of alienation or meaninglessness (Brown, 1996), job involvement seems to tap into the meaning in life portion of eudaimonic wellbeing. Typical job involvement items are, "I eat, live, and breathe my job," "The most important things that happen to me involve my present job," and "Usually I feel detached from my job" (Kanungo, 1982; Lodahl & Kejner, 1965; Saleh & Hosek, 1976).

*Work engagement* has become a very popular term over the past decade, though it means different things to different scholars (Macey & Schneider, 2008). Some conceptualizations of engagement appear to tap eudaimonic wellbeing, as the focus is on meaning, intrinsic motivation, and flow experiences. Kahn (1990, 1992) uses the term "personal engagement" to refer to the amount of authentic physical, cognitive, and emotional self that individuals devote to their work and the feelings of attentiveness, connection, integration, and focus they experience. The most commonly used conceptualization in organizational research describes engagement as

> a positive, fulfilling, work-related state of mind that is characterized by vigor, dedication, and absorption. Vigor is characterized by high levels of energy and mental resilience while working. Dedication refers to being strongly involved in one's work and experiencing a sense of significance, enthusiasm, and challenge. Absorption is characterized by being fully concentrated and happily engrossed in one's work, whereby time passes quickly and one has difficulties with detaching oneself from work.
>
> Bakker & Demerouti (2008), pp. 209–210

It is most often measured by the Utrecht Work Engagement Scale (Schaufeli, Salanova, González-romá, & Bakker, 2002). Sample items include, "At my work, I feel bursting with energy" (vigor), "I find the work that I do full of meaning and purpose" (dedication), and "When I am working, I forget everything else around me" (absorption). Vigor could also be viewed as belonging to the positive affect component of subjective wellbeing.

In sharp contrast, the Gallup Workplace Audit measure of engagement (Harter, Schmidt, & Hayes, 2002) asks for cognitive judgments of workplace conditions rather than the subjective experience of meaning, immersion, or flow. It includes items on role clarity, availability of recognition and praise, opportunities for learning and development, and caring relationships with others at work. While these may be among the antecedents of eudaimonic and social wellbeing at work, this operationalization of engagement is probably more similar to job satisfaction.

Spreitzer's concept of *thriving at work* has both subjective wellbeing and eudaimonic wellbeing components. Thriving is a second-order factor made up of feelings of vitality and the belief that one is learning, developing, and making progress toward self-actualization (Porath, Spreitzer, Gibson, & Garnett, 2012; Spreitzer, Sutcliffe, Dutton, Sonenshein, & Grant, 2005; Spreitzer & Sutcliffe, 2007). A revised 10-item thriving scale sums hedonic statements such as "I feel alive and vital" and "I feel alert and awake" with eudaimonic ones such as "I find myself learning often" and "I have developed a lot as a person" (Porath et al., 2012).

*Flow* occurs when one is totally absorbed in using one's skills to progress on a challenging task. Flow requires feelings of learning, development, and mastery, but is also hedonically very pleasurable (Csikszentmihalyi, 1990; Csikszentmihalyi, Abuhamdeh, & Nakamura, 2005). Measures of flow at work have been developed (Bakker, 2001; Jackson & Marsh, 1996), though some seem to confound the experience of flow with its hypothesized antecedents. *Intrinsic motivational states* are also deeply enjoyable, while meeting eudaimonic needs for competence and self-determination (Deci & Ryan, 1985; Ryan & Deci, 2000). Intrinsic motivation is often measured as the subjective experience of interest or enjoyment while engaged in a task, which may overlap with subjective wellbeing.

Another aspect of eudaimonic wellbeing, *meaning in work*, has attracted fragmented attention from a variety of disciplines, and has taken on greater importance with the rise of positive psychology. Rosso, Dekas, and Wrzesniewski (2010) provide a review. Pratt and Ashforth (2003) discuss two aspects of workplace meaning. They suggest that both contribute to identity, and that when both are present, identities are integrated and transcendent meaning is experienced. The first aspect is meaning *in* work, which is related to the work role itself—doing something important and self-actualizing. The second aspect is meaning *at* work, encompassing identification with social entities, such as the organization or other individuals or collectives encountered in the workplace. The latter may include some aspects of social wellbeing. A current operational definition of meaning in work is found in Steger, Dik, and Duffy's (2012) Work and Meaning Inventory (WAMI). This instrument contains 10 items in three subscales, which can be summed to create a total meaning score if desired. The subscales are positive meaning (e.g., "I understand how my work contributes to my life's meaning"), meaning-making through work (e.g., "My work helps me better understand myself"), and greater good motivation (e.g., "The work I do serves a greater purpose"). Another measure is the Comprehensive Meaningful Work Scale (CMWS) by Lips-Wiersma and Wright (2012).

A closely related concept is *calling at work*. Individuals may view their work activities as merely a job pursued to meet financial needs, as a career satisfying needs for achievement, advancement, and status, or as a calling in which the work is pursued for its own sake or for the purpose of contributing to a greater good (Bellah, Madsen, Sullivan, Swidler, & Tipton, 1985). Research on feeling a calling for one's work has accelerated in the past five years, with vocational psychologists particularly active in this area (Dik & Duffy, 2009; Duffy & Dik, 2012; Hall & Chandler, 2005; Wrzesniewski, McCauley, Rozin, & Schwartz, 1997). Elangovan, Pinder, and McLean (2010, p. 430) define calling as "A course of action in pursuit of prosocial intentions embodying the convergence of an individual's sense of what he or she would like to do, should do, and actually does." Dik, Eldridge, Steger, and Duffy (2012) have developed a 24-item measure of calling at work. The scale contains six subscales related to three aspects of calling. Each aspect is assessed as to the extent to which it is presently experienced, and then to the extent that the respondent wants or is seeking that aspect of calling. Sample items for the presence of calling subscales for the three aspects are: transcendent summons (e.g., "I was drawn by something beyond myself to pursue my current line of work"), purposeful work (e.g., "I see my career as a path to purpose in life"), and prosocial orientation (e.g., "Making a difference for others is the primary motivation in my career").

The feeling that one is living a calling for work, or that one's work is meaningful, is clearly part of eudaimonic wellbeing. There is evidence that these concepts are closely related to each other and to other measures of various aspects of wellbeing at work such as job satisfaction and career commitment (Duffy, Bott, Allan, Torrey, & Dik, 2012). As such, calling or meaning should be included in a comprehensive conceptualization of wellbeing at work. When meaning or calling includes serving or benefiting others, there may be overlap with social wellbeing, which will be discussed next.

## Social Wellbeing at Work

Social wellbeing at work is the third leg in the wellbeing tripod. While early researchers paid attention to social relationships at work (e.g., the Hawthorn studies), the era of behaviorism and the subsequent cognitive revolution paid little heed to this aspect of worklife. Grant and Parker (2009) point out a parallel history in research on job design, with early work including consideration of sociotechnical systems and required and optional interaction at work. However, these aspects were subsequently ignored in research focusing solely on the effects of non-social task characteristics on individual reactions and behavior. The pendulum has begun to swing back, with social, relational, and prosocial aspects of job design again gaining attention (Grant, 2007, 2008; Humphrey, Nahrgang, & Morgeson, 2007; Morgeson & Humphrey, 2006).

Ragins and Dutton (2007) have criticized the apparent belief of organizational scholars that relationships are important in the rest of life but that this need is somehow suspended in the workplace. Recent writing on "quality connections" as sources of energy and wellbeing at work have begun to counter this belief (Dutton, 2003; Dutton & Heaphy, 2003). Quality connections can include both positive short-term transactions and longer term relationships with others encountered while working. Spreitzer et al. (2005) explain that "heedful relating" to others at work in a climate of trust and respect is integrally related to eudaimonic wellbeing as it enables growth and thriving. Rath and Harter's trade book on wellbeing (2010) reports that individuals are more engaged at work when their boss cares about them as a person, they have a best friend at work, and they are able to spend time at work with others whose company they enjoy.

The conceptualization and measurement of social wellbeing at work is in its infancy, though some existing constructs may provide a modest start in this direction. These include satisfaction with peers as well as satisfaction and exchange relationships with leaders. Another relevant construct is social support, which has been studied as a potential buffer against workplace stress, or a predictor of wellbeing, but is less often considered a part of wellbeing in itself. Social support is often conceptualized as having two main dimensions: emotional support and instrumental support. There is evidence that giving as well as receiving social support is important for wellbeing (e.g., Shakespeare-Finch & Obst, 2011). None of these constructs quite captures the critical concept of having strong and satisfying relationships with others in the workplace. An additional aspect of social wellbeing at work might include feelings of belonging to and being embedded in work communities, be they teams, departments, or the whole of the organization. Affective and normative organizational commitment and group cohesion may be relevant constructs. Finally, experiencing transient but satisfying and helpful social encounters with others such as customers may also be important for social wellbeing at work, especially for individuals with strong social or prosocial motives. A great deal more research is needed to better conceptualize social wellbeing in the workplace and to determine its antecedents and consequences.

## Other Models of Wellbeing at Work

Nash and Stevenson (2004, p. 104) studied hundreds of managers and professionals to uncover the causes of lasting personal and professional fulfillment. They describe four critical aspects:

> happiness (feelings of pleasure or contentment about your life); achievement (accomplishments that compare favorably against similar goals others have strived for); significance (the sense that you've made a positive impact on people you care about); and legacy (a way to establish your values or accomplishments so as to help others find future success).

Furthermore, they point out that it is not possible to maximize all four together, and that attempts to maximize one or two invariably come at a cost to some of the others. The key to "success that lasts" appears to be maintaining a healthy balance across all four aspects of wellbeing.

## Measuring Wellbeing at Work

Measures and conceptualizations of wellbeing at work may vary in time frame and in breadth (Warr, 2013). In terms of time frame, the typical approach of organizational scholars is to think in terms of relatively stable differences between people. Wellbeing might be measured once and expected to remain constant over a considerable period of time, as is usually the case for measures of job satisfaction, organizational commitment, or calling. When comprehensive measurement of wellbeing is contemplated, including subjective, eudaimonic, and social aspects, this stable level is probably most appropriate. An alternative is to measure wellbeing in a shorter time frame, such as weekly or daily, or even at a momentary level (Reis, Sheldon, Gable, Roscoe, & Ryan, 2000), using diary or experience-sampling methods. Meaningful variance exists at all levels, with the flow states and the affective components of subjective wellbeing particularly likely to fluctuate over shorter periods of time (Fisher, 2010). Job satisfaction, engagement, and thriving have also been found to vary within person from day to day (e.g., Ilies & Judge, 2004; Niessen, Sonnentag, & Sach, 2012; Sonnentag, 2003).

Breadth is a key issue in conceptualizing and measuring wellbeing. Figure 2.1 and the discussions above suggest a number of aspects of wellbeing, far more than are usually assessed in organizational research on wellbeing. Those studying wellbeing at work have defined the construct in many and inconsistent ways. It will be helpful to reach consensus on the components of overall wellbeing and to adopt consistent terminology for different aspects of wellbeing. This will enable researchers to be very clear on exactly what part of total wellbeing they are theorizing about and measuring. There is a place for both separate measures of components of wellbeing, and for general measures that combine many aspects to index overall wellbeing.

Judge and Kammeyer-Mueller (2012) provide a cogent discussion of the use of general versus specific measures in organizational research. (See Ones and Viswesvaran (1996) for a similar discussion of the bandwidth versus fidelity trade-off in the case of personality dimensions.) Judge and Kammeyer-Mueller suggest that most psychological constructs are hierarchical in nature. A higher order factor such as overall wellbeing at work may be indicated by a number of more specific lower order dimensions. In the case of wellbeing, research suggests that subjective wellbeing, eudaimonic wellbeing, and social wellbeing may be key dimensions, and that each of these in turn has subdimensions.

Whether to adopt broadband or specific measures depends on the research questions being asked. If the other constructs in the research model are specific and narrow, then specific and narrow measures of aspects of wellbeing might be most appropriate. A number of measures of specific aspects of wellbeing have been mentioned earlier in this chapter. If the other constructs in the model are broad, then general measures of wellbeing may be most suitable. Note that often the most predictive power and ability to generalize is supplied by research using broad measures (Judge & Kammeyer-Mueller, 2012). For instance, Harrison, Newman, and Roth (2006) found that a higher order construct comprising both satisfaction and commitment quite strongly predicted a behavior composite consisting of core job performance, contextual performance, lateness, absenteeism, and turnover.

Fisher (2010) suggested that a complete measure of overall happiness at work would consist of overall job satisfaction, affective organizational commitment, and work engagement. This combination would assess attitudes toward the organization as a whole (affective commitment), attitudes about the job including contextual elements (job satisfaction), and intrinsic engagement and enjoyment of the work itself (engagement). A comprehensive measure of wellbeing at work should be broader still. In addition to the

**Table 2.1.**  Flourishing Scale Applied to Work.

| Diener et al. items | Suggested rewording for flourishing at work |
|---|---|
| I lead a purposeful and meaningful life | My work life is purposeful and meaningful |
| My social relationships are supportive and rewarding | My social relationships at and through work are supportive and rewarding |
| I am engaged and interested in my daily activities | I am engaged and interested in my daily work activities |
| I actively contribute to the happiness and wellbeing of others | I actively contribute to the happiness and wellbeing of others through my work |
| I am competent and capable in the activities that are important to me | I am competent and capable in the work activities that are important to me |
| I am a good person and live a good life | I am a good employee and have a good work life |
| I am optimistic about my future | I am optimistic about my future at work |
| People respect me | People at work respect me |

From Diener et al. (2010).

above indicators of happiness, a complete measure should also assess aspects of both eudaimonic and social wellbeing.

Broad measures of wellbeing will inherently tap a variety of different experiences and might look quite messy to those accustomed to tidy, single-factor measures. Comprehensive wellbeing at work scales assessing all the aspects shown in Figures 2.1 and/or 2.2 do not appear to exist at this point in time. However, there are a few existing scales that could be a starting point for building such a measure. One option for researchers wanting an overall wellbeing at work measure would be to modify the Diener et al. (2010) short scale to assess flourishing. This scale is quite broadband and includes items relevant to basic human needs for competence, relatedness, self-acceptance, purpose, and optimism. It appears to have some overlap with core self-evaluations, psychological capital, and engagement, while adding the important dimension of social wellbeing and prosocial impact. Diener and colleagues' (2010) items are shown on the left side of Table 2.1. It is possible that this scale could be adapted for the workplace with minor rewording similar to that suggested on the right side of Table 2.1. However, the flourishing scale does not include the subjective wellbeing aspects of overall satisfaction or positive and negative affect, so it may need to be supplemented with other measures of these aspects. Diener et al. (2010)

**Table 2.2.** Work Satisfaction Items from the Work Well-Being Questionnaire.

Is your work fulfilling?
Do your daily work activities give you a sense of direction and meaning?
Does your work bring a sense of satisfaction?
Does your work increase your sense of self-worth?
Does your job allow you to recraft your job to suit your strengths?
Does your work make you feel that, as a person, you are flourishing?
Do you feel capable and effective in your work on a day-to-day basis?
Does your work offer challenges to advance your skills?
Do you feel you have some level of independence at work?
Do you feel personally connected to your organization's values?

From Parker and Hyett (2011).

provide such a measure, the SPANE, though it is not specific to the workplace. As mentioned above, workplace measures of affect are available from Burke et al. (1989), Daniels (2000), Gee et al. (2012), van Katwyk et al. (2000), and Warr (1990).

Another starting point is the Parker and Hyett (2011) Work Well-Being Questionnaire. This instrument was designed to provide the elusive complete measure of workplace wellbeing. It includes four dimensions: work satisfaction, organizational respect for the employee (e.g., "Do you feel that your organization respects the staff?"), employer care (e.g., "Is your boss caring?"), and intrusion of work into private life. The latter three scales appear to deal more with antecedents of wellbeing rather than the experience of wellbeing itself. However, the first scale, despite being called work satisfaction, does include both hedonic and eudaimonic wellbeing items (Table 2.2) Additional items on affective experience and on social wellbeing would be needed to round out this measure.

## Conclusion

Other than Diener's (1984) well-accepted three aspects of subjective well-being, we seem to have little consensus on how best to define and measure wellbeing. Wellbeing at work has meant whatever each researcher defined it as in his or her study. For instance, one recent article used a single-item measure of job satisfaction together with a measure of emotional exhaustion to operationalize wellbeing. I suggest that it is time to agree on a more comprehensive definition of overall wellbeing at work, perhaps the one shown in Figure 2.2. The component of subjective wellbeing at work parallels Diener's conceptualization and consists of judgments of satisfaction and similar attitudes, plus the experience of more positive and less negative moods and emotions at work. Eudaimonic wellbeing is also important, and includes the experience of growth, meaning/purpose, engagement, and competence through work. While there are existing measures of some aspects of eudaimonic wellbeing, we do not yet have well-accepted instruments for measuring the entirety of this component of wellbeing in the workplace. Finally, social wellbeing at work should also be included. This component has received the least attention in our literature to date. It consists of feeling embedded in meaningful communities and having satisfying short-term interactions and long-term relationships with others. It will be useful to have a single instrument to assess all of these components, both dimensionally and perhaps in a composite overall wellbeing score. A broader conceptualization of wellbeing at work will encourage research on how to best maximize this desirable state for employees (Grant et al., 2007). It will also allow researchers to document the extent to which overall wellbeing at work predicts important outcomes for organizations.

# References

Bakker, A. B. (2001). *Questionnaire for the assessment of work-related flow: The WOLF*. Utrecht: Department of Social and Organizational Psychology, Utrecht University.

Bakker, A., & Demerouti, E. (2008). Towards a model of work engagement. *Career Development International, 13*, 209–223.

Bakker, A. B., & Oerlemans, W. (2011). Subjective well-being in organizations. In K. S. Cameron & G. M. Spreitzer (Eds.), *The Oxford handbook of positive organizational scholarship* (pp. 178–189). New York: Oxford University Press.

Baumeister, R. F., & Leary, M. R. (1995). The need to belong: Desire for interpersonal attachments as a fundamental human motivation. *Psychological Bulletin, 117*, 497–529.

Bellah, R. N., Madsen, R., Sullivan, W. M., Swidler, A., & Tipton, S. M. (1985). *Habits of the heart: Individualism and commitment in American life*. New York: Harper & Row.

Bradburn, N. M. (1969). *The structure of psychological well-being*. Chicago: Alpine.

Brief, A. (1998). *Attitudes in and around organizations*. Thousand Oaks, CA: Sage.

Brief, A. P., Burke, M. J., George, G. M., Robinson, B. S., & Webster, J. (1988). Should negative affectivity remain an unmeasured variable in the study of job stress? *Journal of Applied Psychology, 73*, 193–198.

Brief, A., & Roberson, L. (1989). Job attitude organization: An exploratory study. *Journal of Applied Social Psychology, 19*, 717–727.

Brief, A. P., & Weiss, H. M. (2002). Organizational behavior: Affect in the workplace. *Annual Review of Psychology, 53*, 279–308.

Brown, S. P. (1996). A meta-analysis and review of organizational research on job involvement. *Psychological Bulletin, 120*(21), 235.

Buckingham, M., & Clifton, D. O. (2001). *Now, discover your strengths*. New York: Free Press.

Burke, M. J., Brief, A. P., George, J. M., Roberson, L., & Webster, J. (1989). Measuring affect at work: Confirmatory analyses of competing mood structures with conceptual linkage to cortical regulatory systems. *Journal of Personality and Social Psychology, 57*, 1091–1102.

Cameron, K. S., Dutton, J. E., & Quinn, R. E. (Eds.) (2003). *Positive organizational scholarship*. San Francisco: Berrett-Kohler.

Cameron, K. S., & Spreitzer, G. M. (2011). *The Oxford handbook of positive organizational scholarship*. New York: Oxford University Press.

Cook, J. D., Hepworth, S. J., Wall, T. D., & Warr, P. B. (1981). *The experience of work*. London: Academic Press.

Csikszentmihalyi, M. (1990). *Flow: The psychology of optimal experience*. New York: Harper Perennial.

Csikszentmihalyi, M., Abuhamdeh, S., & Nakamura, J. (2005). Flow. In A. J. Elliot & C. S. Dweck (Eds.), *Handbook of competence and motivation* (pp. 598–608). New York: The Guilford Press.

Daniels, K. (2000). Measures of five aspects of affective well-being at work. *Human Relations, 53*, 275–294.

Deci, E. L., & Ryan, R. M. (1985). *Intrinsic motivation and self-determination in human behavior*. New York: Plenum.

Diener, E. (1984). Subjective well-being. *Psychological Bulletin, 95*, 542–575.

Diener, E. (2000). Subjective well-being. *American Psychologist, 55*, 34–43.

Diener, E., Emmons, R. A., Larsen, R. J., & Griffin, S. (1985). The satisfaction with life scale. *Journal of Personality Assessment, 49*, 71–75.

Diener, E., Sandvik, E., & Pavot, W. (1991). Happiness is the frequency, not the intensity, of positive versus negative affect. In F. Strack, M. Argyle, & N. Schwarz (Eds.), *Subjective well-being: An interdisciplinary perspective* (pp. 119–139). New York: Pergamon.

Diener, E., Wirtz, D., Tov, W., Kim-Prieto, C., Choi, D. W., Oishi, S., & Biswas-Diener, R. (2010). New well-being measures: Short scales to assess flourishing and positive and negative feelings. *Social Indicators Research, 97*, 143–156.

Dik, B., & Duffy, R. (2009). Calling and vocation at work: Definitions and prospects for research and practice. *The Counseling Psychologist, 37*, 424–450.

Dik, B. J., Eldridge, B. M., Steger, M. F., & Duffy, R. D. (2012). Development and validation of the calling and vocation questionnaire (CVQ) and brief calling scale (BCS). *Journal of Career Assessment*, *20*, 242–263.

Duffy, R. D., Bott, E. M., Allan, B. A., Torrey, C. L., & Dik, B. J. (2012). Perceiving a calling, living a calling, and job satisfaction: Testing a moderated, multiple mediator model. *Journal of Counseling Psychology*, *59*, 50–59.

Duffy, R. D., & Dik, B. J. (2012). Research on work as a calling: Introduction to the special issue. *Journal of Career Assessment*, *20*, 239–241.

Dutton, J. E. (2003). *Energize your workplace: How to create and sustain high-quality connections at work*. San Francisco: Jossey-Bass.

Dutton, J. E., & Heaphy, E. (2003). High quality connections. In K. S. Cameron, J. E Dutton, & R. E. Quinn (Eds.), *Positive organizational scholarship: Foundations of a new discipline* (pp. 263–278). San Francisco: Berrett-Koehler Publishers.

Elangovan, A. R., Pinder, C. C., & McLean, M. (2010). Callings and organizational behavior. *Journal of Vocational Behavior*, *76*, 428–440.

Fields, D. L. (2002). *Taking the measure of work*. Thousand Oaks, CA: Sage.

Fisher, C. D. (1997). *What do people feel and how should we measure it?* Paper presented at the Second Biennial Australian Industrial and Organisational Psychology Conference, Melbourne.

Fisher, C. D. (2000). Mood and emotions while working: Missing pieces of job satisfaction? *Journal of Organizational Behavior*, *21*, 185–202.

Fisher, C. D. (2010). Happiness at work. *International Journal of Management Reviews*, *12*, 384–412.

Fredrickson, B. L., & Losada, M. F. (2005). Positive affect and the complex dynamics of human flourishing. *American Psychologist*, *60*, 678–686.

Gallagher, M. W., Lopez, S. J., & Preacher, K. J. (2009). The hierarchical structure of well-being. *Journal of Personality*, *77*, 1025–1050.

Gee, P., Ballard, T., Yeo, G., & Neal, A. (2012). Measuring affect over time: The momentary affect scale. In N. M. Ashkanasy, C. E. J. Härtel, & W. J. Zerbe (Eds.), *Research on emotion in organizations, Volume 8: Experiencing and managing emotions in the workplace* (pp. 141–173). Bingley: Emerald Group.

Grant, A. M. (2007). Relational job design and the motivation to make a prosocial difference. *Academy of Management Review*, *32*, 393–417.

Grant, A. M. (2008). Designing jobs to do good: Dimensions and psychological consequences of prosocial job characteristics. *Journal of Positive Psychology*, *3*, 19–39.

Grant, A. M., Christianson, M. K., & Price, R. H. (2007). Happiness, health, or relationships? Managerial practices and employee well-being tradeoffs. *Academy of Management Perspectives*, *21*, 51–63.

Grant, A. M., & Parker, S. K. (2009). Redesigning work design theories: The rise of relational and proactive perspectives. *Academy of Management Annals*, *3*, 317–375.

Hall, D., & Chandler, D. (2005). Psychological success: When the career is a calling. *Journal of Organizational Behavior, 26*, 155–176.

Harrison, D. A., Newman, D. A., & Roth, P. L. (2006). How important are job attitudes? Meta-analytic comparisons of integrative behavioral outcomes and time sequences. *Academy of Management Journal, 49*, 305–325.

Harter, J. K., Schmidt, F. L., & Hayes, T. L. (2002). Business-unit-level relationship between employee satisfaction, employee engagement, and business outcomes: A meta-analysis. *Journal of Applied Psychology, 87*, 268–279.

Humphrey, S. E., Nahrgang, J. D., & Morgeson, F. P. (2007). Integrating motivational, social, and contextual work design features: A meta-analytic summary and theoretical extension of the work design literature. *Journal of Applied Psychology, 92*, 1332–1356.

Huppert, F. A., & So, T. T. C. (2013). Flourishing across Europe: Application of a new conceptual framework for defining well-being. *Social Indicators Research, 110*, 837–861.

Ilies, R., & Judge, T.A. (2004). An experience-sampling measure of job satisfaction and its relationships with affectivity, mood at work, job beliefs, and general job satisfaction. *European Journal of Work and Organizational Psychology, 13*, 367–389.

Jackson, S. A., & Marsh, H. (1996). Development and validation of a scale to measure optimal experience: The flow state scale. *Journal of Sport & Exercise Psychology, 18*, 17–35.

Judge, T. A., & Kammeyer-Mueller, J. D. (2012). General and specific measures in organizational behavior research: Considerations, examples, and recommendations for researchers. *Journal of Organizational Behavior, 33*, 171–174.

Kahn, W. A. (1990). Psychological conditions of personal engagement and disengagement at work. *Academy of Management Journal, 33*, 692–724.

Kahn, W. A. (1992). To be fully there: Psychological presence at work. *Human Relations, 45*, 321–349.

Kanungo, R. N. (1982). Measurement of job and work involvement. *Journal of Applied Psychology, 67*, 341–349.

Kashdan, T. B., Biswas-Diener, R., & King, L. A. (2008). Reconsidering happiness: The costs of distinguishing between hedonics and eudaimonia. *Journal of Positive Psychology, 3*, 219–233.

Kesebir, P., & Diener, E. (2008). In pursuit of happiness: Empirical answers to philosophical questions. *Perspectives on Psychological Science, 3*, 117–125.

Keyes, C. L. M. (1998). Social well-being. *Social Psychology Quarterly, 61*, 121–140.

Keyes, C. L. M. (2002). The mental health continuum: From languishing to flourishing in life. *Journal of Health and Social Behavior, 43*, 207–222.

Keyes, C. L. M. (2005). Mental illness and/or mental health? Investigating axioms of the complete state model of health. *Journal of Consulting and Clinical Psychology, 73*, 539–548.

King, L. A., Hicks, J. A., Krull, J. L., & Del Gaiso, A. K. (2006). Positive affect and the experience of meaning in life. *Journal of Personality and Social Psychology, 90*, 179–196.

Kunin, T. (1955). The construction of a new type of attitude measure. *Personnel Psychology*, *9*, 65–78.

Lips-Wiersma, M., & Wright, S. (2012). Measuring the meaning of meaningful work: Development and validation of the Comprehensive Meaningful Work Scale (CMWS). *Group & Organization Management*, *37*, 655–685.

Locke, E. A. (1976). The nature and causes of job satisfaction. In M. D. Dunnette (Ed.), *Handbook of Industrial and Organizational Psychology* (pp. 1297–1349). Chicago: Rand McNally.

Lodahl, T. M., & Kejner, M. (1965). The definition and measurement of job involvement. *Journal of Applied Psychology*, *49*, 24–33.

Luthans, F. (2002). The need for and meaning of positive organizational behavior. *Journal of Organizational Behavior*, *23*, 695–706.

Lyubomirsky, S., King, L., & Diener, E. (2005). The benefits of frequent positive affect: Does happiness lead to success? *Psychological Bulletin*, *131*, 803–855.

Lyubomirsky, S., & Lepper, H. S. (1999). A measure of subjective happiness: Preliminary reliability and construct validation. *Social Indicators Research*, *46*, 137–155.

Macey, W. H., & Schneider, B. (2008). The meaning of employee engagement. *Industrial and Organizational Psychology*, *1*, 3–30.

Meyer, J. P., Allen, N. J., & Smith, C. A. (1993). Commitment to organizations and occupations: Extension and test of a three-component conceptualization. *Journal of Applied Psychology*, *78*, 538–551.

Morgeson, F. P., & Humphrey, S. E. (2006). The Work Design Questionnaire (WDQ): Developing and validating a comprehensive measure for assessing job design and the nature of work. *Journal of Applied Psychology*, *91*, 1321–1339.

Mowday, R. T., Steers, R. M., & Porter, L. W. (1979). The measurement of organizational commitment. *Journal of Vocational Behavior*, *14*, 224–247.

Nash, L., & Stevenson, H. (2004). Success that lasts. *Harvard Business Review*, *82*, 102–109.

Nelson, D., & Cooper, C. P. (Eds.) (2007). *Positive organizational behavior*. London: Sage.

Niessen, C., Sonnentag, S., & Sach, F. (2012). Thriving at work—A diary study. *Journal of Organizational Behavior*, *33*, 468–487.

Ones, D. S., & Viswesvaran, C. (1996). Bandwidth-fidelity dilemma in personality measurement: Implications for personnel selection. *Journal of Organizational Behavior*, *17*, 609–626.

Organ, D. W., & Near, J. P. (1985). Cognition vs affect in measures of job satisfaction. *International Journal of Psychology*, *20*, 241–253.

Page, K. M., & Vella-Brodrick, D. A. (2009). The 'what,' 'why' and 'how' of employee well-being: A new model. *Social Indicators Research*, *90*, 441–458.

Parker, G. B., & Hyett, M. P. (2011). Measurement of well-being in the workplace: The development of the work well-being questionnaire. *Journal of Nervous and Mental Disease*, *199*, 394–397.

Porath, C., Spreitzer, G., Gibson, C., & Garnett, F. G. (2012). Thriving at work: Toward its measurement, construct validation, and theoretical refinement. *Journal of Organizational Behavior*, *33*, 250–275.

Pratt, M., & Ashforth, B. (2003). Fostering meaningfulness in working and at work. In K. Cameron, J. Dutton & R. Quinn (Eds.), *Positive organizational scholarship* (pp. 309–327). San Francisco: Berrett-Koehler Publishers.

Ragins, B. R., & Dutton, J. E. (2007). Positive relationships at work: An introduction and invitation. In J. E. Dutton, & B. R. Ragins (Eds.), *Exploring positive relationships at work* (pp. 3–25). Mahwah, NJ: Lawrence Erlbaum.

Raibley, J. (2012). Happiness is not well-being. *Journal of Happiness Studies*, *13*, 1105–1129.

Rath, T., & Harter, J. (2010). *Well being: The five essential elements*. New York: Gallup Press.

Reis, H. T., Sheldon, K. M., Gable, S. L., Roscoe, J., & Ryan, R. M. (2000). Daily well-being: The role of autonomy, competence, and relatedness. *Personality and Social Psychology Bulletin*, *26*, 419–435.

Rosso, B. D., Dekas, K. H., & Wrzesniewski, A. (2010). On the meaning of work: A theoretical integration and review. *Research in Organizational Behavior*, *30*, 91–127.

Russell, J. A. (1980). A circumplex model of affect. *Journal of Personality and Social Psychology*, *39*, 1161–1178.

Ryan, R. M., & Deci, E. L. (2000). Self-determination theory and the facilitation of intrinsic motivation, social development, and well-being. *American Psychologist*, *55*, 68–78.

Ryan, R. M., & Deci, E. L. (2001). On happiness and human potentials: A review of research on hedonic and eudaimonic well-being. *Annual Review of Psychology*, *52*, 141–166.

Ryff, C. D. (1989). Happiness is everything, or is it? Explorations on the meaning of psychological well-being. *Journal of Personality and Social Psychology*, *57*, 1069–1081.

Ryff, C. D., & Singer, B. H. (2008). Know thyself and become what you are: A eudaimonic approach to psychological well-being. *Journal of Happiness Studies*, *9*, 13–39.

Saleh, S. D., & Hosek, J. (1976). Job involvement: Concepts and measurements. *Academy of Management Journal*, *19*, 213–224.

Schaufeli, W. B., Salanova, M., González-romá, V., & Bakker, A. B. (2002). The measurement of engagement and burnout: A two sample confirmatory factor analytic approach. *Journal of Happiness Studies*, *3*, 71–92.

Schimmack, U. (2007). Methodological issues in the assessment of the affective component of subjective well being. In A. Ohn & M. van Dulmen (Eds.), *Handbook of methods in positive psychology* (pp. 96–110). Oxford: Oxford University Press.

Seligman, M. E. P. (2002). *Authentic happiness: Using the new positive psychology to realize your potential for lasting fulfillment*. New York: Free Press.

Seligman, M. (2011). *Flourishing*. New York: Free Press.

Seligman, M. E. P., & Csikszentmihalyi, M. (2000). Positive psychology: An introduction. *American Psychologist*, 55, 5–14.

Seligman, M. E. P., Steen, T. A., Park, N., & Peterson, C. (2005). Positive psychology progress: Empirical validation of interventions. *American Psychologist*, 60, 410–421.

Shakespeare-Finch, J., & Obst, P. L. (2011). The development of the 2-way social support scale: A measure of giving and receiving emotional and instrumental support. *Journal of Personality Assessment*, 93, 483–490.

Sheldon, K. M., & Elliot, A. J. (1999). Goal striving, need satisfaction, and longitudinal well-being: The self-concordance model. *Journal of Personality and Social Psychology*, 76, 482–497.

Sheldon, K. M., Ryan, R., & Reis, H. T. (1996). What makes for a good day? Competence and autonomy in the day and in the person. *Personality and Social Psychology Bulletin*, 22, 1270–1279.

Shirom, A. (2003). Feeling vigorous at work? The construct of vigor and the study of positive affect in organizations. In D. Ganster & P. L. Perrewe (Eds.), *Research in organizational stress and well-being* (pp. 135–165). Greenwich: JAI Press.

Shirom, A. (2011). Vigor as a positive affect at work: Conceptualizing vigor, its relations with related constructs, and its antecedents and consequences. *Review of General Psychology*, 15, 50–64.

Sonnentag, S. (2003). Recovery, work engagement, and proactive behavior: A new look at the interface between nonwork and work. *Journal of Applied Psychology*, 88, 518–528.

Spreitzer, G. M., & Sutcliffe, K. M. (2007). Thriving in organizations. In D. L. Nelson, & C. L. Cooper (Eds.), *Positive organizational behavior* (pp. 74–85). Thousand Oaks, CA: Sage Publications.

Spreitzer, G., Sutcliffe, K., Dutton, J., Sonenshein, S., & Grant, A. M. (2005). A socially embedded model of thriving at work. *Organization Science*, 16, 537–549.

Steger, M. F., Dik, B. J., & Duffy, R. D. (2012). Measuring meaningful work: The Work and Meaning Inventory (WAMI). *Journal of Career Assessment*, 20, 322–337.

Steger, M. F., Frazier, P., Oishi, S., & Kaler, M. (2006). The meaning in life questionnaire: Assessing the presence of and search for meaning in life. *Journal of Counseling Psychology*, 53, 80–93.

Steyer, M. F., Kashdan, T. B., & Oishi, S. (2008). Being good by doing good: Daily eudaimonic activity and well-being. *Journal of Research in Personality*, 42, 22–42.

Thompson, E. R. (2007). Development and validation of an internationally reliable short-form of the positive and negative affect schedule (PANAS). *Journal of Cross-Cultural Psychology*, 38, 227–242.

Van Katwyk, P. T., Fox, S., Spector, P. E., & Kelloway, E. K. (2000). Using the job-related affective well-being scale (JAWS) to investigate affective responses to work stressors. *Journal of Occupational Health Psychology*, 5, 219–230.

Warr, P. (1990). The measurement of well-being and other aspects of mental health. *Journal of Occupational Psychology, 63*, 193–210.

Warr, P. (2007). *Work, happiness, and unhappiness.* Mahwah, NJ: Lawrence Erlbaum.

Warr, P. (2013). How to think about and measure psychological well-being. In M. Wang, R. R. Sinclaire, & L. E. Tetrick (Eds.), *Research methods in occupational health psychology: Measurement, design, and data analysis* (pp. 76–90). New York: Psychology Press/Routledge.

Waterman, A. S. (2008). Reconsidering happiness: A eudaimonist's perspective. *Journal of Positive Psychology, 3*, 234–252.

Watson, D., Clark, L. A., & Tellegen, A. (1988). Development and validation of brief measures of positive and negative affect: The PANAS scale. *Journal of Personality and Social Psychology, 54*, 1063–1070.

Watson, D., & Tellegen, A. (1985). Toward a consensual structure of mood. *Psychological Bulletin, 98*, 219–202.

Weiss, H. M. (2002). Deconstructing job satisfaction: Separating evaluations, beliefs, and affective experiences. *Human Resource Management Review, 12*, 173–194.

Weiss, H. M., & Brief, A. P. (2001). Affect at work: an historical perspective. In R. L. Payne, & C. L. Cooper (Eds.), *Emotions at work: Theory, research, and application* (pp. 133–164). London: Wiley.

Wright, T. A. (2006). The emergence of job satisfaction in organizational behavior: A historical overview of the dawn of job attitude research. *Journal of Management History, 12*, 262–277.

Wrzesniewski, A., McCauley, C., Rozin, P., & Schwartz, B. (1997). Jobs, careers, and callings: People's relations to their work. *Journal of Research in Personality*, 21–33.

# Part 2

# Resources, Coping, and Control

# 3

# Job Demands–Resources Theory

## Arnold B. Bakker

Erasmus University Rotterdam, The Netherlands and
Lingnan University, Hong Kong

## Evangelia Demerouti

Eindhoven University of Technology, The Netherlands

## Introduction

Why do some employees burn out or get bored by their work, whereas others are so enthusiastic about their work that time seems to fly? The question of what causes job stress and what motivates people has received a lot of research attention during the past five decades. Job design theory has played an important role in this respect. "Job design" was originally defined as the set of opportunities and constraints structured into assigned tasks and responsibilities that affect how an employee accomplishes and experiences work (Hackman & Oldham, 1980). Thus, job design scholars tried to unravel which job characteristics make people feel satisfied with their job, and motivated to reach organizational goals. Nowadays, job design is defined more broadly as "encapsulating the processes and outcomes of how work is structured, organized, experienced, and enacted" (Grant, Fried, & Juillerat, 2010, p. 418). According to Grant and his colleagues, this broader definition opens the door for dynamic, emergent roles as opposed to merely emphasizing static job descriptions composed of fixed tasks assigned by management (see also, Parker, Wall, & Cordery, 2001).

*Work and Wellbeing: Wellbeing: A Complete Reference Guide*, Volume III.
Edited by Peter Y. Chen and Cary L. Cooper.
© 2014 John Wiley & Sons, Ltd. Published 2014 by John Wiley & Sons, Inc.
DOI: 10.1002/9781118539415.wbwell03

In this chapter, we discuss job demands–resources (JD-R) theory, which represents an extension of the job demands–resources model (Bakker & Demerouti, 2007; Demerouti, Bakker, Nachreiner, & Schaufeli, 2001) and is inspired by job design and job stress theories. Whereas job design theories have often ignored the role of job stressors or demands, job stress models have largely ignored the motivating potential of job resources. JD-R theory combines the two research traditions, and explains how job demands and resources have unique and multiplicative effects on job stress and motivation. In addition, JD-R theory proposes reversed causal effects: whereas burned-out employees may create more job demands over time for themselves, engaged workers mobilize their own job resources to stay engaged. Before we outline the building blocks of JD-R theory and possible JD-R interventions, we will discuss four early models that have had an important impact on our thinking.

# Early Models

Interestingly, early models of work motivation and job stress have largely ignored each other's literatures. Since JD-R theory combines principles from both literatures, we briefly discuss four influential models, namely two-factor theory (Herzberg, 1966), the job characteristics model (Hackman & Oldham, 1980), the demand–control model (Karasek, 1979), and the effort–reward imbalance model (Siegrist, 1996).

*Two-factor theory.*
Herzberg's (1966; Herzberg, Mausner, & Snyderman, 1959) two-factor theory suggests that there are two independent sets of circumstances that drive employee satisfaction and motivation, namely *hygiene factors* and *motivator factors*. Whereas hygiene factors (also called dissatisfiers), if absent, are postulated to make employees unsatisfied at work, motivator factors (also called satisfiers) are postulated to make employees feel good about their jobs. Using data from engineers and accountants, Herzberg found the following hygiene factors: company policies, supervision, salary, interpersonal relations, and working conditions. He compiled this list from responses given to the question "What makes you feel bad about your job?" The items in this list needed to be present to avoid dissatisfaction. In contrast, motivator factors included achievement, recognition, nature of work, responsibility, and advancement, all of which presumably promote satisfaction. Thus, an

increase in hygiene factors is expected not to promote satisfaction and a lack of one or more of them will promote dissatisfaction. For example, a low salary, or one perceived as lower than one's coworkers, would be expected to increase dissatisfaction. However, once a fair level of pay is established, money is no longer a significant motivator for job satisfaction and performance. According to the two-factor theory, without motivators, employees will perform their jobs as required, but with motivators, employees will increase their effort and exceed the minimum requirements.

Research on the two-factor theory has challenged the validity of distinguishing between hygiene factors and motivators. The critique boils down to the contention that evidence for the two-factor model depends on the method used, and that the model has received limited support for predicting job satisfaction (Ambrose & Kulik, 1999). However, an important contribution of Herzberg's work is that he made researchers and practitioners aware of the potential of job enrichment; jobs can be redesigned, enlarged, and enriched to increase motivation and job satisfaction (Grant et al., 2010).

*The job characteristics model.*
The job characteristics model (Hackman & Oldham, 1976, 1980) examines individual responses to jobs (e.g., job satisfaction, sickness absenteeism, personnel turnover) as a function of job characteristics, moderated by individual characteristics (Roberts & Glick, 1981). Hackman and Lawler (1971) define the core job characteristics as: skill variety (breadth of skills used at work), task significance (impact that the work has on the lives or work of others), task identity (opportunity to complete an entire piece of work), feedback (amount of information provided about effectiveness of job performance), and autonomy (degree to which the job provides substantial freedom, independence, and discretion in determining goal-directed behavior at work).

Core job characteristics are expected to influence job satisfaction and intrinsic work motivation through the attainment of three critical psychological states (CPSs; Hackman & Lawler, 1971; Hackman & Oldham, 1976, 1980): experienced meaningfulness of the work, experienced responsibility for outcomes, and knowledge of the results of work activities. However, most research has omitted the critical psychological states from the model, focusing instead on the direct impact of the core job characteristics on the outcomes. Meta-analyses have demonstrated that the presence of the core job characteristics, in particular job autonomy, leads to positive employee attitudinal outcomes (Fried & Ferris, 1987; Parker & Wall, 1998). Further, research on the mediating role of the three CPSs in the relationship between job characteristics and attitudinal outcomes offers only partial support for this hypothesis (e.g., Renn & Vandenberg, 1995; see, for a meta-analysis, Behson, Eddy, & Lorenzet, 2000). The model further suggests that the relationship between job characteristics and CPSs as well as between CPSs and outcomes is stronger for individuals with high growth need strength (i.e., those who are highly motivated to learn and grow on the job). Evidence for the latter hypothesis is inconsistent (Graen, Scandura, & Graen, 1986).

*The demand–control model.*

A central hypothesis in the demand–control model (DCM; Karasek, 1979; Karasek & Theorell, 1990) is that strain will be highest in jobs characterized by the combination of high job demands and low job control. Such jobs are called "high-strain jobs." In contrast, the active learning hypothesis in the DCM states that task enjoyment, learning, and personal growth will be highest in jobs characterized by the combination of high job demands and high job control. Although such jobs are intensively demanding, employees with sufficient decision latitude are expected to use all available skills, enabling a conversion of aroused energy into action through effective problem solving. Karasek has labeled these jobs "active-learning jobs." Like the job characteristics model, the DCM has acquired a prominent position in the literature. However, the empirical evidence for the model is mixed (De Lange, Taris, Kompier, Houtman, & Bongers, 2003; Van der Doef & Maes, 1999). Additive effects of job demands and job control on employee wellbeing and motivation have often been found, but many studies failed to produce the interaction effects proposed by the DCM. Moreover, in a reanalysis of the 64 studies reviewed by Van der Doef and Maes (1999), Taris (2006) showed that only 9 out of 90 tests provided support for the demand × control interaction effect. Several scholars attribute this lack of evidence to the conceptual and methodological limitations of the model (e.g., Carayon, 1993; De Jonge, Janssen, & Breukelen, 1996; Taris, Kompier, De Lange, Schaufeli, & Schreurs, 2003).

*The effort–reward imbalance model.*

Finally, the effort–reward imbalance (ERI) model (Siegrist, 1996) emphasizes the reward, rather than the control structure of work. The ERI model assumes that job stress is the result of an imbalance between effort (extrinsic job demands and intrinsic motivation to meet these demands) and reward (in terms of salary, esteem reward, and security/career opportunities—i.e., promotion prospects, job security, and status consistency). The basic assumption is that a lack of reciprocity between effort and reward (i.e., high effort/low reward conditions) will lead to arousal and stress (cf. equity theory; Walster, Walster, & Berscheid, 1978), which may, in turn, lead to cardiovascular risks and other stress reactions. Thus, having a demanding but unstable job, and achieving at a high level without being offered any promotion prospects, are examples of a stressful imbalance. The combination of high effort and low reward at work was indeed found to be a risk factor for cardiovascular health, subjective health, mild psychiatric disorders, and burnout (Siegrist, 2008; Tsutsumi & Kawakami, 2004). Unlike the DCM, the ERI model introduces a personal component in the model as well. Overcommitment is defined as a set of attitudes, behaviors, and emotions reflecting excessive striving in combination with a strong desire for approval and esteem. According to the model, overcommitment may moderate the association between effort–reward imbalance and employee wellbeing. Thus, personality is expected to be able to further qualify the interaction between effort and reward. Some evidence for this pattern has been reported (e.g., De Jonge, Bosma, Peter, & Siegrist, 2000).

## Critique on Early Models

There are four, partly overlapping problems with earlier models of job stress and work motivation. First, each of the models has one-sided attention for either job stress or work motivation. A second point of critique is that each of the models is relatively simple, and does not take into consideration the viewpoints of other existing models. Often, only a few variables are expected to describe all possible working environments. Third, each of the early models is static: it is assumed that the models with the specific variables hold across all possible work environments. Finally, the nature of jobs is rapidly changing, and existing job stress or motivation models do not take this volatility into account. Below, we discuss each of these points in a little more detail.

### *One-sidedness.*
Research on job stress and work motivation has typically developed in two separate literatures. This means that research on motivation often ignores research on stress and vice versa. We see similar trends in organizations, where human resources managers focus on employee motivation and job satisfaction, and where company doctors and medical officers focus on

job stress and sickness absence. However, it is evident that job stress is significantly related to work motivation. For example, Leiter (1993) has argued and found that employees who are stressed by their work and become chronically exhausted become demotivated and are inclined to withdraw psychologically from their work. Exhausted employees become cynical about whether their work contributes anything and wonder about the meaning of their work (see also, Bakker, Van Emmerik, & Van Riet, 2008). Furthermore, we will see later in this chapter that working conditions fostering job stress interact with working conditions fostering motivation.

*Simplicity.*
The basic assumption of both the DCM and the ERI model is that job demands often lead to job stress when certain job resources are lacking (autonomy in the DCM; salary, esteem reward, and security/career opportunities in the ERI model). In general, one may argue that the strength of these models lies in their simplicity. This can also be seen as a weakness, since the complex reality of working organizations is reduced to only a handful of variables. This simplicity does no justice to reality. Indeed, research on job stress and burnout has produced a laundry list of job demands and (lack of) job resources as potential predictors, not only including high psychological and physical job demands, lack of rewards, and lack of autonomy, but also emotional demands, low social support, lack of supervisory support, and lack of performance feedback, to name just a few (Alarcon, 2011; Lee & Ashforth, 1996). This raises the question whether the early models are applicable to the universe of job positions, and whether in certain occupations other combinations of demands and (lack of) resources than the ones incorporated in the models may be responsible for job stress (Bakker & Demerouti, 2007). Whereas the DCM and the ERI model have as their basic premise that specific job demands (particularly work overload, work pressure) interact with certain resources, the motivational models only incorporate certain job resources and do not reserve any role for job demands. We would argue that in all jobs some challenging demands are needed, because otherwise work engagement may be thwarted and job performance undermined.

*Static character.*
A third point of critique is the static character of the models. Thus, it is unclear why autonomy is the most important resource for employees in the DCM (and social support in the extended demand–control–support

model; Johnson & Hall, 1988). Would it not be possible that in certain work environments totally different job resources prevail (for example inspirational leadership in an Internet start-up, or open communication among reporters of a TV station)? Remarkable in this context is that the ERI model (Siegrist, 2008) postulates salary, esteem reward, and status control as the most important job resources that may compensate for the impact of job demands on strain. In a similar vein, it is unclear why work pressure or (intrinsic and extrinsic) effort should always be the most important job demands, whereas other aspects are neglected. This is a drawback, since we know that in certain occupations (e.g., teachers, nurses, doctors, waitresses), emotional demands are extremely important (Bakker & Demerouti, 2007), whereas in other occupations these demands are less prevalent. For example, the work of software engineers and air-traffic controllers is more about the processing of information than about working with people (Demerouti et al., 2001), and therefore cognitive job demands are more important in these occupations. Similarly, the job characteristics model (Hackman & Oldham, 1980) focuses exclusively on five specific job characteristics, namely skill variety, task significance, task identity, feedback, and autonomy. Although Hackman and Oldham had good reasons to choose these five job resources as important "enrichers" of one's work environment, it is not very difficult to come up with other valuable job resources. For example, several studies have shown that opportunities for development and supervisory coaching are important motivators (Bakker & Demerouti, 2007), and research on the ERI model has indicated the importance of job security and distributive as well as procedural fairness.

*Changing nature of jobs.*
A fourth point of critique concerns the fact that the nature of jobs is changing rapidly. Contemporary jobs seem to be more complex in terms of functions and networking structures, with the role of information technology being more important than ever to execute one's job (Demerouti, Derks, Ten Brummelhuis, & Bakker, in press), and with individuals negotiating own work content and conditions. This changing nature of jobs also means that different working conditions might prevail than was the case four or five decades ago, when the early models were developed. Cognitive work has come to be an important demanding work characteristic that is relevant for many jobs, while opportunities for development and learning are resources that individuals seek in their jobs nowadays. Moreover, in order for organizations to keep valuable employees they negotiate with them distinct working

conditions (i.e., idiosyncratic deals; Rousseau, 2005) such that they can retain them in their workforce. Consequently, it is an illusion to think that identifying a few work characteristics in a model on job stress or motivation would be sufficient to describe the complexity of contemporary jobs. Theories that allow more flexibility in terms of the work-related factors that are potentially relevant offer a more realistic representation of the work reality.

## Conclusion

Early models of job stress and motivation have produced valuable insights with regard to what influences employee wellbeing. However, influential models in both the stress and motivation literatures have largely neglected each other. We argue that stress and motivation should be considered simultaneously, and that the four main points of critique on the early models should be addressed: the one-sidedness, simplicity, and static character of the models, as well as the changing nature of jobs.

## Job Demands–Resources Theory

During the past decade, the number of studies with the job demands–resources (JD-R) model (Bakker & Demerouti, 2007; Demerouti & Bakker, 2011; Demerouti et al., 2001) has steadily increased. The model has been used to predict job burnout (e.g., Bakker et al., 2005, 2008; Demerouti et al., 2001), organizational commitment, work enjoyment (Bakker, Van Veldhoven, & Xanthopoulou, 2010), connectedness (Lewig, Xanthopoulou, Bakker, Dollard, & Metzer, 2007), and work engagement (Bakker, Hakanen, Demerouti, & Xanthopoulou, 2007; Hakanen, Bakker, & Schaufeli, 2006). In addition, the JD-R model has been used to predict consequences of these experiences, including sickness absenteeism (e.g., Bakker, Demerouti, De Boer, & Schaufeli, 2003a; Clausen, Nielsen, Gomes Carneiro, & Borg, 2012; Schaufeli, Bakker, & Van Rhenen, 2009), and job performance (e.g., Bakker et al., 2008; Bakker, Demerouti, & Verbeke, 2004). In fact, we have now seen so many studies, new propositions, and several meta-analyses on the JD-R model (Crawford, LePine, & Rich, 2010; Halbesleben, 2010; Nahrgang, Morgeson, & Hofmann, 2011) that the model has matured into a theory. With JD-R theory, we can understand, explain, and make predictions about employee wellbeing (e.g., burnout, health, motivation, work engagement) and job performance. In this section, we discuss the most important building blocks of JD-R theory.

## Flexibility

One important reason for the popularity of the JD-R theory is its flexibility. According to the theory, all working environments or job characteristics can be modeled using two different categories, namely job demands and job resources. Thus, the theory can be applied to all work environments and can be tailored to the specific occupation under consideration. Job demands refer to those physical, psychological, social, or organizational aspects of the job that require sustained physical and/or psychological effort and are therefore associated with certain physiological and/or psychological costs (Demerouti et al., 2001). Examples are a high work pressure and emotionally demanding interactions with clients or customers. Although job demands are not necessarily negative, they may turn into hindrance demands when meeting those demands requires high effort from which the employee has not adequately recovered (Meijman & Mulder, 1998). Job resources refer to those physical, psychological, social, or organizational aspects of the job that are: (a) functional in achieving work goals; (b) reduce job demands and the associated physiological and psychological costs; or (c) stimulate personal growth, learning, and development (Bakker, 2011; Bakker & Demerouti, 2007). Hence, resources are not only necessary to deal with job demands, but they are also important in their own right. Whereas meaningful variations in levels of certain specific job demands and resources can be found in almost every occupational group (like work pressure, autonomy), other job demands and resources are unique. For example, whereas physical demands are still very important job demands nowadays for construction workers and nurses, cognitive demands are much more relevant for scientists and engineers.

## Two Processes

A second proposition of JD-R theory is that job demands and resources are the triggers of two fairly independent processes, namely a health impairment process and a motivational process (Figure 3.1). Thus, whereas job demands are generally the most important predictors of such outcomes as exhaustion, psychosomatic health complaints, and repetitive strain injury (RSI) (e.g., Bakker, Demerouti, & Schaufeli, 2003b; Hakanen et al., 2006), job resources are generally the most important predictors of work enjoyment, motivation, and engagement (Bakker et al., 2007, 2010). The reasons for these unique effects are that job demands basically cost effort and consume energetic resources, whereas job resources fulfil basic psychological needs,

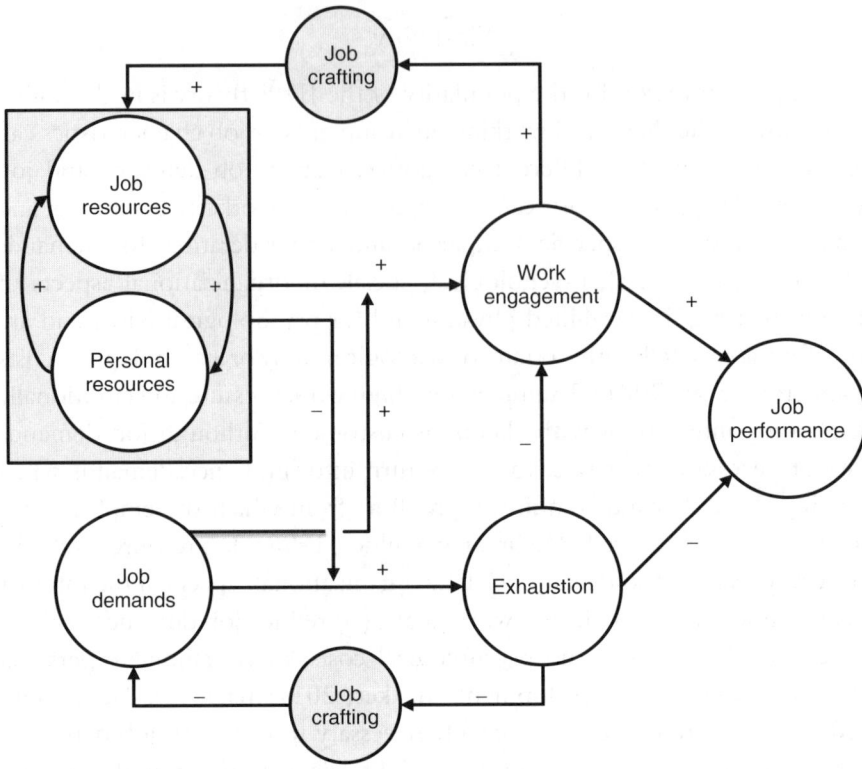

**Figure 3.1.** The Job Demands–Resources Model.

like the needs for autonomy, relatedness, and competence (Bakker, 2011; Deci & Ryan, 2000; Nahrgang et al., 2011).

A number of studies have supported the dual pathways to employee well-being proposed by JD-R theory, and showed that it can predict important organizational outcomes. Bakker et al. (2003b) applied the JD-R model to call center employees of a Dutch telecom company, and investigated its predictive validity for self-reported absenteeism and turnover intentions. Results of a series of structural equation modeling (SEM) analyses largely supported the dual processes. In the first energy-driven process, job demands (i.e., work pressure, computer problems, emotional demands, and changes in tasks) were the most important predictors of health problems, which, in turn, were related to sickness absence (duration and long-term absence). In the second motivation-driven process, job resources (i.e., social support, supervisory coaching, performance feedback, and time control) were the only predictors of dedication and organizational commitment, which, in turn, were related to turnover intentions.

Hakanen et al. (2006) found comparable results in their study among Finnish teachers. More specifically, they found that burnout mediated the effect of job demands on ill-health, and that work engagement mediated the effect of job resources on organizational commitment. Furthermore, Bakker et al. (2003a) applied the JD-R model to nutrition production employees, and used the model to predict future company-registered absenteeism. Results of SEM analyses showed that job demands were unique predictors of burnout and indirectly of absence *duration*, whereas job resources were unique predictors of organizational commitment, and indirectly of absence *spells*. Finally, Bakker et al. (2004) used the JD-R model to examine the relationship between job characteristics, burnout, and other ratings of performance. They hypothesized and found that job demands (e.g., work pressure and emotional demands) were the most important antecedents of the exhaustion component of burnout, which, in turn, predicted *in-role* performance. In contrast, job resources (e.g., autonomy and social support) were the most important predictors of *extra-role* performance, through their relationship with (dis)engagement. Taken together, these findings support JD-R theory's claim that job demands and job resources initiate two different psychological processes, which eventually affect important organizational outcomes.

## Job Demands × Resources Interactions

Job demands and resources initiate different processes, but have also joint effects (see Figure 3.1). The third proposition put forward by JD-R theory is that job demands and resources interact in predicting occupational wellbeing. There are two possible ways in which demands and resources may have a combined effect on wellbeing, and indirectly influence performance. The first interaction is the one where job resources buffer the impact of job demands on strain. Thus, several studies have shown that job resources like social support, autonomy, performance feedback, and opportunities for development can mitigate the impact of job demands (work pressure, emotional demands, etc.) on strain, including burnout (e.g., Bakker et al., 2005; Xanthopoulou et al., 2007b). Employees who have many job resources available can cope better with their daily job demands. The second interaction is the one where job demands amplify the impact of job resources on motivation/engagement. Thus, research has shown that job resources become salient and have the strongest positive impact on work engagement when job demands are high. In particular, when a worker is confronted with challenging job demands, job resources become valuable and foster dedication to the tasks at hand.

Hakanen, Bakker, and Demerouti (2005) tested the latter interaction hypothesis in a sample of Finnish dentists employed in the public sector. It was hypothesized that job resources (e.g., variability in the required professional skills, peer contacts) are most beneficial in maintaining work engagement under conditions of high job demands (e.g., workload, unfavorable physical environment). The dentists were split into two random groups in order to cross-validate the findings. A set of hierarchical regression analyses resulted in 17 out of 40 significant interactions (40%), showing, for example, that variability in professional skills boosted work engagement when qualitative workload was high, and mitigated the negative effect of qualitative workload on work engagement.

Conceptually similar findings have been reported by Bakker et al. (2007). In our study among Finnish teachers working in elementary, secondary, and vocational schools, we found that job resources act as buffers and diminish the negative relationship between pupil misbehavior and work engagement. In addition, we found that job resources particularly influence work engagement when teachers are confronted with high levels of pupil misconduct. A series of moderated structural equation modeling analyses resulted in 14 out of 18 possible two-way interaction effects (78%). In particular, supervisor support, innovativeness, appreciation, and organizational climate were important job resources for teachers that helped them cope with demanding interactions with students.

Finally, in a large study among more than 12,000 employees from different occupational groups, Bakker et al. (2010) found that task enjoyment and organizational commitment were also the result of combinations of many different job demands and job resources. Task enjoyment and commitment were highest when employees were confronted with challenging and stimulating tasks, and had sufficient resources at their disposal (e.g., performance feedback, high-quality relationships with colleagues). In sum, previous research with the JD-R model clearly indicates that job demands and resources interact and have a multiplicative impact on employee wellbeing.

## Personal Resources

An important extension of the original JD-R model (Bakker et al., 2004; Demerouti et al., 2001) is the inclusion of personal resources in the model and theory. Personal resources are positive self-evaluations that are linked to resiliency and refer to individuals' sense of their ability to control and impact upon their environment successfully (Hobfoll, Johnson, Ennis,

& Jackson, 2003). It has been argued and shown that such positive self-evaluations predict goal-setting, motivation, performance, job and life satisfaction, and other desirable outcomes (for a review, see Judge, Van Vianen, & De Pater, 2004). The reason for this is that the higher an individual's personal resources, the more positive the person's self-regard and the more goal self-concordance is expected to be experienced (Judge, Bono, Erez, & Locke, 2005). Individuals with goal self-concordance are intrinsically motivated to pursue their goals and as a result they trigger higher performance and satisfaction (see also Luthans & Youssef, 2007).

Xanthopoulou, Bakker, Demerouti, and Schaufeli (2007a) examined the role of three personal resources (self-efficacy, organizational-based self-esteem, and optimism) in predicting work engagement and exhaustion. Results of SEM analyses showed that personal resources did *not* manage to offset the relationship between job demands and exhaustion. In contrast, personal resources were found to partly mediate the relationship between job resources and work engagement, suggesting that job resources foster the development of personal resources. The longitudinal study by Xanthopoulou, Bakker, Demerouti, and Schaufeli (2009) also suggested that personal resources were reciprocal with job resources and work engagement over time. Thus, job resources predicted personal resources and work engagement; and personal resources and work engagement, in turn, predicted job resources (see also Figure 3.1).

To date, there is only limited evidence for the interaction between personal resources and job demands. In a survey study among military chaplains, Tremblay and Messervey (2011) hypothesized that compassion satisfaction could buffer the impact of job demands on job strain (anxiety and depression). Compassion satisfaction was defined as the fulfillment professional caregivers (e.g., social workers, fire fighters, clergy) feel from helping those who have experienced a traumatic event. The results of regression analyses showed that compassion satisfaction buffered the impact of role overload on job strain. Furthermore, in their study among nurses, Bakker and Sanz-Vergel (in press; study 2) tested the boosting effect of personal resources. Specifically, they hypothesized that weekly emotional job demands could facilitate the positive impact of personal resources (self-efficacy and optimism) on weekly work engagement. They asked 63 nurses to fill in a questionnaire at the end of the working week during three consecutive weeks. Results of hierarchical linear modeling showed that emotional job demands strengthened the effect of personal resources on weekly work engagement—confirming that these demands act as a challenge demand for nurses who particularly enjoy caring for other people.

## Reversed Causal Relationships

As already indicated, the relationship between (self-reported and observed) job demands (e.g., workload and emotional demands) and health-related outcomes (e.g., exhaustion) has been observed frequently (see Bakker & Demerouti, 2007; Demerouti et al., 2001; Lee & Ashforth, 1996). Moreover, recent research shows that job resources may have a strong (longitudinal) impact on motivational outcomes, including work engagement (Xanthopoulou et al., 2009). Conversely, some studies have shown that job strain, including burnout, may also have an impact on job demands over time. In their review, Zapf, Dormann, and Frese (1996) identified that 6 out of 16 longitudinal studies showed reversed causal relationships between working conditions and strain. Later studies provide additional evidence for reversed causation, such as between depersonalization and the quality of the doctor–patient relationship (Bakker, Schaufeli, Sixma, Bosveld, & Van Dierendonck, 2000), and between exhaustion and work pressure (Demerouti, Bakker, & Bulters, 2004).

One possible explanation for reversed causal effects is that employees experiencing strain or disengagement show behaviors that place additional demands upon them, like exhausted employees who fall behind with their work (Demerouti et al., 2004) or depersonalized employees evoking more stressful and more difficult interactions with their future clients (e.g., Bakker et al., 2000). Another explanation is that job demands may also be affected by employees' *perceptions* of the working environment (Zapf et al., 1996). For instance, burned-out employees may evaluate job demands more critically and complain more often about their workload, thus creating a negative work climate (Bakker & Schaufeli, 2000). In support of this, we found that job demands were related to burnout, and that burnout was related to job demands over time (Demerouti, Le Blanc, Bakker, Schaufeli, & Hox, 2009).

Recent studies have also suggested reversed causal relationships between job (and personal) resources and employee psychological wellbeing. For instance, De Lange, Taris, Kompier, Houtman, and Bongers (2005) found positive effects of mental health on supervisory support. Furthermore, Wong, Hui, and Law (1998) reported that job satisfaction was positively related to several organizational resources (e.g., autonomy, skill variety, and feedback) assessed 2 years later. In a similar vein, Salanova, Bakker, and Llorens

(2006), in their 1-year follow-up study among Spanish teachers, found that work-related flow experiences were associated with organizational resources and self-efficacy over time.

Taken together, these findings suggest that work engagement may facilitate the mobilization of job resources. This is consistent with the notion that in the absence of threats, people are motivated to create resources (Hobfoll, 2002). Engaged employees, who are intrinsically motivated to fulfill their work objectives, will activate or create job resources (e.g., ask colleagues for help) to use as means to achieve these objectives. Furthermore, vigorous, dedicated, and absorbed employees are more likely to fulfill their work goals (Demerouti & Cropanzano, 2010). Consequently, this will generate positive feedback, more rewards, and a more positive work climate in terms of relations with supervisors and colleagues. Similarly, Fredrickson (2003; Vacharkulksemsuk & Fredrickson, 2013) proposes that positive affective states have the ability to broaden employees' momentary thought–action repertoires and build enduring personal, social, and psychological resources. For instance, work engagement, as a positive motivational-affective state, broadens by creating the urge to expand the self through learning and goal fulfillment, and as such builds resources. In support of this, Xanthopoulou et al. (2009) found that not only were job resources predictors of work engagement but also work engagement was positively related to job resources over time.

Thus, rather than being deterministic, JD-R theory recognizes and integrates the fact that individuals' levels of exhaustion and work engagement may also influence their job demands and resources, which makes the JD-R theory a dynamic theory (see Figure 3.1). The question is, however, how these reversed relationships develop. This will be handled in the next section, where we discuss the final building block of JD-R theory.

## Job Crafting

It is clear that the availability of well-designed jobs and working conditions facilitates employee motivation and reduces stress, but what if these favorable working conditions are not available? Employees may actively change the design of their jobs by choosing tasks, negotiating different job content, and assigning meaning to their tasks or jobs (Parker & Ohly, 2008). This process of employees shaping their jobs has been referred to as "job crafting" (Wrzesniewski & Dutton, 2001). Job crafting is defined as the physical and cognitive changes individuals make in their task or relational boundaries. Physical changes refer to changes in the form, scope, or number of job tasks, whereas cognitive changes refer to changing how one sees the job. Wrzesniewski and Dutton note that job crafting is not inherently "good" or "bad" for an organization. Its effect depends on the situation.

According to Wrzesniewski and Dutton (2001), the motivation for job crafting arises from three individual needs. First, employees engage in job crafting because they have the need to take control over certain aspects of their work in order to avoid negative consequences such as alienation from work. Second, employees are motivated to change aspects of their work in order to enable a more positive sense of self to be expressed and confirmed by others. Third, job crafting allows employees to fulfill their basic human need for connection to others. In addition, Petrou, Demerouti, Peeters, Schaufeli, and Hetland (2012) suggested that individuals craft their job in order to create conditions in which they can work healthily and be well motivated.

Tims, Bakker, and Derks (2012) recently defined job crafting as the changes employees may make regarding their *job demands* and *job resources*. This conceptualization takes JD-R theory as a starting point. According to Tims and her colleagues, job crafting can take the form of four different types of behaviors: (a) increasing structural job resources; (b) increasing social job resources; (c) increasing challenging job demands; and (d) decreasing hindrance job demands. The study found evidence for four proposed job crafting dimensions, which could be reliably measured with 21 items. In terms of convergent validity, job crafting was positively correlated with the "active" construct of personal initiative, and negatively with the "inactive" construct cynicism. In support of criterion validity of the job crafting conceptualization and measurement, results indicated that self-reports of job crafting correlated positively with colleague ratings of work engagement, employability, and performance. Finally, self-rated job crafting behaviors correlated positively with peer-rated job crafting behaviors, which indicates that job crafting represents behaviors that others can also observe.

In an attempt to integrate job crafting in the JD-R theory, Tims, Bakker, and Derks (2013) hypothesized that job crafting would predict future job demands and job resources and indirectly have a positive impact on work engagement and job satisfaction. Data was collected among employees working in a chemical plant at three time points with 1 month in between the measurement waves. The results of SEM analyses showed that employees who crafted their job resources in the first month of the study showed an increase in their structural and social resources over the course of the study (2 months). This increase in job resources was related to increased work engagement and job satisfaction. Crafting job demands did not result in a change in job demands, but results revealed direct effects of crafting challenging demands on increases in wellbeing. In a similar vein, Petrou et al. (2012) found in their diary study that on days that work pressure and autonomy were both high (i.e., active jobs), employees increased their resources more and lowered their demands less. Interestingly, it was shown that the more employees sought job resources and challenges on a specific day, the more engaged they were in their job. In contrast, the more employees simplified their work on a specific day, the less engagement they experienced on that day. Thus, job crafting, or the bottom-up adjustments of demands and resources, seems to play a substantial role in the mechanisms suggested by the JD-R theory.

## JD-R Interventions

JD-R studies have consistently shown that employees achieve the best job performance in challenging, resourceful work environments, since such environments facilitate their work engagement. This implies that organizations should offer their employees sufficient job challenges, and job resources, including feedback, social support, and skill variety. Research indeed suggests that management can influence employees' job demands and resources (Nielsen, Randall, Yarker, & Brenner, 2008), and may indirectly influence employee engagement and performance.

However, it may be equally important that employees mobilize their own job resources. Managers are not always available for feedback, and organizations that are confronted with economic turmoil may set other priorities. Under such conditions, it may be particularly important for employees to mobilize their own resources, and to show proactive behavior in the form of job crafting.

In addition, JD-R theory acknowledges the importance of the person. Organizations can decide to invest in training their employees so that they are better able to deal with the job demands and to develop themselves during work. Organization-driven interventions aiming at increasing individual employees' personal resources can take the form of in-company training, while individual-driven interventions can take the form of capitalizing on one's strengths. In this chapter, we briefly discuss the four possible JD-R interventions displayed in Figure 3.2, namely (a) job redesign; (b) job crafting; (c) training; and (d) strengths-based intervention. These interventions can be organized on two dimensions: (1) *intervention level*:

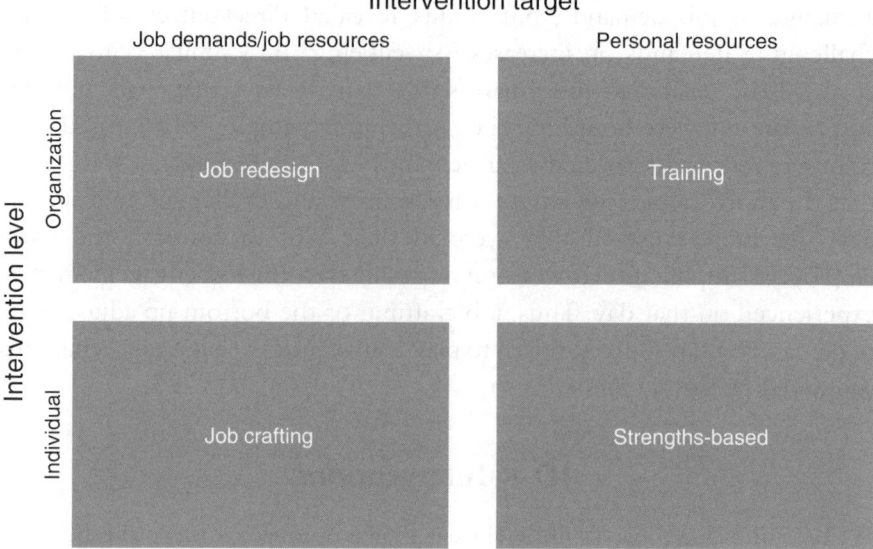

**Figure 3.2.** Interventions on the Basis of JD-R Theory Classified in Terms of Intervention Target and Level.

individual versus organization, and (2) *intervention target*: the work environment (job demands and resources) versus the individual (personal resources).

## Job Redesign

Job redesign is a structural intervention at the organizational level that aims to change the source of employee wellbeing—their job demands and job resources. Job design describes "how jobs, tasks, and roles are structured, enacted, and modified, as well as the impact of these structures, enactments, and modifications on individual, group, and organizational outcomes" (Grant & Parker, 2009, p. 319). Job design usually represents a top-down process in which organizations create jobs and form the conditions under which the job holders/incumbents execute their tasks. Job redesign is usually seen as the process through which the organization or supervisor changes something in the job, tasks, or the conditions of the individual. An example of a traditional work redesign effort is the increase of individual and team autonomy in the production process. A more contemporary example concerns the introduction of project work where individuals within and outside an organization work interdependently on the development of a product—often under time pressure. In each case, the structure and content of the work can be redesigned by the organization or by employees

54

themselves, with the ultimate goal to improve outcomes such as employee wellbeing, work engagement, and job performance.

Note that it is also possible to ask employees to fill in an electronic version of the JD-R questionnaire and to offer them online and personalized feedback on their computer or smartphone about their most important job demands and resources (Bakker, Oerlemans, & Ten Brummelhuis, 2012). The feedback may include histograms of and written information about the specific demands and resources identified as important for engagement in the organization under study. The personal JD-R profile can be used as input for interviews with human resources managers and personal coaches. In this way, it becomes also possible to optimize the working environment for individual employees.

## Job Crafting Interventions

In contrast with traditional job redesign, job crafting is an individual-level intervention that is usually initiated by the individual employee. Employees may actively change the design of their jobs by choosing tasks, negotiating different job content, and assigning meaning to their tasks or jobs (Parker & Ohly, 2008). From a JD-R perspective, they may proactively change their own job demands and job resources. Organizations can stimulate job crafting behavior that is beneficial for both the employees and the organizations by showing individuals how they can craft their job. Van den Heuvel, Demerouti, and Peeters (2012) developed and tested such an intervention among police officers. Through various explanations and exercises during workshops, employees got to know the concept of job crafting and were instructed to develop their own personal crafting plan (PCP). The PCP consisted of specific crafting actions that the participants had to undertake. During a period of four consecutive weeks, participants increased their job resources, increased their challenge demands, and decreased their hindrance job demands. Participants also exchanged their crafting experiences during a reflection meeting where they discussed successes, problems, and solutions. The intervention was found to increase two job resources (contact with the supervisor and opportunities for professional development), one personal resource (self-efficacy), and wellbeing as participants reported more positive emotions and less negative emotions.

Bakker et al. (2012) suggested that a job crafting intervention may also use the Internet to instruct participating employees, and to follow them on a weekly basis (e.g., 6 weeks). At the start of each week, participants can be instructed through email to align their work with their skills and needs by changing the work content or their work environment. Participants can also be provided with examples, such as changing the way they work, when they work, and with whom they work (clients, colleagues); changing the frequency of feedback and coaching; simplifying their work versus looking for more challenges; and carrying out additional tasks. The instruction could additionally provide clear examples of employees in certain jobs who successfully mobilized their job resources or increased/reduced their job demands. To facilitate the job crafting behaviors, participants can be asked to list up to five aspects of their work they would like to change during the upcoming week. In addition, they can be asked—for example, via email or smartphone, or initiated by a personal coach—to indicate for each activity how and when they intend to engage in job crafting. Such implementation intentions will facilitate the success of the job crafting intervention.

## Training

Training and development of employees is one of the cornerstones of human resources management, and can be seen as an organizational level intervention. Through training, employees may acquire new skills, technical knowledge, and problem-solving abilities. Whereas improved knowledge and skills may facilitate personal resources such as self-efficacy, resilience, and optimism, training may also directly focus on personal resources. Peterson, Luthans, Avolio, Walumbwa, and Zhang (2011) have shown that positive change in personal resources (they call this "psychological capital") is related to positive change in supervisor-rated performance and financial performance (i.e., individual sales revenue). Demerouti, van Eeuwijk, Snelder, and Wild (2011) showed that such interventions not only increase self-reported personal resources; external raters can also observe increases in personal resources. Thus, personal resources are malleable and can be increased in order to improve work engagement and performance.

Luthans, Avey, Avolio, and Peterson (2010) assigned participants randomly to treatment or control groups. The treatment groups received a 2-hour training intervention conducted by training facilitators that utilized a series of exercises and group discussions designed to impact the participants' level of efficacy, hope, optimism, and resilience. In the intervention training, the facilitators used a series of writing, discussion, and reflective exercises specific to each of the four personal resources. Examples of the exercises used included one that focused on broadening the hope-oriented self-regulating capacity and pathways thinking toward a specific goal. First, each participant was asked to consider and then write down personal goals. The facilitator led participants through a series of techniques to set and phrase goals to increase agentic capacity (Bandura, 2008). This included parceling large goals into manageable units, thereby also increasing efficacy over smaller subgoals. Next, participants were asked to considering multiple pathways to accomplishing each goal and to share those pathways in small discussion groups within the intervention session. Thus, the capacity for pathway generation was expected to be increased through vicarious learning and in turn to enhance participants' level of efficacy in utilizing the hope application of deriving multiple pathways to accomplish a given goal. In addition, by increasing their efficacy in accomplishing the goal, the participants were expected to increase their positive expectations of goal accomplishment (i.e., their optimism). For more details, see Luthans et al. (2010).

## Strengths-Based Interventions

Work engagement is most probably dependent on the match between individual strengths possessed by employees, and the degree to which they can draw from their strengths in their daily work activities. Individual strengths can be defined as positive traits reflected in thoughts, feelings, and behaviors (Park, Peterson, & Seligman, 2004). Examples are curiosity, bravery, kindness, and gratitude. It has been argued that working with one's strengths is fulfilling and engaging, and induces a feeling of acting in an authentic manner and being true to oneself (Peterson & Seligman, 2004). Employees who can use their strengths at work are expected to be self-efficacious. This intervention can thus be seen as an individual-level intervention aimed at increasing personal resources.

Although strengths-based interventions within the context of work have—to the best of our knowledge—not yet been scientifically evaluated, research on wellbeing in general has produced some promising findings. For example, in one strength-based intervention, participants were asked to first identify their top individual strengths. Subsequently, they were encouraged to use one of their strengths in a new or different way every day for at least one week (Seligman, Steen, Park, & Peterson, 2005). Participants were randomly assigned to an experimental or control group, and were followed over time. Results showed that this intervention led to significant increases in happiness and significant reductions of depressive symptoms at 1 week, 1 month, 3 months, and 6 months follow-up.

57

There may be various ways to "translate" strengths-based interventions to a workplace context. One possibility is to provide individual feedback to employees (e.g., through online modules) about their most important strengths. Thereafter, an option would be to give employees more insight with regard to the frequency with which they use their top character strengths on a daily basis while performing work-related activities (e.g., through keeping a work-related diary). If it turns out that employees use their strengths insufficiently, a next step would be to provide employees with specific pathways that lead them to use their strengths within the work context in a new way. This may lead employees to (re)consider how to use their strengths during specific types of job-related activities, which, in turn, may enhance their levels of personal resources and work engagement.

# Conclusion

The present chapter introduced job demands–resources theory, which is an extension of the job demands–resources model. Overcoming the restricted, static, and one-sided early models of stress and motivation, JD-R theory suggests that work characteristics can be organized in two categories: job demands and job resources. These two categories of work characteristics can be found in virtually every job and are therefore important because they are initiators of two different processes: the health impairment and motivational process. Demands and resources not only have unique effects on employee health and motivation, they also have joint (interactive) effects on employee wellbeing. Rather than being mechanistic, the model suggests that personal resources are also important predictors of motivation, and can buffer the unfavorable effects of job demands.

In addition, JD-R theory proposes that work characteristics and employee health and motivation influence each other mutually over time. Thus, employee health and motivation also change the work environment, which underscores the dynamic nature of the issue of work environment and wellbeing relationships. Finally, JD-R theory also explains the way that these reversed effects occur. Job crafting or individual adjustment of the demands and resources seems to explain how employees change their environment such that they can make it more engaging and less exhausting. JD-R theory can be used to inform interventions driven by the individual or the organization, and these interventions can target personal resources, or job demands and resources. We hope that JD-R theory will be used to guide future research and practice such that employees can work in healthier, more engaging, and more productive working environments.

# References

Alarcon, G. M. (2011). A meta-analysis of burnout with job demands, resources, and attitudes. *Journal of Vocational Behavior*, *79*, 549–562.

Ambrose, M. L., & Kulik, C. T. (1999). Old friends, new faces: Motivation in the 1990s. *Journal of Management*, *25*, 231–292.

Bakker, A. B. (2011). An evidence-based model of work engagement. *Current Directions in Psychological Science*, *20*, 265–269.

Bakker, A. B., & Demerouti, E. (2007). The job demands-resources model: State of the art. *Journal of Managerial Psychology*, *22*, 309–328.

Bakker, A. B., Demerouti, E., De Boer, E., & Schaufeli, W. B. (2003a). Job demands and job resources as predictors of absence duration and frequency. *Journal of Vocational Behavior*, *62*, 341–356.

Bakker, A. B., Demerouti, E., & Euwema, M. C. (2005). Job resources buffer the impact of job demands on burnout. *Journal of Occupational Health Psychology*, *10*, 170–180.

Bakker, A. B., Demerouti, E., & Schaufeli, W. B. (2003b). Dual processes at work in a call centre: An application of the Job Demands–Resources model. *European Journal of Work and Organizational Psychology*, *12*, 393–417.

Bakker, A. B., Demerouti, E., & Verbeke, W. (2004). Using the Job Demands–Resources model to predict burnout and performance. *Human Resource Management*, *43*, 83–104.

Bakker, A. B., Hakanen, J. J., Demerouti, E., & Xanthopoulou, D. (2007). Job resources boost work engagement, particularly when job demands are high. *Journal of Educational Psychology*, *99* , 274–284.

Bakker, A. B., Oerlemans, W., & Ten Brummelhuis, L. L. (2012). Becoming fully engaged in the workplace: What individuals and organizations can do to foster work engagement. In R. Burke & C. Cooper (Eds.), *The fulfilling workplace: The organization's role in achieving individual and organizational health*. Farnham: Gower.

Bakker, A. B., & Sanz-Vergel, A. I. (in press). Weekly work engagement and flourishing: The role of hindrance and challenge demands. *Journal of Vocational Behavior*.

Bakker, A. B., & Schaufeli, W. B. (2000). Burnout contagion processes among teachers. *Journal of Applied Social Psychology*, *30*, 2289–2308.

Bakker, A. B., Schaufeli, W. B., Sixma, H., Bosveld, W., & Van Dierendonck, D. (2000). Patient demands, lack of reciprocity, and burnout: A five-year longitudinal study among general practitioners. *Journal of Organizational Behavior*, *21*, 425–441.

Bakker, A. B., Van Emmerik, H., & Van Riet, P. (2008). How job demands, resources, and burnout predict objective performance: A constructive replication. *Anxiety, Stress, and Coping*, *21*, 309–324.

Bakker, A. B., Van Veldhoven, M. J. P. M., & Xanthopoulou, D. (2010). Beyond the Demand-Control model: Thriving on high job demands and resources. *Journal of Personnel Psychology, 9,* 3–16.

Bandura, A. (2008). An agentic perspective on positive psychology. In S. J. Lopez (Ed.), *Positive psychology* (Vol. 1, pp. 167–196). Westport, CT: Greenwood.

Behson, S. J., Eddy, E. R., & Lorenzet, S. J. (2000). The importance of the critical psychological states in the job characteristics model: A meta-analytic and structural equations modeling examination. *Current Research in Social Psychology, 5,* 170–189.

Carayon, P. (1993). A longitudinal test of Karasek's job strain model among office workers. *Work and Stress, 7,* 299–314.

Clausen, T., Nielsen, K., Gomes Carneiro, I., & Borg, V. (2012). Job demands, job resources and long-term sickness absence in the Danish eldercare services: A prospective analysis of register-based outcomes. *Journal of Advanced Nursing, 68,* 127–136.

Crawford, E. R., LePine, J. A., & Rich, B. L. (2010). Linking job demands and resources to employee engagement and burnout: A theoretical extension and meta-analytic test. *Journal of Applied Psychology, 95,* 834–848.

Deci, E. L., & Ryan, R. M. (2000). The "what" and "why" of goal pursuits: Human needs and the self-determination of behavior. *Psychological Inquiry, 11,* 227–268.

De Jonge, J., Bosma, H., Peter, R., & Siegrist, J. (2000). Job strain, effort-reward imbalance and employee well-being: A large-scale cross-sectional study. *Social Science & Medicine, 50,* 1317–1327.

De Jonge, J., Janssen, P. P. M., & Breukelen, J. P. van (1996). Testing the Demand–Control–Support model among health care professionals: A structural equations approach. *Work and Stress, 10,* 209–224.

De Lange, A. H., Taris, T. W., Kompier, M. A. J., Houtman, I. L. D., & Bongers, P. M. (2003). "The *very* best of the millennium": Longitudinal research and the Demand-Control-(Support) model. *Journal of Occupational Health Psychology, 8,* 282–305.

De Lange, A. H., Taris, T. W., Kompier, M. A. J., Houtman, I. L. D., & Bongers, P. M. (2005). Different mechanisms to explain the reversed effects of mental health on work characteristics. *Scandinavian Journal of Work, Environment, and Health, 31,* 3–14.

Demerouti, E., & Bakker, A. B. (2011). The Job Demands–Resources model: Challenges for future research. *South African Journal of Industrial Psychology, 37,* 1–9.

Demerouti, E., Bakker, A. B., & Bulters, A. J. (2004). The loss spiral of work pressure, work-home interference and exhaustion: Reciprocal relations in a three-wave study. *Journal of Vocational Behavior, 64,* 131–149.

Demerouti, E., Bakker, A. B., Nachreiner, F., & Schaufeli, W. B. (2001). The job demands-resources model of burnout. *Journal of Applied Psychology, 86,* 499–512.

Demerouti, E., & Cropanzano, R. (2010). From thought to action: Employee work engagement and job performance. In A. B. Bakker & M. P. Leiter (Eds.), *Work engagement: A handbook of essential theory and research* (pp. 147–163). New York: Psychology Press.

Demerouti, E., Derks, D., Ten Brummelhuis, L. L., & Bakker, A. B. (in press). New ways of working: Impact on working conditions, work-family balance, and well-being. In P. Hoonakker & C. Karunka (Eds.), *Acceleration: Information technology and quality of working life*. Berlin: Springer Science.

Demerouti, E., Le Blanc, P. M., Bakker, A. B., Schaufeli, W. B., & Hox, J. (2009). Present but sick: A three-wave study on job demands, presenteeism and burnout. *Career Development International*, *14*, 50–68.

Demerouti, E., Van Eeuwijk, E., Snelder, M., & Wild, U. (2011). Assessing the effects of a "personal effectiveness" training on psychological capital, assertiveness and self-awareness using self-other agreement. *Career Development International*, *16*, 60–81.

Fredrickson, B. L. (2003). Positive emotions and upward spirals in organizations. In K. Cameron, J. Dutton, & R. Quinn (Eds.), *Positive organizational scholarship* (pp. 163–175). San Francisco: Berrett-Koehler.

Fried, Y., & Ferris, G. R. (1987). The validity of the Job Characteristics Model: A review and meta-analysis. *Personnel Psychology*, *40*, 287–322.

Graen, G. B., Scandura, T. A., & Graen, M. (1986). A field experimental test of the moderating effects of growth need strength on productivity. *Journal of Applied Psychology*, *71*, 484–491.

Grant, A. M., Fried, Y., & Juillerat, T. (2010). Work matters: Job design in classic and contemporary perspectives. In S. Zedeck (Ed.), *APA handbook of industrial and organizational psychology* (Vol. 1; pp. 417–453). Washington, DC: American Psychological Association.

Grant, A. M., & Parker, S. K. (2009). Redesigning work design theories: The rise of relational and proactive perspectives. *Academy of Management Annals*, *3*, 273–331.

Hackman, J. R., & Lawler, E. E. (1971). Employee reactions to job characteristics. *Journal of Applied Psychology*, *55*, 259–286.

Hackman, J. R., & Oldham, G. R. (1976). Motivation through the design of work: Test of a theory. *Organizational Behavior & Human Decision Processes*, *16*, 250–279.

Hackman, J. R., & Oldham, G. R. (1980). *Work redesign*. Reading, MA: Addison-Wesley.

Hakanen, J. J., Bakker, A. B., & Demerouti, E. (2005). How dentists cope with their job demands and stay engaged: The moderating role of job resources. *European Journal of Oral Sciences*, *113*, 479–487.

Hakanen, J., Bakker, A. B., & Schaufeli, W. B. (2006). Burnout and work engagement among teachers. *Journal of School Psychology*, *43*, 495–513.

Halbesleben, J. R. B. (2010). A meta-analysis of work engagement: Relationships with burnout, demands, resources and consequences. In A. B. Bakker

& M. P. Leiter (Eds.), *Work engagement: A handbook of essential theory and research* (pp. 102–117). New York: Psychology Press.

Herzberg, F. (1966). *Work and the nature of man.* Cleveland, OH: Holland.

Herzberg, F., Mausner, B., & Snyderman, B. B. (1959). *The motivation to work.* New York: Wiley.

Hobfoll, S. E. (2002). Social and psychological resources and adaptation. *Review of General Psychology, 6,* 307–324.

Hobfoll, S. E., Johnson, R. J., Ennis, N., & Jackson, A. P. (2003). Resource loss, resource gain, and emotional outcomes among inner city women. *Journal of Personality and Social Psychology, 84,* 632–643.

Johnson, J. V., & Hall, E. M. (1988). Job strain, work place social support and cardiovascular disease: A cross-sectional study of a random sample of the Swedish working population. *American Journal of Public Health, 78,* 1336–1342.

Judge, T. A., Bono, J. E., Erez, A., & Locke, E. A. (2005). Core self-evaluations and job and life satisfaction: The role of self-concordance and goal attainment. *Journal of Applied Psychology, 90,* 257–268.

Judge, T. A., Van Vianen, A. E. M., & De Pater, I. (2004). Emotional stability, core self-evaluations, and job outcomes: A review of the evidence and an agenda for future research. *Human Performance, 17,* 325–346.

Karasek, R. A. (1979). Job demands, decision latitude, and mental strain: Implications for job redesign. *Administrative Science Quarterly, 24,* 285–308.

Karasek, R. A., & Theorell, T. (1990). *Healthy work.* New York: Basic Books.

Lee, R. T., & Ashforth, B. E. (1996). A meta-analytic examination of the correlates of the three dimensions of job burnout. *Journal of Applied Psychology, 81,* 123–133.

Leiter, M. P. (1993). Burnout as a developmental process: Consideration of models. In W. B. Schaufeli, C. Maslach, & T. Marek (Eds.), *Professional burnout: Recent developments in theory and research* (pp. 237–250). Washington, DC: Taylor & Francis.

Lewig, K., Xanthopoulou, D., Bakker, A. B., Dollard, M., & Metzer, J. (2007). Burnout and connectedness among Australian volunteers: A test of the Job Demands-Resources model. *Journal of Vocational Behavior, 71,* 429–445.

Luthans, F., Avey, J. B., Avolio, B. J., & Peterson, S. J. (2010). The development and resulting performance impact of positive psychological capital. *Human Resource Development Quarterly, 21,* 41–67.

Luthans, F., & Youssef, C. M. (2007). Emerging positive organizational behavior. *Journal of Management, 33,* 321–349.

Meijman, T. F., & Mulder, G. (1998). Psychological aspects of workload. In P. J. Drenth, H. Thierry, & C. J. de Wolff (Eds.), *Handbook of work and organizational psychology* (2nd ed.; pp. 5–33). Hove, U.K.: Erlbaum.

Nahrgang, J. D., Morgeson, F. P., & Hofmann, D. A. (2011). Safety at work: A meta-analytic investigation of the link between job demands, job resources, burnout, engagement, and safety outcomes. *Journal of Applied Psychology, 96,* 71–94.

Nielsen, K., Randall, R., Yarker, J., & Brenner, S. O. (2008). The effects of transformational leadership on followers' perceived work characteristics and psychological well-being: A longitudinal study. *Work & Stress, 22,* 16–32.

Park, N., Peterson, C., & Seligman, M. E. P. (2004). Strengths of character and well-being. *Journal of Social and Clinical Psychology, 23,* 603–619.

Parker, S. K., & Ohly, S. (2008). Designing motivating jobs. In R. Kanfer, G. Chen, & R. Pritchard (Eds.), *Work motivation: Past, present, and future.* SIOP Organizational Frontiers Series. London: Psychology Press.

Parker, S. K., & Wall, T. D. (1998). *Job and work design: Organizing work to promote well-being and effectiveness.* San Francisco, CA: Sage.

Parker, S. K., Wall, T. D., & Cordery, J. (2001). Future work design research and practice: Towards an elaborated model of work design. *Journal of Occupational and Organizational Psychology, 74,* 413–440.

Peterson, C., & Seligman, M. E. P. (2004). *Character strengths and virtues: A handbook and classification.* Washington, DC: American Psychological Association.

Peterson, S. J., Luthans, F., Avolio, B. J., Walumbwa, F. O., & Zhang, Z. (2011). Psychological capital and employee performance: A latent growth modeling approach. *Personnel Psychology, 64,* 427–450.

Petrou, P., Demerouti, E., Peeters, M. C. W., Schaufeli, W. B., & Hetland, J. (2012). Crafting a job on a daily basis: Contextual correlates and the link to work engagement. *Journal of Organizational Behavior, 33,* 1020–1141.

Renn, R. W., & Vandenberg, R. J. (1995). The critical psychological states: An underrepresented component in job characteristics model research. *Journal of Management, 21,* 279–303.

Roberts K. H., & Glick, W. (1981). The job characteristics approach to task design: A critical review. *Journal of Applied Psychology, 66,* 193–217.

Rousseau, D. M. (2005). *I-deals: Idiosyncratic deals employees bargain for themselves.* New York: M. E. Sharpe.

Salanova, M., Bakker, A. B., & Llorens, S. (2006). Flow at work: Evidence for an upward spiral of personal and organizational resources. *Journal of Happiness Studies, 7,* 1–22.

Schaufeli, W. B., Bakker, A. B., & Van Rhenen, W. (2009). How changes in job demands and resources predict burnout, work engagement, and sickness absenteeism. *Journal of Organizational Behavior, 30,* 893–917.

Seligman, M. E. P., Steen, T. A., Park, N., & Peterson, C. (2005). Positive psychology progress: Empirical validation of interventions. *American Psychologist, 60,* 410–421.

Siegrist, J. (1996). Adverse health effects of high effort-low reward conditions. *Journal of Occupational Health Psychology, 1,* 27–41.

Siegrist, J. (2008). Effort-reward imbalance and health in a globalized economy. *Scandinavian Journal of Work, Environment & Health, 6,* 163–168.

Taris, T. W. (2006). Bricks without clay: On urban myths in occupational health psychology. *Work & Stress, 20,* 99–104.

Taris, T. W., Kompier, M. J., De Lange, A. H., Schaufeli, W. B., & Schreurs, P. J. G. (2003). Learning new behaviour patterns: A longitudinal test of

Karasek's active learning hypothesis among Dutch teachers. *Work & Stress, 17,* 1–20.

Tims, M., Bakker, A. B., & Derks, D. (2012). Development and validation of the job crafting scale. *Journal of Vocational Behavior, 80,* 173–186.

Tims, M., Bakker, A. B., & Derks, D. (2013). The impact of job crafting on job demands, job resources, and well-being. *Journal of Occupational Health Psychology, 18,* 230–240.

Tremblay, M. A., & Messervey, D. (2011). The Job Demands-Resources model: Further evidence for the buffering effect of personal resources. *South African Journal of Industrial Psychology, 37,* 1–10.

Tsutsumi, A., & Kawakami, N. (2004). A review of empirical studies on the model of effort–reward imbalance at work: Reducing occupational stress by implementing a new theory. *Social Science & Medicine, 59,* 2335–2359.

Vacharkulksemsuk, T., & Fredrickson, B. L. (2013). Looking back and glimpsing forward: The broaden-and-build theory of positive emotions as applied to organizations. In A. B. Bakker (Ed.), *Advances in positive organizational psychology* (Vol. 1, pp. 45–60). Bingley: Emerald.

Van den Heuvel, M., Demerouti, E., & Peeters, M. (2012). Succesvol job craften door middel van een groepstraining [Successful job crafting through group training]. In J. de Jonge, M. Peeters, S. Sjollema, & H. de Zeeuw (Eds.), *Scherp in werk: 5 routes naar optimale inzetbaarheid* (pp. 27–49). Assen: Koninklijke van Gorcum.

Van der Doef, M., & Maes, S. (1999). The Job Demand-Control(-Support) Model and psychological well-being: A review of 20 years of empirical research. *Work and Stress, 13,* 87–114.

Walster, E., Walster, G. W., & Berscheid, E. (1978). *Equity: Theory and research.* Boston: Allyn & Bacon.

Wong, C. S., Hui, C., & Law, K. S. (1998). A longitudinal study of the job perception-job satisfaction relationship: A test of the three alternative specifications. *Journal of Occupational and Organizational Psychology, 71,* 127–146.

Wrzesniewski, A., & Dutton, J. E. (2001). Crafting a job: Revisioning employees as active crafters of their work. *Academy of Management Review, 26,* 179–201.

Xanthopoulou, D., Bakker, A. B., Demerouti, E., & Schaufeli, W. B. (2009). Reciprocal relationships between job resources, personal resources, and work engagement. *Journal of Vocational Behavior, 74,* 235–244.

Xanthopoulou, D., Bakker, A. B., Demerouti, E., & Schaufeli, W. B. (2007a). The role of personal resources in the job demands-resources model. *International Journal of Stress Management, 14,* 121–141.

Xanthopoulou, D., Bakker, A. B., Dollard, M. F., Demerouti, E., Schaufeli, W. B., Taris, T. W., & Schreurs, P. J. G. (2007b). When do job demands particularly predict burnout? The moderating role of job resources. *Journal of Managerial Psychology, 22,* 766–786.

Zapf, D., Dormann, C., & Frese, M. (1996). Longitudinal studies in organizational stress research: A review of the literature with reference to methodological issues. *Journal of Occupational Health Psychology, 1,* 145–169.

# 4

# Positive Psychology and Coping

## *Towards a Better Understanding of the Relationship*

Philip Dewe

Birkbeck, University of London, U.K.

## Introduction

Since Seligman and Csikszentmihalyi (2000) first published their semi-nal paper on positive psychology "quite a lot has happened in what has become known as the positive psychology movement" (Gable & Haidt, 2005, p. 103). Seligman and Csikszentmihalyi (2000, p. 5) describe positive psychology in terms of three themes: "a science of positive subjective expe-rience, positive individual differences and positive institutions." Together these three themes represent a psychology of positive development and positive individual performance. The positive psychology movement has, of course, attracted considerable attention. Its ideas continue to be vigorously debated as commentators explore what is new about it (Lazarus, 2003a), what it means in terms of understanding the work experience, and how well it confronts the methodological difficulties that all researchers face when trying to unravel the complexities of individual wellbeing (Lazarus, 2003b). At the heart of this debate is the question of balance, of just how much the idea of a positive psychology has "passed unrecognized" (Linley et al., 2006, p. 4) and been "short changed" (Lazarus, 2003a, p. 105) because psychol-ogy has, for too long, allowed its preoccupation with individual vulnerability

*Work and Wellbeing: Wellbeing: A Complete Reference Guide*, Volume III.
Edited by Peter Y. Chen and Cary L. Cooper.
© 2014 John Wiley & Sons, Ltd. Published 2014 by John Wiley & Sons, Inc.
DOI: 10.1002/9781118539415.wbwell04

to dominate the research agenda. Within this debate the role of positive psychology may, as Rand and Snyder (2003, p. 148) suggest, be to act as a catalyst for change; to refocus research to consider not only the demanding aspects of life but also those aspects that allow individuals to flourish and "build positive qualities." While the issue of balance will continue to be robustly debated, by provoking such a debate then, as Csikszentmihalyi (2003, p. 113) suggests, positive psychology will have "served a useful end."

So if, as Csikszentmihalyi (2003, p. 114) goes on to suggest, the goal of positive psychology is "to legitimate the study of positive aspects of human experience in their own right" then what has been the influence of the positive psychology movement on the study of work-related coping? It is important when considering the question of influence to acknowledge the intensity of the debate surrounding the question of balance (Dewe & Cooper, 2012), to accept that exploring the positive and the negative has always been what psychology has been about (Lazarus, 2003a), to consider how much we have learnt about how people flourish (Sheldon & King, 2001) and what we know about human strengths (Snyder & Lopez, 2005), and to recognize that what positive psychology offers is an opportunity to redress any sense of imbalance in a way that expresses "a more complete and balanced scientific understanding of the human experience" (Seligman, Steen, Park, & Peterson 2005, p. 410). Nevertheless it still remains difficult to distinguish between spheres of influence, as boundaries inevitably blur and timings do not always appear as clear-cut as first thought. And when coping research is the focus, there is the added dimension that the word "coping" by its very nature carries with it connotations of success and positive outcomes.

However, despite these caveats it is possible to identify a number of trends in coping research that have, one way or another, emphasized a route through which the positive can be emphasized, offering what must be a better understanding of the nature of coping. These themes include: (a) the move away from the troublesome word "stress" to focusing more on those positive and negative emotions that best express the work experience; (b) a greater emphasis on the process of appraisals in the stress process and, when appraisals are viewed as the channel through which the emotion flows, then how this transactional view offers a more explicit causal pathway for research; (c) the acceptance of the importance of positive emotions and the role they play as a coping resource; (d) the shift from reactive coping to proactive coping; and (e) the need to better understand what is meant by coping effectiveness.

# A Brief Interlude on Coping Research

Coping research is not without its own controversies and debates. The sheer volume of research directed toward understanding the nature of coping and its role in the stress process has, as our knowledge develops, drawn attention to not just the complexity that surrounds such a construct (Snyder, 2001), but the difficulties associated with studying it (Aldwin, 2009). It is not surprising then that controversies emerge (Dewe, O'Driscoll, & Cooper, 2010). This is no more than you would expect from a maturing field where traditional approaches are questioned, alternative approaches promoted, and boundaries redefined, and a field where researchers are constantly presented with not just opportunities for reflecting on the state of our knowledge but also the progress that needs to be made. Two not mutually exclusive tensions have emerged. The first concerns whether the boundaries for determining what constitutes coping have been too narrowly set and that definitions of coping no longer capture the richness of what is actually being done (Dewe et al., 2010; Dewe & Cooper, 2012). Defining coping cannot be separated from how it is measured. So the most intense debate has been around how coping should be measured. This debate has not simply been limited to considering where current measurement practices are taking us and what alternative measures can provide, but has, naturally and quite correctly, extended to debating whether the analysis that flows from such measures limits interpretation and by association our knowledge of the coping process.

Turning to how coping has been defined, the debate can be neatly captured by asking "Where do the boundaries of what actually constitutes coping lie?" (Dewe & Cooper, 2012 p. 135). In attempting to answer this question researchers have considered whether it is now time to broaden our view of coping by extending the definition first offered by Folkman and Lazarus (1991), who defined coping in terms of "cognitive and behavioural efforts to manage specific external and/or internal demands that are appraised as taxing or exceeding the resources of the person" (p. 210). Researchers have drawn attention to two issues with this definition that they believe necessarily limit the array of coping strategies people use. These include the idea that coping strategies require effort (Snyder, 2001) and that strategies are intentionally triggered by a stressful encounter (Coyne & Gottlieb, 1996). When coping is defined in this way, what do you do with those ordinary adaptive behaviors, routines, and habits that simply help people get along (Coyne & Gottlieb, 1996)? What role do they have in helping to shape our definition of coping? As Coyne and Gottlieb (1996, p. 962) go on to argue, this is a "serious omission," because if they are not coping then what are they? If coping is, as Folkman and Lazarus (1991) suggest, a particular type of adaptation, then where do you draw the line when attempting to distinguish one from the other in order to capture the richness of what constitutes coping? The debate as to how broadly coping should be defined will continue. Such a debate simply illustrates the complexity of a construct like coping and cannot be separated from the issue of measurement. It is to these issues that we now turn.

When it comes to how coping is measured then the debate reaches its "greatest intensity when self-report coping questionnaires or checklists become the focus of attention" (Dewe et al., 2010, p. 32). What is at stake is not the utility of checklists but the limits that such a measurement tool places on the power to describe and explain (Oakland & Ostell, 1996, p. 151). For some, little can be gained "by developing better checklists" (Coyne & Gottlieb, 1996, p. 961). However, the key issue when drawing attention to such limitations must be to prevent such measures being seen as an easy convenience (Coyne & Gottlieb, 1996; Dewe & Cooper, 2012) to be used uncritically (Coyne & Gottlieb, 1996), insensitive to when their use is appropriate (Lazarus, 1995), and to recognize that if such measures are to be improved then the effort to do so must come from us (Folkman, 1992). Taking up the last of these challenges, researchers have been urged to consider a range of issues before considering the use of checklists. A synthesis of these issues includes, for example, how the instructions are expressed, the way items are derived and worded, their relevance, how they may be interpreted, the ambiguity they may produce, their number, and the suitability of the scoring key (see Coyne & Gottlieb, 1996; Dewe & Cooper, 2012; Dewe et al., 2010; Folkman & Moskowitz, 2004; Somerfield, 1997a, 1997b). As the debate continues to swirl around the use of checklists, it should not be forgotten that researchers are, as Lazarus (2000) points out, continually engaged in creatively developing more person-centered and process-focused measures to capture the nature of coping and the richness of the coping process.

The debate surrounding measurement practices cannot be separated from analysis and interpretation as each relates to the other, so "when preparing data for analysis researchers need to consider the impact that measurement has on interpretation" (Dewe & Cooper, 2012, p. 145). Whether it is a primary goal or not, one of the first steps researchers will take when transforming their data will be to determine whether it is possible to identify underlying patterns of coping components. Reviewers suggest the need for pragmatism (Folkman, 1992), but also caution researchers (Aldwin, 2000) to consider the impact that data reduction procedures such as factor analysis have on the comprehensiveness and completeness of coping components. The issue centers on the conventions that govern factor loadings. Researchers are advised to first consider the variety of ways in which coping strategies are used, how they relate to each other, and the different functions they perform (Aldwin, 2009; Billings & Moos, 1981; Coyne & Gottlieb, 1996; Dewe & Cooper, 2007; Stone & Kennedy-Moore, 1992). Then they need to consider whether the criteria they use for determining what item loads on a component by, for example, simply exploring the status of an item in terms of the size of its factor loading or its loading across factors (Dewe et al., 2010; Folkman & Moskowitz, 2004), what impact this has on capturing the nature and richness of a particular strategy and the various ways in which it is being used.

Making decisions about whether or not an item loads on a particular coping component and, by inference, the structure of that component draws attention to the difficulties when trying to balance statistical rigor against how a particular strategy is being used or "the range of ways a person may be thinking and acting in a particular encounter" (Dewe & Cooper, 2012, p. 146). Coupled with this difficulty is the question of how exactly coping mean scores should be interpreted. When coping items are aggregated into mean scores then, notwithstanding that they are "often vaguely worded" and "thin descriptions of coping" (Coyne & Gottlieb, 1996, p. 976), there is also the question of whether, if two people share the same score, they are actually using the same sort of coping strategies. This is not to suggest that we should abandon mean scores, but it does suggest that we need to draw attention to the issue of whether a clearer understanding of how a person is coping may come from exploring the patterns that lie behind mean scores (Dewe & Cooper, 2012). Extending our level of analysis to the way coping items pattern may well be a more subtle indicator of how coping strategies are being used and provide a better understanding of how different strategies relate to one another. The debate as to how coping strategies should be measured and the interpretive consequences that follow from such measures will continue. Such debates reflect a field moving forward and the need to decide, as our knowledge advances, what sort of questions should now be asked and how they should best be answered. We will continue to require researchers to reflect on what traditional measures are providing, where they are leading us, and what can be gained by using, as many researchers are, alternative methods. Some of these may now be better placed to provide the more nuanced answers that today's advances in our knowledge require.

## From Stress to Emotions

Coping research is not, however, all about definitional debates or struggling with the difficulties of measurement, although these are issues that must be confronted (Suls & David, 1996). It is clear that for some time coping research has been heading in new directions, acknowledging the depth and rigor of what it has to build on, recognizing where strengths and weaknesses lie, accepting the need for change, witnessing the ebb and flow of ideas, their influence, and their role in reshaping theories and practice, and instilling in researchers the need to be innovative and creative in ways that best express the nature of the work experience. What emerges are a number of themes that reflect this enterprise. We turn now to the first of these and explore how the troublesome word "stress" is now losing ground, if not being abandoned completely, as researchers recognize the significance of those causal pathways that shift attention to the explanatory potential that resides in discrete emotions.

It is almost a tradition for those who write in this field to draw attention to the ambiguity and arguments surrounding the term stress. Despite the warnings that the continual failure of the term to capture the essence of what it is that is being experienced would trivialize the nature of those encounters (Brief & George, 1991) the term stress has survived (Jones & Bright, 2001). But doubts as to the word's meaning have, of course, remained. For some time, concerns with traditional stress definitions that simply describe stress in terms of its structural components (stimulus, response, or an interaction between the two) have led to researchers questioning how such definitions advance our understanding of the stress process (Lazarus, 1990) and more particularly those underlying processes that link the individual to the environment. Perhaps, as reviewers suggest, it is now time to shift attention back to "stress the concept" and away from "stress the word," in this way giving greater clarity to what is being defined and "how that definition informs research" (Dewe & Cooper, 2012, p. 75) and captures the essence of what is being experienced.

When the focus turns away from the more traditional structural approaches to a definition of stress toward defining it in process terms, then it is clear that the "transactional, process, contextual and meaning-centred approach" that has long been associated with the work of Lazarus (1966, 1990, 1991) needs to be more closely aligned with work stress research. Lazarus (1990, p. 3) makes two points clear. The first is that "stress measurement has almost never been truly theory driven" and the second is that through considering stress in terms of the way the individual transacts with the environment provides the theoretical basis for focusing on the "quality of the emotions of daily living . . . greatly expanding our understanding of how individuals handle both positive and negative experiences." Researchers have debated Lazarus' transactional theory of stress with its "requirement" that as stress "essentially occurs at the individual level" it is this "intraindividual" level that needs to become the focus of analysis. What is questioned is the utility of this approach when set against the duty that work stress researchers have to more generally "discover working conditions which are likely to adversely affect *most* workers exposed to them" (Brief & George, 1991, p. 16). While this debate continues, reviewers agree that "the occupational stress field will benefit from the thoughtful application of the transactional process model" (Harris, 1991, p. 28) and rather than an "either or" debate "we can study *all* of the relevant issues of the stress process" (Frese & Zapf, 1999, p. 764).

So, what is it about transactional theory that leads researchers away from thinking in terms of stress to thinking in terms of emotions? The power of Lazarus' theory in supporting this shift lies not just in the idea that transaction implies process, reflected in the "constantly changing interplay between the person and the environment" (Lazarus, 1990, p. 4), but in the way that appraisals operate both as the process that links the person to the environment and, more significantly, by providing the theoretical route through which the emotional response is captured (Lazarus, 2001). It is the appraisal process that offers a "rich and important" (Park & Folkman, 1997, p. 132) causal pathway for understanding work-related emotions. If, as is made clear, "stress always implies emotions" and "an emotional reaction depends on an *appraisal*" (Lazarus & Cohen-Charash, 2001, p. 53), then by investigating those discrete emotions that are triggered by the appraisal process a more focused understanding of the nature of the experience emerges, making researchers better able to loosen their grip on the bothersome ambiguity and bluntness that surrounds the term stress (Kasl, 1983; Lazarus, 1999). Lazarus (1999) discusses two types of appraisal: *primary appraisal* where an individual appraises what "is at stake," where meaning is given to a particular encounter, and *secondary appraisal* where the focus is on "what can be done about it" and where "coping processes are brought into play to manage the troubled person–environmental relationship" (Lazarus, 1990, p. 3). At this stage it is the way in which a person appraises an encounter that is of interest. "It is essential," as Lazarus points out, "to consider how the individual person appraises what is happening to understand his or her emotional reactions" (Lazarus, 1991, p. 4).

Lazarus (2001) refers to primary appraisals in terms of whether they are negatively or positively toned. Negatively toned appraisals are those involving harm, loss or the threat of harm or loss and produce negative emotions. Positively toned appraisals and by inference positive emotions are those that Lazarus describes under the rubric of challenge and involve "a positive, optimistic, mobilized and eager attitude about overcoming obstacles" (Lazarus, 1990, p. 3). Later in his writings, Lazarus (2001) refers to another kind of positive appraisal that he describes as *benefit*, involving the search for or the recognition of some sort of benefit flowing from an encounter. Lazarus (2001) takes the relationship between appraisals and emotions one stage further through his concept of "core relational meanings," arguing that to understand negatively and positively toned emotions it is important to think of different emotions as having, or being connected to, their own discrete pattern of appraising, providing even more reason for Lazarus to marshal his efforts to "transpose his stress theory to the emotions" (Lazarus, 2001, p. 54).

Viewing appraising as "being the conceptual key to our emotions" (Lazarus & Cohen-Charash, 2001, p. 53) means, according to Lazarus and Cohen-Charash (2001, p. 45), that emotions are best placed to reveal the nature of what it is a person is experiencing at work and so "constitute the coin of the realm" in advancing our understanding of working lives. Emotions and appraisals are intimately linked. For researchers interested in the work experience the message and the emphasis are absolutely clear. Investigating appraisals is not "simply *important*" but "*essential*" (Perrewe & Zellars, 1999, p. 749) if we are to acknowledge the significance of emotions in organizational life, capture both the negative and positive qualities of the work experience, and recognize the limitations imposed on our understanding if we persist with the term stress. To fail to take up the challenge would be to fail to recognize the explanatory potential that resides in a concept like primary appraisal, the understanding it offers and its role as an organizing concept (Liddle, 1994) around which future research may wish to unite (Dewe & Cooper, 2012).

## The Role of Positive Emotions

There is, despite the fact that more and more researchers are engaged in exploring the role of emotions at work, a feeling that more needs to be done to promote the role of positive emotions. Indeed, in her seminal article Fredrickson (1998, p. 300) points to our understanding regarding positive emotions as being "so thin that satisfying answers to the question 'What good are positive emotions?' have yet to be articulated." This, as Fredrickson goes on to argue, is regrettable, as positive emotions have a quality that greatly enriches people's lives. Underlying this argument is, of course, the belief that our discipline has been drawn, somewhat by necessity perhaps, more and more into a problem-solving mode. As a result a greater emphasis has been given to exploring the consequences of negative emotions, leaving an "uneven knowledge base" (Fredrickson, 1998, p. 300) that now needs realigning. Why? So that our work can offer a richer, more balanced description of the experience of work, build and develop an understanding of individual flourishing (Fredrickson, 1998, 2001) and acknowledge the capacity-building characteristics of the positive (Fredrickson, 2000).

Fredrickson's work certainly expresses and is consistent with the aspirations of the positive psychology movement and the role that positive emotions can play in such a movement with their focus on "flourishing, or optimal well-being" (Fredrickson, 2001, p. 218). The power of Fredrickson's work lies as much in her theoretical development of the idea as to how positive emotions "*broaden and build*" as it does in how such emotions "build enduring personal resources" (p. 219). The message is clear: "positive emotions are worth cultivating" (p. 218) and provide another lens through which researchers can best explore the work experience. It is clear that positive emotions should be viewed as distinct from negative emotions. They emerge from a mindset that prompts individuals to engage in a broader range of thoughts and actions that have, in all probability, an adaptive quality, are more flexible and growth sustaining, and that build more long-term resources "like social connections, coping strategies and environmental knowledge" (p. 219) that can be drawn on to manage. They are, in short, an essential element in providing wellbeing, growth, and health (Fredrickson, 2005). The evidence, when it comes to coping, suggests that experiencing positive emotions is associated with a "broad-minded" coping style that involves being able to stand back and view an encounter from a range of perspectives (Fredrickson, 2001; Fredrickson & Branigan, 2005).

Other reviewers suggest that focusing on positive emotions "has opened up a new avenue for coping research" (Folkman & Moskowitz, 2004, p. 764). Commenting on the role these broad-minded qualities may play led Folkman and Moskowitz (2004, p. 766) to suggest that such qualities may also lie behind positive reappraisals, "goal-directed problem-focused coping," and "perceiving benefit as a coping strategy." The usefulness of positive emotions to coping has also been reviewed by Tugade (2011). Her review pointed to positive emotions helping to regulate negative emotions (Tugade & Fredrickson, 2004), dissipating their lingering effects (Fredrickson, 2003), enhancing "one's ability to adapt to subsequent stressors" (Tugade, 2011, p. 191), encouraging more "novel and creative thoughts and actions" (Tugade & Fredrickson, 2004, p. 331), and expanding one's coping repertoire (Tugade & Fredrickson, 2004). When linking positive emotions with coping there are still many questions that need to be explored, including what particular coping strategies are associated with and flow from positive emotions (Fredrickson, 2006), how do these strategies differ from other coping strategies, and is their use just related to positive emotions (Folkman & Moskowitz, 2004)? Nevertheless, the importance of positive emotions is "one of the most exciting developments in coping theory and research" (Folkman & Moskowitz, 2004, p. 767). Couple these developments with the more general call for researchers to focus their work on discrete emotions, exploring them within the context of appraisals, is further evidence, if evidence is needed, that this is the direction coping research should now be headed if we wish to capture the richness and unravel the complexity of the coping process.

## Coping Strategies

Although those interested in coping research will have a range of research objectives, all will need to engage at the preliminary data analysis stage in classifying different coping strategies (Dewe et al., 2010; Dewe & Cooper, 2012. In approaching this task researchers have been drawn to the schema first developed by Folkman and Lazarus (1984). These authors distinguished between "two theory-based functions" of coping: problem-focused and emotion-focused. This distinction provided a helpful "broad-brushstrokes" approach and provided "a good starting point" (Folkman & Moskowitz, 2004, pp. 751–752) when considering the range of different strategies. Other researchers have built on this schema, continuing to explore not just the question of function (Folkman, 2011; Folkman & Moskowitz, 2004) but whether, when developing a comprehensive scheme for classifying coping, such a scheme should also take into account issues of mode (Latack & Havlovic, 1992; Lazarus, 1999) and timing (Greenglass, 2002; Schwarzer, 2001, 2004). It is when one coping strategy is distinguished from another on the basis of timing that has led researchers to consider the difference between reactive and proactive coping (Schwarzer, 2001, 2004) and whether, when such a distinction is made, proactive coping represents not just "an important addition to the stress and coping model" (Folkman, 2011, p. 458) but also all those qualities that are reflected in the positive psychology movement.

It is one thing to distinguish reactive from proactive coping at the theoretical level, but quite another when clarifying the nature of this distinction to acknowledge the difficulties that are involved when coping strategies are examined within the context of a stressful encounter, particularly in deciding exactly how a coping strategy is being used, whether all coping strategies have a proactive element, and what motivates the use of a particular coping strategy (Dewe, 2008; Dewe et al., 2010). Nevertheless, the fact that such a distinction has been proposed, has generated a considerable amount of interest, is clearly associated with the positive psychology movement, and resonates with the idea of resource accumulation (Hobfoll, 2001, 2011) indicates that such a distinction warrants closer attention. It is when a time dimension is introduced, argues Schwarzer (2001, 2004), that it is possible to distinguish four types of coping. Schwarzer describes these in terms of whether they are reactive (dealing with ongoing or an encounter that has already happened), anticipatory (dealing with a perceived impending demand), preventive (building up resources to deal with a possible uncertain demand in the future), or proactive (building up resources that facilitate opportunities for individual growth) (Schwarzer, 2004, pp. 348–349).

What makes proactive coping different from the other three is that it is future oriented, where effort is expended to "build up general resources that facilitate promotion toward challenging goals and personal growth" (Schwarzer, 2001, p. 406), it is more aligned to goal management rather than risk management (Greenglass, 2001, 2002), and it is driven by a motivation to meet challenges and a commitment to achieving high personal standards (Schwarzer, 2001, 2004). At the heart of "what makes a difference" is that proactive coping springs from challenge appraisals, whereas the others come from appraisals of threat or harm (Greenglass, 2002). The proactive coper is described by Schwarzer (2001, p. 406) as a person who "strives for improvement of work or life and builds up resources that assure progress and quality of functioning." Proactive coping is "the prototype" of positive coping and "in line with the contemporary trend toward a 'positive psychology'" (Schwarzer, 2004, p. 354).

So what does proactive coping involve? The Proactive Coping Scale (Greenglass, 2001, 2002), developed from the work of Schwarzer (1999), measures 14 items that together express "autonomous goal setting with self-regulatory goal attainment cognitions and behaviours" (Greenglass, Fiksenbaum, & Eaton, 2006, p. 19). Examples of individual strategies that reflect this proactivity include "After attaining a goal, I look for a more challenging one," "I turn obstacles into positive experiences," "I try to pinpoint what I need to succeed," and "I visualize my dreams and try to achieve them" (Greenglass et al., 2006, p. 31).

Researchers continue to explore and refine the dimensions of the Proactive Coping Inventory, drawing distinctions between proactive and reactive coping (Roesch et al., 2009), and point to

- how positive constructs like proactive coping contribute to improved psychological functioning (Greenglass & Fiksenbaum, 2009);
- how resources like social support lead to the development of proactive coping (Greenglass et al., 2006);
- how proactive coping can be promoted by designing interventions that focus on accumulating resources and goal setting (Sohl & Moyer, 2009);
- how individuals who look to, make plans for, and see possibilities in the future, and set themselves goals make more use of proactive coping (Ouwehand, de Ridder, & Bensing, 2008);
- how proactive coping enables individuals to appraise demanding situations more in terms of challenge (Gan, Yang, Zhou, & Zhang, 2007);
- how our understanding of proactive coping would benefit from exploring it in relation to other forms of future-oriented actions and behaviors including how positive emotions may influence how individuals think

76

about the future and their reactions to future events (Aspinwall, 2005); and

- how future research may wish to explore the way in which individuals decide to use proactive coping, use proactive behaviors more effectively, and how such behaviors relate to organizational outcomes (Crant, 2000).

What lies at the heart of much of this work is that it is now time "for broadening the focus in stress and coping research to include positive emotions and cognitions as well as their promotion by coping strategies" (Ziegelmann & Lippke, 2009, p. 3). Broadening our understanding of coping raises the question of whether something is coping if it falls outside a demanding event or whether "coping can occur in the absence of a stress appraisal" (Folkman, 2009, p. 73). While this question will continue to be debated, Folkman (2009, p. 73) goes on to suggest that "there seems to be good reason to assume that proactive coping is a response to anticipated stress of some sort, even if the intensity of the appraisal is low." Similarly Schwarzer and Taubert (2002, p. 24) suggest that proactive coping adds to the transactional appraisal approach of Lazarus by broadening and extending the concept of coping by including "other dimensions" like "personal strivings." Researchers would agree that there is still much to do in developing our understanding of proactive coping. While proactivity is bound up in how individuals actively create, shape, and modify the work they do, the way they shape and develop interpersonal relationships and social interactions, the impact they have, and the goals they set (Grant & Ashford, 2008), definitions of proactivity still differ in terms of "the nature and timings of the behaviours described as well as in their fundamental goal" (Aspinwall, 2011, p. 335). Aspinwall (2011) goes on to illustrate how, from time to time, researchers have used a range of ways of describing proactivity using terms like proactive coping, proactive adaptations, corrective adaptations, preventive coping, personal initiative, and the proactive individual (Greenglass & Fiksenbaum, 2009). Yet despite all these different terms a number of themes emerge that help to capture the character of proactive coping.

These themes would include the idea that proactive coping is built around individuals actively shaping their environment, having relatively strong beliefs in their own competence, in how change has the potential to improve oneself (Greenglass et al., 2006), combined with a sense of optimism, self-determinism, and goal attainment (Roesch et al., 2009). Then there are the themes of time and motivation. Although terms like "anticipatory" (Schwarzer, 1999) and "prevention" (Aspinwall & Taylor, 1997) creep into different definitions when defining proactive coping, it is worth asking whether such terms blur the distinction as to what proactive coping is and whether all forms of coping have some proactive element (Dewe, 2008). To deal with these questions researchers have turned first to the issue of time. Grant and Ashford (2008, p. 9), for example, suggest that the "distinctive characteristic of proactive behaviour is *acting in advance.*" So timing becomes a key discriminator. What determines whether behavior is proactive "is its timing rather than its specific form" (Aspinwall, 2011, p. 336). Interestingly, this suggests that reactive and proactive coping may both involve the same behavior but that the difference lies in their timing (Aspinwall, 2011; Roesch et al., 2009). As Aspinwall (2011) points out, this suggestion needs to be considered carefully so that it does not limit the search for those future-oriented forward-looking behaviors and modes of thinking that help to capture the essence of proactivity.

The theme of motivation has also been used to distinguish proactive coping from other forms of coping (Schwarzer & Taubert, 2002). This theme captures both the motivational efforts to meet the challenge and achieve a positive outcome (Aspinwall, 2011) and the recognition of the developmental potential that lies in accumulating resources and mobilizing them to meet challenges (Aspinwall, 2011; Hobfoll, 1989; Roesch et al., 2009). Aspinwall (2011) distinguishes between proactive coping as prevention-focused coping and as promotion-focused coping. Preventive-focused proactive coping refers to the accumulation of resources and "general resistance" that diminish the demanding potential of possible future events, whereas promotion-focused proactive coping is where effort is directed toward the accumulation of resources that promote goal attainment and individual development (Aspinwall, 2011, p. 336). It is interesting to speculate (Dewe, 2008) whether preventive-focused proactive coping would include exercise, relaxation, meditation, biofeedback, and a balanced approach to life, which are all strategies designed to develop one's capacity to deal with a demanding event should a demanding event occur. When the emphasis is on the idea of promotion-focused activities it is clear that coping by stimulating positive emotions produces a cycle in which such emotions themselves contribute to building "enduring personal resources" that "fuel resilience" (Fredrickson, 2001, p. 219). On the other hand, Aspinwall suggests that preventive-focused behaviors may represent more "clearly coping" as their focus is on reducing the potential harm of future events. Because promotional activities do not "necessarily carry the idea" of dealing with a demanding event, their fit with the stress and coping literature needs careful consideration (Aspinwall, 2011, p. 336). Clearly this debate will continue.

Developing these different themes may require future research to explore

- how individuals decide whether and what priority they give to engagement in proactive coping;
- what are the boundaries to using proactive coping and what limits their use;
- the impact of culture and socialization processes on developing and using proactive coping;
- the importance of communal coping and how, in understanding this type of coping, we can broaden the idea of proactive coping and challenge its individualistic qualities (Aspinwall, 2011, p. 360).

Other directions may include: continuing to explore the impact of individual differences and dispositional factors on proactive coping as they appear to be intimately linked to how proactive coping is defined, profiles that may characterize proactive coping, situational antecedents of proactivity, the costs associated with proactive coping, and the influence of past experiences, successes, and setbacks and how they feed back into the use and initiation of proactive coping (Grant & Ashford, 2008, pp. 21–25). Then, as in coping research more generally, we still need to continue to learn more about why and in what way a coping strategy is being used, how it is being used, the expectation of what should be achieved and how coping strategies should be evaluated by whom and in what way (Dewe, 2008, p. 96).

Determining the nature of a coping strategy is complex and not always as straightforward when strategies are considered in relation to the context within which they are being used. Future researchers may also like to consider how best coping should be measured and the creative person-centered techniques available to capture the richness of such a process (Dewe, 2008). If, as Roesch and his colleagues suggest, "proactive coping is a unique positive psychological construct" that "is a consequence of other positive psychological constructs," then research in the future may "need to explore proactive coping emphasizing its uniquely positive qualities that include its ability to accumulate resources, its potential for individual development and the opportunities it creates for understanding the role, impact and significance of other positive constructs" (Roesch et al., 2009, p. 328). Notwithstanding all these challenges, the addition of proactive coping to "the purview of coping research" does advance our understanding of how people manage the stress in their lives (Folkman, 2011, p. 73).

## Coping Effectiveness

How do we know, Folkman (2011) asks, when coping has an effect? More importantly, what progress has been made in understanding what is meant by coping effectiveness and does asking such a question simply remind us of the work that still needs to be done if we are to answer the question (Folkman, 2009; Ziegelmann & Lippke, 2009)? Two theories have guided how we approach coping effectiveness (Folkman & Moskowitz, 2000, 2004). The first focuses on the relationship between outcomes and coping, whereas the second proposes that coping effectiveness can be determined in terms of the "goodness of fit" between the characteristics of the event and the coping strategies used. When it comes to exploring outcomes, the research has prompted reviewers to consider what is meant by an appropriate outcome, particularly when set against the dictum of "effectiveness for whom and what cost" (Dewe et al., 2010), who is making the judgment (Folkman & Moskowitz, 2004), whether there is a need to be more discriminating between outcomes shifting toward a more focused approach that embraces discrete emotions (Dewe et al., 2010), whether there is a need to distinguish between coping effort and/or use and coping effectiveness (Aldwin, 2000; Bar-Tal & Spitzer, 1994), and how coping actually resolves an encounter (Koeske, Kirk, & Koeske, 1993). Researchers are also urged to consider whether there is a need to distinguish between resolution and conclusion (Folkman & Moskowitz, 2004), whether as an alternative to outcomes a greater emphasis should be given to understanding the goals individuals have in mind when coping with a stressful encounter (Aldwin, 2000), and what needs to be done in terms of measurement to capture how changes in coping relate to changes in outcomes (Folkman, 2011). Perhaps, as Folkman (2011, p. 459) suggests, what is now needed is for research to focus on identifying "plausible pathways of effect from stress through coping to health outcomes," adding that to get the full picture attention must be given to positive as well as negative effect.

Determining whether or not coping is effective is also heavily dependent on the context, and so when the emphasis shifts to "goodness of fit" reviewers have pointed to a number of issues that need to be explored. These include, for example, the role of appraisals in terms of the meaning given to events, as well as the perceived availability of resources (Lazarus, 2001), the nature and influence of the situation (O'Brien & DeLongis, 1996), the influence of individual differences not just in terms of predispositions toward particular types of coping, but also goals and values (Coyne & Racioppo, 2000; Suls, David, & Harvey, 1996), as well as the range of strategies used (Suls & David, 1996), how competent individuals are when using a particular strategy (Suls et al., 1996), and the consistency with which they are used (Suls et al., 1996). It is also interesting to note that in 1996 Suls and his colleagues were pointing to the "positive aspects of adversity" and how coping should be viewed in terms of its potential for building resources and enhancing mastery and self-esteem (p. 728). Although these issues draw attention to aspects of context, they are not to be thought of as mutually exclusive from or not adding to our understanding of what is needed when researching coping outcomes. Irrespective of the research focus, coping effectiveness cannot be understood independently of the context within which it occurs, even though custom and practice has, from time to time, led to the belief that emotion-focused coping should be regarded as somewhat less effective than problem-focused coping. This, as Lazarus makes clear, is an "erroneous conclusion" (2001, p. 49). As context always matters, then, determining the effectiveness of any particular coping strategy should not be made in terms of its inherent qualities but on the basis of the context in which it is being used. In this way researchers should be left to decide the best way forward, accepting that irrespective of whether an outcome or fit focus is adopted both depend on issues of context.

How individuals evaluate their coping efforts is crucial to our understanding of the stress process. Perhaps in endeavoring to understand effective coping, research became somewhat preoccupied by the search for universally effective strategies (Lazarus, 1999), set unrealistic expectations as to just how effective different coping strategies may be (Somerfield & McCrae, 2000), failed to build on the knowledge that could be gained by exploring other areas of psychology (Somerfield & McCrae, 2000), and placed too much emphasis on what could be inferred from a relationship where coping effectiveness was the focus (Dewe et al., 2010). Despite the models for researching coping effectiveness, we still do not know how individuals evaluate the effectiveness of their coping, what criteria they use, how consistent those criteria are, what stakes are involved, the values they aim to preserve and the images of self, what compromises they make, how ideal they judge their coping to be, what alternative coping strategies were available, how they express and gauge what they see as the costs to themselves, others, and the organization, what benefits they perceive emerging from their coping, whether they engage in the process of reappraisal and when, whether others believe they are coping effectively, what ethical issues may be involved, and how and when they determine that closure has been reached.

## Other Developments

Whether it was the influence of the positive psychology movement with its powerful message emphasizing individual flourishing, or whether interesting new findings in coping research had already nudged researchers toward the positive aspects of individual functioning remains a moot point. Whatever the catalyst and whenever it began and whatever it can be traced back to, this "historic shift opened up new horizons" (Zautra & Reich, 2011, p. 173) and initiated what is now a well-established theme in coping research. This theme is present in coping research in a number of guises. Some we have already mentioned, like, for example, the positive appraisals of challenge and benefit (Lazarus, 2001), the role of positive emotions with their broadening and building qualities (Fredrickson, 2000), accumulation of resources (Hobfoll, 2001, 2011), and, of course, proactive coping (Greenglass et al., 2006; Schwarzer, 1999). Despite the difficulty, as Zautra and Reich (2011, p. 182) suggest, in predicting the direction that a "new set of thoughts will take," a number of clear trends are emerging from coping research. The last decade has seen a "surge of interest" in meaning-making coping, where individuals search for some positive meaning from stressful events (Folkman, 2011, p. 457).

Meaning-centered coping is not just to be viewed in the more traditional sense of managing demanding conditions, but more in terms of how, during such an encounter, this type of coping has the potential to sustain individuals by creating, actively cultivating, and maintaining positive states that help them through the experience (Folkman, 2011). This searching for something good from something bad, as Folkman (2011) describes it, now needs researchers to identify those "positive effect pathways" and explore how their sustaining and restoring qualities give positive benefits. In this way, suggests Folkman, researchers can "pursue fascinating questions" about how such coping functions in terms of its adaptational significance, just how influenced it is by personality and aspects of the situation, when during a stressful encounter it is more likely to be used, what impact such positivity has, and how intense and lasting, in comparison to negative emotions, such positive states are (Folkman, 2009, p. 76). Examining a similar but, as Folkman and Moskowitz (2004) suggest, slightly different question is the work of Tennen and Affleck (1999, 2005), who extend the idea of benefit to "benefit finding" (appraisal) and "benefit reminding" (coping). Benefit reminding coping is where individuals remind themselves of the positive benefits that flow from a stressful encounter. Both "taking the time to search for evidence of benefits" is coping, as is "taking the time to remind oneself of these perceived benefits" (Tennen & Affleck, 2005, p. 589). However, Tennen and Affleck (2005, p. 590) make it clear that benefit reminding is only coping when an individual has, during a stressful encounter, "discovered benefits from their adversity" and can make use of that "discovery" to help them through such demanding times. There is, as Tennen and Affleck (2005) make clear, still much to be done in developing our understanding of benefit reminding coping.

Another theme running through coping research is the concept of stress-related growth (Park, Cohen, & Murch, 1996). This concept couples the idea that something positive can come out of stressful encounters with individual development where individuals have the capacity to grow from such encounters. Although there is still considerable debate and discussion surrounding what is meant by growth and how to measure it (Park, 2004), growth is perhaps captured by viewing where individual development occurs over and above what was present before the experience of a stressful encounter (Tedeschi & Calhoun, 2004). This development may, for example stem from enhanced coping skills, a greater sense of self, and the accumulation of personal and social resources, and may over time help to develop different ways of viewing life (Park et al., 1996, pp. 72–73). If we are to understand and appreciate the nature of growth from stress-related encounters then there is still a need to approach the idea cautiously to ensure we are not placing a burden on individuals to expect that some sort of growth will occur from adversity (Wortman, 2004). There is much still to be done and much still to be learnt about how coping identifies, sustains, and maintains positive states in the midst of stressful encounters, and the benefits that flow from such coping (Folkman, 1997, p. 1218).

# Conclusions

This chapter has explored the role positive psychology has played in our understanding of coping. It is possible when exploring coping research to argue that the positive has always been present not just through the connotations of success or managing that accompany the word "cope" but through concepts like appraisal and resources. Researchers would agree that the presence of the positive has always been present in coping research but for many the issue is summed up by Linley and his colleagues when they say that "it has passed unrecognized" (Linley, Joseph, Harrington, & Wood, 2006, p. 4). The argument now lies less in when and what stimulated an interest in the positive, and more in accepting that the positive psychology movement, with its powerful emphasis on individual flourishing, restored the balance, allowing "a more complete and balanced scientific understanding of the human experience" (Seligman, Steen, Park, & Peterson, 2005, p. 410). It gave credibility to the "other side of the coin" (Gable & Haidt, 2005, p. 105) and through its newfound legitimacy allowed researchers to recognize the value of researching the positive (Sheldon & King, 2001).

Set against this backdrop, coping research has achieved a number of important milestones. It has recognized the importance of shifting attention away from the word "stress" toward discrete emotions. It has provided a pathway through which this can be achieved. By focusing on the meanings that individuals give to stressful encounters (appraisals) we have begun to identify pathways that allow us to better understand the role of emotions, the nature and place of resources, and the subtleties of coping strategies. Coping research also offers a more comprehensive approach that balances the negative against the positive and allows the role of the positive to be explored in ways that capture the intimacy with which it is linked to stressful encounters and the myriad of ways in which it expresses itself. It is now time to put appraisals at the center of our research. To ignore this most powerful explanatory variable is to ignore the concept around which the stress process is organized, and through which our knowledge and understanding grows. If we are to fulfill our moral responsibility to those whose working lives we study, and if we are to capture the nature of that experience, both good and bad, and if our aim is to better understand the richness and complexity of coping, then there is no better place to start than by setting our research within the context of appraisal.

# References

Aldwin, C. M. (2000). *Stress, coping and development: An integrative perspective.* London: Guilford Press.

Aldwin C. M. (2009). *Stress, coping, and development: An integrative perspective* (2nd ed.). New York: Guilford Press.

Aspinwall, L. G. (2005). The psychology of future-oriented thinking: From achievement to proactive coping, adaptation and aging. *Motivation and Emotion, 29,* 203–235.

Aspinwall, L. G. (2011). Future-oriented thinking, proactive coping and the management of potential threats to health and well-being. In S. Folkman (Ed.), *The Oxford handbook of stress, health, and coping* (pp. 334–365). Oxford: Oxford University Press.

Aspinwall, L. G., & Taylor, S. (1997). A stitch in time: Self-regulation and pro-active coping. *Psychological Bulletin, 121,* 417–436.

Bar-Tal, Y., & Spitzer, A. (1994). Coping use versus effectiveness as moderating the stress-strain relationship. *Journal of Community and Applied Social Psychology, 4,* 91–100.

Billings, A. G., & Moos, R. H. (1981). The role of coping responses and social resources in attenuating the stress of life events. *Journal of Behavioral Medicine, 4,* 139–157.

Brief, A. P., & George, J. M. (1991). Psychological stress and the workplace: A brief comment on Lazarus' outlook. In P. L. Perrewé (Ed.), *Handbook on job stress* [Special Issue]. *Journal of Social Behaviour and Personality, 6,* 15–20.

Coyne, J. C., & Gottlieb, B. H. (1996). The mismeasure of coping by checklist. *Journal of Personality, 64,* 959–991.

Coyne, J. C., & Racioppo, M. W. (2000). Never the twain shall meet? Closing the gap between coping research and clinical intervention research. *American Psychologist, 55,* 655–664.

Crant, J. M. (2000). Proactive behavior in organizations. *Journal of Management, 26,* 435–462.

Csikszentmihalyi, M. (2003). Legs or wings? A reply to Richard Lazarus. *Psychological Inquiry, 14,* 113–115.

Dewe, P. (2008). Positive coping strategies at work. In A. Kinder, R. Hughes, & C. L. Cooper (Eds.), *Employee well-being support: A workplace resource* (pp. 91–98). Chichester: John Wiley & Sons.

Dewe, P., & Cooper, C. (2007). Coping research and measurement in the context of work related stress. *International Review of Industrial and Organizational Psychology, 22,* 141–191.

Dewe, P., & Cooper, C. (2012). *Well-being and work: Towards a balanced agenda.* Basingstoke: Palgrave Macmillan.

Dewe, P., O'Driscoll, M., & Cooper, C. (2010). *Coping with work stress: A review and critique.* Chichester: Wiley-Blackwell.

Folkman, S. (1992). Improving coping assessment: Reply to Stone and Kennedy-Moore. In H. S. Friedman (Ed.), *Hostility coping and health* (pp. 215–223). Washington, DC: American Psychological Association.

Folkman, S. (1997). Positive psychological states and coping with severe stress. *Social Science and Medicine, 45*, 1207–1221.

Folkman, S. (2009). Questions, answers, issues and next steps in stress and coping research. *European Psychologist, 14*, 72–77.

Folkman, S. (2011). Conclusions and future directions. In S. Folkman (Ed.), *The Oxford handbook of stress, health and coping* (pp. 453–462). Oxford: Oxford University Press.

Folkman, S., & Lazarus, R. (1984). *Stress, appraisal and coping*. New York: Columbia University Press.

Folkman, S., & Lazarus, R. S. (1991). Coping and emotion. In A. Monat & R. S. Lazarus (Eds.), *Stress and coping: An anthology* (pp. 207–227). New York: Columbia University Press.

Folkman, S., & Moskowitz, J. T. (2000). The context matters. *Personality and Social Psychology Bulletin, 26*, 150–151.

Folkman, S., & Moskowitz, J. T. (2004). Coping: Pitfalls and promise. *Annual Review of Psychology, 55*, 745–774.

Fredrickson, B. L. (1998). What good are positive emotions? *Review of General Psychology, 2*, 300–319.

Fredrickson, B. L. (2000). Cultivating research on positive emotions. *Prevention & Treatment, 3*, Article 7, 1–5.

Fredrickson, B. L. (2001). The role of positive emotions in positive psychology. *American Psychologist, 56*, 218–226.

Fredrickson, B. L. (2003). The value of positive emotions. *American Scientist, 91*, 330–335.

Fredrickson, B. L. (2005). Positive emotions. In C. R. Snyder & S. J. Lopez (Eds.), *Handbook of positive psychology* (pp. 120–138). Oxford: Oxford University Press.

Fredrickson, B. L. (2006). Unpacking positive emotions: Investigating the seeds of human flourishing. *Journal of Positive Psychology, 1*, 57–59.

Fredrickson, B. L., & Branigan, C. (2005). Positive emotions broaden the scope of attention and thought-action repertoires. *Cognition & Emotion, 19*, 313–332.

Frese, M., & Zapf, D. (1999). On the importance of the objective environment in stress and attribution theory. Counterpoint to Perrewe and Zellars. *Journal of Organizational Behavior, 20*, 761–765.

Gable, S. L., & Haidt, J. (2005). What (and why) is positive psychology? *Review of General Psychology, 9*, 102–110.

Gan, Y., Yang, M., Zhou, Y., & Zhang, Y. (2007). The two-factor structure of future-oriented coping and its mediating role in student engagement. *Personality and Individual Differences, 43*, 851–863.

Grant, A. M., & Ashford, S. J. (2008). The dynamics of proactivity at work. *Research in Organizational Behavior, 28*, 3–34.

Greenglass, E. R. (2001). Proactive coping, work stress and burnout. *Stress News*, *13*, 1–5.

Greenglass, E. R. (2002). Proactive coping and quality of life management. In E. Frydenberg (Ed.), *Beyond coping: Meeting goals, visions, and challenges* (pp. 37–62). Oxford: Oxford University Press.

Greenglass, E. R., & Fiksenbaum, L. (2009). Proactive coping, positive affect, and well-being: Testing for mediation using path analysis. *European Psychologist*, *14*, 29–39.

Greenglass, E. R., Fiksenbaum, L., & Eaton, J. (2006). The relationship between coping, social support, functional disability, and depression in the elderly. *Anxiety, Stress and Coping*, *19*, 15–31.

Harris, J. R. (1991). The utility of the transactional approach for occupational stress research. In P. L. Perrewé (Ed.), *Handbook on job stress* [Special Issue]. *Journal of Social Behavior and Personality*, *6*, 21–29.

Hobfoll, S. E. (1989). Conservation of resources: A new attempt at conceptualizing stress. *American Psychologist*, *44*, 513–524.

Hobfoll, S. E. (2001). The influence of culture, community, and the nested-self in the stress process: Advancing conservation of resources theory. *Applied Psychology: An International Review*, *50*, 337–421.

Hobfoll, S. E. (2011). Conservation of resources theory: Its implications for stress, health, and resilience. In S. Folkman (Ed.), *The Oxford handbook of stress, health, and coping* (pp. 127–147). Oxford: Oxford University Press.

Jones, F., & Bright, J. (2001). *Stress: Myth, theory and research*. Harlow: Pearson-Prentice Hall.

Kasl, S. V. (1983). Perusing the link between stressful life experiences and disease: A time for reappraisal. In C. L. Cooper (Ed.), *Stress research: Issues for the eighties* (pp. 79–102). Chichester: John Wiley & Sons.

Koeske, G. F., Kirk, S. A., & Koeske, R. D. (1993). Coping with job stress: Which strategies work best? *Journal of Occupational and Organizational Psychology*, *66*, 319–335.

Latack, J. C, & Havlovic, S. J. (1992). Coping with job stress: A conceptual evaluation framework for coping measures. *Journal of Organizational Behavior*, *13*, 479–508.

Lazarus, R. S. (1966). *Psychological stress and the coping process*. New York: McGraw-Hill.

Lazarus, R. S. (1990). Theory-based stress measurement. *Psychological Inquiry*, *1*, 3–13.

Lazarus, R. S. (1991). Psychological stress in the workplace. In P. L. Perrewé (Ed.), *Handbook on job stress* [Special Issue]. *Journal of Social Behavior and Personality*, *6*, 1–13.

Lazarus, R. S. (1995). Vexing research problems inherent in cognitive-mediational theories of emotion—and some solutions. *Psychological Inquiry*, *6*, 183–196.

Lazarus, R. S. (1999). *Stress and emotion: A new synthesis*. London: Free Association Books.

Lazarus, R. (2000). Toward better research on stress and coping. *American Psychologist*, *55*, 665–673.

Lazarus, R. S. (2001). Relational meaning and discrete emotions. In K. R. Scherer, A. Schorr, & T. Johnstone (Eds.), *Appraisal processes in emotion* (pp. 37–67). Oxford: Oxford University Press.

Lazarus, R. S. (2003a). Does the positive psychology movement have legs? *Psychological Inquiry*, *14*, 93–109.

Lazarus, R. S. (2003b). The Lazarus manifesto for positive psychology and psychology in general. *Psychological Inquiry*, *14*, 173–189.

Lazarus, R., & Cohen-Charash, Y. (2001). Discrete emotions in organizational life. In R. Payne & C. Cooper (Eds.), *Emotions at work: Theory, research and applications for management* (pp. 45–81). Chichester: John Wiley & Sons.

Liddle, H. A. (1994). Contextualizing resiliency. In M. C. Wong & E. W. Gordon (Eds.), *Educational resilience in inner-city America* (pp. 167–177). Hillsdale, NY: Earlbaum.

Linley, P. A., Joseph, S., Harrington, S., & Wood, A. M. (2006). Positive psychology: Past, present, and (possible) future. *Journal of Positive Psychology*, *1*, 3–16.

Oakland, S., & Ostell, A. (1996). Measuring coping: A review and critique. *Human Relations*, *49*, 133–155.

O'Brien, T. B., & DeLongis, A. (1996). The interactional context of problem-, emotion-, and relationship-focused coping: The role of the big-five personality factors. *Journal of Personality*, *64*, 775–813.

Ouwehand, C., de Ridder, D. T. D., & Bensing, J. M. (2008). Individual differences in the use of proactive coping strategies by middle-aged and older adults. *Personality and Individual Differences*, *45*, 28–33.

Park, C. J. (2004). The notion of growth following stressful life experiences: Problems and prospects. *Psychological Inquiry*, *15*, 69–76.

Park, C. L., & Folkman, S. (1997). Meaning in the context of stress and coping. *Review of General Psychology*, *1*, 115–144.

Park, C. L. Cohen, L. H., & Murch, R. L. (1996). Assessment and prediction of stress-related growth. *Journal of Personality*, *64*, 71–105.

Perrewe, P. L., & Zellars, K. L. (1999). An examination of attributions and emotions in the transactional approach to the organizational stress process. *Journal of Organizational Behavior*, *20*, 739–752.

Rand, K. L., & Snyder, C. R. (2003). A reply to Dr Lazarus, the evocator emeritus. *Psychological Inquiry*, *14*, 148–153.

Roesch, S. C., Aldridge, A. A., Huff, T. L. P., Langner, K., Villodas, F., & Bradshaw, K. (2009). On the dimensionality of the proactive coping inventory. *Anxiety, Stress & Coping*, *22*, 327–340.

Schwarzer, R. (1999). *Proactive coping theory*. Paper presented at the 20th International Conference of Stress and Anxiety Research Society (STAR) Cracow, Poland, July 12–14.

Schwarzer, R. (2001). Stress, resources, and proactive coping. *Applied Psychology: An International Review*, *50*, 400–407.

Schwarzer, R. (2004). Manage stress at work through preventive and proactive coping. In E. A. Locke (Ed.), *The Blackwell handbook of principles of organizational behavior* (pp. 342–355). Oxford: Blackwell.

Schwarzer, R., & Taubert, S. (2002). Tenacious goal pursuits and strivings: Toward personal growth. In E. Frydenberg (Ed.), *Beyond coping: Meeting goals, visions, and challenges* (pp. 19–35). Oxford: Oxford University Press.

Seligman, M. E. P., & Csikszentmihalyi, M. (2000). Positive psychology: An introduction. *American Psychologist*, 55, 5–14.

Seligman, M. E. P., Steen, T. A., Park, N., & Peterson, C. (2005). Positive psychology progress: Empirical validation of interventions. *American Psychologist*, 60, 410–421.

Sheldon, K. M., & King, L. (2001). Why positive psychology is necessary. *American Psychologist*, 56, 216–217.

Snyder, C. R. (Ed.). (2001). *Coping with stress: Effective people and processes*. Oxford: Oxford University Press.

Snyder, C. R., & Lopez, S. J. (2005). The future of positive psychology: A declaration of independence. In C. R. Snyder & S. J. Lopez (Eds.), *Handbook of positive psychology* (pp. 751–767). Oxford: Oxford University Press.

Sohl, S. J., & Moyer, A. (2009). Refining the conceptualization of a future-oriented self-regulatory behavior: Proactive coping. *Personality and Individual Differences*, 47, 139–144.

Somerfield, M. R. (1997a). The utility of systems models of stress and coping for applied research. *Journal of Health Psychology*, 2, 133–151.

Somerfield, M. R. (1997b). The future of coping research as we know it. *Journal of Health Psychology*, 2, 173–183.

Somerfield, M. R., & McCrae, R. R. (2000). Stress and coping research: Methodological challenges, theoretical advances. *American Psychologist*, 55, 620–625.

Stone, A. A., & Kennedy-Moore E. (1992). Assessing situational coping: Conceptual and methodological consideration. In H. S. Friedman (Ed.), *Hostility coping and health* (pp. 203–214). Washington, DC: American Psychological Association.

Suls, J., & David, P. D. (1996). Coping and personality: Third time's the charm? *Journal of Personality*, 64, 993–1005.

Suls, J., David, J. P., & Harvey, J. H. (1996). Personality and coping: Three generations of research. *Journal of Personality*, 64, 711–735.

Tedeschi, R. G., & Calhoun, L. G. (2004). Posttraumatic growth: Conceptual foundations and empirical evidence. *Psychological Inquiry*, 15, 1–18.

Tennen, H., & Affleck, G. (1999). Finding benefit in adversity. In C. R. Snyder (Ed.), *Coping: The psychology of what works* (pp. 279–304). New York: Oxford University Press.

Tennen, H., & Affleck, G. (2005). Benefit-finding and benefit-reminding. In C. R. Snyder & S. J. Lopez (Eds.), *Handbook of positive psychology* (pp. 564–597). Oxford: Oxford University Press.

Tugade, M. M. (2011). Positive emotions and coping: Examining dual-process models of resilience. In S. Folkman (Ed.), *The Oxford handbook of stress, health, and coping* (pp. 186–199). Oxford: Oxford University Press.

Tugade, M. M., & Fredrickson, B. L. (2004). Resilient individuals use positive emotions to bounce back from negative experiences. *Journal of Personality and Social Psychology, 86,* 320–333.

Wortman, C. B. (2004). Posttraumatic growth: Progress and problems. *Psychological Inquiry, 14,* 81–90.

Zautra, A. J., & Reich, J. W. (2011). Resilience: The meanings, methods, and measures of a fundamental characteristic of human adaption. In S. Folkman (Ed.), *The Oxford handbook of stress, health, and coping* (pp. 173–185). Oxford: Oxford University Press.

Ziegelmann, J. P., & Lippke, S. (2009). Theory-based approaches to stress and coping: Emerging themes and contemporary research. *European Psychologist, 14,* 3–6.

# 5

# The Role of Workplace Control in Positive Health and Wellbeing

## Erin M. Eatough and Paul E. Spector
### University of South Florida, U.S.A.

## Introduction

Control both inside and outside the workplace has long played a prominent role in research and thinking about stress and health. The focus on job control has been largely on how its lack can contribute to ill-health, as often it is low job control that has been shown to relate to disease and impaired wellbeing, and how it might buffer the adverse effects of stressful job conditions (i.e., stressors). Indeed low levels of job control have been linked to both physical illness such as cardiovascular disease (Bosma, Stansfeld, & Marmot, 1998; Karasek, 1979) and psychological distress (Spector, 1986). Certainly job control would be important if it merely buffered the ill-effects of adverse environmental conditions and events. However, job control also has the potential to contribute to positive health and wellbeing beyond the mere absence of physical or psychological disorder or illness. In this chapter we will explore the potential role job control plays in positive happiness, health, and wellbeing, as well as occupational adjustment and success.

*Work and Wellbeing: Wellbeing: A Complete Reference Guide*, Volume III.
Edited by Peter Y. Chen and Cary L. Cooper.
© 2014 John Wiley & Sons, Ltd. Published 2014 by John Wiley & Sons, Inc.
DOI: 10.1002/9781118539415.wbwell05

# The Nature of Control

Control can be conceptualized as both an environmental condition (e.g., one has the authority to purchase needed items from a department account) and a perception about those conditions, with both being important. Heckhausen and Schulz (1995) noted that humans are motivated to achieve behavior-event contingencies, and that the loss or even threat of loss of that ability is stressful. From the perceptual side, control is the belief that one can achieve desired outcomes and avoid undesirable ones (Thompson, 2009). In both cases, control is defined in terms of the connection between one's efforts and the results, both positive and negative, with the latter being the main focus of control-health research. For example, Thompson (1981) provided an in-depth analysis of the connection between control and response to aversive events. Her review suggested that the ability to avoid aversive events, most notably pain, results in less aversiveness and greater tolerance for the event. She concludes that the most likely explanation can be found in Miller's (1979) minimax hypothesis, which suggests that control allows the person the ability to minimize the maximum danger or discomfort. According to Miller, the person with control can attribute the cause of relief from the aversive event to a stable internal source, the self, rather than a less stable external source. Having perceptions of control provides more certainty that the severity of the aversive event can be kept within tolerable limits.

Another important distinction is between primary and secondary control (Rothbaum, Weisz, & Snyder, 1982). Primary control, both environmental and perceived, is the extent to which people can or believe they can affect the environment as defined in the previous paragraph. Secondary control is the extent to which an individual can control his or her response to the environment, for example, by enhancing the ability to predict what will happen in the future or by associating with powerful others to vicariously enhance feelings of control (Rothbaum et al., 1982). Whereas primary control is directed toward the external environment and involves mainly direct action, secondary control is directed toward the self and involves more cognitive activity (Heckhausen & Schulz, 1995).

In addition to perceptual control over the specific environment, there are personality characteristics that reflect people's predispositions to believe they have control across situations. Locus of control is the tendency to believe in control, with internal control beliefs reflecting personal control and external control beliefs reflecting control by luck, fate, or powerful others (Rotter,

1966). Spector (1988) developed the work locus of control construct to reflect locus of control specific to the workplace.

Self-efficacy is the extent to which individuals believe they are capable of performing well on specific classes of tasks, such as being good at fixing computers or writing papers (Bandura, 1977). Although focused toward self-appraised abilities, self-efficacy is considered a form of control (Thompson, 2009) in that the belief in one's ability to accomplish tasks is a belief in one being able to control certain aspects of the work environment.

In the workplace there are different ways in which control can manifest. Employee autonomy concerns control over how, when, and where job tasks are performed. Breaugh (1999) distinguished method autonomy (control over how job tasks are done), schedule autonomy (control over the hours worked), and criteria autonomy (control over goals and which tasks are done), although in most studies autonomy is measured globally (e.g., Hackman & Oldham, 1975; Spector, Dwyer, & Jex, 1988). Other forms of employee control include participation in decision making, which concerns allowing employees input into organizational decisions that might or might not affect them (Mikkelsen & Gundersen, 2003), and empowerment, which concerns enhancing employee feelings of competence and ability to impact the workplace (Spreitzer, Kizilos, & Nason, 1997). Although there are distinctions among these constructs, they all reflect employee perceptions of control.

## Lack of Control and Stress

Low levels of control at work have been associated with adverse effects on employees, generally thought to be the result of reactions to stressful job conditions. If we accept that people are highly motivated to seek and maintain control (Heckhausen & Schulz, 1995; Thompson, 2009), perceptions of not having control are likely to be stressful themselves. Thus it is not surprising that lack of control has been found to relate to a variety of physical and psychological measures of poor health and wellbeing. For example, in a cross-sectional survey study, Spector et al. (1988) found that perceptions of low control at work were associated with feelings of anxiety when control was assessed by employees (perceived control) or by their supervisors (environmental control). Lack of control has also been associated with emotional distress and physical symptoms such as digestive distress and headache (see meta-analysis by Spector, 1986). In 5-year prospective studies,

Ganster, Fox, and Dwyer (2001) linked lack of control to use of medical services, and Bosma, Stansfeld, and Marmot (1998) linked lack of control to cardiovascular disease.

In addition to additive effects, Karasek's (1979) control–demand model posits that control can buffer the adverse effects of stressful job conditions on health and wellbeing. According to the theory, under conditions of low control job stressors will lead to ill-health. Although there have been many tests of this model, evidence for buffering has been inconsistent (Terry & Jimmieson, 1999), with some studies finding support and others failing to do so. A number of methodological issues, however, have been noted as contributing to the inconsistent support, such as inadequate statistical power to detect moderator effects in many studies, and the lack of correspondence between job stressors and control of those stressors (Spector, 2009).

Taken together, the evidence clearly supports a connection between low levels of work control, in all its forms, and high levels of physical and psychological symptoms of ill-health, as well as disease itself. What this line of research does not demonstrate, however, is that high control will do anything beyond helping to protect from ill-health. Equally important is the question of whether having control contributes to positive outcomes for employees in terms of better work happiness and satisfaction at work and beyond, as well as career and personal success.

## Control and Positive Outcomes at Work

Control over work is undoubtedly an important precursor to positive outcomes for employees. Researchers have recognized the importance of control in employee wellbeing and satisfaction for many decades. Indeed, the literature has confirmed that a sense of control is a robust predictor of wellbeing and positive outcomes (Skinner, 1996). The theoretical notions as to why it could be expected that control at work relates to positive employee outcomes is an important discussion. First, we focus on why control may impact positive feelings such as work and life satisfaction, next we briefly mention the control–health outcome link, and finally we explore why control may be tied to employee motivation and career success-related outcomes.

Satisfaction with work may be related to amount of control on the job both directly and indirectly. First, control may directly relate to positive work attitudes because with control, in particular with autonomy, comes the ability to structure one's schedule and environment to personal liking and preferences. For example, when high levels of autonomy are given to employees, they may be able to set their own work schedules according to personal choice or determine the exact hours of the day in which they are at work. One can imagine an employee who is able to elect to go in to work at a time which allows him or her to drop their children off at school, leave work midday to run an errand, and schedule tasks during the day in order to complete them in the most time-efficient manner. These types of freedoms may accumulate to significant reductions in daily hassles and inefficiencies, and enhancements to typical non-work life domains such as social life or family life. In other words, when high levels of control are afforded, individuals may be able to achieve a better work–life or work–family balance, an idea that has indeed been supported in research (Geurts, Beckers, Taris, Kompier, & Smulders, 2009; Jang, Park, & Zippay, 2011; Parris, Vickers, & Wilkes, 2008; Valcour, 2007).

Furthermore, having control over the physical work space, such as ability to adjust the lighting, temperature, and décor to personal liking or display personal photos or art, may be aspects of the work environment that can directly lead to more positive feelings while at work and when reflecting upon work. In sum, power over personal schedule and environment may directly impact job satisfaction and life satisfaction by allowing employees simply to maximize the amount of satisfaction that can be derived from their daily lives and their environment.

In fact, the prominent job characteristics theory (Hackman & Oldham, 1975) suggests that high control can lead to positive employee wellbeing indicators such as job satisfaction. The theory also suggests that high levels of autonomy at work can translate into choice over job tasks and/or the structure of the actual work, and this kind of autonomy or control cultivates a sense of responsibility over job outcomes. When individuals have an experienced responsibility for the outcomes of their job, such as the quality or quantity of the work produced, accomplishing that work leads to greater job satisfaction. Perceptions of the characteristics of the job, such as level of job autonomy, are thought to precede affective states, a notion that has been well supported in research (Champoux, 1991; Fried & Ferris, 1987; Hackman & Oldham, 1976; Loher, Noe, Moeller, & Fitzgerald, 1985). Thus, the idea that autonomy or control on the job is tied to employee wellbeing, specifically job satisfaction, is not a stranger to theoretical or empirical study and has received substantial support.

Second, control may be indirectly related to positive psychological or physical outcomes. It may be associated with health outcomes simply based on the human physiological response to unfavorable or uncontrollable conditions in the environment. For example, when control at work is high, stress-related hormones such as catecholamines and cortisol are lower than when control is low (Frankenhaeuser & Johansson, 1986). Prolonged exposure to high levels of these hormones can result in impaired immune systems (Stephen, 2003). Furthermore, control may allow individuals to take necessary breaks or obtain appropriate equipment to prevent injuries or illness. Some work has found that control at work is associated with fewer work-related musculoskeletal complaints (Eatough, Way, & Chang, 2012), perhaps because control allows employees to take self-directed breaks from repetitive movement. Autonomy at work may also allow individuals to care for their personal health. For example, control over daily work schedule may allow an employee to leave work to have a doctor's visit, which prevents physical or psychological health needs from being neglected. When a person is deprived of such liberty with their time, options for scheduling or attending appointments may be much more limited. These reasons may in part be responsible for the linkages between low control and poor health found in the literature, such as with somatic complaints and cardiovascular disease (Landsbergis, Schnall, & Dobson, 2009; van der Doef & Maes, 1998). The experience of poor health is associated with negative feelings that adversely affect satisfaction and general happiness.

Career and personal success may also be associated with high control. Several explanations for this are possible. High control may simply lead to more effectiveness on the job. For example, when control is high an employee may be better able to find innovative ways to complete job tasks, seek assistance, or delegate tasks, and may be able to manage their time in a way that maximizes efficiency. Warr (1987) suggests the possibility that jobs that do not provide sufficient opportunities for task control will also rob employees of opportunities to use their full range of skills. Reduced opportunity for skill utilization can in turn prevent employees from developing new work capabilities or expertise. In fact, job control has been shown to relate to the concept of work engagement. In a recent study, job control was related to increased engagement (vigor, dedication, and absorption) in work (Parker, Jimmieson, & Amiot, 2010). Similarly, as described in Karasek's job demands–control model (1979), high control may lead to learning and an expansion of one's knowledge on how to predict, cope with, and maintain high performance during high job demands. Even more, job control may actually improve one's home life via increased work–family facilitation. Using a daily diary design, Butler, Grzywacz, Bass, and Linney (2005) found daily job control promoted more work–family facilitation, perhaps by allowing the job to be a resource that employees could draw upon at home. Thus, through these various mechanisms, job control may lead to increased effectiveness and, potentially, career and personal success outcomes.

In addition, control in the forms of personal characteristics such as locus of control and self-efficacy are likely to coincide with success indicators. It is probable that possessing a general sense of control over one's life and one's ability to succeed at meeting goals leads an individual to make more success-prone decisions. For example, when goals are thought to be achievable, the actual occupations or jobs selected may be appropriately matched to the upper bound of one's skill level, allowing for full use of one's potential. A highly self-efficacious individual may also feel more inclined to choose a job in line with personal interests. Appropriate or well-suited vocational choices may directly relate to positive feelings about work (Mount & Muchinsky, 1978). In addition, it may not only be that individuals that have a high sense of personal control select occupations in which the opportunity for high career success is likely, but they may also be more able to successfully secure a job offer when seeking employment. For example, high internal work locus of control can lead to more favorable interview impressions (Silvester, Anderson-Gough, Anderson, & Mohamed, 2002) and interview outcomes (Cook, Vance, & Spector, 2000).

Control in the form of participation in decision making may also be important for positive career outcomes. Career and personal success may be better achieved when participation in decision making is high as this signals that employees have more instrumental control over the conditions, functions, or requirements of their own job. Having influence over actual job tasks or the specifics of one's role at work may allow an employee to shape their job tasks, evaluation metrics, and performance standards in such a way that they are achievable for them, creating an environment where career success is more likely.

Furthermore, career and personal success may arise from job control because high control encourages intrinsic motivation to work (Barney & Elias, 2010). Being afforded personal freedoms at work may make work more appealing and lead to more effort on job duties. When work is more intrinsically driven and more effort is expended, success indicators such as performance evaluations, goal attainment, and pay raises are likely to follow.

In other words, performance at work (Dodd & Ganster, 1996) and higher quality work (Kauffeld, Jonas, & Frey, 2004) may emerge from employees with high control. Moreover, employees with high job control may also be given the opportunities to perform above and beyond their formal job requirements (Morgeson, Delaney-Klinger, & Hemingway, 2005), which may be another mechanism by which control prompts rewards on the job such as promotions (Allen, 2006). Thus, several explanatory pathways are possible when thinking about control–positive outcome relationships.

## Perceived Control and Objective Control

When discussing the role of control in wellbeing, it is natural to think of the actual control an individual has over the environment, their schedule, their demands, or their job tasks. However, in empirical research, it is often difficult to measure the objective or actual control an individual has. Rather, researchers tend to measure perceptions of control as a proxy of true or objective control. This raises the question of whether perceptions of control are as powerful as actual control, or if perceived and actual control are similar predictors of wellbeing. Some research addressing the issue has suggested that perceived control may actually be a stronger predictor of outcomes than actual control (e.g., Spector & Fox, 2003). Spector and Fox (2003) compared the relationship between a measure of control specifically geared to tap into actual control, the Factual Autonomy Scale (FAS), and a popular measure of control that tends to capture more subjective assessments, the autonomy subscale of the Job Diagnostic Survey (JDS; Hackman & Oldham, 1975). While the FAS asks about things such as needing permission to change the hours one works, the JDS includes perception-based items such as "The job gives me a chance to use my personal initiative . . .." In fact, the perception-based scale was more strongly correlated with job satisfaction than was the fact-based scale and self-reports converged more with coworker and supervisor reports on the FAS, illustrating that perceptions can be quite an individual experience that may or may not be totally tied to reality, and that these perceptions about control may be the more meaningful factor in predicting employee wellbeing.

Thus, because perceived control tends to be the construct measured in research and may be just as, if not more important than actual control, the focus of the rest of this chapter is primarily on the impact of perceptions of control in positive employee wellbeing. Theoretically, perceptions should be quite important antecedents to wellbeing. As mentioned, the minimax hypothesis suggests that individuals strive to maintain their ability to minimize the maximum possible aversiveness of outcomes of demands or stressors. Along these lines, researchers (e.g., Spector, 1998; Terry & Jimmieson, 1999) have discussed perceptions of control as a mechanism for reducing the damage of high demands. Avoiding aversive outcomes can transpire by allowing the individual to both sense control over the amount of exposure to the stressor (e.g., feeling able to control the completion of tasks regarding deadline in order to keep stressor level manageable) or eliminate the demand if the strain becomes too great (e.g., feeling able to decline tasks, delegate to others, or even quit the job). However, it may also be the sheer knowledge (or perception) of being able to manage or terminate an aversive stimulus that can in and of itself reduce the strain response and promote positive wellbeing.

## Evidence for Control–Positive Outcome Relationships

The importance of perceptions of control on the job has been studied in relation to positive feelings about work, positive feelings about life, motivation, and career success. In general, findings have pointed toward perceptions of control leading to greater employee wellbeing. However, the complete nomological network of control and positive psychology-related outcomes has been far from comprehensively examined. For example, as of the beginning of 2012, searching the keywords "job control" and "happiness" returned only three relevant studies on a PsychInfo literature search, highlighting the need for research examining broader personal wellbeing outcomes related to control at work. Nevertheless, a brief summary of a selection of control–positive outcome relationships discovered to date follows. Both perceived control (from here on the terms "perceived control" and "job control" represent a general construct representing autonomy, participation in decision making, and empowerment when self-rated unless otherwise specified) and personal characteristics associated with control (namely locus of control and self-efficacy) will be discussed.

Perceptions of control tend to be related to positive feelings such as job satisfaction, life satisfaction, and happiness. Job satisfaction is the most widely studied positive outcome related to perceived control. Perceived control tends to be robustly associated with job satisfaction levels, both when job satisfaction is approached globally and when individual job satisfaction facets are considered. In fact, in a meta-analysis by Spector (1986), 101 samples were used to examine the overall relationship between job control and job satisfaction. Control was found to be related to general job satisfaction (mean $r = .30$), and facets of job satisfaction (mean $r$ between .19 and .49), with growth, work, and supervision facets showing the largest relationships. Interestingly, similar patterns of relationships between control and job satisfaction were found when autonomy at work and participation in decision making were analyzed separately, suggesting each form of control has meaning for job satisfaction levels. In a more recent study by Liu, Spector, and Jex (2005), perceptions of control were related to job satisfaction, but nonsignificant relationships were reported when independent raters provided control ratings for that job or the O*NET ratings of autonomy were used, underscoring the potential importance of *perceptions* themselves in positive outcomes like job satisfaction. Furthermore, the control–job satisfaction relationship seems to be quite robust over time. For example, in a 3-year longitudinal study, perceptions of job control stably predicted job satisfaction across three time points (Mansell, Brough, & Cole, 2006). Some work has sought to better understand the mechanisms by which job control may lead to satisfaction and has found support for the idea that perceptions of control may lead to great use of one's skills at work and this leads to more positive job attitudes (Morrison, Cordery, Girardi, & Payne, 2005).

Broader measures of employee wellbeing may also be particularly relevant to perceived job control. Specifically, life satisfaction and happiness have received support as outcomes linked to perceived control. For example, in a study of fashion models, Meyer, Enström, Harstveit, Bowles, and Beevers (2007) found that autonomy needs satisfaction, or the degree to which an individual's preferences for control are satisfied at work, was related to life satisfaction (.53) and happiness (.48). In one study using a large Canadian organization, reports of job control was the only factor to account for unique variance in life satisfaction when included in a model with other role-related job characteristics (Day & Jreige, 2002). This study underscores the uniqueness and importance of control at work as a contributor to overall life satisfaction. Similarly, in a large study of office workers perceptions of control at work were related to employee reports of happiness (Piotrkowski, Cohen, & Coray, 1992).

As mentioned earlier, motivation may also be an important positive outcome of job control. Specific work investigating perceptions of control and motivation at work have received considerable research attention. In a study of public sector employees, perceptions of control predicted job satisfaction as well as an outcome termed "work wellbeing," a construct which included emotions (such as tension at work) and motivation at work (Mansell & Brough, 2005). In Spector's meta-analysis (1986), perceptions of job control were related to motivation at work, in this case conceptualized as how important an employee feels it is to do their job well, at a .29 level, similar to the meta-analytic relationship between job control and job satisfaction.

Furthermore, as one might expect given the theoretical discussion above, perceived control has also been found to predict career-related outcomes. In a study using a random sample of individuals in the welfare system, Sullivan (2005) found perceived control predicted whether individuals were employed and if employed, whether the job was high paying or not. In a large Dutch sample, control at work has been shown to also lead to personal growth and development opportunities (Van Ruysseveldt, Verboon, & Smulders, 2011). Thus, employment status, pay, and growth and development opportunities at work have been demonstrated to be relevant potential outcomes of job control.

## Control-Related Personality Variables

Finally, personality characteristics related to control are predictors of positive employee outcomes. Undoubtedly, personal factors such as locus of control and self-efficacy interact with the environment to influence perceptions of control (Spector, 1998) and thus the impact of control perceptions is not a process independent from individual differences. However, we can think about the importance of these personal factors as meaningful precursors themselves as research has shown that they also have direct relationships with outcomes. As discussed, personality characteristics—specifically locus of control and self-efficacy—are conceptualized somewhat differently than actual job control or perceptions of job control, as they represent individual difference factors rather than situational or contextual factors. Research aimed specifically at these personal characteristics has also explored the resulting impact on positive employee outcomes of locus of control and self-efficacy. Similar to the state of the literature regarding perceptions of job control, holistically, research suggests high internal locus of control and high self-efficacy are beneficial for positive wellbeing.

Meta-analytic research has demonstrated internal work locus of control to be related to job satisfaction at a mean level of .33 and to be related to life satisfaction at a mean level of .35 (Ng, Sorensen, & Eby, 2006). Ng et al. (2006) also demonstrated that mental ($r = .36$) and physical ($r = .26$) health have relationships with work locus of control. Spector and O'Connell (1994) used a longitudinal design in which they showed that locus of control assessed in college students prior to employment predicted job satisfaction approximately a year after graduation. Noor (1995) examined locus of control in relation to happiness. Happiness was measured by the combined score on the Oxford Happiness Inventory subscales "positive cognition" and "positive affect" and the relationship between this score and locus of control was .47. In addition, Noor demonstrated that when support at work was high, internal locus of control served to protect the happiness of employees by preventing challenges on the job from degrading positive affect levels. Self-efficacy has demonstrated similar relationships. For example, self-efficacy has positively predicted life satisfaction and positive thinking (Caprara & Steca, 2006). While these studies serve only as examples, locus of control and self-efficacy are linked to a positive outlook, expectations of the future, job and life satisfaction, and general happiness.

Interestingly, research also supports the notion that greater overall career success may be in part determined by locus of control and self-efficacy. The greater success achieved by internally oriented or highly self-efficacious individuals may be in part due to their expectation of effort to outcome relationships. For example, individuals with high self-efficacy tend to do more job search planning and job search behaviors (Fort, Jacquet, & Leroy, 2011). Furthermore, aligning personal interests with work may be more likely when a sense of personal control is high. Some work shows that individuals with high internal locus of control make vocational choices more in line with their career interests. For example, Luzzo and Ward (1995) demonstrated that locus of control can predict the congruence between career aspirations and the current occupation of college students. Werbel, Landau, and DeCarlo (1996) similarly showed that locus of control and reports of person–job congruence were significantly related in a sample of employees from a financial institution. Thus, recognizing and obtaining well-fitting jobs are more likely when these personal characteristics are present. In addition, procuring an employment offer may be more likely. When an internal locus of control is displayed during job interviews, interviewers are more likely to leave with a positive impression of the candidate (Cook et al., 2000; Silvester et al., 2002). Similarly, more internal, controllable attributions for negative events or information lead to more successful graduate recruitment interview outcomes (Silvester, 1997). Thus, possessing high internal locus of control or high self-efficacy can have meaningful impacts on career success via behaviors associated with identifying and attaining worthy vocations.

It is perhaps in part a result of these beneficial vocational behaviors that locus of control and self-efficacy have also been shown to translate into objective and subjective career success markers. For example, in a meta-analysis by Ng, Eby, Sorensen, and Feldman (2005), locus of control was found to significantly predict salary (mean $r = .06$) and career satisfaction (mean $r = .47$). In addition, internal locus of control has been associated with better promotion opportunities (Sharma & Chaudhary, 1980). Furthermore, some longitudinal evidence points to the notion that self-efficacy can predict salary, hierarchical status, and career satisfaction well into the future of recent graduates (Abele & Spurk, 2009). Thus, individual characteristics representing a personal sense of control are significant correlates of positive outcomes relevant to the satisfaction and success of employees.

## Conclusions and Future Directions

Although the literature we have reviewed suggests clear linkages between control and positive health and wellbeing, there are a number of unanswered questions that deserve attention; we note three here. First, how much perceived control is sufficient to potentially impact positive outcomes, and do people vary in their optimal level of control? Under many of the current frameworks such as the job characteristics theory (Hackman & Oldham, 1976) and the job demand–control theory (Karasek, 1979), complex nonlinear relationship patterns have yet to be incorporated. However, future investigations might be able to refine these theories by considering more complex patterns of relationships. For example, although enhancing job characteristics like autonomy may in general be quite beneficial for employee satisfaction, perhaps there is a point of diminishing returns after an optimal level of control is reached. Furthermore, individual differences, such as growth need strength, certainly play a moderator role when it comes to positive wellbeing (Spector, 1985), so that the ideal level varies between people.

Second, and relatedly, is there a point at which too much control becomes a burden and begins to degrade wellbeing? It may be that when demands are high and these high demands are coupled with extreme levels of control (perhaps to the point of lack of guidance or support), control's expected buffering effects as outlined in the job demand–control model (Karasek, 1979) may be reversed. In other words, when the pressure is high and autonomy in managing the demands leaves an employee feeling overwhelmed, control may no longer be so appealing. Indeed, Narayanan, Menon, and Spector (1999) showed how too little direction (having too much autonomy) was considered a stressor in a sample of Indian employees. Gaining a better understanding of the linear or perhaps nonlinear relationship between control and positive outcomes could result in more specific recommendations for managers and supervisors to maximize the benefits of offering autonomy to employees.

Third, how do employees develop their perceptions of control; perhaps via idiosyncratic internal standards (Spector & Jex, 1991) or perhaps via social comparison (Salancik & Pfeffer, 1978)? At this time, it is not well understood whether perceptions of control are formed independent of comparative others or if control is sensed by examining and comparing the autonomy levels of relevant others. If perceptions of control are in fact formed in part via social comparison, it would be interesting to know who the comparative others often are. For example, comparisons may be localized to others at one's own workplace, expand to others outside the organization in similar jobs, or even apply to spouses or individuals in one's social network. Understanding the process by which control perceptions are formed could have important practical implications. For example, if social comparison to others at work is one primary input for forming control perceptions, managers may be urged to evaluate procedures used to distribute autonomy at work so fairness is preserved. Or, if perceptions of control are quite independent of social comparison, perhaps effort should simply be allocated to highlighting and enhancing the true realms of autonomy individuals possess in the workplace. Whereas these questions may be left generally unrequited at this point, future work is expected to begin to unravel some of these more complex questions regarding how perceptions of control develop and influence positive outcomes.

In sum, workplace control plays an important role in positive employee outcomes and wellbeing. It is important to keep in mind that the concept of "workplace control" as discussed in this chapter has been referred to at different times as actual job control, job autonomy, participation in decision making, perceived control, locus of control, self-efficacy, and empowerment. Each has important theoretical and empirical contributions to the discussion of control as a precursor of positive employee outcomes and wellbeing, topics that were explored here. As detailed, it is expected and supported that control at work has established ties to positive feelings, job satisfaction, life satisfaction, motivation, and career and personal success. Continued efforts toward a more complete understanding of the theory, process, and positive outcomes associated with work control are encouraged and anticipated.

# References

Abele, A. E., & Spurk, D. (2009). The longitudinal impact of self-efficacy and career goals on objective and subjective career success. *Journal of Vocational Behavior, 74*(1), 53–62.

Allen, T. D. (2006). Rewarding good citizens: The relationship between citizenship behavior, gender, and organizational rewards. *Journal of Applied Social Psychology, 36*(1), 120–143.

Bandura, A. (1977). Self-efficacy: Toward a unifying theory of behavioral change. *Psychological Review, 84*(2), 191–215.

Barney, C. E., & Elias, S. M. (2010). Flex-time as a moderator of the job stress–work motivation relationship: A three nation investigation. *Personnel Review, 39*(4), 487–502.

Bosma, H., Stansfeld, S. A., & Marmot, M. G. (1998). Job control, personal characteristics, and heart disease. *Journal of Occupational Health Psychology, 3*(4), 402–409.

Breaugh, J. A. (1999). Further investigation of the work autonomy scales: Two studies. *Journal of Business and Psychology, 13*(3), 357–373.

Butler, A. B., Grzywacz, J. G., Bass, B. L., & Linney, K. D. (2005). Extending the demands-control model: A daily diary study of job characteristics, work-family conflict and work-family facilitation. *Journal of Occupational and Organizational Psychology, 78*(2), 155–169.

Caprara, G. V., & Steca, P. (2006). The contribution of self-regulatory efficacy beliefs in managing affect and family relationships to positive thinking and hedonic balance. *Journal of Social and Clinical Psychology, 25*(6), 603–627.

Champoux, J. E. (1991). A multivariate test of the Job Characteristics Theory of Work Motivation. *Journal of Organizational Behavior, 12*(5), 431–446.

Cook, K. W., Vance, C. A., & Spector, P. E. (2000). The relation of candidate personality with selection-interview outcomes. *Journal of Applied Social Psychology, 30*(4), 867–885.

Day, A. L., & Jreige, S. (2002). Examining Type A behavior pattern to explain the relationship between job stressors and psychosocial outcomes. *Journal of Occupational Health Psychology, 7*(2), 109–120.

Dodd, N. G., & Ganster, D. C. (1996). The interactive effects of variety, autonomy, and feedback on attitudes and performance. *Journal of Organizational Behavior, 17*(4), 329–347.

Eatough, E. M., Way, J. D., & Chang, C.-H. (2012). Understanding the link between psychosocial work stressors and work-related musculoskeletal complaints. *Applied Ergonomics, 43*(3), 554–563.

Fort, I., Jacquet, F., & Leroy, N. (2011). Self-efficacy, goals, and job search behaviors. *Career Development International, 16*(5), 469–481.

Frankenhaeuser, M., & Johansson, G. (1986). Stress at work: Psychobiological and psychosocial aspects. *International Review of Applied Psychology, 35*(3), 287–299.

Fried, Y., & Ferris, G. R. (1987). The validity of the Job Characteristics Model: A review and meta-analysis. *Personnel Psychology, 40*(2), 287–322.

Ganster, D. C., Fox, M. L., & Dwyer, D. J. (2001). Explaining employees' health care costs: A prospective examination of stressful job demands, personal control, and physiological reactivity. *Journal of Applied Psychology, 86*(5), 954–964.

Geurts, S. A. E., Beckers, D. G. J., Taris, T. W., Kompier, M. A. J., & Smulders, P. G. W. (2009). Worktime demands and work-family interference: Does worktime control buffer the adverse effects of high demands? *Journal of Business Ethics, 84*(Suppl2), 229–241.

Hackman, J., & Oldham, G. R. (1975). Development of the Job Diagnostic Survey. *Journal of Applied Psychology, 60*(2), 159–170.

Hackman, J. R., & Oldham, G. R. (1976). Motivation through the design of work: Test of a theory. *Organizational Behavior & Human Performance, 16*(2), 250–279.

Heckhausen, J., & Schulz, R. (1995). A life-span theory of control. *Psychological Review, 102*(2), 284–304.

Jang, S. J., Park, R., & Zippay, A. (2011). The interaction effects of scheduling control and work–life balance programs on job satisfaction and mental health. *International Journal of Social Welfare, 20*(2), 135–143.

Karasek, R. A. (1979). Job demands, job decision latitude, and mental strain-implications for job redesign. *Administrative Science Quarterly, 24*(2), 285–308.

Kauffeld, S., Jonas, E., & Frey, D. (2004). Effects of a flexible work-time design on employee- and company-related aims. *European Journal of Work and Organizational Psychology, 13*(1), 79–100.

Landsbergis, P. A., Schnall, P. L., & Dobson, M. (2009). The workplace and cardiovascular disease. In P. L. Schnall, M. Dobson, & E. Rosskam (Eds.), *Unhealthy work: Causes, consequences, cures* (pp. 89–111). Amityville, NY: Baywood Publishing.

Liu, C., Spector, P. E., & Jex, S. M. (2005). The relation of job control with job strains: A comparison of multiple data sources. *Journal of Occupational and Organizational Psychology, 78*(3), 325–336.

Loher, B. T., Noe, R. A., Moeller, N. L., & Fitzgerald, M. P. (1985). A meta-analysis of the relation of job characteristics to job satisfaction. *Journal of Applied Psychology, 70*(2), 280–289.

Luzzo, D. A., & Ward, B. E. (1995). The relative contributions of self-efficacy and locus of control to the prediction of vocational congruence. *Journal of Career Development*, *21*(4), 307–317.

Mansell, A., & Brough, P. (2005). A comprehensive test of the job demands-control interaction: Comparing two measures of job characteristics. *Australian Journal of Psychology*, *57*(2), 103–114.

Mansell, A., Brough, P., & Cole, K. (2006). Stable predictors of job satisfaction, psychological strain, and employee retention: An evaluation of organizational change within the New Zealand Customs Service. *International Journal of Stress Management*, *13*(1), 84–107.

Meyer, B., Enström, M. K., Harstveit, M., Bowles, D. P., & Beevers, C. G. (2007). Happiness and despair on the catwalk: Need satisfaction, well-being, and personality adjustment among fashion models. *Journal of Positive Psychology*, *2*(1), 2–17.

Mikkelsen, A., & Gundersen, M. (2003). The effect of a participatory organizational intervention on work environment, job stress, and subjective health complaints. *International Journal of Stress Management*, *10*(2), 91–110.

Miller, S. M. (1979). Controllability and human stress: Method, evidence and theory. *Behaviour Research and Therapy*, *17*(4), 287–304.

Morgeson, F. P., Delaney-Klinger, K., & Hemingway, M. A. (2005). The importance of job autonomy, cognitive ability, and job-related skill for predicting role breadth and job performance. *Journal of Applied Psychology*, *90*(2), 399–406.

Morrison, D., Cordery, J., Girardi, A., & Payne, R. (2005). Job design, opportunities for skill utilization, and intrinsic job satisfaction. *European Journal of Work and Organizational Psychology*, *14*(1), 59–79.

Mount, M. K., & Muchinsky, P. M. (1978). Person–environment congruence and employee job satisfaction: A test of Holland's theory. *Journal of Vocational Behavior*, *13*(1), 84–100.

Narayanan, L., Menon, S., & Spector, P. E. (1999). A cross-cultural comparison of job stressors and reactions among employees holding comparable jobs in two countries. *International Journal of Stress Management*, *6*, 197–212.

Ng, T. W. H., Eby, L. T., Sorensen, K. L., & Feldman, D. C. (2005). Predictors of objective and subjective career success. A meta-analysis. *Personnel Psychology*, *58*(2), 367–408.

Ng, T. W. H., Sorensen, K. L., & Eby, L. T. (2006). Locus of control at work: A meta-analysis. *Journal of Organizational Behavior*, *27*(8), 1057–1087.

Noor, N. M. (1995). Job-role quality and women's psychological well-being: Locus of control and social support as moderators. *Journal of Community & Applied Social Psychology*, *5*(4), 259–272.

Parker, S. L., Jimmieson, N. L., & Amiot, C. E. (2010). Self-determination as a moderator of demands and control: Implications for employee strain and engagement. *Journal of Vocational Behavior*, *76*(1), 52–67.

Parris, M. A., Vickers, M. H., & Wilkes, L. (2008). Caught in the middle: Organizational impediments to middle managers' work-life balance. *Employee Responsibilities and Rights Journal*, *20*(2), 101–117.

Piotrkowski, C. S., Cohen, B. G., & Coray, K. E. (1992). Working conditions and well-being among women office workers. *International Journal of Human–Computer Interaction, 4*(3), 263–281.

Rothbaum, F., Weisz, J. R., & Snyder, S. S. (1982). Changing the world and changing the self: A two-process model of perceived control. *Journal of Personality and Social Psychology, 42*(1), 5–37.

Rotter, J. B. (1966). Generalized expectancies for internal versus external control of reinforcement. *Psychological Monographs: General & Applied, 80*(1), 1–28.

Salancik, G. R., & Pfeffer, J. (1978). A social information processing approach to job attitudes and task design. *Administrative Science Quarterly, 23*, 224–253.

Sharma, U., & Chaudhary, P. N. (1980). Locus of control and job satisfaction among engineers. *Psychological Studies, 25*(2), 126–128.

Silvester, J. (1997). Spoken attributions and candidate success in graduate recruitment interviews. *Journal of Occupational and Organizational Psychology, 70*(1), 61–73.

Silvester, J., Anderson-Gough, F. M., Anderson, N. R., & Mohamed, A. R. (2002). Locus of control, attributions and impression management in the selection interview. *Journal of Occupational and Organizational Psychology, 75*(1), 59–76.

Skinner, E. A. (1996). A guide to constructs of control. *Journal of Personality and Social Psychology, 71*(3), 549–570.

Spector, P. E. (1985). Higher-order need strength as a moderator of the job scope-employee outcome relationship: A meta-analysis. *Journal of Occupational Psychology, 58*, 119–127.

Spector, P. E. (1986). Perceived control by employees: A meta-analysis of studies concerning autonomy and participation at work. *Human Relations, 39*(11), 1005–1016.

Spector, P. E. (1988). Development of the Work Locus of Control Scale. *Journal of Occupational Psychology, 61*(4), 335–340.

Spector, P. E. (1998). A control model of the job stress process. In C. L. Cooper (Ed.), *Theories of organizational stress* (pp. 153–169). London: Oxford University Press.

Spector, P. E. (2009). The role of job control in employee health and well-being. In C. L. Cooper, J. C. Quick, & M. J. Schabracq (Eds.), *International handbook of work and health psychology* (3rd ed., pp. 173–195). Chichester: Wiley-Blackwell.

Spector, P. E., Dwyer, D. J., & Jex, S. M. (1988). Relation of job stressors to affective, health, and performance outcomes: A comparison of multiple data sources. *Journal of Applied Psychology, 73*(1), 11–19.

Spector, P. E., & Fox, S. (2003). Reducing subjectivity in the assessment of the job environment: Development of the factual autonomy scale (FAS). *Journal of Organizational Behavior, 24*(4), 417–432.

Spector, P. E., & Jex, S. M. (1991). Relations of job characteristics from multiple data sources with employee affect, absence, turnover intentions, and health. *Journal of Applied Psychology, 76*, 46–53.

Spector, P. E., & O'Connell, B. J. (1994). The contribution of personality traits, negative affectivity, locus of control and Type A to the subsequent reports of job stressors and job strains. *Journal of Occupational and Organizational Psychology*, 67(1), 1–12.

Spreitzer, G. M., Kizilos, M. A., & Nason, S. W. (1997). A dimensional analysis of the relationship between psychological empowerment and effectiveness, satisfaction, and strain. *Journal of Management*, 23(5), 679–704.

Stephen B, P. (2003). Stress and the immune system. *Pathophysiology*, 9(3), 133–153.

Sullivan, M. (2005). Welfare reform transitions: The effects of emotional well-being on job status in current TANF recipients. *Journal of Human Behavior in the Social Environment*, 12(2–3), 1–15.

Terry, D. J., & Jimmieson, N. L. (1999). Work control and employee well-being: A decade review. In C. L. Cooper & I. T. Robertson (Eds.), *International review of industrial and organizational psychology* (pp. 95–148). Chichester: John Wiley.

Thompson, S. C. (1981). Will it hurt less if I can control it? A complex answer to a simple question. *Psychological Bulletin*, 90(1), 89–101.

Thompson, S. C. (2009). The role of personal control in adaptive functioning. In C. R. Snyder & S. J. Lopez (Eds.), *Oxford handbook of positive psychology* (2nd ed., pp. 271–278). New York: Oxford University Press.

Valcour, M. (2007). Work-based resources as moderators of the relationship between work hours and satisfaction with work-family balance. *Journal of Applied Psychology*, 92(6), 1512–1523.

van der Doef, M., & Maes, S. (1998). The job demand–control(–support) model and physical health outcomes: A review of the strain and buffer hypotheses. *Psychology & Health*, 13(5), 909–936.

Van Ruysseveldt, J., Verboon, P., & Smulders, P. (2011). Job resources and emotional exhaustion: The mediating role of learning opportunities. *Work & Stress*, 25(3), 205–223.

Warr, P. (1987). *Work, unemployment, and mental health*. New York: Oxford University Press.

Werbel, J., Landau, J., & DeCarlo, T. E. (1996). The relationship of pre-entry variables to early employment organizational commitment. *Journal of Personal Selling & Sales Management*, 16(2), 25–36.

# Part 3

# Happy Workers and Happy Organizations

# 6

# The Happy Worker
## *Revisiting the "Happy–Productive Worker" Thesis*

### Peter Hosie
Curtin University, Australia

### Nada ElRakhawy
Al Garhoud Private Hospital, United Arab Emirates

*When you feel good about yourself, you perform better. And when you perform well, you feel good about yourself. Neither can endure without the other.*

*Tracey (1993), p. 69*

## Introduction

For over half a century, the universal happy–productive worker thesis has captured and held the imagination of organizational researchers and practitioners. Proponents of this idea believe that "a happy worker is a good worker." Support for this commonsense theory is based on the belief that happy workers perform better on the job than their unhappy colleagues. Decades of research have attempted to establish a firm link between workers' happiness and performance. A thorough review is undertaken here into the impact of two important aspects of job happiness: affective wellbeing and intrinsic job satisfaction. Qualified support for the happy–productive worker

*Work and Wellbeing: Wellbeing: A Complete Reference Guide*, Volume III.
Edited by Peter Y. Chen and Cary L. Cooper.
© 2014 John Wiley & Sons, Ltd. Published 2014 by John Wiley & Sons, Inc.
DOI: 10.1002/9781118539415.wbwell06

thesis was found by linking the conceptual bases relating to workers' affective wellbeing, intrinsic job satisfaction, and performance. Practical outcomes of this investigation are addressed, such as how workers' jobs can be changed to enhance or prevent a decline in happiness, and how these findings might be integrated with workplace initiatives to improve workers' job performance.

In the twenty-first century, happiness in the workplace is well and truly back in vogue. There has been an explosion of literature and research into workers' (employees') happiness, optimism, and positive character traits. There has long been lay and academic adherence to the intuitively appealing notion that happy workers perform better. But decades of research have been unable to establish a clear empirical link between job satisfaction and performance. Perhaps the happy–productive worker thesis is actually a self-sustaining "urban myth," founded in opinion but lacking empirical support? So what is driving this renewed interest in workers' job happiness and performance? Pressures to deal with increasingly complex local, national, and global workplace dynamics are greater than ever before. Successful organizations are dependent on workers' capacity to achieve and maintain high levels of individual job performance. As a consequence, predictors of improvements or deterioration in workers' performance are critical to the success of organizations.

## How are Happy Workers Conceptualized?

In his book *Work, happiness, and unhappiness*, Warr (2007, p. 2) posed a seminal question: "Why are some people at work happier or unhappier than others?" Drawing on decades of research, Warr concluded that happy workers have a job with desirable features that match individual needs and wants, where cognition and personal traits combine to create a happy state. This line of reasoning supports the view that people are partly genetically predisposed to being happy (Bartels & Boomsma, 2009). As mentioned earlier, "happiness" has been defined and operationalized in various ways. However, "(un)happiness" has generally been exchanged for the terms "affect" and "wellbeing," where the term "happiness" focuses on a connotative meaning that emphasizes "implied associations based on personal and sociocultural interpretations" (Warr, 2007, p. 9) by further enhancing the subjective nature of happiness (Page & Vella-Brodrick, 2009).

In this conceptualization, happiness includes both objective and subjective dimensions. The objective element is regarded by philosophers as those features that are not under the influence of an individual. These elements may be translated into the workplace as the environment, and its effect on the development of a worker's abilities that utilize skills (Warr, 2007). The subjective aspect of happiness is considered to be the abundance of positive emotions over negative ones, accounting for naming "happiness" as "wellbeing," as subjective (Diener & Oishi, 2005; Lyubomirsky, King, & Diener, 2005; T. A. Wright, Cropanzano, Denney, & Moline, 2002). Thus, in order to experience higher levels of wellbeing, workers should experience both higher levels of positive emotions and lower levels of negative ones (T. A. Wright et al., 2002).

In this conceptualization being "happy" does not exclude exposure to negative instances or emotions. Thus, a "happy worker" may be regarded as an individual with high levels of subjective wellbeing, in the context of the workplace. Paradoxically, our experience of happiness must also include a measure of darkness, as its opposing force loses its meaning if not balanced by sadness (Jung, 1933). Marcel Proust believed that "Happiness serves hardly any other purpose than to make unhappiness possible," in agreement with Mark Twain, who in 1909 observed that "happiness ain't a thing in itself—it's only a contrast with something that ain't pleasant." Happiness is essentially a feeling, a state of mind that is an individualistic experience, since "what brings happiness to one person ill fits another" (Epicurus, cited in Waterfield, 1993, p. 9). The question posed here is: "Are happy workers good workers?"

## The Happy–Productive Worker Thesis

The origins of the happy–productive worker thesis can be traced to the seminal Hawthorne studies (Roethlisberger & Dickson, 1939), where higher levels of job-related performance were attributed to happy workers, compared to their unhappy counterparts. Research into emotions and affect in the workplace were initiated and peaked in the 1930s (C. D. Fisher, 1980; V. E. Fisher & Hanna, 1931; Hoppock, 1935; Kornhauser & Sharp, 1932; Roethlisberger & Dickson, 1939). Hersey's (1932) research represented seminal research into emotions and performance in the workplace which coincided with the Hawthorne studies and Hoppock's (1935) investigations into job satisfaction. Hersey (1932) was arguably the first researcher to demonstrate a definite relationship between emotional state and productivity in the workplace (Weiss & Cropanzano, 1996). He maintained that the primary causes of satisfaction and dissatisfaction were specific work

115

events. Research into the links between affective job states and performance has evolved over decades as the definitions, measures, dimensions, and terminology have been refined.

Studies from the 1930s onwards had found only modest support for the link between worker satisfaction and improved job performance (Organ & Paine, 1999). Belief in the happy–productive worker thesis also has its roots in the Human Behaviour School of the 1950s (Coyle-Shapiro, Kessler, & Purcell, 2004). Improving workers' morale was believed to result in higher productivity. Proponents of the 1970s Human Relations Movement had a significant influence on job redesign and quality-of-life initiatives through Herzberg, Mausner, and Snyderman's classic work (1959), which was credited with specifying the original satisfaction–performance relationship (Coyle-Shapiro et al., 2004; King & Peter, 1993; Perrow, 1986; Strauss, 1968).

In the 1970s, the perceived direction of the causal relationship between satisfaction and performance was reversed: workers who performed better were expected to be more satisfied because they received greater rewards (Lawler & Porter, 1967). Tenets of the Human Behavior School and Human Relations Movement now coexist with the productivity doctrines espoused by economic rationalists in the late 1980s and early 1990s (King & Peter, 1993). Interest in the happy–productive worker thesis plateaued in the intervening decades, until being revived in the mid-1980s and 1990s (Brief & Weiss, 2002). From the 1990s onwards there has been a veritable avalanche of research into emotions and affect in organizations (Ashkanasy, 2004). Barsade, Brief, and Spataro (2003) were moved to announce that an "affective revolution" had occurred in industrial and organizational psychology of similar proportions to the cognitive shift depicted a decade earlier by Ilgen, Major, and Tower (1994).

Half a century of active research has been unable to establish a strong link between job satisfaction and performance. Notwithstanding renewed interest, evidence to support the proposition that happy workers perform better is still not compelling, as subsequent studies have found only modest support for this predicted relationship. Despite the lack of empirical evidence, the notion that happy workers are more productive is firmly entrenched in management ideology (Cropanzano & Wright, 1999, 2001; Ledford, 1999; T. A. Wright & Cropanzano, 2000; T. A. Wright, Cropanzano, Denney, & Moline, 2002; T. A. Wright & Staw, 1999a, 1999b). Despite these mixed and often contradictory findings, a veritable stream of research and theory building may be found into the happy–productive worker thesis that is both "important and worthy" of investigation (West, Arnold, Corbett, & Fletcher, 1992, p. 1), as it "begins to make a claim on our attention" (Christensen, Andrews, & Porter, 1982, p. 6).

## Job Satisfaction and Worker Performance

Earlier research has also been unable to establish a close link between job satisfaction and performance (cf. Brayfield & Crockett, 1955; Iaffaldano & Muchinsky, 1985; Locke, 1976; Porter, 1963; Vroom, 1964). Undeterred by these findings, Brief (1998, p. 43) stated, "I still suspect a consistent, significant job satisfaction/task performance relationship is out there to be found." A review of the literature by Spector (1997) indicated that more satisfied workers are more cooperative toward coworkers, punctual, time efficient, have fewer days off work, and remain with organizations longer than their colleagues who had lower levels of job satisfaction. Worker psychological wellbeing has been found to be in the best interests of employers (Harter, Schmidt, & Hayes, 2002).

A meta-analysis by Harter and colleagues (2002) of the relationship between worker perceptions of the workplace and business unit outcomes found a positive relationship between job satisfaction and worker performance, especially aspects of satisfaction with supervisors and satisfaction with work. Later meta-analyses have indicated that there is a stronger relationship between job satisfaction and job performance than was previously evident (Harter, Schmidt, & Hayes, 2002; Judge, Thoresen, Bono, & Patton, 2001). However, overall the average observed relationship between job satisfaction and performance is positive but relatively weak, ranging from 0.14 to 0.25 (Judge et al., 2001). But a strong association ($r = 0.57$) between momentary task satisfaction and momentary task performance, using within-person analysis (i.e., the same person rating both satisfaction and performance) was reported by C. D. Fisher (2003). Satisfaction–performance correlations are usually stronger in more complex jobs, such as those undertaken by highly skilled workers.

Researchers have mainly ceased investigating whether satisfied workers are more productive, possibly as a consequence of using undifferentiated job satisfaction as the predictor variable, instead of more appropriate measures, such as "happiness" (T. A. Wright & Staw, 1999a, 1999b), or using a close proxy, affective wellbeing (Sevastos, 1996). Affective wellbeing and intrinsic job satisfaction may be a more accurate predictor of workers' job performance when compared to undifferentiated job satisfaction. Furthermore, the construct "workers' job performance" previously has not been robustly measured, making associations between these constructs problematic, partly due to conceptual misspecification and the use of inadequate research methodologies. Organ (1977, p. 46) attributed the acceptance of the conventional wisdom that "satisfaction causes performance" to the acceptance of broader conceptualizations of the construct "performance." Rather than being an aberrant stream of investigation, these findings may well result from poorly specified and measured constructs.

## Significance of the Happy–Productive Worker Thesis

T. A. Wright and Staw (1999a, 1999b) reopened the general debate as to whether happy workers are more productive after decades of research had found inadequate evidence to fully support the happy–productive worker thesis (Staw, 1986, p. 41), or the proposition that "a happy worker is a good worker" (Katzell & Thompson, 1995, p. 111). Authors critical of the veracity of the happy–productive worker thesis, such as T. A. Wright, Cropanzano, Denney, and Moline (2002, p. 146), concluded that "despite decades of study, support for this hypothesis remains equivocal . . . these inconsistent findings may also be a consequence of the disparate manner in which happiness has been operationalized." Conversely, lay people are thought to believe in the happy–productive worker thesis despite the indifferent evidence supporting this supposed relationship (C. D. Fisher, 2003).

Happiness has invariably been conceived and measured as job satisfaction, when a more accurate operationalization of happiness is "job-related affect" and "intrinsic job satisfaction." Job satisfaction in general is probably closer to a state of "bovine contentment" than an actual state of "happiness" (T. A. Wright & Staw, 1999a, 1999b). Researchers have previously erroneously conceived and operationalized job satisfaction as being synonymous with affective wellbeing (Cropanzano, James, & Konovsky, 1993; Cropanzano & Wright, 2001; T. A. Wright & Cropanzano, 2000). As a consequence, "happiness" has been mistakenly operationalized as job satisfaction in organizational research. Job (un)happiness has been equated with job (dis)satisfaction when these are actually discrete constructs. In addition, the word job "satisfaction" is more relativistic in character than the word "happy." Furthermore, job-related affect (i.e., feelings relating to specific

118

tasks undertaken by individuals in a particular work setting) has rarely been used as a predictor of job performance outcomes.

A refocus on this debate occurred with evidence to indicate that affective states and the disposition to experience affective states (state personality) influence the way people perform their jobs (George & Zhou, 2002). Organizational researchers have found that affect correlates with worker job performance, but again the associations found were weak and showed ambiguous relationships (Barrick & Mount, 1991; Gardner & Kozsowski, 1993; Saks, 1996). There are also other potential moderators or mediators of the relationship between affect and job performance.

## Commonsense Theory and the Happy–Productive Worker Thesis

Lay people are thought to believe that happy people exhibit better job performance despite indifferent evidence from the literature to corroborate this link. C. D. Fisher (2003, p. 771) has documented the "widespread existence of a strong commonsense theory; that happy workers are more productive workers, or that workers who are satisfied with their jobs are likely to be better performers on those jobs." C. D. Fisher (2003, p. 773) contended that:

> Individuals may believe that satisfied employees are good performers because of their own highly accessible experiences of being more satisfied at moments that they are performing work tasks more efficiently, and less satisfied when they are performing less well.

Students, workers, and supervisors from a diversity of national and cultural backgrounds considered their positive feelings (mood, happiness, or job satisfaction) were related to better performance (C. D. Fisher, 2003). With regard to the satisfaction–performance relationship the momentary mood and task satisfaction may seem to lay people to covary between persons, when compared with more stable measures of job satisfaction and job performance. C. D. Fisher argued that this belief may stem from the lay people's belief that feeling more than usually satisfied at work translates into better job performance. Possibly this may lead lay people to erroneously attribute their experiences of this perceived covariation between satisfaction–performance and then somehow generalize this idea into the notion that satisfied workers perform better.

Kluger and Tikochinsky (2001) have identified the reasons why the lay belief or "commonsense theory" may identify a strong relationship between two variables such as satisfaction/happiness–performance. According to them, using alternative definitions of constructs and units of analysis may result from lay people using different operationalizations of identical or similar constructs (such as happiness or performance) to those used by researchers, based on loose definitions of the constructs involved. For example, productivity usually refers to assessments undertaken at the organizational level, whereas performance is defined and measured at the individual level. Both terms are used inconsistently and interchangeably in the literature. The terms satisfaction, happiness, and performance may be given different meanings by researchers and lay people and this could account for the perceived magnitude of differences in the relationship between the satisfaction/happiness–performance constructs (C. D. Fisher, 1980, 2002; Judge et al., 2001).

## Happier-and-Smarter or Sadder-but-Wiser?

The literature does not consistently support the view that positive affect always has beneficial consequences on job performance. A trial simulation conducted by Staw and Barsade (1993) tested whether people with a positive disposition performed better or worse on decisional and interpersonal tasks. A positive relationship between dispositional affect and performance was found which supported the "happier-and-smarter" (Enthusiasm–Naivety) as opposed to the "sadder-but-wiser" (Depressive–Realism) hypothesis. Research into the Depressive–Realism view of work performance effect indicates depressed people may actually be more inclined, in certain circumstances, to make accurate judgments compared with their less-depressed counterparts.

Subsequent to this study, Weiss and Cropanzano (1996, p. 55) posed a seminal question, by asking "How are the behaviors in the emotion domain related to the behaviors in the job domain?" They argued that behaviors in the emotional domain have the potential to facilitate, interfere, or are simply unrelated with behaviors in the job domain. However, Weiss and Cropanzano (1996) made the countervailing argument by contending that emotional responses tend to produce decrements in performance. These decrements are argued to be the outcome of both positive and negative emotions (affects) which are incompatible with job demands as they consume cognitive resources required to perform job tasks. Activities resulting from a negative state are reasoned by Weiss and Cropanzano (1996) to be more extensive and constantly disruptive than those resulting from a positive state.

This position is consistent with Taylor's (1991) view that reactions to negative events have been found to produce stronger reactions than positive events. Work by Sinclair and Mark (1992) found that people in a positive mood were more likely to engage in simplified heuristic processing when making judgments and decisions. In contrast, people in a negative mood were found to be more likely to employ systematic processing strategies. Individuals reporting negative affect have been found to focus attention on improvements in the quality of decisions made (Forgas, 2002; Schwarz & Bless, 1991).

Perhaps people with negative affect are more rooted to organizational reality. Several studies support the Depressive–Realism effect which indicates that individuals with depressive tendencies tend to avoid a range of biases. These include optimism bias (Lichtenstein, Fischoff, & Phillips, 1982; Martin & Stang, 1978) and the illusion of control (Langer, 1975). Weiss and Cropanzano (1996) present evidence from the literature to suggest that individuals who are least positive in affect may exercise more accurate information processing. A person with depressive tendencies may be less likely to overestimate their capacity to deal with ambiguous task circumstances (Tabacknick, Crocker, & Alloy, 1983).

This counterintuitive position is highly speculative regarding the possible decrements in performance resulting from the emotion–performance relationship. The predicted state emotion–performance relationship may possibly hold for emotionally charged situations. People experiencing volatile emotional states may have extreme performance reactions but these are likely to be short-lived. In this sense the measurement of "performance" is not really objective. The most obvious bias is that generally people respond positively to optimistic and happy people and negatively to those who are melancholic. In this case, a person's affective reaction may be what is being rated.

When induced by everyday events, positive affect has been shown to promote cognitive flexibility, innovation, problem solving, and creativity (Ganster, 2005). In negotiation settings positive affect is reported to lead people to use problem solving that is focused on generating integrative solutions (Isen & Labroo, 2003). Transitory positive affect has been consistently shown to have a beneficial impact on a variety of decision-making processes in a broad range of settings, including organizations (George & Brief, 1996; Isen & Baron, 1991; Staw & Barsade, 1993). State affect occurs over and above stable dispositional affect, which can also influence behavior (Weiss, Nicholas, & Dauss, 1999). Overall, positive affect seems to improve many aspects of the decision-making process, particularly those aspects concerned with generating innovative alternatives.

Moreover, as Weiss and Cropanzano (1996) anticipated, a simple linear relationship between either positive or negative states for affect and performance was indeed "overtly simple." The debate continues over whether emotional responses by workers are "happier-and-smarter" or "sadder-but-wiser." The affect–performance relationship is far more complex than anticipated. Interest in the "happy–performing workers" proposition and the wider "happier-and-smarter" (Enthusiasm–Naivety) and the "sadder-but-wiser" (Depressive–Realism) hypotheses may be seen with the broader context of the movement to Positive Organizational Scholarship.

## Positive Organizational Scholarship

There is a growing movement in psychology to abandon the exclusive focus on the dark side of human existence with a preference to explore a more positive view of the mind (Cameron & Caza, 2004; Snyder & Lopez, 2002). All this bad news about diminished happiness in the workplace needs to be countervailed by the good news of the movement rapidly taking hold: Positive Organizational Scholarship. The emerging movement to Positive Organizational Scholarship is a health model based on the premise that understanding and enabling human potential will create a positive path to human and organizational wellbeing. Seligman puts the case for Positive Organizational Scholarship:

> By working on mental illness we forgot about making the lives of relatively untroubled people happier, more productive and more fulfilling. We didn't develop interventions to make people happier; we developed interventions to make people less miserable (www.edge.org).

Furthermore, Bagnall (2004) concurs with the Positive Organizational Scholarship approach and extends this line of reasoning by arguing that there are sound social and economic reasons for promoting happiness through healthy work. For example, positive psychology has focused attention on the potential benefits of positive feelings in the workplace (Pressman & Cohen, 2005; Seligman & Csikszentmihalyi, 2000). Positive Organizational Scholarship is orientated to investigating and understanding "positive deviance," to discover the ways in which organizations and their members flourish

122

and prosper in extraordinary ways. Positive Organizational Scholarship seeks to understand exemplars of human condition in organizations by studying organizations and organizational contexts characterized by appreciation, collaboration, and vitality. Fulfillment with the purpose of creating abundance and human wellbeing are seen as the key indicators of success in the workforce. As such, employee wellbeing is viewed from an intrinsic goal-orientated perspective, rather than as being the end that all participants in organizational work life should aspire. Positive Organizational Scholarship seeks to rigorously understand what represents the best of the human condition, founded on scholarly research and theory.

## Becoming a Happy Worker

How *does* one become a "happy worker?" Happiness is partly inherited: around 40% of people are predisposed to being "happy" (Bartels & Boomsma, 2009). However, being "happy" can also be partly acquired by adopting certain tactics (Lyubomirsky, Sheldon, & Schkade, 2005). Moreover, there is a strong subjective aspect to being "happy" (Warr & Clapperton, 2010). Levels of happiness need to maintain or exceed certain levels that vary through time, circumstances, and career stages (P. Warr, 2007). Acting happy emphasizes the contagious nature of being happy (Otake, Shimai, Tanaka-Matsumi, Otsui, & Fredrickson, 2006).

The basis of such an approach may be found in social psychology, in terms of "roles" (Myers, 2003) whereby a role is a behavior adopted in a social or occupational setting (Lindgren, 1997). Experiments have further illustrated that people who take on new roles tend to adopt the characteristics of such roles over time, a famous example being the illustrative experiment of role-play by Zimbardo between prisoners and guards (Myers, 2003). Therefore, enacting the role of a happy worker may, over time, lead to actually feeling and acquiring the elements of being a happy worker.

Developing close social relationships (Diener & Oishi, 2005; Otake et al., 2006; T. A. Wright et al., 2002) is a "happy" recipe that includes prioritizing close relationships with others to build a base for ongoing happiness (Diener & Oishi, 2005). A growing number of studies have displayed that the positive effects of exercise and sleep on happiness (Page & Vella-Brodrick, 2009) is a two-way relationship (Myers, 2003). Gratitude—a worker listing and appreciating the blessings in life or work—is another important recipe for "happiness" (Sheldon & Lyubomirsky, 2006). Within the workplace context, this is reflected through improved relationships with coworkers.

Furthermore, the importance of recognition is acknowledged, not only of individuals but also of others in the workplace. This may be viewed as a cycle: contributions to the recognition of a colleague's work in turn enhances levels of happiness, which reflect upon own happiness, due to a "contagious" effect or just the joy of making someone else happy (Otake et al., 2006). Hence, to become a happy worker not only involves focusing on individual interests but also on exhibiting concerns for other workers. In addition, social relationships are nurtured through "self-disclosures" (Myers, 2003), such as sharing life (dis)similarities with coworkers. Eventually, such a practice would perhaps aid in creating a work environment consisting of the ingredients for fostering happy workers (Warr, 2007; Warr & Clapperton, 2010).

## What Factors Would Facilitate and Inhibit in the Course of Being Happy Workers?

In addition to the content and features of a job (Saavedra & Kwun, 2000; Warr, 2007), there seems to be some consensus about other factors that affect a worker's ability to achieve a desirable level of "happiness." One such factor is personality. Numerous studies have shown that individuals who possess certain personality traits tend to be happier (Warr & Clapperton, 2010). Personality development parallels the genetic predisposition of a happy worker (Bartels & Boomsma, 2009; Page & Vella-Brodrick, 2009). In other words, a happy worker is generally predisposed to being happy. This is perhaps closely linked to and further supports personality as a facilitating or inhibiting factor. Since personality is partly inherited, exposure to different life circumstances, such as are found in the workplace, are going to shape a person's personality (Myers, 2003). Accordingly, an individual would have to adopt certain practices and attitudes described earlier in order to utilize a predisposition to achieve a desired state of happiness. As Lyubomirsky, Sheldon, and Schkade (2005) confirm, "happiness is a process, not a place."

Another factor in determining workers' happiness is the quality of social relationships. With healthy relationships comes a sense of belonging (Myers, 2003) and meaningfulness (Harter, Schmidt, & Keyes, 2002); both of these job features contribute to a worker's wellbeing (Warr, 2007; Warr & Clapperton, 2010). As social relationships in the workplace involve interactions with other workers, positive gestures and actions aid in facilitating workers in their journey to become "happy workers." However, it should be noted that for social relationships to serve as a facilitating factor, the possession of largely positive interactions is required (Diener & Oishi, 2005). As mentioned earlier, this is because negative instances tend to yield a larger emotional reaction than positive ones (Diener & Oishi, 2005). Furthermore, social relationships are also fostered by personality traits, such as extraversion and outgoing characteristics (Page & Vella-Brodrick, 2009). As most of these factors overlap, an individual could practice those which need to be acquired, and match it to the nature of the job in an attempt to become happier.

Furthermore, studies such as those by Sheldon and Lyubomirsky (2006) have found that visualizing being happy does in fact lead to higher levels of positive affect. An explanation for such a result may be found in the psychological concept of a "self-fulfilling prophecy" (Myers, 2003). This may also hold the other way around: visualizing negative occurrences or outcomes or even demotivating self through a "can't do" attitude would in fact render a person incapable of happy actions. Thus, positive or negative attitude in "imagining" (Page & Vella-Brodrick, 2009) does result in facilitating or inhibiting the quest to become a happy worker.

Monetary rewards beyond a certain level are not the only cause for happiness in the workplace. In some cases, being paid less to produce more may not necessarily have an adverse effect on a worker's happiness if other conditions of work are adjusted to account for individual differences (Warr & Clapperton, 2010). Adjusting certain job features, as found in Hackman and Oldham's classic Job Characteristic Model (Saavedra & Kwun, 2000) or Warr's Job Features (Warr & Clapperton, 2010), will permit healthier jobs to be created. The perfect mix would depend on the predilections of each worker, given the subjective nature of happiness. For this to occur managers need to conceive and treat each individual worker as unique rather than as simply part of a standard operating procedure.

## Outcomes (Individual, Work, Family, Life, etc.) of Being Happy Workers

As Bagnall (2004) observed (along with Tolstoy), unhappiness may be more interesting, but happy people do better in almost every area of life. Lyubomirsky and colleagues (Lyubomirsky, Sheldon, et al., 2005) found that happy people tend to acquire favorable life circumstances which engender success. A link between happiness and success has been made across many studies, indicating that happy individuals are successful across multiple life domains, such as marriage, friendship, health, and job performance (Lyubomirsky, King, et al., 2005).

From a broader perspective, research into affective wellbeing has consistently shown that the "characteristics and resources valued by society correlate with happiness" (Lyubomirsky, King, et al., 2005, p. 925). Elevated levels of happiness have been found to covary with marriage (Mastekaasa, 1994), a comfortable income (Diener & Biswas-Diener, 2003), superior mental health (Koivumaa-Honkanen et al., 2004), and a long life (Danner, Snowdon, & Friesen, 2001) as "happy people are likely to acquire favourable life circumstances" (Lyubomirsky, King, et al., 2005, p. 803). By rigorously testing the happiness–success link, Lyubomirsky and colleagues demonstrated that happy people tend to be successful and flourish. Positive emotions and chronic happiness were found to be "often associated with resources and characteristics that parallel success and thriving—that is, desirable behaviors and cognitions such as sociability, optimism, energy, originality, and altruism" (Lyubomirsky, King, et al., 2005, p. 846).

The outcome of being a happy worker reflects upon an individual at different levels. Clinical psychology studies indicate positive/negative affect at the individual level of impacts on self-esteem, which in turn determines levels of motivation (T. A. Wright et al., 2002). This further translates into thought processes. In life, this may include the individual's perspective of experiences, as well as family life. Improved social relationships in the workplace are depicted by the tendency for a happy worker to make better decisions (Côté, 1999) and to have enhanced personal competence (Diener & Oishi, 2005). Also, the willingness and quality of participation in the workplace associated with happy workers leads to more effective teamwork (Côté, 1999). Evidence also indicates that improved social relationships resulting from being a happy worker lead to better teamwork (Diener & Oishi, 2005). A happy worker also has the benefit of emitting cues of being happy, which leads to receiving positive impacts on attitude and approach to work, and more positive ratings by peers (Côté, 1999).

However, it should be noted that potential downsides do exist. One such example is that an increased sense of potential can create a false or somewhat distorted sense of confidence, which may hinder logical reasoning and decision making (Lyubomirsky, King, et al., 2005). Furthermore, a potential bias is the possibility of a halo effect upon a happy worker's performance rating. Since improved social functioning is a known outcome for happy workers (T. A. Wright et al., 2002), this may result in a bias in performance ratings, particularly that of peers. One could further extend this point and consider if the bias would be in a negative direction, perhaps due to jealousy of others? In all, considerable evidence has been presented by Lyubomirsky and colleagues to challenge the belief that successful outcomes and desirable characteristics are primarily the causes, not the consequences, of happiness.

## Relationship to Contemporary Workplace Issues

In the twenty-first century, workers are also expected to produce more with less. Better services, quicker response times, more products to market, shorter product cycles, increased sales, and better value for money are demanded. As a direct consequence of globalization, the roles and performance expectations of workers have changed substantially. Workers are operating in a "just in time" mode, teetering on the brink of not having adequate time to complete their work. Such changes to the workplace highlight the need to understand how workers can work smarter and faster, rather than harder and longer, and still retain their affective wellbeing.

Strategically integrated human resource initiatives are likely to contribute to an organization's success (Guest, 1990). Human resource practices have emerged as a key competitive advantage for countries and organizations (Collins, 2001; O'Reilly & Pfeffer, 2000; Schuler & MacMillan, 1984). Decisions about the direction human resource management practices take will ultimately be largely dependent on the world economy. Likewise, workers are dependent on the financial prosperity of the organizations they work for. As such, the financial viability of organizations and nation-states will be in large measure determined by their workers' capacity to contribute to the generation of wealth. In this environment, strategic human resource initiatives that enhance workers' affective wellbeing and intrinsic job satisfaction constitute a way of contributing to workers' performance (Collins, 2001; Forster, 2005; O'Reilly & Pfeffer, 2000).

Organizations seeking to create and maintain a healthy working environment for the benefit of the physical, mental, and social wellbeing of their workers need to implement strategies that promote workplace health and safety (Cooper & Cartwright, 1994). Evidence of the process of how affective wellbeing and intrinsic job satisfaction interact with workers' performance will be invaluable in determining job designs and organizational level interventions. Such an understanding has the potential to translate into improved managerial practices.

Improvements in the quality of people's working lives and their performance resonates and builds insights into how certain human resource management practices have large effects on organizational productivity, as described by Ichniowski, Shaw, and Prennushi (1997) and Patterson et al. (1997). In combination, these benefits may result in more effective organizational outcomes, including increased productivity, reduced organizational costs, and reduced staff turnover. In all, failure to address affective wellbeing issues in the workplace potentially retards an organization's capacity to maximize efficiency and effectiveness (Staw & Barsade, 1993).

Human resource practices targeted at individual performance have been found to be associated with perceptual and financial measures of organizational effectiveness (Becker & Gerhart, 1996; Delaney & Huselid, 1996; Huselid, 1995; Huselid, Jackson, & Schuler, 1997; Snell & Youndt, 1995; Terpstra & Rozell, 1993; Youndt, Snell, Dean, & Lepak, 1996). A strong link has been indicated between people management and business performance (Ichniowski et al., 1997; O'Reilly & Pfeffer, 2000; Patterson et al., 1997; Purcell, 2004). In a groundbreaking study, Huselid (1995) determined that a set of human resource practices (high performance work systems) were related to turnover, accounting profits, and firm market value.

Compared to other management practices (e.g., strategy, quality focus, investment in research and development), human resource practices explained 18% of the variation in productivity and 19% in profitability of companies in the United Kingdom (Patterson et al., 1997). Two clusters of skills—acquisition and development of workers' skills (including the use of appraisals) and job design—were shown to be particularly important. Patterson and colleagues have established an empirically strong argument supporting the relationship between people-management practices and commercial performance. A longitudinal study by Ichniowski and colleagues (1990, 1997) found that clusters of innovative human resource management systems had large effects on workers' performance but changes in individual employment practices had minimal effect.

An optimal bundle or combination of properly applied human resource policies was found by Purcell (2004) to be necessary for the achievement of high performance. Consistent with Ichniowski and colleagues' (1990, 1997) findings, the "human resource bundle" requirements were found to be different for different occupations. Eleven human resource policy areas were associated with achieving the desired ability, motivation, and opportunity to achieve higher levels of organization commitment, job satisfaction, and ultimately performance. Integrated "bundles" or "clusters" of human resource practices are likely to produce greater improvement in organizational effectiveness than isolated interventions (Huselid, 1995; Huselid et al., 1997; Ichniowski, 1990; Ichniowski et al., 1997; Purcell, 2004).

Way (2002, p. 765) boldly stated in the same vein that "Theoretical and empirical HRM research has led to a general consensus that the method used by a firm to manage its workforce can have a positive impact on firm performance." Positive workplace perceptions and feelings were found by Harter, Schmidt, and Hayes (2002) to be associated with higher business unit customer loyalty, higher profitability, higher productivity, and lower rates of turnover. According to Nankervis, Compton, and McCarthy (2004), the mutual contributions of "soft" (people-driven human resource features, such as motivation and leadership) and "hard" (market-driven forces such as strategy formulation and programme evaluation) aspects of management have yet to be established.

A subsequent review of the published literature on human resource practices and organizational performance by Wall and Wood (2005) takes a more sobering position. They claimed that the existing studies have opened up a promising line of inquiry, but methodological limitations preclude making a definitive conclusion about the causal relationship between human resource practices and individual performance and organizational productivity. Further, P. M. Wright, Gardner, Moynihan, and Allen (2005) argued that claims by Huselid and Becker (1997) that existing research suggested a positive link between human resource practices and organizational performance were premature. Research still lacks sufficient methodological rigor to demonstrate a causal relationship between human resource practices and organizational performance. In contrast, P. M. Wright et al. (2005) found human resource practices were strongly related to both future performance and past performance.

Controlling for past or concurrent performance eliminated the correlation of human resource practice with future performance, negating proof that these practices "cause" that high organizational performance. Large amounts of evidence have accumulated to support the human resource management–productivity link (Appelbaum, Bailey, Berg, & Kalleberg, 2000; Harter, Schmidt, & Keyes, 2002; Ichniowski, 1990; Lawler, Mohrman, & Ledford, 1995, 1998). However, evidence is emerging to indicate that management practices designed to humanize the workplace are being reciprocated by improved productivity (Maister, 2001).

# Summary and Conclusion

This chapter revisits a seminal question in management theory and practice: the happy–productive worker thesis. There has long been an adherence to the intuitively appealing notion that happy workers perform better. The conceptualization and analysis in the literature has made substantial progress toward supporting a more evolved "happy–productive worker." Insights are derived from the interrelationships between a number of disciplines, theories, and models related to the field of management. The study of affective wellbeing, intrinsic job satisfaction, and workers' performance is primarily situated in an industrial, organizational, and occupational psychology framework, which is complemented by elements of organizational behavior and strategic human resource management. This research contributes to the emerging movement for Positive Organizational Scholarship, which has begun investigating the link between happy workers and productive organizations.

Recent decades have witnessed two related major structural changes in developed economies: the intensification of global competition and the pervasive dispersal of computer-based technologies. Structural changes in state policies resulting from the emergence of significant competitors in manufacturing industries from low-wage economies has had important consequences for labor markets, particularly pay and working conditions. Radical alterations in work organization have been reinforced by widespread and systematic changes in the workplace. Rising effort requirements of jobs, the changing extent of task discretion, and other forms of job involvement could be expected to affect workers' happiness. A further major change with implications for intrinsic job satisfaction is the rising level of competencies required in jobs, resulting from the adoption of skill-biased technological change.

Work is a pervasive and influential aspect of individual and organizational life. The incidence of work-related affective disorders in the developed world is approaching epidemic proportions. Individuals and organizations are increasingly being forced to acknowledge that this emerging form of social inflation may be attributed to overwork and pressure. The incidence of mental health problems affecting these workforces is increasing. Work-related stress and associated medical ailments are costly hazards for modern society. Mental health problems in the workplace are now regarded as an international problem of considerable magnitude. The "happy performing workers" proposition confronts a wider vista to contemplate how workers' "private troubles" have become structural influences on "public concerns."

Expanding the construct space for both affect and performance in the workplace makes it possible to test potential new linkages between these variables. A more sophisticated understanding of how affective wellbeing and intrinsic job satisfaction interacts with workers' performance is posited to contribute to a better understanding of aspects of the relationships underlying these constructs. There is a case for extending the happy–productive worker thesis to an examination of the extent to which workers' affective wellbeing influences performance, using more robust methodologies to measure these constructs. Reinvigorating this debate may also inform the more general but unproven proposition that happy workers perform more effectively.

Changes to the design of jobs have the potential to either improve or worsen workers' affective wellbeing and intrinsic job satisfaction and, consequently, their performance. Identifying factors that either positively or negatively impact on workers' affective wellbeing and intrinsic job satisfaction will enable recommendations to be made for designing jobs and altering work environments that will then assist workers to achieve optimal performance. Such information may permit the identification of the relevant job characteristics that can be adjusted to assist in promoting positive affective wellbeing and intrinsic job satisfaction. This can be seen as preventative "worker medicine." A challenge exists for researchers and practitioners to explore new models, theories, and measures of workers' happiness and performance by building upon the Positive Organizational Scholarship movement.

# References

Appelbaum, E., Bailey, T., Berg, P., & Kalleberg, A. L. (2000). *Manufacturing advantage: Why high performance work systems pay off*. Ithaca, NY: Cornell University Press.

Ashkanasy, N. M. (2004). Emotions and performance. *Human Performance*, *17*(2), 137–144.

Bagnall, D. (2004, December 15). *Science of happiness: The secret of happiness is the holy grail of the new millennium. The Bulletin Features, Summer Reading*, A6.

Barrick, M. R., & Mount, M. K. (1991). The big five personality dimensions and job performance: A meta-analysis. *Personnel Psychology*, *44*(1), 1–26.

Barsade, S. G., Brief, A. P., & Spataro, S. E. (2003). The affective revolution in organizational behavior: The emergence of a paradigm. In J. Greenberg (Ed.),

*Organizational behavior: The state of the science* (pp. 3–52). Hillsdale, NJ: Lawrence Erlbaum.

Bartels, M., & Boomsma, D. I. (2009). Born to be happy? The etiology of subjective well-being. *Behavior Genetics, 39*(6), 605–615.

Becker, B., & Gerhart, B. (1996). The impact of human resource management on organizational performance: Progress and prospects. *Academy of Management Journal, 39*(4), 779–801.

Brayfield, A. H., & Crockett, W. H. (1955). Employee attitudes and employee performance. *Psychological Bulletin, 52*(5), 396–424.

Brief, A. P. (1998). *Attitudes in and around organizations*. Thousand Oaks, CA: Sage.

Brief, A. P., & Weiss, H. M. (2002). Organizational behavior: Affect at work. *Annual Review of Psychology, 53*, 279–307.

Cameron, K. S., & Caza, A. (2004). Contributions to the discipline of positive organisational scholarship. *American Behavioral Scientist, 47*(6), 731–739.

Christensen, C. R., Andrews, K. R., & Porter, M. E. (1982). *Business policy: Texts and cases* (5th ed.). Homewood, IL: Irwin.

Collins, J. (2001). *Good to great: Why some companies make the leap . . . and others don't*. New York: Harper Collins.

Cooper, C. L., & Cartwright, S. (1994). Healthy mind, healthy organization: A proactive approach to occupational stress. *Human Relations, 47*(4), 455–471.

Côté, S. (1999). Affect and performance in organizational settings. *Current Directions in Psychological Science, 8*(2), 65–68.

Coyle-Shapiro, J., Kessler, I., & Purcell, J. (2004). Reciprocity or "it's my job": Exploring organizationally directed citizenship behavior in a National Health Service Setting. *Journal of Management Studies, 41*(1), 85–106.

Cropanzano, R. S., James, K., & Konovsky, M. A. (1993). Dispositional affectivity as a predictor of work attitudes and job performance. *Journal of Organizational Behavior, 14*(6), 595–606.

Cropanzano, R. S., & Wright, T. A. (1999). A five-year study of the relationship between well-being and performance. *Journal of Consulting Psychology, 51*, 252–265.

Cropanzano, R. S., & Wright, T. A. (2001). When a "happy" worker is really a "productive" worker: A review and further refinements of the happy-productive worker thesis. *Consulting Psychology Journal, 53*(3), 182–199.

Danner, D. D., Snowdon, D. A., & Friesen, W. V. (2001). Positive emotions in early life and longevity: Findings from the nun study. *Journal of Personality and Social Psychology, 80*(5), 804–813.

Delaney, J. T., & Huselid, M. A. (1996). The impact of human resource management practices on perceptions of organizational performance. *Academy of Management Journal, 39*(4), 949–969.

Diener, E., & Biswas-Diener, R. (2003). Will money increase subjective well-being? *Social Indicators Research, 57*, 119–169.

Diener, E., & Oishi, S. (2005). The nonobvious social psychology of happiness. *Psychological Inquiry, 16*(4), 162–167.

Fisher, C. D. (1980). On the dubious wisdom of expecting job satisfaction to correlate with performance. *Academy of Management Review*, 5(4), 607–612.

Fisher, C. D. (2002). Antecedents and consequences of real-time affective reactions at work. *Motivation and Emotion*, 26(1), 3–30.

Fisher, C. D. (2003). Why do lay people believe that satisfaction and performance are correlated? Possible sources of a commonsense theory. *Journal of Organizational Behavior*, 24(6), 753–777.

Fisher, V. E., & Hanna, J. V. (1931). *The dissatisfied worker*. New York: Macmillan.

Forgas, J. P. (2002). Towards understanding the role of affect in social thinking and behavior. *Psychological Inquiry*, 13(1), 90–102.

Forster, N. (2005). *Maximum performance: A practical guide to leading and managing people at work*. Cheltenham: Edward Elgar.

Ganster, D. C. (2005). Executive job demands: Suggestions from a stress and decision-making perspective. *Academy of Management Review*, 30(3), 492–502.

Gardner, P. D., & Kozsowski, S. W. J. (1993). Learning the ropes: Co-ops do it faster. *Journal of Cooperative Education*, 28(3), 30–41.

George, J. M., & Brief, A. P. (1996). Motivational agendas in the workplace: The effects of feelings on focus of attention and work motivation. *Research in Organizational Behavior*, 18(2), 75–109.

George, J. M., & Zhou, J. (2002). Understanding when bad moods foster creativity and good ones don't: The role of context and clarity of feelings. *Journal of Applied Psychology*, 87(4), 687–697.

Guest, D. E. (1990). Human resource management and the American dream. *Journal of Management Studies*, 27(4), 377–397.

Harter, J. K., Schmidt, F. L., & Hayes, T. L. (2002). Business-unit-level relationship between employee satisfaction, employee engagement, and business outcomes: A meta-analysis. *Journal of Applied Psychology*, 87(2), 268–279.

Harter, J. K., Schmidt, F. L., & Keyes, C. L. M. (2002). Well-being in the workplace and its relationship to business outcomes: A review of the Gallup Studies. In C. L. M. Keyes & J. Haidt (Eds.), *Flourishing: The positive person and the good life* (pp. 205–224). Washington, DC: American Psychological Association.

Hersey, R. B. (1932). *Workers' emotions in the shop and home: A study of individual workers from the psychological and physiological standpoint*. Oxford: University of Pennsylvania Press.

Herzberg, F., Mausner, B., & Snyderman, B. (1959). *The motivation to work*. New York: Wiley.

Hoppock, R. (1935). *Job satisfaction*. New York: Harper.

Huselid, M. A. (1995). The impact of human resource management practices on turnover, productivity, and corporate financial performance. *Academy of Management Journal*, 38(3), 635–672.

Huselid, M. A., & Becker, B. E. (1997). *The impact of high performance work systems, implementation effectiveness, and alignment with strategy on shareholder wealth*. Paper presented at the Academy of Management Proceedings.

Huselid, M. A., Jackson, S. E., & Schuler, R. S. (1997). Technical and strategic human resource management effectiveness as determinants of firm performance. *Academy of Management Journal, 40*(1), 171–188.

Iaffaldano, M. T., & Muchinsky, P. M. (1985). Job satisfaction and job performance: A meta-analysis. *Psychological Bulletin, 97*(2), 251–273.

Ichniowski, C. (1990). *Human resource management systems and the performance of U.S. manufacturing businesses.* NBER Working Paper No. 3449. http://www.nber.org/papers/w3449.

Ichniowski, C., Shaw, K., & Prennushi, G. (1997). The effects of human resource management practices on productivity: A study of steel finishing lines. *American Economic Review, 87*(3), 291–313.

Ilgen, D. R., Major, D. A., & Tower, S. L. (1994). The cognitive revolution in organizational behavior. In J. Greenberg (Ed.), *Organizational behavior: The state of the science* (pp. 1–22). Hillsdale, NJ: Lawrence Erlbaum.

Isen, A. M., & Baron, R. A. (1991). Positive affect as a factor in organisational behaviour. *Research in Organizational Behavior, 13*, 1–53.

Isen, A. M., & Labroo, A. A. (2003). Some ways in which positive affect facilitates decision making and judgement. In S. L. Schneider & J. Shanteau (Eds.), *Emerging perspectives on judgment and decision research* (pp. 365–393). New York: Cambridge University Press.

Judge, T. A., Thoresen, C. J., Bono, J. E., & Patton, G. K. (2001). The job satisfaction–job performance relationship: A qualitative and quantitative review. *Psychological Bulletin, 127*(3), 376–407.

Jung, C. G. (1933). *Modern man in search of a soul.* London: Routledge & Kegan.

Katzell, R. A., & Thompson, D. E. (1995). Work motivation: Theory and practice. In D. A. Kolb, J. S. Osland, & I. M. Rubin (Eds.), *The organizational behavior reader* (6th ed., pp. 110–124). Englewood Cliffs, NJ: Prentice Hall.

King, S. P., & Peter, L. (Eds.). (1993). *Economic rationalism: Dead end or way forward?* St Leonards, NSW: Allen & Unwin.

Kluger, A. N., & Tikochinsky, J. (2001). The error of accepting the "theoretical" null hypothesis: The rise, fall, and resurrection of commonsense hypotheses in psychology. *Psychological Bulletin, 127*(3), 408–423.

Koivumaa-Honkanen, H., Koskenvuo, M., Honkanen, R. J., Viinamaki, H., Heikkilae, K., & Kaprio, J. (2004). Life dissatisfaction and subsequent work disability in an 11-year follow-up. *Psychological Medicine, 34*(2), 221–228.

Kornhauser, A. W., & Sharp, A. A. (1932). Employee attitudes: Suggestions from a study in a factory. *Personnel Journal, 10*, 393–404.

Langer, E. (1975). The illusion of control. *Journal of Personality and Social Psychology, 32*(2), 311–328.

Lawler, E. E., Mohrman, S. A., & Ledford, G. E. (1995). *Creating high performance organizations.* San Francisco, CA: Jossey-Bass.

Lawler, E. E., Mohrman, S. A., & Ledford, G. E. (1998). *Strategies for high performance organizations.* San Francisco, CA: Jossey-Bass.

Lawler, E. E., & Porter, L. W. (1967). The effects of performance on job satisfaction. *Industrial Relations, 7*, 20–28.

Ledford, G. E., Jr., (1999). Happiness and productivity revisited. *Journal of Organizational Behavior*, *20*(1), 25–30.

Lichtenstein, S., Fischoff, B., & Phillips, L. D. (1982). Calibration of probabilities: The state of the art in 1980. In D. Kahneman, P. Slovic, & A. Tversky (Eds.), *Judgment under uncertainty: Heuristics and biases* (pp. 306–334). New York: Cambridge University Press.

Lindgren, R. (1997). *Belbin's team roles viewed from the perspective of the Big 5: A content validation*. Oslo: University of Oslo.

Locke, E. A. (1976). The nature and causes of job satisfaction. In M. D. Dunnette (Ed.), *Handbook of industrial and organizational psychology* (pp. 1297–1349). Chicago, IL: Rand McNally.

Lyubomirsky, S., King, L., & Diener, E. (2005). The benefits of frequent positive affect: Does happiness lead to success? *Psychological Bulletin*, *131*(6), 803–855.

Lyubomirsky, S., Sheldon, K. M., & Schkade, D. (2005). Pursuing happiness: The architecture of sustainable change. *Review of General Psyhology*, *9*, 111–131.

Maister, H. (2001). *Practice what you preach: What managers must do to achieve a high performance culture*. New York: Free Press.

Martin, M., & Stang, D. (1978). *The Pollyanna principle*. Cambridge, MA: Schenkman.

Mastekaasa, A. (1994). Marital status, distress, and well-being: An international comparison. *Journal of Comparative Family Studies*, *25*(2), 183–205.

Myers, D. (2003). *Psychology*. New York: Worth Publishers.

Nankervis, A. R., Compton, R. L., & McCarthy, T. E. (2004). *Strategic human resource management: Strategies and processes in strategic human resource management* (5th ed.). South Melbourne, Victoria: Nelson.

O'Reilly, C. A., & Pfeffer, J. (2000). *Hidden value: How great companies achieve extraordinary results with ordinary people*. Boston, MA: Harvard University Press.

Organ, D. W. (1977). A reappraisal and reinterpretation of the satisfaction-causes-performance hypothesis. *Academy of Management Review*, *2*(1), 46–53.

Organ, D. W., & Paine, J. (1999). A new kind of performance for industrial and organizational psychology: Recent contributions to the study of organizational citizenship behavior. In C. L. Cooper & I. T. Robertson (Eds.), *International review of industrial and organizational psychology* (pp. 338–368). Chichester: Wiley.

Otake, K., Shimai, S., Tanaka-Matsumi, J., Otsui, K., & Fredrickson, B. L. (2006). Happy people become happier through kindness: A counting kindnesses intervention. *Journal of Happiness Studies*, *7*(3), 361–375.

Page, K. M., & Vella-Brodrick, D. A. (2009). The 'what,' 'why' and 'how' of employee well-being: A new model. *Social Indicators Research*, *90*(3), 441–458.

Patterson, M., West, M. A., Lawthom, R., & Nickell, S. (1997). Impact of people management practices on business performance. *Issues in People Management*, *22*, 1–28.

Perrow, C. (1986). *Complex organizations: A critical essay* (3rd ed.). New York: Random House.

Porter, L. W. (1963). Where is the organization man? *Harvard Business Review*, *41*(6), 53–61.

Pressman, S. D., & Cohen, S. (2005). Does positive affect influence health? *Psychological Bulletin*, *131*(6), 925–971.

Purcell, J. (2004). *The HRM-Performance link: Why, how and when does people management impact on organisational performance?* John Lovett Memorial Lecture 2004, University of Limerick.

Roethlisberger, F. J., & Dickson, W. J. (1939). *Management and the worker* (3rd ed.). Cambridge, MA: Harvard University Press.

Saavedra, R., & Kwun, S. K. (2000). Affective states in job characteristics theory. *Journal of Organizational Behavior*, *21*(2), 131–146.

Saks, A. M. (1996). The relationship between the amount and helpfulness of entry training and work outcomes. *Human Relations*, *49*(4), 429–451.

Schuler, R. S., & MacMillan, I. C. (1984). Gaining competitive advantage through human resource management practices. *Human Resource Management*, *23*(3), 241–255.

Schwarz, N., & Bless, H. (1991). Happy and mindless, but sad and smart? The impact of effective states on analytic reasoning. In J. P. Forgas (Ed.), *Emotion and social judgement*. Oxford: Pergamon Press.

Seligman, M. E. P., & Csikszentmihalyi, M. (2000). Positive psychology: An introduction. *American Psychologist*, *55*(1), 5–14.

Sevastos, P. P. (1996). *Job-related affective well-being and its relation to intrinsic job satisfaction* (Unpublished PhD). Curtin University, Perth, Western Australia.

Sheldon, K. M., & Lyubomirsky, S. (2006). Achieving sustainable gains in happiness: Change your actions, not your circumstances. *Journal of Happiness Studies*, *7*, 55–86.

Sinclair, R. C., & Mark, M. M. (1992). The influence of mood state on judgement and actions: Effects on persuasion, categorization, social justice, person perception and judgemental accuracy. In L. L. Martin & A. Tesser (Eds.), *The construction of social judgements* (pp. 1165–1193). Hillsdale, NJ: Lawrence Erlbaum.

Snell, S. A., & Youndt, M. A. (1995). Human resource management and firm performance: Testing a contingency model of executive controls. *Journal of Management*, *21*(4), 711–737.

Snyder, C. R., & Lopez, S. J. (Eds.). (2002). *Handbook of positive psychology*. New York: Oxford University Press.

Spector, P. E. (1997). *Job satisfaction: Application, assessment, cause and consequences*. Thousand Oaks, CA: Sage.

Staw, B. M. (1986). Organizational psychology and the pursuit of the happy/productive worker. *California Management Review*, *28*(4), 40–53.

Staw, B. M., & Barsade, S. G. (1993). Affect and managerial performance: A test of the sadder-but-wiser vs. happier-and-smarter hypotheses. *Administrative Science Quarterly*, *38*(2), 304–331.

136

Strauss, G. (1968). Relations—1968 style. *Industrial Relations: A Journal of Economy and Society, 7*(3), 262–276.

Tabacknick, N., Crocker, J., & Alloy, L. B. (1983). Depression, social comparison and the false consensus effect. *Journal of Personality and Social Psychology, 45*(3), 688–699.

Taylor, S. E. (1991). The asymmetrical impact of positive and negative events: The mobilization-minimization hypothesis. *Psychological Bulletin, 110*, 68–85.

Terpstra, D. E., & Rozell, E. J. (1993). The relationship of staffing practices to organizational level measures of performance. *Personnel Psychology, 46*(1), 27–48.

Tracey, B. (1993). *Maximum achievement*. New York: Simon & Schuster.

Vroom, V. H. (1964). *Work and motivation*. New York: Wiley.

Wall, T. D., & Wood, S. J. (2005). The romance of human resource management and business performance, and the case for big science. *Human Relations, 48*(4), 429–462.

Warr, P. (2007). *Work, happiness, and unhappiness*. Mahwah, NJ: Lawrence Erlbaum.

Warr, P., & Clapperton, G. (2010). *The joy of work? Jobs, happiness, and you*. London: Routledge.

Waterfield, R. (1993). *Letter on happiness*. London: Ebury Press.

Way, S. A. (2002). High performance work systems and intermediate indicators of firm performance within the US small business sector. *Journal of Management Studies, 28*(6), 765–785.

Weiss, H. M., & Cropanzano, R. (1996). Affective events theory: A theoretical discussion of the structure, causes and consequences of affective experiences at work. In B. M. Staw & L. L. Cummings (Eds.), *Research in organizational behavior: An annual series of analytical essays and critical reviews* (Vol. 18, pp. 1–74). Greenwich, CT: JAI Press.

Weiss, H. M., Nicholas, J. P., & Dauss, C. S. (1999). An examination of the joint effects of affective experiences and job beliefs on job satisfaction and variations in affective experiences over time. *Organizational Behavior and Human Decision Processes, 78*(1), 1–24.

West, M., Arnold, J., Corbett, M., & Fletcher, B. (1992). Editorial: Advancing understanding about behavior at work. *Journal of Occupational and Organizational Psychology, 65*(1), 1–3.

Wright, P. M., Gardner, T. M., Moynihan, L. M., & Allen, M. R. (2005). The relationship between HR practices and firm performance: Examining causal order. *Personnel Psychology, 58*(2), 404–447.

Wright, T. A., & Cropanzano, R. S. (2000). Psychological well-being and job satisfaction as predictors of job performance. *Journal of Occupational and Health Psychology, 5*(1), 84–94.

Wright, T. A., Cropanzano, R. S., Denney, P. J., & Moline, G. L. (2002). When a happy worker is a productive worker: A preliminary examination of three models. *Canadian Journal of Behavioural Science, 34*(3), 146–150.

137

Wright, T. A., & Staw, B. M. (1999a). Affect and favorable work outcomes: Two longitudinal tests of the happy-productive worker thesis. *Journal of Organizational Behavior, 20*(1), 1–23.

Wright, T. A., & Staw, B. M. (1999b). Further thoughts on the happy-productive worker. *Journal of Organizational Behavior, 20*(1), 31–34.

Youndt, M. A., Snell, S. A., Dean, J. W., & Lepak, D. P. (1996). Human resource management, manufacturing strategy, and firm performance. *Academy of Management Journal, 39*(4), 836–866.

# 7

# Organizational Characteristics of Happy Organizations

## Bret L. Simmons
### University of Nevada, U.S.A.

## Introduction

Do happy organizations have a strategic competitive advantage? Tony Hsieh, the CEO of Zappos, thinks so. In his 2010 book entitled *Delivering happiness: A path to profits, passion, and purpose*, Hsieh states that his vision for Zappos is "delivering happiness to the world" (p. 250). Hsieh even offers a Science of Happiness class to his employees because he believes so strongly that happy employees and customers are the key to the success of his business. Hsieh concludes his book by encouraging entrepreneurs to start their new companies "with happiness at the core of their business models" (Hsieh, 2010, p. 239).

Happiness might seem to work for Zappos; unfortunately, the empirical evidence on the long-term performance of happy organizations is almost nonexistent. That makes sense, because research that links micro-level latent variables like emotions and attitudes to macro-level observable and measurable variables like market share and profit is very difficult to conduct. Organizational happiness is also very vulnerable to the halo effect, where the happiness of organizational members is just as likely to be the result of company performance as it is the cause of excellence (Rosenzweig, 2007).

While the Science of Happiness (Diener & Biswas-Diener, 2008) is relatively well developed, the efficacy of happiness in the workplace is not a "slam-dunk." The claims of recent popular press books on happiness at

*Work and Wellbeing: Wellbeing: A Complete Reference Guide*, Volume III.
Edited by Peter Y. Chen and Cary L. Cooper.
© 2014 John Wiley & Sons, Ltd. Published 2014 by John Wiley & Sons, Inc.
DOI: 10.1002/9781118539415.wbwell07

work are far from conclusive because they are based primarily on proprietary data and anecdotal evidence (e.g., Achor, 2010; Pryce-Jones, 2010). The value of organizational happiness is certainly not total nonsense, but the "hard facts" (Pfeffer & Sutton, 2006) about the meaning, consequences, and causes of happiness at work remain elusive.

This chapter will begin with a look at what it means to be happy, with the assumption being that a happy organization is one full of employees that are happy. I'll then examine how happiness has been measured in peer-reviewed management and organizational psychology journals and discuss the evidence on its consequences and causes. Finally, I will present two frameworks for explaining why happiness should matter and make some recommendations for organizational characteristics to enhance happiness.

My goal is to offer a concise, evidence-based guide on organizational happiness for practicing managers. If we are going to recommend that organizations focus on increasing the happiness levels of employees, we need to be able to show that happy workers are indeed more productive, or that the happiness effect somehow consistently aggregates to produce valued organizational outcomes. In order to do this with some degree of credibility, we need to be specific about what happiness is, and one of the best ways to do that is to look at how it is measured.

## Defining Happiness

The emerging field of positive organizational behavior (POB) attempts to look at the world of work with a focus on positive attributes of people and organizations (Nelson & Cooper, 2007). This move away from traditional models of disease and dysfunction encouraged by POB was championed first by positive psychology (Seligman & Csikszentmihalyi, 2000). Yet defining happiness is as challenging for POB as it is for positive psychology. The best textbook on the topic of positive psychology (Peterson, 2006) devotes an entire chapter to happiness without ever offering one specific definition of the construct.

Happiness is most often conceptualized as subjective wellbeing, or thinking and feeling positively about one's health, relationships, work, and overall life (Diener & Biswas-Diener, 2008; Fisher, 2010; Lyubomirsky, 2008). Relatedly, happiness has been described as "feeling good—enjoying life and wanting the feeling to be maintained" (Layard, 2005, p. 12) and "the total fulfillment of one's potentialities" (Csikszentmihalyi, 2003, p. 28).

At the core of this way of thinking about happiness is the concept that happiness is a pleasant state that results from an ongoing process of experiencing life with a positive attitude, which is not necessarily the result of obtaining desirable circumstances. There is a growing body of evidence in psychology that people with positive feelings are beneficial. "Happiness, then, is itself a resource you can tap to achieve the things you want in life" (Diener & Biswas-Diener, 2008, p. 9). Happy people live longer, are more likely to get married and stay married, are more energetic, more helpful and cooperative, and better liked by others (Lyubomirsky, 2008).

The process of enhancing happiness is driven by what people do in their daily lives and how they think. Research shows that as much as 50% of an individual's happiness is set by genetically determined factors, and another 10% is explained by differences in life circumstances or situations. This means that *behavior*, the thing individuals have the most control over, accounts for the remaining 40% of happiness. Suggested strategies for increasing happiness include expressing gratitude, investing in social connections, managing stress, living in the present, committing to your goals, practicing religion or spirituality, and taking care of your body (Lyubomirsky, 2008). Other routes to positivity include applying your strengths, following your passions, visualizing the future, and opening your mind (Fredrickson, 2009). Recognizing and appreciating happiness are key to savoring the positive experience and leveraging its benefits (Brant & Veroff, 2007).

Enabling and encouraging positive organizational behavior is therefore the key to enhancing happiness at work, but is this really "good business" (Csikszentmihalyi, 2003)? Independent of the ethical merits of the issue, the empirical case for the efficacy of organizational happiness remains equivocal primarily because of problems with how it has been defined and subsequently measured in samples of working individuals. Happiness has been defined as the process of experiencing the presence of the positive; consequently, valid measures of happiness at work should reflect the presence of a positive psychological state, differentiate happiness from other measures of positive concepts, and isolate the experience of happiness as the result of some equally valid and malleable measure of an organizational characteristic.

## Measuring Happiness at Work

Happiness is the result of a process, which means that happiness in the workplace is far from static. Employees can be happy at work at one moment and at a different moment feel unhappy. Measure employee happiness 6 months after a salary cut, layoff, or major achievement and you will likely get a different result than if you measured a few weeks on either side of the event (Ashkanasy, 2011). As I will discuss later in this chapter, paying attention to daily events at work is one of the most effective strategies for regulating what employees think and how they feel about work.

The biggest problem with the evidence on happiness at work is that very few management and organizational researchers have directly measured it in a consistent way. Given the preceding discussion on the definition of happiness, this is hardly a revelation. The problem with defining and measuring happiness as "feeling good" is that it often means little more than "not feeling bad." Emotional states like joy, gratitude, interest, and hope are more precisely defined and measured than generic happiness (Fredrickson, 2009). Unlike other positive states commonly associated with employee performance, there is no distinct measure for happiness at work. What organizational researchers have often called happiness is actually a constellation of positive constructs like subjective wellbeing (SWB), psychological wellbeing (PWB), good mood, satisfaction, commitment, and engagement (Fisher, 2010).

## The Happiness of Wellbeing

Research on wellbeing at work often uses the findings to draw conclusions about employee happiness. This is inherently problematic because there are a variety of ways to assess wellbeing, and many of them involve defining wellbeing as the absence of dysfunction or disease. For example, in one recent and well-designed study, wellbeing was used as a proxy for happiness (Fritz et al., 2010). In this study, wellbeing was operationalized as both emotional exhaustion and life satisfaction. Life satisfaction is one of the most common ways to measure happiness (Peterson, 2006). Although life satisfaction is a positive indicator of wellbeing, questions like "I am satisfied with my life," and "In most ways my life is close to ideal" do not isolate the happiness of an employee derived from and experienced at work.

The items the authors used to measure emotional exhaustion were a subscale of an inventory of burnout, which taps something negative. In a separate and equally well-designed study, wellbeing was measured as the absence of both health complaints and burnout (Fritz & Sonnentag, 2006). Subjective wellbeing, a seemingly positive and desirable state, is most consistently measured as the absence of the negative: anxiety, irritability, depression, and somatic symptoms (e.g., Kossek, Colquitt, & Noe, 2001), even though it is sometimes measured with questions that are similar to general life satisfaction (Judge, Ilies, & Dimotakis, 2010).

Evaluation of the measurement of wellbeing is critical because it is one of the core constructs of the happy–productive worker hypothesis (Taris & Schreurs, 2009; Wright & Staw, 1999; Wright, Cropanzano, & Bonett, 2007). The happy–productive worker hypothesis assumes that "individual well-being leads to high individual-level performance, which should translate into high organizational performance" (Taris & Schreurs, 2009, p. 120). With questions that include asking employees how often they felt "very lonely or remote from other people," or "depressed or very unhappy," psychological wellbeing struggles to live up to claims that it taps something positive (Wright et al., 2009). Measuring happiness as wellbeing renders this approach to establishing the happiness–productivity connection murky at best (Ledford, 1999).

## Happiness as Satisfaction, Commitment, and Engagement

Although there is no distinct measure of happiness at work, and the most common measure of the happy–productive worker hypothesis, wellbeing, is problematic, there are other proxies for happiness at work that are more consistent predictors of performance. Three very promising proxies for happiness at work are job satisfaction, organizational commitment, and engagement (Fisher, 2010). Warr (2009) places heavy emphasis on the efficacy of job satisfaction when making his case for happiness at work. We have known for decades about the power of satisfaction and commitment (Harrison, Newman, & Roth, 2006; Judge, Thoresen, Bono, & Patton, 2001) to drive work performance, and solid evidence about engagement now also exists (Christian, Garza, & Slaughter, 2011; Rich, Lepine, & Crawford, 2010).

Job satisfaction is a "pleasurable emotional state resulting from the appraisal of one's job as achieving or facilitating one's job values" (Locke, 1969, p. 317), and affective organizational commitment represents an individual's positive emotional attachment to the organization's goals and values (Meyer & Allen, 1991). As positive psychological states measured with questions that tap the presence of the positive instead of the absence of the negative, both are reasonable proxies for happiness at work. There is some evidence to suggest that a company's average job satisfaction affects measures of financial productivity (Patterson, Warr, & West, 2004).

A well-designed meta-analysis found that a sound measure of overall job attitude, measured as job satisfaction and affective organizational commitment, is probably the most useful piece of information an organization can have about its employees (Harrison et al., 2006). Employee feelings of satisfaction and commitment are consistently effective predictors of a wide variety of measures of individual effectiveness: task performance, citizenship, and employee withdrawal (tardiness, absenteeism, and turnover).

Until recently, the hype for a link between psychological engagement and employee performance has far exceeded the credible evidence. Studies of psychological engagement will use the terms "work engagement," "employee engagement," and "job engagement" to mean pretty much the same thing: the manifest effect of psychological engagement of an employee as she or he performs job responsibilities in the workplace.

A well-designed study of 245 firefighters and their supervisors found that job engagement was a significant predictor of both organizational citizenship behavior (OCB) and task performance (Rich, Lepine, & Crawford, 2010). This is especially significant because job engagement was tested for its effect on performance and OCB simultaneously with job involvement, job satisfaction, and intrinsic motivation. In the presence of job engagement, these other important factors lost their significance. They also identified three antecedents of job engagement: value congruence, perceived organizational support, and core self-evaluations, such that higher levels of these were associated with higher levels of job engagement.

The researchers defined job engagement as "a multidimensional motivational concept reflecting the *simultaneous* investment of an individual's physical, cognitive, and emotional energy in active, full work performance" (Rich et al., 2010, p. 619). A simple way to remember this is "engagement involves investing the hands, head, and heart in active, full work performance" (Rich et al., p. 619). Most importantly, this research gives us a new measure of job engagement that is in my opinion the best available. This new measure of job engagement has 18 questions, 6 for each of the subdimensions of engagement: physical engagement (e.g., "I exert my full effort to my job"), emotional engagement (e.g., "I feel energetic at my job"), and cognitive engagement ("At work, I focus a great deal of attention on my job"). As you can see by the sample items, the questions on this new measure of engagement are true *effect* indicators in the specific context of an employee performing job responsibilities at work. Contrast this with the most popular measure of engagement, the Gallup Workplace Audit (GWA), whose 12 questions are all *causal* rather than effect indicators (Harter, Schmidt, & Hayes, 2002). Respondents to the GWA are asked how *satisfied* or *dissatisfied* they are with their company as a place to work (e.g., "I have a best friend at work"); consequently, it is not a direct measure of the effect of engagement and could potentially be confounded with satisfaction.

A separate meta-analysis of six different effect measures of engagement found that work engagement predicts work performance over and above job satisfaction and organizational commitment (Christian, Garza, & Slaughter, 2011). It is interesting to note that even though this study focused on engagement, it once again found significant effects for both satisfaction and commitment. The study also found that both characteristics of the job and characteristics of the individual were significant predictors of work engagement. The characteristics of the job that enhanced engagement were task variety and task significance, and the characteristics of the individual were conscientiousness and positive affect. An interesting finding of the study was that autonomy, feedback, and transformational leadership had little effect on employee engagement.

The evidence on job satisfaction, engagement, and commitment is clear: when employees have certain positive thoughts and feelings at work they are likely to perform better and withdraw less. The evidence on wellbeing also makes clear that minimizing negative thoughts and feelings of employees at work also matters. What remains unclear is how well our measures of the presence of the positive and the absence of the negative at work represent a higher order construct we can label happiness, and if the happiness of an organization's employees is really a consistently significant predictor of performance indicators like revenue and growth. Although good evidence establishing the link between employee happiness and revenue is hard to come by, poor employee job performance, absenteeism, and turnover cost organizations money, which makes happiness a bottom-line issue. The specific link between happiness and organizational performance does remain an empirical question; nevertheless, I think we know enough to justify moving employee happiness closer to the top of our list of organizational priorities.

## Enhancing Happiness at Work

Selecting and promoting leaders who understand the importance of attending to their own happiness is probably critical for any organization that aspires to improve the happiness of its employees. Any planned organizational intervention that does not operate at and work for all levels of leadership will ultimately fail because it will not be seen as authentic and legitimate. If the goal is to create happy–productive workers, one of the objectives must be to develop happy–influential leaders. Although the effect of the happy leader is an unanswered empirical question, there is support for the idea that positive, authentic leadership enhances wellbeing and positive attitudes in followers (Macik-Frey, Quick, & Cooper, 2009; Woolley, Caza, & Levy, 2011).

Leaders who have a deep personal commitment to the work they do, pursue their goals with energy and enthusiasm, enjoy their work, and inspire others to do the same are more likely to be satisfied with their own lives and work (Keller & Price, 2011). Leaders that can tap into their own happiness "create positive energy around them, becoming more compelling as role models and more inspiring as communicators" (p. 185). The studies of engagement discussed earlier suggest that conscientiousness and a positive core self-evaluation are two personality traits we could screen for if we are interested in promoting leaders with a propensity for happiness (Christian, Garza, & Slaughter, 2011; Rich, Lepine, & Crawford, 2010).

As leaders experiment with changes intended to enhance organizational happiness, they should keep in mind that change is demanding. If organizational happiness truly is a competitive imperative, then it merits a persistent sense of urgency (Kotter, 1996). The happy–competitive organization will require broad-based empowerment because "the hearts and minds of all members of the workforce are needed to cope with the fast-shifting realities of the business climate" (Kotter, 1996, p. 166). Enabling people to make decisions and take action presents challenges and potentially stress for both leaders and their employees. Organizational transformation requires leaders with an understanding of the psychology of individuals, the psychology of groups, and the psychology of change (Deming, 2000). The route to happiness is more a winding path of uncertainty, risk, and sacrifice than a superhighway of bliss. Consequently, any effort to enhance organizational happiness must reflect an understanding of both stress and motivation.

## The Happiness of Stress and the Stress of Happiness

Work stress can affect employee happiness, but not always in negative ways. Debra Nelson and I have posited that an individual's response to stressors at work can be simultaneously both positive and negative, and in contrast to distress, we think of eustress as the positive response to stress (Simmons & Nelson, 2007). We treat eustress as a higher order construct composed of multiple positive indicators, much the way happiness is treated in practice. Indicators that someone has had a positive response to a demanding situation can be found in their behaviors, their attitudes, and their emotions. In our Holistic Stress model (Figure 7.1), happiness at work is one potential indicator of a positive emotional response to demands. Later I will discuss one explanation for how these positive emotions work together with perceptions and motivations to affect performance behaviors in employees. From a holistic perspective, organizational characteristics intended to produce happy organizations will always have the potential to also produce degrees of negative responses like ambiguity, anxiety, and even burnout.

Eustress reflects the extent to which cognitive appraisal of an event can be seen as beneficial. We expect that most work events elicit a mixed bag of both positive and negative responses in individuals. For example, a recently promoted individual should be expected to experience joy and satisfaction associated with the recognition of achievement and excitement about the opportunity to pursue new goals and challenges at work. At the same time, and as a result of the same event, the individual may also experience a degree of disappointment if the additional compensation associated with the promotion is perceived as inadequate, or may experience the beginnings of the anxiety they anticipate about having to tell friends, family, and colleagues that the new promotion involves relocation to another city. On the other hand, an individual recently downsized out of a job can be expected to experience hostility associated with the loss and anxiety due to the uncertainty of having to find a new job. Yet at the same time the individual could feel relief to be leaving an overworked job in a sinking ship, or may see it as an opportunity to spend more coveted time with family.

Warr (2009) reminds us that similar to eustress and distress, happiness and unhappiness are also interdependent. "By working less hard in a difficult job it is sometimes possible to reduce unhappiness created by that job; conversely, striving to perform well can in some cases give rise to negative feelings accompanying overload or failure" (p. 80). We need to accept that any planned intervention to increase organizational happiness can also in certain situations or for certain people produce unhappiness. Generating active happiness might involve exposing employees to challenges that some find distressful. In contrast, a relaxed happiness resulting from less effort and

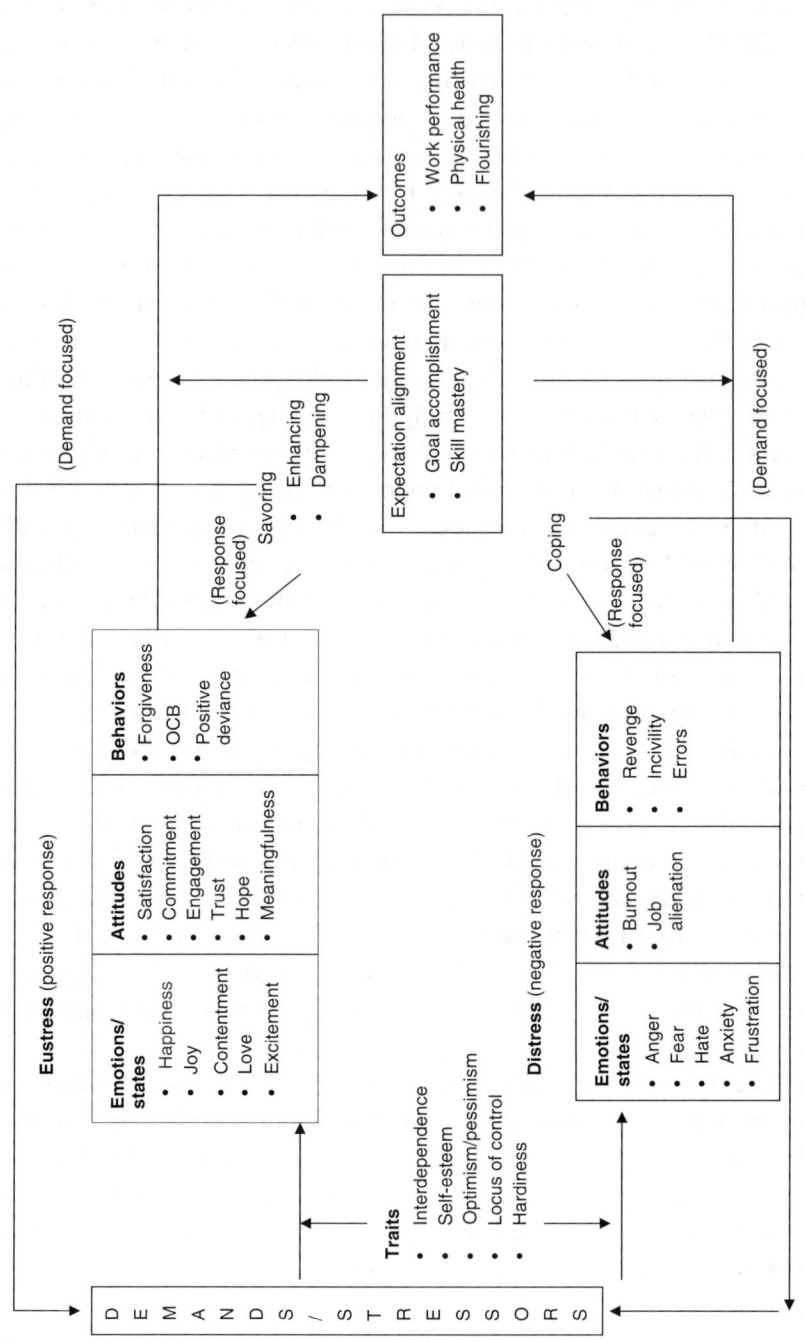

**Figure 7.1.** Holistic Model of Stress.

challenge, while satisfying to some, could be distressful to others. Warr (2009) encourages organizations and individuals to create conditions that permit a balance over time between active and relaxed happiness at work.

A starting point for conditions that create balanced happiness should be research that shows what encourages job satisfaction and affective commitment. Fisher (2010, p. 398) developed the following recommendations for creating a happy workplace that reflect what we know about improving satisfaction and commitment at work:

- Create a healthy, respectful, and supportive organizational culture.
- Supply competent leadership at all levels.
- Provide fair treatment, security, and recognition.
- Design jobs to be interesting, challenging, autonomous, and rich in feedback.
- Facilitate skill development to improve competence and allow growth.
- Select for person–organization fit through the use of realistic job previews and socialization practices.
- Persuade employees to reframe a current less-than-ideal work environment as acceptable.
- Adopt high performance work systems (HPWS).
- Reduce minor hassles and increase daily uplifts.

The final two points on this list are supported by very credible recent evidence. A study of employees and managers in 119 service departments of local government in Wales examined both the direct effect high performance HR practices have on departmental performance, and how these practices affect departmental performance indirectly by influencing employee attitudes and discretionary behaviors (Messersmith, Patel, & Lepak, 2011). The employee attitudes they examined were all good indicators of happiness: job satisfaction, organizational commitment, and empowerment. The study found that HPWS had a significant, positive effect on these attitudes, and these attitudes in turn enhanced the organizational citizenship behavior (OCB) of the employees. Departmental performance was affected both directly by HPWS and indirectly via the citizenship behavior of employees. The authors' explanation of the findings makes a compelling case for organizational happiness:

> The study demonstrates that building an effective HR system may have a powerful influence on the attitudes and behaviors of individual employees.

149

Not only is this likely to create a more positive work place environment but it also seems to have an influence on departmental performance. Investing in the selection, training, information sharing, compensation, and performance management processes may have a positive effect on employee attitudes and behaviors and may pay further dividends with higher service quality and performance. This highlights the importance of not just managing based upon results but also paying attention to the role that attitudes and behaviors play in creating better results.

(Messersmith et al., 2011, p. 1115)

Reducing minor hassles and increasing daily uplifts might be the most significant of Fisher's 10 recommendations for creating a happy workplace (Fisher, 2010). Capturing some very basic principles of employee motivation, this recommendation should probably be an explicit part of the job description of every manager in an organization serious about employee happiness.

## Daily Progress, Happiness, and Performance

In their exceptional evidence-based management book entitled *The progress principle: Using small wins to ignite joy, engagement, and creativity at Work*, Teresa Amabile and Steven Kramer focus on the importance of reducing minor hassles and increasing daily progress. They provide compelling evidence that daily events at work affect how employees think and feel about work, which in turn affects their motivation and ultimately their performance. The book focuses on something the authors call the *inner work life effect*: "people do better work when they are happy, have positive views of the organization and its people, and are motivated primarily by the work itself" (Amabile & Kramer, 2011, p. 47). They go so far as to claim their research shows "as inner work life goes, so goes the company" (p. 3).

The inner work life system comprises perceptions, emotions, and motivation. As a positive emotion, employee happiness is an integral part of the inner work life system. Employee happiness affects job performance because it affects an employee's motivation to work. Perceptions employees have about the organization, the work they do, the people they work for and work with, and their sense of accomplishment affect their happiness, and their happiness or lack of happiness can also affect these same perceptions. Perceptions and emotions affect motivation, and it is motivation that ultimately affects job performance. If we want to improve how people perform,

150

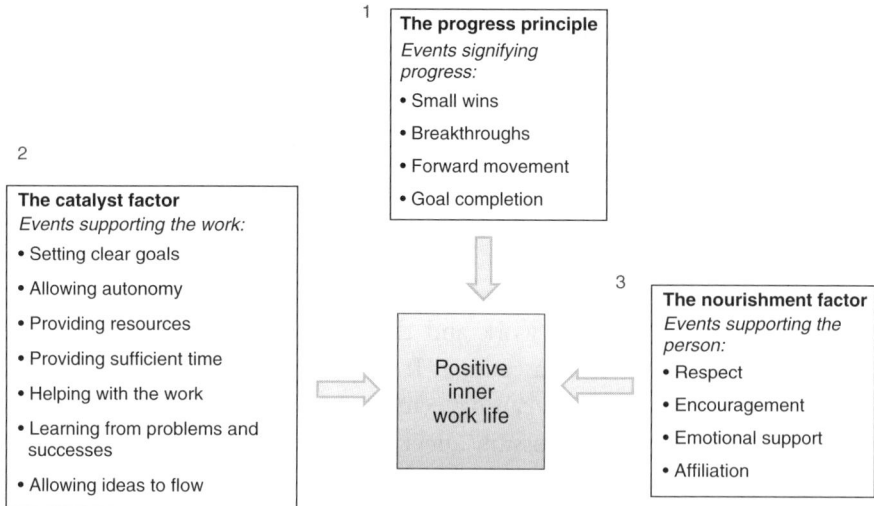

**Figure 7.2.** Daily Events That Support Happiness. Adapted from Amabile & Kramer (2011).

we have to change how they think and feel at work. Changing how people think and feel at work is not accomplished via wishful thinking but rather through planned changes to the characteristics of the organization.

The research of Amabile and Kramer (2011) highlights the power of *events* that are part of every workday. In order of importance, the three events are those that signal progress in meaningful work, events that support the work, and events that support the person doing the work (Figure 7.2). Amabile and Kramer (2011) stress that their research shows that even seemingly small events, such as daily progress or minor setbacks, can have a powerful effect on inner work life, and negative events are more powerful than positive events. They believe this *progress principle* should become a fundamental management principle.

The authors strongly emphasize that efforts to support the progress of employees should focus more on avoiding the negative than accentuating the positive. Leader influence is most effective when it is used to eliminate obstacles rather than create supports, because "small losses can overwhelm small wins" (Amabile & Kramer, 2011, p. 92). The power of setbacks to diminish happiness is more than twice as strong as the power of progress to boost happiness.

Bad leaders and the damage they cause have more impact than the help of good leaders. Leaders also need to be aware of how they rob meaning from people's work. In their research, Amabile and Kramer identified four actions that managers should avoid because they negate the value of work (p. 96):

1. dismiss someone's ideas;
2. make employees doubt the work they do is important;
3. assign people to work for which they are overqualified;
4. keep people from assuming full ownership of their work.

Amabile and Kramer (2011) use the term *catalyst* to describe things that facilitate the completion of work and the term *inhibitor* to describe the absence or negative form of a catalyst. It is very important to keep in mind that "catalysts and inhibitors can have an immediate impact on inner work life, even before they could possibly affect the work itself" (p. 102). Catalysts and inhibitors are a direct product of an organization's culture, which "is created largely by the words and actions of leaders, beginning with the organization's founders" (p. 108). The three main aspects of culture that shape specific catalyst and inhibitor events at work are (p. 109):

- *Consideration for people and their ideas.* Do managers at all levels honor the dignity of employees, value their ideas, and serve as examples of civil discourse?
- *Coordination.* Are systems and procedures (e.g., performance evaluation) designed to facilitate coordination or competition between individuals and groups?
- *Communication.* Open, honest, and respectful communication is perhaps the most powerful force for sustaining progress, coordinating work, establishing trust, and helping people understand that what they think and do matters.

Another category of events that Amabile and Kramer (2011) found affect inner work life are *nourishers,* which are events that support the person doing the work. "The primary way in which nourishers fuel inner work life is by infusing the work with greater meaning" (p. 131). Unfortunately, Amabile and Kramer found in their research that toxins were overwhelmingly more present than nourishers. They identified four categories of nourishers (pp. 131–133) displaying the following characteristics:

- *Respect:* Implicit or explicit expressions of another person's value. Basic civility signifies respect and incivility disrespect.

- *Encouragement*: Helping others find the ability to work through challenges, setbacks, and fears to accomplish meaningful goals.
- *Emotional support*: Validating emotions, including calming fears and reducing frustrations.
- *Affiliation*: Developing bonds of trust, appreciation, support, and cooperation among coworkers.

# Conclusion

Happiness is a messy concept. It is an umbrella term for positive feelings and emotions that have been measured in a variety of ways in the workplace. Even though we are still in the very early stages of understanding characteristics of happy organizations, there is good reason to believe that organizational happiness does provide a competitive edge. Right now, the practice of organizational happiness is probably leading the evidence, but I anticipate we will see a growing body of good research on the causes and consequences of happiness at work in the next decade. I also anticipate we will see a growing number of organizations become interested in and sincere about the pursuit of employee and customer happiness. Truly happy organizations, with leaders like Tony Hsieh, will make it a priority to learn more about how they can use the science of happiness at work to run their organizations more effectively.

I see a real opportunity for researchers to create new conceptualizations and measures of *organizational* happiness. Our current construct definitions and measures that serve as proxies of happiness are primarily at the individual level. Is a happy organization really simply one in which a certain percentage of its employees obtain and consistently maintain over time some degree of happiness? What happens in an organization as the effects of individual happiness begin to aggregate to teams and groups within the organization, and is it possible to directly measure these effects? How do between group differences in happiness affect organizational happiness? Depending on how you define and evaluate organizational happiness, it is quite possible that a happy organization might be one in which some of its teams and groups are unequivocally unhappy. Can chronic organizational happiness buffer episodic organizational unhappiness, and are the chronic effects of episodic unhappiness always negative?

Most of the focus of the science of happiness at work has been on how the happiness of employees ultimately affects the performance of the organization. We know little to nothing about how the performance of the organization affects the happiness of its leaders, and in turn how the happiness of leaders affects the happiness of groups and individual employees. If the happiness of leaders does have a significant effect on members of the organization, how does this work such that we might be able to enhance the effect of the happy leader and constrain the effect of the unhappy leader? These are important but very difficult questions to answer because it is easier to focus on individual attitudes and performance than it is to study the happiness of a significant number of leaders and the performance of their organizations over time. Nevertheless, for leaders and researchers interested in the organizational characteristics of happy organizations, the rewards will ultimately outweigh all of the challenges.

# References

Achor, S. (2010). *The happiness advantage: The seven principles of positive psychology that fuel success and performance at work.* New York: Crown Business.

Amabile, T. M., & Kramer, S. J. (2011). *The progress principle: Using small wins to ignite joy, engagement, and creativity at work.* Boston: Harvard Business Review Press.

Ashkanasy, N. M. (2011). International happiness: A multilevel perspective. *Academy of Management Perspectives, 25*(1), 23–29.

Brant, F. B., & Veroff, J. (2007). *Savoring: A new model of positive experience.* Mahwah, NJ: Lawrence Erlbaum.

Christian, M. S., Garza, A. S., & Slaughter, J. E. (2011). Work engagement: A quantitative review and test of its relations with task and contextual performance. *Personnel Psychology, 64,* 89–136.

Csikszentmihalyi, M. (2003). *Good business: Leadership, flow, and the making of meaning.* New York: Penguin.

Deming, W. Edwards. (2000). *The new economics for industry, government, education* (2nd ed.). Cambridge, MA: MIT Press.

Diener, E., & Biswas-Diener, R. (2008). *Happiness: Unlocking the mysteries of psychological wealth.* Malden, MA: Blackwell.

Fisher, C. D. (2010). Happiness at work. *International Journal of Management Reviews, 12,* 384–412.

Fredrickson, B. L. (2009). *Positivity: Groundbreaking research reveals how to embrace the hidden strength of positive emotions, overcome negativity, and thrive.* New York: Crown.

Fritz, C., & Sonnentag, S. (2006). Recovery, well-being, and performance-related outcomes: The role of workload and vacation experiences. *Journal of Applied Psychology, 91*(4), 936–945.

Fritz, C., Yankelevich, M., Zarubin, A., & Barger, P. (2010). Happy, healthy, and productive: The role of detachment from work during nonwork time. *Journal of Applied Psychology, 95*(5), 977–983.

Harrison, D. A., Newman, D. A., & Roth, P. L. (2006). How important are job attitudes? Meta-analytic comparisons of integrative behavioral outcomes and time sequences. *Academy of Management Journal, 49*(2), 305–325.

Harter, J. K., Schmidt, F. L., & Hayes, T. L. (2002). Business-unit-level relationships between satisfaction, employee engagement, and business outcomes: A meta-analysis. *Journal of Applied Psychology, 87*(2), 268–279.

Hsieh, T. (2010). *Delivering happiness: A path to profits, passion, and purpose.* New York: Business Plus.

Judge, T. A., Ilies, R., & Dimotakis, N. (2010). Are health and happiness the product of wisdom? The relationship of general mental ability and occupational attainment, health, and well-being. *Journal of Applied Psychology, 95*(3), 454–468.

Judge, T. A., Thoresen, C. J., Bono, J. E., & Patton, G. K. (2001) The job satisfaction-job performance relationship: A qualitative and quantitative review. *Psychological Bulletin, 127*, 376–407.

Keller, S., & Price, C. (2011). *Beyond performance: How great organizations build ultimate competitive advantage.* Hoboken, NJ: John Wiley & Sons.

Kossek, E. E., Colquitt, J. A., & Noe, R. A. (2001). Caregiving decisions, well-being, and performance: The effects of place and provider as a function of dependent type and work-family climates. *Academy of Management Journal, 44*(1), 29–44.

Kotter, J. P. (1996). *Leading change.* Boston, MA: Harvard Business School.

Layard, R. (2005). *Happiness: Lessons from a new science.* New York: Penguin.

Ledford, G. E. (1999). Happiness and productivity revisited. *Journal of Organizational Behavior, 20*, 25–30.

Locke, E. A. (1969). What is job satisfaction? *Organizational Behavior and Human Performance, 4*, 309–336.

Lyubomirsky, S. (2008). *The how of happiness: A scientific approach to getting what you want in life.* New York: Penguin.

Macik-Frey, M., Quick, J. C., & Cooper, C. L. (2009). Authentic leadership as a pathway to positive health. *Journal of Organizational Behavior, 30*, 453–458.

Messersmith, J. G., Patel, P. C., & Lepak, D. P. (2011). Unlocking the black box: Exploring the link between high-performance work systems and performance. *Journal of Applied Psychology, 96*(6), 1105–1118.

Meyer, J. P., & Allen, N. J. (1991). A three-component conceptualization of organizational commitment. *Human Resource Management Review, 1*, 61–89.

Nelson, D. L., & Cooper, C. L. (2007). Positive organizational behavior: An inclusive view. In D. L. Nelson & C. L. Cooper (Eds.), *Positive organizational behavior* (pp. 3–8). London: Sage.

Patterson, M. J., Warr, P. B., & West, M. A. (2004). Organizational climate and company productivity: The role of employee affect and employee level. *Journal of Occupational and Organizational Psychology, 77*, 193–216.

Peterson, C. P. (2006). *A primer in positive psychology*. New York: Oxford University Press.

Pfeffer, J., & Sutton, R. I. (2006). *Hard facts, dangerous half-truths, and total nonsense: Profiting from evidence-based management*. Boston, MA: Harvard Business School Press.

Pryce-Jones, J. (2010). *Happiness at work: Maximizing your psychological capital for success*. Chichester: Wiley Blackwell.

Rich, B. L., Lepine, J. A., & Crawford, E. R. (2010). Job engagement: Antecedents and effects on job performance. *Academy of Management Journal*, *53*(3), 617–635.

Rosenzweig, P. (2007). *The halo effect . . . and the eight other business delusions that deceive managers*. New York: Free Press.

Seligman, M. E. P., & Csikszentmihalyi, M. (2000). Positive psychology. *American Psychologist*, *55*, 5–14.

Simmons, B. L., & Nelson, D. L. (2007). Eustress at work: Extending the holistic stress model. In D. L. Nelson & C. L. Cooper (Eds.), *Positive organizational behavior* (pp. 40–53). London: Sage.

Taris, T., & Schreurs, P. (2009). Well-being and organizational performance: An organizational level test of the happy-productive worker hypothesis. *Work and Stress*, *23*(2), 120–136.

Warr, P. (2009). Environmental "vitamins," personal judgments, work values, and happiness. In S. Cartwright & C. L. Cooper (Eds.), *The Oxford handbook of organizational well-being*. Oxford: Oxford University Press.

Woolley, L., Caza, A., & Levy, L. (2011). Authentic leadership and follower development: Psychological capital, positive work climate, and gender. *Journal of Leadership and Organizational Studies*, *18*(4), 438–448.

Wright, T. A., Cropanzano, R., & Bonett, D. G. (2007). The moderating role of employee positive well-being on the relation between job satisfaction and job performance. *Journal of Occupational Health Psychology*, *12*, 93–104.

Wright, T. A., Cropanzano, R., Bonett, D. G., & Diamond, W. J. (2009). The role of employee psychological well-being in cardiovascular health: When the twain shall meet. *Journal of Organizational Behavior*, *30*, 193–208.

Wright, T. A., & Staw, B. M. (1999). Affect and favorable work outcomes: Two longitudinal tests of the happy/productive worker thesis. *Journal of Organizational Behavior*, *20*, 1–23.

# Part 4
# Character and Wellbeing

# 8

# Character and Wellbeing

## Thomas A. Wright
Fordham University, U.S.A.

## Tyler Lauer
Manhattan, Kansas, U.S.A.

*Character is the basis of happiness and happiness the sanction of character.*
*George Santayana (1863–1952)*

The existence of an association between character and wellbeing has long been assumed by academics and practitioners alike (Wright & Quick, 2011a). For many, including Santayana, character is presumed to be an underlying condition, even a necessity, for the occurrence *and* maintenance of one's happiness and general wellbeing. Santayana's basic thesis is highly consistent with the positive psychology and positive organizational behavior movements' recognition that every individual has a portfolio of core strengths, including those involving character, which lead to personal growth and betterment (Luthans, 2002; Wright, 2003; Wright & Quick, 2009). In this chapter, we highlight three primary objectives. First, a brief overview of the organizational research on wellbeing is provided. Second, a working definition of character is introduced. Finally, exciting future directions for applied researchers interested in the relationship between character and wellbeing are presented.

*Work and Wellbeing: Wellbeing: A Complete Reference Guide*, Volume III.
Edited by Peter Y. Chen and Cary L. Cooper.
© 2014 John Wiley & Sons, Ltd. Published 2014 by John Wiley & Sons, Inc.
DOI: 10.1002/9781118539415.wbwell08

## Organizational Research on Wellbeing

Throughout the ages, one of the most persistent topics of human interest has been the pursuit of wellbeing or "happiness" (Russell, 1930; Wright & Cropanzano, 2000). Consistent with this pursuit, the causes and consequences of employee wellbeing have long been of interest to organizational scholars. Such early leading luminaries as Snow (1923), Mayo (1924), Fisher and Hanna (1931), McMurry (1932), and Hersey (1932) were well aware of the prominent role of both positive and negative worker wellbeing on various individual efficiency and health indicators. For example, and focusing on positive wellbeing, Hersey (1932, p. 289) found that "men are more productive in a positive emotional state than in a negative [one]." Alternatively, a number of early applied scholars focused on the negative or unpleasantness end of the wellbeing continuum (Wright & Cropanzano, 2007). As one example, Anderson (1929) determined that a significant number of employees suffered from psychological distress and were "problem" employees. While detailed analysis is beyond the scope of this chapter (see Wright & Cropanzano, 2007 for a further historical overview), a brief point of clarification of "happiness" and "wellbeing" construct terminology is in order.

Generally speaking, when scholars use the term happiness they are typically referring to an individual's psychological wellbeing, emotional wellbeing, subjective wellbeing, life satisfaction, or such objective life conditions as income (Cropanzano & Wright, 2014; Diener, 1984; Wright & Doherty, 1998). These are certainly not identical constructs. Unfortunately, they are all too often used interchangeably. Consistent with Diener (1984) and Wright and Cropanzano (2000), we prefer the term wellbeing to avoid the imprecision and lay connotation captured in the less precise term happiness. Furthermore, as with the happiness and wellbeing distinction, the terms "emotional," "psychological," and "subjective" wellbeing are also not isomorphic concepts. Consistent with the body of extant research that purports to examine a character–wellbeing relationship (cf. Park, Peterson, & Seligman, 2004; Peterson, Park, & Seligman, 2006), we focus our attention on the character–psychological wellbeing relationship (Littman-Ovadia & Steger, 2010).

Psychological wellbeing is best considered to be a type of emotion-based wellbeing that assesses positive and negative affect on a single bipolar scale (Berkman, 1971; Cropanzano & Wright, 2014; Wright, 2005). According to Bradburn (1969, pp. 53–54), psychological wellbeing is distinguished from affect intensity and is limited to the measurement of those feelings that are "pleasurable and unpleasurable in nature."

Psychological wellbeing (PWB) has three primary defining characteristics. First, it is a phenomenological event (Diener, 1994; Parducci, 1995; Wright & Cropanzano, 2000). People are psychologically well when they subjectively believe themselves to be so. Second, it involves how we feel, experience, and process various forms of emotion. In particular, psychologically well individuals are more prone to experience positive emotions and less prone to experience negative emotions (Argyle, 1987; Warr, 1990). Third, it is best considered as a global judgment (Wright, Larwood, & Denney, 2002). This means that psychological wellbeing refers to one's life in the aggregate, that is, considered as a whole (Wright, 2012). These are important distinctions from such other "happiness" constructs as job satisfaction.

Unlike job satisfaction, which is centered about the work context (Wright, 2006), psychological wellbeing is not aligned to any particular situation. Furthermore, it has consistently been shown to demonstrate temporal stability, though it is not so stable that it cannot be influenced by a number of situational circumstances from both work and nonwork contexts (Cropanzano & Wright, 2001; Wright & Cropanzano, 2007). For example, Cropanzano and Wright (1999) reported a 6-month test–retest correlation of 0.76, a 4-year test–retest correlation of 0.68, and a 5-year test–retest correlation of 0.60 for their measure of psychological wellbeing, the Index of Psychological Well-Being (Berkman, 1971). The fact that psychological wellbeing has been shown to be responsive to various therapeutic interventions has relevance to human resource professionals interested in selection, training and development, and placement decisions (Seligman, 2002; Wright, 2012). Considered in this context, someone exhibiting a high level of psychological wellbeing is indicative that the individual is experiencing a greater measure of positive as compared to negative feelings or emotions (Wright, 2010a). Of practical importance, psychological wellbeing has consistently been shown to be related to a number of important individual and organizational health and betterment indicators, including employee job performance (Wright & Cropanzano, 2000), employee retention (Wright & Bonett, 2007), and cardiovascular health (Wright, Cropanzano, Bonett, & Diamond, 2009).

Over the last 20 years, a growing body of empirical research has consistently determined that various measures of psychological wellbeing are associated with employee performance. In a quasi-experimental research design, Staw and Barsade (1993) found that college students higher in wellbeing were better decision makers, showed better interpersonal behaviors, and received higher overall performance ratings. Psychological wellbeing has also been shown to be related to job performance in a number of organizational field studies (Wright & Cropanzano, 2007). For example, in a longitudinal study, Wright and Bonett (1997) supported the hypothesis that wellbeing was a positive predictor of job performance. Considered together, Wright and his colleagues have consistently established this relationship in a number of studies which have also examined a number of possible third variable covariates, including job satisfaction, positive affect, negative affect, and emotional exhaustion (for a further review, see Wright, Cropanzano, & Meyer, 2004; Wright & Staw, 1999). Even controlling for these potential third variables, research has consistently found significant correlations ranging to 0.50.

As with job performance, the importance of employee wellbeing in the prediction of employee retention has long been recognized in organizational research (E. Frost, 1920; Wright, 2012; for a further historical discussion, see Wright & Bonett, 2007). Similar to the findings that while employee turnover or withdrawal can certainly be functional from the organization's perspective, as when dissatisfied, poorly performing workers quit their job, the prevailing human resources approach is that high employee retention (or low turnover) can be viewed as an indicant of organizational health (Quick, 1999). To that end, Wright and Bonett (1992) found a pattern of results consistent with the proposed relationship between psychological wellbeing and employee retention/withdrawal decisions.

Using a longitudinal design, Wright and Bonett (1992) found that employees low in both job satisfaction and psychological wellbeing were much less likely to stay on the job. In addition, those lowest on job satisfaction and psychological wellbeing were most likely to not only change their current job, but also their occupation as well. In a later study, Wright and Bonett (2007) found that 1-point increases in reported psychological wellbeing (measured on Berkman's 7-point scale) doubled the probability of the employee remaining on the job. Given that the average yearly salary for their employee sample was in excess of US$100,000, and using Cascio's (2003) formula for determining turnover cost, the potential cost of turnover in this sample was estimated to range from a minimum of $150,000 to $250,000 per employee.

Recent research indicates the possibility that psychological wellbeing may also be instrumental in the determination of cardiovascular health

(Wright & Diamond, 2006). According to the latest data from the American Heart Association (2012), approximately 81,100,000 Americans and countless hundreds of millions worldwide are affected by one or more types of cardiovascular heart disease (CHD), with the majority suffering from high blood pressure. While high blood pressure has a number of causes, Wright (2012) suggested that, on average, employees involved in stressful work have higher levels of blood pressure. This is unfortunate as the costs associated with CHD are quite consequential for both the employee and organization. More specifically, the American Heart Association recently estimated the direct and indirect costs of cardiovascular disease at \$503.2 billion (American Heart Association, 2012). The problem is not specific to just the United States and is truly global in nature, with an estimated 90% of CHD found in developing countries (Hecht & Hecht, 2005; Wright, 2012).

Incorporating a sample of supervisory level management personnel, Wright et al. (2009) examined the role of psychological wellbeing in predicting cardiovascular health measured as diastolic blood pressure (DBP), systolic blood pressure (SBP), or pulse product. Pulse product, a composite measure of cardiovascular health and efficiency, is defined as the difference between SBP and DBP, multiplied by the pulse rate, and divided by 100. Lower pulse product scores are associated with better cardiovascular health. Wright (2012) suggested that pulse product scores less than 40 are indicative of cardiovascular efficiency. Based upon prior empirical research (Wright et al., 2009), Wright (2012) suggested the important role of psychological wellbeing in cardiovascular health. In particular, Wright et al. (2009) found that while neither SBP nor DBP were related to psychological wellbeing, pulse product was negatively related ($r = -0.27$, $p < 0.01$) to it. That is, when psychological wellbeing was high, pulse product was low (more efficient). In addition, psychological wellbeing was related to pulse product even after controlling for such cardiovascular health risk factors as employee age, gender, weight, employee smoking behavior, and anxiety level. These results provide preliminary evidence that psychological wellbeing may be beneficial in determining employee cardiovascular health. And, as if the established relationships among psychological wellbeing, job performance, employee retention, and cardiovascular are not enough, there is a longstanding basis for a relationship between psychological wellbeing and character. To that end, we next provide the basis for a definition of character.

163

# Character Defined

As with psychological wellbeing, the development of rigorous definitions of character has long challenged scholars in the applied sciences (Hannah & Avolio, 2011; Wright & Quick, 2011a; Wright & Wefald, 2012). Symptomatic of this definition of character dilemma is the early work of Filter (1921). Filter (1921, p. 297) was so distressed by the definitional ambiguity of character in the social sciences that he stated that, "The looseness of meanings attached to names of character traits demands first consideration . . . (and) must be defined in order to be studied intelligently." Filter fell into the same trap as so many others and failed to provide even a rudimentary definition of character in his research. William James (1920) found the task of defining character so daunting that he begrudgingly concluded that character could at best be considered as those particular mental and moral attitudes that leave one feeling most deeply and intensely vibrant and alive. For James, this transcendent moment is best epitomized by one's inner voice stating that "This is the real me!" The James reference to the "real me" emphasizes the importance of being as precise as possible in delineating the character construct.

Although many of these same definitional problems still exist today (Francis, 2012), a more grounded definitional basis for a more precise conceptualization of character can be found in a number of sources. These include Aristotelian thought, the Judeo-Christian beliefs advocated by St. Paul of faith, hope, and charity, Eastern philosophies such as Confucianism (as espoused in the tenets of *jen, yi, li, zhi,* and *xin*), as well as the more modern, secular models such as utilitarian, justice, and social contract (Peterson & Seligman, 2004).

While traditional views of character have been influenced by a range of religious and philosophical sources, they share one important similarity. They typically contain both moral *and* social dimensions. As a consequence, character is best considered as a multidimensional construct, with the following three dimensions the most widely accepted: moral discipline, moral attachment, and moral autonomy (Hunter, 2000; Wright & Goodstein, 2007). An individual exhibits *moral discipline* if he or she suppresses individual, personal needs for those of a greater societal good. The second dimension, *moral attachment,* constitutes a clear affirmation of an individual's commitment to someone or something greater than herself. The third dimension, *moral autonomy,* is exhibited by someone who has the capacity to freely make ethical decisions (Hunter, 2000). Autonomy means that a person has both the necessary discretion *and* the skills of judgment at their disposal to freely act morally.

Building on these three dimensions, Wright and his colleagues (Wright, 2010b; Wright & Goodstein, 2007; Wright & Huang, 2008; Wright & Quick, 2011a) defined character as those interpenetrable and habitual qualities within individuals, and applicable to organizations that both constrain and lead them to desire and pursue personal and societal good.

The most comprehensive classification framework in the social sciences for measuring character is Peterson and Seligman's (2004) VIA-Inventory of Strengths (VIA-IS). Peterson and Seligman identified six core virtues (with the strengths of character common to each virtue listed in parentheses): wisdom and knowledge (creativity, curiosity, critical thinking, love of learning, perspective); courage (valor, integrity, industry, zest); humanity (kindness, love, social intelligence); justice (fairness, leadership, citizenship); temperance (forgiveness, modesty, prudence, self-regulation); and transcendence (appreciation of beauty, gratitude, hope, humor, spirituality). One potentially promising avenue for character research can be found in what Wright (2010b) calls "profiles in character."

Over the past several years, Wright (2010b; Wright & Quick, 2011a) has assigned his undergraduate and graduate level MBA students the task of completing the 240-item VIA questionnaire. After filling out the survey online, the students receive immediate feedback detailing their scores. Responses are averaged within scales, so that the respondents learn the relative (within subject) ranking of their 24 strengths of character. With their scores in hand, students engage in an often spirited exchange on the role of character on a number of topics, including the role of character in employee betterment, wellbeing, and performance.

Building upon Peterson and Seligman's (2004) 24 strengths of character taxonomy and incorporating a focus group approach, Wright (2010b) developed a number of "top-5" profiles (from the population of all 24 VIA-IS strengths) which respondents (both MBA students and actual business people) consider to be the most beneficial in achieving success in a growing number of work occupations. Over time, a number of profiles have been developed for such occupations as manager, college president, entrepreneur, nurse, sales/marketing, accountant, and politician, among others. As one example, the "top-5" character profile for an accountant includes: prudence, integrity, industry, critical thinking, and valor. Along with accountant, a number of MBA students express a career interest in the field of sales/marketing. A consistent top-5 signature strength profile of success emerges, with zest consistently rated as the necessary top signature strength, followed by the strengths of character: social intelligence, creativity, humor, and curiosity.

One potential career option that more and more students are seriously considering is that of entrepreneur. Incorporating input from both students and working adults, class discussions regarding what constitutes the strengths of character for a successful entrepreneur have proven to be very enlightening. Wright and Quick (2011a, p. 977) defined entrepreneurs as "individuals who acquire or exhibit habitual traits, abilities and strengths of character utilized to effectively recognize opportunities, assume risks in a start-up business venture, and overcome obstacles." Entrepreneurs successfully incorporate new ideas and concepts, or bring existing ideas together in new ways. Signature strength optimal profiles for entrepreneurs include the following strengths: hope, curiosity, zest, industry, and self-regulation.

Some very interesting findings indicate that actual top-5 student profiles are consistently and significantly at variance from their proposed or ideal profiles. For example, students assess social intelligence as being one of the top strengths necessary to be an effective manager. Similarly, love of learning is considered as one of the top-5 character strengths to be an effective MBA student. However, both of these strengths of character are actually among those less commonly self-reported by the students (Wright & Quick, 2011a). Similar results have been found among undergraduate business students. In addition, both graduate and undergraduate business students self-rate themselves low in self-regulation and valor. However conceptualized, the relationship between wellbeing and character strength has long been of interest.

## Character and Wellbeing

We propose that employee character is a central and defining feature for the wellbeing of not only the individual employee, but also the employing organization and the greater societal good. In fact, Littman-Ovadia and Steger (2010) proposed that the ways in which individuals deploy their character strengths is instrumental in the achievement of wellbeing. A growing body of evidence indicates possible linkages between wellbeing and such strengths of character as critical thinking, hope, industry, gratitude, kindness, self-regulation, valor, and zest (cf., Avey, Luthans, Smith, & Palmer, 2010; Peterson & Seligman, 2004; Wright & Quick, 2011a, 2011b).

For example, operationalizing wellbeing as life satisfaction, Peterson, Park, Hall, and Seligman (2009) found that zest was associated with work as a calling, work satisfaction and general life satisfaction. Park et al. (2004) found zest, gratitude, hope, love, and curiosity associated with life satisfaction.

These findings are consistent with preliminary results obtained by the current authors from a sample of MBA students. For example, zest was found to be related to positive affect as measured by the PANAS Scale (Watson, Clark, & Tellegen, 1988) and kindness was correlated with the General Happiness Scale (Lyubomirsky & Lepper, 1999). In addition, the benefits of industry and perseverance on the wellbeing of individuals with such physical maladies as cancer (Ferrell, Smith, Cullinane, & Melancon, 2003), arthritis (Lambert, Lambery, Klipple, & Mewshaw, 1989), and HIV/AIDS (Goodman, Chesney, & Tipton, 1995) have been well documented. In addition, research suggests that positive relationships exist among self-regulation (Gross, 2002), integrity (Becker, 1998), and critical thinking (Wu, 2010) with psychological wellbeing. Given the importance of a successful marriage to one's satisfaction with life, it is perhaps no surprise that Yeh, Lorenz, Wickrama, Conger, and Elder (2006) found integrity was instrumental in marital wellbeing and satisfaction. Finally, the relationship of wellbeing with valor is more difficult to interpret, with research on whistle-blowing demonstrating the complex nature of the relationship (Rothschild & Miethe, 1999). Incorporating a case study approach to our profiles in character format, we next use the proposed relationship between valor and wellbeing to suggest future research directions for organizational scholars.

## Future Research Directions

Wright and colleagues (Wright, 2010a; Wright & Quick, 2011a), using their focus group approach composed of actual business and graduate business students, have identified valor as an important strength of character for such varied occupations as accountant and what Hannah, Uhl-Bien, Avolio, and Cavarretta (2009) refer to as military and paramilitary workers in extreme situations. More specifically, building on Wright's (2010a) framework, Quick and Wright (2011) proposed that individuals in extreme contexts are best served with a top-5 signature profile in character which includes the strengths of valor, integrity, industry, critical thinking, and self-regulation. Posing a question that is highly relevant to the present discussion, Park et al. (2004) asked whether it is possible for someone to have "too much" of a particular strength of character. And, if so, what effect does this excess have on their wellbeing?

Incorporating a parallel construct-validating project, Park et al. (2004) conducted interviews asking individuals whether their signature strengths ever "got them into trouble." Over 90% of the respondents said they did, but 100% indicated that they would not change because these strengths were "who they are." From these findings, Park et al. (2004, p. 615) proposed that individuals are willing "to pay the occasional penalty of a signature strength because the benefit was being true to themselves."

A potential problem with this assertion was that Park et al. asked respondents to respond anonymously to hypothetical scenarios. What happens in real-life situations where there are real consequences to one's actions involves different thought processes. In fact, research on whistleblowing indicates that the consequences may be more than many individuals are prepared to pay (Near & Miceli, 1996; Wright & Lauer, 2013).

Research has found that whistleblowers are often fired from their job, have trouble finding subsequent employment, are harassed by work peers, suffer various forms of physical and emotional stress, and even contemplate suicide (Velasquez, 2002). In addition, the harassment is often constant in nature and tends to build over time with the ultimate goal of wearing down the individual. Given these severe consequences, the question becomes one of what should an individual of character do and what price should they be willing to pay to seek justice? Given that whistleblowers typically have a strong belief in universal moral principles (Velasquez, 2002), many report their journey, though often very difficult, to be a powerful experience and one that provided them with a renewed sense of life meaning and purpose.

For Steger (2009) and Littman-Ovadia and Steger (2010, p. 420), our meaning in life refers to "one's ability to perceive oneself and the world as worthwhile and valued, identify a unique niche, and establish a valued life purpose." Central to how one acts in a time of crisis involves how well-articulated is their sense of purpose or meaning (Frankl, 1965). However, Frankl (1984) also noted that many of us are lacking in a sense of purpose and meaning. As a result, we suggest that any relationship between character strength and wellbeing is moderated by one's meaning in life.

Taken in the context of work, applied research has long been interested in optimizing the level of fit between the individual and the organization (Wright, 1991). This degree of suitability between individual employees and their work has been formalized as person–environment (P-E) theory (French, Caplan, & Harrison, 1982). P-E theory suggests that the wellbeing of both the individual and organization suffers when there is an incongruent fit between the characteristics or demands of the job and the characteristics of the employee (Caplan, Cobb, French, Harrison, & Pinneau, 1980). While numerous dimensions of fit have been introduced and examined over the years, the role of employee strengths of character has not received adequate consideration. For example, what role does the strength of character hope play in successfully surviving in a crisis situation? Are there optimal top-5 strengths of character profiles which help people to benefit from crisis situations? Do these optimal top-5 profiles change as a function of time (Wright, 1997)? Can a kind woman prosper in an organization that is toxic and lacks compassion (P. J. Frost, 2011)? Can a man of integrity even minimally survive in a corrupt organization? The research topics are many and varied.

## Concluding Thoughts

As with definitions of wellbeing (Cropanzano & Wright, 2014; Wright & Huang, 2012), how we define character is worthy of further attention. Roughly 90 years ago, Gordon Allport's (1921) goal was to expunge all aspects of "moral" from the social sciences. His famous dictum "to define character as personality evaluated and personality . . . as character devaluated" (Allport, 1961, p. 32) is alive and well in the work of Peterson and Seligman (2004). In particular, like Allport, Peterson and Seligman do not "saddle" character with a moral dimension, as evidenced by their inclusion of such strengths as social intelligence, zest, creativity, creativity, critical thinking, and humor. Alternatively, Hunter (2000) and Wright and his colleagues (Wright, 2010b; Wright & Quick, 2011a) emphasize the moral dimension of character. This highlights the need for future research to further delve into what character *is* and *is not*. Obviously, this is an exciting time for organizational scholars to be interested in psychological wellbeing and character.

## References

Allport, G. W. (1921). Personality and character. *Psychological Bulletin, 18,* 441–455.
Allport, G. W. (1961). *Personality: A psychological interpretation.* New York: Holt (Original work published in 1937).

American Heart Association (2012). *Forecasting the future of cardiovascular disease in the United States.* website: http://circ.ahajournals.org/content/121/7e46.full.

Anderson, V. V. (1929). *Psychiatry in industry.* New York: Harpers.

Argyle, M. (1987). *The experience of happiness.* London: Methuen.

Avey, J. B., Luthans, F., Smith, R. M., & Palmer, N. F. (2010). Impact of positive psychological capital on employee well-being over time. *Journal of Occupational Health Psychology, 15,* 17–28.

Becker, T. W. (1998). Integrity in organizations: Beyond honesty and conscientiousness. *Academy of Management Review, 23,* 154–161.

Berkman, P. L. (1971). Measurement of mental health in a general population survey. *American Journal of Epidemiology, 94,* 105–111.

Bradburn, N. M. (1969). *The structure of psychological well-being.* Chicago, IL: Aldine.

Caplan, R. D., Cobb, S., French, J. R. P. Jr., Harrison, R. Van, & Pinneau, S. R. Jr., (1980). *Job demands and worker health: Main effects and occupational differences.* Ann Arbor, MI: Institute for Social Research.

Cascio, W. F. (2003). *Managing human resources: Productivity, quality of life, profits* (6th ed). New York: McGraw-Hill.

Cropanzano, R., & Wright, T. A. (1999). A five-year study of change in the relationship between well-being and job performance. *Consulting Psychology Journal: Practice and Theory, 51,* 252–265.

Cropanzano, R., & Wright, T. A. (2001). When a 'happy' worker is really a 'productive' worker: A review and further refinement of the happy-productive worker thesis. *Consulting Psychology Journal: Practice and Research, 53,* 182–199.

Cropanzano, R., & Wright, T. A. (2014). The four faces of happiness. In H. M. Weiss (Ed.), *Handbook of work attitudes and affect.* New York: Oxford University Press.

Diener, E. (1984). Subjective well-being. *Psychological Bulletin, 95,* 542–575.

Diener, E. (1994). Assessing subjective well-being: Progress and opportunities. *Social Indicators Research, 31,* 103–157.

Ferrell, B., Smith, S. L., Cullinane, C. A., & Melancon, C. (2003). Psychological well-being and quality of life in ovarian cancer survivors. *Cancer, 98,* 1061–1071.

Filter, R. O. (1921). An experimental study of character traits. *Journal of Applied Psychology, 5,* 297–317.

Fisher, V. E., & Hanna, J. V. (1931). *The dissatisfied worker.* New York: Macmillan.

Francis, C. A. (2012). The mediating force of "face": Supervisor character and status related to perceived organizational support and work outcomes. *Journal of Leadership & Organizational Studies, 19,* 58–67.

Frankl, V. E. (1965). *The doctor and the soul: From psychotherapy to logotherapy.* New York: Vantage Books.

Frankl, V. E. (1984). *Man's search for logotherapy: An introduction to logotherapy.* New York: Touchstone.

French, J. R. P. Jr., Caplan, R. D., & Harrison, R. Van (1982). *The mechanisms of job stress and strain*. London: Wiley.

Frost, E. (1920). What industry wants and does not want from the psychologist. *Journal of Applied Psychology*, *4*, 18–24.

Frost, P. J. (2003). *Toxic emotions at work: How compassionate managers handle pain and conflict*. Boston, MA: Harvard business School Press.

Frost, P. J. (2011). Why compassion counts! *Journal of Management Inquiry*, *20*, 395–401.

Goodman, E., Chesney, M. A., & Tipton, A. C. (1995). Relationship of optimism, knowledge, attitudes, and beliefs to use of HIV antibody testing by at-risk female adolescents. *Psychosomatic Medicine*, *57*, 542–546.

Gross, J. J. (2002). Emotion regulation: Affective, cognitive, and social consequences. *Psychophysiology*, *39*, 281–291.

Hannah, S. T., & Avolio, B. J. (2011). The locus of leader character. *The Leadership Quarterly*, *22*, 979–983.

Hannah, S., Uhl-Bien, M., Avolio, B. J., & Cavarretta, F. (2009). A framework for examining leadership in extreme contexts. *The Leadership Quarterly*, *20*, 897–919.

Hecht, B. K., & Hecht, F. (2005). Heart attack risks around the world. MedicineNet. com. http://www.medicinenet.com/script.main/art.asp?articlekey+38774.

Hersey, R. B. (1932). *Workers' emotions in shop and home: A study in industrial workers from the psychological and physiological standout*. Philadelphia, PA: University of Pennsylvania Press.

Hunter, J. W. (2000). *The death of character: Moral education in an age without good or evil*. New York: Basic Books.

James, W. (1920). In H. James (Ed.), *The letters of William James*. Boston: The Atlantic Monthly Press.

Lambert, V. A., Lambery, C. E., Klipple, G. L., & Mewshaw, E. A. (1989). Social support, hardiness and psychological well-being in women and arthritis. *Journal of Nursing Scholarship*, *21*, 128–131.

Littman-Ovadia, H., & Steger, M. (2010). Character strengths and well-being among volunteers and employees: Toward an integrative model. *Journal of Positive Psychology*, *5*, 419–430.

Luthans, F. (2002). The need for and meaning of positive organizational behavior. *Journal of Organizational Behavior*, *23*, 695–706.

Lyubomirsky, S., & Lepper, H. S. (1999). A measure of subjective happiness: Preliminary reliability and construct validation. *Social Indicators Research*, *46*, 137–155.

Mayo, E. (1924). Revery and industrial fatigue. *Journal of Personnel Research*, *3*, 273–281.

McMurry, R. N. (1932). Efficiency, work satisfaction and neurotic tendency. *Personnel Journal*, *11*, 201–210.

Near, J. P., & Miceli, M. P. (1996). Whistle-blowing: Myth and reality. *Journal of Management*, *22*, 507–526.

Parducci, A. (1995). *Happiness, pleasure, and judgment: The contextual theory and its applications.* Mahwah, NJ: Erlbaum.

Park, N., Peterson, C., & Seligman, M. E. P. (2004). Strengths of character and well-being. *Journal of Social and Clinical Psychology, 23,* 603–619.

Peterson, C., Park, N., Hall, N., & Seligman, M. E. P. (2009). Zest and work. *Journal of Organizational Behavior, 30,* 161–172.

Peterson, C., Park, N., & Seligman, M. E. P. (2006). Greater strength of character and recovery from illness. *Journal of Positive Psychology, 1,* 17–26.

Peterson, C., & Seligman, M. E. P. (2004). *Character strengths and virtues: A handbook and classification.* New York: Oxford University Press/Washington, DC: American Psychological Association.

Quick, J. C. (1999). Occupational health psychology: The convergence of health and clinical psychology with public health and preventive medicine in an organizational context. *Professional Psychology: Research and Practice, 30,* 123–128.

Quick, J. C., & Wright, T. A. (2011). Character-based leadership, context and consequences. *The Leadership Quarterly, 22,* 984–988.

Rothschild, J., & Miethe, T. D. (1999). Whistle-blower disclosures and management retaliation: The battle to control information about organization corruption. *Work and Occupations, 26,* 107–128.

Russell, B. (1930). *The conquest of happiness.* New York: Liveright.

Seligman, M. E. P. (2002). *Authentic happiness.* New York: Free Press.

Snow, A. J. (1923). Labor turnover and mental alertness test scores. *Journal of Applied Psychology, 7,* 285–290.

Staw, B. M., & Barsade, S. G. (1993). Affect and managerial performance: A test of the sadder-but-wiser vs. happier-and-smarter hypotheses. *Administrative Science Quarterly, 38,* 304–331.

Steger, M. (2009). Meaning in life. In S. J. Lopez & C. R. Snyder (Eds.), *Oxford handbook of positive psychology* (pp. 679–687). New York: Oxford University Press.

Velasquez, M. G. (2002). *Business ethics: Concepts and cases.* Upper Saddle River, NJ: Prentice Hall.

Warr, P. (1990). The measurement of well-being and other aspects of mental health. *Journal of Occupational Psychology, 63,* 193–210.

Watson, D., Clark, L. A., & Tellegen, A. (1988). Development and validation of brief measures of positive and negative affect: The PANAS Scales. *Journal of Personality and Social Psychology, 54,* 1063–1070.

Wright, T. A. (1991). The level of employee utilization and its effect on subsequent turnover. *Journal of Applied Business Research, 7,* 25–29.

Wright, T. A. (1997). Time revisited in organizational research. *Journal of Organizational Behavior, 18,* 201–204.

Wright, T. A. (2003). Positive organizational behavior: An idea whose time has truly come. *Journal of Organizational Behavior, 24,* 437–442.

Wright, T. A. (2005). The role of 'happiness' in organizational research: Past, present and future directions. In P. L. Perrewe & D. C. Ganster (Eds.), *Research in occupational stress and well-being* (Vol. 4, pp. 225–268). Amsterdam: JAI Press.

Wright, T. A. (2006). The emergence of job satisfaction in organizational research: A historical overview of the dawn of job attitude research. *Journal of Management History*, 12, 262–277.

Wright, T. A. (2010a). The role of psychological well-being in job performance, employee retention and cardiovascular health. *Organizational Dynamics*, 39, 13–23.

Wright, T. A. (2010b). Character assessment is business ethics education. In D. G. Fisher & D. L. Swanson (Eds.), *Toward assessing business ethics education* (pp. 361–380). Charlotte, NC: Information Age Publishing.

Wright, T. A. (2012). Encouraging employee happiness. In S. A. David, I. Boniwell, & A. M. Conley-Ayers (Eds.), *The Oxford handbook of happiness* (pp. 783–797). Oxford: Oxford University Press.

Wright, T. A., & Bonett, D. G. (1992). The effect of turnover on work satisfaction and mental health: Support for a situational perspective. *Journal of Organizational Behavior*, 13, 603–615.

Wright, T. A., & Bonett, D. G. (1997). The role of pleasantness and activation-based well-being in performance prediction. *Journal of Occupational Health Psychology*, 2, 212–219.

Wright, T. A., & Bonett, D. G. (2007). Job satisfaction and psychological well-being as nonadditive predictors of workplace turnover. *Journal of Management*, 33, 141–160.

Wright, T. A., & Cropanzano, R. (2000). Psychological well-being and job satisfaction as predictors of job performance. *Journal of Occupational Health Psychology*, 5, 84–94.

Wright, T. A., & Cropanzano, R. (2007). The happy/productive worker thesis revisited. In J. Martocchio (Ed.), *Research in personnel and human resource management* (Vol. 26, pp. 269–313). Amsterdam: Elsevier.

Wright, T. A., Cropanzano, R., Bonett, D. G., & Diamond, J. W. (2009). The role of psychological well-being in cardiovascular health: When the twain shall meet. *Journal of Organizational Behavior*, 30, 193–208.

Wright, T. A., Cropanzano, R., & Meyer, D. G. (2004). State and trait correlates of job performance: A tale of two perspectives. *Journal of Business and Psychology*, 18, 365–383.

Wright, T. A., & Diamond, W. J. (2006). Getting the 'pulse' of your employees: The use of cardiovascular research in better understanding behavior in organizations. *Journal of Organizational Behavior*, 27, 395–401.

Wright, T. A., & Doherty, E. M. (1998). Organizational behavior "rediscovers" the role of emotional well-being. *Journal of Organizational Behavior*, 19, 481–485.

Wright, T. A., & Goodstein, J. (2007). Character is not "dead" in management research: A review of individual character and organizational-level virtue. *Journal of Management*, 33, 928–958.

Wright, T. A., & Huang, C.-C. (2008). Character is organizational research: Past directions and future prospects. *Journal of Organizational Behavior, 29*, 981–987.

Wright, T. A., & Huang, C.-C. (2012). The many benefits of employee well-being in organizational research. *Journal of Organizational Behavior, 33*, 1188–1192.

Wright, T. A., Larwood, L., & Denney, P. J. (2002). The different "faces" of happiness-unhappiness in organizational research: Emotional exhaustion, positive affectivity, negative affectivity, and psychological well-being as correlates of job performance. *Journal of Business and Management, 8*, 109–126.

Wright, T. A., & Lauer, T. L. (2013). What is character and why it really matters. *Organizational Dynamics, 42*, 25–34.

Wright, T. A., & Quick, J. C. (2009). The emerging positive agenda in organizations: Greater than a trickle, but not yet a deluge. *Journal of Organizational Behavior, 30*, 147–159.

Wright, T. A., & Quick, J. C. (2011a). The role of character in ethical leadership research. *Leadership Quarterly, 22*, 975–978.

Wright, T., & Quick, J. C. (2011b). *A review of individual character and organizational-level virtue, scale development and preliminary results: Technical Report.* Contract No. W911SD-09-P-0581, March 28, 2011, USACA, United States Military Academy, West Point, NY.

Wright, T. A., & Staw, B. M. (1999). Affect and favorable work outcomes. Two longitudinal tests of the happy-productive worker thesis. *Journal of Organizational Behavior, 20*, 1–23.

Wright, T. A., & Wefald, A. J. (2012). Leadership in an academic setting: A view from the top. *Journal of Management Inquiry, 21*, 180–186.

Wu, C. H. (2010). Meanings of music making experiences among second-generation Chinese string students. *Dissertation Abstracts International Section A: Humanities and Social Sciences, 71*, 6-A.

Yeh, H. C., Lorenz, F. O., Wickrama, K. A. S., Conger, R. D., & Elder, G. H. (2006). Relationships among sexual satisfaction, marital quality, and marital instability at midlife. *Journal of Family Psychology, 20*, 339–343.

# 9

# Stress, Health, and Wellbeing in Practice

## Workplace Leadership and Leveraging Stress for Positive Outcomes

### James Campbell Quick

The University of Texas at Arlington, U.S.A. and
Lancaster University Management School, U.K.

### Joel Bennett

Organizational Wellness and Learning Systems, U.S.A.

### M. Blake Hargrove

Shippensburg University, U.S.A.

There is a deep and ongoing relationship between an employee's stress, level of physical health, and experience of wellbeing. For example, work stress is a significant predictor of heart disease (Kivimäki et al., 2006), chronic stress is associated with obesity (Dallman et al., 2003), and obesity is associated with less wellbeing (Doll, Petersen, & Stewart-Brown, 2000), reduced engagement/productivity (Gates, Succop, Brehm, Gillespie, & Sommers, 2008), and lower participation in the workforce (Klarenbach, Padwal, Chuck, & Jacobs, 2006). Further, positive workplace engagement helps workers to handle stress (Bakker, Hakanen, Demerouti, & Xanthopoulou, 2007). Accordingly, any positive work designs or interventions that target one of these areas also affect the others. This chapter presents a model on

*Work and Wellbeing: Wellbeing: A Complete Reference Guide*, Volume III.
Edited by Peter Y. Chen and Cary L. Cooper.
© 2014 John Wiley & Sons, Ltd. Published 2014 by John Wiley & Sons, Inc.
DOI: 10.1002/9781118539415.wbwell09

the positive aspects of stress, and how workplaces can leverage these aspects to the benefit of health and wellbeing for organizations and for workers. We accentuate the positive with an understanding that negative aspects of stress (e.g., burnout, toxic emotions, trauma, or tragedy) cannot be ignored and that both strengths (protective factors) and weaknesses (risk factors) are intertwined (Cameron, 2007). We return to the issue of obesity and its links with stress at the end of the chapter because it is a growing and serious concern for society and for employers, and because we believe that a greater focus on positive stress management can help to address issues of physical health.

We assume a tremendous upside potential available to employers who leverage the positive aspects of stress, including the reduction of workplace risk factors. We discuss stress as a double-edged sword, ending on a positive note that segues into an exploration of positive pathways through which stress can build a healthy workplace. These five positive pathways are: strength of character, self-awareness, socialized power motivation, requisite self-reliance, and diverse professional supports. Finally, we review the literature on practical interventions—with a focus on best practices—that are available to address negative stress and build health and wellbeing in organizations.

## Stress: A Double-Edged Sword

The dark side of stress as a threat to health and wellbeing has become well understood over the past 70 years (Quick & Quick, 2013a). Stress is linked, directly or indirectly, to seven of the ten leading causes of death in the developed economies. What is less well understood is the positive side of stress, which can lead to extraordinary human acts, overcoming legitimate emergencies and achieving peak performances. Selye (1975) introduced the term *eustress* to describe the positive, functional state resulting from exposure to stressful stimuli. During the past decade, explorations regarding the specific type of stressors related to positive and negative stress responses have received attention. An important theoretical contribution was made by Cavanaugh, Boswell, Roehling, and Boudreau (2000), who distinguished challenge-related from hindrance-related stress. Subsequent scholars have defined challenge stressors as those stimuli appraised as related to job accomplishment or personal development (Podsakoff, 2007). A meta-analysis of hindrance and challenge stressors found that challenge stressors are positively associated with functional outcomes, such as job satisfaction and commitment, and negatively related to dysfunctional outcomes, such as intention to turnover and withdrawal behavior (Podsakoff, LePine, & Lepine, 2007). The results indicate that it is not desirable to eliminate all stressors within the organizational context. The presence of challenge stress is a potentially powerful force in human development and achievement.

Though reducing negative stress remains an important managerial consideration, providing stimuli that appropriately challenge individuals should also receive attention. Building a healthy and happy organization requires both minimizing negative stress and optimizing positive stress. We propose that thoughtful managers or strategically minded leaders proactively seek to provide or manage work stressors that stimulate employee accomplishment and competency development as well as seeking to avoid generating stressful stimuli that create barriers.

## Positive Pathways to Health and Wellbeing

Wellbeing has been a subject of interest for organizational scholars for more than 80 years. One of the earliest inquiries into executive wellbeing was at Ford Motor Company; this study sought to show how every executive could become his own psychologist (Laird, 1929). Laird focused on occupational skills and self-expression through work, on the management of fatigue and energy, on personal development of the executive, and on loyalty and morale.

The body of empirical and clinical research on executives and executive wellbeing led to the conclusion that there are at least five positive pathways that can lead executives to states of positive wellbeing (for themselves as well as for their associates). Associated with positive wellbeing is the accumulation of resource surpluses that benefit the executive, all levels of management and leadership, and those whom these leaders serve. The five positive pathways that we address in this section are: strength of character, self-awareness, socialized power motivation, requisite self-reliance, and diverse professional supports. Each of these makes a unique positive contribution to the development and maintenance of an executive's positive wellbeing and resources. In turn, as an executive exhibits these resources, he or she generates opportunities to promote challenges that support the growth of others. The following discussion of each pathway first describes how it manifests as an asset for leaders. We then describe relevant research on the path, ending with an emphasis on how the path can be leveraged to help transform stress into a positive organizational function (i.e., eustress, challenge stressors).

We should note that the approach to workplace wellbeing described here differs from those that focus on different aspects or domains of wellbeing (e.g., social, financial, community, and physical wellbeing; Rath & Harter, 2010). Instead, we take a practical or practice-oriented perspective and point to functional behaviors that leaders can exhibit that will promote wellbeing. Specifically, the five positive pathways work because, through them, leaders take an intentional orientation to stress as a positive feature of occupational life rather than an inevitable evil or a fixed or immutable cause of poor health and lower productivity. At the same time, we believe that when leaders take these paths, they can help to improve wellbeing across many domains (within workers, between workers, and in the community as well).

Finally, we believe it prudent to state a caveat before we review each pathway. Specifically, the five paths we prescribe are not a "magic bullet," and extra effort and strategy will be required to practically translate the proposed insights into everyday work. There are likely important boundary conditions that can greatly hinder how much leaders and organizations can practically use these pathways, as well as moderating factors that should be considered. For example, more effort may be necessary for occupations in which work is characterized by high job strain (i.e., high demands + low autonomy) and repetitive labor. Alternatively, creative solutions may be required for the increasing number of jobs that are virtual, mobile, or have nontraditional work schedules. Further, disease-type, racial, gender-related, and generational factors may moderate how these pathways are perceived and how workers respond to them. We mention these issues up-front not only because we wish to paint a realistic picture, but also because we invite readers to actively think through these challenges as they consider each path.

## Strength of Character

Strength of character may be defined as a composite set of virtues (e.g., belief in oneself, integrity, courage, concern for the greater good), a willingness to uphold these higher standards in the face of crisis, challenge, or direct attacks, and a commitment to practice these virtues in word, action, and follow-through. Strength of character is anchored in moral philosophy and more specifically within the virtue ethics tradition of Aristotle (310/1998, 2000). The character or virtue ethics tradition is contemporarily interpreted by Solomon (1999), who examined ethics, goodness, and nobility within the American corporate system. More recently, Thompson, Grahek,

Phillips, and Fay (2008) found that the character to lead was one of three cornerstones to excellence in executive performance. For Thompson and his colleagues, character is the integrity, ethics, and courage to earn and maintain stakeholder trust and to be accountable. The Leadership Worth Following executive performance model is one basis for both executive selection and executive development (Thompson et al., 2008).

Goolsby, Mack, and Quick (2010) emphasize positive ethics and character by examining three cases: two executive and one organizational. One of these executive cases is that of Joseph M. Grant who, as chairman and CEO of Texas American Bancshares in the 1980s, lost his bank and his financial worth in the Great Texas Banking Crash. Grant's display of strength of character in this crisis came with his unwillingness to abandon his key executive leadership position within the bank, despite the personal and family cost that ensued. While Grant fought an uphill battle against the collapse of the Texas economy and the Federal Deposit Insurance Corporation (FDIC), he did not act primarily out of self-interest. He simultaneously supported the interests of his executive team, the bank's many stakeholders, his family, and the community of Fort Worth, Texas.

Grant's display of strength of character in the crisis set the stage for his subsequent establishment a decade later of Texas Capital Bank, believed to be the largest start-up bank in U.S. history, with initial capitalization of US $80 million (Goolsby et al., 2010). His integrity and courage were central to the willingness of investors and colleagues to entrust him with significant wealth. Grant was later honored with a Horatio Alger Distinguished American Award at the United States Supreme Court in 2010 for overcoming adversity. His character strength of integrity was crucial to ultimate success.

Several studies have examined strength of character as it applies to organizational leadership (Kets de Vries, 2009a; Steinbrecher & Bennett, 2003; Thun & Kelloway, 2011), including the proposal that love, trust, and forgiveness are central to effective leadership (Caldwell & Dixon, 2010). Insights can also be gleaned from the field of positive psychology, which suggests that fostering character strengths is essential to the development of individual wellbeing (Peterson & Park, 2011). For example, self-directedness, cooperativeness, and self-transcendence have been described as essential for wellbeing (Cloninger, 2006). A recent study among 149 adolescents found that strengths that focus on others rather than oneself, such as kindness and teamwork, predicted a lower instance of depression (Gillham et al., 2011). The same study found that transcendence strengths such as meaning and love predicted improved life satisfaction (Gillham et al.,

2011). The connectedness or alignment between values and behavior also seems to be relevant. Some evidence suggests that interventions designed to connect values with behavior can improve physical fitness and mental wellbeing (Anshel, 2010). Another recent study explored the relationship among character, meaningfulness, and wellbeing. Among a sample of paid workers and volunteers, the study found that deploying character strengths at work improved meaningfulness and improved wellbeing (Littman-Ovadia & Steger, 2010).

## Application to Positive Stress

Following from the above, we propose the dual thesis that a worker's ability to address stressful stimuli is enhanced through character and that the development of character through workplace leadership helps organizations do a better job of not just managing stress but embracing stress as part of workplace health and wellbeing. Indeed, it may be—as seen from the perspective of character strength—that many of the workplace stressors defined in the occupational literature (e.g., job demands, effort–reward imbalance) are not intrinsically problematic and that only a reactive attitude makes them so. Conversely, a proactive sense of ethics (either self-generated or imbued by leadership) may lead workers to see these stressors as opportunities for growth.

## Self-Awareness

While executives often have rather low levels of self-awareness (Kets de Vries, 2009b), self-awareness is a powerful positive pathway to wellbeing. Clinical inquiry with executives and global leaders offers deeper insights into the conflicts, confusions, and dilemmas that so often foil a leader's ability to achieve happiness and positive wellbeing (Kets de Vries, 2009b; Levinson, 1964/1985; Moss, 1981). Research by the Hay Group finds that without self-awareness, executives have a 96% probability of failing to exercise good self-management skills such as self-control. Self-awareness is therefore the basis for self-regulation in action and behavior. In addition, the Hay Group research finds that without self-awareness, executives have an 84% probability of failing to develop good social awareness skills, such as empathy. Hence, self-awareness is a crucial personal and interpersonal attribute critical to executive wellbeing as well as job function. Kets de

Vries (2009b) shows how the struggle with competing demands and inner conflicts within an executive can disturb psychological equilibrium, hinder the pursuit of happiness, and adversely impact wellbeing.

Self-awareness is foremost a guard against negative wellbeing and can offer opportunities for positive action with resulting wellbeing. For example, by creating dissonance and exploring discrepancies between how executives see themselves, how they are seen by family, and how their leaders see them, Moss (1981) enabled executives to better understand their own inner conflicts and tensions. When individuals confront these inner conflicts, they also gain insight into their defense mechanisms, and positive pathways are opened for actions that can lead to success, productive achievements, and happiness (Vaillant, 1977). Mature defenses, or adaptive mechanisms, have functional value in smoothing the way through the threats and challenges in life, as we see when addressing those issues later.

At this time there are few empirical studies published testing the hypothesis that increased self-awareness improves individual wellbeing. One recent study conducted among a sample of mental health professionals suggests that mindfulness mediates the relationship between self-care and wellbeing (Richards, Campenni, & Muse-Burke, 2010). Other research supports the connection between self-leadership and wellbeing. Lovelace, Manz, and Alves (2007) propose a model of self-leadership, citing evidence showing that emotional regulation is predictive of wellbeing (Côté, 2005; Gross, 1998). We suggest that both worker mindfulness and self-regulation (as concomitants of self-awareness) may be critical to wellbeing. This hypothesis presents an opportunity to current scholars interested in wellbeing.

## Application to Positive Stress

Following from the above, we propose that a healthy workplace may intentionally introduce stressful stimuli in the form of executive coaching, performance feedback, 360 evaluations, and leadership practices that embrace rather than avoid conflict. If done well, these types of practices may actually induce greater employee self-awareness that can be contrasted with a defensive or reactive posture in organizations attached to a status quo or unvarying bureaucratic mandate. Seen from the perspective of self-awareness, stressful stimuli may provide workers with the capacity for continuous learning and refinement of their skills in mindfulness and self-regulation. Here again, we propose that stress can be a positive factor in helping an organization—and its workers—stay agile and vigilant.

181

## Socialized Power Motivation

In addition to conflicts and tensions, needs and motivation are powerful inner forces within executives. McClelland (1975) discovered that the best leaders and managers were those who had a high need for power accompanied by a relatively low need for affiliation. This inner need for power was first differentiated from the need for achievement (i.e., doing things well) and the need for affiliation (i.e., close, warm relationships), and defined as a concern for exercising influence and making a difference. Additional research also suggests a distinction between an egoistic need for positional power (i.e., being the one who makes decisions) and interpersonal influence (i.e., knowing one's ideas have an effect on others) (Bennett, 1988; Ulemann, 1972). The experience and expression of power motivation is central to an executive's wellbeing.

McClelland and Burnham (2003) distinguished between those with a high need for personal achievement (imperial power), or self-aggrandizement, and those with a high need for interactive (socialized) power, or institutional advancement. The latter, socialized power motivation is healthier and distinguishes the best leaders and executives. This is consistent with Smith's (1759) emphasis on the social passions that balance the selfish passions. Thus, world-class executives who build positive wellbeing are ones who are motivated to balance their self-interest with the interests of others. By being socialized leaders, these executives deliver top-quartile business results along with high morale because they work with others (Burnham, 2002).

This distinguishing power-oriented characteristic of altruism is consistent with Vaillant's (1977) identification of the Level IV adaptive ego mechanisms that facilitate positive wellbeing outcomes. These mature mechanisms contribute to health and wellbeing and include sublimation, altruism, suppression, anticipation, and humor. While the best executives have a power motivation to make an impact, to influence others, to change events, and to make a difference in life, they channel this energy in socially desirable and constructive ways for the benefit of all concerned. The preoccupation with power and manipulation for personal gain alone is selfish, self-centered, frequently self-defeating, and undermines health and wellbeing.

Imperial power motivation stands in contrast to socialized power motivation. The former leads to a preoccupation with personal power and self-serving interests. When unchecked, personal achievement and imperial power motivation becomes destructive to the interests of others, including colleagues, family members, the organization, and the community. John Goolsby was able to check self-serving behavior as CEO of the Howard Hughes Corporation by putting in place ethics guidelines and standards that included enforcement mechanisms (Goolsby et al., 2010). Goolsby's rejection of imperial power motivation led to positive wellbeing for himself, his family, the company, and importantly for Howard Hughes' heirs.

Recent empirical research supports the notion that there are sex differences in power motivation among executives. In a study of 107 female and 257 male executive managers, women reported significantly higher affiliation scores and men reported significantly higher explicit power scores (Kazén & Kuhl, 2011). In the same study, the authors found that striving for goals without gaining pleasure from doing so impaired wellbeing.

Power motivation may also be a significant predictor of wellbeing among individuals in general. One recent study among an international sample of German, Hong Kong Chinese, and mainland Chinese participants reported that alignment between implicit power motives and explicit power goals positively predicted both life satisfaction and positive affect (Hofer, Busch, Bond, Li, & Law, 2010). The same study found that the negative relationship between power values and wellbeing was mediated by the motive–goal interaction. Taken together, these findings suggest that motive matters in the exercise of power.

Some research indicates that there are risks associated with individuals who place "too much" importance on powerfulness. One study among male cancer patients investigated adherence to masculine power scripts. The findings suggest that patients with lower adherence to masculine power scripts experienced more positive mental health than those patients who adhered to masculine notions of power (Burns, 2006). This study was among a very specific sample of distressed individuals and may not generalize to all populations.

## Application to Positive Stress

Following from above, we propose that an egoistic orientation to power (self-serving or imperial power) may desensitize individuals to stressors in themselves and others and also lead to reductions in wellbeing or in the valuation of health as an important part of the work setting. Research on supervisor abuse and workplace bullying suggests as much (Kivimäki, Elovainio, & Vahtera, 2000). In contrast, an altruistic orientation to positive influence (affiliative or socialized power) may lead workers to be more aware of their common stressors and seek to find solutions that enhance both the social environment and employee wellbeing. Indeed, with a positive emphasis on influence, anyone in the organization can be a leader or a "champion" for dealing with stress and health. When stressful stimuli arise in a work setting characterized by power-driven relations, those stressors may be ignored and, as a result, have a cumulative and negative impact on wellbeing. Alternatively, managers, supervisors, or champions who are sensitive to the impact of stressors on others may seek to use their positive influence to either curb those stressors or find ways to leverage them as positive challenges (Lovelace et al., 2007). Keltner (2009) has also defined this as switching the way we frame situations, from an attitude characterized by "What's in it for me?" to one that asks "How can I bring out the best in you?"

## Requisite Self-Reliance

Quick, Nelson, and Quick (1987) and Nelson, Quick, and Quick (1989) presented in-depth biographical research aimed at understanding healthy executives with positive wellbeing despite the demands on their time, energy, and the stress they encountered. The research showed that these individuals practiced some form of stress management and that all of them had positive personal and professional relationships as a common characteristic. We describe these successful men and women as self-reliant, a paradoxical term referring to the capacity to work and act autonomously when that is appropriate while simultaneously being comfortable asking for support, guidance, help, and counsel when reaching one's limits. As a central part of their self-reliance, all of these managers used stress management, but not all of them shared the same type of stress-reduction methods, such as exercise, meditation, prayer, time management practices, or nutrition. Rather, a central common denominator was good, secure relationships and attachments at work and at home.

Levinson (1996) saw the coming of this new age of self-reliance in which executives must turn to family and personal relationships as secure sources of support. Requisite self-reliance means interdependence in relationships, not independent or overly dependent or co-dependent on the resources of others. The positive resources that accrue through secure interdependent relationships include emotional caring, informational guidance, evaluative feedback, instrumental support, and personal protection. Positive wellbeing results for executives when they have a surplus of these interpersonal resources at their disposal. Importantly, the self-reliant executive is neither reluctant nor anxious to draw on the well of support available within his or her interpersonal world. Requisite self-reliance entails a reciprocal capacity to serve as a secure support for others in their times of need, trial, and tribulation. Requisite self-reliance balances personal power and autonomy with positive interpersonal relationships and collaboration.

As with self-awareness, there have been few empirical studies published testing the hypothesis that increased self-reliance improves individual well-being. However, there are several closely related constructs of self-leadership, help giving, and internal locus of control that have seen moderate to extensive research. In general, these findings suggest that an internal locus of control, in contrast to an external locus of control, is associated with individual wellbeing. These findings have been observed among a wide variety of samples and across cultures. Further, research on self-leadership in a corporate sample showed that it correlates positively with wellbeing and negatively with stress (Dolbier, Soderstrom, & Steinhardt, 2001). These authors define self-leadership as a secure sense of one's core self (e.g., "I trust that I will take care of myself"). Finally, research suggests that providing social support may be more beneficial to health than receiving it (Brown, Nesse,Vinokur, & Smith, 2003). Given theoretical congruence between these constructs (internal locus of control, self-leadership, help giving, and self-reliance), we propose that requisite self-reliance promotes individual wellbeing.

## Application to Positive Stress

The preceding ideas suggest that when faced with stress the self-reliant leader has access to his or her own signature resources for self-management and that these often include the ability to reach out and receive as well as provide support in the interpersonal sphere. Moreover, the self-reliant individual appears to maintain both sets of resources—personal techniques (e.g., exercise, prayer) and interpersonal connection—and uses these proactively to buffer against negative stress. We propose that because healthy leaders do not overly depend on only one approach, they simultaneously role model personal strength while promoting an interpersonal environment that permits help seeking and help giving. Hence, the presence of negative stressors are not seen as overwhelming to the collective (i.e., the team, crew, department) but rather the collective is more apt to mobilize requisite resources (intra- as well as interpersonal) to address the challenge. Furthermore, because of the emphasis on self-sufficiency, the organization strives to have a diverse set of resources available to deal with stress (e.g., internal consultants, organizational development, human resource practices and benefits, wellness programs, and employee assistance).

## Diverse Professional Supports

Related to requisite self-reliance is the positive pathway of diverse professional supports, having a network of others to learn from, exchange ideas, and receive occupational support. Although requisite self-reliance is the capacity to form and maintain healthy interpersonal relationships while maintaining a sense of self-support (that is, it provides access to varied resources), this characteristic is complemented in an executive's environment by the presence of supportive networks (i.e., it provides access to distinct and diverse sets of individuals).

Two key supports are the executive's leadership team and the company's board of directors. The senior leadership team is best when composed of diverse expertise, talents, and perspectives. This is especially important in dynamic, changing environments. For example, the U.S. and global healthcare environment is one of the most challenging, dynamic industries of our day (Management Sciences for Health, 2009). Change is a regular, endemic characteristic of this environment. Change ushers in continuing uncertainty and places constant pressure on executives and executive teams.

When a leadership team includes both optimistic and pessimistic points of view on the dynamic, changing environment, the executive has access to a richer set of information upon which to draw in decision making and action (Seligman, 1991). Thus, an executive team that balances these two contrasting psychological interpretative mechanisms can contribute to the team's fitness, functioning, and wellbeing. The question an executive should ask is whether the team members' styles fit their function (Edwards, 1996). For example, optimism might be very functional in executives responsible for finding new business given the opportunities they seek and exploit. Alternatively, pessimism in chief financial officers may have value if that perspective cues them to keep a constant eye to averting and/or managing negative financial results. So, the executive who assembles a senior team based on diverse perspectives enriches the variance, diversity, and dialogue for good decision making.

A company's board of directors is another central support for executive wellbeing. For example, in restructuring the Howard Hughes Corporation, John Goolsby worked in collaboration with Will Lummis as the chairman of the company's board of directors (Goolsby et al., 2010). Creative tension and heartfelt communication between a chairman and a chief executive carries the positive potential for better decisions, better strategic planning, and improved ethical outcomes. Merging the chairman and CEO roles is to concentrate power inappropriately, whereas splitting these two key roles serves to create more accountability. The Sarbanes–Oxley Act (SOX) of 2002 is a federal law that carries the potential for a positive impact on executive wellbeing through greater accountability. SOX intends to create incentives for boards to be more engaged with executives for the wellbeing of the executive and the company. Diversity and heterogeneity among board members in functional expertise, gender, psychological interpretative mechanisms, and backgrounds may also add value.

Not only do leaders require diverse support, there is strong evidence that social support enhances wellbeing of all individuals and stress is reduced when there is social support (Viswesvaran, Sanchez, & Fisher, 1999). In particular, and as suggested above, it helps to have a diverse social network (Barefoot, Grønbæk, Jensen, Schnohr, & Prescott, 2005; Cromwell & Waite, 2009). A recent qualitative study found that the presence of a kin network enhanced individual wellbeing (Ochieng, 2011). To put it simply, the people surrounding us in our lives make a difference. It has been well understood for decades that there is a significant relationship between perceived social support and individual emotions and perceived quality of life (Abbey, Abramis, & Caplan, 1985; Lincoln, 2000). In addition, social support is related to the impact of stress on wellbeing. One recent study found that social support significantly moderated the relationship between stress and wellbeing (Chao, 2011).

The relationship between social support and wellbeing is not only significant for adults; social support impacts wellbeing throughout the human development process. A recent meta-analysis of 246 studies found a significant relationship between social support and wellbeing among children and adolescents (Chu, Saucier, & Hafner, 2010). The same meta-analysis reported another interesting finding even more relevant to individuals within organizations: the effects of social support on wellbeing tended to increase with age. In other words, social support is not only relevant to individuals as they develop during childhood, its importance increases as they age. Individuals who fail to develop strong social skills and the ability to access social support may be more susceptible to negative outcomes associated with stress.

Social support may be especially significant among populations at risk. In a study among combat veterans suffering from posttraumatic stress disorders

(PTSD), findings suggest that veterans who have high levels of social anxiety had lower levels of wellbeing and experienced more day-to-day variance of wellbeing than veterans with lower levels of social anxiety (Kashdan, Julian, Merritt, & Uswatte, 2006). A similar finding among 327 Kenyan AIDS orphans found that lower perceived social support was associated with higher rates of depressive symptoms and lower rates of self-esteem (Okawa et al., 2011).

Some findings suggest that the relationship between social support and wellbeing among workers is complex and nuanced. For example, social support may interact with other factors as a predictor of wellbeing. A recent study using a sample of Indian men and women reported that social support moderated the relationship between positive psychological strengths (operationalized by psychological capital) and wellbeing (Khan & Husain, 2010). Social support may also interact with self-reliance and locus of control, as the following empirical finding illustrates. A study among women with breast cancer found that social support was less important than life stress among subjects who were more self-reliant (Funch & Marshall, 1984). In another study, mainly among women, social support was shown to be particularly important to the psychological wellbeing for individuals with an external locus of control (Vanderzee, Buunk, & Sanderman, 1997). In a subsequent study, the same authors identified a potential sex difference. They reported that locus of control did not moderate the relationship between social support and psychological wellbeing among men (Vanderzee et al., 1997).

Other studies suggest that the source and nature of social support is significant when considering wellbeing. In study of 89 information systems professionals, nonwork sources of social support were more predictive of wellbeing than work sources (Love, Irani, Standing, & Themistocleous, 2007). Similarly, a study of 119 two-career couples found that work support was associated with job satisfaction, whereas spousal support was associated with life satisfaction (Parasuraman, Greenhaus, & Granrose, 1992). Other studies indicate that social support may interact with social exchange. There is evidence that social support impacts most positively on wellbeing when individuals feel that the amount of support they give is reciprocated by the amount of support they receive (Luo, 1997). The author of this study suggests that there can be a downside to helping others if the help you give far exceeds the help you receive. A similar recent finding supports the idea of reciprocity but argues that general reciprocity is important. Empirical findings suggest that the effect of social support on wellbeing can be attenuated by an imbalance of reciprocity in either direction (Nahum-Shani, Bamberger, & Bacharach, 2011). Social support has less impact as the distance between even exchange increases. In other words, either giving more than you get or getting more than you give reduces the effect of social support on wellbeing.

## Application to Positive Stress

The preceding review—both for leadership and in the general population—suggests that social support and access to diverse social networks buffer the negative effects of stress on health. More importantly, for the purpose of this chapter, the reverse also appears to be true: when we have social support we may be more likely to frame stressful stimuli in a positive manner and potentially address the stressor as a challenge to be met rather than a hindrance to be overcome. This particular path also follows from two previous lines of research. First, studies on team leadership suggest that when faced with adversity, highly cohesive teams persist at the task (Zaccaro, Rittman, & Marks, 2001). Second, studies on resilience suggest that having access to a community is associated with greater resilience (Clausen, 1993; Friborg et al., 2003; Masten, Obradovic, & Burt, 2006). In the workplace setting, positive leadership and a strong sense of teamwork often go hand in hand with a sense of being part of a larger vision, of contributing to something greater than oneself, sometimes called civic responsibility. We propose that eustress is enhanced when workplace practices communicate that workers belong to, are part of, and contribute to this greater good. We also propose that when executives and leadership at all levels role model this sense of belonging (by using networks themselves), they are more likely to promote stronger social ties among their associates. As a result, when stressful stimuli inevitably arise and accumulate, the entire group is ready and willing to use the stressor as something to help them become stronger.

## Summary and Integration of the Five Pathways

Table 9.1 summarizes the five pathways, displaying both the core qualities of the path and its orientation to stress. Again, the goal was to show how stress can be a positive resource for workplaces. (See Quick & Quick, 2013b for application of these pathways to executives.) The preceding descriptions

189

**Table 9.1.** The Five Pathways: Core Qualities and Orientation to Stress.

| Pathway | Core qualities | Orientation to stress |
|---|---|---|
| Strength of character | Presence of a range of virtue-based qualities and ethical standards that lead an individual to remain strong in the face of stress. Strengths referenced include integrity, love, trust, forgiveness, wisdom, cooperativeness | An attitude toward stress as a challenge and opportunity for growth, something that can be embraced, build character, and used to help the organization |
| Self-awareness | A proactive willingness to self-reflect, stay mindful of one's actions and impact on others, and subsequently regulate one's behavior | The introduction, use, and institutionalization of evaluation processes (surveys, relevant meetings) in order to proactively surface and address issues (including potential stressors); this includes a willingness to embrace rather than avoid conflict |
| Socialized power motivation | An altruistic motivation to positive social influence at work that overrides a more egoistic, positional desire to dominate, especially in decision-making contexts; a desire to channel power for constructive social ends | A mindful or vigilant orientation to how stressful stimuli may impact workers and an empathic response to curb or leverage such stressors for the greater good |
| Requisite self-reliance | A secure sense of oneself and one's ability to utilize, as required by the situation, either an internal set of personal stress management or reliance on others; this orientation may be described more as a capacity for interdependence than overly independent or dependent | With a balance between a climate of self-sufficiency and one that promotes help seeking and help giving, stressors are viewed as opportunities to build strength in the interpersonal sphere at work; this includes access to a diverse set of resources and the secure knowledge that the organization has the resources it needs |
| Diverse professional supports | The presence of sufficient levels of social support and access to diverse social networks that enhances the quality of work life and buffers the negative effects of stress on health | A tendency to frame adverse events, crises, or stressors as factors that can be embraced or "taken on" by the group, workplace community, or particular group (specialty group) or network within the organization |

alternately viewed each pathway as an approach to leadership development as well as a resource in the work setting, one that may be cultivated through effective executive performance and leadership skill. However, we also believe they convey qualities in the work environment proper and operate independently of executive influence. For example, an entire organization can display strength of character by how it embraces and sustains core values (Collins & Porras, 1994); it may display self-awareness through its commitment to quality and excellence (Peters & Waterman, 1982); and it may practice altruistic motives through empowerment philosophies (Conger & Kanungo, 1988). Leaders may initiate such practices but, over time, an organization's positive response to stress must become institutionalized or systemic. Social norms, workplace climate, and culture should promote an individual worker's positive response to stress.

Hence, we present orientation to stress (Table 9.1) as not merely as a manager-driven initiative, but as an orientation to be enacted by the organization as a whole. The organization itself becomes "people-centered" and supports learning, trust, loyalty, respect, and belongingness (Sisodia, Wolfe, & Sheth, 2007). The organization exists not only to do business but also, simultaneously, to build strength of character, to encourage self-reflection and self-regulation, to invite multiple leaders rather than centralize power, to provide resources for self-sufficiency, and to promote a collective sense that everyone has access to the people and social networks to help get the job done. When these goals are taken together as a whole, the result is an approach to stress that incorporates both cultural or systemic and individual strategies. As we shall see in the next section, it is precisely this approach that the research suggests is most effective.

## Stress and Health Promotion Interventions

This section summarizes several reviews that point to effective approaches for health promotion and stress reduction within the work setting (see also Quick, Wright, Adkins, Nelson, & Quick, 2013, for a preventive stress management approach to distress prevention coupled with eustress and heath promotion). We begin with a summary of a systematic review of the stress intervention literature conducted by LaMontagne, Keegel, Louie, Ostry, and Lansbergis (2007). This review contained a detailed appendix supplement that described each of the 30 "high" intervention studies compiled in the review. A high rating was given to "systemic" interventions that were both organizationally and individually focused, versus moderate (organizational only), and low (individual only). We reviewed the methodologies across these systemic interventions and extracted detailed information about the main intervention types that appeared to be most effective according to the review. Following this review we summarize some recent reviews that point to best practices in workplace health promotion. In both the stress and health promotion reviews, we make some connections with the five positive pathways and discuss possibilities for future research.

## Practical Guidelines from Stress Interventions

LaMontagne et al. (2007) provide an appendix (appendix table I) of 30 different interventions. A review of these interventions shows that they operate across three levels: (1) they enhance the work environment and production flow; (2) they create methods for positive communication over time; and (3) they provide individuals with coping skills through education. The research suggests that the most effective interventions integrate all three of these levels and that the degree of integration predicts effectiveness. Indeed, one can look at the five positive pathways discussed in the previous section as promoting these three operations. The following bullet points summarize five major practical guidelines gleaned primarily from the LaMontagne review, with the addition of other recent reviews (Parks & Steelman, 2008; Richardson & Rothstein, 2008).

- Integrated approaches work. Most importantly, the program should focus and integrate both individual- and workplace-level changes. The more systemic or integrated the program the better.
- Individual-level changes should include education on cognitive-behavioral strategies for dealing with stress. This education can include: (a) identifying workplace stressors; (b) discussing strategies for dealing with the stressors; (c) promoting innovative ways of coping; (d) developing action plans for coping; (e) appraising those plans realistically; and (f) following up and revising to improve. Other techniques that reduce arousal are beneficial as well, such as meditation or relaxation response.
- Workplace-level changes should include one or more of the following: (a) improvements in communication; (b) commitment to ongoing improvements through committees and support work; (c) giving employees opportunities to be physically active at work and/or during the work

day; this may include a variety of group activities including wellness days or regular group programs that could be incorporated into the work culture (sports, competitions, wellness challenges); and (d) modification of work stressors through positive changes in increased work control for employees, work schedules, workloads, job rotation, opportunities for work breaks (e.g., stretch periods), enhanced performance appraisals, and possible changes in production work flows and mechanics.

- Improvements in communication can occur through one or more of the following: (a) setting up an ongoing steering, advisory, or wellness committee whose suggestions are seriously reviewed and acted upon by management; (b) use of focus groups to ascertain employee perceptions of stress; (c) use of anonymous comments (suggestion boxes) that specifically request pointers on stress reduction; (d) opportunities for management–employee interaction; and (e) opportunities for managers to clarify their roles and responsibilities.
- Assessments are critical in implementing most of the above strategies. These assessments are typically done in the early stages of the systemic intervention and can include: (a) ergonomic analysis of the work space (how work is conducted, mechanics, physical environment, and constraints); (b) health risk or wellness appraisals; (c) work communication assessments; (d) perceptions of work stress and work climate; (e) individual assessments of role stressors; and (f) use of established stress analyses (e.g., job strain, effort–reward imbalance).

## Essential Elements and Promising Practices from Health Promotion Interventions

Over the past decade, researchers and practitioners have accumulated both scientific data and case studies in an effort to identify best practices in the field of workplace health promotion. A review of these practices reveals some overlap with the guidelines derived from the above review of the stress intervention literature. Three recent reports include recommendations for "what works" in health promotion. These reports come from an expert panel (NIOSH, 2008), from a literature review of five best-practice studies (Goetzel, Shechter, Ozminkowski, Marmet, & Tabrizi, 2007), and from a synthesis of over 130 studies from obesity programs in the work setting (Archer et al., 2011). Importantly, in the latter case, there is enough evidence accumulating to start to identify programs that might be considered "evidence-based" or practices that have been tested in rigorous research trials.

We examine these reports side by side for two reasons (Table 9.2). First, they point to different gradations or a continuum of standard for defining "what works" (from broad claims made by experts to specific operational insights gleaned from research). Second, across these reviews we believe that we can identify overlap not only with effective stress interventions but also with the five positive pathways identified in the first section of this chapter. To be sure, evidence of these pathways is not explicit in these studies, but we propose that the pathways work "behind the scenes" to bring these best practices to the fore. As we said above, an organization's positive response to stress must become institutionalized or systemic. Health promotion practices are more likely to be woven into the work culture when the five pathways are in operation.

### Essential Elements of Effective Workplace Programs and Policies for Improving Worker Health and Wellbeing

A group of experts were convened by the National Institute of Occupational Safety and Health (NIOSH, 2008) to identify the essential elements for workplace health promotion. The resulting document is considered a key part of the NIOSH WorkLife Initiative, and the group offered 20 recommendations across three categories: organizational culture/leadership, program design, and program implementation (see Table 9.2). Culture, leadership, employee participation, and communication are all considered essential. Specifically, for the recommendation to develop a "human-centered culture" the report states: "Effective programs thrive in organizations with policies and programs that promote respect throughout the organization and encourage active worker participation, input, and involvement. A human-centered culture is built on trust, not fear." This emphasis on trust, input, and involvement is similar to positive pathways that seek to engage the social network and promote a positive orientation to handling stress as a collective (i.e., requisite self-reliance and diverse professional supports).

### Promising Practices in Employer Health and Productivity Management

To derive best practices, Goetzel and colleagues (2007) reviewed the literature from five best-practice studies, held site visits with nine promising practice employers, and conducted interviews with subject matter experts. Among the best practices were an organizational commitment to health, the

**Table 9.2.** Studies Showing Different and Promising Practices for Workplace Health Promotion.

| Example of broad recommendations | Example of specific benchmarks | Evidence-based criteria |
|---|---|---|
| BROAD ← | | → OPERATIONAL |
| **Essential elements of effective workplace programs and policies for improving worker health and wellbeing** (NIOSH, 2008) | **Promising practices in employer health and productivity management efforts: findings from a benchmarking study** (Goetzel et al., 2007) | **Promising practices for the prevention and control of obesity in the worksite** (Archer et al., 2011) |
| List derived by panel of experts | Literature review of five best-practice studies, site visits to nine promising practice employers, interviews with SMEs | Synthesis of empirical results from 136 studies, each weighted on the basis of study design, quality, and effect size |
| Note. Incomplete; list below is example of 20 recommendations | Note. Incomplete; following are from table 1 (*number of 5 best-practice studies that showed evidence for the characteristic shown in parentheses*) | Note. List below shows all studies found and those that were deemed of "Greatest Suitability" due to high quality and positive outcomes. |
| **Organizational culture/leadership** Develop a "human-centered culture" Demonstrate leadership | Organizational commitment (*all 5*) Identification of wellness champions (3) Data collection, measurement, reporting, and evaluation (including ROI) (3) | Enhanced access to opportunities for physical activity combined with health education (*5 studies, 3 suitable*) Exercise prescriptions alone (*14 studies, 10 suitable*) Multicomponent educational practices (*25 studies, 13 suitable*) |

*(Continued overleaf)*

**Table 9.2.** (*Continued*)

| Example of broad recommendations | Example of specific benchmarks | Evidence-based criteria |
|---|---|---|
| Engage mid-level management | Ongoing program evaluation (3) | Weight loss competitions and incentives (*16 studies, 6 suitable*) |
| | Program linked to business objectives (2) | |
| **Program design** | Effective communication (2) | Behavioral practices with incentives (*17 studies, 8 suitable*) |
| Establish clear principles | Effective operation plan (2) | |
| Integrate relevant systems | Program goals include productivity and morale (2) | Behavioral practices without incentives (*47 studies, 26 suitable*) |
| Eliminate occupational hazards | | |
| Promote employee participation | Interdisciplinary team focus (2) | |
| Tailor programs to *specific* workplace | Incentives to participate (2) | |
| Find and use the right tools | Effective screening and triage (2) | |
| Adjust the program as needed | State-of-the-art interventions (2) | |
| **Program implementation** | | |
| Be willing to start small and scale up | | |
| Communicate strategically | | |
| Build accountability into program implementation | | |

identification and support of wellness champions, effective communication, and program goals that made sure to include productivity and morale. As with the previous reviews, communication and an emphasis on a positive participatory culture emerge as critical common elements. Importantly, in both the Goetzel and NIOSH reviews, leadership commitment and a willingness to lead by example and incorporate health into the business plan were seen as important elements. Leaders have to be willing to stand up for the value of wellbeing and health and to commit to these values in both their words and their actions. This is akin to the strength of character described above. Caldwell and Dixon (2010), in making the case for the virtues of love and care in leadership, quote from Townsend (1982, p. 24):

> Perhaps the most obvious thing that leadership and love have in common is the act of caring about the welfare of others—an act that is central to both. One's love for another implies caring for the wellbeing, physical and mental, of the other.

The evidence—across dozens of studies we have briefly reviewed—is clear: care for the wellbeing of employees appears to be the common, if not the core, element in successful workplace stress management and health promotion programs. Strong positive leadership may be defined by care for the common wellbeing, and putting that care into practice. It should be noted that Goetzel and colleagues also found an emphasis on evaluation and monitoring performance as a common best practice. We believe this is representative of the pathway of self-awareness described above. Organizations committed to positive health make an effort to evaluate how well their programs are addressing risks and promoting positive strengths.

## Promising Practices for the Prevention and Control of Obesity in the Worksite

Toward the beginning of this chapter, we discussed obesity—and its reduction through workplace practices—as a key example of concern for employers. Fortunately, through a systemic compilation and synthesis of empirical results from 136 studies (each weighted on the basis of study design, quality, and effect size), Archer and colleagues (2011) have identified several domains of best practices, especially six areas that yielded studies deemed of "greatest suitability" due to high quality of the research and the most positive outcomes (see Table 9.2). Among these practices were enhanced access to opportunities for physical activity, combined with health education, weight loss competitions, as well as other resources (education, incentives). An employer who provides different types of resources sends a clear message to workers that their health matters. Moreover, following from the description of requisite self-reliance and the LaMontagne review, the employer does not depend on only one approach to achieve the aims of managing stress but simultaneously promotes both individual self-care and social support practices. Put another way, the organization does "whatever it takes" to promote health and wellbeing. The synthesis by Archer and colleagues is very important in this regard because employee weight problems and obesity have grown to epidemic proportions in recent years, driving health-care costs for employers to crisis levels.

# Conclusion

Stress, in and of itself, is not a negative force that must inevitably lead to poor health outcomes. We propose the exact opposite, and the evidence bears this out: when stress is embraced and leveraged as an opportunity for challenge, employers can build a work environment and social network that thrives, flourishes, and becomes stronger in the face of stress. We propose that this is an inside-out practice. Leadership has to be willing to demonstrate strength of character, implement self-awareness practices, practice socialized influence, show requisite self-reliance, and promote diverse social supports. A review of the research literature suggests that these may be—from a leadership perspective—common elements of effective health promotion practices. It is possible that as the evidence continues to accumulate on these effective practices future employers may adopt them without fully embracing the five positive pathways. In other words, they may simply follow operational guidelines for "what works" in other settings or from other studies. We believe that these employers will not be optimally effective in their approach and may even be doomed to failure in the long run.

As we have seen, leadership commitment, positive communication, employee morale, social support, and a healthy culture all appear to be so essential that they appear again and again in the research literature. We offer the five positive pathways as a way to integrate this literature with findings on stress management and leadership success. More importantly, as workplaces face lean times, financial crises, and rising health-care costs, we believe the five pathways offer a model for simultaneously building leadership and promoting workplace health. In the end, it will be up to everyone in the work setting—employers and employees working side by side—to find the requisite resources both within themselves and from identified best practices to leverage stressful stimuli for the common good.

# References

Abbey, A., Abramis, D. J., & Caplan, R. D. (1985). Effects of different sources of social support and social conflict on emotional wellbeing. *Basic & Applied Psychology, 6*(2), 111–129.

Anshel, M. (2010). The disconnected values model improves mental wellbeing and fitness in an employee wellness program. *Behavioral Medicine, 36*(4), 113–122.

Archer, W. R., Batan, M. C., Buchanan, L. R., Soler R. E., Ramsey, D. C., Kirchhofer, A., & Reyes, M. (2011). Promising practices for the prevention and control of obesity in the worksite. *American Journal of Health Promotion, 25*(3), e12–e26.

Aristotle (310/1998). *Nicomachean ethics* (D. Ross, Trans.) (Revised by J. L. Ackrill & J. O. Urmson). Oxford: Oxford World Classics.

Aristotle (2000). *The Nicomachean ethics* (R. Crisp, Trans.). Cambridge: Cambridge University Press.

Bakker, A. B., Hakanen, J. J., Demerouti, E., & Xanthopoulou, D. (2007). Job resources boost work engagement, particularly when job demands are high. *Journal of Educational Psychology, 99*(2), 274–284.

Barefoot, J. C., Grønbæk, M., Jensen, G. Schnohr, P., & Prescott, E. (2005). Social network diversity and risks of ischemic heart disease and total mortality: Findings from the Copenhagen city heart study. *American Journal of Epidemiology, 161*(10), 960–967.

Bennett, J. B. (1988). Power and influence as distinct personality traits: Development and validation of a psychometric measure. *Journal of Research in Personality, 22*, 361–394.

Brown, S. L., Nesse, R. M., Vinokur, A. D., & Smith, D. M. (2003). Providing social support may be more beneficial than receiving it: Results from a perspective study of mortality. *Psychological Science, 14*(4), 320–327.

Burnham, D. H. (2002). *Inside the mind of the world-class leader*. Boston: Burnham Rosen Group.

Burns, S. R. (2006). Physical health, self-reliance, and emotional control as moderators of the relationship between locus of control and mental health among men treated for prostate cancer. *Journal of Behavioral Medicine, 29*(6), 561–572.

Caldwell, C., & Dixon, R. D. (2010). Love, forgiveness, and trust: Critical values of the modern leader. *Journal of Business Ethics, 93*(1), 91–101.

Cameron, K. S. (2007). Forgiveness in organizations. In D. L. Nelson & C. L. Cooper (Eds.), *Positive organizational behavior* (pp. 129–142). Thousand Oaks, CA: Sage.

Cavanaugh, M. A., Boswell, W. R., Roehling, M. V., & Boudreau, J. W. (2000). An empirical examination of self-reported work stress among U.S. managers. *Journal of Applied Psychology, 85*(1), 65–74.

Chao, R. (2011). Managing stress and maintaining wellbeing: Social support, problem-focused coping, and avoidant coping. *Journal of Counseling & Development, 89*(3), 338–348.

Chu, P., Saucier, D. A., & Hafner, E. (2010). Meta-analysis of the relationships between social support and wellbeing in children and adolescents. *Journal of Social and Clinical Psychology, 29*(6), 624–645.

Clausen, J. (1993). *American lives: Looking back at the children of the Great Depression.* New York: Free Press.

Cloninger, C. (2006). The science of well being: An integrated approach to mental health and its disorders. *Psychiatria Danubina, 18*(3–4), 218–224.

Collins, J. C., & Porras, J. I. (1994). *Built to last.* New York: HarperCollins.

Conger, J. A., & Kanungo, R. N. (1988). The empowerment process: Integrating theory and practice. *Academy of Management Review, 13*(3), 471–482.

Côté, S. (2005). A social interaction model of the effects of emotion regulation on work strain. *Academy of Management Review, 30*(3), 509–530.

Cromwell, E. Y., & Waite, L. J. (2009). Social disconnectedness, perceived isolation, and health among older adults. *Journal of Health and Social Behavior, 50*(1), 31–48.

Dallman, M. F., Pecoraro, N., Akana, S. F., la Fleur, S. E., Gomez, F., Houshyar, H., Bell, M. E., Bhatnagar, S., Laugero, K. D., & Manalo, S. (2003). Chronic stress and obesity: A new view of 'comfort food.' *Proceedings of the National Academy of Sciences of the United States of America, 100*(20), 11696–11701.

Dolbier, C. L., Soderstrom, M., & Steinhardt, M. A. (2001). The relationship between self-leadership and enhanced psychological, health, and work outcomes. *Journal of Psychology, 135*(5), 469–485.

Doll, H. A., Petersen, S. E. K., & Stewart-Brown, S. L. (2000). Obesity and physical and emotional well-being: Associations between body mass index, chronic illness, and the physical and mental components of the SF-36 Questionnaire. *Obesity Research, 8,* 160–170.

Edwards, J. R. (1996). An examination of competing versions of the person-environment fit approach to stress. *Academy of Management Journal, 39,* 292–339.

Friborg, O., Hjemdal, O., Rosenvenge, J. H., & Martinussen, M. (2003). A new rating scale for adult resilience: What are the central protective resources behind healthy adjustment? *International Journal of Methods in Psychiatric Research, 12*(2), 65–76.

Funch, D. P., & Marshall, J. R. (1984). Self-reliance as a modifier of the effects of life stress and social support. *Journal of Psychosomatic Research, 28*(1), 9–15.

Gates, D. M., Succop, P., Brehm, B. J., Gillespie, G. L., & Sommers, B. D. (2008). Obesity and presenteeism: The impact of body mass index on workplace productivity. *Journal of Occupational and Environmental Medicine*, *50*(1), 39–45.

Gillham, J., Adams-Deutsch, Z., Werner, J., Reivich, K., Coulter-Heindl, V., Linkins, M., & . . . Seligman, M. P. (2011). Character strengths predict subjective wellbeing during adolescence. *Journal of Positive Psychology*, *6*(1), 31–44.

Goetzel, R. Z., Shechter, D., Ozminkowski, R. J., Marmet, P. F., & Tabrizi, M. J. (2007). Promising practices in employer health and productivity management efforts: Findings from a benchmarking study. *Journal of Occupational Environmental Medicine*, *49*, 111–130.

Goolsby, J. L., Mack, D. A., & Quick, J. C. (2010). Winning by staying in bounds: Good outcomes from positive ethics. *Organizational Dynamics*, *39*, 248–257.

Gross, J. J. (1998). Antecedent- and response-focused emotion regulation: Divergent consequences for experience, expression, and physiology. *Journal of Personality and Social Psychology*, *74*(1), 224–237.

Hofer, J., Busch, H., Bond, M., Li, M., & Law, R. (2010). Effects of motive-goal congruence on wellbeing in the power domain: Considering goals and values in a German and two Chinese samples. *Journal of Research in Personality*, *44*(5), 610–620.

Kashdan, T. B., Julian, T., Merritt, K., & Uswatte, G. (2006). Social anxiety and posttraumatic stress in combat veterans: Relations to wellbeing and character strengths. *Behaviour Research and Therapy*, *44*(4), 561–583.

Kazén, M., & Kuhl, J. (2011). Directional discrepancy between implicit and explicit power motives is related to wellbeing among managers. *Motivation and Emotion*, *35*(3), 317–327.

Keltner, D. (2009). *Born to be good: The science of a meaningful life*. New York: W. W. Norton.

Kets de Vries, M. (2009a). *Reflections on character and leadership*. Chichester: John Wiley & Sons.

Kets de Vries, M. (2009b). *Sex, money, happiness and death: The quest for authenticity*. Basingstoke: Palgrave Macmillan.

Khan, A., & Husain, A. (2010). Social support as a moderator of positive psychological strengths and subjective wellbeing. *Psychological Reports*, *106*(2), 534–538.

Kivimäki, M., Elovainio, M., & Vahtera, J. (2000). Workplace bullying and sickness absence in hospital staff. *Occupational Environmental Medicine*, *57*, 656–660.

Kivimäki, M., Virtanen, M., Elovainio, M., Kouvonen, A., Väänänen, A., & Vahtera, J. (2006). Work stress in the etiology of coronary heart disease—a meta-analysis. *Scandinavian Journal of Work, Environment & Health*, *32*(6), 431–442.

Klarenbach, S., Padwal, R., Chuck, A., & Jacobs, P. (2006). Population-based analysis of obesity and workforce participation. *Obesity*, *14*, 920–927.

Laird, D. (1929). *Psychology and profits*. New York: B.C. Forbes.

Lamontagne, A. D., Keegel, T., Louie, A. M., Ostry, A., & Lansbergis, P. A. (2007). A systematic review of the job-stress intervention evaluation literature,

1990–2005. *International Journal of Occupational and Environmental Health*, *13*, 268–820.

Levinson, H. (1964/1985). *Executive stress*. New York: New American Library.

Levinson, H. (1996). A new age of self-reliance. *Harvard Business Review*, July–August, 162–173.

Lincoln, K. D. (2000). Social support, negative social interactions, and psychological wellbeing. *Social Service Review*, *74*(2), 231.

Littman-Ovadia, H., & Steger, M. (2010). Character strengths and wellbeing among volunteers and employees: Toward an integrative model. *Journal of Positive Psychology*, *5*(6), 419–430.

Love, P. D., Irani, Z., Standing, C., & Themistocleous, M. (2007). Influence of job demands, job control and social support on information systems professionals' psychological wellbeing. *International Journal of Manpower*, *28*(6), 513–528.

Lovelace, K. J., Manz, C. C., & Alves, J. C. (2007). Work stress and leadership development: The role of self-leadership, shared leadership, physical fitness and flow in managing demands and increasing job control. *Human Resource Management Review*, *17*(4), 374–387.

Luo, L. (1997). Social support, reciprocity and well-being. *Journal of Social Psychology*, *137*(5), 618–628.

Management Sciences for Health. (2009). *Annual report*. Cambridge, MA: MSH.

Masten, A. S., Obradovic, J., & Burt, K. B. (2006). Resilience in emerging adulthood: Developmental perspectives on continuity and transformation. In J. Arnett & L. Tanner (Eds.), *Emerging adults in America: Coming of age in the 21st century* (pp. 172–190). Washington, DC: American Psychological Association.

McClelland, D. C. (1975). *Power: The inner experience*. New York: Irving.

McClelland, D. C., & Burnham, D. H. (2003). Power is the great motivator. *Harvard Business Review*, January–February, 1–10.

Moss, L. (1981). *Management stress*. Reading, MA: Addison-Wesley.

Nahum-Shani, I., Bamberger, P. A., & Bacharach, S. B. (2011). Social support and employee wellbeing: The conditioning effect of perceived patterns of supportive exchange. *Journal of Health and Social Behavior*, *52*(1), 123–139.

NIOSH (National Institute for Occupational Safety and Health) (2008). *Essential elements of effective workplace programs and policies for improving worker health and wellbeing*. http://www.cdc.gov/niosh/TWH/essentials.html.

Nelson, D. L., Quick, J. C., & Quick, J. D. (1989). Corporate warfare: Preventing combat stress and battle fatigue. *Organizational Dynamics*, *18*, 65–79.

Ochieng, B. N. (2011). The effect of kin, social network and neighbourhood support on individual wellbeing. *Health & Social Care in the Community*, *19*(4), 429–437.

Okawa, S., Yasuoka, J., Ishikawa, N., Poudel, K. C., Ragi, A., & Jimba, M. (2011). Perceived social support and the psychological wellbeing of AIDS orphans in urban Kenya. *AIDS Care*, *23*(9), 1177–1185.

Parasuraman, S., Greenhaus, J. H., & Granrose, C. (1992). Role stressors, social support, and wellbeing among two-career couples. *Journal of Organizational Behavior, 13*(4), 339–356.

Parks, K. M., & Steelman, L. A. (2008). Organizational wellness programs: A meta-analysis. *Journal of Occupational Health Psychology, 13*, 58–68.

Peters, T. J., & Waterman, R. H. (1982). *In search of excellence*. New York: Warner Books.

Peterson, C., & Park, N. (2011). Character strengths and virtues: Their role in wellbeing. In S. I. Donaldson, M. Csikszentmihalyi, & J. Nakamura (Eds.), *Applied positive psychology: Improving everyday life, health, schools, work, and society* (pp. 49–62). New York: Routledge/Taylor & Francis.

Podsakoff, N. P. (2007). *Challenge and hindrance stressors in the workplace: Tests of linear, curvilinear, and moderated relationships with employee strains, satisfaction, and performance* (Dissertation). University of Florida.

Podsakoff, N. P., LePine, J. A., & LePine, M. A. (2007). Differential challenge stressor-hindrance stressor relationships with job attitudes, turnover intentions, turnover, and withdrawal behavior: A meta-analysis. *Journal of Applied Psychology, 92*(2), 438–454.

Quick, J. C., Nelson, D. L., & Quick, J. D. (1987). Successful executives: How independent? *Academy of Management Executive, 1*, 139–145.

Quick, J. C., & Quick, J. D. (2013a). Stress and stress management. In D. Guest & D. Needle (Eds.), *Wiley encyclopedia of human resource management*. London: Wiley Blackwell.

Quick, J. C., & Quick, J. D. (2013b). Executive wellbeing. In K. Cameron & A. Caza (Eds.), *Part VII—Happiness and organizations, Handbook of happiness* (pp. 798–813). New York and Oxford: Oxford University Press.

Quick, J. C., Wright, T. A., Adkins, J. A., Nelson, D. L., & Quick, J. D. (2013). *Preventive stress management in organizations* (2nd ed.). Washington, DC: American Psychological Association.

Rath, T., & Harter, J. (2010). *Well being: The five essential elements*. New York: Gallup Press.

Richards, K. C., Campenni, C. E., & Muse-Burke, J. L. (2010). Self-care and wellbeing in mental health professionals: The mediating effects of self-awareness and mindfulness. *Journal of Mental Health Counseling, 32*(3), 247–264.

Richardson, K. M., & Rothstein, H. R. (2008). Effects of occupational stress management intervention programs: A meta-analysis. *Journal of Occupational Health Psychology, 13*, 69–93.

Sarbanes–Oxley Act of 2002. (2002). http://www.soxlaw.com.

Seligman, M. E. P. (1991). *Learned optimism*. San Francisco, CA: Barrett-Koehler.

Selye, H. (1975). Confusion and controversy in the stress field. *Journal of Human Stress, 1*(2), 37–44.

Sisodia, R. S., Wolfe, D. B., & Sheth, J. N. (2007). *Firms of endearment*. Upper Saddle River, NJ: Wharton School.

Smith, A. (1759). *The theory of the moral sentiments*. Edinburgh: A. Kincaid and J. Bell.

Solomon, R. C. (1999). *A better way to think about business*. New York: Oxford University Press.

Steinbrecher, S., & Bennett, J. B. (2003). *Heart-centered leadership: An invitation to lead from the inside out*. Memphis, TN: Black Pants Publishing.

Thompson, A. D., Grahek, M., Phillips, R. E., & Fay, C. L. (2008). In search of worthy leadership. *Consulting Psychology Journal: Practice and Research*, 60(4), 366–382.

Thun, B., & Kelloway, E. K. (2011). Virtuous leaders: Assessing character strengths in the workplace. *Canadian Journal of Administrative Sciences*, 28, 270–283.

Townsend, P. L. (1982). Love and leadership. *Marine Corps Gazette*, February, p. 24.

Ulemann, J. S. (1972). The need for influence: Development and validation of a measure, and comparison with the need for power. *Genetic Psychology Monograph*, 85, 157–214.

Vaillant, G. E. (1977). *Adaptation to life*. Boston, MA: Little, Brown.

Vanderzee, K. I., Buunk, B. P., & Sanderman, R. (1997). Social support, locus of control, and psychological wellbeing. *Journal of Applied Social Psychology*, 27(20), 1842–1859.

Viswesvaran, C., Sanchez, J. I., & Fisher, J. (1999). The role of social support in the process of work stress: A meta-analysis. *Journal of Vocational Behavior*, 54(2), 314–334.

Zaccaro, S. J., Rittman, A. L., & Marks, M. A. (2001). Team leadership. *Leadership Quarterly*, 12, 451–483.

# Part 5

# Organizational Strategies to Promote Wellbeing

# 10

# Cancer, Work, and the Quality of Working Life

## *A Narrative Review*

### Tom Cox

Birkbeck, University of London, U.K.

### Sara MacLennan and James N'Dow

University of Aberdeen, U.K.

## Overview

Much of the research published in occupational health psychology on the relationship between work and health has a negative focus on the alleged detrimental effects of work on employee health (for a variety of reviews, see, for example, Cox, 1993; Cox, Griffiths, & Rial-Gonzalez, 2000; Michie, 2002; Michie & Williams, 2003; Quinlan, Mayhew, & Bohle, 2001; Sparks & Cooper, 1997). However, this perspective represents only one interpretation of the dynamic relationship between work and health, which is central to the definition of both occupational health and occupational health psychology (Cox, Baldurrson, & Rial-Gonzalez, 2000). There are other perspectives, including one that considers the role of work and working life in relation to the management of chronic ill health. This encompasses issues such as the nature and management of sickness absence (e.g., Collins et al., 2005; Kivimäki et al., 1997; Munir, Yarker, & Haslam, 2008), the challenges of a return to work after injury or illness (e.g., Feuerstein, 1991; Franche & Krause, 2002), and the impact of working on the quality of

*Work and Wellbeing: Wellbeing: A Complete Reference Guide*, Volume III.
Edited by Peter Y. Chen and Cary L. Cooper.
© 2014 John Wiley & Sons, Ltd. Published 2014 by John Wiley & Sons, Inc.
DOI: 10.1002/9781118539415.wbwell10

life of those with chronic ill health (e.g., Dongen, 1996; Silver, 1982). In the case of life-threatening chronic illness, there is also the question of the role that work can play in the quality of survival (Silver, 1982). Much of this particular story can be positive, at least when the focus is on interventions to promote the quality of survival and, in that sense, wellbeing.

One important conceptual framework for all these different considerations of the work health relationship is arguably the *person × environment* interaction (e.g., Caplan, 1983, 1987). This framework has been developed in many different publications over at least 50 years and is the basis of many contemporary theories of work-related stress, employee health, and wellbeing, particularly those of a transactional nature (Cooper, 1998; Cooper, Dewe, & O'Driscoll, 2001; Cox, 1993; Cox, Griffiths, & Rial-Gonzalez, 2000). The person × environment framework focuses on the interaction between the person and their psychosocial work and organizational environments in relation both to the etiology of organizational behavior and work-related health and to their management. Logically, the framework suggests three different approaches to the management of outcomes: those situated with the individual, those situated with the organization and its work, and those reflecting the fit between these two sets of factors (the *person−environment fit*). Often the weakness in the management of problems at work is that we consider the first two of these three approaches separately and fail to understand or exploit the third: their integration through the concept of fit.

This chapter considers the relationship between work and a particular life-threatening form of chronic illness, cancer. It does so within the framework of the person × environment model. It attempts a narrative review of a relatively small but growing literature and, in doing so, describes the authors' development of a new intervention strategy to promote and support working in those with cancer. Working is seen as a potentially positive influence on the quality of cancer survival and wellbeing. The Accommodation Adaptation Intervention Paradigm is being developed through the METIS Collaboration, which is a research program involving the Academic Urology Unit, University of Aberdeen, the charity UCAN, and the Centre for Sustainable Working Life, Birkbeck University of London. It was established in 2008 to consider psychological, social, and organizational issues relating to the patient journey and survivorship.

# The Accommodation Adaptation Intervention Paradigm

The Accommodation Adaptation Intervention Paradigm is an intervention program being developed for the optimal management of those working or returning to work after a diagnosis of cancer. It is an organizational level strategy set in the wider context of the patient journey, care pathways, and cancer survival. It represents a positive approach to the challenge of ensuring that the person's ability to work and work involvement is optimal for them and their organization, that their experience of work is positive and that their health and wellbeing (and prognosis) is enhanced where possible. This narrative review discusses what is known about the way that organizations might adjust work and work environments to optimize the involvement and health of employees with cancer and optimize those employees' experience of working (accommodation). In parallel, it also considers what the organization might do to encourage and support the employee's adjustment to work, so changed, and to working (adaptation). Logically, the intervention process is focused on the organization first, exploring what it can do, then the employee determining their adaptation to the changed conditions of work and, finally, an evaluation of how these two processes fit together: their integration. Ideally, what is being described here is an ongoing sequence of actions—a cycle of development—with the objective of engineering an optimal fit between the person with cancer, and the organization, its work, and requirements. The research and planning involved are essential in shaping success. Illingworth, Hubbard, and Stoddart (2009) have highlighted studies suggesting that the obvious lack of such planning by organizations in relation to those with cancer increases the latter's reluctance to request or apply for work adjustments.

The separate concepts of accommodation and adaptation are strongly represented in the literature on employee health across a number of different areas. This coverage includes the organization's legal duties in relation to accommodating those with disability in work or in relation to the management of the return to work of those with chronic conditions (see, for example, Allaire, 2000; Harlan & Robert, 1998). Interestingly, legislation in many countries treats cancer as a disability. Coverage also includes employees' adaptation to the demands and stresses of work (see, for example, Isaksson & Johansson, 2000; Michie, 2002; Rosse & Hulin, 1984). However, few researchers have put the two concepts together to define an integrated approach to the challenge of managing people working or returning to work with chronic conditions. The main exceptions appear to be Feuerstein (2009) and Daly and Bound (1996), although others have come close (Munir, Yarker, & McDermott, 2009).

## Background: Cancers and Work

Despite advances in diagnostics, treatment, and care, cancer remains a major threat to health and wellbeing, and to the quality of life and longevity. In 2008, the annual incidence of cancer worldwide was estimated at 12.7 million *new* cases by the World Health Organization's International Agency for Research on Cancer (IARC). IARC also estimated that worldwide there were 7.6 million deaths due to cancer annually. These figures exclude nonmelanoma skin cancers. A number of common cancers in developed countries appear to be associated with reasonably high survival rates. These include prostate, breast, and colorectal cancers. At the same time, several cancers with poorer prognoses are common in less-developed countries. These include liver, stomach, and esophageal cancers. Based on IARC data, there were 304,235 new cases of cancer in the United Kingdom in 2008, with a predicted rise to 331,557 new cases in 2015. In 2008, somewhere in the region of 30% of new cases in the United Kingdom involved people of working age. This figure is consistent with Amir, Wynn, Whitaker, and Luker's (2009) estimation that currently 90,000 people of working age in the United Kingdom are diagnosed with cancer every year.

The METIS Collaboration has a particular but not exclusive interest in urological cancers. These represent an important grouping on the cancer landscape. The five main urological cancers are: prostate, testicular, penile, bladder, and kidney cancer. As a group, urological cancers account for 16.5% of all new cases of cancer in the United Kingdom (excluding nonmelanoma skin cancer) and for 11.7% of cancer deaths (NICE, 2002; Office for National Statistics, 2002; Quinn, Babb, Brock, Kirby, & Jones, 2001). Bradley, Neumark, Luo, Bednarek, and Schenk (2005) predicted that the increasing emphasis on screening for prostate cancer would result in an increase in the number of men diagnosed and at a younger age. As a result, the proportion of men of working age with prostate cancer will increase. Happily, the advances that have been achieved in diagnosis and treatment, and in cancer care, mean that we can now talk with confidence about "cancer survival" and "survivorship" (The U.S. National Cancer Institute defines cancer survival in terms of the period of time from the time of diagnosis through the balance of the person's life. Some define a cancer survivor in terms of survival past 5 years after diagnosis.)

Verdecchia and colleagues (2007) have reported improvements in cancer survival. For all cancers, age-adjusted 5-year period survival had improved for patients diagnosed in 2000–2002, especially for patients with colorectal, breast, prostate, and thyroid cancer, Hodgkin's disease, and non-Hodgkin's lymphoma. Survival for patients diagnosed in 2000–2002 was generally highest for those in northern European countries and lowest for those in eastern European countries, although patients in eastern European had the highest improvement in survival for major cancer sites during 1991–2002. It was noted that a number of factors probably contributed to this improvement in cancer survival, including cancer service infrastructure, prevention and screening programs, access to diagnostic and treatment facilities, tumor-site-specific protocols, multidisciplinary management, and application of evidence-based clinical guidelines. Estimates now suggest that at the end of the present decade, a person in the United Kingdom with cancer will have a 46.2% chance of being alive 10 years after diagnosis, compared with a 23.6% chance only 30 years ago.

Many people with cancer continue to be involved with work, some returning after a period of absence for treatment and others continuing through and beyond treatment. Spelten, Sprangers, and Verbeek (2002) have reported that the mean rate of return to work of cancer survivors in the studies that they reviewed was 62% with a range from 30% to 93%. Slightly earlier, Peteet (2000) reported that between 27% and 95% of those diagnosed with cancer return to previous employment. The actual rates depended on the cancer site.

In 2005, Taskila-Abrandt and colleagues reported a study of *all* cancer survivors in Finland who were alive on December 31, 1997 (Taskila-Abrandt, Pukkala, Martikainen, Karjalainen, & Hietanen, 2005). They found that 50% of cancer survivors were employed, compared to 55% of a referent group appropriately matched by age and gender. There was considerable variation across types of cancer but the most prevalent cancers were associated with employment rates only marginally below those of their referent groups. These were, in Taskila-Abrandt and colleagues' (2005) study terms: breast cancer, female and male genital cancers, and urinary cancers (relative risk 0.92–0.93). In 2009, de Boer and her colleagues published a meta-analysis of 36 studies, which, together, compared 20,366 survivors with 157,603 healthy controls. Their data came from 16 studies in the United States, 15 in Europe, and 5 from other countries. Overall, cancer survivors were shown to be more likely to be unemployed than healthy controls (33.8% against 15.2%; pooled relative risk 1.37). These findings are not necessarily at odds with those of Taskila-Abrandt et al. (2005). The two study samples were very different and, furthermore, employment rates and patterns can differ markedly across time with changes in the economic situation. What the study by de Boer and colleagues (2009) tells us is that about two thirds of cancer survivors in the United States and Europe are employed.

One of the interesting findings of this study relates to the pattern of unemployment across cancer sites. Cancer survivors with the highest likelihood of unemployment compared to healthy controls were those with breast cancer, gastrointestinal cancers, and cancers of the female reproductive organs. Survivors with similar rates of unemployment to healthy controls were those with blood cancers, prostate cancer, and testicular cancer. Apparent differences between the United States and Europe disappeared after adjustment for diagnosis, age, and background unemployment rate. An earlier study by Bradley, Bednarek, and Neuman (2001) might be used to develop these findings further. Bradley and her colleagues (2001), using data from the U.S. Health & Retirement study, examined differences between breast cancer survivors and noncancer controls. They reported that while having breast cancer had a negative impact on the decision to work, survivors who worked tended to work longer hours and have higher annual earnings than noncancer controls. The authors discussed potential biases in their study.

It can now be suggested with some confidence that a majority of cancer survivors are eventually able to return to work, although it is noted that a significant minority do not (Amir & Brocky, 2009; Taskila & Lindbohm, 2007).

It is argued here and elsewhere (e.g., Spelten et al., 2003) that work can be a factor determining the success (or otherwise) of treatment and care. In many evaluations of treatment and survivorship, continued working and return to work are taken as key markers of success (Peteet, 2000). At the same time, loss of work related to cancer diagnosis, treatment, or care has been shown to be a potential source of psychosocial and economic stress (see, for example, Emanuel, Fairclough, Slutsman, & Emanuel, 2000; Yun et al., 2005), and a threat to mental health, in particular to a sense of self and value, and to self identity (Peteet, 2000). It has been suggested that continuing in work or returning to work may mitigate any such effects of having cancer and allow the individual to retain a sense of normalcy (Amir, Neary, & Luker, 2008; Ferrell, Grant, Funk, Otis-Green, & Garcia,

1997). In this context, Talcott (2005) has suggested that consideration of the impact of treatment on involvement with work should be a factor in treatment decision making for localized prostate cancer, given that key treatments do not otherwise differ significantly in efficacy (NICE, 2002 and http://guidance.nice.org.uk/CG58).

Steiner, Cavender, Main, and Bradley (2004), on the basis of their systematic review of 18 studies, stated that at that time we did not understand sufficiently the impact of diagnosis and treatment on work-related outcomes. Their motivation appears to have been the design of interventions to improve work ability to mitigate the economic effects of cancer and to improve the quality of life for those with cancer. The present review uses an informed synthesis of the published research evidence on cancer, work, and the quality of working life in the context of available clinical and organizational experience. It is scaffolded by the Accommodation Adaptation Intervention Paradigm as an organizational intervention to promote and support working among those with cancer. The questions that structure this review are "What do organizations do to accommodate the needs of those with cancer through changes to the design and management of work?" and "What are the key aspects of individual adaptation to the demands and constraints of work and what can organizations do to support individuals in adapting?" These two questions both explore the role of the organization and imply the interaction between the organization and the individual.

## Review Method

The literature on cancer, the patient journey, and involvement with work is growing through its infancy. It is sparse, diverse, and somewhat fractured. The majority of the studies that have been conducted have been for research purposes: there have been few organizational interventions that have been successfully conducted and evaluated within the workplace (de Boer et al., 2008; de Boer & Frings-Dresen, 2009; Hoving, Broekhuizen, & Frings-Dresen, 2009; Joyce, Pabayo, Critchley, & Bambra, 2010). As a body of evidence, it is vested in a variety of methods, both qualitative and quantitative, and is published through a diverse set of journals by discipline, and through formal reports. Possibly as a result, the application of a strict systematic review methodology, as described for example, by Clarke, Oxma, Paulsen, Higgins, and Green (2010), fails to capture all the publications known to be part of this particular body of evidence. As a result, this methodology was adapted here to allow greater flexibility in the search mechanisms, broader inclusion criteria for publications, and a much greater emphasis on cross-checking references from the papers identified in the search and elsewhere. There was an emphasis throughout on general consistency with received knowledge derived from clinical and organizational experience. The current review also drew more heavily than traditional systematic reviews on synthesizing a narrative-based understanding. Such adapted methodologies have been used and reported elsewhere (see, for example, Illingworth et al., 2009). Popay has offered a discussion on the synthesis of diverse sources of evidence (Popay, 2006; Popay et al., 2003–2005).

The main review was carried out in late 2010 and early 2011. It was updated for the purpose of this chapter in 2012. Three clusters of search terms were used:

- those relating to work (examples: work; employment; working life; work ability; work limitations; work disability; absenteeism; return to work; sick leave; vocational rehabilitation; organization; management; intervention);
- those relating to cancer, including urological cancers (examples: cancer; neoplasms; urologic cancer/neoplasms; kidney cancer/neoplasms; prostatic cancer/neoplasms; urinary bladder cancer/neoplasms; penile cancer/neoplasms; testicular cancer/neoplasms);
- those relating to survivor and work outcomes and moderators (examples: survival, survivor; survivorship; patient; patient journey; after diagnosis; after treatment; care).

Forty-three relevant primary sources were identified along with six reviews. Five were systematic reviews and one was a narrative review. Four reviews were conducted in 2009, one was conducted in 2004, and one was conducted in 2002. The evidence base for the reviews varied from 124 articles (Illingworth et al., 2009) to 4 articles (Hoving et al., 2009). This could be a reflection of the growth in the literature but is also related to the use of somewhat different review methodologies. Forty articles relevant to cancer and work were included in the final version of this chapter.

Despite the current and obvious weaknesses in the evidence base, there is arguably sufficient information available to support the future development of the Accommodation Adaptation Intervention Paradigm. This is the purpose of the review. The review is fit for purpose (Cox, Karanika, Griffiths, & Houdmont, 2007).

## Accommodation by the Organization

Here accommodation is defined as the organization changing the design or management of work, modifying the workplace or adjusting work systems and procedures to facilitate a return to work or continued working by those with cancer. In a sense, it is a primary intervention and, among other things, is intended to make working less stressful. There is growing evidence that accommodation by the organization, or at least survivors' perceptions that their organization is "accommodating," appears to be important and positive in relation to a return to work. Bouknight, Bradley, and Luo (2006) interviewed 416 employed women with newly diagnosed identified breast cancer from the U.S. Metropolitan Detroit Cancer Surveillance System. These women were largely employed in white-collar jobs (85%) and many were in professional, managerial, or technical and related positions (61%). They were interviewed 12 and 18 months after diagnosis. They were asked a general question about their organization being accommodating. The data shows that more than 80% of these women with breast cancer returned to work during the period of the study. Eighty-seven percent reported that their organization was accommodating to their cancer and its treatment. After appropriate control for health and work-related variables, perception of the organization as accommodating was positively associated with a return to work at 12 months and also at 18 months. This study makes a general point but one of its limitations is the lack of information about the nature of organizations' accommodations.

Chan, da Silva Cardoso, Copeland, Jones, and Fraser (2011) have discussed workplace accommodations in the United States for those with cancer in the context of the 1990 Americans with Disabilities Act (ADA). Since 1994, this Act has included consideration of those with cancer. In the United Kingdom, the 1995 Disability Discrimination Act was extended in 2005 to include, inter alia, those with cancer. This Act was replaced in 2010 by broader legislation (the Equality Act) that continued to cover those with cancer. There is a question here about whether those with cancer are best conceived of and treated as disabled. However, the extension of both Acts has provided a legal framework for accommodation in those countries. The ADA places a legal obligation on employing organizations with 15 or more employees to provide "reasonable" accommodations for those who are disabled. There is a second question here about the definition of "reasonable" but the Act states that such accommodation might include two things. First, it might involve making existing facilities accessible to and usable by an individual with disability. Second, it might involve the redesign and restructuring of work and jobs, for example, providing part-time work, modifying work schedules, modifying work equipment, or acquiring new equipment, or relocating work tasks and modifying training. Unreasonable accommodations might, according to the ADA, place undue hardship on the employing organization, be too costly, or too difficult to implement.

There is evidence from the literature that at least four aspects of work design and management are important in relation to the organization better accommodating those with cancer returning to work or continuing to work through. A fifth might be added on logical grounds although it is underresearched. The four established factors involve the redesign and restructuring of work and jobs, the education of employers, managers and colleagues, greater flexibility in work organization and greater control over work, and better communication around chronic conditions and work within the organization. The fifth relates to the design of and access to existing facilities and, in particular, toilet facilities. Here it is argued that the first factor, the imperative to redesign and restructure jobs, is made clear in both U.S. and U.K. legislation and is a very individual, organizational and job-specific issue. Furthermore, it tends to subsume the other factors identified in the literature, especially those of flexibility and control. As a result, it is not strongly represented there per se. This review focuses on the other factors. All may be usefully considered in terms of contemporary stress theory and within the conceptual framework of the person × environment fit. Their influence in relation to accommodation might be mediated, at least in part, through a reduction of work-related stress. Furthermore, there is general evidence that such improvements might benefit those employees who suffer other chronic conditions (or who are healthy) as well as those with cancer.

## Education of Employers, Managers, and Colleagues

A number of studies have recommended more and better education of employers, managers, and colleagues to facilitate return to work after ill-health. Lack of understanding among these groups has been long cited as a barrier to effective return to work in cancer survivors (Barofsky, 1989; Feldman, 1978). A systematic review by Spelten et al. (2002) provided evidence that, in this context, understanding and a positive attitude on the part of colleagues appears to be associated with an effective return to work. Illingworth et al. (2009) have suggested that three particular things are required: a greater awareness and a better understanding of the nature of cancer, of the patient journey, and of the issues surrounding working on and returning to work. Earlier, Short, Vasey, and Tunceli (2005) argued that there must be recognition within the organization that the effects of cancer treatment and care can extend beyond the first year of survivorship. This point is important and has been repeated by Amir et al. (2008) and by Yarker, Munir, Bains, Kalawsky, and Haslam (2009).

The challenge would appear to be twofold: first, to ensure that the organization and its managers and employees approach the overall challenge in an educated and positive way but, second, that all of this is reflected and given substance in planning and subsequent actions. Illingworth et al. (2009) emphasize the importance of effective planning for all stakeholders. It is suggested here that the overarching aim is to develop an informed culture in organizations that balances support with pragmatism and that positively influences the reality of working life.

## Greater Flexibility and Control at Work

The evidence, drawn not only from studies on cancers but also from those on other chronic conditions and from the general occupational health literature, suggests that flexibility in the organization of work and control over work are important positive factors for employee health and wellbeing. The recent systematic review of intervention studies by Joyce et al. (2010) concludes that, although the evidence base with regard to cancers is small, interventions focused on increasing flexibility in work do bring benefits in terms of both physical and mental health. A range of different types of flexibility was considered; these included temporal flexibility (work scheduling), spatial flexibility (working away from the organization), and contractual flexibility (e.g., part-time work, fixed-term contracts, and early retirement). Of these, the evidence suggested that interventions involving control over the scheduling of work (temporal flexibility) and gradual (partial) retirement (contractual scheduling) were associated with health improvements.

The question of whether control at work (often referred to more narrowly as job control) is related to cancer etiology and prognosis has not been fully addressed, although there are a small number of studies that suggest some association between lack of job control and, at least, the incidence of colon and colorectal cancers (e.g., Courtney, Longnecker, & Peters, 1996; Spiegelman & Wegman, 1985). A case–control study by Spiegelman and Wegman (1985) drew on several different population databases to generate and test hypotheses about associations between colorectal cancer and workplace exposures, both physical and psychosocial. The Third U.S. National Cancer Survey interview sample was used by the authors to select 343 male and 208 female cancer cases and 626 male and 1,235 female noncancer controls. Potential work exposures were then assigned with the use of data from the U.S. National Institute for Occupational Safety and Health and from the U.S. Health National Occupational Hazard Survey. Dietary factors were modeled from the U.S. National Health and Nutrition Examination Survey data. Work-related stress was assessed using a model based on the U.S. Department of Labor's Quality of Employment Survey. Other risk factors were taken into account. Logistic analysis suggested increased colon cancer risk in males with potentially high exposure to solvents, abrasives, and fuel oil and in those in jobs that combined high demand with low control (high strain or stress). Earlier research by Courtney, Longnecker, and Peters (1996), also a case–control study, suggested that low job control was associated with a modestly increased risk of colon cancer but that high job demand was not. The mechanisms underpinning such effects remain unclear and the findings have been challenged. For example, a more recent longitudinal study (Achat, Kawachi, Byrne, Hankinson, & Colditz, 2000; Schernhammer et al., 2004) appears to present contradictory findings in relation to job stress. However, there are differences between the Spiegelman and Achat studies. The more recent longitudinal study was focused on breast cancer, whereas the earlier study concerned colorectal cancer. The authors of the former also failed to disentangle the separate effects of job demands and job control within the model of job stress that they used. Despite these possibly contradictory findings, the systematic review by Spelten, Sprangers, and Verbeek (2002) suggested that (more focused) control over work hours or amount of work is positively associated with an effective return to work. Here control can be equated with flexibility.

Similar findings have emerged from research with other chronic conditions and health challenges (e.g., inflammatory bowel disease: S. J. MacLennan et al., unpublished work). On the basis of the qualitative data collected in this is study, it was recommended that to facilitate working with the conditions under consideration attention be paid to control over the nature of the tasks and the demands placed on the person, to control over working hours, and to flexible working. Also of importance for working people with irritable bowel disorder were communication within their organization and the availability and design of toilets and control over access to them (MacLennan et al., unpublished paper). The latter is discussed below.

## Better Communication within the Organization

Improved communication within organizations in relation to those working with chronic conditions emerges as a common recommendation from many different studies. Key elements appear to be good communication between the person with the condition and their colleagues, managers, and employers and good communication among employers, managers, and the occupational health and primary care services (Hoving et al., 2009; Illingworth et al., 2009; Nieuwenhuijsen, Bos-Ransdorp, Uitterhoeve, Sprangers, & Verbeek, 2006; Pryce, Munir, & Haslam, 2007; Spelten et al., 2002; Yarker et al., 2009). What may be needed is evidence of the possible beneficial effects of joined-up organizational thinking and of consistency of approach.

## Improved Toilet Facilities and Access

Two of the acknowledged side effects of treatment for urological cancers are urinary and fecal incontinence (NICE, 2002). To cope with either at work, it is obvious that a person must have easy access to adequate toilet facilities and sufficient control over their work to allow them to use those facilities as required. These were among the recommendations of the recent study on working with irritable bowel disorder by MacLennan et al. (unpublished paper). Two other related issues were highlighted in that study: first, the need for suitably designed toilet cubicles to ensure privacy (high walls and a door) and an understanding and supportive attitude on the part of managers and colleagues towards frequent and unpredictable use of such toilet facilities. These findings are likely to generalize beyond bowel incontinence in those working with irritable bowel disorder to those with urological cancers. This is an underresearched area and this lack of research may be partly due to a stubborn taboo around the discussion of toilets and toilet habits.

The evidence available so far highlights the importance of organizational accommodation of five aspects of work design and management. It can be seen from this discussion that there is much interplay and some overlap among them. Questions remain about how such accommodation might be made manifest by the translation of an appropriately positive organizational culture into management practice. There are also questions to be addressed in relation to disclosure on the part of the person with cancer (e.g., Pryce et al., 2007), to individual needs for accommodation in job design and restructuring, and to an individual's desire not to be picked out and identified by their condition or the organization's reaction to them (MacLennan et al., unpublished paper).

## Individual Adaptation: An Organizational Perspective

Not all of those with cancer will require accommodations to be made by their organizations in order for them to work (Kennedy, Haslam, Munir, & Pryce, 2007). It is unlikely, however, that many will not have to adapt in some way to working after cancer diagnosis and treatment. Adaptation is defined here as the changes that the person with cancer makes to facilitate returning to work or working on in terms of their perceptions, cognitions, and emotions, their attitudes and beliefs, coping strategies and behavior, and social relations. This section is concerned with the organizational perspective on adaptation and how the person's organization might support their adaptation to work.

On the basis of the published evidence, it appears that the areas for consideration in relation to the organization's support for individual adaptation are help in building a positive attitude to work, providing social support for adaptation in the workplace, and the provision of effective occupational health services and vocational rehabilitation with timely and appropriate information and advice. The latter point is returned to later.

### A Positive Attitude to Work

The evidence suggests that changed attitudes to work involving reduced importance given to working and a decrease in work aspirations are negatively associated with an effective return to work by women with breast cancer (Maunsell, Brisson, Dubois, Lauzier, & Fraser, 1999). In an earlier study of men with testicular cancer by Edbril and Rieker (1989), many participants reported that they became less confident about their physical ability in relation to their work and others reported that they became less interested in work achievements as a result of having cancer. It is possible that developing or maintaining a positive attitude to work and building self-confidence in work ability may be important for successful return to work and adaptation to working in those with cancer independent of age or clinical factors (de Boer et al., 2008). Peteet (2000) has advocated screening following a diagnosis of cancer to identify those struggling with issues of identity, normalcy, and perceived fairness in relation to work. This could allow the targeting of help in support of adaptation. Taskila and Lindbohm (2007) present a similar argument in relation to limited work ability. It would seem logical that return to work procedures should include programs that address these issues.

## Support at Work

The evidence suggests that good support for those with cancer from colleagues and managers in the workplace is associated with job satisfaction and increased productivity. This is possibly because of related feelings of increased control over work and the experience of less work-related stress (Berry, 1993; Nachreiner et al., 2007; Spelten et al., 2002). Lack of support has been reported to have a negative effect on those working with cancer. Such findings are consistent with the general literature on the effects of social support at work especially if such support is conceptualized as assistance with coping (for example: Dewe, Cox, & Ferguson, 1993; Ell, 1996; Thoits, 1986). The timing of such support and the continued provision of support following the initial return to work period have been highlighted as issues (Yarker et al., 2009).

Research originating in the Nordic Study Group of Cancer and Work Life (NOCWO) has focused, in part, on the effects of social support at work for cancer survivors. It has extended the analysis of social support in two ways: by distinguishing between the levels of support needed and received by cancer survivors and by also distinguishing between that provided by colleagues, supervisors and occupational health services. For example, Taskila et al. (2006) reported that women survivors both needed and received more support at work than men survivors. However, about a third of each group reported needing more support than they received. Gudbergsson, Fossa, Lindbohm, and Dahl (2009) failed to replicate this finding but used a different measurement instrument for social support and one that was only weakly correlated with that used by Taskila et al. (2006). Interestingly, Gudbergsson et al. (2009) showed significant differences between the support landscapes for Norwegian and Finnish women cancer survivors at work. The Norwegian survivors reported significantly more support from supervisors than did the Finns but less support from occupational health services. Gudbergsson et al. (2009) explained this difference in terms of differences in the benefit systems of the two countries and differences in the structures of occupational health provision. It may also reflect cultural differences within the Nordic region.

It is reassuring that strengthening social support at work can have a positive effect for those returning to work and working with cancer. It is interesting that much of this effect appears to originate with colleagues and supervisors or managers or in occupational health provision, although this might be a largely Nordic perspective. It is not clear whether this effect varies with cancer site. Support is conceptualized here largely in terms of assistance with coping and is required beyond the initial return to work period or period following diagnosis (Yarker et al., 2009).

## Occupational Health Services

Only 14% of workers in the United Kingdom benefit from comprehensive occupational health support and only 12% have access to occupational physicians (Nicholson, 2004). The situation is substantively better in some other European countries such as Norway, Finland, and the Netherlands. Occupational health support is therefore limited and mainly only available in larger organizations either on an in-house or bought-in basis (Amir et al., 2009). In the absence of access to occupational health, employees with cancer usually have to seek health advice on work-related issues from their general practitioners. General practitioners may play a key role at least in the United Kingdom.

Amir et al. (2009) argue that improved communication between occupational health services, where they exist, and general practice might ensure that those in occupational health develop a better understanding of cancer prognosis, treatment and care, side effects, and functional outcomes. At the same time, general practice may develop a better understanding of the role of work, vocational rehabilitation, and employment law as it relates to employee health and the role of occupational health in relation to line management. However, Wynn (2009) points out that general practitioners' experience of new cases of cancer is limited as is that of occupational health physicians. Although approximately 300,000 new cases of cancer are now diagnosed in England and Wales each year, the frequency with which any general practitioner or occupational health physician will see a patient with a new diagnosis is low. Taking as an example lung cancer, Wynn (2009) estimates that, on average, a general practitioner only sees between 1 and 2 new cases each year. This cannot help but affect their understanding of the issues involved in those patients returning to work or working on with cancer. Not surprisingly, Wynn (2009) states that opportunities to advise newly diagnosed patients with cancer about work are therefore often missed despite their importance. The system available to the working person diagnosed with cancer must be judged to be far from adequate. However, Macmillan, the major cancer charity in the United Kingdom, has now made advice giving a priority target for both its research and service delivery (see www.macmillan.co.uk).

In addition to better communication between occupational health and general practice, there needs to be better communication among occupational health, line managers, and employees, including those with cancer (Grunfeld, Rixon, Eaton, & Cooper, 2008). Both Grunfeld et al. (2008) and Yarker et al. (2009) have highlighted the need to raise employee awareness of the availability of occupational health support and services where offered.

## Vocational Rehabilitation

One of the services that might be offered or recommended by occupational health is vocational rehabilitation. Multidisciplinary planning for and delivery of vocational rehabilitation has been identified as important for those working with cancer (Illingworth et al., 2009). Despite this, Amir et al. (2009) have argued that there is a general lack of awareness about the need for vocational rehabilitation and uncertainty as to who should provide such a service. Hoving et al. (2009) have drawn attention to the rehabilitation strategies that have been established as important to cancer patients, for example, the use of graded activity and of goal setting.

## Information and Advice

The provision of timely and appropriate information and advice is a key issue for those with cancer and for their families. There would appear to be two areas of possible difficulty, at least in the United Kingdom. The first is the nature of the advice given in relation to working (see above) and the other is the consistency of the advice given by health and social care professionals. Anecdotal evidence suggests that, in the United Kingdom at least, well-meaning advice given by health and social care professionals to those diagnosed with cancer tends to minimize the importance of work, focusing on "taking time out to recover." The implication is, possibly, that working is not helpful to their situation. Such advice might inadvertently undermine the patient's attitudes to work and their own feelings of adequacy in relation to work.

No matter how well meaning advice might be, if it conveys an unhelpful message (against the available evidence) or if it is inconsistent across professionals, it may not serve the purpose for which it is intended: supporting coping, improving the quality of survivors' lives, and possibly aiding survival.

Advice is given by different health and social care groups across the patient journey, including their general (primary) medical practitioners. If the survivor is working then it may also be provided by functions such as human resources and occupational health. Much of the published literature focuses on the possible role of occupational health and general practitioners in the provision of advice about cancer and work. Such advice is often given to support the person's decision making about treatment and their forward planning, for example, in relation to time away from work (Bradley et al., 2005; Bradley, Oberst, & Schenk, 2006). The timely delivery of such advice is seen as important (Illingworth et al., 2009). Talcott (2005) has suggested that consideration of the impact of treatment on involvement with work could be a factor in treatment decision making for localized prostate cancer, given that key treatments do not differ significantly in efficacy. Interestingly, however, clinical care plans for those diagnosed with cancer do not routinely include planning for working or a return to work, nor are they routinely covered by general practice (Amir et al., 2008, 2009). An important area of research is indicated here.

## Discussion

There is sufficient evidence available within this review to inform the development of the Accommodation Adaptation Intervention Paradigm for those working on or returning to work with cancer. As this area develops, more and better evidence should become available and this will help refine, implement, and evaluate this organizational-level approach.

It was possible from the evidence reviewed to suggest some of the possible elements that could define both accommodation and adaptation. For accommodation, these are: education of employers, managers, and colleagues, education of health professionals on how they could help and the timing of such help, flexibility in work and control at work, communication within the organization, and the design of and access to toilet facilities. For adaptation, these are: building a positive attitude to work, providing social support in the workplace for adaptation, the provision of effective occupational health services, vocational rehabilitation, and timely advice. Obviously, given the acknowledged nature of the evidence base, the detail of this strategy might be challenged, hopefully through research, or evaluated and found wanting in intervention studies. Whatever, this review will have served a useful purpose in stimulating and guiding further work in the area.

Interestingly, the elements that might define accommodation appear to be interrelated with the possibility of one of their common effects being the reduction of stress relating to working. There is evidence, dating back to the 1970s and properly reviewed elsewhere, that the experience of stress, through psycho-neuro-immune mechanisms might affect, at least, prognosis for those with cancer (for example, Cox & Mackay, 1982). Furthermore, many of these elements, presented as recommendations, appear to arise in many other studies of chronic conditions. One possible exception is the design and access to toilets but, even here, there is wider relevance beyond urological and bowel cancers. The fact that many of the elements of accommodation find utility beyond the urological cancers strengthens the argument for considering them in the workplace and this argument is further strengthened because many also have positive relevance for the wider workforce.

Much of the discussion of adaptation, from the organizational perspective, has focused on the provision of adequate occupational health services, something which is not happening in the United Kingdom. There is obviously a case here for considering the arguments for the provision of more such services across organizations. If this is not possible, then consideration must be given to their provision on a community basis, perhaps as a charitable initiative or through general practitioners.

## Integration and Research

The question of the interaction between accommodation and adaptation is implicit in much research but has rarely been addressed directly and explicitly. This observation strongly indicates a future research need. Future research needs in this area have been discussed in some detail by Feuerstein (2011), who sets out a broad agenda based around the need to develop cancer-specific work disability models. These, he argues, should take account of the natural history of different types of cancer and of work disability and be as parsimonious as possible. These arguments are sound and might be sensibly added to in terms of the need for a framework which combines the best of clinical and organizational experience and practice with the developing scientific evidence. The interaction between accommodation and adaptation is alluded to across Feuerstein's (2011) agenda. Here we give an example from the present review of one way in which they interact. It is about the role that education and training can play and how that can (and should) provide the scaffolding for much of what has been discussed above. Perhaps it is one of the keys to further progress.

Education and training appear to be important in at least three respects. First, health and social care professionals who support those with cancer may benefit from further education and training which helps them build a more positive attitude to work in those in their care, provide more informed advice on working, and ensure the consistency of that advice. Second, occupational health (and possibly human resource) professionals might benefit from education and training around the Accommodation Adaptation Intervention Paradigm and share such training with primary care (general) practitioners. The aim here would be to develop a stronger shared understanding and also be more aware of each other's position and concerns. Finally, managers and staff in organizations, as colleagues of the person with cancer, might benefit from a better understanding of cancer and cancer survival in relation to working. In all cases, such education and training serves to ensure that accommodation is effected in a reasonable way, from the organization's point of view, and helps the person with cancer continue working or return to work without unnecessary challenge and stress and performs well to reasonable expectations to their and the organization's benefit. Part of this is about the design and management of work, part of it is about effective advice and support, and part of it is about enhanced individual coping. Here knowledge empowers progress. In some senses, education and training provide one example of a macro- or bridging-factor within the Accommodation Adaptation Intervention Paradigm.

## Particular Implications for Cancer Care Practice

The findings of this narrative review of the literature on cancer, work, and the quality of life makes a number of important points for practice not only in relation to work organizations but also to health and social care professionals.

The learning points are obvious for organizations. First, working with cancer is not only possible but, in reality, affects a substantial number of people in the United States, the United Kingdom, and the rest of Europe. Cancer survivors are a real part of the workforce. Their engagement in work is possible and their contribution to the economy important. Second, work itself may have positive effects on the survivors' journeys, not only financially but also psychologically and socially. Finally, organizations can relatively easily accommodate the needs of survivors returning to or continuing to work and they can equally easily support the individuals' adaptation to work. An interesting point here, mentioned earlier, is that much of what is indicated here by way of possible organizational interventions will benefit not only cancer survivors but probably those with other chronic conditions and also the healthy.

The implications for health and social care professionals should also be obvious. First, working may be good for survivors and may be a significant positive factor in determining the quality of their survival and possibly contributing indirectly to their prognosis. This has to be understood and built into the thinking of such professionals and reflected in the advice that they give and the planning that they encourage in survivors. At the same time, partly because this message may be new in many quarters, advice given around it tends to be inconsistent or nuanced in different ways. In addition to perhaps being unhelpful, inconsistent advice is worrying and can be stressful in itself. There is a major area of research and development indicated here. One of the possible ways forward is through the design and implementation of a patient advice and information system that will both involve the different stakeholder groups and unfold across the whole of the patient journey. The effectiveness of such a system will depend on the education and training of the stakeholder groups, their sharing of information, and a method of recording and reviewing the advice given to patients. An example of the latter might be afforded by the notion of an "information passport" which is completed by the stakeholders but held by the patient. The authors are involved with Macmillan in Scotland in developing such a patient advice and information system.

## Final Comments

Not every person with cancer wants to work on or is able to work on but a majority do and can. Some will not have employment to return to. In our enthusiasm to promote working as a positive factor, we must not unintentionally create a situation in which all those with cancer feel under pressure to work or seek work. Caution here is necessary but not a sufficient reason to draw back from research in this area or attempts to design effective practices to promote working for those who wish to work and can work.

# References

Achat, H., Kawachi, I., Byrne, C., Hankinson, S., & Colditz, G. (2000). A prospective study of job strain and risk of breast cancer. *International Journal of Epidemiology, 29,* 622–628.

Allaire, S. H. (2000). Update on work disability in rheumatic diseases. *Disability & Rehabilitation, 22,* 578–582.

Amir, Z., Neary, D., & Luker, K. (2008). Cancer survivors' views of work 3 years post diagnosis: A UK perspective. *European Journal of Oncology Nursing, 12,* 190–197.

Amir, Z., & Brocky, J. (2009). Cancer survivorship and employment: Epidemiology. *Occupational Medicine, 59,* 373–377.

Amir, Z., Wynn, P., Whitaker, S., & Luker, K. (2009). Cancer survivorship and return to work: UK occupational physician experience. *Occupational Medicine, 59,* 390–396.

Barofsky, I. (1989). *Work and illness: The cancer patient.* New York: Praeger.

Berry, D. L. (1993). Return to work experiences of people with cancer. *Oncology Nursing Forum, 20,* 905–911.

Bouknight, R. R., Bradley, C. J., & Luo, Z. (2006). Correlates of return to work for breast cancer survivors. *Journal of Clinical Oncology, 24,* 345–352.

Bradley, C. J., Bednarek, H., & Neuman, D. (2001). *Breast cancer, survival, work and earnings.* NBER Working paper no: 8134. National Bureau of Economic Research.

Bradley, C. J., Neumark, D., Luo, Z., Bednarek, H., & Schenk, M. (2005). Employment outcomes of men treated for prostate cancer. *Journal of National Cancer Institute, 97,* 958–965.

Bradley, C. J., Oberst, K., & Schenk, M. (2006). Absenteeism from work: The experience of employed breast and prostate cancer patients in the months following diagnosis. *Psycho-Oncology, 15,* 739–747.

Caplan, R. D. (1983). Person–environment fit: Past, present, future. In C. L. Cooper (Ed.), *Stress research: Issues for the eighties.* Chichester: John Wiley & Sons.

Caplan, R. D. (1987). Person–environment fit theory and organizations: Commensurate dimensions, time perspectives, and mechanisms. *Journal of Vocational Behavior, 31,* 248–267.

Chan, F., da Silva Cardoso, E., Copeland, J., Jones, R., & Fraser, R. T. (2011). Workplace accommodations. In M. Feuerstein (Ed.), *Work and cancer survivors.* New York: Springer Science & Business.

Clarke, M., Oxma, A. D., Paulsen, E., Higgins, J. P. T., & Green, S. (2010). *Guide to the contents of a Cochrane Methodology protocol and review.*

http://www.mrc-bsu.cam.ac.uk/cochrane/handbook/index.htm#appendix_
a/appendix_a_guide_to_the_contents_of_a_cochrane_methodology.htm.

Collins, J. C., Baase, C. M., Sharda, C. E., Ozminkowski, R. J., Nicjolson, S., Billotti, G. M., Turpin, R. S., Olson, M., & Berger, M. L. (2005). The assessment of chronic health conditions on work performance, absence and total economic impact for employers. *Journal of Occupational & Environmental Health, 47,* 547–557.

Cooper, C. L. (1998). *Theories of organisational stress.* Chichester: John Wiley & Son.

Cooper, C. L., Dewe, P., & O'Driscoll, M. P. (2001). *Organisational stress: A review and critique of theory, research and applications.* London: Sage.

Courtney, J. G., Longnecker, M. P., & Peters, R. K. (1996). Psychosocial aspects of work and the risk of colon cancer. *Epidemiology, 7,* 175–181.

Cox, T. (1993). *Stress research and stress management: Putting theory to work.* Sudbury: HSE Books.

Cox, T., Baldurrson, E., & Rial-Gonzalez, E. (2000). Occupational health psychology. *Work & Stress, 14,* 101–104.

Cox, T., Griffiths, A. J., & Rial-Gonzalez, E. (2000). *Work-related stress.* Luxembourg: Office for Official Publications of the European Communities.

Cox, T., Karanika, M., Griffiths, A., & Houdmont, J. (2007). Evaluating organizational-level work stress interventions: Beyond traditional methods. *Work & Stress, 21,* 348–362.

Cox, T., & Mackay, C. J. (1982). Psychosocial factors and psychophysiological mechanisms in the aetiology and development of cancers. *Social Science & Medicine, 16,* 381–396.

Daly, M. C., & Bound, J. (1996). Worker adaptation and employer accommodation following the onset of a health impairment. *Journal of Gerontology, 51B,* S53–S60.

de Boer, A. G. E. M., & Frings-Dresen, M. H. W. (2009). Employment and the common cancers: Return to work of cancer survivors. *Occupational Medicine, 59,* 378–380.

de Boer, A. G. E. M., Taskila, T., Ojajarvi, A., van Dijk, F. J. H., & Verbeek, J. H. A. M. (2009). Cancer survivors and unemployment: A meta-analysis and meta-regression. *Journal of the American Medical Association, 301,* 753–762.

de Boer, A. G. E. M., Verbeek, J. H. A. M., Spelten, E. R., Uitterhoeve, A. L. J., Ansink, A. C., de Reijke, T. M., Mammeijer, M., Sprangers, M. A. G., & van Dijk, F. J. H. (2008). Work ability and return-to-work in cancer patients. *British Journal of Cancer, 98,* 1342–1347.

Dewe, P., Cox, T., & Ferguson, E. (1993). Individual strategies for coping with stress at work: A review. *Work & Stress, 7,* 5–15.

Dongen, C. J. (1996). Quality of life and self-esteem in working and nonworking persons with mental illness. *Community Mental Health Journal, 32,* 535–548.

Edbril, S. D, & Rieker, P. P. (1989). The impact of testicular cancer on the work lives of survivors. *Journal of Psychosocial Oncology, 7,* 17–29.

Ell, K. (1996). Social networks, social support and coping with serious illness: The family connection. *Social Science & Medicine, 42*, 173–183.

Emanuel, E. J., Fairclough, D. L., Slutsman, J., & Emanuel, L. L. (2000). Understanding economic and other burdens of terminal illness: The experience of patients and their caregivers. *Annals of Internal Medicine, 132*, 451–459.

Feldman, F. L. (1978). *Work and cancer health histories: A study of experiences of recovered blue collar workers*. San Francisco: American Cancer Society California Division.

Ferrell, B. R., Grant, M. M., Funk, B., Otis-Green, S., & Garcia, N. (1997). Quality of life in breast cancer survivors as identified by focus groups. *Psycho-Oncology, 6*, 13–23.

Feuerstein, M. (1991). A multidisciplinary approach to the prevention, evaluation, and management of work disability. *Journal of Occupational Rehabilitation, 1*, 5–12.

Feuerstein, M. (2009). *Work and cancer survivors*. New York: Springer Science & Business.

Feuerstein, M. (2011). The Journal of Cancer Survivorship: retrospective and future directions. *Journal of Cancer Survivorship, 5*, 315–319.

Franche, R.-L., & Krause, N. (2002). Readiness for return to work following injury or iIllness: Conceptualizing the interpersonal impact of health care, workplace, and insurance factors. *Journal of Occupational Rehabilitation, 12*, 233–256.

Grunfeld, E. A., Rixon, L., Eaton, E., & Cooper, A. F. (2008). The organisational perspective on the return to work of employees following treatment for cancer. *Journal of Occupational Rehabilitation, 18*, 381–388.

Gudbergsson, S. B., Fossa, S. D., Lindbohm, M.-J., & Dahl, A. A. (2009). Received and needed social support at the workplace in Norwegian and Finnish stage 1 breast cancer survivors: A study from the Nordic Study group of Cancer and Work (NOWCO). *Acta Oncologica, 48*, 67–75.

Harlan, S. L., & Robert, P. M. (1998). Why employers resist reasonable accommodation. *Work and Occupations, 25*, 397–435.

Hoving, J. L., Broekhuizen, M. L. A., & Frings-Dresen, M. H. W. (2009). Return to work of breast cancer survivors: A systematic review of intervention studies. *BMC Cancer, 9*, 117.

Illingworth, N., Hubbard, G., & Stoddart, K. (2009). *Employment following cancer diagnosis: A narrative summary of the evidence*. Cancer Care Research Centre, University of Stirling.

Isaksson, K., & Johansson, G. (2000). Adaptation to continued work and early retirement following downsizing: Long-term effects and gender differences. *Journal of Occupational and Organizational Psychology, 73*, 241–256.

Joyce, K., Pabayo, R., Critchley, J. A., & Bambra, C. (2010). Flexible working conditions and their effects on employee health and wellbeing: A review. *The Cochrane Collaboration, 2*, 89.

Kennedy, F., Haslam, C., Munir, F., & Pryce, J. (2007). Returning to work following cancer: A qualitative exploratory study into the experience of returning to work following cancer. *European Journal of Cancer Care, 16*, 17–25.

Kivimäki, M., Vahtera, J., Thompson, L., Griffiths, A., Cox, T., & Pentti, J. (1997). Psychosocial factors predicting employee sickness absence during economic decline. *Journal of Applied Psychology*, *82*, 858–872.

Maunsell, E., Brisson, C., Dubois, L., Lauzier, S., & Fraser, A. (1999). Work problems after breast cancer: An exploratory qualitative study. *Psycho-Oncology*, *8*, 467–473.

Michie, S. (2002). Causes and management of stress at work. *Occupational and Environmental Medicine*, *59*, 67–72.

Michie, S., & Williams, S. (2003). Reducing work related psychological ill health and sickness absence: A systematic literature review. *Occupational and Environmental Medicine*, *60*, 3–9.

Munir, F., Yarker, J., & Haslam, C. (2008). Sickness absence management: Encouraging attendance or "Risk-taking" presenteeism in employees with chronic illness? *Disability and Rehabilitation*, *30*, 1461–1472.

Munir, F., Yarker, J., & McDermott, H. (2009). Employment and the common cancers: Correlates of work ability during or following cancer treatment. *Occupational Medicine*, *59*, 381–389.

Nachreiner, N. M., Dagher, R. K., McGovern, P. M., Baker, B. A., Alexander, B. H., & Gerberich, S. G. (2007). Successful return to work for cancer survivors. *AAOHN*, *7*, 290–295.

NICE (National Institute of Clinical Excellence). (2002). *Guidance on cancer services—Improving outcomes in urological cancer: The manual*. London: NICE.

Nicholson, P. J. (2004). Occupational health services in the UK—challenges and opportunities. *Occupational Medicine*, *54*, 147–152.

Nieuwenhuijsen, K., Bos-Ransdorp, B., Uitterhoeve, L. L., Sprangers, M. A., & Verbeek, J. H. (2006). Enhanced provider communication and patient education regarding return to work in cancer survivors following curative treatment: A pilot study. *Journal of Occupational Rehabilitation*, *16*, 647–657.

Office for National Statistics (2002). *New cases of cancer diagnosed in England, 1998*. London: Office for National Statistics.

Popay, J. (2006). *Moving beyond effectiveness in evidence synthesis: Methodological issues in the synthesis of diverse sources of evidence*. London: National Institute for Clinical Excellence (NICE).

Peteet, J. R. (2000). Cancer and the meaning of work. *General Hospital Psychiatry*, *22*, 200–205.

Popay, J., Roen, K, Sowden, A., Rodgers, M., Roberts, H., Arai, L., Petticrew, M., & Baldwin, S. (2003–2005). *Developing methods for the narrative synthesis of quantitative and qualitative data in systematic reviews of effectiveness*. ccsr.ac.uk/methods/projects/posters/popay.shtml.

Pryce, J., Munir, F., & Haslam, C. (2007). Cancer survivorship and work: Symptoms, supervisor response, co-worker disclosure and work adjustment. *Journal of Occupational Rehabilitation*, *17*, 83–92.

Quinn, M., Babb, P., Brock, A., Kirby, L., & Jones, J. (2001). *Cancer trends in England and Wales 1950–1999*. London: The Stationery Office.

231

Quinlan, M., Mayhew, C., & Bohle, P. (2001). The global expansion of precarious employment, work disorganization, and consequences for occupational health: A review of recent research. *International Journal of Health Services, 31,* 335–414.

Rosse, J. G., & Hulin, C. L. (1984). Adaptation to work: An analysis of employee health, withdrawal and change. *Organisational Behaviour and Human Decision Processes, 36,* 324–347.

Schernhammer, E. S., Hankinson, S. E., Rosner, E., Kroenke, C. H., Willett, W. C., Colditz, G. A., & Kawachi, I. (2004). Job stress and breast cancer risk: The Nurses' Health Study. *American Journal of Epidemiology, 160,* 1079–1086.

Short, P. F., Vasey, J. J., & Tunceli, K. (2005). Employment pathways in a large cohort of adult cancer survivors. *Cancer, 103,* 1292–1301.

Silver, A. S. (1982). Resuming the work with a life-threatening illness. *Contemporary Psychoanalysis, 18,* 314–326.

Sparks, K., & Cooper, C. L. (1997). The effects of hours of work on health: A meta-analtyic review. *Journal of Occupational & Organisational Psychology, 70,* 391–408.

Spelten, E. R., Sprangers, M. A. G., & Verbeek, J. H. A. M. (2002). Factors reported to influence the return to work of cancer survivors: A literature review. *Psycho-Oncology, 11,* 124–131.

Spelten, E. R., Verbeek, J. H. A. M., Uitterhoeve, A. L. J., Ansink, A. C., van der Leslie, J., de Reijke, T. M., Kammeijer, M., de Haes, J. C. J. M., & Sprangers, M. A. G. (2003). Cancer, fatigue and the return of patients to work–a prospective cohort study. *European Journal of Cancer, 39,* 1562–1567.

Spiegelman, D., & Wegman, D. H. (1985). Occupation-related risk for colorectal cancer. *Journal of the National Cancer Institute, 75,* 813–821.

Steiner, J. F., Cavender, T. A., Main, D. S., & Bradley, C. J. (2004). Assessing the impact of cancer on work outcomes: What are the research needs? *Cancer, 101,* 1703–1711.

Talcott, J. (2005). Employment after therapy for localized prostate cancer: Widening the perspective. *Journal of the National Cancer Institute, 97,* 948–949.

Taskila, T., Lindbohm, M.-L., Martikainen, R., Lehto, U.-S., Hakanen, J., & Hietanen, P. (2006). Cancer survivors' received and needed social support from their work place and the occupational health services. *Support Care Cancer, 5,* 427–435.

Taskila, T., & Lindbohm, M. L. (2007). Factors affecting cancer survivors' employment and work ability. *Acta Oncology, 46,* 446–451.

Taskila-Abrandt, T., Pukkala, E., Martikainen, R., Karjalainen, A., & Hietanen, P. (2005). Employment status of Finnish cancer patients in 1997. *Psycho-Oncology, 14,* 221–226.

Thoits, P. A. (1986). Social support as coping assistance. *Journal of Consulting and Clinical Psychology, 54,* 416–423.

Verdecchia, A., Francisci, S., Brenner, H., Gatta, G., Micheli, A., Mangone, L., & Kunkler, I. (2007). Recent cancer survival in Europe: A 2000–02 period analysis of EUROCARE-4 data. *Lancet Oncology, 8,* 784–796.

Wynn, P. (2009). Employment and the common cancers: Overview. *Occupational Medicine, 59,* 369–372.

Yarker, J., Munir, F., Bains, M., Kalawsky, K., & Haslam, C. (2009). The role of communication and support in return to work following cancer-related absence. *Psycho-Oncology, 19,* 1078–1085.

Yun, Y. H., Rhee, Y. S., Kang, I. O., Lee, J. S., Bang, S. M., Lee, W. S., Kim, J. S., Kim, S. Y., Shin, S. W., & Hong, Y. S. (2005). Economic burdens and quality of life of family caregivers of cancer patients. *Oncology, 68,* 107–114.

# 11

# Lead Well, Be Well

## *Leadership Behaviors Influence Employee Wellbeing*

### Jennifer Robertson
Western University, Canada

### Julian Barling
Queen's University, Canada

## Introduction

The notion that a bad boss can cause undue stress is not new. Indeed, millions of workers come home from work each day and complain to their families and friends about their dreaded boss. Comments such as "My boss is driving me crazy" and "My boss will drive me to drink" are legendary, as bad bosses and their negative effects are commonplace. The ubiquity of bad bosses is frequently reflected in North American popular culture. Starting in the 1990s, for example, Scott Adams' satiric cartoon strip "Dilbert" parodied the effects of bad leadership, and became widely popular. More recently, TV shows and movies, such as *The Office* and *Horrible Bosses*, have been very well received. Similarly, there has been a tremendous focus on poor management within the professional world, such that a plethora of mainstream books have surfaced. Titles such as *A survival guide for working with bad bosses: Dealing with bullies, idiots, back-stabbers, and other managers from hell* (Scott, 2006) and Robert Sutton's (2007) popular *The no asshole rule: Building a civilized workplace and surviving one that isn't* eloquently make the point.

*Work and Wellbeing: Wellbeing: A Complete Reference Guide*, Volume III.
Edited by Peter Y. Chen and Cary L. Cooper.
© 2014 John Wiley & Sons, Ltd. Published 2014 by John Wiley & Sons, Inc.
DOI: 10.1002/9781118539415.wbwell11

As the attention paid to bad bosses has increased, so too has the availability of resources to cope with the negative effects of poor leadership. Typing "coping with a bad boss" into google.com results in about 230,000 results that range from websites such as individual blogs to wiki "how-to" guides, YouTube videos, and online magazine and news articles. There is even a website with the domain name www.badbossology.com. Suffice it to say, employees are plagued by bad bosses whose negative effects on employee wellbeing has resulted in an explosion of interest in this topic.

## Academic Focus on Leadership and Employee Wellbeing

All of this attention has been paralleled by considerable interest from researchers in general on the nature and effects of bad leadership, and this interest has been especially pronounced within the fields of occupational health psychology and organizational behavior. However, while it is obviously important to understand the detrimental effects of leadership, a complete understanding of the effects of leadership requires that we also ask whether positive leadership has a positive effect on employee wellbeing, and research on this question is in its infancy. Accordingly, the purpose of this chapter is to review the literature that links both poor and good leadership to employee wellbeing. Specifically, we begin by considering the empirical evidence for any negative effects of poor leadership on employee wellbeing. We then turn our attention to the brighter side of management, and consider whether positive leadership styles can positively affect employee wellbeing. Thereafter, we conclude by providing directions for future research on the effects of positive leadership on employee wellbeing. In all cases, we have reached the point where there are simply too many studies to allow for a discussion of every available study; instead of inclusiveness, our discussion is guided by ensuring that general lessons from research are appropriately highlighted.

## Construct Definitions

Before embarking on our substantive discussion, we pause briefly to clarify the primary constructs under discussion. First, defining leadership is difficult to say the least, not because of the absence of any definitions, but because of the plethora of available definitions. For this chapter, we follow Kelloway and Barling (2010) and define leadership as "a process of social influence that is enacted by designated individuals who hold formal leadership roles in organizations" (p. 261). Categorizing leadership as positive or negative is often accomplished by focusing on its outcomes. Eschewing this circular and amoral approach, we consider transformational leadership to reflect a positive style because of its foundation in positive values and focus on the development of employees. In contrast, abusive supervision and laissez-faire reflect poor leadership because they consist of leadership behaviors that are abusive toward, or dismissive of, employees.

Second, like leadership, wellbeing suffers from a glut of broad and diverse definitions (Danna & Griffin, 1999). Thus, in this chapter we follow Sivanathan, Arnold, Turner, and Barling (2004) and define wellbeing as comprising physical (e.g., general health, occupational safety, health-related behaviors) and psychological (e.g., mental illness, stress, self-efficacy, self-esteem, affective wellbeing) health at work.

## Leadership and Employee Wellbeing

Kelloway and Barling (2010) suggest that leaders can affect their subordinates' wellbeing through several different paths: (a) they serve as role models for their subordinates and can model (un)healthy and (un)safe working practices; (b) leaders' power to reward or punish their subordinates assumes a considerable importance for employee wellbeing; and (c) the decision leaders make can produce additional stress for their subordinates (e.g., assigning an abundance of tasks to one employee can result in role overload), or as we will emphasize, enhance the quality of their work experiences. It is through these mechanisms that leaders affect employees' wellbeing, and there is a substantial body of literature supporting this claim. For example, one recent meta-analysis found that specific leadership styles were related to employee stress and affective wellbeing (Skakon, Nielsen, Borg, & Guzman, 2010). Similarly, another meta-analysis reported a moderate positive relationship between (a) good leadership styles (e.g., considerate, supportive and transformational leadership) and employee psychological wellbeing, and (b) a negative relationship with decreased sick absences and disability pensions (Kuoppala, Lamminpaa, Liira, & Vainio, 2008). Collectively, these meta-analyses offer considerable empirical support for the link between leadership styles and employee wellbeing. We first turn our attention to the literature that links poor management to impaired employee wellbeing.

## Abusive Supervision

Abusive supervision has attracted increasing empirical attention ever since Tepper first defined it as "subordinates' perceptions of the extent to which supervisors engage in the sustained display of hostile verbal and nonverbal behaviors, excluding physical contact" (Tepper, 2000, p. 178). Leaders exhibit abusive leadership behaviors when they publicly ridicule subordinates, blame subordinates for mistakes they are not responsible for (Tepper, Duffy, & Shaw, 2001), and/or intimidate and call subordinates derogatory names (Keashly, 1998). There are now sufficient studies from which we can draw substantive conclusions about the effects of abusive supervision on employees.

### Employees' Physical Wellbeing

Empirical evidence suggests that abusive leaders negatively impact diverse aspects of employee physical wellbeing, including their overall general health, their sleep, and their health risk and safety behaviors. Research now tends to focus on the moderators and mediators of these relationships. For example, a recent study found that the negative relationship between abusive supervision and employees' general physical health was moderated by perceived responsibility, such that it was weaker for those who felt they were personally responsibly for the abusive behavior (Bowling & Michel, 2011). Bamberger and Bacharach (2006) showed that abusive supervision was positively linked to subordinate problem drinking. Consistent with a resistance-based explanation (i.e., employees engage in drinking behaviors as a form of covert resistance to their supervisor), these authors also found that the relationship between abusive supervision and employee problem drinking was moderated by employee personality, such that the relationship was attenuated for employees high in conscientiousness and/or agreeableness. Examining employees' sleep, Rafferty, Restubog, and Jimmieson (2010) reported an indirect relationship between leaders' abusive behaviors and subordinate insomnia; specifically, abusive supervision affected employee insomnia through subordinates' psychological distress.

Although it is scant, research has also focused on abusive supervision and employee safety behaviors. For example, in a qualitative study based on employees whose work posed a moderate risk for injury, Mullen (2004) identified abusive supervision behaviors (e.g., ridicule, intimidation) as a

238

determinant of unsafe employee behaviors, including failure to use safety equipment. Mullen and Fiset (2008) subsequently refined this finding, showing that abusive supervision negatively impacted employees' safety participation, and that this relationship was mediated by perceptions of safety climate.

## Employees' Psychological Wellbeing

The negative effects of abusive supervision extend well beyond physical wellbeing to include effects on employees' psychological wellbeing. For example, early research found some support for a positive link between leaders' abusive behaviors and employee frustration, stress, and helplessness (Ashforth, 1997). Subsequently, three studies demonstrated a positive link between abusive supervision and aspects of employee psychological distress (e.g., anxiety, depression, emotional exhaustion; Rafferty et al., 2010; Restubog, Scott, & Zagenczyk, 2011; Tepper, 2000). Research also showed that this relationship was (a) mediated by organizational justice, (b) moderated by job mobility, such that it was stronger for employees with less job mobility (Tepper, 2000) and who thus may feel they cannot leave their jobs, and (c) also moderated by employee self-esteem, such that it was stronger for employees with high self-esteem (Rafferty et al., 2010).

Focusing on different psychological outcomes, other data suggests that abusive supervision is related to employees' general life satisfaction (Bowling & Michel, 2011; Tepper, 2000), self-efficacy, and somatic complaints, such as headaches, dry mouth, and clammy hands (Duffy, Ganster, & Pagon, 2002). With respect to self-efficacy and somatic complaints, Duffy et al. (2002) found that supervisors' social undermining was negatively related to subordinate self-efficacy and positively related to employee somatic complaints, and these relationships were stronger than the relationship between supervisor support, self-efficacy, and somatic complaints. These authors also found that employees whose supervisor demonstrated both social undermining and positive support had the lowest levels of self-efficacy and the most somatic complaints. In a similar vein, data from experimental research replicated these general findings, by showing a negative effect between abusive supervision and state self-esteem, especially for females (Burton & Hoobler, 2006).

Finally, research has linked leaders' abusive behaviors to employee burnout as an indicator of psychological wellbeing. For example, Yagil

(2006) showed a relationship between abusive supervision and two indicators of burnout (e.g., emotional exhaustion and depersonalization), and Grandey, Kern, and Frone (2007) found a link between supervisor verbal abuse and job-related exhaustion. Harvey, Stoner, Hochwarter, and Kacmar (2007) replicated the relationship between abusive supervision and emotional exhaustion, but showed that this relationship was buffered by employee ingratiation (i.e., tactics used to advance personal interests) and positive affect. More recently, Wu and Hu (2009) found that the positive relationship between abusive supervision and employee emotional exhaustion was intensified for employees susceptible to emotional contagion, and surprisingly, when coworker support was high. Taken together, these studies provide strong support for the negative relationship between abusive supervision and various aspects of employees' physical and psychological wellbeing.

## Laissez-Faire Leadership

In contrast to abusive supervision, in which leaders actively display hostile behaviors, laissez-faire leadership is a passive management style in which leaders are disengaged, and often avoid and deny responsibility even in the face of dire situations (Bass & Riggio, 2006). Although it seems logical to assume that a lack of leadership would be neither positively nor negatively related to employee wellbeing, research findings suggests otherwise, and there are several reasons for this. Specifically, as data shows, laissez-faire leadership negatively impacts employees' physical wellbeing because it decreases employees' awareness of safety issues (e.g., safety consciousness) and their perceptions that safety behaviors are rewarded and supported (e.g., safety climate; Kelloway, Mullen, & Francis, 2006). Laissez-faire leadership also negatively impacts employees' psychological wellbeing because it increases workplace stressors (e.g., role conflict, role ambiguity, and conflict with coworkers) and bullying at work (Skogstad, Einarsen, Torsheim, Aasland, & Hetland, 2007), and decreases trust in leaders (Kelloway, Turner, Barling, & Loughlin, 2012).

### Employees' Physical Wellbeing

Largely as a function of the research conducted by Kelloway and his colleagues, we now know that there is a link between laissez-faire leadership and

240

different aspects of employees' occupational safety. In their earlier research, Kelloway et al. (2006) showed that safety-specific passive leadership (i.e., laissez-faire leadership) was indirectly related to an increase in safety-related events and employee injuries through employees' safety consciousness and perceptions of safety climate. They also demonstrated that safety-specific passive leadership accounted for significantly more variance than safety-specific transformational leadership in safety-related events and injuries. Mullen, Kelloway, and Teed (2011) replicated and extended these earlier findings by showing that leaders' *inconsistent* leadership (defined as the interaction of safety-specific transformational and passive leadership) was associated with employees' reports of lower levels of safety behaviors than employees whose leaders exhibited safety-specific transformational leadership, or safety-specific laissez-faire leadership.

## Employees' Psychological Wellbeing

Somewhat similar to the effects on employee physical safety, most of the research shows negative effects of laissez-faire leadership on employee psychological wellbeing. Skogstad et al. (2007) found that laissez-faire leadership was indirectly linked to employee psychological distress through bullying at work and workplace stressors. Similarly, Kelloway and colleagues (2012) showed more recently that laissez-faire leadership was negatively related to employee psychological wellbeing, and that this relationship was mediated by lower trust in the leader. Examining emotional exhaustion, Kanste, Kyngas, and Nikkila (2007) demonstrated that laissez-faire leadership was positively related to emotional exhaustion and negatively related to a sense of personal accomplishment (both indicators of burnout), and that these relationships were stronger for temporary nursing staff and nurses in supervisory positions. Likewise, Hetland, Sandal, and Johnsen (2007) found that passive–avoidant leadership was positively related to the emotional exhaustion and cynicism indicators of burnout.

In contrast, data from a study on public high school teachers and principals yielded no association between laissez-faire leadership and burnout (Mazur & Lynch, 1989). Similarly, no relationship emerged between laissez-faire leadership and job-related stress amongst a sample of mentor–protégé dyads in Sosik and Godshalk's (2000) study.

In sum, there is a large body of well-designed empirical research linking poor management to lower levels of employee wellbeing. Despite support for these relationships, several questions emerge. First, the corollary does not necessarily hold true: Just because poor leadership results in poor employee wellbeing, we cannot take for granted that high-quality leadership will be positively associated with employees' wellbeing; it is possible that poor leadership has negative effects, but positive leadership has no effects on employee wellbeing. Second, focusing solely on negative leadership cannot provide a comprehensive understanding of both the negative *and* positive effects of leadership on employee wellbeing. Shifting explicit attention to positive leadership fundamentally raises a new set of questions, which are beginning to attract empirical scrutiny, and we now turn our attention to this issue. More specifically, as transformational leadership has been considered the closest management style to positive leadership (Liu, Siu, & Shi, 2010), research is now focusing on whether transformational leadership exerts any positive effects on employees' wellbeing.

## Transformational Leadership

Since Burns' (1978) and Bass's (1985) early work, transformational leadership has received widespread scholarly attention, such that it has become the most widely studied of all leadership theories in the last 20 years (Barling, Christie, & Hoption, 2011). Transformational leadership includes four behaviors: idealized influence, inspirational motivation, intellectual stimulation, and individualized consideration (Bass & Riggio, 2006). Transformational leadership is inherently positive because of its focus on ethical behavior (idealized influence), elevating employees' motivation (inspirational motivation), encouraging and allowing employees to think for themselves (intellectual stimulation), and demonstrating real concern for individuals' needs (individualized consideration). It is through these positive behaviors that transformational leaders positively affect employee wellbeing, and there are several reasons why these leaders have these effects. For example, transformational leaders provide role clarity (Nielsen, Randall, Yarker, & Brenner, 2008), meaningful work (Arnold, Turner, Barling, Kelloway, & McKee, 2007), and enable employees to develop self-efficacy (Nielsen & Munir, 2009; Nielsen, Yarker, Randall, & Munir, 2009) and trust in their leaders (Kelloway et al., 2012), all of which positively impact employee wellbeing.

## Employees' Physical Wellbeing

Extending our understanding of the effects of leadership on physical well-being, research has investigated whether transformational leadership is associated with aspects of occupational safety. Within this research, findings consistently demonstrate a link between transformational leadership and employee safety. For example, Zohar (2002) showed that the preventative action subdimension of safety climate mediated this link, and that the link between transformational leadership and preventative action was moderated by assigned safety priority, such that transformational leadership was more strongly related to employee safety when the organization assigned low priority to safety. Later, Inness, Turner, Barling, and Stride (2010) demonstrated that transformational leadership was positively related to subordinates' safety participation among a sample of "moonlighters" (i.e., individuals who simultaneously work two different jobs and have two different supervisors); however, these effects did not spill over between jobs.

Unlike the vast majority of research on transformational leadership, research on transformational leadership and subordinate safety has also investigated the effects of safety-specific transformational leadership, in which the behaviors involved in transformational leadership focus specifically on positive safety practices (Mullen & Kelloway, 2009). Two studies initially showed that safety-specific transformational leadership was indirectly linked to a reduction in safety events and injuries though its positive effects on individual safety consciousness and perceptions of safety climate (Barling, Loughlin, & Kelloway, 2002; Kelloway et al., 2006). More recently, Conchie and Donald (2009) found that the relationship between safety-specific transformational leadership and employees' safety citizenship behaviors was moderated by safety-specific trust, while Conchie, Taylor, and Donald (2012) reported that the relationship between safety-specific transformational leadership and employees' safety voice behaviors was sequentially mediated by affect-based trust beliefs and disclosure trust intentions. However, the relationship between disclosure of trust intentions and safety voice behaviors was only significant when employees' intentions to rely on their leaders were moderate to high. Finally, Mullen and Kelloway (2009) have shown that safety-specific transformational leadership can be taught.

Intriguingly, there seems to have been no research investigating whether transformational leadership is associated with other indicators of positive physical wellbeing. At least two reasons might account for this. First, as is evident from media attention and popular culture, it is far more appealing to ask whether negative leadership hurts people. Second, the dominant focus within occupational health psychology and work stress research remains on the effects of negative work experiences on ill-health, or the absence of ill-health.

## Employees' Psychological Wellbeing

Scholars have also focused their attention on understanding the beneficial effect of transformational leadership on a variety of psychological wellbeing indicators. For example, Sosik and Godshalk (2000) examined the effect of transformational leadership on job-related stress, and showed that when mentors exhibited transformational leadership, protégés' job-related stress was reduced, especially when protégés received social support. Similarly, a study on employees from two Chinese cities focused on perceived work stress and general stress symptoms, and found that transformational leadership was negatively and indirectly related to these psychological wellbeing indicators through employees' trust in their leader and self-efficacy. In contrast, Arnold and colleagues (2007) focused on positive affective wellbeing and mental health as indicators of psychological wellbeing. Data from their two studies supported both a partially and fully mediated model, in which transformational leadership was directly and indirectly related to employee positive affective wellbeing and mental health, through its effect on employees' perceptions of having meaningful work. Three other studies also focused on mental health as an indicator of psychological health, and showed that transformational leadership was directly related to reduced depressive symptoms (Munir, Nielsen, & Gomes Carneiro, 2010), and indirectly related to employee mental health through its positive effects on employees' sense of community in the workplace (McKee, Driscoll, Kelloway, & Kelley, 2011) and trust in their leader (Kelloway et al., 2012).

Focusing on affective wellbeing as an indicator of psychological wellbeing, there is a consistent and positive link between transformational leadership and employee affective wellbeing. For example, health-care workers whose leaders rated high on transformational leadership experienced more positive emotions (e.g., optimism, happiness, enthusiasm) throughout the day compared to their counterparts whose leaders did not rate high on transformational leadership (Bono, Foldes, Vinson, & Muros, 2007). Partially replicating Arnold and colleagues' (2007) findings, other research has shown that the relationship between transformational leadership and employees' affective wellbeing is partially mediated by meaningful work (Nielsen et al., 2008) and perceived work characteristics (e.g., role clarity, meaningfulness, and opportunities for development; Nielsen, Yarker, Brenner, Randall, & Borg, 2008), and fully mediated by self-efficacy and team efficacy (Nielsen & Munir, 2009; Nielsen et al., 2009). Likewise, a longitudinal study on Swedish social service workers revealed that the positive effects of transformational leadership on affective wellbeing were fully mediated by climate for innovation (Tafvelin, Armelius, & Westerberg, 2011). Clearly, transformational leadership is associated with opportunities for positive work experiences for employees, which result in psychological wellbeing.

The positive effects of transformational leadership extend to include effects on employee burnout. Although one study failed to find a negative relationship between transformational leadership and emotional exhaustion (Stordeur, D'hoore, & Vandenberghe, 2001), several other studies provide support for this relationship. In particular, Kanste and colleagues (2007) found that transformational leadership prevented nurses, especially temporary nursing staff, from experiencing emotional exhaustion, while Hetland and colleagues (2007) reported that transformational leadership prevented two components of burnout (e.g., high cynicism and low professional efficacy) among employees working in an information technology firm. Further, a study on senior managers from an Australian law-enforcement organization showed that inspirational motivation (one of the behaviors comprising transformational leadership) was negatively related to the emotional exhaustion and depersonalization indicators of burnout, and positively related to the personal accomplishment indicator (Densten, 2005).

All these studies have focused on transformational leadership as a unidimensional construct. However, focusing on the individual components of transformational leadership is equally important, as they might exert different effects on different aspects of employee wellbeing (Franke & Felfe, 2011), and a couple of studies have investigated the differential effects of the individual components. Specifically, one study found that after controlling for idealized influence and individualized consideration, intellectual stimulation was related to an increase in burnout symptoms (Seltzer, Numerof, & Bass, 1989). Separately, research has shown that individualized consideration and idealized influence (attributed) were negatively related to employees' perceptions of strain, and that idealized influence (behavior) was positively related to strain (Franke & Felfe, 2011). Nonetheless, focusing on the individual components limits the extent we can learn from these studies. First, there are still very few studies addressing these relationships.

Second, different aspects of idealized influence (attributed versus behavior) were assessed in this research. Third, the consistently high relationships yielded between the four transformational leadership components (Barling et al., 2011) substantially limit our ability to make independent conclusions about their separate effects. Fourth, while the consequences of intellectual stimulation are indeed negative in the short term, there may be positive benefits in the long term as employees become accustomed to a style of leadership that challenges them.

## Looking to the Future

As research turns its attention toward understanding the positive or "bright" side of leadership and employee wellbeing, the potential for future research in this area is virtually unlimited, and we conclude this chapter by offering several avenues for future research. First, while research has focused appropriately on identifying moderators and mediators, more longitudinal and experimental research is now needed to enable causal inferences in the relationship between transformational leadership and employee wellbeing. Second, based on consistent evidence that leadership development initiatives influence leadership skills and behaviors (e.g., Avolio, Reichard, Hannah, Walumbwa, & Chan, 2009), we echo Kelloway and Barling's (2010) call for future research to investigate whether leadership development initiatives influence not only employee performance (Barling, Weber, & Kelloway, 1996), but also diverse aspects of employee wellbeing. Third, we suggest that future research begin to investigate the antecedents of the specific leadership styles that affect employee wellbeing in the first place. One possibility is that leaders' own wellbeing influences whether they will provide positive or negative leadership to their employees in the first instance (e.g., Dionisi et al., 2013), which in turn, influence employees' wellbeing. Understanding why leaders engage in transformational leadership or abusive supervision, or are generally disengaged (laissez-faire leadership) is certainly worthy of empirical attention, and research should now be extended to include leaders' own wellbeing as an antecedent.

Extending our focus to leaders' own wellbeing, future research should also investigate whether engaging in positive behaviors may be beneficial for the leaders themselves, and consequently, influence the leadership behaviors they enact. For example, some research has shown that apologizing after a transgression is positively associated with leaders' own wellbeing (Byrne, Barling, & Dupré, 2013), while other data suggests that engaging in pro-environmental initiatives (e.g., reducing consumption) might have positive effects on individuals' wellbeing (Swim, Clayton, & Howard, 2011). Extending these findings, future research should investigate the indirect relationships between apologies and workplace pro-environmental behaviors (Robertson & Barling, 2013) and various leadership styles.

Last, a general comment is in order. Constraints in writing a chapter of this nature preclude us from discussing all manifestations of positive leadership. As but one example, there is a very large body of research on the effects of what is often referred to as "supervisor support" and employee wellbeing, with findings consistently showing a positive effect (Kelloway & Barling, 2010; Kuoppala et al., 2008). Future research might profitably investigate whether different aspects of positive (e.g., supervisor support, LMX) or negative leadership cumulatively exert additive, exacerbating, or inuring (Raver & Nishii, 2010) effects on wellbeing. Likewise, understanding the possible effects of both positive and negative leadership styles simultaneously, either from the same or different leaders, should be a goal of future research.

## Conclusion

An overwhelming number of employees must work with a bad boss on a daily basis, and research over several decades has helped to identify the negative consequences of different aspects of poor leadership. Nonetheless, knowing this cannot tell us whether exposure to positive leadership behaviors enhances employees' wellbeing. Recently, research has started to identify beneficial effects of transformational leadership on employee wellbeing; however, research needs to expand our understanding of the effects of positive leadership, as well as our understanding of leaders' own wellbeing. As research moves in these directions, a more comprehensive understanding of leadership will emerge, new questions will open for researchers, and new opportunities will be presented for organizations looking to benefit their employees and themselves.

## References

Arnold, K. A., Turner, N., Barling, J., Kelloway, E. K., & McKee, M. C. (2007). Transformational leadership and psychological well-being: The mediating role of meaningful work. *Journal of Occupational Health Psychology, 12,* 193–203.

Ashforth, B. E. (1997). Petty tyranny in organizations. A preliminary examination of antecedents and consequences. *Canadian Journal of Administrative Sciences*, *14*, 126–140.

Avolio, B. J., Reichard, R. J., Hannah, S. T., Walumbwa, F. O., & Chan, A. (2009). A meta-analytic review of leadership impact research: Experimental and quasi-experimental studies. *The Leadership Quarterly*, *20*, 764–784.

Bamberger, P., & Bacharach, S. (2006). Abusive supervision and subordinate problem drinking: Taking resistance, stress and subordinate personality into account. *Human Relations*, *59*, 723–752.

Barling, J., Christie, A., & Hoption, C. (2011). Leadership. In S. Zedeck (Ed.), *APA handbook of industrial and organizational psychology*. Vol. 1: *Building and developing the organization* (pp. 183–240). Washington, DC: American Psychological Association.

Barling, J., Loughlin, C., & Kelloway, E. K. (2002). Development and test of a model linking safety-specific transformational leadership and occupational safety. *Journal of Applied Psychology*, *87*, 488–496.

Barling, J., Weber, T., & Kelloway, E. K. (1996). Effects of transformational leadership training on attitudinal and financial outcomes: A field experiment. *Journal of Applied Psychology*, *81*, 827–832.

Bass, B. M. (1985). *Leadership and performance beyond expectations*. New York: Free Press.

Bass, B. M., & Riggio, R. E. (2006). *Transformational leadership* (2nd ed.). Hillsdale, NJ: Erlbaum.

Bono, J. E., Foldes, H. J., Vinson, G., & Muros, J. P. (2007). Workplace emotions: The role of supervision and leadership. *Journal of Applied Psychology*, *92*, 1357–1367.

Bowling, N. A., & Michel, J. S. (2011). Why do you treat me badly? The role of attributions regarding the cause of abuse in subordinates' responses to abusive supervision. *Work & Stress*, *25*, 309–320.

Burns, J. M. (1978). *Leadership*. New York: Harper & Row.

Burton, J., & Hoobler, J. (2006). Subordinate self-esteem and abusive supervision. *Journal of Managerial Issues*, *18*, 340–355.

Byrne, A., Barling, J., & Dupré, K. E. (2013). Leader apologies and employee and leader well-being. *Journal of Business Ethics*, DOI: 10.1007/s10551-013-1685-3.

Conchie, S. M., & Donald, I. J. (2009). The moderating role of safety-specific trust on the relation between safety-specific leadership and safety citizenship behaviors. *Journal of Occupational Health Psychology*, *14*, 137–147.

Conchie, S. M., Taylor, P. J., & Donald, I. J. (2012). Promoting safety voice with safety-specific transformational leadership: The mediating role of two dimensions of trust. *Journal of Occupational Health Psychology*, *17*, 105–115.

Danna, K., & Griffin, R. W. (1999). Health and well-being in the workplace: A review and synthesis of the literature. *Journal of Management*, *25*, 357–384.

Densten, I. L. (2005). The relationship between visioning behaviors of leaders and follower burnout. *British Journal of Management*, *16*, 105–118.

Dionisi, A., Byrne, A., Barling, J., Bergenwall, A., Robertson, J. L., Lys, R., Dupre, K., & Wylie, J. (2013). The depleted leader: The influence of leaders' diminished psychological resources on leadership behaviors. *The Leadership Quarterly* (in press).

Duffy, M. K., Ganster, D. C., & Pagon, M. (2002). Social undermining in the workplace. *The Academy of Management Journal, 45,* 331–351.

Franke, F., & Felfe, J. (2011). How does transformational leadership impact employees' psychological strain? Examining differentiated effects and the moderating role of affective organizational commitment. *Leadership, 7,* 295–316.

Grandey, A. A., Kern, J. H., & Frone, M. R. (2007). Verbal abuse from outsiders versus insiders: Comparing frequency, impact on emotional exhaustion, and the role of emotional labor. *Journal of Occupational Health Psychology, 12,* 63–79.

Harvey, P., Stoner, J., Hochwarter, W., & Kacmar, C. (2007). Coping with abusive supervision: The neutralizing effects of ingratiation and positive affect on negative employee outcomes. *The Leadership Quarterly, 18,* 264–280.

Hetland, H., Sandal, G. M., & Johnsen, T. B. (2007). Burnout in the information technology sector: Does leadership matter? *European Journal of Work and Organizational Psychology, 16,* 58–75.

Inness, M., Turner, N., Barling, J., & Stride, C. B. (2010). Transformational leadership and employee safety performance: A within-person, between-jobs design. *Journal of Occupational Health Psychology, 15,* 279–290.

Kanste, O., Kyngas, H., & Nikkila, J. (2007). The relationship between multidimensional leadership and burnout among nursing staff. *Journal of Nursing Management, 15,* 731–739.

Keashly, L. (1998). Emotional abuse in the workplace: Conceptual and empirical issues. *Journal of Emotional Abuse, 1,* 85–117.

Kelloway, E. K., & Barling, J. (2010). Leadership development as an intervention in occupational health psychology. *Work & Stress, 24,* 260–279.

Kelloway, E. K., Mullen, J., & Francis, L. (2006). Divergent effects of transformational and passive leadership on employee safety. *Journal of Occupational Health Psychology, 11,* 76–86.

Kelloway, E. K., Turner, N., Barling, J., Loughlin, C. (2012). Transformational leadership, transactional leadership and employee psychological well-being: The mediating role of trust. *Work & Stress, 26,* 39–55.

Kuoppala, J., Lamminpaa, A., Liira, J., & Vainio, H. (2008). Leadership, job well-being, and health effects: A systematic review and meta-analysis. *Journal of Occupational and Environmental Medicine, 60,* 904–915.

Liu, J., Siu, O., & Shi, K. (2010). Transformational leadership and employee well-being: The mediating role of trust in the leader and self-efficacy. *Applied Psychology, 59,* 454–479.

Mazur, P. J., & Lynch, M. D. (1989). Differential impact of administrative, organizational, and personality factors on teacher burnout. *Teaching and Teacher Education, 5,* 337–353.

McKee, M. C., Driscoll, C., Kelloway, E. K., & Kelley, E. (2011). Exploring linkages among transformational leadership, workplace spirituality and well-being in health care workers. *Journal of Management, Spirituality & Religion, 8,* 233–255.

Mullen, J. (2004). Investigating factors that influence individual safety behavior at work. *Journal of Safety Research, 35,* 275–285.

Mullen, J. E., & Fiset, J. (2008). *The effects of abusive suspension on employee occupational health and safety outcomes.* Paper presented at the 9th World Conference an Injury Prevention and Safety promotion. Merida, Mexico.

Mullen, J. E., & Kelloway, E. K. (2009). Safety leadership: A longitudinal study of the effects of transformational leadership on safety outcomes. *Journal of Occupational and Organizational Psychology, 82,* 253–272.

Mullen, J., Kelloway, E. K., & Teed, M. (2011). Inconsistent style of leadership as a predictor of safety behaviour. *Work & Stress, 25,* 41–54.

Munir, F., Nielsen, K., & Gomes Carneiro, I. (2010). Transformational leadership and depressive symptoms: A prospective study. *Journal of Affective Disorders, 120,* 235–239.

Nielsen, K., & Munir, F. (2009). How do transformational leaders influence followers' affective well-being? Exploring the mediating role of self-efficacy. *Work & Stress, 23,* 313–329.

Nielsen, K., Randall, R., Yarker, J., & Brenner, S. (2008). The effects of transformational leadership on followers' perceived work characteristics and psychological well-being: A longitudinal study. *Work & Stress, 22,* 16–32.

Nielsen, K., Yarker, J., Brenner, S., Randall, R., & Borg, V. (2008). The importance of transformational leadership style for the well-being of employees working with older people. *Journal of Advanced Nursing, 63,* 465–475.

Nielsen, K., Yarker, J., Randall, R., & Munir, F. (2009). The mediating effects of team and self-efficacy on the relationship between transformational leadership, and job satisfaction and psychological well-being in healthcare professionals: A cross-sectional questionnaire survey. *International Journal of Nursing Studies, 46,* 1236–1244.

Rafferty, A. E., Restubog, S. L. D., & Jimmieson, N. L. (2010). Losing sleep: Examining the cascading effects of supervisors' experience of injustice on subordinate's psychological health. *Work & Stress, 24,* 36–55.

Raver, J. L., & Nishii, L. H. (2010). Once, twice, or three times as harmful? Ethnic harassment, gender harassment, and generalized workplace harassment. *Journal of Applied Psychology, 95,* 236–254.

Restubog, S. L. D., Scott, K. L., & Zagenczyk, T. J. (2011). When distress hits home: The role of contextual factors and psychological distress in predicting employees' responses to abusive supervision. *Journal of Applied Psychology, 96,* 713–729.

Robertson, J. L., & Barling, J. (2013). Greening organizations through leaders' influence on employees' pro-environmental behaviors. *Journal of Organizational Behavior, 34,* 176–194.

Scott, G. G. (2006). *A survival guide for working with bad bosses: Dealing with bullies, idiots, back-stabbers and other managers from hell*. New York: AMACOM.

Seltzer, J., Numerof, R. E., & Bass, B. M. (1989). Transformational leadership: Is it a source of more or less burnout or stress? *Journal of Health and Human Resources Administration, 12,* 174–185.

Sivanathan, N., Arnold, K. A., Turner, N., & Barling, J. (2004). Leading well: Transformational leadership and well-being. In A. Linley & S. Joseph (Eds.), *Positive psychology in practice* (pp. 241–255). New York: Wiley.

Skakon, J., Nielsen, K., Borg, V., & Guzman, J. (2010). Are leaders' well-being, behaviors, and style associated with the affective well-being of their employees? A systematic review of three decades of research. *Work & Stress, 24,* 107–139.

Skogstad, A., Einarsen, S., Torsheim, T., Aasland, M. S., & Hetland, H. (2007). The destructiveness of laissez-faire leadership behavior. *Journal of Occupational Health Psychology, 12,* 80–92.

Sosik, J. J., & Godshalk, V. M. (2000). Leadership styles, mentoring functions received, and job-related stress: A conceptual model and preliminary study. *Journal of Organizational Behavior, 21,* 365–390.

Stordeur, S., D'Hoore, W., & Vandenberghe, C. (2001). Leadership, organizational stress, and emotional exhaustion among hospital nursing staff. *Journal of Advanced Nursing, 35,* 533–542.

Sutton, R. I. (2007). *The no asshole rule: Building a civilized workplace and surviving one that isn't*. New York: Warner Business Books.

Swim, J. K., Clayton, S., & Howard, G. S. (2011). Human behavioral contributions to climate change: Psychological and contextual drivers. *American Psychologist, 66,* 251–264.

Tafvelin, S., Armelius, K., & Westerberg, K. (2011). Toward understanding the direct and indirect effects of transformational leadership on well-being: A longitudinal study. *Journal of Leadership & Organizational Studies, 18,* 480–492.

Tepper, B. J. (2000). Consequences of abusive supervision. *The Academy of Management Journal, 43,* 178–190.

Tepper, B. J., Duffy, M. K., & Shaw, J. D. (2001). Personality moderators of the relationship between abusive supervision and subordinates' resistance. *Journal of Applied Psychology, 86,* 974–983.

Wu, T., & Hu, C. (2009). Abusive supervision and employee emotional exhaustion. *Group & Organization Management, 34,* 143–169.

Yagil, D. (2006). The relationship of abusive and supportive workplace supervision to employee burnout and upward influence tactics. *Journal of Emotional Abuse, 6,* 49–65.

Zohar, D. (2002). The effects of leadership dimensions, safety climate, and assigned priorities on minor injuries in work groups. *Journal of Organizational Behavior, 23,* 75–92.

# 12

# Organizational Coping Strategies and Wellbeing

## Gordon Tinline and Matthew Smeed
### Robertson Cooper, U.K.

Coping strategies vary in terms of their range and stage of implementation. In terms of range they can be broad pan-organizational, through groups and teams, to individually specific interventions. The stage of use can be from the no symptom preventative to treatment application for highly stressed individuals. Figure 12.1 summarizes the range and stage dynamic in an adapted stressor–strain framework (Hurrell, Nelson, & Simmons, 1998).

Coping strategies are required at all stages of the stressor–strain chain. The later they are applied the narrower and more targeted they need to be. This chapter will provide an overview of coping strategies applied in organizations and summarize their practical benefits and limitations.

## Early-Stage Broad Strategies

In theory, if broad coping strategies were applied consistently across organizations there would be little or no need for more focused later stage interventions! In practice this never happens, primarily as a result of the variation that individuals experience cognitively and emotionally, and demonstrate behaviorally, when facing the same work pressures. Broad strategies intended to either block or remove organizational stressors or to mitigate their impact across the organization are essentially preventative, but need to

*Work and Wellbeing: Wellbeing: A Complete Reference Guide*, Volume III.
Edited by Peter Y. Chen and Cary L. Cooper.
© 2014 John Wiley & Sons, Ltd. Published 2014 by John Wiley & Sons, Inc.
DOI: 10.1002/9781118539415.wbwell12

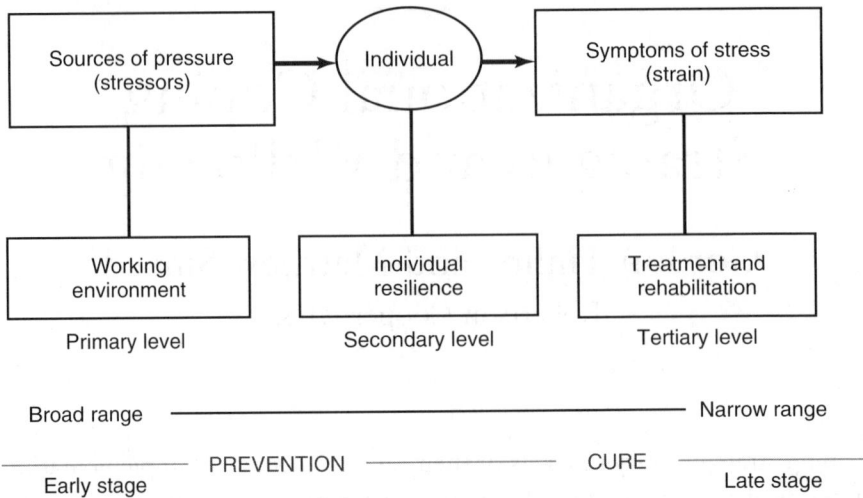

**Figure 12.1.** Range and Stage of Intervention.

be structured to tackle key sources of pressure. One model that categorizes organizational pressures and their impact is Robertson Cooper's 6 Essentials (http://www.robertsoncooper.com/what-we-do/the-6-essentials-of-workplace-well-being), as illustrated in Figure 12.2.

This model demonstrates the relationship between sources of pressure in organizations and their outcomes. When pressure in these areas is positive, or when employees are coping well with negative pressures, the outcome cycle will be positive, whereas when the 6 Essential pressures are more negative than positive, the manifestation is often negative outcomes. The 6 Essentials in this model are similar to stressors highlighted in other approaches such as the U.K. Health and Safety Executive's Stress Management Standards (see http://www.hse.gov.uk/stress/standards/). They are drawn from a shared and well-established research base on sources of pressure and work-related stress.

As a broad, early-stage strategy, organizations can consider what support is available to help all employees cope with work-related pressures. To illustrate this, consider two of the drivers in the 6 Essentials model: "balanced workload" and "job security and change." A common perception among managers can be that workloads are increasing exponentially and there is little that can be done to control this pressure. However, this position is essentially a form of learned helplessness (Abramson, Seligman, & Teasdale, 1978) that can and should be challenged. For example, when was the last

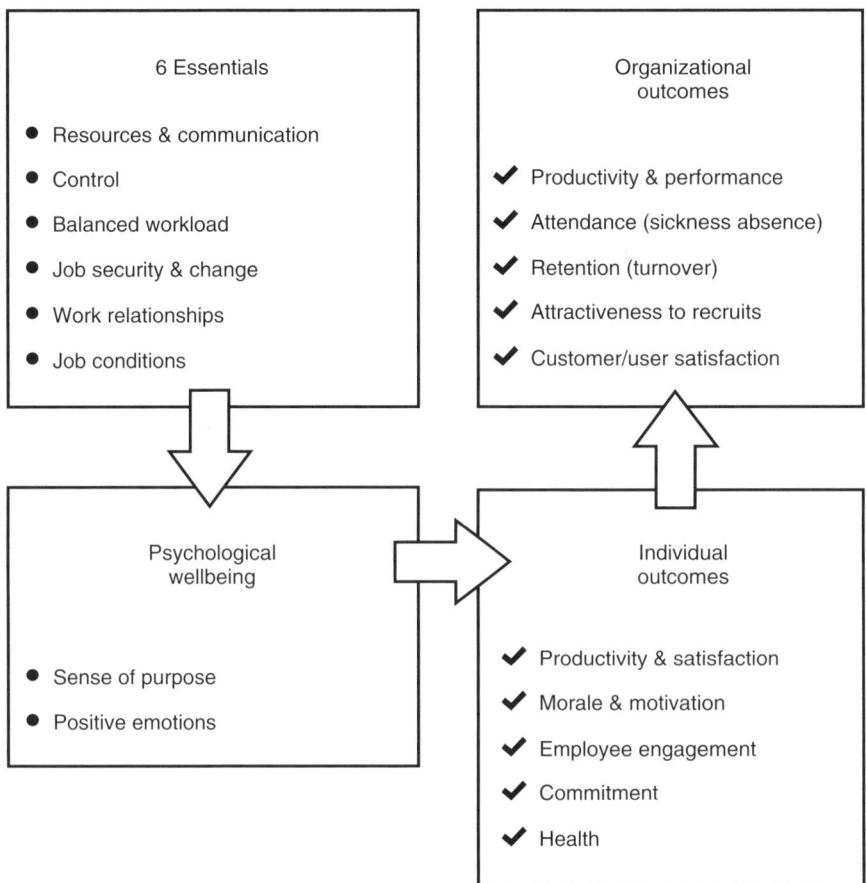

**Figure 12.2.** Robertson Cooper's 6 Essentials.

time the organization did a systematic review of its work distribution system (Kumar, Van Der Aalst, & Verbeek, 2001)? Many organizations seem to be at risk of burning out their best people by overloading them. Clearly there is a need for flexibility and adaptability in organizational systems; in most cases it would be suboptimal to design very rigid work planning procedures. Nevertheless, a complete lack of a systematic approach in this area is likely to be neither efficient nor maximally productive.

Economic uncertainty clearly has a major impact on perceived job security in many industry sectors at different times. However, organizations can play a role in mitigating this by actively managing to be more resilient to economic fluctuations and by sharing their approach to doing so with employees. In terms of major organizational change, such as restructuring or merger, effective change management and implementation can go some way to helping employees cope. Some senior managers and executives seem to take the view that the future is completely uncertain, therefore there is little that can be done to reassure employees that they have secure jobs. In some cases this may be true. However, it is more likely that there are a small number of discrete possible options likely to form the future for most organizations. Scenario planning around these in an open and transparent manner may help to reassure employees that although major change may occur this does not mean there is nothing that can be done to exert some control and cope with different possibilities.

Psychological wellbeing in the 6 Essentials model has two core components: "sense of purpose" and "positive emotions." The first of these is primarily related to goals. Being connected to goals that are clear and valued is important, not just for performance reasons but also because it influences aspects of self-worth such as self-efficacy (Mone, Baker, & Jeffries, 1995). Positive emotional experience is also a key aspect of psychological wellbeing and this is discussed below in relation to resilience. This is not just about having fun, although the value of that tends to be underrated! It can be about deeper emotions such as contentment and pride. Emotional experience is essentially the hedonic component of psychological wellbeing and sense of purpose the eudaimonic (Ryan & Deci, 2001). The 6 Essentials will have a direct impact on psychological wellbeing. For example, if relationships with colleagues are positive this is likely to make you feel happy but may also help you stay connected to your goals.

A range of individual and organizational outcomes are influenced by positive psychological wellbeing and the research base around these is fairly extensive (Robertson & Cooper, 2011). One area that has had a high profile in the last decade is employee engagement. Engagement is usually identified as motivated employees willingly releasing their discretionary effort. Data gathered using Robertson Cooper's ASSET tool shows that engagement levels are a significant predictor of productivity. However, engagement and psychological wellbeing in combination have a much stronger relationship with productivity than engagement alone (Robertson & Cooper, 2011, p. 36). Therefore, organizations focusing on improving employee engagement levels are likely to gain larger and more sustainable benefits from also improving psychological wellbeing.

# Mid-Stage Group and Individual Strategies

Mid-stage strategies are those implemented when strain is being experienced by groups and individuals, but this may not have resulted in high levels of severe stress. They tend to be more narrowly focused to specific groups and individuals rather than being intended to impact the whole organization. The focus is on active, rather than reactive, psycho-social coping skills.

There has been an increased emphasis in the last few years on the development of personal resilience. Resilience is the capacity to maintain work performance and wellbeing when facing challenging situations and to recover, or bounce back, from setbacks. There are likely to be a number of factors that influence personal resilience. For example, Dennis Charney (quoted by Milne, 2007) advocates a "resilience prescription" based on his research on factors that influence a resilient response, and argues that many of these can be developed as coping mechanisms. These include factors with a known link to personality, such as optimism (Wrosch & Scheier, 2003), as well as established coping techniques such as reframing through cognitive behavioral techniques or therapy (CBT) and social support. To some extent, the focus on resilience seems like a new label for established coping techniques. However, it differs in emphasis and also the extent to which it draws on newer trends in positive psychology.

Resilience is not a single quality or attribute which you either have or do not have. In terms of personality there are a number of different facets related to personal resilience. Robertson Cooper, using a "Big Five" personality factor approach, assesses four broad areas of personal resilience in their i-resilience model (www.robertsoncooper.com) (Figure 12.3).

As well as providing a diagnostic framework for understanding an individual's resilience strengths and risks, the model can be used as a structure for development. Each of the four areas in the model has a personality link but each can be improved through learning and development. For example, purposefulness can be improved by using goal-based motivational and coaching approaches. This could be an area to address, not just to improve coping skills but to focus on developing actively regardless of whether the individual is experiencing strain associated with a lack of purpose. As organizations expose people to greater levels of uncertainty and change, staying connected to a strong underlying purpose can not only help individuals cope but also improve their ability to react positively to change by being able to frame it anchored by their fundamental goals.

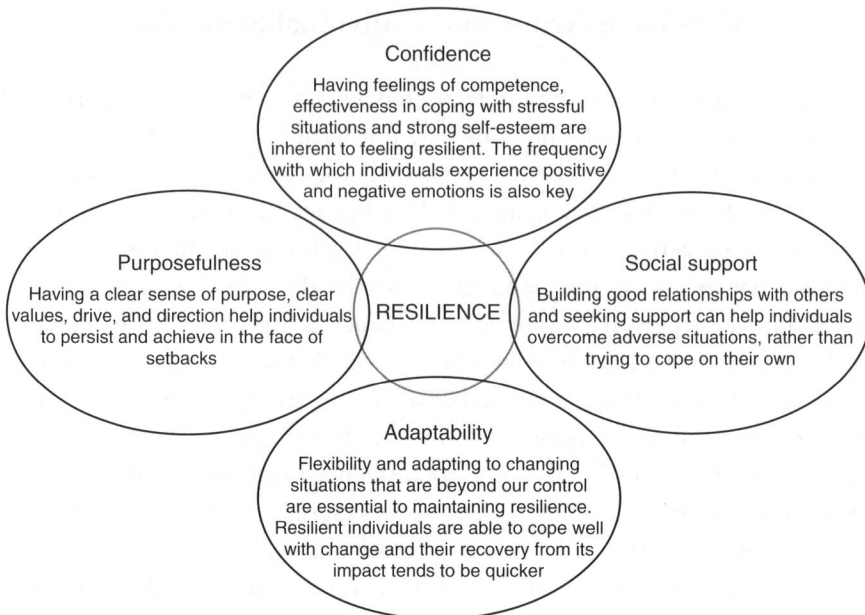

**Figure 12.3.** i-resilience Model.

The main contribution to resilience drawn from the work of positive psychologists such as Martin Seligman and Barbara Fredrickson is the emphasis on positive emotions and playing to strengths. A core argument behind the positive psychology movement is that we tend to underestimate the importance of positive experiences and their associated emotions. For example, Fredrickson (2001) argues that positive emotions broaden and build our thought–action repertoire. When we frequently experience emotions such as contentment and pride we open out in terms of our capacity to attend and respond to a wider range of stimuli (*broaden*) and as a result more effectively *build* personal resources (e.g., coping, problem solving).

The strengths approach (e.g., Luthans, 2002) advocated by positive psychologists can be used to help groups and individuals cope when facing negative hindrance pressures and to use positive challenge pressures as active learning experiences. The distinction between hindrance and challenge pressures or stressors is an important one (LePine, Podsakoff, & LePine, 2005). Hindrance pressures are viewed as barriers to learning and performance, whereas challenge pressures are job demands that are difficult, but are viewed as positive learning experiences and regarded as likely to bring positive outcomes when tackled. Hindrance pressures tend to lead to negative outcomes and challenge pressures to positive ones. For example, Rodell and Judge (2009) demonstrated that challenge pressures can increase attentiveness, which has a positive impact on citizenship behaviors. Focusing on strengths when facing hindrance and challenge pressures may bolster resilience in different ways.

We can spend a lot of time in organizations attending to what is not working and on trying to develop our weaknesses. To some extent this seems inevitable. We need to fix what is not working, particularly if it is job, career, or business critical. However, there is a risk that we spend so much time concentrating on failure that we do not understand and learn well from successes and the strengths that they can indicate. Playing to our strengths enables us to spend more time doing what we are naturally good at, which is very likely to stimulate positive emotions. When facing significant hindrance pressures or stressors, keeping some focus on drawing on what the team or individuals naturally do well is likely to be important in coping with the negative aspects.

## Late-Stage Narrow Strategies

When individuals are experiencing and exhibiting severe signs and symptoms of stress, targeted specific strategies usually need to be applied. These might include counselling, CBT, and other behavioral therapies. Such individual support is often provided in large organizations in the form of employee assistance programs (EAPs). Typically these provide a confidential gateway to counseling and other psychological therapies. There are a range of views regarding the effectiveness of EAPs and it is important to evaluate them well using relevant service provision criteria (Winwood & Beer, 2008). However, there is little doubt that they can provide access to useful individual support for employees experiencing stress symptoms. One advantage of EAPs is that they usually provide support for those dealing with stressors that are not work related or only partially so, such as family relationships or financial problems. This can be an important ingredient in comprehensive coping support provision, as few other interventions have the legitimacy to provide direct support to those facing nonwork pressures. In our experience, some organizations have excellent late-stage narrow support in place but little broader, earlier stage provision. This is like providing good recovery services for those experiencing stress and illness but doing next to nothing to address root causes!

**Table 12.1.** Practical Benefits and Limitations of a Range of Coping Strategies and Support.

| Level | Examples | Benefits | Risks |
|---|---|---|---|
| Early-stage broad strategies | Work planning/distribution review | Potentially reach a wide range of employees | Operationally disruptive—requires strong business case |
| | Scenario planning to reduce uncertainty | Early-stage preventative avoiding later costs | Deals with situational causes but not intrapersonal (e.g., personality influences) |
| | Team-working process improvement interventions targeted at strengthening interpersonal relationships (e.g., introducing processes to improve in-formal communication in virtual teams) | Likely to produce broader unintended benefits (e.g., improve innovation) | |
| | Introduction of enhanced flexible working options to improve work–life balance and control | | |
| Mid-stage group and individual strategies | Resilience training | Build coping capacity in employees that helps facing future uncertainty and challenge | May overemphasize the expectation that individuals just need to toughen up as negative aspects of the organizational context cannot be addressed |
| | Coaching | | |
| | Specific skills training (e.g., assertiveness, time management) | Address situational and intrapersonal factors | |
| Late-stage narrow strategies | Individual counseling, accessed through an EAP | In-depth tailored individual support. Capacity to deal with nonwork-related stressors | Mainly treating symptoms rather than root causes |

## Summary of Benefits and Limitations

Table 12.1 summarizes the practical benefits and limitations of different levels of organizational coping strategies and support.

In 2003, one of the authors was involved in a review for the U.K. Health and Safety Executive (HSE), looking at what defined excellence in organizational stress management (http://www.hse.gov.uk/research/rrpdf/rr133.pdf). A conclusion at the time was that many organizations demonstrated excellent practices but rarely were they well integrated across functional boundaries (e.g., HR, health and safety, learning, and development) to maximize benefits. It seems to us that this remains a major challenge as the emphasis has switched toward wellbeing. The prime wellbeing stakeholders in organizations (HR, occupational health, health and safety) need a strategic integrated approach to ensure they deliver maximum benefits for their organizations. This requires an approach that addresses wellbeing at different levels of intervention and across organizational boundaries in a coherent and coordinated manner, with clear shared goals and business benefits. A strong wellbeing brand within the organization can help to achieve this, as can director-level responsibility and board-level reporting. Wellbeing can and should be mainstreamed into people processes (e.g., induction, performance management, learning, and development) and not seen as an occasional disconnected initiative. This requires senior-level vision and ownership, as well as clarity and measurement of desired individual and organizational outcomes from wellbeing improvements.

## References

Abramson, L. Y., Seligman, M. E. P., & Teasdale, J. D. (1978). Learned helplessness in humans: Critique and reformulation. *Journal of Abnormal Psychology, 87,* 49–74.

Fredrickson, B. L. (2001). The role of positive emotions in positive psychology: The broaden-and-build theory of positive emotions. *American Psychologist, 56*(3), 218–226.

Hurrell, J. J., Nelson, D. L., & Simmons, B. L. (1998). Measuring job stressors and strains. *Journal of Occupational Health Psychology, 3,* 368–389.

Kumar, A., Van Der Aalst, W. M. P., & Verbeek, E. M. W. (2001). Dynamic work distribution in workflow management systems. *Journal of Management Information Systems, 18*(3), 157–193.

LePine, J. A., Podsakoff, N. P., & LePine, M. A. (2005). A meta-analytic test of the Challenge Stressor–Hindrance Stressor Framework. *Academy of Management Journal*, *48*(5), 764–775.

Luthans, F. (2002). Positive organizational behavior: Developing and managing psychological strengths. *Academy of Management Executive*, *16*(1), 57–72.

Milne, D. (2007). People can learn markers on road to resilience (interview with Dennis Charney). *Psychiatric News*, *42*(2).

Mone, M. A., Baker, D. A., & Jeffries, F. (1995). Predictive validity and time dependency of self-efficacy, self-esteem, personal goals, and academic performance. *Educational and Psychological Measurement*, *55*(5), 716–727.

Robertson, I., & Cooper, C. (2011). *Well-being: Productivity and happiness at work*. Basingstoke: Palgrave Macmillan.

Rodell, J. B., & Judge, T. A. (2009). Can good stressors spark bad behaviours? The mediating role of emotions in links of challenge and hindrance stressors with citizenship and counterproductive behaviours. *Journal of Applied Psychology*, *94*(6), 1438–1451.

Ryan, R. M., & Deci, E. L. (2001). A review of research on hedonic and eudaimonic well-being. *Annual Review of Psychology*, *52*, 141–166.

Winwood, M. A., & Beer, S. (2008). What makes a good employee assistance programme? In A. Kinder, R. Hughes, & C. Cooper (Eds.), *Employee well-being support* (pp. 183–200). Chichester: John Wiley & Sons.

Wrosch, C., & Scheier, M. F. (2003). Personality and quality of life: The importance of optimism and goal adjustment. *Quality of Life Research*, *12*, 59–72.

# 13

# Workplace Mistreatment

## Recent Developments in Theory, Research, and Interventions

### Michael Hanrahan and Michael P. Leiter

Acadia University, Canada

## Introduction

Most people can provide a definition of workplace incivility. For most, that definition starts with a personal experience. Memories of being left out of a meeting, not being asked to sit in on a call relevant to your work, catching a coworker slip out an exaggerated sigh as you express your opinion, can all be quickly recalled and likely come with an emotional sting that highlights the meaning incidents of incivility can hold for us. Sometimes it is how something is said, or a certain look that seems to have a deeper meaning, or even the outwardly rude remarks, that we use to define our interpersonal experiences. Although a more academic or inclusive definition of workplace incivility may escape us when put on the spot, the experiences that represent incivility seem etched in the memories of those who experience or observe it.

This chapter addresses the topic of incivility in the workplace and its relationship to wellbeing. It is intended that by the end of the chapter readers will have a better understanding of what workplace incivility is, how it interferes with the ability of individuals, workgroups, and entire organizations to meet their full potentials, and how people can counteract the dysfunction and recover the productivity incivility often costs us.

*Work and Wellbeing: Wellbeing: A Complete Reference Guide*, Volume III.
Edited by Peter Y. Chen and Cary L. Cooper.
© 2014 John Wiley & Sons, Ltd. Published 2014 by John Wiley & Sons, Inc.
DOI: 10.1002/9781118539415.wbwell13

This chapter is made up of six sections. In the first, we summarize the nature of workplace incivility, in part by distinguishing it from other more intensive and intended disruptive behaviors. Next we consider theories to explain the origin of incivility in the workplace and how such behaviors can spread and be maintained within workgroups and organizations. In the third section we briefly examine how workplace incivility has been measured. The fourth section will address the cost that individuals, workgroups, and organizations pay for incivility in the workplace. In the fifth section we examine recommendations that have been proposed to avoid incivility taking hold in the workplace. We also consider an intervention that has been designed and implemented to reverse the impact incivility has by re-establishing or developing new patterns of civility to replace uncivil behavior. The last section concludes with thoughts about future directions in addressing workplace incivility as a practical and research issue.

## Incivility: What It Is and What It Is Not

When people consider the multitude of negative, harmful, and inappropriate behaviors that can occur in the workplace it can be difficult to appreciate the importance of differentiating the behavior captured with the phrase "workplace incivility" from other, more dramatic and overt workplace behaviors. At first this seems a reasonable oversight. After all, if you were a journalist trying to capture the attention of your audience, the headline "Life sentence without parole for Md. woman who beat, stabbed co-worker to death at yoga shop" ("Life Sentence," 2012) is more appealing than a headline describing rude comments someone makes while a coworker gives a presentation. On the surface, it would seem easier to sell an executive the idea of spending time and money addressing acts of vandalism or physical assault compared to pitching the need to address less intense acts such as workers ignoring their colleagues' feedback on a team project. Yet in their book *The cost of bad behavior*, Pearson and Porath (2009) provide a formula to estimate the cost of workplace incivility. For a health-care organization with nearly US$1 billion income, they calculated that the organization lost approximately $71 million dealing with the consequences of incivility; this is hardly something to be overlooked as insignificant.

In their initial definition of workplace incivility, Andersson and Pearson (1999) stressed the importance of viewing the phenomenon as a social interaction. In doing so they immediately identified workplace incivility as involving and influencing the instigator, the targets or recipients, any observers, and the social context in which the interaction occurs. They defined workplace incivility as "low intensity deviant behavior with ambiguous intent to harm the target, in violation of workplace norms for mutual respect. Uncivil behaviors are characteristically rude and discourteous, displaying a lack of regard for others" (p. 457). Andersson and Pearson (1999) also observed that previous research had indeed focused on acts of inappropriate behaviors that had a clear intent to cause harm. However, there was evidence that many employees were being exposed to rudeness and negative gestures of ambiguous intent (e.g., Ehrlich & Larcom, 1994; Neuman & Baron, 1997) and the authors questioned how these less intense behaviors of ambiguous intent were related to the more serious acts of aggression and violence (Andersson & Pearson, 1999).

Andersson and Pearson (1999) described workplace incivility as one type of workplace mistreatment that falls under the larger scope of antisocial behaviors. Antisocial behaviors were previously defined as "any behavior that brings harm, or is intended to bring harm to an organization, its employees, or its stakeholders" (Giacalone & Greenberg, 1997, p. vii). Obviously, antisocial behaviors in the workplace can include actions with clear intent and a wide range of intensity, including acts of violence and aggression, and perhaps is the broadest of the workplace mistreatment concepts, as it only requires that harm occur or be intended, with no specific restrictions on the intensity, duration, or frequency of the behavior. Nor are there any restrictions placed on the relationship between the target and perpetrator of antisocial behaviors, unlike abusive supervision (Tepper, 2000), for example, which defines a relationship between a supervisor and supervisee in which the former uses sustained verbal and nonverbal (excluding physical contact) behaviors to ridicule and invade the supervisee's personal space.

Andersson and Pearson (1999) viewed workplace incivility as existing under the umbrella of antisocial behaviors, which they considered to include deviant behaviors, violence, aggression, and, at the lowest level of intensity, workplace incivility. The first point of specification is that deviant behaviors are antisocial behaviors that, in addition to being harmful to an organization or its individual members, also violate the norms that have been established within an organization (Robinson & Bennett, 1997). Workplace aggression adds to the definition of deviant behaviors by requiring intent to harm and represents a higher intensity behavior than workplace incivility, and violence is a specific case of workplace aggression encompassing high-intensity acts of physical aggression intended to cause physical harm to the target

(Schat & Kelloway, 2005). Although aggression in the workplace may take the form of vandalism, verbal abuse, or harassment and cause harm that is physical or psychological (Neuman & Baron, 1997), it is only when aggression is expressed through physical acts that intentionally physically harm the target that the term "workplace violence" applies. Incivility is distinguished from these constructs primarily by the ambiguity of the intent to harm (Andersson & Pearson, 1999). Although there are aggressive acts that are in the same intensity range as incivility, when those behaviors are clearly and undeniably intended to cause harm to an individual or the organization in violation of norms, they can no longer be classified as incivility. So although a manager ignoring an email from a team leader may be defined as incivility, if that same manager decides to ignore that employee's email in order to prevent the employee from getting information she needs to perform her job, and the manager acknowledges this, it crosses a line and is an act of workplace aggression. As we will discuss in more detail later, when considering acts of incivility, the ability of the perpetrator to avoid acknowledging intent, the ability of the target to accept that the behavior was not intended to harm them, or the ability of anyone aware of the incident to consider the behavior to fall within the norms of the workplace in which the behavior is occurring, can have drastic impact on how people perceive and label behaviors (Jex, Burnfield Geimer, Clark, Guidroz, & Yugo, 2010).

In addition to Andersson and Pearson's (1999) definition of workplace incivility, there are several other forms of mistreatment that occur within organizations that have been described and seem to capture behaviors similar to those described in workplace incivility research. Multiple definitions may serve as enriching the construct or muddying the waters. For example, Hershcovis (2011) discusses the proliferation of constructs reflective of workplace mistreatment, whereas Bowling and Beehr (2006) considered forms of workplace harassment. Both papers considered some of the same constructs (e.g., bullying and interpersonal conflict), which would also fall under Andersson and Pearson's (1999) conceptualization of aggression. Hershcovis put forward the perspective that workplace mistreatment research has resulted in a high degree of construct overlap, negatively influencing the development of the field. She argued that current research measures often fail to capture the distinguishing features of various mistreatment constructs, and suggested that a broader construct underlies most assessed with these various measures. Using a sample of workplace mistreatment constructs that included incivility

(Andersson & Pearson, 1999), bullying (Einarsen, 2000), abusive supervision (Tepper, 2000), and interpersonal conflict (Spector & Jex, 1998), Hershcovis (2011) conducted a meta-analysis to determine if these constructs were related to several outcome variables in the manner predicted by the distinguishing features contained in the construct definitions. As previously noted, abusive supervision is differentiated from incivility and other mistreatment concepts by its focus on one particular perpetrator (the supervisor). The definition also requires that the mistreatment be sustained. As is the case with workplace incivility, abusive supervision excludes physical acts of aggression, but it does not specify that the intensity of the behavior is low (Hershcovis, 2011; Tepper, 2000). Bullying is defined as repeated exposures to negative acts from another member of the organization (superior, peer, or subordinate), but there is generally a power imbalance between the perpetrator and target based on a wide variety of variables such as age, gender, or social position (Hershcovis, 2011). It is also implied that bullying requires the negative acts to persist for a sustained period of time; unlike incivility, which does not place any restrictions on the persistence of the behavior. Interpersonal conflict (Spector & Jex, 1998) encompasses mutually stressful disagreement between organizational members ranging from low to high intensity and is not easily discernible from the other mistreatment concepts as it is defined loosely enough to overlap with all of the previous discussed concepts to some extent, including incivility (Hershcovis, 2011).

It was predicted that if the constructs being tested were truly distinct, as their definitions imply, bullying and abusive supervision would result in stronger adverse impact on attitudes and behaviors compared to incivility. In addition, Hershcovis examined the patterns of relationships among the four types of workplace mistreatment noted above, and the outcome measures (i.e., job satisfaction, turnover intention, affective commitment, psychological wellbeing, and physical wellbeing). The findings, which reflected a total of 60 samples reported in 53 studies, supported Hershcovis's perspective: bullying and abusive supervision were not found to have stronger adverse impacts than incivility, as the distinguishing traits implied in the definitions would predict. However, there was also evidence that incivility has a degree of distinctness, as there were significant differences on some outcome variables between incivility and the three other forms of workplace mistreatment that were investigated. More specifically, incivility was found to have a significantly more negative relationship with job satisfaction than interpersonal conflict, was significantly less related to physical wellbeing than was bullying, and had a stronger relationship with turnover intention than both bullying and interpersonal conflict (Hershcovis, 2011). Although these results indicate a degree of overlap among these constructs, incivility also appears to have distinct relationships with outcome variables, which supports considering incivility as a distinct form of workplace mistreatment. Although the results of Hershcovis' meta-analysis highlight that there is redundancy in the construct definitions proposed to represent forms of workplace mistreatment, she advocated that moving forward the task is to actually develop more precise construct definitions, rather than abandon investigating them and focus on the broader construct of mistreatment.

Whereas Andersson and Pearson described workplace incivility as a single concept, Cortina (2008) discusses incivility in the workplace in terms of "general incivility" and "selective incivility." Selective workplace incivility encompasses covert forms of gender and racial discrimination in the workplace. This perspective holds that some forms of incivility can reflect unconscious prejudices the perpetrator holds against members of the gender or ethnic group to which the target of the specific incident of incivility belongs. Although there is evidence that gender (Cortina, Magley, Williams, & Langhout, 2001; Cortina, 2008) and, to a lesser degree, ethnicity, influence the likelihood an individual experiences incivility, and specifically less overt forms of incivility (Cortina, 2008), the actual behaviors have not been shown to be different from those behaviors considered to represent "general incivility." Ultimately, although it may be true that some incidences of incivility represent a form of racial or gender discrimination, it is not clear that this distinction would drastically impact measurement of incivility behaviors, as the intention would still remain ambiguous. Furthermore, although there may be gender or racial biases in the frequency with which incivility is experienced, there is no evidence that the impact of incivility is of a different intensity based on gender or ethnicity. As Cortina (2008) indicates, further research is required in this area, but at this point and for the purposes of this chapter, incivility is considered to reflect all low-intensity behaviors that violate the organizational norms for mutual respect, where the intent to harm a target remains ambiguous (Andersson & Pearson, 1999; Cortina, Magley, Williams, & Langhout, 2001).

It should also be noted that although Andersson and Pearson's definition of workplace incivility is the most commonly cited, and perhaps most accepted, other definitions have been proposed. For example, Zauderer (2002) provided a definition that varied slightly, by emphasizing

**Table 13.1.** Definitions of Workplace Mistreatment.

| Source | Construct | Source | Intensity | Frequency | Intent |
|---|---|---|---|---|---|
| Andersson & Pearson (1999) | Incivility | Anyone | Low | Undefined | Ambiguous |
| Leymann (1996) | Bullying | Anyone | Moderate to high | Weekly for six months | Deliberate |
| Tepper (2000) | Abusive supervision | Authority figure | Moderate to high | Weekly for six months | Deliberate |
| Spector & Jex (1998) | Interpersonal conflict | Anyone | Undefined | Undefined | Deliberate |
| Duffy, Ganster, & Pagon (2002) | Social under-mining | Anyone | Undefined | Undefined | Deliberate |

the affective reaction of recipients of incivility and by setting the comparison of appropriateness to the expectations the recipient has for how he or she should be treated, rather than the norms of the organization. Under Zauderer's definition, actions would only be labeled as incivility in instances when the recipient reacts negatively (Jex et al., 2010) and precludes defining workplace incivility from anyone's perspective other than the recipient. As we will discuss in a later section of this chapter, the research on the impact of workplace incivility has measured consequences for both perpetrators and recipients of uncivil behavior and suggest that Zauderer's definition is too limiting. In addition, this definition does not alter the behaviors that would be considered uncivil, only the circumstances in which they would reflect incivility.

Although the potential for new conceptualization of workplace incivility to emerge must be acknowledged, it is our intent to discuss workplace incivility as defined by Andersson and Pearson (1999). Table 13.1 provides an overview of relevant constructs. For the most part this chapter refers to incivility as the primary construct, acknowledging that its commonalities with other forms of workplace mistreatment are likely more salient than its differences. In the next section of the chapter we discuss the means through which workplace incivility has been studied.

## Measurement

The original definition formulated by Andersson and Pearson, although the most widely accepted, has not been universally adopted and work continues that may ultimately change how workplace incivility is conceptualized. This poses the first problem in measuring incivility. Variability in categorizing the experiences described by research participants would make reliable and valid measurement of the underlying construct a considerable challenge. In addition, as workplace behavioral norms evolve, the behaviors that reflect incivility may become more or less extreme, and it is possible that acts labeled as incivility today could be deemed normative and acceptable in the future. As a result, the measurement of specific behaviors as a means of identifying workplace incivility would require ongoing adjustment to adapt to evolving workplace norms. On the one hand, this makes the measurement of incivility a difficult task, but on the other hand, it highlights the strength of the Andersson and Pearson (1999) definition of workplace incivility. As their definition does not prescribe a particular set of behaviors, and instead places the emphasis on the context in which the behavior occurs and how the action relates to the norms of the environment, it is a definition that can tolerate changes in workplace normative behaviors over time.

It is similarly adaptable to varying workplaces. Although it is reasonable to expect that the behaviors reflective of incivility will be similar across the vast majority of workplace settings, it also obvious that some workplaces have a culture of normative social interaction and personal conduct that fall in the extremes. Places where employees are constantly in competition, where collaboration is tolerated rather than embraced and dominance over others is rewarded would be expected to have different expectations for respect than settings where the normative social interaction is extreme politeness and where employees measure success in terms of team performance instead of individual achievements. In such divergent settings, the need to accommodate for the unique norms of specific workplaces is evident.

Accepting workplace incivility to be "low intensity deviant behavior with ambiguous intent to harm the target, in violation of workplace norms for mutual respect" which are "characteristically rude and discourteous, displaying a lack of regard for others" (Andersson & Pearson, 1999, p. 457) provides the criteria to evaluate a wide variety of situations. However, workplace incivility is described as a social interaction (Andersson & Pearson, 1999; Cortina et al., 2001; Pearson, Andersson, & Porath, 2000; Pearson

& Porath, 2009) involving at least two individuals. This leads to potential interpretation differences dependent on the point of view from which a situation is observed or experienced (Jex et al., 2010). Initial efforts relied on structured and semi-structured interviews to gather experiences of recipients of incivility in the workplace (Jex et al., 2010; Pearson & Porath, 2009) and such interpretational differences could be accounted for and addressed by the interviewer (Spector & Rodopman, 2010). These interviews provided a wealth of detailed personal experiences and testimonies to the consequences incivility had for individual recipients. For example, in their 2009 book, Pearson and Porath recount a number of incidents of incivility described by their interview participants, ranging from the personal experiences of health-care workers and their patients, to retail employees and their customers. Such interviews began to identify the behaviors most often being experienced during incidences of incivility (Pearson, Andersson, & Porath, 2000). This led to the development of questionnaires that could be distributed more widely, in order to more effectively collect larger samples of information regarding the frequency of the behaviors repeatedly related to experienced incivility. These questionnaires could also be used to evaluate workplace incivility's relationships with other mistreatment variables and outcome measures needed to further understand workplace incivility.

The first, and most widely used (Martin & Hine, 2005) questionnaire to measure instances of workplace incivility was the Workplace Incivility Scale (WIS; Cortina et al., 2001). This measure initially included seven items that asked employees to rate the frequency with which they had experienced each of the uncivil acts in the previous 5 years from superiors or their coworkers. The items reflected uncivil acts including devaluation of work and work effort, insulting comments, and social exclusion. Validated on a sample of nearly 1,200 public sector employees, the WIS was found to fit a single-factor model very well, and an alpha of 0.89 in the validation sample indicated the measure had good internal reliability. Cortina et al. (2001) noted that the time frame of 5 years they used in their initial version of the WIS was likely to result in an underestimation of workplace incivility, as would the brevity of the measure, which had a limited number of uncivil behaviors for respondents to consider. Variations of the original WIS have been constructed by adding (e.g., Cortina & Magley, 2009) or removing items, or repeating the items for supervisors and coworkers separately (e.g., Leiter, Laschinger, Day, & Gilin-Oore, 2011). In such cases the reliability and factor structure of the WIS has been repeatedly demonstrated (Cortina & Magley, 2009; Martin & Hine, 2005). Blau and Andersson (2005) flipped the perspective of the original WIS in order to measure instances of instigated workplace incivility. Their measure of instigated workplace incivility was found to be distinct from experienced workplace incivility and demonstrated good reliability (alpha $= 0.89$).

Martin and Hine (2005) considered the one dimension of the WIS to be inadequate, and endeavored to develop a measure more encompassing of the incivility construct. They developed the Uncivil Workplace Behavior Questionnaire (UWBQ), which ultimately contained 17 items, resulting in four subscales, to measure incivility in the workplace. The UWBQ four subscales include hostility (e.g., "Raised their voice while speaking to you"), privacy invasion (e.g., "Opened our desk drawers without prior permission"), exclusionary behavior (e.g., "Avoided consulting you when they would normally be expected to do so"), and gossiping (e.g., "Talked about you behind your back"). Although they reported that their findings confirmed that their 17 items fit a four-factor model better than a single-factor model, the UWBQ total score demonstrated better internal consistency (overall alpha $= 0.92$) than did all subscales (alphas ranging between 0.84 and 0.87). The UWBQ total score was significantly correlated with the WIS. The privacy invasion subscale had the weakest correlation with the WIS [$r$ (339) $= .28$, $p < .01$], while the remaining subscale correlations with the WIS were stronger [hostility: $r$ (339) $= .65$, $p < .01$; exclusionary behavior: $r$ (339) $= .64$, $p < .01$; gossiping: $r$ (339) $= .64$, $p < .01$]. This suggests perhaps that a two-factor model might fit the UWBQ better, with the privacy invasion subscale being distinct from the WIS-like domain. However, given that the privacy invasion subscale had relatively weak correlations with most measures in their study, it may not be capturing an essential dimension of incivility. Although not part of Martin and Hine's study, it seems reasonable to expect that reversing the perspective of the UWBQ items could be used to measure instigated acts of workplace incivility to complement the measurement of experienced incivility (Blau & Andersson, 2005).

Interviews and surveys have been the primary forms of collecting information about experiences of incivility, and each has its own strengths and weaknesses. Although surveys are efficient, usually offer participants anonymity and convenience, and can become easily established, they also are vulnerable to biases such as social desirability (Spector & Rodopman, 2010). On the other hand, interviews are not usually time or cost effective, and considerable training is required to develop competent interviewers capable of overcoming the challenges of interviewee resistance to discussing sensitive topics, which might be more easily measured when the respondent is able to remain anonymous. It has been recommended by Spector and Rodopman (2010) that integrating these methods more routinely, as well as incorporating other methods, such as diary studies, can provide valuable information that not only identifies the frequency of specific behaviors, but would also provide a better context against which specific incidents could be compared.

# Origin

The focus of research involving workplace incivility to date has been on understanding how it can be detected and measured, how it influences those individuals and groups involved, and how it can be addressed effectively (e.g., Pearson, 2010). Relatively little attention has been paid to how incivility has infiltrated the workplace, how it is activated during workplace interactions, and how such rude and discourteous behaviors spread and evolve in the work environment. Numerous scholars have suggested that today's social culture supports individuals' right to freely express themselves over mutual respect for each other (Andersson & Pearson, 1999). Essentially, it is argued that the expectations of civility in everyday interactions have deteriorated, and that a shift to a more informal expectation for behavior and social interactions has subsequently invaded the workplace. With no obvious cues or clear expectations as to what constitutes proper workplace behavior, individuals are acting with less consideration for those around them. In the best case, these behaviors are committed without obvious awareness of the negative impact on others, and at the very worst they are committed by individuals able to deny a malicious intent (e.g., Andersson & Pearson, 1999; Pearson, Andersson, & Porath, 2000).

Pearson and Porath (2009) looked to the causes of incivility in broader society to explain its appearance in the workplace. Less involvement in community, changes toward indulgent parenting, the sensationalizing of vulgarity and conflict through modern media, whether it be as part of a scripted film or a televised political debate, and the ever-increasing stressful nature of today's world all are likely contributors to the erosion of social norms that protected against the growth of incivility in past decades. Research in these respective domains has identified negative consequences that are consistent with an increasing tone of incivility.

Research indicates that decreased participation in one's community is related to significant impairment in social skills and development of healthy peer relationships. In a recent study involving 317 German students from grade seven to grade nine, Wolfer, Bull, and Scheithauer (2012) found, not surprisingly, that increasing levels of social isolation were negatively associated with social skills. They also reported that the benefits of support and resources were more evident in socially integrated youths than in their less socially integrated counterparts. Although these youths were not actively bullied or actively teased, not being actively integrated with a defined social group precludes development of the skills required to adapt to the social norms that exist, and would also limit their ability to accurately ascertain the norms of any new environment they may encounter. Furthermore, longitudinal research has demonstrated that lack of social contact can have a negative impact on physical wellbeing (Caspi, Harrington, Moffitt, Milne, & Poulton, 2006), leading to additional life stresses, which Pearson and Porath (2009) also suggested as a factor responsible for reduced incivility.

Although there have been suggestions that the rapid expansion of social networking and increased access to sophisticated personal communication devices have improved social connectedness (Valkenburg & Peter, 2007), the research remains divided, and others have reported that the use of new social networking technologies has had negative impacts on social relationships and wellbeing (Schiffrin, Edelman, Falkenstern, & Stewart, 2010). Schiffrin et al. (2010) also reported that although computer-mediated communication was frequently used, despite the ample opportunities and ease of face-to-face communication for their sample of college students, participants perceived non-face-to-face communication to be less effective. A shift to less personal forms of communication increases the likelihood of miscommunication and ambiguity and decreases inhibition (Baruch, 2005), conditions expected to increase incidences of incivility (Jex et al., 2010). O'Kane and Hargie (2007) reported that although employee use of email has been linked to improved efficiency of communication, unintended consequences such as an increased ability for employees to avoid having difficult conversations face to face and more opportunities for individuals to be excluded from conversations relevant to their work (intentionally or unintentionally) have also been observed. It has been long accepted that face-to-face interactions are best suited for communications that involve potentially high levels of ambiguity due to the ability of all participants to observe and interpret nonverbal cues (Westmyer, DiCioccio, & Rubin, 1998).

The changes in parenting styles suggested by Pearson and Porath (2009) would intuitively result in changes in the characteristics of young adults who enter the workforce. Parenting research has identified a variety of parenting styles, including the authoritative and indulgent or permissive parenting styles (Nelson, Padilla-Walker, Christensen, Evans, & Carroll, 2011). Authoritative parents are characterized as having high expectations, which they communicate clearly to their children, and display high levels of warmth. Rules are clear and rational and any punishment is consistently administered based on those rules. Parents who are categorized as indulgent or permissive express high levels of warmth through overindulgence and have low levels of demands and avoid correcting inappropriate behavior or setting boundaries. Study results indicate that children raised by authoritative parents are more likely to score higher on measures of psychological wellbeing, lower on depressive symptoms and alcohol abuse. In contrast, children raised by parents who are more indulgent are more likely to have poorer social skills, perform less effectively, and have a lower sense of autonomy, but a higher sense of entitlement (Nelson et al., 2011). Such a constellation does not suggest well-adjusted individuals ready to work as part of workgroups, or being able to identify with and act within social norms without sufficient cues.

Another contributing factor suggested to be related to the erosion of civility in society is increased exposure to more profane and uncivil language. If one looks to the political arena, the lack of civility in public debate is easily observed, and is often cited as a potential cause for citizen disengagement from the political process, although it does make for good television viewing (Forgette & Morris, 2006). The increased use of curse words by high school students also indicates an increasing tolerance for vulgarity, as use of curse words, particularly among peer groups, is no longer automatically perceived to reflect negative intentions or malice (Plank, McDill, McPartland, & Jordan, 2001). Today you may be as likely to hear curse words in a local televised city council meeting, in a post game sports interview, or in an award acceptance speech. Although it is true that such instances do draw attention and complaints, and fines are levied, today there is an equally large group of individuals who point to those offended by such language as overreacting and being too sensitive. Perhaps due to this, the frequency of such language has increased dramatically. For example, during the 1989/1990 television season in the United States, there was less than one use of rough, not necessarily profane, language per one prime time television hour averaged across all broadcast networks. In the 1999/2000 season there were almost five profanities per television hour (Parents Television Council, 2002). Vulgar language is becoming more common in our daily interactions (DuFrene & Lehman, 2002). Although encountering such language in the workplace is not always unexpected, it remains outside normative workplace experience in many work environments (Baruch & Jenkins, 2007). As profane language normalizes in less formal settings and individuals act more informally at work, the collision of increased use of such language in a setting where it remains atypical potentially contributes to increased incidents of experienced incivility (Baruch & Jenkins, 2007; Pearson & Porath, 2009).

Although the exact causes of incivility in society are not known for certain, the factors reviewed above suggest that the experiences of individuals outside of work have changed over time. The consequences of these changes identify possible explanations for increased friction between individual behaviors and the normative expectations that exist in the workplace. We now look at theories of how incivility is potentially activated and maintained in the workplace.

In an effort to meaningfully expand the theory of incivility, Leiter, Laschinger, Day, and Gilin-Oore (2010) proposed that workplace incivility is influenced by workgroup interactions and personal cognitions and they explored mechanisms through which incivility continues in the workplace. As employees interact, they observe each other and come to understand the culture and norms of a particular workplace. In an effort to conform, individuals mimic what they observe others doing (Sechrist & Stangor, 2001) and this might be one mechanism through which acts of incivility are replicated. In cases when an individual is a recipient of incivility, they may mirror such interactions and begin to respond to uncivil behavior in kind (Dabos & Rousseau, 2004). In instances when one behaves outside the limits of the accepted behavior of a workplace, the individual must resolve the conflict that arises in having acted in a manner contrary to the norms that previously governed his or her behavior. Under such circumstances Leiter et al. (2010) suggested that three rationales are used to justify acts of incivility in the face of the normative standards of the workplace. These include the pressure rationale, the toughness rationale, and the sensitive rationale.

The *pressure rationale* would occur in instances when individuals reduce or limit their own responsibility for an uncivil act by attributing blame to situational factors. It acknowledges that the behavior itself may have been a violation of the work setting norms, but disperses blame from the self to the pressures of a particular situation, including incivility recipients who may have contributed to the pressures of the situation. In adopting such a stance individuals can view themselves less critically, and the need for change is externalized to causes of work pressures and stress.

The *toughness rationale* justifies acts of incivility as being a way of acting with individuals who require external motivation and aggressive direction in order to function successfully at work, as they lack sufficient internal motivation. In this way, acts of incivility are framed as being a set of behaviors reserved for those individuals who require such treatment. This may include individuals who are perceived to have aggressive intentions, in which case the instigator of incivility is acting in self-defense of a perceived threat, which would also suggest that certain individuals are in need of very specific treatment, and would allow the instigator to maintain a view of themselves as acting within the workplace norms except in dealing with those who require atypical treatment (Leiter et al., 2010).

The final rationale described by Leiter et al. (2010) is the *sensitive rational*. This rationale denies an act of incivility and places blame entirely on the recipients of incivility, reasoning that the instigator's actions were appropriate to the workplace norms, and the recipient's own sensitivities and misinterpretations are responsible for his or her incivility experiences.

To assess these rationales, Leiter et al. (2010) developed the Rudeness Rationale Scale, composed of eight items (four pressure items, two tough items, and two sensitive items) rated on a seven-point Likert scale ranging from $0 =$ "never" to $6 =$ "daily" in terms of how often individuals experienced work-related feelings. The three-factor structure was confirmed on a study sample of 729 nurses from Nova Scotia and Ontario, Canada. In addition to the Rudeness Rationale Scale, respondents also completed the WIS (Cortina et al., 2001) to report instances of experienced incivility from supervisors and coworkers separately, and also reported on the frequency of behaviors they considered to be uncivil, but which did not describe a specific behavior as did the WIS. Nurses also reported on their own instigated acts of incivility as recommended by Blau and Andersson (2005), using the same behaviors described for experienced supervisor and coworker incivility.

Results of this study revealed that the sensitive rationale was endorsed most frequently, the toughness rationale was endorsed less often, and the pressure rationale was reported least frequently. One possible explanation for this finding is that by externalizing responsibility to recipients of incivility, instigators minimize the risk to their own self-image (Leiter et al., 2010).

Despite differences in the degree to which each rationale was utilized by the nurses, all three rationales were found to be moderators between experiences of incivility and instigated incivility. When participants did not endorse a rationale, instigated incivility remained consistently low regardless of the level of coworker incivility. When the rationales were endorsed,

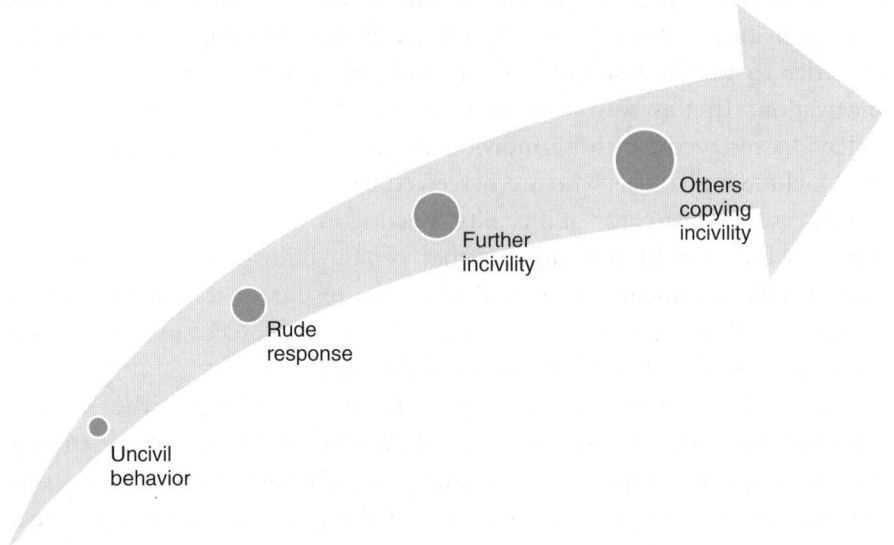

**Figure 13.1.** Incivility Spiral.

instigated incivility increased from low coworker incivility experiences to high coworker incivility experiences. The same pattern of results was observed when considering experiences of supervisor incivility. In both instances, the results suggest that individuals attempt to conform to the behavior they observe in the workplace, and when their actions can be justified, potentially minimizing the challenge to self-image, they engage in these behaviors more frequently. These conditions describe an "incivility spiral" (Andersson & Pearson, 1999), whereby acts of incivility spread throughout a workplace, potentially to the point of escalating to more serious forms of mistreatment (Figure 13.1).

Basing the "incivility spiral" on similar observations for organizational decline and tyrannical leadership, Andersson and Pearson (1999) describe a series of workplace interactions that begin with an initiating action that is experienced or observed as being in violation of the social norms of the work-place. It is suggested that this creates a sense of interactional injustice (Caza & Cortina, 2007) that creates negative affect in the recipient(s) of incivility, and simultaneously creates a desire to reciprocate the uncivil act. In this manner, repeated cycles of uncivil behavior may form between individuals, each taking their turn as instigator then recipient. Although in some cases this desire to reciprocate may be for the purposes of retribution (i.e., to return the unpleas-antness of their experience to the instigator), it is also possible that the urge to react to incivility with more incivility is an attempt to conform to social norms (Dabos & Rousseau, 2004), particularly if the incivility is instigated by someone who the recipient had looked to for cues of what constituted normative behavior (Pearson, 2010). Andersson and Pearson (1999) offer that the recipient may also make a decision to ignore an act of incivility, or the instigator may apologize before the incivility is reciprocated, and in doing so possibly prevent the spiral from continuing, at least between those two individuals.

Cortina and Magley (2009) identified coping strategies used by recipients of incivility, and noted that the largest group of individuals in their sample coped with incivility by detaching from the stressful situations and did little to actually address uncivil incidents. Another coping strategy utilized was to minimize and avoid aversive interactions with the instigator. This group also tended not to seek support. Although these coping mechanisms may prevent the spiral from developing further in this instance, there is little to suggest that these strategies would protect the recipients from negative consequences of the experienced incident.

Observers of uncivil acts may also perceive interactional injustice, and they would have the same potential to react with a desire to reciprocate (Andersson & Pearson, 1999), either toward the instigator of the observed incident, the direct recipient, or toward other bystanders. It is easy to see how incivility can dominate the experience of workgroups if left uninterrupted. To make matters worse, a tipping point is suggested, when an individual reaches a breaking point. Following a series of experienced incivility, the "last straw" triggers a more intense affective response that requires a more intense reaction, where intent to harm the target is no longer ambiguous (Andersson & Pearson, 1999). In this manner, repeated experiences of incivility can escalate into more intense forms of workplace mistreatment (Hershcovis, 2011). It is worth considering that the rationales for uncivil behavior described by Leiter et al. (2010), particularly those that displace the most blame for incivility to the recipient, might also influence the affective experience of the recipient, and could conceivably increase the perception of the recipient that a stronger response is warranted and might remove the ambiguity of the instigator's intent if the rationale became known to the recipient.

Although the focus of most research is on workplace experiences of incivility involving other employees, it is worth noting that incivility between employees and customers might also contribute to the overall experience of workplace incivility. Through an investigation of incivility employees experienced from customers, van Jaarsveld, Walker, and Skarlicki (2010) demonstrated that the incivility is reciprocated between customers and employees as it is between employees. Although the expectations of normative social interactions with customers would likely be different from those with coworkers (i.e., the same behavior from a coworker may be perceived differently than that from a customer), incivility in one domain may influence the probability one would react with incivility in the other. The results of van Jaarsveld and colleagues' study (2010) also indicated that emotional exhaustion mediated the positive relationship between customer incivility and employee incivility toward customers. Such findings suggest circumstances in which the pressure rational described by Leiter et al. (2010) may be utilized more frequently.

Although there remains much work in determining the exact causes of incivility in the workplace and in general, the friction between changes in societal norms and traditional work expectations fit with research findings. Research is also beginning to determine the cognitive processes that might allow individuals to justify uncivil action. Identifying such processes is a valuable tool in stopping the incivility spiral. Before turning our attention to methods to reduce and eliminate incivility, the next section of this chapter will discuss the consequences of workplace incivility.

## Consequences of Incivility

Although workplace incivility is characterized by low-intensity behaviors, its influence on the wellbeing of those who experience it is anything but low in intensity. In much the same way that one can consider individual uncivil acts, uncivil group dynamics, or the overall organizational experience of incivility, one can also examine the consequences of incivility from the individual, workgroup, or organization's perspective. A variety of consequences of incivility (Reio & Ghosh, 2009) have been identified, including consequences for an individual's job satisfaction, physical and psychological wellbeing, work attitudes and engagement in work. As incivility spreads, these consequences spread as well, deteriorating workgroup dynamics and ultimately interfering with organizations' ability to meet their goals.

Cortina et al. (2001) surveyed nearly 1,600 public sector employees in the U.S. court system. Their findings indicate that women experienced incivility more frequently than men did, and that the status an individual holds within the organization influences incivility experiences. Experiences of incivility were found to have significantly negative associations with individuals' reported job satisfaction, as well as their satisfaction with coworkers and supervisors. Reio and Ghosh (2009) surveyed 402 individuals from 11 organizations, representing a wide variety of industries in the United States, who were attending training seminars. Their findings also indicated that incivility had negative associations with overall job satisfaction.

Cortina et al. (2001) noted that increased incivility was related to employees reporting lower satisfaction with pay, benefits, and advancement opportunities within their organization. Lim and Cortina (2005) too found that in their sample of female public sector employees, incivility experiences were correlated with negative job, supervisor, and coworker satisfaction scores, as well as reward and advancement opportunities satisfactions.

Cortina et al. (2001) reported that recipients of incivility were more likely to have considered quitting their job and had significantly more reported symptoms of psychological distress (depression and anxiety). Reio and Ghosh (2009) additionally reported that incivility experiences were related to negative perceptions of an individual's own physical health.

Laschinger, Leiter, Day, and Gilin (2009) studied 612 Canadian nurses and found that experiences of supervisor incivility and coworker incivility were each significant negative predictors of job satisfaction, as well as organizational commitment. Supervisor incivility was a more important predictor of intentions for individuals to leave the organization. In a large-scale study of over 34,000 employees across 179 organizations in New Zealand and Australia, Griffin (2010) revealed that an organizational environment defined by higher incidents of incivility significantly predicted lower intention to stay, even after controlling for the relationship between personal experiences of incivility and intention to stay. This, consistent with the incivility spiral (Andersson & Pearson, 1999), demonstrates the vicarious effect incivility can have.

Incivility was positively associated with considerations of quitting in Lim and Cortina's study as well. Increased incivility had a significant correlation with more frequent report of symptoms of psychological distress (depression and anxiety) and lower levels of life and health satisfaction (Lim & Cortina, 2005). Furthermore, they demonstrated that increasing levels of mistreatment were associated with increased negative consequences, which supports the "incivility spiral" (Andersson & Pearson, 1999) and the importance of addressing incivility as early in the "spiral" as possible.

Caza and Cortina (2007) surveyed over 1,000 university students and measured the frequency of uncivil acts over the course of the previous year. The results of this study indicated that 76% of the sample had experienced at least one act of incivility in the past year, and of those individuals, close to one third described incivility as the most notable form of mistreatment on campus. For each uncivil act, students were asked to identify the status of the instigator (student staff or administrator). The respondents indicated that they experienced acts of incivility from both peers and those with higher status at the institution. As Caza and Cortina (2007) had predicted, the results of their study supported a model whereby instances of experienced workplace incivility led to perceptions of injustice and ostracism, which in turn contributed to psychological distress and institutional dissatisfaction. These in turn led to academic disengagement and predicted decreased academic performance as measured by self-reported grade point average. Caza and Cortina (2007) additionally found that incivility experienced from individuals with higher status within the institution's hierarchy had a stronger link to perceptions of injustice than did incivility experienced at the hands of those at the same level of institutional status.

Lim, Cortina, and Magley (2008) tested a theoretical model of the personal and work consequences of incivility. In their first study (using the same sample as Cortina et al., 2001), they showed that experiences of incivility significantly reduced job satisfaction, coworker satisfaction, and supervisor satisfaction. Supervisor satisfaction and work satisfaction were also found to be negatively associated with turnover intentions. Incivility experiences were also found to have a direct positive association with turnover intentions, indicating that supervisor and work satisfaction only partially mediated this relationship. Their results also indicated that experienced incivility was associated with increased experiences of depression and anxiety, which fully mediated the relationship between incivility and negative physical health outcomes. In a second study, with a sample of 271 municipal employees from the Midwestern United States, the researchers distinguished between personally experienced incivility and incivility of the workgroup (the incivility experiences of all an individual's workgroup minus the individual's personal experiences of incivility). Their findings were consistent with their first study, and additionally suggested that vicarious incivility also has significant negative consequences for job satisfaction and psychological wellbeing, which in turn fully mediates the consequences of workgroup incivility in terms of turnover intention and physical health.

Lim and Lee (2011) explored workplace incivility across a variety of work environments in Singapore. In addition to attempting to replicate findings from Western studies of incivility in relation to the role instigator status plays in the personal and professional wellbeing of recipients of workplace incivility, they also investigated the impact workplace incivility had on work-to-family conflict. Lim and Lee (2011) found that in their sample of

180 men and women from different industries (e.g., banking and finance, construction, real estate, government, education, and more), 91% had experienced instances of incivility from superiors, coworkers, or subordinates sometime in the previous 5 years. The level of incivility was found to vary significantly relative to the status of the instigator. Specifically, respondents indicated that they had experienced the greatest level of incivility from superiors and the least from subordinates. Incivility experiences involving coworkers (i.e., at the same status level) fell between the superior and subordinate level, and $t$-tests confirmed all pair-wise comparisons to be statistically significant. Incivility experienced from superiors was negatively related to supervisor satisfaction and positively associated with work-to-family conflict. Coworker incivility was negatively associated with perceptions of fairness and coworker satisfaction, and was linked to increased reports of depression. Incivility experienced from coworkers was not significantly related to any of the measured outcomes in this study. The researchers also found that when family support was high, the relationships between superior incivility and work-to-family conflict and between coworker incivility and depression were stronger than when family support was low. Given the significant amount of time that employees spend immersed in the work environment, it should come as no surprise that job satisfaction has been found to be significantly related to life satisfaction (Rice, Near, & Hunt, 1980) and perceived quality of marital relationships (Rogers & May, 2003).

The research described above clearly demonstrates that individuals experience significant consequences not only when subjected to incivility directed toward themselves, but also when working in an environment where incivility occurs. The organizational consequences of incivility are a direct result of the personal consequences experienced by individuals and groups. For example, Pearson and Porath (2009) note that organizations that develop reputations as being uncivil environments will have difficulty recruiting top prospects, as mistreated employees spread the damage by telling those outside the organization of their negative experiences. When these employees leave the organization, this negative description of the working environment could continue to spread, even if the organization takes steps to change. Customers of uncivil organizations will simply choose to take their business to a more pleasant organization, as it has been reported that observing employee-to-employee incivility is as negative an experience for customers as experiencing it themselves (Pearson & Porath, 2009).

Reduction in productivity is another consequence organizations experience once incivility takes hold. Johnson and Indvik (2001) note that 12%

of employees quit their job to avoid further targeted incivility. More than half of recipients of incivility lose time from their work worrying about past or anticipated acts of incivility. An astounding 22% of employees report that their experiences of incivility cause them to intentionally decrease their work effort. Again, considering the interconnectedness of most worker environments, when one person reduces their effort, intentionally or as a symptom of their distress, this will place higher demands on others to "pick up the slack." Such demands can increase burnout and prompt additional withdrawal, including reduced work efforts, higher absenteeism, and higher turnover rates (Chiaburu & Harrison, 2008).

In considering the economic cost of incivility to organizations, Pearson and Porath (2009) include estimates for the reduced production of employees struggling with the burden of uncivil encounter. They also consider the cost of reduced production by the observers of incivility as well as replacing those who left the organization as a response. As noted in the introduction to this chapter, one organization estimated that approximately $71 million of their $1 billion of income was spent addressing the consequences of incivility. Given what likely remains to be discovered about incivility, this very well could be an underestimation. Alleviating the negative consequences experienced by individuals makes sense from a humanistic point of view, but it also makes good business sense.

## Solving the Incivility Problem

As we have described in previous sections of this chapter, workplace incivility has become an important and significantly detrimental risk to the wellbeing of individuals and organizations. Given that the study of incivility is relatively new in comparison to other forms of workplace mistreatment (Andersson & Pearson, 1999), investigations of how to most effectively address the incivility problem are few. In this section of the chapter, recommendations that have been made to address workplace incivility will be reviewed. Many of these recommendations are based on the current understanding of workplace incivility; however, in many cases the effectiveness of instituting such recommendations, while making intuitive sense in light of what is known, has not been empirically evaluated to date. We then shine the spotlight on one intervention that has been empirically found to positively impact the social dynamics of the workplace in a manner that reduces the occurrence and impact of workplace incivility.

In order to manage incivility, the general consensus seems to be that it requires more than simply stopping uncivil behavior. Recommendations focus on setting clear and understandable expectations for civil behavior (Pearson & Porath, 2009). Pearson and Porath (2005, 2009) put forward recommendations to change the workplace culture in a manner that excludes incivility in favor of civility. The first of these is to set a zero tolerance expectation that flows from the highest levels throughout an organization. Those in positions of power who have the highest degree of influence should be responsible for setting a standard for civil interactions. These standards should then be reinforced through behavioral modeling, as well as being reflected in available written policies. Such actions will set a defined norm that excludes incivility. As an example, an organization's mission statement or introductions to mandatory orientation material presents an opportunity to clearly articulate an expectation of mutual respect accessible to all employees (Pearson & Porath, 2009).

Their second recommendation is for those in positions of authority to evaluate themselves more thoroughly and honestly. Although more research is required in this area, some research has demonstrated that incivility is more likely to be directed at those individuals of lower status (Lim & Lee, 2011), and coping responses typically do not involve communicating up the organizational hierarchy (Cortina & Magley, 2009). A third recommendation is to prevent incivility from entering a workplace. To accomplish this, organizational management can make efforts to refuse exposing employees to uncivil customers, and to take the extra step in screening new employees. Pearson and Porath comment that "Incivility leaves a trail" (Pearson & Porath, 2009, p. 143) and note that one third of organizations do not perform background checks despite the wide availability of information that would reveal individuals with histories of uncivil behavior.

The fourth recommendation is to actively teach civility. This implies going beyond defining civility and modeling it, but expands into investing in the difficult task of priming individuals to react with civility. In their fifth point, Pearson and Porath (2009) recommend providing training for employees and managers alike to assist in identifying signals of incivility in order to act as early in the potential "spiral" (Andersson & Pearson, 1999) as possible. A sixth recommendation discussed by Pearson and Porath (2005, 2009) is to be comprehensive in evaluating claims of an employee instigating incivility. Soliciting anonymous perspectives from subordinates, peers, and superiors will likely result in differing, but more complete understanding of specific

incidents and the workplace culture in whole. In addition, obtaining varying perspectives of the same incident can point to the most likely means
of addressing the problem. In terms of responding to instances of workplace incivility, Pearson and Porath's seventh recommendation is to respond
swiftly and with conviction. To not react to an identified occurrence of incivility sends a message that the behavior was acceptable and can lead to other
workgroup members acting similarly (Dabos & Rousseau, 2004; Sechrist &
Stangor, 2001). This leads to the eighth recommendation, to act on all warning signals and take all complaints seriously. The ninth recommendation is to
never make excuses for incivility instigated by powerful or otherwise valuable
employees, as this again sends the message that incivility is acceptable in certain situations. The final recommendation relates to gathering information
from departing employees. As noted, not all instances of workplace incivility
are visible throughout the organization, despite being well known to specific
workgroups. The apparent hesitation of recipients of incivility to seek support
from higher levels of the organization is evident (Cortina & Magley, 2009)
and some recipients may suffer in silence before making the decision to leave.
In such cases, the loss of the experiences of recipients prevents action from
being taken and allows incivility to continue to spread and potentially escalate
into more serious forms of mistreatment (Andersson & Pearson, 1999).

These recommendations are supported by findings that the most consistent predictors of workplace mistreatment relate to lack of clear guidelines for
expectations for treating peers and authoritarian leadership styles (Aquino
& Thau, 2009). So the solution involves making changes that impact the
patterns of social interaction in the workplace that are no longer permissive
of incivility, and are supported by an organization's management. Next we
examine the only intervention program empirically supported to specifically
address workplace incivility by changing the way workers react to uncivil
behavior and establishing new normative expectations for mutual respect.

Civility training may influence behavior through forms of reciprocity
because both positive and negative reciprocity perpetuate the quality of social
relationships (Bowling et al., 2004). Therefore, effective interventions would
include a means of interrupting negative social interactions like incivility. By
interrupting the cycle, negative consequences can be limited before uncivil
behaviors are reciprocated. Interventions can utilize employees' tendency to
mimic behaviors they observe in others (Dabos & Rousseau, 2004; Sechrist
& Stangor, 2001) in order to promote positive exchanges among colleagues,
inspiring reciprocal actions that improve the overall tone of social exchange
throughout the group.

Osatuke, Moore, Ward, Dyrenforth, and Belton (2009) reported the results of an intervention that specifically targeted workplace civility in Veterans Hospital Administration (VHA) settings (i.e., Civility, Respect, and Engagement in the Workplace; CREW). Their program design approach involved employees, management, and researchers. This resulted in a 6-month process in which facilitators worked cooperatively with employees to address issues related to social interactions among the workgroup members. A key aspect of this approach was the ability to tailor the specific approaches to address the specific issues of concern for each unit. Workgroups, with assistance from researchers and facilitators, identified specific areas of workplace social interactions to be addressed. Through discussion they would then develop and activate a plan, which could be then evaluated for success. In a review of interventions intended to address disruptive workplace behaviors, Rogers-Clark, Pearce, and Cameron (2009) reported that the majority of studies focused on local interventions. Although such studies provided valuable information, the results were of limited utility in terms of applying the same procedures in other settings. As CREW was designed with flexibility in mind, the model could be applied in varying settings, allowing the employees to cooperatively work out the details.

The defining principles of the CREW are that: (1) building civility requires direct conversations based upon accurate evaluations of the group's pre-intervention social environment, specifically the extent of incivility; (2) exercises that help participants explore new ways of interacting drive the process; (3) leadership from facilitators helps participants move out of their established patterns of social behavior; (4) explicit support for the process from management is essential to the program's success; and (5) employees must own the process in order for it to be successful (Osatuke et al., 2009). In other words, the key aspects of CREW are that employees facilitate and activate the change themselves, based on each participant's unique situation.

In their final analysis, Osatuke et al. (2009) compared 23 workgroups who participated in the CREW intervention to matched comparison groups that did not participate in the CREW interventions. CREW group scores on a measure of civility before and after intervention participation was compared to the same scores collected from the comparison group over the same time period. Results demonstrated that workgroup levels of civility significantly increased between pre-intervention and post-intervention. As expected, there were no significant changes in civility ratings for the comparison groups over the same time period. Qualitative data collected with CREW groups' post-intervention survey data suggested that participants

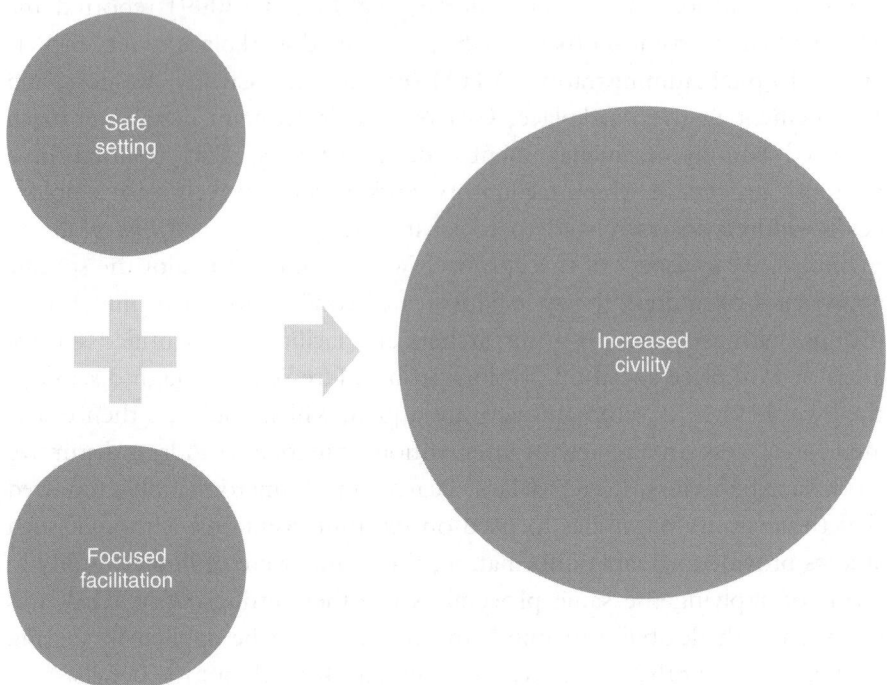

**Figure 13.2.** The CREW Process.

accepted that civility was connected to positive outcomes in their work tasks. Participants in CREW interventions also noted that the combination of exposure to new information and experiential learning positively influenced this acceptance of the utility of civility (Figure 13.2).

Leiter et al. (2011) extended the research on the CREW intervention in several ways. They studied Canadian health-care workers from 41 workgroups, evaluating a combination of variables reflecting the social environment of workgroups (civility, coworker incivility, supervisor incivility, instigated incivility, and respect), burnout and turnover intentions, job attitudes (organizational commitment, personal efficacy, and job satisfaction), trust in management, and absenteeism. These variables were assessed before the CREW intervention and after the CREW intervention for 8 participating workgroups and 33 control groups which did not participate in the CREW intervention.

Results were consistent with those of Osatuke et al. (2009), and demonstrated that the CREW intervention has additional benefits not directly measured in the Osatuke et al. (2009) study. Leiter et al. (2011) found that workgroups that participated in the CREW intervention experienced improvements in workgroup civility, job attitudes, and trust in management. Reductions in burnout experiences, absenteeism, and incivility were also identified. This last finding supports the notion that fostering a culture of civility contradicts growth of, and can actually reduce a culture of incivility. In addition, Leiter et al. (2011) noted that the degree to which workgroups implemented CREW significantly predicted higher levels of civility. That is to say, the more workgroups bought into CREW and made it their own through cohesive and creative involvement, the more likely it was that higher levels of workgroup civility were reported post intervention.

These two studies provide compelling evidence that improving the social interactions employees experience at work, in addition to being possible, can have tangible benefits for individual workgroups and organizations. Although significant work remains in order to more precisely identify and articulate the processes that best enhance the social interactions of employees, there is strong support that one can turn the table on incivility. In essence, it seems that by utilizing the same mechanisms through which incivility spreads, it is possible to eradicate cycles of rude and discourteous behavior and replace them with a culture of self-perpetuating civility.

## Future Directions and Concluding Remarks

As researchers continue adding to the existing knowledge about workplace incivility, it will deserve more attention from the general population of workers. The discussion may prompt people to see and label incivility in their work environments. A shift from subjective experience to objective understanding may in itself cause an individual to pause to reconsider reciprocating an act of incivility. Alternatively, being more aware of incivility could also have the paradoxical effect of making incivility a more available response within an incivility spiral. Improving civility requires more than an awareness of it. As noted by participants in the Osatuke et al. (2009) study, the combination of information and experiential learning was key to changing patterns of social interactions to be more civil. Little is known about the impact of simply increasing awareness of incivility without providing opportunities for experiential learning to combat the process.

Moving forward, the research field must refine what it can offer those who endure the consequences of incivility, and better still seek definitive explanations for how to prevent incivility from infecting our workplaces in the first place. Although encouraged by evidence that targeted interventions can improve the social interactions of workgroups (Leiter et al., 2011; Osatuke et al., 2009), further study is required to examine how these improvements are maintained in the long term. This is particularly relevant as it seems that the cultural themes contributing to workplace incivility are unlikely to disappear or spontaneously change.

This field of research is relatively new, and future research efforts are encouraged to explore more effective and inclusive ways to measure incivility. Looking to document the frequency of behaviors may be an efficient way of collecting information about incivility but it lacks the richness of detail needed to truly understand the process. Moving to more integrated research approaches that consider multiple points of view, and include varied methods of data collection within the same study, would provide such richness (Spector & Rodopman, 2010). Of particular interest would be methods that offer the most insight into the processes involved in a "live" incivility incident (as could be captured through a diary study).

Lastly, the work of Osatuke et al. (2009) and Leiter et al. (2011) should be replicated in a larger variety of organizations, and in regions with different culture norms. These works have demonstrated that civility is a pathway to more positive social environments which can exclude incivility. Given the extent to which incivility has taken root in organizations today, there is a lot of catching up needed.

In conclusion, when people experience mistreatment at work, the workplace becomes a riskier place. The experience diverts attention and energy away from pursuing the workgroup's mission toward managing the risks of potential isolation or humiliation. Organizational interventions that can move an uncivil culture toward one of respect and support can contribute to productivity and wellbeing.

# References

Andersson, L. M., & Pearson, C. M. (1999). Tit for tat? The spiraling effect of incivility in the workplace. *Academy of Management Review, 24*(3), 542–471.

Aquino, K., & Thau, S. (2009). Workplace victimization: Aggression from the target's perspective. *Annual Review of Psychology, 60*, 1–18.

Baruch, Y. (2005). Bullying on the net: Adverse behavior on e-mail and its impact. *Information & Management, 42*, 361–371.

Baruch, Y., & Jenkins, S. (2007). Swearing at work and permissive leadership culture: When anti-social becomes social and incivility is acceptable. *Leadership, & Organization Development Journal, 28*(6), 492–507.

Blau, G., & Andersson, L. (2005). Testing a measure of instigated workplace incivility. *Journal of Occupational and Organizational Psychology, 78*, 595–614.

Bowling, N. A., & Beehr, T. A. (2006). Workplace harassment from the victim's perspective: A theoretical model and meta-analysis. *Journal of Applied Psychology, 91*, 998–1012.

Bowling, N. A., Beehr, T. A., Johnson, A. L., Semmer, N. K., Hendricks, E. A., & Webster, H. A. (2004). Explaining potential antecedents of workplace social support: Reciprocity or attractiveness? *Journal of Occupational Health Psychology, 9*, 339–350.

Caspi, A., Harrington, H. L., Moffitt, T. E., Milne, B. J., & Poulton, R. (2006). Socially isolated children 20 years later: Risk of cardiovascular disease. *Archives of Pediatrics & Adolescent Medicine, 160*, 850–811.

Caza, B. B., & Cortina, L. M. (2007). From insult to injury: Explaining the impact of incivility. *Basic and Applied Social Psychology, 29*(4), 335–350.

Chiaburu, D. S., & Harrison, D. A. (2008). Do peers make the place? Conceptual synthesis and meta-analysis of co-worker effects on perceptions, attitudes, OCB's, and performance. *Journal of Applied Psychology, 93*, 1082–1103.

Cortina, L. M. (2008). Unseen injustice: Incivility as modern discrimination in organizations. *Academy of Management Review, 33*(1), 55–75.

Cortina, L. M., & Magley, V. J. (2009). Patterns and profiles of response to incivility in the workplace. *Journal of Occupational Health Psychology, 14*(3), 272–288.

Cortina, L. M., Magley, V. J., Williams, J. H., & Langhout, R. D. (2001). Incivility in the workplace: Incidence and impact. *Journal of Occupational Health Psychology, 6*(1), 64–80.

Dabos, G. E., & Rousseau, D. M. (2004). Mutuality and reciprocity in the psychological contracts of employees and employers. *Journal of Applied Psychology, 89*, 52–72.

Duffy, M. K., Ganster, D. C., & Pagon, M. (2002). Social undermining in the workplace. *Academy of Management Journal, 45*, 331–351.

DuFrene, D. D., & Lehman, C. M. (2002). Persuasive appeal for clean language. *Business Communication Quarterly, 65*(1), 48–55.

Ehrlich, H. J., & Larcom, B. E. K. (1994). *Ethnoviolence in the workplace*. Baltimore, MD: Center for the Applied Study of Ethnoviolence.

Einarsen, S. (2000). Harassment and bullying at work: A review of the Scandinavian approach. *Aggression and Violent Behavior: A Review Journal, 5*, 371–401.

Forgette, R., & Morris, J. S. (2006). High-conflict television news and public opinion. *Political Research Quarterly, 59*(3), 447–456.

Giacalone, R. A., & Greenberg, J. (Eds.) (1997). *Antisocial behavior in organizations*. Thousand Oaks, CA: Sage.

Griffin, B. (2010). Multilevel relationships between organizational-level incivility, justice and intention to stay. *Work & Stress, 24*(4), 309–323.

Hershcovis, M. S. (2011). "Incivility, social undermining, bullying . . . oh my!": A call to reconcile constructs within workplace aggression research. *Journal of Organizational Behavior, 32*, 499–519.

Jex, S. M., Burnfield Geimer, J. L., Clark, O., Guidroz, A., & Yugo, J. E. (2010). Challenges and recommendations in the measurement of workplace incivility. In J. Greenberg (Ed.), *Insidious workplace behavior* (pp. 239–271). New York: Taylor & Francis.

Johnson, P. R., & Indvik, J. (2001). Slings and arrows of rudeness: Incivility in the workplace. *Journal of Management Development*, *20*(8), 705–713.

Laschinger, H. K. S., Leiter, M. P., Day, A., & Gilin, D. (2009). Workplace empowerment, incivility, and burnout: Impact on staff recruitment and retention outcomes. *Journal of Nursing Management*, *17*, 302–311.

Leiter, M. P., Laschinger, H. K. S., Day, A., & Gilin-Oore, D. (2011). The impact of civility interventions on employee social behavior, distress, and attitudes. *Journal of Applied Psychology*, *96*(6), 1258–1274.

Leiter, M. P., Laschinger, H. K. S., Day, A., & Gilin-Oore, D. (2010). *Rudeness rationales: Whatever were they thinking?* Presentation at the Annual Conference of the Academy of Management, Montreal, Canada.

Leymann, H. (1996). The content and development of mobbing at work. *European Journal of Work and Organizational Psychology*, *5*(2), 165–184.

Life sentence without parole for Md. woman who beat, stabbed co-worker to death at yoga shop. (2012, January 27). *The Washington Post*. Retrieved from http://www.washingtonpost.com.

Lim, S., & Cortina, L. M. (2005). Interpersonal mistreatment in the workplace: The interface and impact of general incivility and sexual harassment. *Journal of Applied Psychology*, *90*(3), 483–496.

Lim, S., Cortina, L. M., & Magley, V. J. (2008). Personal and workgroup incivility: Impact on work and health outcomes. *Journal of Applied Psychology 93*(1), 95–107.

Lim, S., & Lee, A. (2011). Work and nonwork outcomes of workplace incivility: Does family support help? *Journal of Occupational Health Psychology*, *16*(1), 95–111.

Martin, R. J., & Hine, D. W. (2005). Development and validation of the uncivil workplace behavior questionnaire. *Journal of Occupational Health Psychology*, *10*(4), 477–490.

Nelson, L. J., Padilla-Walker, L. M., Christensen, K., J., Evans, C. A., & Carroll, J. S. (2011). Parenting in emerging adulthood: An examination of parenting clusters and correlates. *Journal of Youth and Adolescence*, *40*, 730–743.

Neuman, J. H., & Baron, R. A. (1997). Aggression in the workplace. In R. A. Giacalone & J. Greenberg (Eds.), *Antisocial behavior in organizations* (pp. 37–67). Thousand Oaks, CA: Sage.

O'Kane, P., & Hargie, O. (2007). Intentional and unintentional consequences of substituting face-to-face interaction with e-mail: An employee-based perspective. *Interacting with Computers*, *19*, 20–31.

Osatuke, K., Moore, S. C., Ward, C., Dyrenforth, S., & Belton, L. (2009). Civility, Respect, Engagement in the Workforce (CREW): Nationwide Organization Development Intervention at Veterans Health Administration. *Journal of Applied Behavioral Science*, *45*, 384–410.

Parents Television Council (2002). *Wired for raunch: A content analysis of basic cable's original prime-time series*. Retrieved from http://www.parentstv.org/ptc/publications/reports/cablestudy/main.asp.

Pearson, C. M. (2010). Research on workplace incivility and its connection to practice. In J. Greenberg (Ed.), *Insidious workplace behavior* (pp. 149–173). New York: Taylor & Francis.

Pearson, C. M., Andersson, L. M., & Porath, C. L. (2000). Assessing and attacking workplace incivility. *Organizational Dynamics, 29*(2), 123–137.

Pearson, C. M., & Porath, C. L. (2005). On the nature, consequences and remedies of workplace incivility: No time for "nice"? Think again. *The Academy of Management Executive, 19*(1), 7–18.

Pearson, C., & Porath, C. (2009). *The cost of bad behavior: How incivility is damaging your business and what to do about it*. New York: Penguin Books.

Plank, S. B., McDill, E. L., McPartland, J. M., & Jordan, W. J. (2001). Situation and repertoire: Civility, incivility, cursing, and politeness in an urban high school. *Teachers College Record, 103*(3), 504–524.

Reio, T. G., Jr., & Ghosh, R. (2009). Antecedents and outcomes of workplace incivility: Implications for human resource development research and practice. *Human Resource Development Quarterly, 20*(3), 237–264.

Rice, R. W., Near, J. P., & Hunt, R. G. (1980). The job-satisfaction/life satisfaction relationship. A review of empirical research. *Basic & Applied Social Psychology, 1*(1), 37–64.

Robinson, S. L., & Bennett, R. J. (1997). Workplace deviance: Its definition, its manifestations, and its causes. In R. Lewicki, B. Sheppard, & R. Bies (Eds.), *Research on negotiation in organizations* (Vol. 6, pp. 3–27). Greenwich, CT: JAI Press.

Rogers, S. J., & May, D. C. (2003). Spillover between marital quality and job satisfaction; Long-term patterns and gender differences. *Journal of Marriage and Family, 65*(2), 482–495.

Rogers-Clark, C., Pearce, S., & Cameron, M. (2009). Management of disruptive behaviour within nursing work environments: A comprehensive systematic review of the evidence. *The JBI Database of Systematic Reviews and Implementation Reports, 7*, 615–678.

Schat A. C. H., & Kelloway E. K. (2005). Workplace violence. In J. Barling, E. K. Kelloway, & M. Frone (Eds.), *Handbook of work stress* (pp. 189–218). Thousand Oaks, CA: Sage.

Schiffrin, H., Edelman, A., Falkenstern, M., & Stewart, C. (2010). The associations among computer-mediated communication, relationships, and well-being. *Cyberpsychology, Behavior, and Social Networking, 3*(13), 299–306.

Sechrist, G., & Stangor, C. (2001). Perceived consensus influences intergroup behavior and stereotype accessibility. *Journal of Personality and Social Psychology, 80*, 645–654.

Spector, P. E., & Jex, S. M. (1998). Development of four self-report measures of job stress and strain: Interpersonal conflict at work scale, organizational constraints scale, quantitative workload inventory, and physical symptoms inventory. *Journal of Occupational Health Psychology, 3*, 356–367.

Spector, P. E., & Rodopman, O. B. (2010). Methodological issues in studying insidious workplace behavior. In J. Greenberg (Ed.), *Insidious workplace behavior* (pp. 273–306). New York: Taylor & Francis.

Tepper, B. J. (2000). Consequences of abusive supervision. *Academy of Management Journal, 43*, 178–190.

Valkenburg, P., & Peter, J. (2007). Online communication and adolescent well being: Testing the stimulation versus the displacement hypothesis. *Journal of Computer-Mediated Communication, 12*, 1169–1182.

van Jaarsveld, D. D., Walker, D. D., & Skarlicki, D. P. (2010). The role of job demands and emotional exhaustion in the relationship between customer and employee incivility. *Journal of Management, 36*, 1486–1504.

Westmyer, S. A., DiCioccio, R. L., & Rubin, R. B. (1998). Appropriateness and effectiveness of communication channels in competent interpersonal communication. *Journal of Communication, 48*, 27–48.

Wolfer, R., Bull, H. D., & Scheithauer, H. (2012). Social integration in youth: Insights from a social network perspective. *Group Dynamics: Theory, Research, and Practice, 16*(2), 138–147.

Zauderer, D. G. (2002). Workplace incivility and the management of human capital. *Public Manager, 31*, 36–43.

# 14

# The Sustainable Workforce
## *Organizational Strategies for Promoting Work–Life Balance and Wellbeing*

## Ellen Ernst Kossek
Purdue University Krannert School of Management, U.S.A.

## Monique Valcour and Pamela Lirio
EDHEC Business School, France

What is it like to be part of a sustainable workforce? Just ask employees. Browsing employee comments about the employers recently identified as the top 25 companies for work–life balance by the online employment and career community of current employees and job seekers Glassdoor.com reveals the following picture:

> [The company] respects and values its employees and their families. Work–life balance is very real and everyone is encouraged to take time off and keep their work hours under control. The work environment is much less stressful than the competition.
>
> Professional and personal development are highly encouraged for all employees.
>
> [The company] strongly believes in supporting the local community.
>
> Pros: freedom, autonomy, respect, a real life. When you love your job and the company values your contributions, everything is easy.

*Work and Wellbeing: Wellbeing: A Complete Reference Guide*, Volume III.
Edited by Peter Y. Chen and Cary L. Cooper.
© 2014 John Wiley & Sons, Ltd. Published 2014 by John Wiley & Sons, Inc.
DOI: 10.1002/9781118539415.wbwell14

By contrast, employees at companies that rank low on work–life balance describe their workplaces on Glassdoor.com with comments like these:

> Twelve- and fourteen-hour days with no lunch breaks, not much flexibility with scheduling and always pressured to work extra days.
>
> The company's focus on activity metrics and growth expectations over team morale creates a hostile work environment.
>
> The company doesn't demonstrate that it values employees. [We are] hemorrhaging experience and expertise . . . as formerly loyal employees who no longer feel valued by the company, as a result of increased work-loads, budget cutbacks and pay-cuts, [choose to leave].

As these opening examples suggest, organizations vary in their ability to create, support, and maintain a sustainable workforce. Research is needed to develop an understanding of organizational strategies to foster a sustainable workforce. We argue that a sustainable workforce is created and nurtured via employment practices that link employee work–life balance and wellbeing to employment experiences over the course of employees' working lives, enabling them to perform well over time while also thriving in their personal and family lives.

Yet work–life balance, wellbeing, and sustainability are not well linked in research and practice, despite the fact they are growing in importance in the scholarly and managerial literatures. This disconnect is a critical problem. Creating stronger connections between these domains in the design of work and workplaces will not only enhance the long-term effectiveness of employees over their working lives but will also enhance the health and resource munificence of institutions and society. Employment practices that sustain work–life balance and wellbeing in workplace experiences are critical pathways to long-term workforce effectiveness.

In this chapter, we briefly define sustainable workforce, work–life balance, and wellbeing, and examine how they are related. Then, in order to make these connections actionable for organizational researchers and practitioners, we identify three organizational strategies that can be employed to improve these linkages: promoting sustainable careers, increasing workplace social support, and safeguarding against work intensification. We close with a research agenda. A main tenet is that enacting human resource strategies to build stronger connections between work–life balance and wellbeing will help promote the development of sustainable workforces in organizations, and will foster long-term social benefits.

# Sustainable Workforce, Work–Life Balance, and Wellbeing: Conceptualization and Linkages

Just as there is growing concern about promoting the sustainability of environmental resources, there should be similar concern for fostering the sustainability of human resources (Pfeffer, 2010). However, the sustainability of people, their work–life balance, and wellbeing has been undervalued relative to other targets of sustainability in the management and organizations literatures (Ehnert, 2009).

## Sustainable Workforce

In order to understand what a sustainable workforce is, it is helpful to begin with discussion of what it is not. Many employment settings are designed in ways that do not link support for employee wellbeing and work–life balance to organizational business strategy and performance. As Kalleberg (2009) observes, the employment relationship between workers and employers is in transition in many countries at present. Environmental, social, economic, and political shifts over recent decades nationally and globally have converged to make work experiences more "precarious." By "precarious work" Kalleberg (2009, p. 2) means employment conditions that are more "uncertain, unpredictable, risky from the perspective of the employee." He and others (Lambert, 2008; Kossek, Kaillaith, & Kaillaith, 2012) note that precarious working conditions are characterized by weakening attachment between employers and employees, nonstandard and/or unpredictable work schedules, little or no job security, and compensation and benefits systems that transfer risk and shifts in customer and market demands from the organization to the worker (Lambert, 2008). The impact of this shift has been felt in higher levels of stress, and in the overall degradation of employees' working conditions and their physical and mental health.

Even when employees voice concern about sustaining the wellbeing of the workforces, the discourse often suggests that employers are not responsible for nor benefit from workforce wellbeing. One example is the growing attention to rising employer-based health-care costs in the United States and gaps in coverage of individuals who are not covered by employer-linked health insurance. Health-care costs are seen as a threat to economic competitiveness and therefore as a target for reduction. Jobs are increasingly offered with no or limited benefits. Employers react by slashing benefits,

297

increasing employee co-payments, and/or offering jobs with limited or no benefits, thereby passing on the risk and expenses to employees. Lambert (2008) refers to this approach as "passing the buck."

Another example is from a study of 27 public sector organizations in the United Kingdom (Lewis & Anderson, 2013). These organizations are cutting work–life balance policies. They are also trying to model high performance work system practices and are moving toward lean production approaches to work organization. Employees are increasingly expected to work harder, faster, and smarter (Lewis & Anderson, 2013). The interviews manifested a growing employer expectation that individuals should take more responsibility to ensure their own health and wellbeing rather than relying on supportive organizational initiatives.

A final example comes from the recent tragedy of Hurricane Sandy in the eastern United States. Low-wage workers are hardest hit economically by disasters, as they are most likely to have to forego pay if they cannot get to work (Shapiro, Knafo, & Hindman, 2012). Many New York area employees in lower economic jobs (e.g., hairdressers, restaurant workers, health-care aides) risked life and limb to go to work. Rather than jeopardize employment, pay, or benefits, employees showed up despite school closings, fallen electrical lines, flooded homes, and disrupted public transportation systems (Rohde, 2012).

In contrast to the preceding discussion, a sustainable workforce is one where the work environment is caring and supports employee wellbeing. Employees are not seen as primarily resources that can be deployed (and depleted) to serve employers' economic ends. Their skills, talents, and energies are not overused or overly depleted. They are not faced with excessive workload nor with an unrelentless pace of work for weeks or years on end. During times of crisis (e.g., natural disasters, sickness), employees are given time to recover or seek the extra resources they need to be able to perform in the future. Burnout is avoided and workers are given time for renewal.

When human resources are used in a sustainable way, employees are not only able to perform in-role or requisite job demands, but also to flourish, be creative, and innovate. Sustainable human resource management practices develop positive social relationships at work, which enhances business performance (Cooperider & Fry, 2012), including greater cohesion among organizational members, commitment to common purpose, hope for success, resilience, knowledge sharing, and collaborative capacity. Enrichment and synergies from nonwork roles can improve performance at work (Demerouti, Bakker, & Voydanoff, 2010). For example, employees who have happy personal lives and are active and contributing members of their communities bring skills and positive energies from home to work (Ruderman, Ohlett, Panzer, & King, 2002).

Pfeffer (2010, p. 35) argues that human sustainability considers:

> how organizational activities affect people's physical and mental health and well-being—the stress of work practices on the human system—as well as effects of management practices such as work hours and behaviors that produce workplace stress on groups and group cohesion and also the richness of social life, as exemplified by participation in civic, voluntary, and community organizations.

Van Engen, Vinkenburg, and Dikkers (2012) argue that a focus on human sustainability "requires that employers take the present and future well-being and performance of their employees into account."

Building on the preceding discussion, we define a sustainable workforce as one whose employees have the positive energy, capabilities, vitality, and resources to meet current and future organizational performance demands while sustaining their economic and mental health on and off the job. We argue that organizational facilitation of employee work–life balance and wellbeing are the pillars needed to support sustainable careers, sustainable families, and a sustainable workforce.

## Work–Life Balance

Scholars have debated the meaning of the term "work–life balance" in the literature for a number of years. Some authors prefer to use the more traditional label of "work–family" in recognition of the fact that for many people, the job and the nuclear family constitute the role domains that demand the greatest amount of time, attention, and energy and are most likely to come into conflict with one another. These scholars note that the term work–family grew out of early policy efforts in industrialized nations to countervail gender discrimination and ensure that care for young children did not deter female labor market participation (Kossek, Baltes, & Matthews, 2011). Yet the term "work–family" can oversimplify people's work and nonwork roles; some scholars (Valcour, 2007) believe it fails to do justice to the diversity of work and life circumstances of working people, such as single individuals and those in nontraditional family structures. Recently, increasing numbers of authors have adopted the term "work–life" out of conviction that it recognizes the numerous social roles people occupy in both the work (e.g., subordinate, supervisor, coworker, mentor) and nonwork (e.g., parent, child, spouse, friend, community member) domains as well as the diversity of role configurations represented by members of the workforce. However, we recognize the term "work–life" is not ideal, as work is part of life (Kossek, Baltes, et al., 2011). Further, the term work–life has sometimes been used by large employers as a public relations tool to lessen backlash from employees without current family demands or reduce beliefs of employer responsibility for supporting the family demands of employees (Kossek, Kaillaith, & Kaillaith, 2012). Despite these challenges, consistent with recent trends in the literature, we adopt the more inclusive term "work–life."

There is also little consensus among scholars about what is meant by the word "balance." Many authors do not explicitly state their definition of the concept, leaving the measurement instrument to stand in for a proper definition. For instance, measures of work–life conflict are often used to operationalize work–life balance, reflecting an assumption that these two concepts are opposite ends of a continuum and that people with low conflict between work and life roles necessarily experience good work–life balance. Although work–life conflict and balance are inversely related, empirical research does not support the assumption that they are opposite sides of the same coin, nor that low work–life conflict fully captures the construct of work–life balance. Furthermore, work–life balance is unique among work–life constructs in referring to a global experience of combining multiple roles, rather than to a strictly cross-domain process such as the transfer of strain generated in the work domain to a nonwork domain.

Some authors implicitly adopt the metaphor of a physical balance or scale, emphasizing an equal allocation of one's time and attention to the different roles in one's life. For instance, Greenhaus, Collins, and Shaw (2003) define work–family balance as equal engagement (both in terms of time and psychological involvement) in and equal satisfaction derived from work and family roles. This definition is unusually prescriptive in that it specifies an equal division of time, involvement, and satisfaction between the work and nonwork domains as the ideal scenario. By contrast, other authors favor definitions that refer to the fit of individuals' work–life demands and resources to their own values, goals, and needs as well to their external work and life circumstances. For example, Kofodimos (1993, p. 8) wrote that balance consists of "finding the allocation of time and energy that fits your values and needs, making conscious choices about how to structure your life and integrating inner needs and outer demands and . . . honoring and living by your deepest personal qualities, values and goals." This definition exemplifies what Reiter (2007) characterizes as a situationalist definition (i.e., one that seeks an optimum outcome for each worker, regardless of his or her work and life circumstances).

We agree with Reiter's (2007) argument that the way in which work–life balance is defined influences the development and implementation of organizational work–life initiatives, with important consequences for employees and organizations. We further assert that organizations must approach work–life balance initiatives broadly and creatively enough to develop a suite of approaches that support positive, high-quality integration of work and nonwork roles for all of their employees over the long term, regardless of age, life or career stage, family circumstances, occupation, or socioeconomic status. In particular, organizations must foster workplace cultures and structures that not only support diversity in values that align work and personal life, but enable employees to exert schedule and boundary control in order to synthesize work–life demands in alignment with needs and preferences (Kossek, Ruderman, Braddy, & Hannum, 2012).

Building on these perspectives, we define work–life balance as satisfaction and perceptions of success in meeting work and nonwork role demands, low levels of conflict among roles, and opportunity for inter-role enrichment, meaning that experiences in one role can improve performance and satisfaction in other roles as well (Frone, 2003; Greenhaus & Allen, 2010; Valcour, 2007). Our use of the term "balance" is not intended to prescribe an equal division of time and attention to each of the roles in a person's role system, but to support the pattern of role investment that is appropriate to each individual at any given time. That is, work–life balancing can mean different things to different people depending on the demands and values of their work and the personal identities that are most salient and meaningful (Kossek, Ruderman, et al., 2012). We emphasize that work–life balance is a broad issue with relevance for all working people, because it is fundamentally about being able to do well at things we care about. There is no single ideal model of work–life balance; it depends upon people's values, priorities, the demands they face in the different areas of their lives, and the resources they can access and use to meet those demands. The picture of work–life balance looks different from one person to another, as well as at different points in a person's career and life. Since work–life balance is highly valued by nearly all employees and linked to important performance-related outcomes, yet also challenging to achieve, it also has broad applicability to employers.

301

Employing organizations who seek to foster overall workforce sustainability must approach work–life balance broadly. While not overlooking the needs of working mothers with young children, employers should support involvement of all employees' needs for work–life balance. Examples might include support of fathers who want to take an active role in child care or shared care (where fathers and mothers are involved in parent care), elder care, and involvement in community, regular exercise, education, and social and religious involvement. Those firms that take a very narrow view of who is entitled to work–life balance facilitation and do not seek ways to enhance positive linkages between all employees' involvement in multiple roles performance and wellbeing over their working lives miss out on opportunities to fully engage and develop their workforce. They also deplete the organization of resources for sustainability, as workers with family demands may resent the lack of support, while those without visible family demands feel overworked or that they are always carrying the workload (whether this reflects reality or not) by picking up the slack (Rothausen, Gonzalez, Clarke, & O'Dell, 1998).

## Wellbeing

Wellbeing is important for both organizational effectiveness and individual mental and physical health (Diener, 2000). Fisher's review of wellbeing at work (Chapter 2 in this volume) defines wellbeing as being multidimensional, comprising subjective wellbeing (positive affect), social wellbeing (friends at work), and feelings of engagement and involvement toward self-actualization. Employees may come to work with different personality proclivities, but once there they are nested in organizational environments that can foster or deplete wellbeing. The structure of work has consequences for employees both on and off the job. Of the five life domains comprising general wellbeing, career wellbeing is the most important for the wellbeing of most individuals (Rath & Harter, 2010).

Related to the growth in research on wellbeing is an exploding redeveloping interest in positive approaches to the psychology of work, and particularly in promoting wellbeing. Wellbeing at work has received renewed attention as a vehicle for organizational effectiveness, social change, and a managerial lever for ensuring performance (cf. Golden-Biddle & Dutton, 2012). Managerial awareness of the importance of employee wellbeing is growing, along with human resource programs designed to foster it, such as employee assistance, flexible work arrangements, and fitness initiatives. Best-selling books with titles like *Wellbeing: The five essential elements* (Rath & Harter, 2010), *Feeling good: The new mood therapy* (Burns, 1999), and *Flow: The psychology of optimal experience* (Csikszentmihalyi, 1990) provide evidence of popular interest in cultivating wellbeing. Even some governments have begun to put stock in measures of gross national happiness along with more traditional social and economic indicators of the wellbeing of their citizens (Blanchflower & Oswald, 2011).

Employers have jumped on the bandwagon to promote engagement and wellbeing by measuring engagement via the Gallup surveys. This survey, called the Gallup Q-12, includes items measuring whether an employee "has a close friend at work" or "feel involved in their jobs" (http://www.well-beingindex.com/), which are indicators that map closely to the definitions of wellbeing at work noted above. Some companies link their leaders' compensation to employee engagement based on research that has shown that engagement is associated with quality, turnover, and customer service (Towers Watson, 2012).

## Summary of Linkages

Table 14.1 summarizes the definitions and highlights where there are convergence and divergence in concepts. Work–life balance, wellbeing, and sustainability all include notions of positive appraisals of energy at work. Wellbeing also includes satisfaction with work and nonwork roles. Both work–life balance and workforce sustainability include notions of maintaining resources and having an equilibrium. Regarding differences, wellbeing and work–life balance are momentary states. In contrast, sustainability involves short-term action to use human resources in ways that do not deplete resources and also facilitate capabilities to perform in the future.

## Organizational Strategies to Foster a Sustainable Workforce

Organizational strategies designed to foster a sustainable workforce include safeguarding against work intensification, promoting workplace social support, and fostering sustainable careers. Table 14.2 gives an overview of activities and outcomes related to these organizational strategies. Highlights of the table are discussed below.

303

**Table 14.1.** Comparison of Work–Life Balance, Wellbeing, and Sustainability.

| Construct | Definition | Similarity (conceptual connections) | Distinctiveness (examples of temporal and content differences) |
|---|---|---|---|
| Work–life balance | Satisfaction and perceptions of success in meeting work and nonwork role demands, low levels of conflict among roles, opportunity for inter-role enrichment | Includes positive emotions and appraisals of wellbeing at work<br><br>Includes notions of positive energy | Momentary state<br><br>Linkage between multiple roles as positive and having multiple roles is seen as synergistic |
| Work well-being | Subjective and social wellbeing at work, work involvement toward self-actualization | Wellbeing is a term that reflects not only one's health but also satisfaction with work and life | Momentary state<br><br>Summative concept deriving from state of health and quality of working life<br><br>Known to be related to productivity levels among individuals, organizations, and societies |
| Workforce sustainability | Positive energy, capabilities, vitality, and resources to meet current and future organizational performance demands without harming economic and mental health on and off the job | Resource stance: Like the notion of work–life balance, resources are used in equilibrium and not depleted<br><br>Involves positive work–nonwork relationships<br><br>Involves health (like wellbeing) | Time frame differences: Unlike balance and wellbeing, which seem to be states, sustainability takes more of a long-term perspective<br><br>Energy, and notion of maintaining and restoring resources and capabilities |

Table 14.2. Organizational Strategies for Enhancing Work–Life Balance and Wellbeing to Enhance a Sustainable Workforce.

| Organizational strategy | Definition | Examples of activities | Effects on increasing work–life balance and wellbeing linkages |
|---|---|---|---|
| Sustainable career management | Practices and policies enabling employees to maintain positive involvement in career, family, and personal roles over the life course | Career breaks<br>Part-time work<br>Part-year work<br>Ongoing personal and work development<br>Employee say over career changes without penalty<br>Leave control for time off work, vacations, sabbaticals | Allows total life resources to be adapted to promote equilibrium in total life space over time<br>Promotes positive synergies<br>Ability to be advanced in career and be involved in community and family |
| Culture of positive workplace social support | The degree to which individuals perceive that their wellbeing is valued by workplace sources, such as supervisors, and the broader organization in which individuals are embedded | Designing work to foster high social support<br>Cross-training employees to back each other up<br>Rewarding helping behavior<br>Developing leaders to care about workers and workers to care about each other | Positive emotions and wellbeing at work<br>Workers are freed up to learn new things on the job and are not burnt out<br>Workers' personal time is freed up to handle personal life demands<br>Positive work and nonwork social support spillover |

(Continued overleaf)

Table 14.2. (*Continued*)

| Organizational strategy | Definition | Examples of activities | Effects on increasing work–life balance and wellbeing linkages |
|---|---|---|---|
| Safeguarding against work intensification to promote job control | Striving to prevent the heightened focus and engagement demanded of employees at work, usually experienced as: time pressure (e.g., tightening of deadlines), increased pace (speeding up the rate at which work is performed), and/or work overload (trying to accomplish more work in same amount of time) | Setting realistic deadlines and planning work activities accordingly<br>Striving for synergies in the work process by streamlining necessary procedural steps (e.g., working "smarter")<br>Establishing a standard range for employee performance that is attainable and sustainable with reasonable engagement and effort<br>Valuing quality over quantity or speed and allowing employees to perform to the best of their abilities<br>Allowing for a measure of job control or discretion over one's work and performance<br>Creating and fostering a culture of healthy work practices (e.g., teleworkers not "overworking" to compensate for unique work arrangement) and normalizing the use of flexibility (e.g., evaluations based on results not "face time") | Allows employees and managers to contain workloads so individual and organizational goals can be achieved in harmony<br>Tapping into employees' engagement at work without exploiting their work effort fosters workforce wellbeing<br>Permits valuing of restorative time to counteract possible work overload and assist employees in maintaining overall wellbeing at work and home |

## Preventing Work Intensification

One important aspect of work design that promotes wellbeing in the workplace is related to sources of employee stress stemming from a required output at work, or job demands (Karasek, 1979). In settings where decision latitude or job control (discretion) over job demands is largely absent, the wellbeing of employees is adversely affected. An example of this would be when employees work in a high-strain job which has high demands–low control conditions. The Job Demand–Control (JDC) model has been widely accepted and tested within the stress and coping literature (Doef & Maes, 1999) and has now expanded into the work and family literature as well (Gronlund, 2007; Joudrey & Wallace, 2009).

Lack of control or discretion at work is stress-provoking for employees regardless of the specific job demands (Berset, Semmer, Elfering, Amstad, & Jacobshagen, 2009). Berset et al. (2009) confirmed this by testing the levels of participants' stress hormones during workdays and during weekends. They found that the level of control participants enjoyed at work alleviated their stress levels and enabled them to recover better on their days off and return to work less stressed. Recently, Chiang, Birtch, and Kwan (2010) found that the additional presence of work–life practices in the workplace along with high job control alleviated stress among employees working in high demand jobs. However, employers' interests in wellbeing may be largely self-serving. Ortega (2009) found in his study of Western European employees that organizations permitted employees to have discretion over their work as a mechanism to improve performance in the workplace, rather than as a result of a desire to assist employees in improving their work–life balance. As the boundaries between work and personal life become increasingly blurred through the use of mobile technology and flexible work practices, researchers are beginning to find that total discretion to self-regulate the work–life interface can be harmful if organizational norms encourage employees to remain continuously connected and responsive to work. The phenomenon of constant connection to work has increasingly been linked to attention deficit disorder, stress, and depletion of resources (Kossek & Lautsch, 2007; Turkle, 2011).

Increased workload can be examined in terms of amount of time spent at work (or "work hours"), which is largely where the work and family literature has focused to date (cf. Kossek, Lautsch, & Eaton, 2006; Valcour, 2007). Control at work has been more readily interpreted within the literature in relation to executing individual discretion in where, when, and how work

307

is done (e.g., teleworking) and not in how much work is done, given the job duties. Some researchers have approached this issue from a perspective of "psychological job control" over how and when their work gets done (Kossek et al., 2006), whereas other researchers have examined the quantity of work accomplished (i.e., amount of work or "workload") and the qualities by which work is done in terms of the focus and engagement demanded at work (i.e., "work intensification").

Looking at the employee's ability to "push back" on work demands or have discretion in deciding the amount of work they do remains under-researched. However, this becomes important to consider with globalization and technology speeding up and intensifying the pace of business due to continual connectivity across spatial and temporal boundaries (Ladner, 2008). And in the era of managers staying connected to work (Towers, Duxbury, Higgins, & Thomas, 2006), it becomes increasingly important to examine *work overload* and *work intensification*. This is particularly important given that managers can often avail themselves of flexibility to accommodate personal or family needs more readily than most staff employees (e.g., by shifting their work schedules as needed or ad hoc working from home). Managers do not, however, as easily reduce their workload as a means of coping with work–family conflict or stress, although research on professionals and managers with reduced-load work arrangements has shown some evidence of this (Lee, MacDermid, & Buck, 2002).

Moreover, Skinner and Pocock (2008) see the problem of containing work in terms of assessing work overload. There are three dimensions of demands experienced at work, namely: (1) time pressure (e.g., deadlines), (2) high speeds (e.g., pace), and (3) overload (e.g., quantity). Typically, both the number of hours of work and the amount of work to be completed are related to work–life conflict (here, measured in terms of negative spillover and conflict from work to nonwork aspects of life); however, work overload has been shown to be more strongly related (Allan, Loudoun, & Peetz, 2007; Wallace, 1997). Along this vein, Macky and Boxall (2008) advocate working smarter, not longer or more intensely. They found that being more *engaged* in work does not necessarily lead to increased stress and lower balance between work and nonwork activities (based on family, friends, and other aspects of personal life). Yet, in an environment where pressure exists to work longer and harder, and personal time is infringed upon in the name of work, employees report less job satisfaction, higher stress, and lower work–life balance. Recently, Parker, Jimmieson, and Amiot (2010) found that job control can be effective in stress management for those who are highly engaged in their work (meaning that they are working intensely and are highly motivated).

Kelliher and Anderson (2010) investigated the notion of "work intensification" among those who are working differently through remote and reduced-load work flexible work arrangements to manage work and family demands. Here, work intensification is conceptualized as energy and effort that is put forth in doing work, typically in a concentrated manner (e.g., having too much work to do in the time normally allotted for work). The authors identify three ways by which work intensification arises: (1) it can be *imposed*, due to organizational change such as downsizing and other resource cutbacks, (2) it can be *enabled*, when employees work harder during work time because they have fewer distractions when remote working, and (3) through an *exchange*, which stems from employees working harder to reward the organization for allowing them certain flexibilities. What can be problematic here among flexworkers is that although they may report high job satisfaction for having the flexibility they desire, they may experience a more intense work setting which over time could be detrimental to their overall wellbeing.

*Examples of work-intensification reduction activities and outcomes.*
As Table 14.2 shows, managers can increase job control and prevent work intensification by setting realistic deadlines and planning work activities accordingly. They can also strive for synergies in the work process by identifying ways to get rid of low-value work that does not help productivity and is unnecessary, such as poorly run meetings. They can have a range for employee performance that looks at productivity that is maintained on outcomes and quality and is assessed over a period of time. Overworking, such as teleworkers trying to be available 24/7, in order to have access to flexibility is not rewarded. Taking breaks, vacations, and time for recovery from work is valued.

## Sustainable Careers

Sustainable careers allow individuals to have positive career experiences over the long term in ways that promote organizational and individual effectiveness. We define a sustainable career as providing: (1) security to meet economic needs; (2) fit with one's core career and life values; (3) flexibility and capability of evolving to suit one's changing needs and interests; and (4) renewal so that individuals have regular opportunities for rejuvenation. Thus, a sustainable career is dynamic and flexible; it features continuous learning, periodic renewal, the security that comes from employability, and a harmonious fit with the individual's skills, interests, and values (Newman, 2011; Valcour, 2013). Sustainable career strategies help individuals to maintain an evolving sequence of work experiences over time (Arthur, Hall, & Lawrence, 1989) in ways that allow an employee to have positive career experiences in the present and over the long term. This avoids burnout and allows positive emotions (wellbeing) to be linked to career success over time. Sustainable careers can sometimes involve reduced-load work strategies to prevent intensification and overload. A longitudinal study by Hall, Lee, Kossek, and Las Heras (2012) examined the objective and subjective career success of 73 managers and high-level professionals who decided to reduce their workloads to support higher involvement in family and other personal activities. What they found was that taking time out to reduce career demands did not necessarily harm long-term economic and social success, with one exception: individuals who remained part time for more than 7 years were less likely to be promoted than individuals who returned to full-time employment over the period. The study also found very little relationship between objective and subjective success. Comparing extreme cases of individuals who were higher or lower on perceptions of career success was also informative. The use of flexible work–life arrangements such as reduced-load work was not a panacea in and of itself for sustainable careers. Rather it was the psychological meaning of wellbeing and the ability to remain involved in family life while having a career and vice versa that allowed these high-talent individuals to craft lives that work for them, fostering cross-domain success.

Studies such as this remind us how important it is to look at the nonwork side of the work–nonwork equation to see how restorative time helps experiences in the work or nonwork domains. Leisure time is crucial for employee wellbeing and performance (Fritz & Sonnentag, 2006; Fritz, Sonnentag, Spector, & McInroe, 2010), and especially for those working in intense and stressful environments, such as the lawyers Joudrey and Wallace (2009) study. Having the ability to control working time affects a person's ability to restore his- or herself over a career. Like work intensification, job control is also important for the enactment of sustainable careers. Having control not only over the number and scheduling of work hours (i.e., flextime), but also over the overall amount of work expected is important for a sustainable career (Geurts, Beckers, Taris, Kompier, & Smulders, 2009) because control over the prevention of work overload allows individuals to maintain the resources needed for career success (Grebner, Elfering, & Semmer, 2010) and to have a life outside of work.

This leads us to another emergent strategy for sustainable careers: "leave control." Enabling adequate time off and respecting vacation time improves employee work–life balance. Leave control has the effect of taking workload "off one's plate" or freeing one's agenda. In their study, Geurts et al. (2009) found that leave control in particular contributed to a lower incidence of work interfering with family and fostered employee wellbeing.

Leave control is needed not only to sustain involvement in caregiving over career, but also to give time for continual lifelong learning and education. Having time to make friends, have hobbies, and be involved in one's community while developing a career enables a successful retirement (Newman, 2011). Leave control promotes economic wellbeing because people do not feel forced to retire, a consideration that is particularly important for the millions of older workers who lack adequate financial resources for retirement. It also enhances social wellbeing because individuals do not perceive their careers as hurting their health or their ability to be successful parents, spouses, children, and community members. In a sustainable workforce, taking care of health and engaging in community and other important roles is not devalued relative to work demands.

*Examples of activities and outcomes.*
As Table 14.2 shows, examples of sustainable career activities are permitting career breaks without losing one's job, part-time and part-year work, regular time off for personal and professional development, and giving employees the ability to ramp up or ramp down their career intensity without penalty. With the growth in electronic communication making it more difficult for employees to take a break from 24/7 availability, increasing leave control to have time off work, vacations, and sabbaticals is increasingly important to prevent burnout and exhaustion and the rise of health problems (Fritz, Yankelevich, Zarubin, & Barger, 2010). The benefits of these strategies are that they allow total life resources to be adapted to promote equilibrium in total life space over time. Synergies and positive energies are promoted between work and nonwork. Individuals also have greater positive wellbeing as they feel they are able to advance in their careers and be involved in community and family without sacrificing their values or health.

*Workplace social support.*

Creating organizational cultures that foster positive workplace social support as an ongoing aspect of the work environment is a key element of building a sustainable workforce. A recent meta-analysis (Kossek, Pichler, Bodner, & Hammer, 2011) defines "workplace social support" as the degree to which employees perceive that supervisors, coworkers, or employers care about their global wellbeing on the job through providing positive social interaction or resources. The authors note that workplace social support can be content-general or content-specific. General support is defined as overall communication of concern, such as emotional support or instrumental support to ensure the wellbeing of an employee. Most organizational research has focused on the benefits of general social support for job performance. Research on positive relational interactions on work is growing and suggests that when employees feel their wellbeing is cared for by others at work, they are more likely to care about the recipients of their work tasks. Some scholars go as far as to argue that jobs can actually be designed to increase workplace social support and the act of caring (Grant, 2007).

Workplace social support can also be content-specific, pertaining to individual perceptions of receiving care to carry out a specific role demand (e.g., dependent care, healthy behaviors such as exercise) (Kossek, Hammer, et al., 2012). For example, a randomized study by Hammer, Kossek, Bodner, Anger, and Zimmerman (2011) found leaders and coworkers can be trained to demonstrate these behaviors and increase positive social interaction and resources to be able to carry out family demands. The authors showed that depressive symptoms were reduced, job satisfaction increased, and work–family conflict decreased. A multilevel study of the group dynamics of having leaders who are seen as more supportive of personal life shows that individuals in workgroups with more supportive leaders are more likely to follow safety procedures, have higher sleep quality, and perform better.

*Examples of workplace social support activities and outcomes.*

As shown in Table 14.2, examples of workplace social support activities include relational task design to foster high social support on the job (Grant, 2007). Employees are motivated to voluntarily cross-train and back each other up. Helping behavior is rewarded. Leaders are trained, rewarded, and developed to care about workers' lives on and off the jobs. Leaders themselves are cared for so they do not burn out and are able to care for workers. This role modeling facilitates workers to care more about each other as they build a culture of care and bench strength for future leaders.

The outcomes of such activities are enhancement of positive emotions and wellbeing at work. Positive spillover from work to home occurs. Workers feel empowered to learn new things on the job and are not burnt out. Employees' personal time is freed up to handle personal life demands so less negative spillover from personal life to work occurs.

## Conclusions and Future Directions

Examining wellbeing and work–life balance as levers for creating a sustainable workforce is an important vein of inquiry warranting further investigation. Countervailing the growing trends toward work intensification, reducing career sustainability over the life course, and the depletion of workplace social support on and off the job is critical to ensure the long-term health of workers and society. We have also demonstrated in our discussion of these concepts how much they are overlapping yet potentially synergistic.

Future research should build on recent studies suggesting that measurement of employee influence over how work gets accomplished is important to consider in mitigating strain from work and family demands (cf. Berset et al., 2009). Research is also needed to better understand how not only total work hours relate to employee wellbeing, but also the sustainability of work hours, that is, the amount and intensity of the work experienced during working time as well. What is also not clearly understood, however, are the absolute standards and the role of individual agency in containing the scope of jobs. This entails a study of increasing employee ability to have greater choice to determine what should reasonably be expected of them to accomplish in their work role, within an acceptable amount of time. This could be relevant, for instance, for those who travel as part of their job duties, with varying degrees of input as to when and for how long they are away from home. Similarly, it would be beneficial for individuals with night work, which has been shown to be deleterious to health, to be able to place limits on the amount of night working time without jeopardizing their jobs.

As the preceding paragraph suggests, workforce sustainability demands greater attention to and respect for the individual's voice in determining the intensity with which work is approached. In an era of global competition and economic crises, needing to do more work with less organizational resources is not uncommon. The availability of 24/7 connectivity via technology creates a society where employees are less able to release themselves from the ongoing demands of the workplace. Increasingly, work may creep into evenings or weekend time formerly reserved for the family, as well as other restorative periods such as vacations and sabbaticals. So what remains unclear is what mechanisms may facilitate an employee's ability to contain or control the demanding nature of their work. For example, can norms around technology use or supportive work–family cultures help in these instances?

Studies might examine journals or time diary research to see how employees spend their time and on what activities. For each activity, employees could reord their physical state and/or emotions as well as their overall feeling of wellbeing in the moment. This would help scholars to better understand the connection between work activities and nonwork activities (e.g., duration, intensity) and the effects on wellbeing while on and off the job over time.

Longitudinal studies could be conducted with employees over time to identify peak moments of positive career experience and examine if higher periods of job control and reduced-load work preceded such experiences and were linked to overall wellbeing through periods of work and nonwork. A control group might include other professionals where work was not contained to be more sustainable but had constant crunch times and/or cycles of intensity.

Workplace intervention studies might set up a workload "bank" within a team of employees doing similar kinds of work or working on a project together. Employees of a similar skill set could be socialized to increase social support for each other and trade-off workload and hours. Employees could log when they estimate having a window of time/energy free (creating credits in the system) and others can request their time (help) if they are overloaded at the moment, or log that they need help. Those that return the favor of sharing are rewarded as role models in the cultural system.

Lastly, we urge scholars to work with organizations to investigate how to use internal social media platforms to post success stories and best practices that optimize workflow, wellbeing, and work–life balance to help their employees "work smarter." Job analysis and scoping work to determine reasonable time frames or energy targets for task performance in different work roles could be a continuous improvement target that is evaluated on a regular basis. Work intensification could be tracked and measured in terms of work performance (and then measured against the guidelines set by HR, in consultation with employees who know the job). Similarly, sustainable career development could also be examined and refined by tracking how wellbeing and work–life balance over time, taking breaks when needed, slowing down and speeding up career progression in order to accommodate the needs of other life roles, are linked to long-term career success, and to overall effectiveness and satisfaction on and off the job.

# References

Allan, C., Loudoun, R., & Peetz, D. (2007). Influences on work/non-work conflict. *Journal of Sociology*, *43*(3), 219–239.

Arthur, M. B., Hall, D. T., & Lawrence, B. S. (Eds.). (1989). *Handbook of career theory*. Cambridge: Cambridge University Press.

Berset, M., Semmer, N. K., Elfering, A., Amstad, F. T., & Jacobshagen, N. (2009). Work characteristics as predictors of physiological recovery on weekends. *Scandinavian Journal of Work, Environment & Health*, *35*(3), 188–192.

Blanchflower, D. G., & Oswald, A. J. (2011). International happiness: A new view on the measure of performance. *Academy of Management Perspectives*, *25*(1), 6–22.

Burns, D. D. (1999). *Feeling good: The new mood therapy* (Revised and updated ed.). New York: Avon.

Chiang, F. F. T., Birtch, T. A., & Kwan, H. K. (2010). The moderating roles of job control and work-life balance practices on employee stress in the hotel and catering industry. *International Journal of Hospitality Management*, *29*(1), 25–32.

Cooperider, D., & Fry, R. (2012). Minor flourishing and the positive psychology of sustainability. *Journal of Corporate Citizenship*, *46*, 3–12.

Csikszentmihalyi, M. (1990). *Flow: The psychology of optimal experience*. New York: Harper & Row.

Demerouti, E., Bakker, A. B., & Voydanoff, P. (2010). Does home life interfere with or facilitate job performance? *European Journal of Work and Organizational Psychology*, *19*(2), 128–149.

Diener, E. (2000). Subjective well-being. *American Psychologist*, *55*, 34–43.

Doef, M. v. d., & Maes, S. (1999). The job demand-control (-support) model and psychological well-being: A review of 20 years of empirical research. *Work & Stress*, *13*(2), 87–114.

Ehnert, I. (2009). *Sustainable human resource management: A conceptual and exploratory analysis from a paradox perspective*. Berlin–Heidelberg: Physica-Verlag.

Fritz, C., & Sonnentag, S. (2006). Recovery, well-being, and performance-related outcomes: The role of workload and vacation experiences. *Journal of Applied Psychology*, *91*(4), 936–945.

Fritz, C., Sonnentag, S., Spector, P. E., & McInroe, J. A. (2010). The weekend matters: Relationships between stress recovery and affective experiences. *Journal of Organizational Behavior*, *31*(8), 1137–1162.

Fritz, C., Yankelevich, M., Zarubin, A., & Barger, P. (2010). Happy, healthy, and productive: The role of detachment from work during nonwork time. *Journal of Applied Psychology, 95*(5), 977–983.

Frone, M. R. (2003). Work-family balance. In J. C. Quick & L. E. Tetrick (Eds.), *Handbook of occupational health psychology* (pp. 143–162). Washington, DC: American Psychological Association.

Geurts, S. A. E., Beckers, D. G. J., Taris, T. W., Kompier, M. A. J., & Smulders, P. G. W. (2009). Worktime demands and work-family interference: Does worktime control buffer the adverse effects of high demands? *Journal of Business Ethics, 84,* 229–241.

Golden-Biddle, K., & Dutton, J. (2012). *Using a positive lens to explore social change and organizations: Building a theoretical and research foundation.* New York: Routledge.

Grant, A. M. (2007). Relational job design and the motivation to make a prosocial difference. *Academy of Management Review, 32,* 393–417.

Grebner, S., Elfering, A., & Semmer, N. K. (2010). The success resource model of job stress. In P. L. Perrewé & D. C. Ganster (Eds.), *New developments in theoretical and conceptual approaches to job stress* (Vol. 8, pp. 61–108). Bingley: Emerald Books.

Greenhaus, J. H., & Allen, T. D. (2010). Work-family balance: A review and extension of the literature. In L. E. Tetrick & J. C. Quick (Eds.), *Handbook of occupational health psychology* (2nd ed., pp. 165–183). Washington, DC: American Psychological Association.

Greenhaus, J. H., Collins, K. M., & Shaw, J. D. (2003). The relation between work-family balance and quality of life. *Journal of Vocational Behavior, 63*(3), 510–531.

Gronlund, A. (2007). More control, less conflict? Job demand-control, gender and work-family conflict. *Gender, Work and Organization, 14*(5), 476–497.

Hall, D. T., Lee, M. D., Kossek, E. E., & Heras, M. L. (2012). Pursuing career success while sustaining personal and family well-being: A study of reduced-load professionals over time. *Journal of Social Issues, 68*(4), 742–766.

Hammer, L. B., Kossek, E. E., Bodner, T., Anger, K., & Zimmerman, K. (2011). Clarifying work-family intervention processes: The roles of work-family conflict and family supportive supervisor behaviors. *Journal of Applied Psychology, 96*(1), 134–150.

Joudrey, A. D., & Wallace, J. E. (2009). Leisure as a coping resource: A test of the job demand-control-support model. *Human Relations, 62*(2), 195–217.

Kalleberg, A. L. (2009). Precarious work, insecure workers: Employment relations in transition. *American Sociological Review, 74*(1), 1–22.

Karasek, R. A., Jr. (1979). Job demands, job decision latitude, and mental strain: Implications for job redesign. *Administrative Science Quarterly, 24*(2), 285–308.

Kelliher, C., & Anderson, D. (2010). Doing more with less? Flexible working practices and the intensification of work. *Human Relations, 63*(1), 83–106.

Kofodimos, J. R. (1993). *Balancing act: How managers can integrate successful careers and fulfilling personal lives.* San Francisco: Jossey-Bass.

Kossek, E., Baltes, B., & Matthews, R. (2011). How work-family research can finally have an impact on organizations. *Industrial and Organizational Psychology: Perspectives on Science and Practice, 4,* 352–369.

Kossek, E., Hammer, L., Bodner, T., Petty, R., Michel, J., & Yragui, N. (2012). *A multi-level model of antecedents of work-family support, conflicts & effectiveness.* Paper presented at the Academy of Management meetings, Boston, August.

Kossek, E., Kaillaith, T., & Kaillaith, P. (2012). Achieving employee wellbeing in a changing work environment: An expert commentary on current scholarship. *International Journal of Manpower, 33*(7), 738–753.

Kossek, E., & Lautsch, B. (2007). *CEO of Me: Creating a life that works in the flexible job age.* Upper Saddle River, NJ: Pearson.

Kossek, E. E., Lautsch, B. A., & Eaton, S. C. (2006). Telecommuting, control, and boundary management: Correlates of policy use and practice, job control, and work-family effectiveness. *Journal of Vocational Behavior, 68*(2), 347–367.

Kossek, E., Pichler, S., Bodner, T., & Hammer, L. (2011). Workplace social support and work-family conflict: A meta-analysis clarifying the influence of general and work-family specific supervisor and organizational support. *Personnel Psychology, 64,* 289–313.

Kossek, E., Ruderman, M., Braddy, P., & Hannum, K. (2012). Work–nonwork boundary management profiles: A person-centered approach. *Journal of Vocational Behavior, 81,* 112–128.

Ladner, S. (2008). Laptops in the living room: Mobile technologies and the divide between work and private time among interactive agency workers. *Canadian Journal of Communication, 33*(3), 465–489.

Lambert, S. (2008). Passing the buck: Labor flexibility practices that transfer risk onto hourly workers. *Human Relations, 61,* 1203–1227.

Lee, M. D., MacDermid, S. M., & Buck, M. L. (2002). Reduced-load work arrangements: Response to stress or quest for integrity of functioning? In D. L. Nelson & R. J. Burke (Eds.), *Gender, work stress, and health* (pp. 169–190). Washington, DC: American Psychological Association.

Lewis, S., & Anderson, D. (2013). *Work-life balance in the context of public section cuts.* Paper presented at the annual meeting of Divisional Occupational Psychology Annual meeting, Chester, U.K. January.

Macky, K., & Boxall, P. (2008). High-involvement work processes, work intensification and employee well-being: A study of New Zealand worker experiences. *Asia Pacific Journal of Human Resources, 46*(1), 38–55.

Newman, K. L. (2011). Sustainable careers: Lifecycle engagement in work. *Organizational Dynamics, 40*(2), 136–143.

Ortega, J. (2009). Why do employers give discretion? Family versus performance concerns. *Industrial Relations, 48*(1), 1–26.

Parker, S. L., Jimmieson, N. L., & Amiot, C. E. (2010). Self-determination as a moderator of demands and control: Implications for employee strain and engagement. *Journal of Vocational Behavior*, 76(1), 52–67.

Pfeffer, P. (2010). Building sustainable organizations: The human factor. *Academy of Management Perspectives*, February, 34–45.

Rath, T., & Harter, J. (2010). *Well being: The five essential elements*. New York: Gallup Press.

Reiter, N. (2007). Work life balance: What DO you mean? The ethical ideology underpinning appropriate application. *Journal of Applied Behavioral Science*, 43(2), 273–294.

Rohde, D. (2012, October 31). The hideous inequality exposed by Hurricane Sandy. *The Atlantic*. http://www.theatlantic.com/business/archive/2012/10/the-hideous-inequality-exposed-by-hurricane-sandy/264337/.

Rothausen, T. J., Gonzalez, J. A., Clarke, N. E., & O'Dell, L. L. (1998). Family-friendly backlash: Fact or fiction? The case of organizations' on-site child care centers. *Personnel Psychology*, 51(3), 685–706.

Ruderman, M. N., Ohlott, P. J., Panzer, K., & King, S. N. (2002). Benefits of multiple roles for managerial women. *Academy of Management Journal*, 45(2), 369–386.

Shapiro, L., Knafo, S., & Hindman, N. C. (2012). Hourly workers are hit in Hurricane Sandy aftermath. *Huffington Post*. http://www.huffingtonpost.com/2012/11/01/hourly-workers-hurricane-sandy-aftermath_n_2060235.html.

Skinner, N., & Pocock, B. (2008). Work-life conflict: Is work time or work overload more important? *Asia Pacific Journal of Human Resources*, 46(3), 303–315.

Towers, I., Duxbury, L., Higgins, C., & Thomas, J. (2006). Time thieves and space invaders: Technology, work and the organization. *Journal of Organizational Change Management*, 19(5), 593–618.

Towers Watson (2012). *2012 Global workplace study*. New York: Towers Watson.

Turkle, S. (2011). *Alone together: Why we expect more from technology and less from each other*. New York: Basic Books.

Valcour, M. (2007). Work-based resources as moderators of the relationship between work hours and satisfaction with work-family balance. *Journal of Applied Psychology*, 92(6), 1512–1523.

Valcour, M. (2013). *Craft a sustainable career*. http://blogs.hbr.org/cs/2013/07/craft_a_sustainable_career.html.

Van Engen, M., Vinkenburg, C., & Dikkers, J. S. E. (2012). Sustainability in combining career and care: Challenging normative beliefs about parenting. *Journal of Social Issues*, 68(4), 645–664.

Wallace, J. E. (1997). It's about time: A study of hours worked and work spillover among law firm lawyers. *Journal of Vocational Behavior*, 50(2), 227–248.

# 15

# Development of a Theoretically Grounded Model of Sexual Harassment Awareness Training Effectiveness

## Lisa M. Kath

San Diego State University, U.S.A.

## Vicki J. Magley

University of Connecticut, U.S.A.

Sexual harassment is a serious and costly problem for organizations, with documented mental health effects on victims (e.g., depression, anxiety; Willness, Steel, & Lee, 2007). Organizations and governments tend to view sexual harassment as a legal issue (McDonald, 2012), and they look to government bodies for guidance on how to comply with national and local laws concerning harassment. The United States, courts typically prescribe sexual harassment awareness (SHA) training as a method of preventing and remedying harassment, as well as a way to shield organizations from liability in harassment cases (Bisom-Rapp, 1999, 2001; Grossman, 2003). A case in point is the enactment of California's state law AB 1825, which mandates that supervisors receive 2 hours of SHA training every 2 years.

*Work and Wellbeing: Wellbeing: A Complete Reference Guide*, Volume III.
Edited by Peter Y. Chen and Cary L. Cooper.
© 2014 John Wiley & Sons, Ltd. Published 2014 by John Wiley & Sons, Inc.
DOI: 10.1002/9781118539415.wbwell15

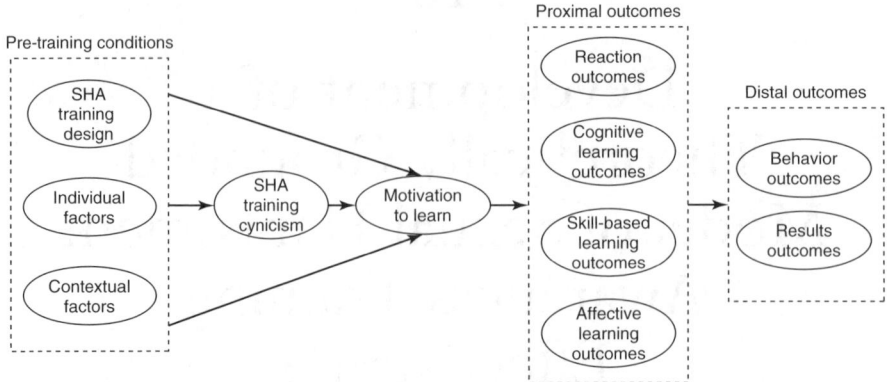

**Figure 15.1.** General Model of SHA Training Effectiveness.

The presumption is that training helps protect employees from sexual harassment.

Despite such emphasis, SHA training has been under-studied as an organizational intervention deterring occurrences of sexual harassment (Fitzgerald & Shullman, 1993; Grundmann, O'Donohue, & Peterson, 1997). The few studies that do evaluate SHA training have shown both positive *and negative* training effects (cf. Bingham & Scherer, 2001; Goldberg, 2007; Perry, Kulik, & Schmidtke, 1998; Robb & Doverspike, 2001; York, Barclay, & Zajack, 1997). In addition to this lack of consistent support for the effectiveness of SHA training, published studies are largely atheoretical and do not draw from the available, maturing literature on workplace training effectiveness.

Because other published work has very recently reviewed the SHA training literature (Goldberg, 2011), our goal with the present chapter is to articulate a general model of SHA training effectiveness (Figure 15.1). As such, we first summarize workplace training effectiveness models and training outcome taxonomies, and we draw upon these models to broadly describe our model of SHA training effectiveness. We then make the case that cynicism and motivation are critical factors that can influence SHA training effectiveness and identify possible training design, individual factors, and contextual factors that may influence trainees' cynicism, motivation, and outcomes. Next, we detail a number of possible SHA training outcomes that may be used in evaluation. Finally, we propose directions for future research on SHA training effectiveness.

# General Model of SHA Training Effectiveness

## Workplace Training Effectiveness Models

Training effectiveness researchers have typically focused on either training design issues (e.g., content, delivery mode, instructional approaches; reviews include Arthur, Bennett, Edens, & Bell, 2003; Goldstein & Ford, 2002) or internal psychological processes (e.g., motivation, learning; reviews include Ford, 1997; Salas & Cannon Bowers, 2001). The latter is generally framed in terms of three components: training motivation, proximal training outcomes (i.e., reaction and learning), and distal training outcomes (i.e., transfer of learning outside the training context). Models and frameworks proposed for each of these components of training effectiveness are detailed and extensive (e.g., Baldwin & Ford, 1988; Cannon Bowers, Salas, Tannenbaum, & Mathieu, 1995; Colquitt, LePine, & Noe, 2000; Mathieu & Martineau, 1997; Noe, 1986), but not unified.

To more easily apply current training models to the study of SHA training effectiveness, we generalized existing models to create a broad heuristic model of training effectiveness. *Training design* (e.g., group composition, training content, and training format), *individual factors* (e.g., pre-training attitudes and beliefs, conscientiousness, anxiety, cognitive abilities), and *contextual factors* (e.g., climate, support from others, materials and supplies) have all been theorized and shown to influence three components of training effectivess: *training motivation* (e.g., Colquitt et al., 2000; Mathieu & Martineau, 1997), *proximal training outcomes* (e.g., Goldstein & Ford, 2002), and *distal training outcomes* (e.g., Baldwin & Ford, 1988; Cannon Bowers et al., 1995; Facteau, Dobbins, Russell, & Ladd, 1995; Ford, Quinones, Sego, & Sorra, 1992; Noe, 1986). There is a notable overlap among individual and contextual factors that have been shown to influence these three components of training effectiveness. Thus, although the arrows suggest full mediation through motivation to learn, please note that pre-training conditions can also have direct influences on proximal and distal outcomes (Figure 15.1).

## Workplace Training Outcomes Models

It is vitally important to assess training effectiveness along a number of dimensions. Kirkpatrick's ubiquitous model of training evaluation (Kirkpatrick, 1959a, 1959b, 1960a, 1960b) includes four levels of criteria:

321

reaction, learning, behavior, and results. Proximal outcomes include reactions, which are intended to measure the employees' satisfaction with training. Learning outcomes measure the knowledge and skills acquired in the training program. Kraiger, Ford, and Salas (1993) have noted that learning outcomes are complex, and they offer a taxonomy of learning outcomes that encompasses cognitive outcomes, skill-based outcomes, and affective outcomes. Cognitive learning outcomes focus on knowledge about training topics. Skill-based learning outcomes emphasize technical or motor skills as a result of training. Affective learning outcomes encompass attitudes and beliefs. Distal outcomes include behaviors, which are a measure of training transfer (i.e., the extent to which employees actually change their job behavior). Results outcomes include organizational-level success measures, such as profitability or safety record. All of these categories of outcomes are included in Figure 15.1.

The application of training effectiveness models to the study of SHA training effectiveness is a significant step forward for the literature on this type of training evaluation. Although this application is long overdue, research in the area of SHA training effectiveness has only recently begun to formally consider such well-established components of training effectiveness, such as training motivation. We shift next to considering the central roles of motivation and cynicism as precursors to SHA training outcomes.

## Centrality of Motivation and Cynicism

### Training Motivation

The bulk of the research done on workplace training effectiveness has focused on job-skills training. These job skills can range from concrete (or "hard") skills like operating a new piece of equipment to less tangible (or "soft") skills like negotiation. Job-skills training, or any training whose desired outcomes contribute directly to the personal job performance of the trainee, is more likely to be extrinsically rewarded through pay-for-performance programs. In addition, according to Schneider's Attraction-Selection-Attrition model (Schneider, 1987; Schneider, Goldstein, & Smith, 1995), job-skills training is likely to be intrinsically interesting to employees as well.

SHA training, on the other hand, belongs to a subset of workplace training that is focused on socialization and includes other training programs such as diversity training, workplace violence reduction training, and civility training. Organizational socialization has been defined as a "process by which an individual acquires the social knowledge and skills necessary to assume an organizational role" (Van Maanen & Schein, 1979, p. 211). Although most researchers have primarily focused their efforts on the socialization process for new organizational members (e.g., Fisher, 1986), we define socialization training more broadly: it is any kind of *formal* training (cf. socialization as unstructured training; Chao, 1997; Chao, O'Leary-Kelly, Wolf, & Klein, 1994) where the organization wishes to develop employees' social knowledge and skills to inform them about organizational climate and/or culture. Because of this emphasis on the broad goal of learning a cultural perspective, SHA training outcomes are achieved through a process by which organizations communicate cultural values and expected behaviors based on a standard of basic respect.

Because SHA training does not involve the acquisition of job skills, it is often not readily apparent why trainees should be motivated to pay attention during training. Adult learning theory (Knowles, 1990) indicates that adults need to know why they are learning something. Based on this principle, we believe that training motivation for socialization training in general, and SHA training in specific, is expected to be a particularly influential factor in achieving desired training outcomes.

A number of researchers have noted that a key predictor of training outcomes is training motivation (see Figure 15.1; Baldwin & Ford, 1988; Noe, 1986; Salas & Cannon Bowers, 2001). If employees are not motivated to perform well in training or to utilize their training in their workplace, the training will not be effective. When this principle is applied to SHA training, the result is that unmotivated employees will be less likely to pay attention to trainers and learn about sexual harassment policies in their organizations. In addition, employees who are not motivated will be unlikely to transfer anything they might have learned in training to the job. Because intrinsic motivation for SHA training is expected to be relatively low, and because sexual harassment is a sensitive topic, in the next section we make the case that cynicism is an important factor influencing motivation to learn in SHA training.

## Cynicism as a Key Predictor of Motivation

Drawing again from adult learning theory (Knowles, 1990), we noted that adults prefer to bring their own work experiences into learning situations. Most people do not engage in sexual harassment themselves, and those who

**Table 15.1.** Pre-Training Conditions and Possible Proximal Training Outcomes for SHA Training.

| Pre-training conditions | Possible proximal training outcomes |
| --- | --- |
| **Training design factors** | **Reactions** |
| Goals—focus on awareness or behavior/skills? | Training satisfaction |
| Trainer—male or female? | **Cognitive learning outcomes** |
| Content—which topics will be covered? | Knowledge of organizational policies |
| Framing—legal or ethical perspective? | Knowledge of sexual harassment laws |
| Mode—online or face to face? | |
| **Individual factors** | **Skills-based learning outcomes** |
| Trainee sex | Interpersonal communication |
| Trainee perceptions of organization's integrity | Bystander intervention |
| Trainee cynicism about organizational change | Harassment reporting |
| **Contextual factors** | **Affective learning outcomes** |
| Training transfer climate (manager, coworker support) | Attitude direction: sexual harassment myth endorsement |
| Climate for sexual harassment | Attitude strength: sexual harassment importance |
| | Perceptions of climate for sexual harassment |

do would probably be even less interested in learning about it. In addition, employees may experience sexual harassment, but they may not label their experiences as such (e.g., Magley, Hulin, Fitzgerald, & DeNardo, 1999; Magley & Shupe, 2005). Thus, personal reasons for being motivated to learn in SHA training are expected to be few and far between.

Organizations, however, may be extremely motivated to host such training. They may truly seek only to shield themselves against liability claims of sexual harassment from their employees. More positively, though, organizations may also seek to assist employees' wellbeing by providing a safer climate in which to work. These reasons are not mutually exclusive; organizations can reasonably conduct training for both legal and humanistic motives. Theoretically, social exchange theory (Blau, 1964; Gouldner, 1960) would suggest that if employees believe the organization is conducting SHA training with their best interests in mind (i.e., for humanistic reasons), they are more likely to respond in kind with increased motivation. Similarly, when employees perceive that SHA training is conducted in a less-than-sincere manner and solely to shield the organization from liability, employees are likely to be cynical about the organization's SHA training efforts.

In addition to the organizational rationale underlying the implementation of SHA training, sexual harassment can be an emotionally charged training topic, which means the potential for attitudinal backlash may be especially high (see Stockdale, Bisom-Rapp, O'Connor, & Gutek, 2004). Both authors of the present chapter have heard numerous anecdotal stories/comments about employees being cynical about SHA training, ranging from complaints about SHA training as "a necessary evil" to SHA training being "another way to ram PC [politically correct] thinking down our throats." Despite receiving little attention by SHA training research thus far, we posit that training cynicism is likely to be a primary factor influencing SHA training motivation and effectiveness. More specifically, it is expected that higher levels of cynicism about SHA training will lead to decreased training motivation.

In this next section, we move to a discussion of the training design, individual, and contextual factors (i.e., pre-training conditions) that may influence SHA training effectiveness. A summary of these pre-training conditions can be found in the left side of Table 15.1.

## Pre-Training Conditions Influencing SHA Training Effectiveness

### Training Design Factors

There has been very little research focused on training design specifically for SHA training. However, much more research has been done on diversity training design. Because we consider SHA training to be a specific type of diversity training, we draw upon that literature as well in creating a list of training design factors that may influence SHA training effectiveness.

A recent review indicates that diversity training can be designed to influence awareness, behavior/skills, or both (Bezrukova, Jehn, & Spell, 2012). This concept can be easily applied to SHA training. The literature is far from clear about which approach is best, although Bezrukova and colleagues noted that diversity training fell into "awareness only" or "both" categories, with none focusing solely on behavior/skills. Roberson, Kulik, and Pepper (2003) suggest that careful needs assessment be conducted at organizations to determine the best approach for designing diversity training, and we echo that suggestion for those designing SHA training.

Other factors commonly discussed in diversity training literature are whether the trainees should be a homogeneous or heterogeneous group and whether the trainer should be in the majority or minority group (Bezrukova et al., 2012; Roberson et al., 2003). Because the mere existence of SHA training can make men feel persecuted, we do not recommend that training be conducted in a same-sex group. Regarding the trainer's sex, we agree with Roberson and colleagues that a careful needs assessment can go a long way in helping make the decision about how important this factor may be, and we additionally concur with Perry and colleagues (2009) that what is most important is that the trainer is highly skilled.

Care must be taken in terms of deciding what topics to include in designing SHA training. Some topics may be required by law (such as in California's AB 1825 law). Goldberg (2007) reported on a study that suggested that inclusion of information about the negative effects to victims for reporting sexual harassment (such as retaliation and alienation) might have led to a decrease in likelihood to voice complaints after training.

Another design factor we would like to highlight is the suggestion by O'Leary-Kelly and Bowes-Sperry (2001) to conduct SHA training from an ethical perspective, as opposed to the more traditional legal perspective. More specifically, they assert that organizations could improve the effectiveness of their training by teaching employees that sexual harassment is an ethical as well as a legal issue (see also Bowes-Sperry & O'Leary-Kelly, 2005; Bowes-Sperry & Powell, 1999). Legally focused SHA training is compliance-oriented, and it tends to teach employees about sexual harassment law and their obligations to avoid illegal behavior. In contrast, ethically focused SHA training is value-oriented, teaching employees to engage in respectful interactions, avoid harassing behaviors, and help harassment targets because it is the right thing to do. This concept was tested by Yamashita, Kath, and Bowes-Sperry (2009), and initial empirical support was found for the benefits of adopting an ethical perspective in SHA training.

Finally, we are aware (anecdotally) of an increase in organizations' interest in utilizing online (Web-based) SHA training to fulfill their SHA training requirements. Although we certainly are not naïve in thinking that online training is problematic across the board, in that plenty of research supports its use in the workplace (Kraiger, 2013), to our knowledge there is no empirical research on SHA training that considers its use in lieu of face-to-face training.

We argue that the nature of the training goals, as guided by a thorough needs assessment, is most important in guiding organizations' choice on mode of training. In particular, we hypothesize that face-to-face training would be equivalent to online training if the goals of the SHA training were solely centered on cognitive learning outcomes (e.g., What are the legal parameters surrounding sexual harassment?; What are the organization's policies and procedures?). However, we hypothesize that attitude change, skill development and/or behavioral change outcomes would suffer with online training approaches. Clearly, additional research is badly needed in this arena. In light of its paucity, we encourage organizations/practitioners to pay careful attention to the evaluation of any online SHA training used.

## Individual or Trainee Factors

Trainee sex is a commonly studied factor that has been found to influence SHA training effectiveness (e.g., Beauvais, 1986; Blakely, Blakely, & Moorman, 1998; Moyer & Nath, 1998). We believe this is likely to be a proxy for a number of different individual factors that are correlated with trainee sex. For example, women are more likely to have experienced harassing behaviors (McDonald, 2012), and as a result, they may have more knowledge about the laws and policies, be more likely to believe sexual harassment is an important issue, and endorse fewer myths about sexual harassment. Because the two published studies that report SHA trainings actually made things worse were conducted with male trainees (Bingham & Scherer, 2001; Robb & Doverspike, 2001), we suggest that researchers focus their efforts on understanding what makes SHA training more effective for men in particular, but we also encourage the explicit study of the causal mechanisms underlying these sex differences, such as knowledge and attitudes. Practitioners more often are required to train men and women equally in organizations, so attending to trainee sex may not be a possibility from their perspective.

In addition to gender-related factors that may influence SHA training effectiveness, there are also likely to be sources of training cynicism that are based on integrity evaluations of the organization, from the employees' perspectives. Two factors that we argue are particularly relevant are perceived organizational support and cynicism about organizational change. Perceived organizational support (Eisenberger, Huntington, Hutchison, & Sowa, 1986) could operate through social exchange theory (Blau, 1964; Gouldner, 1960), whereby a sense that the organization supports the personal values of the employee (which hopefully includes a value to avoid harassment!) would initiate an exchange where the employee would be less cynical toward and more motivated about SHA training. Similar results may be found when considering other constructs that represent a connection between the employee and the organization, such as organizational trust, affective organizational commitment, or organizational identification.

Regarding cynicism about organizational change, it is important to consider how SHA training is used in light of the organization's status before SHA training is/was implemented (Kath, 2005). Sometimes SHA training is designed to *maintain* a climate that does not tolerate sexual harassment. However, sometimes SHA training is implemented to address a problem with sexual harassment in an organization. In this situation, an organization will communicate that sexual harassment is unacceptable through the creation of policies and procedures for dealing with sexual harassment, followed by company-wide training to disseminate that information (Bisom-Rapp, 2001). In this case, training is expected to engender *organizational change* by decreasing the acceptability and incidence of sexual harassment.

Wanous, Reichers, and Austin (2000) define cynicism about organizational change as "a pessimistic viewpoint about change efforts being successful because those responsible for making change are blamed for being unmotivated, incompetent, or both" (p. 133). Most interestingly, cynicism about organizational change has also been reported to predict training generalization (Tesluk, Farr, Mathieu, & Vance, 1995). Training generalization is considered to be one step beyond training transfer, pertaining to the transfer of those learning outcomes to a different context than was originally intended. Tesluk and colleagues found that employees' cynicism about organizational change, in addition to their participation in training and their commitment to the organization, was predictive of the spillover effects of the training outside the training context. Because SHA training is often implemented to bring about change in the organization's climate for harassment, cynicism about organizational change has the potential to be an interesting factor affecting such training (Kath, 2005).

## Contextual or Situational Factors

Training models indicate that training does not occur in a vacuum, and care must be taken to understand the organizational environment where the training transfer is to occur (e.g., Baldwin & Ford, 1988). A supportive training transfer climate is one that has management and coworker support for training transfer (Tracey, Hinkin, Tannenbaum, & Mathieu, 2001). Thus, management and coworker attitudes about sexual harassment could be very important contextual factors that may influence the transfer for SHA training. Similarly, the climate for sexual harassment (i.e., the extent to which sexual harassment is tolerated in a workgroup or organization) is another contextual factor that may influence SHA training effectiveness.

The mechanism by which any of these contextual influences would occur is that the contextual factor could encourage conformity through either normative or informational influence (Deutsch & Gerard, 1955). For example, individuals in a workgroup that has poor managerial support for SHA training transfer may decide to be cynical about SHA training because they wish to avoid rejection or gain acceptance (i.e., normative influence) or because they accept the workgroup climate as reflective of reality (i.e., informational influence). Even though contextual influences on training effectiveness have long been theorized (e.g., Baldwin & Ford, 1988) and demonstrated (e.g., Facteau et al., 1995; Ford et al., 1992), we assert that the influence of contextual factors is particularly influential in the effectiveness of SHA training because of its lack of tangible contribution to the trainees' skill set.

## Possible SHA Training Outcomes

We have reviewed two major frameworks for classifying SHA training outcomes, which are summarized on the right side of Figure 15.1. Now we apply this summary to the identification of specific outcomes that could be included when evaluating SHA training effectiveness. A summary of these possible training outcomes can be found on the right side of Table 15.1.

### Proximal Training Outcomes

Typical proximal outcomes in published SHA training studies include the ability for participants to recognize sexual harassment in scenarios (e.g., Barak, 1994; Keyton & Rhodes, 1999; Moyer & Nath, 1998; York et al., 1997); knowledge about sexual harassment laws, policies, and procedures (e.g., Knapp & Heshizer, 2001; Licata & Popovich, 1987; Perry et al., 1998); and attitudes about sexual harassment (e.g., Beauvais, 1986). As in most training evaluations, reaction outcomes are the most likely to be measured in evaluations of SHA training effectiveness. Reaction outcomes for SHA training can be measured by simply assessing the employee's satisfaction with the training.

Cognitive learning outcomes of SHA training often include knowledge of organizational policies and practices about sexual harassment. Supervisors are often targeted for additional training because they have special responsibilities under the law to provide protection for subordinates against harassment (e.g., Eberhardt, Moser, & McFadden, 1999). Therefore, supervisors/managers need to know what to do if an employee comes to them with a complaint of harassment. Training for supervisors may also focus on legal definitions of sexual harassment (e.g., Howard, 1991). Those not in supervisory roles also benefit from cognitive outcomes of SHA training, as they may learn to recognize what are considered to be sexually harassing behaviors (e.g., Moyer & Nath, 1998), what mechanisms the organization has in place to address those unwanted behaviors (e.g., Barak, 1994), and how perpetrators (i.e., harassers) are punished (Dekker & Barling, 1998). Cognitive outcomes are frequently targeted in training designed for supervisory and nonsupervisory employees alike; these outcomes are measurable using a test of knowledge about sexual harassment laws and policies. It is unlikely that a validated measure will be published because of the need to tailor these tests to the laws and specific organizational policies for each country/region/organization.

Identifying skills-based learning outcomes for SHA training is a bit tricky, because this type of outcome often focuses on technical or motor skills. Nevertheless, diversity training researchers have often focused on the development of appropriate communication skills as a key training outcome (Bezrukova et al., 2012). Another set of skills-based learning outcomes are rooted in the Bowes-Sperry and O'Leary-Kelly (2005) typology of observer intervention behaviors in sexual harassment: bystander intervention and harassment reporting. Again, needs assessment is critical in identifying the most appropriate skills to be included in an evaluation of SHA training effectiveness.

Affective learning outcomes are another important goal in SHA training. Attitudes toward sexual harassment can be measured in terms of their direction and their strength. To measure direction, we noted that some SHA training programs focus on debunking myths (i.e., inaccurate beliefs) about sexual harassment, such as "Most women who are sexually insulted by a man provoke his behavior by the way they talk, act, or dress" (Beauvais, 1986). Therefore, we suggest decreased sexual harassment myth endorsement as a critical attitudinal outcome resulting from SHA training. A measure of sexual harassment myth endorsement has been published by Lonsway, Cortina, and Magley (2008). To measure strength, we suggest that the importance of sexual harassment be included as well. Although there is no published measure of this construct, Yamashita and colleagues (2009) reported on a sexual harassment importance measure based on work by Krosnick, Boninger, Chuang, and Berent (1993).

In addition, training is expected to cultivate attitudes that sexual harassment is unacceptable behavior in an organization (e.g., Licata & Popovich, 1987); thus the very existence of a SHA training program may communicate that the organization is serious about this issue and is supportive of those who are targeted with unwanted behaviors (Armenakis & Bedeian, 1999). These goals lead to the identification of perceptions of the climate for sexual harassment as another affective learning outcome. A common measure of climate for sexual harassment is the Organizational Tolerance for Sexual Harassment Inventory (Hulin, Fitzgerald, & Drasgow, 1996).

## Distal Training Outcomes

Distal training outcomes are often neglected in workplace training evaluation (Goldstein & Ford, 2002), and SHA training is no exception. Wilkerson (1999) identified distal goals for SHA training, which include decreased incidence of harassment, decreased litigation, increased compliance with organizational policies, improved employee morale, and improved reputation of the organization. Legal counsel in the employ of the organization may even recommend against the measurement of distal training outcomes, because the information will then become discoverable if a sexual harassment lawsuit is filed. A field study by Magley, Fitzgerald, Salisbury, Drasgow, and Zickar (2013) examined harassment incidence and harassment reporting rates (in addition to several proximal training outcomes). Incidence did not change after the training, although employees were slightly *more* likely to file complaints of sexual harassment. It is possible that distal outcomes may get a bit worse after training before they get better. Clearly more research on these "gold standard" outcomes is needed; we remain optimistic that researchers and practitioners will continue to evaluate these important outcomes, particularly considering the possible temporal factors at play. Simply put, because our knowledge of the effectiveness of SHA training is especially weak with regards to distal training outcomes, any time distal training outcomes can be included, they should be.

## Implications and Future Directions

In this chapter, we have proposed a model of SHA training effectiveness that includes training design, individual, and contextual factors; training cynicism and motivation as critical factors for success; and a wide array of possible training outcomes. A strong case was made for the centrality of cynicism and motivation in understanding SHA training effectiveness.

Researchers are encouraged to continue understanding individual factors that influence effectiveness, because anything that can be understood about the toughest trainees could be critical for maximizing effectiveness. However, we note that practitioners are likely working with a broad range of target employees. As a result, their focus would likely be to minimize the influence of stable individual factors like ability, personality, and demographic variables on SHA training effectiveness. To do so, the focus would be on training design, such that the content and delivery of training would minimize the impact of relevant individual factors.

In addition, the recommendation to include contextual factors in our model of SHA training effectiveness indicates it is not enough to simply conduct SHA training in an organization without first considering the history and the context of the organization. If, as may be the case in a number of organizations, employees have negative residual feelings from past organizational change efforts that have failed, they may be suspicious of the next organizational change effort. This suspicion can translate into cynical attitudes about future organizational change, at either the individual or workgroup level.

Another contribution is the identification of a broad array of possible SHA training outcomes. The need for construing training outcomes broadly has been repeatedly noted in the training evaluation literature (for a review, see Arthur et al., 2003). The SHA training outcomes presented represent different facets of effectiveness, and they may show different relationships that could shed light on our theoretical base for SHA training.

Finally, we note that the vast majority of studies on SHA training effectiveness focus on improving participants' ability to recognize sexual harassment in scenarios (e.g., Keyton, 1996; Moyer & Nath, 1998; Wilkerson, 1999), despite any empirical evidence that this training objective actually helps reduce the occurrence of sexual harassment in organizations. On the other hand, there are numerous studies supporting a relationship between climate for sexual harassment and experiences of sexual harassment (Cohorn,

Sims, & Drasgow, 2002; Dekker & Barling, 1998; Fitzgerald, Drasgow, Hulin, Gelfand, & Magley, 1997; Fitzgerald, Drasgow, & Magley, 1999; Glomb et al., 1997; Hesson-McInnis & Fitzgerald, 1997; O'Connell & Korabik, 2000), such that this is now a well-established relationship in the literature. As a result, we strongly recommend that researchers and SHA training evaluators include climate for sexual harassment as a key SHA training outcome.

In sum, we believe that our knowledge about SHA training is limited but important. We have made a number of suggestions for researchers and practitioners alike to work toward an increased understanding of how to design, implement, and evaluate SHA training to maximize its effectiveness. SHA training will never be a panacea for the problem of sexual harassment in organizations, but it will be a very important tool for helping to educate employees about this pernicious problem, which will hopefully set the stage for a climate that does not tolerate sexual harassment in the workforce.

# References

Armenakis, A. A., & Bedeian, A. G. (1999). Organizational change: A review of theory and research in the 1990s. *Journal of Management*, 25(3), 293–315.

Arthur, W., Jr., Bennett, W., Jr., Edens, P. S., & Bell, S. T. (2003). Effectiveness of training in organizations: A meta-analysis of design and evaluation features. *Journal of Applied Psychology*, 88(2), 234–245.

Baldwin, T. T., & Ford, J. K. (1988). Transfer of training: A review and directions for future research. *Personnel Psychology*, 41(1), 63–105.

Barak, A. (1994). A cognitive-behavioral educational workshop to combat sexual harassment in the workplace. *Journal of Counseling and Development*, 72(6), 595–602.

Beauvais, K. (1986). Workshops to combat sexual harassment: A case study of changing attitudes. *Signs*, 12(1), 130–145.

Bezrukova, K., Jehn, K. A., & Spell, C. S. (2012). Reviewing diversity training: Where we have been and where we should go. *Academy of Management Learning & Education*, 11(2), 207–227.

Bingham, S. G., & Scherer, L. L. (2001). The unexpected effects of a sexual harassment educational program. *Journal of Applied Behavioral Science*, 37(2), 125–153.

Bisom-Rapp, S. (1999). Discerning form from substance: Understanding employer litigation prevention strategies. *Employee Rights and Employment Policy Journal*, 3, 1–64.

Bisom-Rapp, S. (2001). Fixing watches with sledgehammers: The questionable embrace of employee sexual harassment training by the legal profession. *University of Arkansas at Little Rock Law Review*, 24, 147–163.

Blakely, G. L., Blakely, E. H., & Moorman, R. H. (1998). The effects of training on perceptions of sexual harassment allegations. *Journal of Applied Social Psychology*, 28(1), 71–83.

Blau, P. M. (1964). *Exchange and power in social life*. New York: Wiley.

Bowes-Sperry, L., & O'Leary-Kelly, A. M. (2005). To act or not to act: The dilemma faced by sexual harassment observers. *Academy of Management Review*, 30(2), 288–306.

Bowes-Sperry, L., & Powell, G. N. (1999). Observers' reactions to social-sexual behavior at work: An ethical decision making perspective. *Journal of Management*, 25(6), 779–802.

Cannon Bowers, J. A., Salas, E., Tannenbaum, S. I., & Mathieu, J. E. (1995). Toward theoretically based principles of training effectiveness: A model and initial empirical investigation. *Military Psychology*, 7(3), 141–164.

Chao, G. T. (1997). Unstructured training and development: The role of organizational socialization. In J. K. Ford (Ed.), *Improving training effectiveness in work organizations* (pp. 129–152). Mahwah, NJ: Lawrence Erlbaum Associates.

Chao, G. T., O'Leary-Kelly, A. M., Wolf, S., & Klein, H. J. (1994). Organizational socialization: Its content and consequences. *Journal of Applied Psychology*, 79, 730–743.

Cohorn, C. A., Sims, C. S., & Drasgow, F. (2002, April). *Organizational climate, sexual harassment, and outcomes on United States military installations*. Paper presented at the Society for Industrial and Organizational Psychology, Toronto.

Colquitt, J. A., LePine, J. A., & Noe, R. A. (2000). Toward an integrative theory of training motivation: A meta-analytic path analysis of 20 years of research. *Journal of Applied Psychology*, 85(5), 678–707.

Dekker, I., & Barling, J. (1998). Personal and organizational predictors of workplace sexual harassment of women by men. *Journal of Occupational Health Psychology*, 3(1), 7–18.

Deutsch, M., & Gerard, H. B. (1955). A study of normative and informational social influence upon individual judgment. *Journal of Abnormal and Social Psychology*, 51, 629–636.

Eberhardt, B. J., Moser, S. B., & McFadden, D. (1999). Sexual harassment in small government units: An investigation of policies and attitudes. *Public Personnel Management*, 28(3), 351–364.

Eisenberger, R., Huntington, R., Hutchison, S., & Sowa, D. (1986). Perceived organizational support. *Journal of Applied Psychology*, 71(3), 500–507.

Facteau, J. D., Dobbins, G. H., Russell, J. E. A., & Ladd, R. T. (1995). The influence of general perceptions of the training environment on pretraining motivation and perceived training transfer. *Journal of Management*, 21(1), 1–25.

Fisher, C. D. (1986). Organizational socialization: An integrative review. In K. M. Rowland & G. R. Ferris (Eds.), *Research in personnel and human resources management* (Vol. 4, pp. 101–145). Greenwich, CT: JAI Press.

Fitzgerald, L. F., Drasgow, F., Hulin, C. L., Gelfand, M. J., & Magley, V. J. (1997). Antecedents and consequences of sexual harassment in organizations: A test of an integrated model. *Journal of Applied Psychology*, *82*(4), 578–589.

Fitzgerald, L. F., Drasgow, F., & Magley, V. J. (1999). Sexual harassment in the armed forces: A test of an integrated model. *Military Psychology*, *11*(3), 329–343.

Fitzgerald, L. F., & Shullman, S. L. (1993). Sexual harassment: A research analysis and agenda for the 1990s. *Journal of Vocational Behavior*, *42*(1), 5–27.

Ford, J. K. (1997). *Improving training effectiveness in work organizations*. Mahwah, NJ: Lawrence Erlbaum Associates.

Ford, J. K., Quinones, M. A., Sego, D. J., & Sorra, J. S. (1992). Factors affecting the opportunity to perform trained tasks on the job. *Personnel Psychology*, *45*(3), 511–527.

Glomb, T. M., Richman, W. L., Hulin, C. L., Drasgow, F., Schneider, K. T., & Fitzgerald, L. F. (1997). Ambient sexual harassment: An integrated model of antecedents and consequences. *Organizational Behavior and Human Decision Processes*, *71*(3), 309–328.

Goldberg, C. B. (2007). The impact of training and conflict avoidance on responses to sexual harassment. *Psychology of Women Quarterly*, *31*(1), 62–72.

Goldberg, C. B. (2011). What do we really know about sexual harassment training effectiveness? In M. A. Paludi, C. A. Paludi, & E. R. DeSouza (Eds.), *Praeger handbook on understanding and preventing workplace discrimination* (Vols 1 & 2, pp. 45–48). Santa Barbara, CA: Praeger.

Goldstein, I. L., & Ford, J. K. (2002). *Training in organizations: Needs assessment, development, and evaluation* (4th ed.). Belmont, CT: Wadsworth.

Gouldner, A. W. (1960). The norm of reciprocity: A preliminary statement. *American Sociological Review*, *25*, 161–178.

Grossman, J. L. (2003). The culture of compliance: The final triumph of form over substance in sexual harassment law. *Harvard Women's Law Journal*, *26*, 1–75.

Grundmann, E. O. H., O'Donohue, W., & Peterson, S. H. (1997). The prevention of sexual harassment. In W. O'Donohue (Ed.), *Sexual harassment: Theory, research, and treatment* (pp. 175–184). Needham Heights, MA: Allyn & Bacon.

Hesson-McInnis, M. S., & Fitzgerald, L. F. (1997). Sexual harassment: A preliminary test of an integrative model. *Journal of Applied Social Psychology*, *27*(10), 877–901.

Howard, S. (1991). Organizational resources for addressing sexual harassment. *Journal of Counseling and Development*, *69*(6), 507–511.

Hulin, C. L., Fitzgerald, L. F., & Drasgow, F. (1996). Organizational influences on sexual harassment. In M. S. Stockdale (Ed.), *Sexual harassment in the workplace: Perspectives, frontiers, and response strategies* (pp. 127–150). Thousand Oaks, CA: Sage.

Kath, L. (2005). How cynicism about organizational change can influence the effectiveness of socialization training: Sexual harassment awareness training as exemplar. *Dissertation Abstracts International*, *66* (6-B).

335

Keyton, J. (1996). Sexual harassment: A multidisciplinary synthesis and critique. In B. R. Burleson (Ed.), *Communication yearbook* (Vol. 19, pp. 93–155). Thousand Oaks, CA: Sage.

Keyton, J., & Rhodes, S. C. (1999). Organizational sexual harassment: Translating research into application. *Journal of Applied Communication Research, 27*(2), 158–173.

Kirkpatrick, D. L. (1959a). Techniques for evaluation training programs. *Journal of ASTD, 13*(11), 3–9.

Kirkpatrick, D. L. (1959b). Techniques for evaluation training programs: Part 2—Learning. *Journal of ASTD, 13*(12), 21–26.

Kirkpatrick, D. L. (1960a). Techniques for evaluation training programs: Part 3—Behavior. *Journal of ASTD, 14*(1), 13–18.

Kirkpatrick, D. L. (1960b). Techniques for evaluation training programs: Part 4—Results. *Journal of ASTD, 14*(2), 28–32.

Knapp, D. E., & Heshizer, B. P. (2001). Outcomes of requests for summary judgments in federal sexual harassment cases: Policy capturing revisited. *Sex Roles, 44*(3/4), 109–128.

Knowles, M. (1990). *The adult learner* (4th ed.). Houston: Gulf Publishing.

Kraiger, K. (2013). Understanding and facilitating learning: Advancements in training and development. In I. B. Weiner, N. W. Schmitt, & S. Highhouse (Eds.), *Handbook of psychology: Industrial and organizational psychology* (Vol. 12, pp. 244–261). Hoboken, NJ: Wiley.

Kraiger, K., Ford, J. K., & Salas, E. (1993). Application of cognitive, skill-based, and affective theories of learning outcomes to new methods of training evaluation. *Journal of Applied Psychology, 78*(2), 311–328.

Krosnick, J. A., Boninger, D. S., Chuang, Y. C., & Berent, M. K. (1993). Attitude strength: One construct or many related constructs? *Journal of Personality and Social Psychology, 65*(6), 1132–1151.

Licata, B. J., & Popovich, P. M. (1987). Preventing sexual harassment: A proactive approach. *Training and Development Journal, 41*(5), 34–38.

Lonsway, K. A., Cortina, L. M., & Magley, V. J. (2008). Sexual harassment mythology: Definition, conceptualization, and measurement. *Sex Roles, 58*(9–10), 599–615.

Magley, V. J., Fitzgerald, L. F., Salisbury, J., Drasgow, F., & Zickar, M. J. (2013). Changing sexual harassment within organizations via training interventions: Suggestions and empirical data. In R. Burke & C. Cooper (Eds.), *The fulfilling workplace: The organization's role in achieving individual and organizational health* (pp. 225–246). Surrey, U.K.: Gower.

Magley, V. J., Hulin, C. L., Fitzgerald, L. F., & DeNardo, M. (1999). Outcomes of self-labeling sexual harassment. *Journal of Applied Psychology, 84*(3), 390–402.

Magley, V. J., & Shupe, E. I. (2005). Self-labeling sexual harassment. *Sex Roles, 53*(3), 173–189.

Mathieu, J. E., & Martineau, J. W. (1997). Individual and situational influences on training motivation. In J. K. Ford (Ed.), *Improving training effectiveness in work organizations* (pp. 193–222). Mahwah, NJ: LEA.

McDonald, P. (2012). Workplace sexual harassment 30 years on: A review of the literature. *International Journal of Management Reviews, 14*(1), 1–17.

Moyer, R. S., & Nath, A. (1998). Some effects of brief training interventions on perceptions of sexual harassment. *Journal of Applied Social Psychology, 28*(4), 333–356.

Noe, R. A. (1986). Trainees' attributes and attitudes: Neglected influences on training effectiveness. *Academy of Management Review, 11*(4), 736–749.

O'Connell, C. E., & Korabik, K. (2000). Sexual harassment: The relationship of personal vulnerability, work context, perpetrator status, and type of harassment to outcomes. *Journal of Vocational Behavior, 56*(3), 299–329.

O'Leary-Kelly, A. M., & Bowes-Sperry, L. (2001). Sexual harassment as unethical behavior: The role of moral intensity. *Human Resource Management Review, 11*(1–2), 73–92.

Perry, E. L., Kulik, C. T., & Field, M. P. (2009). Sexual harassment training: Recommendations to address gaps between the practitioner and research literatures. *Human Resource Management, 48*(5), 817–837.

Perry, E. L., Kulik, C. T., & Schmidtke, J. M. (1998). Individual differences in the effectiveness of sexual harassment awareness training. *Journal of Applied Social Psychology, 28*(8), 698–723.

Robb, L. A., & Doverspike, D. (2001). Self-reported proclivity to harass as a moderator of the effectiveness of sexual harassment-prevention training. *Psychological Reports, 88*(1), 85–88.

Roberson, L., Kulik, C. T., & Pepper, M. B. (2003). Using needs assessment to resolve controversies in diversity training design. *Group & Organization Management, 28*(1), 148–174.

Salas, E., & Cannon Bowers, J. A. (2001). The science of training: A decade of progress. *Annual Review of Psychology, 52*, 471–499.

Schneider, B. (1987). The people make the place. *Personnel Psychology, 40*(3), 437–453.

Schneider, B., Goldstein, H. W., & Smith, D. B. (1995). The ASA framework: An update. *Personnel Psychology, 48*(4), 747–773.

Stockdale, M. S., Bisom-Rapp, S., O'Connor, M., & Gutek, B. A. (2004). Coming to terms with zero tolerance sexual harassment policies. *Journal of Forensic Psychology Practice, 4*(1), 65–78.

Tesluk, P. E., Farr, J. L., Mathieu, J. E., & Vance, R. J. (1995). Generalization of employee involvement training to the job setting: Individual and situational effects. *Personnel Psychology, 48*, 607–632.

Tracey, J. B., Hinkin, T. R., Tannenbaum, S., & Mathieu, J. E. (2001). The influence of individual characteristics and the work environment on varying levels of training outcomes. *Human Resource Development Quarterly, 12*(1), 5–23.

Van Maanen, J., & Schein, E. H. (1979). Toward a theory of organizational socialization. In B. M. Staw (Ed.), *Research in organizational behavior* (Vol. 1, pp. 209–264). Stamford, CT: JAI Press.

Wanous, J. P., Reichers, A. E., & Austin, J. T. (2000). Cynicism about organizational change. *Group and Organization Management*, 25(2), 132–153.

Wilkerson, J. M. (1999). The impact of job level and prior training on sexual harassment labeling and remedy choice. *Journal of Applied Social Psychology*, 29(8), 1605–1623.

Willness, C. R., Steel, P., & Lee, K. (2007). A meta-analysis of the antecedents and consequences of workplace sexual harassment. *Personnel Psychology*, 60(1), 127–162.

Yamashita, H., Kath, L. M., & Bowes-Sperry, L. (2009). *Effectiveness of ethics-based sexual harassment awareness training*. Paper presented at the annual meeting of the Society for Industrial and Organizational Psychology, New Orleans, LA.

York, K. M., Barclay, L. A., & Zajack, A. B. (1997). Preventing sexual harassment: The effect of multiple training methods. *Employee Responsibilities and Rights Journal*, 10(4), 277–289.

# 16

# The Working Wounded
## *Stigma and Return to Work*

Lori Francis, James E. Cameron,
E. Kevin Kelloway, Victor M. Catano,
and Arla L. Day
Saint Mary's University, Canada

C. Gail Hepburn
University of Lethbridge, Canada

Economic and legislative realities place pressure on organizations to return individuals to the workplace as soon as is safely possible following a lost time injury. The need for the early return of injured workers is likely to intensify as shifting societal demographic groups (e.g., an aging population) result in worker shortages (Krause & Lund, 2004). Beyond these factors, the view that being engaged in work contributes to health and wellbeing (e.g., Jahoda, 1982, 1988; Kelloway, Gallagher, & Barling, 2004) further encourages the goal of quickly returning injured workers. The fact that personal and financial costs of a lost time injury increase with the length of the disability leave also adds to the goal of early and sustained return to work.

In light of these pressures to return injured workers to work, the use of modified work to facilitate early reentry is a widely adopted practice (Krause, Dasinger, & Neuhauser, 1998; Krause & Lund, 2004) that in some jurisdictions is formalized into the workers' compensation process (Eakin, 2005; Eakin, MacEachen, & Clarke, 2003). With these practices, injured workers are returned to the workplace early, perhaps before they have recovered fully, to jobs that have been adapted to accommodate their work limitations (e.g.,

*Work and Wellbeing: Wellbeing: A Complete Reference Guide*, Volume III.
Edited by Peter Y. Chen and Cary L. Cooper.
© 2014 John Wiley & Sons, Ltd. Published 2014 by John Wiley & Sons, Inc.
DOI: 10.1002/9781118539415.wbwell16

assigning the worker to a different job, light or shared duties in the original job, reduced hours). With an increasing focus on early return to work and the costs and negative outcomes associated with unsuccessful attempts to return (Franche et al., 2005, 2007; Krause & Lund, 2004), research on the factors that affect the success of return-to-work programs is vital. Return to work has been the subject of an increasing amount of research (Franche et al., 2005, 2007; Hepburn, Kelloway, & Franche, 2010; Krause et al., 1998; Krause & Lund, 2004; Leyshon, & Shaw, 2012; MacEachen, Kosny, Ferrier, & Chambers, 2010; Stewart, Polak, Young, & Schultz, 2012). The severity of the condition prompting the leave (Shaw, Segal, Polatajko, & Harburn, 2002) and the physical demands of the job have long been established as important predictors of initial and sustained return to work (see Krause & Lund, 2004, for a review). More recent research has illustrated that workplace-based strategies such as the provision of workplace accommodations and the presence of return-to-work coordinators within an organization can help return injured employees to the workplace successfully (Franche et al., 2005, 2007; Hepburn, Franche, & Francis, 2010; Krause et al., 1998; Krause & Lund, 2004). A smaller body of research has pointed to the importance of psychological aspects of work and the social context of the workplace in successful return to work. Not surprisingly, low-quality jobs (i.e., jobs that are characterized by a lack of control, high job demands, and stress; see, for example, Krause et al., 2001) and monotonous work (Kristensen, 1991) are associated with delayed return to work.

An organizational culture that is supportive of injured workers is also associated with early and successful return to work. For example, Amick et al. (2000) found that disability leave was shortened following carpal tunnel surgery in organizations that valued strong interpersonal relations and safety. It also appears that supervisor (e.g., Krause et al., 1997, 2001) and coworker support may be related to the length of disability leaves. That said, findings regarding the nature of supervisor and coworker support in return to work are mixed, likely because support can manifest in multiple ways, including not only encouraging return to work but also encouraging injured workers to take adequate time to recover (Krause et al., 1997).

We propose that a full understanding of the success of an employee's return to work following an injury requires attention to the social context of the workplace. It seems reasonable that social characteristics of the workplace, such as whether or not returning employees are accepted by coworkers, would impact the success of reentry. The potential for stigma faced by returning workers is one core aspect of this social context. In fact, the stigma that injured workers experience throughout the compensation and return-to-work processes may be "anti-therapeutic" (Lippel, 2007) and contribute to failed return to work and chronic disability (Eakin, 2005; Tarasuk & Eakin, 1995).

## Stigma and Return to Work

In his seminal book, Goffman (1963) defined stigma as "an attribute that is deeply discrediting," which reduces the afflicted individual to a "tainted, discounted" person (p. 3). More recent social psychological perspectives (e.g., Crocker, Major, & Steele, 1998; Heatherton, Kleck, Hebl, & Hull, 2000; Klein & Snyder, 2003; Major & O'Brien, 2005) situate stigma in relationships between perceiver and target. Crocker and colleagues' (1998) definition reflects this attention to the social setting: "stigmatized individuals possess (or are believed to possess) some attribute or characteristic that conveys a social identity that is devalued in a particular social context" (p. 505). Given that the workplace is one such context, we view the stigma of the "working wounded" as a socially constructed phenomenon that emerges and is reproduced in a situated process. Following Link and Phelan's (2001) approach, we suggest that this process unfolds as individuals label differences, and then apply negative stereotypes about and categorize people based on those differences (e.g., Tajfel, 1969), resulting in discrimination and status loss for the target.

The designation "injured worker" alone sets these individuals apart from their coworkers. A need for modified work likely serves to distinguish them further from their workgroups. Many injured workers report being treated as either malingers or criminals who are attempting to misuse the workers' compensation system (Lippel, 2007; Roberts-Yates, 2003; Strunin & Boden, 2004), the health-care system (Reid, Ewan, & Lowy, 1991), and their coworkers and organizations in the return-to-work process (Eakin, 2005; Roberts-Yates, 2003; Tarasuk & Eakin, 1995). Injured workers might be viewed as lower status employees who are unable to perform their work and have less to offer the organization (Strunin & Boden, 2000). Certainly, there is a power imbalance in the return-to-work process where the injured worker is one, potentially devalued, person interacting with groups of coworkers, the employing organization, and the health-care and workers' compensation systems (Lippel, 2007).

341

Stigmatized individuals face several predicaments (Crocker et al., 1998). Knowing that their injury and their ability to work are negatively evaluated and that some aspects of their self-identity (e.g., honest person recovering from a legitimate injury) are questioned can lead to negative outcomes for injured workers. The prejudice and discrimination that results from a negative assessment of one's self-identity can negatively influence self-esteem and psychological wellbeing (e.g., Branscombe, Schmitt, & Harvey, 1999; Major, Quinton, & McCoy, 2002). It is also possible that injured workers experience stereotype threat (e.g., Steele, 1997; Steele & Aronson, 1995), whereby the anxiety arising from the possibility of confirming a negative stereotype can become a self-fulfilling prophecy and actually impede performance at work. They may also experience attributional ambiguity (Crocker & Major, 1989) if they question whether they are best described in terms of the stigmatizing characteristic (e.g., injured worker) or some other attribute (e.g., good worker).

A body of empirical research illustrates that injured workers do feel stigmatized in their interactions with workers' compensation systems, physicians, coworkers, and employers (Eakin, 2005; Eakin, MacEachen, & Clarke, 2003; Lippel, 1999, 2007; MacEachen et al., 2010; Roberts-Yates, 2003; Strunin & Boden, 2004; Tarasuk & Eakin, 1995). Some injured workers report that being on workers' compensation in and of itself is stigmatizing and that it is perhaps the "greatest disability of all" (Roberts-Yates, 2003, p. 904). Injured workers commonly speak of feeling humiliation (Strunin & Boden, 2004), negative emotions, anxiety, and depression (Lippel, 2007; Roberts-Yates, 2003). Lippel (2007) reported that the majority of injured workers she interviewed said that their experiences with the workers' compensation system had a negative effect on their mental health, with some workers reporting suicidal thoughts.

A breakdown in social relations at work also appears to be a common theme reported by injured workers. Even before their reentry to the workplace, returning employees worry about social aspects of their return (Shaw et al., 2002) and feel anxious about how their coworkers will react to them upon their reintegration into the workplace. Adversarial (Roberts-Yates, 2003) and demeaning (Strunin & Boden, 2004) relationships with coworkers and other stakeholders have been reported throughout the experience of the injury and return to work. Negative workplace relationships reported by injured workers have been associated with an erosion of trust between injured employees and their employers (Eakin, 2005). Some workers indicated that their coworkers viewed the job modifications necessary for early return to work as a privilege that these colleagues ultimately resented (Eakin et al., 2003).

## Predicting Stigma for Returning Workers

Having illustrated that injured workers are the targets of stigma and that this stigma reflects a socially constructed set of beliefs that injured workers are malingerers (Lippel, 2007) who aim to abuse the support offered by public or private insurers and their employers (Eakin, 2005), we turn our attention to identifying the circumstances under which a returning worker will be particularly vulnerable to stigma.

### Visibility of the Injury

One key feature of stigmatized qualities is whether the target is marked in an apparent way that is visible to perceivers (Jones et al., 1984). From a social-cognitive perspective, the visibility of a stigmatized quality is crucial because various psychological and behavioral responses in the perceiver rely on categorization of the target as a member of a devalued group (Crocker et al., 1998). Thus, generally, the more visible a stigmatized feature is the more vulnerable the target becomes (Jones et al., 1984). Research focusing on individuals with disabilities suggests that those with unconcealed disabilities will experience more negative treatment in the workplace (Stone & Colella, 1996). Some take advantage of the concealability of an element of themselves (e.g., cancer) to reduce the experience of stigma (Corrigan & Matthews, 2003). However, invisibility can be double-edged (Goffman, 1963) because individuals with concealed qualities worry about the backlash and stigma they will experience if others became aware of the stigmatized quality.

Returning injured workers cannot always conceal the fact they sustained an injury. Thus, the question becomes how visible is the condition that everyone is already aware of? Given the well-documented issue of perceived legitimacy with workplace injuries (Krause & Lund, 2004; Tarasuk & Eakin, 1995), we suggest that individuals with invisible injuries, such as soft tissue damage, will be more likely to experience stigma than are those with visible injuries, such as a broken arm, because in such a case the visible injuries may be perceived as a more legitimate basis for leave, compensation, and workplace accommodation. Invisible injuries open the target to questions of malingering and abuse of the system.

## Aesthetic Qualities of the Injury

We suggest that in the case of visible injuries, with all else being equal, those whose visible injuries involve aesthetically unappealing physical qualities (e.g., loss of limb, disfigurement, burns) will be subjected to increased stigmatization relative to those whose visible injuries do not involve devalued physical marks (e.g., broken limb, minor scars). This hypothesis regarding the impact of aesthetics in the experience of stigma for employees returning to work is in line with the well-documented findings in the social psychology literature (Jones et al., 1984) and reflects proposed relationships regarding the treatment of disabled individuals in organizations (Stone & Colella, 1996).

## Sensitivity, Identification, and Goals

Individuals vary in the degree to which they are sensitive to stigma (Major & O'Brien, 2005). In particular, individuals may become sensitized to stigma as a result of being treated based on the group, rather than their personal, identity. In an organizational context, the returning worker who is treated as a special case as a result of being injured may become increasingly sensitized to, and feel increasing threatened by, coworker or institutional reactions. To the extent that an injured worker feels particularly threatened by the negative stereotypes associated with their status (Steele & Aronson, 1995), the resultant anxiety may become a self-fulfilling prophecy and impede work performance, launching a vicious circle of poor performance and further stigmatization for the injured worker.

The degree to which an individual identifies with the organizational context or the work role may also influence how a returning worker perceives stigmatization due to an injury. Alienated or disaffected workers may not be threatened by organizational messages that suggest a lack of performance or competence. In contrast, the highly job-involved individuals, who see work as central to self-esteem, may be threatened by the perception that they are not as capable or competent as they once were (Rabinowitz & Hall, 1977; Saal, 1978).

## Job Performance and Status

The ability of the returning injured worker to perform at work also likely influences the treatment they receive from coworkers. There appears to be

344

consensus in the literature on workers with disabilities that high-performing individuals receive better treatment than low performers (Stone & Colella, 1996) and that other workers judge accommodations to be more reasonable when they are offered to high, rather than low, performers (Honig, 1999). Stone and Colella (1996), for example, suggested that a high performer who becomes disabled will still be viewed as qualified, recommended for promotion, and assigned to challenging tasks. In contrast, when prior performance is ambiguous or not as good there is a greater likelihood of negative stereotypes being invoked. Organizations value good work, and high performance may offer an injured worker a degree of immunity to stigma. In their study of workers returning to the workplace following a lost time back-injury, Tarasuk and Eakin (1995) found that those who had more seniority and held higher social status in an organization faced fewer questions about the legitimacy of their injuries.

## Course of the Injury

The course of a stigmatized quality reflects its change over time; it may progress, recur, disappear, or remain unchanged. Estimating the influence that the course of a condition will have on stigma is difficult and nuanced (Jones et al., 1984). Examining the experience of workers with disabilities, some have proposed that chronic or incurable conditions are associated with negative reactions from coworkers (Stone & Colella, 1996). In the case of return to work, the influence of course likely relates to coworkers' perceptions of the injured worker's improvement. If a returning employee's condition is perceived to be improving, coworkers may perceive that this individual is rightfully back to work and view any accommodations as appropriate and temporary and therefore legitimate. Alternatively, in the case of a similar injury, but with a constant or worsening course, coworkers might question the return and judge negatively accommodations that appear long standing. Thus, we suggest that those whose conditions are constant or worsening will experience more stigma than those whose health is improving.

## Origin of the Injury

Judgments about when and how an injury occurred have important impli-cations for the perceiver's affective and behavioral responses, because they can implicate the target as more or less responsible for the condition (Jones et al., 1984). In general, individuals whose conditions are perceived to be the fault of their own actions are more frequently targets of stigma than are those who have conditions perceived to be beyond their control (e.g., Powell, Christensen, Abbott, & Katz, 1998; Weiner, Perry, & Magnusson, 1988). We propose that this view generalizes to the work setting, as do other researchers (e.g., Stone & Colella, 1996).

In the case of on-the-job accidents, however, there are several factors that influence how blame is attributed that might influence stigma. Drawing on research related to eyewitness testimony (e.g., Fisher, 1995; Haber & Haber, 2000; Wells & Olson, 2003), Kelloway, Stinson, and MacLean (2004) argued that coworkers have, at best, imperfect recall of workplace accidents and that memories are fragile, malleable, and susceptible to forgetting, even in optimal conditions (for reviews see Cutler & Penrod, 1995; Loftus & Doyle, 1997; Ross, Read, & Toglia, 1994). Individuals who witness accidents actively sort through and reorganize information in order to make sense of complex information (e.g., Dekker, 2002; Weick, 1995) and tend to blame individual rather than system causes (e.g., Dekker, 2002). These observations suggest that coworkers may be motivated to attribute the causes of workplace injuries to weaknesses or carelessness on the part of the individuals involved (Kelloway et al., 2004).

## Disruption Stemming from Return to Work

A disruptive injury is one that "hinders, strains, and adds to the difficulty of interpersonal relationships" (Jones et al., 1984, p. 46). The return of employees following injury will likely be viewed as disruptive when it interrupts or largely changes the routine of their coworkers. The accommodation needs of a returning worker, if substantial, can prompt anxiety, fear, uncertainty, and fairness judgments among coworkers. If, to accommodate the needs of returning employees, the employer has to make major changes to the job content, team composition, or work schedules of other people, returning employees may be negatively viewed among their coworkers. Substantial accommodations for injured workers may increase perceptions of unfairness among coworkers (Colella, 2001; Eakin et al., 2003) and prompt them to question the legitimacy of the individual's return to work, or in the case of invisible conditions such as soft tissue injury, the legitimacy of the injury itself.

The degree of disruption caused by the return of an injured worker may be influenced by the size of the organization. Eakin and her colleagues (Eakin & MacEachen, 1998; Eakin et al., 2003) examined occupational health and return to work in small enterprises. Small businesses have lower rates of return to work than larger firms (Oleinick, Gluck, & Guire, 1995). Fewer human and economic resources in small organizations increase the likelihood that a return to work is governed in an ad hoc, or potentially disruptive, manner. The close social relations that typify many small workplaces also add to the difficulty surrounding return to work when the employer views the process primarily in business terms, but the injured worker views it through the lens of established interpersonal relationships (Eakin et al. 2003).

## Threat

Peril represents the real or imagined dangers associated with devalued social categories (Jones et al., 1984). Perceivers can be threatened by or fear possible contamination by illness or physical harm (Coverdale, Nairn, & Claasen, 2002; Schulze & Angermeyer, 2003; Sieff, 2003) and thus distance themselves from an afflicted individual. Peril can also be experienced more indirectly, via awareness of one's own frailty or mortality (Jones et al., 1984). Threatening stigmas are likely to be particularly disruptive to interpersonal relations and organizational functioning. If coworkers perceive that a returning employee is incapable of working safely, either because of the degree of injury or because the injury prompted a reputation as an unsafe worker, those coworkers may feel that working with the returning employee is dangerous and thus stigmatize him or her. These responses are likely to be most prevalent in contexts where there are safety hazards and potentially dangerous conditions. In addition, people can be threatened by the negative experiences of others because it reminds them that they too are vulnerable to similar harm. To escape such psychological threat people may avoid interacting with the targeted person or even derogate or blame the victim via a just world bias (Lerner & Miller, 1978), even in cases where objective evidence does not support that conclusion.

## Coworker Experiences

Perceptions of legitimacy may be related to the amount of personal or vicarious experience coworkers have with workplace injury. Greater understanding may be expected from individuals who have experienced a return to work following injury themselves. With respect to mental illness, people who have more frequent contact with individuals with a mental illness are less likely to possess prejudicial beliefs about mental illness (e.g., Link &

Cullen, 1986) and are less likely to engage in stigmatizing behavior toward the mentally ill (e.g., Corrigan et al., 2003). Thus, increased contact with injured workers may increase coworkers' understanding of their status and increase their perceptions of legitimacy around injury and accommodations.

## Safety Climate

Safety climate refers to employees' shared understanding of their organization's safety policies, procedures, and practices; and ultimately, their understanding of safety as a priority in their organization (Zohar, 2003). Zohar's conceptual framework for safety climate indicates that workers build their understanding of safety as a priority by making observations of top managers' actions with regard to the implementation of safety policies and procedures, and supervisory practices of supervisors. For example, workers note if their management invests in safety training and takes safety into consideration when making production-related decisions. Workers recognize if their supervisors emphasize safety even during times of work pressure, reward safe work behaviors, and regularly discuss safety issues. It is not surprising that there is a link between safety climate and employee safety behaviors (e.g., Griffin & Neal, 2000; Hofmann & Stetzer, 1996; Zohar & Luria, 2005) and injuries (e.g., Zohar, 2000, 2002). We would expect that compared to a workplace scoring low on safety climate, a workplace with a high level of safety climate will likely have fewer workers seriously injured on the job and, therefore, fewer injured workers to return to the workplace. However, despite their lower numbers, we would argue that stigmatization is less for these few injured workers.

Employees in workplaces high in safety climate recognize that the responsibility for safety is shared with their supervisors and top management, and it seems likely that injured workers will not be unfairly blamed as the cause of their injury, thereby reducing the likelihood of stigmatization. The origin of invisible injuries may also be clarified as workers are more likely to have an understanding of all injury types, even invisible ones such as soft tissue injuries. They will also have an appreciation for the fact that injuries can and do develop over time at work, rather than as the result of a specific, acute, incident.

It is also likely that in workplaces with a positive safety climate that threat may be diminished because incidents resulting in a workplace injury will be investigated properly and any working conditions or lapse in training deemed to be contributing factors addressed quickly. As a result, coworkers should not fear for their own safety as a result of a similar accident. Further, because safety concerns and efforts to correct hazards are part of the day-to-day business in such workplaces, communication about the causes of workplace incidents will be thorough. Coworkers will not needlessly fear that their returning colleague is an unsafe worker. It also seems reasonable that, given their strong attention to safety in general, workplaces with high levels of safety climate will have policies and procedures in place related to return to work. Certainly, policies and procedures regarding work accommodations for returning injured workers will take into account the safety of not only the injured workers, but also their coworkers. No workers will be put in the position of having to perform jobs that they cannot perform safely, reducing coworker fear that they will be working with someone who may cause a safety incident. Further, it seems unlikely that offered accommodations will cause disruptions that may put coworkers at risk. Regardless, workplaces with high levels of safety climate will encourage employees to raise any safety concerns that arise during the accommodation, and supervisors and top management will be inclined to address them quickly.

## Managing Stigma in Return to Work

Given that organizations in many jurisdictions have a legal duty to accommodate the needs of employees with disabilities, including those obtained through an occupational injury, employers must look for ways to manage the stigma and accompanying negative outcomes. As noted in the previous section, a positive safety climate can help to alleviate some of the sources of stigma for returning employees. Thus, one viable option to manage stigma in return-to-work is to work toward a positive organizational safety climate. Another source of ideas for organizational interventions to address issues of stigma in return to work situations is the social psychology literature on reducing stigma. Three avenues for changing people's perceptions of some stigmatized characteristics, such as mental illness, that have been emphasized in social psychology research are education, protest, and contact (e.g., Corrigan & Matthews, 2003; Corrigan et al., 2001; Penn et al., 1994).

Education programs aimed at reducing the stigma associated with particular stigmatized mental health conditions have attempted to replace myths and emotionally charged public perceptions about the mental illness with accurate information (Corrigan et al., 2001). For instance, an education program might target the myth that people with mental illness tend to be dangerous to others. Research in this area suggests that education programs can improve people's attributions about and attitudes toward people with psychiatric conditions (Corrigan et al., 2001; Pinfold et al., 2003).

Strategies involving protest emphasize that stigmas are unfair and appeal to people on a moral level to suppress stigmatizing attitudes and avoid engaging in discriminatory behavior (Corrigan & Matthews, 2003; Corrigan et al., 2001). Evidence for the impact of protest on reducing the stigma associated with mental illness is mixed. Some studies indicate that protest is not effective in changing attitudes (e.g., Corrigan et al., 2001). Others show that asking people to suppress stereotypes can reduce the extent to which individuals engage in stereotype consistent behavior, suggesting that stereotype suppression may be a viable strategy for reducing the stigma associated with injured employees (Penn & Corrigan, 2002). However, other studies illustrate that instructing individuals to suppress stereotypes may make them more likely to engage in prejudiced behavior in future situations: a finding commonly labeled the "rebound effect" (e.g., McCrae, Bodenhausen, Milne, & Jetten, 1994; Monteith, Spicer, & Toorman, 1998). Given the equivocal nature of the findings on the effectiveness of protest strategies in reducing discriminatory behavior in general we refrain from making suggestions regarding the use of protest in the return-to-work arena. However, we do propose that the relationship between protest activities and stigma for injured employees be empirically examined.

Strategies to reduce stigma that rely on contact promote direct interaction between the targets and perceivers of stigma (Corrigan et al., 2001). Research indicates that contact strategies are successful in reducing stigma and discrimination (Corrigan & Matthews, 2003). For example, with respect to mental illness, people who have more frequent contact with individuals who have a mental illness are less likely to possess prejudicial beliefs about mental illness (e.g., Link & Cullen, 1986) and less likely to engage in stigmatizing behavior toward the mentally ill (e.g., Corrigan et al., 2003). It therefore appears that increased contact between injured employees and their coworkers may reduce the extent to which returning employees are stigmatized. As such, organizations might promote situations in which returning employees and their colleagues interact on a social basis. For instance, an employee who has been on extended leave might be invited to partake in work-related social events shortly before the official reentry into the workplace. To the extent that coworkers are able to talk with and get to know the situation of a returning employee they may be less likely to exclude the individual. This strategy may also help coworkers predict the types of accommodations that the returning employee will require, allowing them an opportunity to adjust to the situation beforehand and perhaps feel less threatened by the employee's official return.

Another potential intervention strategy to reduce the effects of stigma is social support. The social support literature has consistently demonstrated the value of support from supervisors and coworkers in individual wellbeing and productivity (Cohen & Wills, 1985; Frese, 1999). It seems reasonable to extend these findings to the return-to-work situation and state that a high degree of support from coworkers and supervisors will facilitate an injured employee's return. On this basis we propose that a supportive environment can help to reduce the stigma experienced by returning employees. There is also a considerable body of evidence suggesting social support moderates the experience of stress (e.g., Cohen & Wills, 1985; House, 1981). That is, being surrounded by supportive people can make a person less vulnerable to workplace stressors. In the return-to-work situation, the experience of stigma is likely a stressor for the returning employee. Even if some coworkers stigmatize, simply having a supervisor or group of colleagues who are willing to bolster the stigmatized individual may help that person be more resistant to the stigma and in turn reduce negative outcomes such as depression or reduced self-esteem (Ritsher, Otilingam, & Grajales, 2003). Certainly, recent research on return to work has recognized the importance of supervisor support in realizing positive outcomes (e.g., Munir, Yarker, Hicks, & Donaldson-Fielder, 2012).

## Conclusion

To be devalued is to be discounted, marginalized, not to belong, not to be a full member of the group or organization, and ultimately, as Goffman (1963) argued, to be denied status as a complete human being. This is the experience of the stigmatized individual. Injured workers experience negative treatment throughout their experiences with workers' compensation (e.g., Lippel, 2007) and upon return to work (e.g., Eakin, 2005). Examining return to work through the lens of stigma, we considered how qualities of the injured individual, situation, and organization might come together to influence the stigma experienced by injured workers upon return to work. Although necessarily subject to future empirical investigation and further elaboration, we suggest that the ideas outlined in this chapter can lay the groundwork for research on the stigmatization of injured workers and how this affects return-to-work outcomes.

# References

Amick, B., Habeck, R. V., Hunt, A., Fossel, A. H., Chapin, A., & Keller, R. B. (2000). Measuring the impact of organizational behaviors on work disability prevention and management. *Journal of Occupational Rehabilitation, 10,* 21–38.

Branscombe, N. R., Schmitt, M. T., & Harvey, R. D. (1999). Perceiving pervasive discrimination among African-Americans: Implications for group identification and well-being. *Journal of Personality and Social Psychology, 77,* 135–149.

Cohen, S., & Wills, T. A. (1985). Stress, social support and the buffering hypothesis. *Psychological Bulletin, 98,* 310–357.

Colella, A. (2001). Coworker distributive fairness judgments of the workplace accommodation of employees with disabilities. *Academy of Management Review, 26,* 100–116.

Corrigan, P. W., & Matthews, A. K. (2003). Stigma and disclosure: Implications for coming out of the closet. *Journal of Mental Health, 12,* 235–248.

Corrigan, P. W., Larson, J. E., & Kuwabara, S. A. (2007). Mental illness stigma and the fundamental components of supported employment. *Rehabilitation Psychology, 52,* 452–457.

Corrigan, P. W., River, L. P., Lundin, R. K., Penn, D. L. Uphoff-Wasowski, K., Campion, J., . . . Kubiak, M. A. (2001). Three strategies for changing attributions about severe mental illness. *Schizophrenia Bulletin, 27,* 187–195.

Corrigan, P. W., Rowan, D, Green, A., Lundin, R. K., River, L. P., Uphoff-Wasowski, K., et al. (2003). Challenging two mental illness stigmas: Personal responsibility and dangerousness. *Schizophrenia Bulletin, 28,* 296–310.

Coverdale, J., Nairn, R., & Claasen, D. (2002). Depictions of mental illness in print media: A prospective national sample. *Australian and New Zealand Journal of Psychiatry, 36,* 697–700.

Crocker, J., & Major, B. (1989). Social stigma and self-esteem: The self-protective properties of stigma. *Psychological Review, 96,* 608–630.

Crocker, J., Major, B., & Steele, C. (1998). Social stigma. In D. T. Gilbert, S. T. Fiske, & G. Lindzey (Eds.), *Handbook of social psychology* (4th ed., Vol. 2, pp. 504–553). Boston: McGraw-Hill.

Cutler, B. L., & Penrod, S. D. (1995). *Mistaken identification: The eyewitness, psychology, and the law.* New York: Cambridge University Press.

Dekker, S. W. A. (2002). Reconstructing human contribution to accidents: The new view on error and performance. *Journal of Safety Research, 33,* 371–385.

Eakin, J. M. (2005). The discourse of abuse in return to work: A hidden epidemic of suffering. In C. L. Peterson & C. Mayhew (Eds.), *Occupational health and safety: International influences and the "new" epidemics* (pp. 159–174). Amityville, NY: Baywood.

Eakin, J. M., & MacEachen, E. (1998). Health and the social relations of work: A study of the health-related experiences of employees in small workplaces. *Sociology of Health & Illness, 20*(6), 896–914.

Eakin, J., MacEachen, E., & Clarke, J. (2003).'Playing it smart' with return to work: Small workplace experience under Ontario's policy of self reliance and early return. *Policy and Practice in Health and Safety, 1*(2), 19–42.

Fisher, R. P. (1995). Interviewing victims and witnesses of crime. *Psychology, Public Policy, and Law, 1*, 732–764.

Franche, R.-L., Cullen, K., Clarke, J., Irvin, E., Sinclair, S., Frank, J., et al. (2005). Workplace-based return-to-work interventions: A systematic review of the quantitative literature. *Journal of Occupational Rehabilitation, 15*, 607–631.

Franche, R.-L., Severin, C., Hogg-Johnson, S., Côté, P., Vidmar, M., & Lee, H. (2007). The impact of early workplace-based return-to-work strategies on work absence duration: A 6-month longitudinal study following an occupational musculoskeletal injury. *Journal of Occupational and Environmental Medicine, 49*, 960–974.

Frese, M. (1999). Social support as a moderator of the relationship between work stressors and psychological dysfunctioning: A longitudinal study with objective measures. *Journal of Occupational Health Psychology, 4*, 179–192.

Goffman, E. (1963). *Stigma: Notes on the management of spoiled identity*. Englewood Cliffs, NJ: Prentice Hall.

Griffin, M. A., & Neal, A. (2000). Perceptions of safety at work: A framework for linking safety climate to safety performance, knowledge, and motivation. *Journal of Occupational Health Psychology, 5*, 347–58.

Haber, R. N., & Haber, L. (2000). Experiencing, remembering and reporting events. *Psychology, Public Policy and Law, 6*, 1057–1097.

Heatherton, T. F., Kleck, R. E., Hebl, M. R., & Hull, J. G. (Eds.) (2000). *The social psychology of stigma*. New York: Guilford.

Hepburn, C. G., Franche, R.-L., & Francis, L. (2010). Successful return to work: The role of fairness and workplace-based strategies. *International Journal of Workplace Health Management, 3*, 7–24.

Hepburn, C. G., Kelloway, E. K., & Franche, R.-L. (2010). Early employer response to workplace injury: What injured workers perceive as fair and why these perceptions matter. *Journal of Occupational Health Psychology, 15*, 409–420.

Hofmann, D. A., & Stetzer, A. (1996). A cross-level investigation of factors influencing unsafe behaviors and accidents. *Personnel Psychology, 49*, 307–339.

Honig, H. A. (1999). Reasonable employment accommodations for persons with disabilities: A policy capturing approach. *Dissertation Abstracts International: Section B: The Sciences and Engineering, 60*(3-B), 1336.

House, J. S. (1981). *Work stress and social support*. Reading, MA: Addison-Wesley.

Jahoda, M. (1982). *Employment and unemployment and social psychological analysis*. Cambridge: Cambridge University Press.

Jahoda, M. (1988). Economic recessions and mental health: Some conceptual issues. *Journal of Social Issues, 44*, 13–24.

353

Jones, E. E., Farina, A., Hastorf, A. H., Markus, H., Miller, D. T., & Scott, R. A. (1984). *Social stigma: The psychology of marked relationships*. New York: Freeman.

Kelloway, E. K., Gallagher, D., & Barling, J. (2004). Work, employment and the individual. In B. Kaufman (Ed.), *Theoretical advances in industrial relations*. Madison, WI: Industrial Relations Research Association.

Kelloway, E. K., Stinson, V., & MacLean, C. (2004). Eyewitness testimony in occupational accident investigations: Towards a research agenda. *Law and Human Behavior, 28*, 115–132.

Klein, O., & Snyder, M. (2003). Stereotypes and behavioral confirmation: From interpersonal to intergroup perspectives. In M. P. Zanna (Ed.), *Advances in experimental social psychology* (Vol. 35, pp. 153–234). San Diego, CA: Academic Press.

Krause, N., Dasinger, L. K., Deegan, L. J., Brand, R. J., & Rudolph, L. (2001). Psychosocial job factors and RTW after low back injury: A disability phase-specific analysis. *American Journal of Industrial Medicine, 40*, 374–392.

Krause, N., Dasinger, L. K., & Neuhauser, F. (1998). Modified work and return to work: A review of the literature. *Journal of Occupational Rehabilitation, 8*, 113–139.

Krause, N., & Lund, T. (2004). Returning to work after occupational injury. In J. Barling & M. R. Frone (Eds.), *The psychology of workplace safety* (pp. 265–295). Washington, DC: American Psychological Association.

Krause, N., Lynch, J., Kaplan, G. A., Cohen, R. D., Goldberg, D. E., & Salonen, J. T. (1997). Predictors of disability retirement. *Scandinavian Journal of Work, Environment, and Health, 23*, 403–413.

Kristensen, T. S. (1991). Sickness absence and work strain among Danish slaughter house workers: An analysis of absence from work regarded as coping behaviour. *Social Science and Medicine, 32*, 15–27.

Lerner, M. J., & Miller, D. T. (1978). Just world research and the attribution process: Looking back and ahead. *Psychological Bulletin, 85*, 1030–1051.

Leyshon, R., & Shaw, L. (2012). Using multiple stakeholders to define a successful return to work: A concept mapping approach, *Work: A Journal of Prevention, Assessment and Rehabilitation, 41*, 397–408.

Link, B. G., & Cullen, F. T. (1986). Contact with the mentally ill and perceptions of how dangerous they are. *Journal of Health and Social Behavior, 27*, 289–302.

Link, B. G., & Phelan, J. C. (2001). Conceptualizing stigma. *Annual Review of Sociology, 27*, 363–385.

Lippel, K. (1999). Therapeutic and anti-therapeutic consequences of workers' compensation systems. *International Journal of Law and Psychiatry, 22*(5–6), 521–546.

Lippel, K. (2007). Workers describe the effect of the workers' compensation process on their health: A Québec study. *International Journal of Law and Psychiatry, 30*, 427–443.

Loftus, E. F., & Doyle, J. M. (1997). *Eyewitness testimony: Civil and criminal* (3rd ed.). Charlottesville, VA: Lexis Law.

MacEachen, E., Kosny, A. Ferrier, S., & Chambers, L. (2010). The toxic dose of systems problems: Why some injured workers don't return to work as expected. *Journal of Occupational Rehabilitation, 20*, 349–366.

Major, B., & O'Brien, L.T. (2005). The social psychology of stigma. *Annual Review of Psychology, 56*, 393–421.

Major, B., Quinton, W. J., & McCoy, S.K. (2002). Antecedents and consequences of perceiving the self as a target of discrimination: Theoretical and empirical advances. In M. P. Zanna (Ed.), *Advances in experimental social psychology* (Vol. 34, pp. 251–330). San Diego, CA: Academic Press.

McCrae, C. N., Bodenhausen, G. V., Milne, A. B., & Jetten, J. (1994). Out of mind but back in sight: Stereotypes on the rebound. *Journal of Personality and Social Psychology, 67*: 808–817.

Monteith, M. J., Spicer, C. V., & Toorman, G. D. (1998). Consequences of stereotype suppression: Stereotypes on AND not on the rebound. *Journal of Experimental Social Psychology, 34*, 355–377.

Munir, F. Yarker, J., Hicks, B., & Donaldson-Fielder. E. (2012). Returning employees back to work: Developing a measure for Supervisors to Support Return to Work (SSRW). *Journal of Occupational Rehabilitation, 22*, 196–208.

Oleinick, A., Gluck, J., & Guire, K. (1995). Establishment size and risk of occupational injury. *American Journal of Industrial Medicine, 28*, 1–21.

Penn, D. L., & Corrigan, P. W. (2002). The effects of stereotype suppression on psychiatric stigma. *Schizophrenia Research, 55*, 269–276.

Penn, D. L., Guynan, K., Daily, T., Spaulding, W. D., Garbin, C. P., & Sullivan, M. (1994). Dispelling the stigma of schizophrenia: What sort of information is best? *Schizophrenia Bulletin, 20*, 567–578.

Pinfold, V., Huxley, P., Thornicroft, G., Farmer, P., Toulmin, H., & Graham, T. (2003). Reducing psychiatric stigma and discrimination: Evaluating an educational intervention with the police force in England. *Social Psychiatry and Psychiatric Epidemiology, 38*, 337–344.

Powell, J. L., Christensen, C., Abbott, A. S., & Katz, D. S. (1998). Adding insult to injury: Blaming persons with HIV disease. *AIDS and Behavior, 2*, 307–317.

Rabinowitz, S., & Hall, D. (1977). Organizational research on job involvement. *Psychological Bulletin, 84*, 245–258.

Reid, J., Ewan, C., & Lowy, E. (1991). Pilgrimage of pain: The illness experiences of women with repetition strain injury and the search for credibility. *Social Science & Medicine, 32*(5), 601–612.

Ritsher, J. B., Otilingam, P. G., & Grajales, M. (2003). Internalized stigma of mental illness: Psychometric properties of a new measure. *Psychiatry Research, 121*, 31–49.

Roberts-Yates, C. (2003). The concerns and issues of injured workers in relation to claims/injury management and rehabilitation: The need for new operational frameworks. *Disability and Rehabilitation, 25*(16), 898–907.

Ross, D. F., Read, J. D., & Toglia, M. P. (1994). *Adult eyewitness testimony: Current trends and developments*. New York: Cambridge University Press.

Saal, F. E. (1978). Job involvement: A multivariate approach. *Journal of Applied Psychology, 63*, 53–61.

Schulze, B., & Angermeyer, M. C. (2003). Subjective experiences of stigma: A focus group study of schizophrenic parties, their relatives and mental health professionals. *Social Science and Medicine, 56*, 299–312.

Shaw, L., Segal, R., Polatajko, H., & Harburn, K. (2002). Understanding return to work behaviours: Promoting the importance of individual perceptions in the study of return to work. *Disability and Rehabilitation, 24*, 185–195.

Sieff, E. M. (2003). Media frames of mental illness: The potential impact of negative frames. *Journal of Mental Health, 12*, 259–269.

Steele, C. M. (1997). A threat in the air: How stereotypes shape intellectual identity and performance. *American Psychologist, 52*, 613–629.

Steele, C. M., & Aronson, J. (1995). Stereotype threat and the intellectual test performance of African Americans. *Journal of Personality and Social Psychology, 69*, 797–811.

Stewart, A. M., Polak, E., Young, R., & Schultz, I. Z. (2012). Injured workers' construction of expectations of return to work with sub-acute back pain: The role of perceived uncertainty. *Journal of Occupational Rehabilitation, 22*, 1–14.

Stone, D. L., & Colella, A. (1996). A model of factors affecting the treatment of disabled individuals in organizations. *Academy of Management Review, 21*, 352–401.

Strunin, L., & Boden, L. I. (2000). Paths of reentry: Employment experiences of injured workers. *American Journal of Industrial Medicine, 38*, 373–384.

Strunin, L., & Boden, L. I. (2004). The workers' compensation system: Worker friend or foe? *American Journal of Industrial Medicine, 45*, 338–345.

Tajfel, H. (1969). Cognitive aspects of prejudice. *Journal of Social Issues, 25*, 79–97.

Tarasuk, V., & Eakin, J. (1995). The problem of legitimacy in the experience of work-related back injury. *Qualitative Health Research, 5*(2), 204–221.

Weick, K. (1995). *Sensemaking in organizations*. Thousand Oaks, CA: Sage.

Weiner, B., Perry, R. P., & Magnusson, J. (1988). An attributional analysis of reactions to stigmas. *Journal of Personality and Social Psychology, 55*, 738–748.

Wells, G. L., & Olson, E. A. (2003). Eyewitness testimony. *Annual Review of Psychology, 54*, 277–295.

Zohar, D. (2000). A group level model of safety climate: Testing the effect of group climate on micro-accidents in manufacturing jobs. *Journal of Applied Psychology, 85*, 587–596.

Zohar, D. (2002). The effects of leadership dimensions, safety climate and assigned priorities on minor injuries in work groups. *Journal of Organizational Behavior, 23*, 75–92.

Zohar, D. (2003). Safety climate: Conceptual and measurement issues. In J. C. Quick & L. Tetrick (Eds.), *Handbook of occupational health psychology* (pp. 123–142). Washington, DC: American Psychological Association.

Zohar, D., & Luria, G. (2005). A multi-level model of safety climate: Cross-level relationships between organization and group-level climates. *Journal of Applied Psychology, 90*, 616–628.

# 17

# Job Stress in University Academics

## *Evidence from an Australian National Study*

### Anthony H. Winefield

University of South Australia, Australia

## Introduction

It is universally recognized that universities play a vital role in the economic and social life of all developed nations. They train the nation's scientists, engineers, lawyers, doctors, and other professionals and produce much of its cutting-edge research. In order to fulfill this role successfully they need to attract and retain high-quality staff and provide a supportive working environment. Their ability to do so has been threatened over the past few decades by deteriorating working conditions resulting from cuts to their operating grants. In Australia, for example, the average student-to-staff ratio increased steadily from around 13:1 in 1990 to around 19:1 in 2000 (Senate Committee, 2001) and continues to rise, exceeding 20:1 in 2012. This has led to increased pressure and high reported stress levels that generally exceed those reported in normative data from the general population (Akerlind & McAlpine, 2009; Catano et al., 2010; McClenahan, Giles, & Mallett, 2007; Tytherleigh, Webb, Cooper, & Ricketts, 2005; Watts & Robertson, 2011).

University teaching has traditionally been regarded as a low-stress occupation. Although not highly paid, academics have been envied because they

*Work and Wellbeing: Wellbeing: A Complete Reference Guide*, Volume III.
Edited by Peter Y. Chen and Cary L. Cooper.
© 2014 John Wiley & Sons, Ltd. Published 2014 by John Wiley & Sons, Inc.
DOI: 10.1002/9781118539415.wbwell17

enjoyed tenure, light workloads, flexibility, "perks" such as overseas trips for study and/or conference purposes, and the freedom to pursue their own research interests.

During the past 20 years most of these advantages have been eroded in many countries. Academic salaries have fallen in real terms in countries such as the United States, the United Kingdom, Australia, and New Zealand (Winefield, 2000, 2003). Increasing numbers of academic positions are now untenured, workloads have increased, and academics are under increased pressures to attract external funds for their research and to "publish or perish." Universities and academic departments are being subjected to external "quality" audits—for example the Research Assessment Exercise (RAE) in the United Kingdom and the Excellence in Research Australia (ERA)—which scrutinize their research output in terms of quantity, quality, and impact as well as teaching. Future funding support is determined by the outcomes of such audits. As Shirley Fisher (1994) says in relation to British universities in her book *Stress in academic life*: "The demands on academics have risen rapidly over the last ten years . . . there has been a steady erosion of job control. All the signs are that this will continue" (p. 61). Several U.K. studies have supported Fisher's contention, including those by Hind and Doyle (1996) and Daniels and Guppy (1992).

It is now well recognized that workplace stress in universities worldwide is increasing and has a multitude of detrimental effects on individuals and organizations. Clearly, given the role that universities play in education and training, it is important that they are able to obtain creative solutions from a well-educated workforce. One way in which this may be done is through assisting staff to overcome their stress.

Research from the United States indicates that the phenomenon of academic stress is alarmingly widespread. In a survey of almost 2000 faculty members, Melendez and de Guzman (1983) found that 62% acknowledged severe or moderate job stress. In his review of the literature, Seldin (1987) states that the academic environment of the 1980s has imposed surprisingly high levels of job stress on academics, and that the level of stress will continue to increase in future decades.

The impact of faculty stress is less well documented. In their study on faculty stress in the United States, Bowen and Schuster (1985, 1986) characterized faculty morale as "very poor" at a quarter of the campuses they researched. They further reported that many of the senior faculty members they interviewed were angry, embittered, and felt devalued and abandoned.

358

High levels of faculty stress have also been associated with high academic turnover.

In the early 1990s, the Carnegie Foundation for the Advancement of Teaching sponsored an international survey of the academic profession in which 14 countries participated (Australia, Brazil, Chile, England, Germany, Hong Kong, Israel, Japan, Korea, Mexico, The Netherlands, Russia, Sweden, United States). The data were collected from 1991 to 1993 (Altbach, 1996). According to Altbach:

> For a number of years, the professoriate has been undergoing change and has been under strain almost everywhere. Fiscal problems for higher education are now evident in all of these fourteen countries . . . In most of the nations, the somewhat unprecedented phenomenon of increasing enrollments has been allowed to supersede allocated resources . . . At the same time, professors in a number of countries are being asked to be more entrepreneurial—for example, in bringing research grants and contracts to their institutions.
>
> Altbach (1996), pp. 4–5

Somewhat surprisingly, despite widespread complaints about their working conditions, most of the respondents said that their overall morale was high because of the intellectual pleasure provided by their work, with 63% (England) to 85% (Israel) disagreeing with the proposition "If I had it to do over again, I would not become an academic." A major source of dissatisfaction was institutional leadership: "An unusually large number express dissatisfaction with and doubts about the quality of the leadership provided by top-level administrators at their colleges and universities" (Altbach, 1996, pp. 28–29). On the other hand, Armour (1987) found that a high percentage of academics planned to leave academia, which they attributed to the high levels of stress encountered in the profession. The research literature further indicates that faculty stress significantly affects the quality of both teaching and research. Research has highlighted that some of the effects of faculty stress, such as detachment, low job satisfaction, and low job commitment can be contagious for students and colleagues (Armour, 1987). It is apparent that the consequences of academic stress may be far more wide ranging than the occasional stress illness.

A recent systematic literature review on burnout by Watts and Robertson (2011) in the United Kingdom found that

> staff exposure to high numbers of students, especially tuition of postgraduates, strongly predicts the experience of burnout. Other predictive variables included

gender, with higher depersonalisation scores found in male teachers and female teachers typically scoring higher on the emotional exhaustion dimension. Age also demonstrated an association, with younger staff appearing more vulnerable to emotional exhaustion.

Watts and Robertson (2011), p. 33

Twelve studies were included in the review: 5 from the United States, 2 from the United Kingdom, and 1 each from Canada, South Africa, Spain, Turkey, and The Netherlands, although with the exception of the U.K. study by Doyle and Hind (1998), which sampled 85 universities, the studies were all based at a single university.

Although the bulk of the research on academic stress has been conducted in the United Kingdom and the United States, the problem is clearly worldwide with recent reports from Australia (Akerlind & McAlpine, 2009; Bakker et al., 2010; Boyd et al., 2011; Gillespie, Walsh, Winefield, Dua, & Stough, 2001; Winefield, Boyd, Saebel, & Pignata, 2008a, 2008b; Winefield, Gillespie, Stough, Dua, & Hapuarachchi, 2002; Winefield et al., 2003; Winefield & Jarrett, 2001), Canada (Catano et al., 2010), China (Sun, Wu, & Wang, 2011), Holland (Taris, Schreurs, & Van Iersal-Van Silfhout, 2001), and South Africa (Barkhuizen & Rothmann, 2008; Rothmann & Barkhuizen, 2008).

In contrast to the volume of research conducted in the United Kingdom and the United States, there has been very little research on the job-related stress experienced by academic staff in Australian universities. In the late 1980s, Australian universities underwent major restructuring similar to what happened to universities in England in the early 1990s. In both countries, the binary system which distinguished between universities and less prestigious tertiary institutions was abolished, so that former teachers' colleges and polytechnics/institutes of technology were granted university status. These changes took somewhat different forms. In Australia, for example, but not in England, tertiary institutions were encouraged to merge, which resulted in major disruptions and numerous multi-campus universities. In England, many of the new universities lacked a research tradition and were seen as inferior to the traditional universities. In both countries, the restructuring was inevitably disruptive and augmented the ongoing problems associated with reduced funding.

In a study assessing the level of stress of both academic and general staff, Winefield and Jarrett (2001) surveyed all staff at the University of Adelaide. The survey attracted more than 2,000 replies, which represented an overall response rate of 72% of noncasual staff (77% for general staff and 65% for academic staff). The overall level of psychological distress was very high, particularly among academic staff, even though their overall level of job satisfaction was moderately high. Indeed, dissatisfaction was reported with only 2 (out of 15) aspects of work: "Your chance of promotion/ reclassification" and "The way the University is managed."

Similar studies have been reported at Monash (Sharpley, Dua, Reynolds, & Acosta, 1995) and the University of New England (Dua, 1994). At Monash, stress was perceived as a major problem for about 25% of staff, with lack of feedback on performance, lack of promotion opportunities, worries about amalgamations, and lack of equipment and/or infrastructure support identified as frequent sources of stress. At New England, Dua found: (a) staff at more junior levels reported more stress than those at more senior levels; (b) stress was associated with poor self-reported health; (c) staff who perceived high levels of control over their work environment experienced less stress than those who perceived low levels of control.

Finally, several key researchers have suggested that while stress is an inevitable part of academia, universities must bear the responsibility for assisting employees to manage job-related stress (Seldin, 1987). Certainly, with the increasing frequency of stress-related claims and the resultant costs (Armour, 1987), it is in a university's best interest to be proactive rather than reactive in managing faculty stress.

Recent research has highlighted the need to include both positive and negative work-related events in our understanding of the stress coping process (Wearing & Hart, 1996). However, few theoretical models of stress and wellbeing have attempted to incorporate both these factors. Indeed, there is currently little research demonstrating the theoretical relationship between cognitive appraisal of positive and negative work events and other well-known moderators of stress, namely personality, coping resources, and coping strategies.

Surprisingly, even less theoretical development has focused on the direct effect stressors and uplifts have on meaningful organizational (productivity, absenteeism, turnover, morale, commitment) and individual (psychological wellbeing, physical health) outcome variables.

To assist organizations with assessing and managing workplace stress, researchers have devised a number of general stress scales (e.g., Holmes & Rahe, 1967; Kanner, Coyne, Schaefer, & Lazarus 1981; Nowack, 1990) and occupational stress scales (e.g., Cooper, Sloan, & Williams., 1988). In recent years researchers have argued that occupation-specific and industry-specific stress scales are more reliable and valid predictors of stress and effects of stress than general occupational stress scales. As a result of this argument, a great deal of recent stress research on various occupational groups (e.g., teachers, nurses, and police officers) has used occupational stress scales specifically designed for these groups. Dua (1994), for example, has used scales specifically designed for university staff.

Though workplace stress can lead to strains (negative effects on health and quality of work), researchers have identified a number of moderating variables which can reduce the experience of stress or reduce the negative effects of stress. Some examples of these variables are coping strategies, social support, and hardiness. The last of these variables comprises control, commitment, and challenge. Research has shown that social support, positive coping, problem-focused coping, and hardiness reduce the level of stress and the impact of stress on health, and negative coping and type A behaviors increase the level of stress and its impact on health (e.g., Bernard & Krupat, 1994; Brannon & Feist, 1992; Sharpley et al., 1995). Moreover, it has been shown recently that personality dimensions such as neuroticism (or negative affectivity) may also act to moderate the stress–health relationship (Bakker et al., 2010).

## The Sources of Work Stress in Universities

University academics are not traditionally an occupational group noted for making compensation claims or for showing high sickness, absenteeism, or turnover rates. On the other hand, there is evidence that they are being subjected to an increasingly stressful work environment. Much of the increase is related to reduced government funding and increased demands for "accountability." In countries such as Australia, New Zealand, and the United Kingdom, salaries have been eroded, as has job security (tenure), workloads have increased, and additional demands have been imposed. At the same time, academics have experienced reduced control/autonomy as "collegiality" has been replaced by "managerialism."

Cooper (1998) describes a range of contemporary theories of organizational stress, each focusing on different aspects of the work environment. Five of the best known are Maslach's burnout theory (Maslach & Jackson, 1981), Karasek's demand–control theory (Karasek, 1979), the job demands—resources model (Demerouti, Bakker, Nachreiner, & Schaufeli, 2001), Siegrist's effort-reward imbalance theory (Siegrist, 1998) , Hobfoll's conservation of resources theory (Hobfoll, 2001), and person–environment fit theory (French, Caplan, & van Harrison, 1984). It is readily apparent how the changes to the work roles of academics in recent years would be conceptualized within each of these theories.

For example, burnout theory has been applied principally to members of the caring professions and to teachers, and teaching is one of the core activities of most university academics (the exceptions being those involved in research only or those who have moved into administration). Demand–control theory is clearly relevant to the situation in which the demands on academics are increasing (increased teaching loads arising from worsening student–staff ratios, increased demands to publish and attract external funding) and control is decreasing because of increased managerialism, and loss of tenure. Similarly, the job demands–resources model is applicable given the increased demands and reduced resources experienced by academics. Effort–reward imbalance theory refers to disequilibrium between the amount of effort involved in performing a job and the reward received. Again, the relevance is clear in a situation where academic workloads are becoming intolerable, yet academic salaries are falling relative to other groups. Conservation of resources theory assumes that people strive to maintain their resources and experience negative outcomes (e.g., strain, burnout) when these are threatened by excessive demands. Taris et al. (2001) have applied this theory in a study of job stress in Dutch university staff. Finally, person–environment fit predicts that strain will occur when there is a mismatch between the individual and the work environment. The mismatch can arise either because the worker is unable to meet the demands of the job or because the job fails to satisfy the needs of the worker. There are good reasons to suppose that both kinds of mismatch are increasing in relation to academics.

Future research on academic stress will be informed by the theories outlined above but needs also to explore the possibility and potential of intervention strategies. Unless academic stress can be reduced, there will be significant costs both to the effectiveness of universities and to the psychological and physical wellbeing of the academics responsible for their core activities of research and teaching. Universities themselves will find it increasingly difficult to attract and retain high-quality academics. Bright young people are likely to be attracted to professions offering better, less stressful working conditions. Good, productive academics are likely to be attracted to other careers, or to academic careers in overseas countries offering better working conditions and remuneration (the "brain drain").

There is already evidence of both these trends in Australian universities, where many of the best students are choosing to study subjects such as information technology rather than physics or chemistry, and commerce and accountancy rather than economics, and where some of the best academics are going overseas.

The strategy adopted by several Australian universities of offering voluntary redundancy or early retirement packages is often counterproductive. Such packages are generally most attractive to those staff who are able to get other jobs: the very people whom the university least wishes to lose.

The costs to the university of maintaining a workforce of stressed academics are also obvious. Academics who are experiencing psychological strain are unlikely to perform at a high level. Consider their core activities: teaching and research. An outstanding university teacher is one who keeps abreast of current developments in the field, and who is able to communicate effectively with students, and inspire them by enthusiasm and excitement. Such qualities are unlikely to be found in people suffering from work overload and burnout.

The other core activity of academics is research. In order to perform research that is creative and original, researchers need time to be able to devote to reading, thinking, and discussing their ideas. These fundamental requirements are unlikely to be achieved in an environment where there is never-ending pressure to produce, as much and as quickly as possible.

Dollard and Winefield (1996) have drawn attention to the fact that Sweden and the United States have both recognized occupational stress as a national health issue. For example, Levi (1990) reported that the Swedish Government had established a Commission for Work Environment and Health to identify present and predict future work-related illnesses and to propose recommendations and strategies to remove or reduce the risks.

In the United States, the National Institute for Occupational Safety and Health (NIOSH) recognizes psychological disorders as one of the 10 leading occupational diseases and generally refers to them under the rubric of "job stress" (Sauter, Murphy, & Hurrell, 1990).

By contrast, Australian mental health experts seem less willing to acknowledge the role of job stress as a determinant of mental health. This is revealed in a recent monograph *Promotion, prevention and early intervention for mental health* published by the Commonwealth Government (Commonwealth of Australia, 2000). In the section headed "Psychosocial determinants of health and mental health" the authors refer to "The benchmark Whitehall studies of British civil servants (Marmot et al., 1984)" (p. 11) which identifies the following factors associated with ill-health: "low socioeconomic status, high stress levels, hardship or risk exposure in early life, social exclusion, high stress in the workplace, job insecurity, low social support, addictive behaviours, unhealthy food choices and unhealthy transport practices" (p. 11). However, the authors only list three (psychosocial) factors as contributing to health in the Australian context: poverty, ethnicity, and gender. These three no doubt subsume several of the 10 listed by the Whitehall researchers. For example, "poverty" and "ethnicity" would no doubt subsume "low socioeconomic status, hardship or risk exposure in early life, social exclusion, low social support, addictive behaviours, unhealthy food choices, and unhealthy transport practices," but two of the factors associated with job stress, "high stress in the workplace" and "job insecurity," do not seem to be regarded as important by the Australian mental health experts who wrote the monograph.

Fisher (1994) has drawn attention to the problems facing universities in Britain and reports results from studies conducted over the period 1988–1993 showing high levels of stress experienced by academic staff following a decade of reductions in government funding. In Australia a similar decline in government funding has occurred, particularly between 1994 and the present. The current situation in Australia has been documented in a Senate Committee Report "Universities in Crisis" (Senate Committee, 2001). Government statistics show that, despite increases in student enrolments, the Commonwealth government's contribution to university operating grants has declined from AU\$4,772 million in 1994 to AU\$4,461 million in 2000. Moreover, the student-to-staff ratio has gradually increased from 13:1 in 1990 to more than 19:1 in 2000 and exceeded 20:1 in 2012.

Reduced funding has also led most Australian universities effectively to abolish academic tenure since the mid-1990s. In many Western countries academic freedom has been highly valued because the role (and responsibility) of the academic has been seen as the fearless pursuit and dissemination of knowledge and, where appropriate, as acting as social critic. Tenure has been regarded as the only guarantee of academic freedom. Consequently, although academic work has not been highly paid, academics have traditionally enjoyed high levels of autonomy and freedom to publish and to speak openly, even when their views are unpopular with authority, whether it be the university administration, the scientific establishment, or the government.

Critics of tenure have pointed out that it protects the lazy, incompetent, and unproductive and denies opportunities to talented young scholars.

During the past 4 or 5 years, in response to increasing financial pressures, many Australian universities have abandoned tenure (Coady, 2000; Molony, 2000). So-called tenured staff can (and have been) made "involuntarily redundant" and there has been an increase in contract (as opposed to tenure track) appointments.

Higher stress levels among academic staff than general staff were reported by Winefield and Jarrett (2001) in their study of staff at the University of Adelaide. Similar findings were reported from the National University Stress Study, described in more detail later.

## Effects of Work Stress in Universities

What are the consequences of the apparent widespread increase in academic stress? The impact of job-related stress on general employee performance (not specific to academia) has been well documented. Job-related stress has been found to increase turnover of staff, absenteeism, non-productivity, inefficiency, frustration, tiredness, and burnout (Melendez & de Guzman, 1983).

Employees experiencing high levels of job-related stress also report lower levels of job satisfaction, morale, and general wellbeing, which in turn may negatively affect work performance (Nowack, 1989; Terry, Tonge, & Callan, 1995). Thus workplace stress takes its toll upon the health of the organization and the health of the workers (Matteson & Ivancevich, 1988).

Stress is often accompanied by negative feelings, anxiety, depression, sadness, hopelessness, helplessness, anger, and/or a sense of worthlessness. Stressed persons are more likely to be psychologically distressed and stress has been linked to a number of physical illnesses.

## Interventions

Organizational stress researchers generally distinguish three levels of intervention: primary, secondary, and tertiary (Murphy, 1988). Primary and secondary interventions are generally seen as preventative, whereas tertiary interventions involve taking steps to help the individual who has experienced an adverse reaction to workplace stressors, either psychological or physical or both.

Primary interventions involve attempts to reorganize or restructure the work environment so as to make it less stressful. For example, they could involve improving the physical environment through introducing more efficient heating/cooling systems, or increasing space in order to reduce crowding, or purchasing new equipment, or more comfortable chairs, etc. Other kinds of primary intervention involve changes to work organization aimed at reducing known sources of stress, such as role overload, role conflict, and role ambiguity. They may be aimed at specific, identified sources of stress, arising from complaints by workers, or they may be theoretically inspired. For example, Karasek's theory assumes that stress is caused by a combination of high demand and low autonomy, so a primary intervention might aim to reduce demand or increase autonomy.

Secondary interventions, on the other hand, are oriented to individual workers and designed to help them cope with potential stressors in their work environment. For example, time management and relaxation are widely used stress management techniques that can be taught to workers so as to help them combat a stressful work environment.

Other sorts of secondary interventions may be theoretically based. For example, the Person–Environment Fit theory (French, Caplan, & van Harrison, 1984) assumes that job stress can be a consequence of two kinds of mismatch: a mismatch between the requirements of the job and the ability of the worker to meet those requirements; and a mismatch between the worker's expectation of what the job involves and what it actually involves.

The first kind of mismatch could be addressed by helping the worker to acquire or develop relevant skills. The second kind of mismatch could be more difficult to address and may require the worker to find different work.

Tertiary intervention is aimed at helping workers who are suffering as a consequence of work pressures, which may lead to other problems, such alcohol addiction, family problems, etc. Employee assistance programs (EAPs) were first introduced in the United States around 1970 largely to counsel employees suffering from alcoholism, but more in recent years they have developed a wider orientation.

## Methodological Critique of Work Stress Research in the Academic Profession

As with much of the reported research on occupational stress, the work stress research carried out on academics has relied largely on cross-sectional analyses of self-report data. As many critics have observed, such data are often difficult to interpret because they are vulnerable to the problem of method variance (leading to spurious correlations) and do not readily permit causal inference.

Improvements to such research designs include the collection of longitudinal data and the use of "objective" data, in addition to "subjective" self-report data. It is important to recognize, however, that self-report data are often an invaluable source of information and, in some situations, the only source of information. Critics of self-report data tend to overlook the fact that they are used by audiologists and optometrists for prescribing hearing and visual aids. Also, soft tissue injuries where there is no internal bleeding are not amenable to objective observation and may rely on self-report for their diagnoses.

In behavioral research, the most sensible approach to self-reporting is to assume that it is likely to be valid, unless the person has a good reason to mislead, or is distracted, or where there is reason to suspect that judgment may be impaired (say, through fatigue or drug or alcohol use). On the other hand, self-report measures taken on a single occasion may be biased because of a temporary mood state leading to spurious correlations as referred to above. As Frese and Zapf (1988) have pointed out, "the use of subjective judgments of stressors can lead to an overestimate of the correlation between stressors and dysfunctioning . . . On the other hand, the use of objective (observers') judgments of stressors leads to an underestimate of the 'true' correlation" (p. 381).

Because of this, it is desirable to utilize data from a variety of sources. In organizational stress research it is often possible to assess the levels of strain experienced by workers by measuring absenteeism, turnover, sick leave, and stress claims. These measures can be used to verify self-report measures indicating low levels of job satisfaction, strain, etc. Similarly, the pressures within the work environment may also be assessed independently. In relation to academic stress, for example, the workload for academics involved in teaching can be estimated from the student-to-staff ratio. In general, most commentators agree that stress researchers should use multiple measures, including both "objective" and "subjective" measures and longitudinal designs in order to tease out the often complex relations between organizational stressors and their impact on individual workers.

# National University Stress Study

The data reported here come from national surveys conducted at 17 established Australian metropolitan universities in 2000 and in 2004. The research was supported by a collaborative grant from the Australian Research Council, with the National Tertiary Education Union as the industry partner and cash contributions from vice chancellors of the 17 participating universities. The support from the vice chancellors was obtained in response to a letter from the Vice Chancellor of the University of Adelaide, inviting them to join her in supporting the project.

## Phase 1: Focus Group Interviews

The first phase comprised 22 focus group interviews carried out with 178 academic and general staff at 15 Australian universities in 2000. Both groups reported a dramatic increase in stress over the past 5 years with academic staff reporting higher levels than general staff. Five major sources of stress were identified: insufficient funding and resources; work overload; poor management practice; job insecurity; and insufficient recognition and reward (Gillespie et al., 2001).

## Phase 2: Staff Survey

The second phase comprised a survey distributed to all staff at the 17 participating universities of whom 8,732 responded, giving a response rate of 25%. Those responding were representative of the population in terms of demographic group (age, gender, work role, etc.). The survey included measures of psychological strain, job satisfaction, organizational commitment, work pressure, work–family conflict, job insecurity, job involvement, job autonomy, procedural fairness, trust in departmental heads, trust in senior management, measures of personality, and negative affectivity as well as stress-related symptoms and medical conditions. Finally, for academics, we measured satisfaction with resources and perceptions of the academic work environment. These questions were informed by the results of the focus group study (Gillespie et al., 2001). Full details of the measures are reported in Winefield et al. (2002).

*Overview of results.*

The results showed that the overall level of strain was very high in both academic and general staff using the well-validated GHQ-12 (Goldberg & Williams, 1988) by comparison with national and occupational norms. Job satisfaction was low in academic staff but average in general staff. Most academic staff reported dissatisfaction with five aspects of their job: university management; hours of work; industrial relations; chance of promotion; rate of pay. By contrast, general staff expressed dissatisfaction with only one aspect: chance of promotion. The groups most at risk (experiencing the highest strain and lowest job satisfaction were: (a) academic staff involved in teaching; (b) middle-ranked academic staff; and (c) academic staff in the Humanities and Social Sciences.

At the individual level, the strongest predictors of psychological strain were: (a) job insecurity; (b) work pressure; (c) lower levels of autonomy; (d) teaching and research demands (for academic staff); and (e) procedural fairness (for general staff). The strongest predictors of job satisfaction were: (a) procedural fairness; (b) trust in head of department; and (c) higher levels of autonomy. The strongest predictor of commitment to the university was trust in senior management (however only 19% agreed that senior management is trustworthy). At the university level, psychological strain was predicted by percentage cut in government grants to the university (for general staff) and investment income (for academic staff). Job satisfaction was predicted by percentage cut in full-time staff (for general staff) and student-to-staff ratio (for academic staff).

*Recommendations.*

The following recommendations (similar to those by Gillespie et al., 2001) were formulated, designed to reduce stress and enhance wellbeing in university staff, and conveyed to the vice chancellors (CEOs) of the 17 universities: (1) Review the fairness of procedures and processes related to promotion, redundancy, and performance appraisal, with the aim of increasing staff perceptions of the fairness of these procedures. (2) Review the adequacy of current pay promotion, reward and recognition systems. (3) Review teaching and research demands, particularly for middle-ranked academics. (4) Develop processes and programs to reduce job insecurity, and/or assist staff to cope with job insecurity. (5) Develop leadership capabilities.

## Phase 3: Follow-Up Survey

The first survey was not intended to include longitudinal observations, therefore no attempt was made to identify responses. The second survey was part of a longitudinal study, therefore, although responses were anonymous, all participants were asked to provide a code identifier so that the researchers could match responses from time 1 (2000) to time 2 (2004).

Although all of the vice chancellors of the 17 universities had initially agreed to take part in the follow-up, in the event, 4 declined to do so. The follow-up survey in 2004 was thus distributed to 13 of the original 17 universities. More than 6,000 staff participated at each time, of whom 969 (stayers) participated at both times. The results are summarized below, first the cross-sectional data, second the longitudinal data for the 969 participants who responded at both times. More details are reported by Winefield and colleagues (2008a, 2008b).

*Overview of cross-sectional data.*
Overall, the cross-sectional data from all participants showed some encouraging improvements. For example, there were increases in organizational commitment, job involvement, job autonomy, procedural fairness, and trust in senior management, as well as decreases in work pressure and job insecurity. However, there were also increases in psychological strain and work–home conflict.

*Overview of longitudinal data.*
Longitudinal results from the stayers showed a similar pattern. These participants also showed increases in job involvement, job autonomy, belief in procedural fairness, and trust in senior management, and a decrease in job insecurity, together with increased work–home conflict and increased psychological strain. However, they did not show improvements in organizational commitment or work pressure, and also reported reduced job satisfaction.

*Conclusions and limitations.*
Attrition analyses revealed some time 1 differences between the stayers and dropouts that might explain the discrepant findings. Neither the cross-sectional nor longitudinal changes were uniform across all universities, or all categories of staff. The improvements were more marked for nonacademic than for academic staff, and for female than for male staff. Regression

analyses found that for academic staff, trust in senior management predicted both psychological strain and organizational commitment, while procedural fairness predicted both job satisfaction and organizational commitment. On the other hand, for general staff the best predictors were individual difference (personality) variables, such as negative affectivity, rather than workplace variables.

### Phase 4: Analysis of Workplace Interventions Introduced between 2000 and 2004

Pignata (2011) has attempted to analyze and evaluate the effectiveness of stress-reduction intervenions on employee wellbeing, perceptions of senior management trustworthiness, and procedural justice using the social-exchange theoretical framework. A question included in the 2004 survey was: "During the past 3 years has your university undertaken any measures to reduce stress among its employees?" Analyses indicated that employees who reported that stress-reduction interventions had been undertaken scored lower on psychological strain and higher on job satisfaction and commitment than those who were unaware of the interventions. She concluded that simply the awareness of stress interventions is linked to positive employee outcomes. The study further revealed that trust in senior management and perceived procedural justice both mediated the relationship between awareness and wellbeing.

## Conclusions

Two of the main challenges for future researchers (in Australia at least) will be to persuade the Government first that job stress in general poses a threat to the psychological and physical health of workers, and second that academics in particular are experiencing increasingly high levels of job stress (even though the same may well be true for other workers). Perhaps the most effective means of persuasion will be to argue that job performance, as well as physical and psychological health, is likely to be adversely affected by job stress (increased strain and reduced job satisfaction). The recent meta-analytic finding of a .30 correlation between job satisfaction and job performance (accounting for 9% of the variance) and .52 for high complexity jobs (accounting for 27% of the variance) reported by Judge et al. (2001) is very much higher than the correlation of .17 (accounting for less than 3%

of the variance) reported by Iaffaldano and Muchinsky (1985) and is likely to stimulate further research designed to explicate the relationship between them.

Finally, it is particularly important for senior university administators and government policy makers to be aware of the increasingly high levels of psychological strain/burnout being experienced by university staff. They need to recognize the high costs, both to individuals and to universities (in terms of reduced performance, high turnover, stress claims) and attempt to implement stress-reduction interventions. Giga, Cooper, and Faragher (2003) provide a useful account of what interventions are likely to prove most effective.

# References

Akerlind, G., & McAlpine, L. (2009). Academic practice: How is it changing? *International Journal for Researcher Development*, *1*, 4–10.

Altbach, P. G. (Ed.) (1996). *The international academic profession*. Princeton, NJ: Carnegie Foundation for the Advancement of Teaching.

Armour, R. A. (1987). Academic burnout: Faculty responsibility and institutional climate. *New Directions for Teaching and Learning*, *29*, 3–11.

Australian Vice-Chancellors' Committee (AVCC). (2006). Table 1: Actual Student: Staff ratios by AVCC Institution and Academic Organisational Unit (AOU) Group, 1999, All Student/Staff in AOU's. Unpublished data extracted from DEST's (1999) final Student and final Staff Publications.

Bakker, A. B., Boyd, C. M., Dollard, M., Gillespie. N., Winefield, A. H., & Stough, C. (2010). The role of personality in the Job Demands–Resources model: A study of Australian academic staff. *Career Development International*, *15*, 622–636.

Barkhuizen, N., & Rothmann, S. (2008). Occupational stress of academic staff in South African higher education institutions. *South African Journal of Psychology* *38*, 321–336.

Bernard, L. C., & Krupat, E. (1994). *Health psychology: Biopsychosocial factors in health and illness*. Orlando, FL: Harcourt Brace.

Bowen, H. R., & Schuster, J. H. (1985). Outlook for the academic profession. *Academe-Bulletin of the AAUP*, *71*, 8–15.

Bowen, H. R., & Schuster, J. H. (1986). *American professors: A national resource imperiled*. New York: Oxford University Press.

Boyd, C. M., Bakker, A. B., Pignata, S., Winefield, A. H., Gillespie, N., & Stough C. (2011). A longitudinal test of the job demands-resources model among Australian university academics. *Applied Psychology: An International Review*. *60*, 112–140.

Brannon, L., & Feist, J. (1992). *Health psychology: An introduction to behavior and health*. Belmont, CA: Wadsworth.

Catano, V., Francis, L., Haines, T., Kirpalani, H., Shannon, H., Stringer, B., & Lozanski, L. (2010). Occupational stress in Canadian universities: A national survey. *International Journal of Stress Management*, *17*, 232–258.

Coady, T. (2000). Universities and the ideals of inquiry. In T. Coady (Ed.), *Why universities matter* (pp. 3–25). St Leonards, NSW: Allen & Unwin.

Cohen, J. (1988). *Statistical power analysis for the behavioral sciences*. New York: Erlbaum.

Commonwealth of Australia (2000). *Promotion, prevention and early intervention for mental health: A monograph*. Canberra: Commonwealth Department of Health and Aged Care.

Cooper, C. L. (Ed.) (1998). *Theories of organizational stress*. Oxford: Oxford University Press.

Cooper, C. L., Sloan, S. J., & Williams, S. (1988). *Occupational stress indicator: Management guide*. Windsor, U.K.: NFER-Nelson.

Costa, P. T. (1996). Work and personality: Use of the NEO-PI-R in industrial/organizational psychology. *Applied Psychology: An International Review*, *45*, 225–241.

Daniels, K., & Guppy, A. (1992). Control, information-seeking preferences, occupational stressors and psychological well-being. *Work and Stress*, *6*, 347–353.

Demerouti, E., Bakker, A. B., Nachreiner, F., & Schaufeli, W. B. (2001). The job demands-resources model of burnout. *Journal of Applied Psychology*, *86*, 499–512.

Dollard, M. F., & Winefield, A. H. (1996). Managing occupational stress: A national and international perspective. *International Journal of Stress Management*, *3*, 69–83.

Doyle, C., & Hind, P. (1998). Occupational stress, burnout and job status in female academics. *Gender, Work and Organizations*, *5*, 67–82.

Dua, J. K. (1994). Job stressors and their effects on physical health, emotional health, and job satisfaction in a university. *Journal of Educational Administration*, *32*, 59–78.

Fisher, S. (1994). *Stress in academic life*. London: The Society for Research into Higher Education and Open University Press.

French, J. R. P. Jr., Caplan, R. D., & van Harrison, R. (1984). *The mechanisms of job stress and strain*. New York: Wiley.

Frese, M., & Zapf, D. (1988). Methodological issues in the study of work stress: Objective versus subjective measurement of work stress and the question of longitudinal studies. In C. L. Cooper & R. Payne (Eds.), *Causes, coping and consequences of stress at work*. Chichester: Wiley.

Giga, S. I., Cooper, C. L., & Faragher, B. (2003). The development of a framework for a comprehensive approach to stress management interventions at work. *International Journal of Stress Management*, *10*, 280–296.

Gillespie, N. A., Walsh, M., Winefield, A. H., Dua, J., & Stough, C. (2001). Occupational stress within Australian universities: Staff perceptions of the determinants, consequences and moderators of stress. *Work and Stress, 15,* 53–72.

Goldberg, D. P., & Williams, P. (1988). *A user's guide to the GHQ*. London: NFER-Nelson.

Hind, P., & Doyle, C. (1996). A cross cultural comparison of perceived occupational stress in academics in higher education. Paper given at XXVI International Congress of Psychology, Montreal.

Hobfoll, S. E. (2001). The influence of culture, community, and the nested-self in the stress process: Advancing conservation of resources theory. *Applied Psychology: An International Review, 50,* 337–370.

Holmes, T. H., & Rahe, R. H. (1967). The social readjustment rating scale. *Psychosomatic Medicine, 11,* 213–218.

Iaffaldano, M. T., & Muchinsky, P. M. (1985). Job satisfaction and job performance: A meta-analysis. *Psychological Bulletin, 97,* 251–273.

Judge, T. A., Thoreson, C. J., Bono, J. E., & Patton, G. K. (2001). The job satisfaction–job performance relationship: A qualitative and quantitative review. *Psychological Bulletin, 127,* 376–407.

Kanner, A. D., Coyne, J. C., Schaefer, C., & Lazarus, R. S. (1981). Comparison of two modes of stress measurement: Daily hassles and uplifts versus major life events. *Journal of Behavioral Medicine, 4,* 1–39.

Karasek, R. A. (1979). Job demands, job decision latitude, and mental strain: Implications for job redesign. *Administrative Science Quarterly, 24,* 285–308.

Levi, L. (1990). Occupational stress: Spice of life or kiss of death? *American Psychologist, 45,* 1142–1145.

Marmot, M. G., Shipley, M. J., & Rose, G. (1984). Inequalities in death—specific explanations of a general pattern? *Lancet, 1,* 1003–1006.

Maslach, C., & Jackson, S. E. (1981). The measurement of experienced burnout. *Journal of Occupational Behavior, 2,* 99–113.

Matteson, M. T., & Ivancevich, J. M. (1988). Worksite health promotion: Some important questions. *Health Values, 12,* 23–29.

McClenahan, C., Giles, M. L., & Mallett, J. (2007). The importance of context specificity in work stress research: A test of the demand–control–support model in academics. *Work and Stress, 21,* 85–95.

Melendez, W., & de Guzman, R. M. (1983). *Burnout: The new academic disease. ASHE-ERIC Higher Education Research Report, No. 9.* Washington, DC: Association for the Study of Higher Education.

Molony, J. (2000). Australian universities today. In T. Coady (Ed.), *Why universities matter* (pp. 72–84). St Leonards, NSW: Allen & Unwin.

Murphy, L. R. (1988). Workplace interventions for stress reduction and prevention. In C. L. Cooper and R. Payne (Eds.), *Causes, coping and consequences of stress at work.* Chichester: Wiley.

Nowack, K. M. (1989). Coping style, cognitive hardiness, and health status. *Journal of Behavioral Medicine, 12,* 145–158.

Nowack, K. M. (1990). Initial development of an inventory to assess any health risk. *American Journal of Health Promotion, 4,* 173–180.

Pignata, S. (2011). *Effect and ethical implications of stress-reduction interventions on health and well-being, and attitudes of procedural fairness, trust in senior management and commitment in university staff* (Unpublished PhD thesis). University of South Australia.

Rothmann, S., & Barkhuizen, N. (2008). Burnout of academic staff in South African higher education institutions. *South African Journal of Higher Education, 22*, 439–456.

Sauter, S. L., Murphy, L. R., & Hurrell, Jr., J. J. (1990). Prevention of work-related psychological disorders. *American Psychologist, 45*, 1146–1158.

Seldin, P. (1987). Research findings on causes of academic stress. *New Directions for Teaching and Learning, 29*, 13–21.

Senate Committee (2001). *Universities in crisis. Senate Committee Report*. Canberra: Australian Government.

Sharpley, C. F., Dua, J. K., Reynolds, R., & Acosta, A. (1995). The direct and relative efficacy of cognitive hardiness, Type A behavior pattern, coping behaviour and social support as predictors of stress and ill-health. *Scandinavian Journal of Behaviour Therapy, 24*, 15–29.

Siegrist, J. (1998). Adverse health effects of effort-reward imbalance at work. In C. L. Cooper (Ed.), *Theories of organizational stress* (pp. 190–204). Oxford: Oxford University Press.

Sun, W., Wu, H., & Wang, L. (2011). Occupational stress and its related factors among university teachers in China. *Journal of Occupational Health, 53*, 280–286.

Taris, T. W., Schreurs, P. J. G., & Van Iersal-Van Silfhout, I. J. (2001). Job stress, job strain, and psychological withdrawal among Dutch university staff: Towards a dual-process model for the effects of occupational stress. *Work and Stress, 15*, 283–296.

Terry, D. J., Tonge, L., & Callan, V. J. (1995). Employee adjustment to stress: The role of coping resources, situational factors and coping responses. *Anxiety, Stress, and Coping, 8*, 1–24.

Tytherleigh, M. Y., Webb, C., Cooper, C. L., & Ricketts, C. (2005). Occupational stress in UK higher education institutions: A comparative study of all staff categories. *Higher Education Research & Development, 24*, 41–61.

Watts, J., & Robertson, N. (2011). Burnout in university teaching staff: A systematic literature review. *Educational Research, 53*, 33–50.

Wearing, A. J., & Hart, P. M. (1996). Work and non-work coping strategies: Their relation to personality, appraisal and life domain. *Stress Medicine, 12*, 93–103.

Winefield, A. H. (2000). Stress in academe: Some recent research findings. In D. T. Kenny, J. G. Carlson, F. J. McGuigan, & J. L. Sheppard (Eds.), *Stress and health* (pp. 437–446). Amsterdam: Harwood Academic Publishers.

Winefield, A. H. (2003). Stress in university academics. In M. F. Dollard, A. H. Winefield, & H. R. Winefield (Eds.), *Occupational health in the service professions* (pp. 237–260). London: Taylor & Francis.

Winefield, T., Boyd, C., Saebel, J., & Pignata, S. (2008a). Update on National University Stress Study. *Australian Universities Review, 50*, 20–29.

Winefield, A. H., Boyd, C. Saebel, J., & Pignata, S. (2008b). *Job stress in university staff: An Australian research study* (pp. 197). Bowen Hills, Queensland: Australian Academic Press.

Winefield, A. H., Gillespie, N. A., Stough, C. K., Dua, J. K., & Hapuarachchi, J. R. (2002). *Occupational stress in Australian Universities: A national survey 2002.* Melbourne, Victoria: National Tertiary Education Union Publication.

Winefield, A. H., Gillespie, N., Stough, C., Dua, J., Hapuarachchi, J. R., & Boyd, C. (2003). Occupational stress in Australian university staff: Results from a national survey. *International Journal of Stress Management*, *10*, 51–63.

Winefield, A. H., & Jarrett, R. J. (2001). Occupational stress in university staff. *International Journal of Stress Management*, *8*, 285–298.

# Part 6

# From Research to National Policy

# 18

# Longitudinal Research in Occupational Stress
## *A Review of Methodological Issues*

### Robert C. Brusso
Old Dominion University, U.S.A. and ICF International

### Konstantin P. Cigularov and Rachel C. Callan
Old Dominion University, U.S.A.

Occupational stress researchers are interested in the physiological, behavioral, and psychological responses of employees (i.e., strains) to job characteristics and work environment factors (i.e., stressors) in order to (a) predict the outcomes of exposure to stressors, and (b) better design and organize work or to intervene to reduce the presence of stressors and the experiences of strains (Cooper, 1998; Sonnentag & Frese, 2003; Tetrick & Quick, 2011). Although research in occupational stress continues to dominate the field of occupational health psychology (Macik-Frey, Quick, & Nelson, 2007), it has not been spared by criticisms of methodological shortcomings and deficiency of rigorous longitudinal studies, thus limiting its theoretical and practical contributions (Frese & Zapf, 1988; Kasl, 1987; Sonnentag & Frese, 2003; Zapf, Dormann, & Frese, 1996).

In fact, the prevalence of cross-sectional studies and the need for longitudinal research have been highlighted as key limitations of the occupational stress literature by both methodological (e.g., de Lange, Taris,

*Work and Wellbeing: Wellbeing: A Complete Reference Guide*, Volume III.
Edited by Peter Y. Chen and Cary L. Cooper.
© 2014 John Wiley & Sons, Ltd. Published 2014 by John Wiley & Sons, Inc.
DOI: 10.1002/9781118539415.wbwell18

Kompier, Houtman, & Bongers, 2003; Zapf et al., 1996) and meta-analytic reviews (e.g., Amstad, Meier, Fasel, Elfering, & Semmer, 2011; Crawford, LePine, & Rich, 2010; Eatough, Chang, Miloslavic, & Johnson, 2011). Thus, we agree that for occupational stress research to truly progress and provide meaningful and valid information about causal relationships between stressors and strains, researchers must consider design issues in their studies (Chen, Cigularov, & Menger, 2013; Kasl & Jones, 2011), and more specifically the use of rigorous longitudinal designs (Zapf et al., 1996).

Although there is general agreement regarding the necessity and benefits of longitudinal occupational stress studies in examining hypothesized causal relationships between occupational stressors and strains (Kasl, 1987; Sonnentag & Frese, 2003), there is less consensus on what exactly qualifies as longitudinal research. To complicate the issue further, actual practices tend to deviate from acceptable standards for implementing longitudinal research designs and analyses (Frese & Zapf, 1988; Zapf et al., 1996). In addition, researchers have voiced concerns regarding common misunderstandings and erroneous assumptions about the powers and limitations of longitudinal research designs in occupational health psychology (Taris & Kompier, 2003), as well as the underrealization of the advantages such designs can offer (de Lange et al., 2003; Zapf et al., 1996).

For example, in their influential 1996 paper (cited 285 times since publication), Zapf and his colleagues reviewed the methodological quality of 43 longitudinal studies of occupational stress and observed that (a) although the number of published longitudinal studies of occupational stress had increased during the 1978–1995 period, the number was still substantially low relative to cross-sectional research, and (b) a large number of the longitudinal studies used weak designs and/or did not examine issues related to reverse/reciprocal causation and third variables. In conclusion, Zapf et al. provided recommendations for conducting methodologically sound longitudinal research and explicitly called for the use of "more systematic longitudinal designs of organizational stress studies that make it possible to test reverse causal hypotheses and a series of third variable explanations" (p. 158).

Similar methodological recommendations were made by de Lange and colleagues (2003), who reviewed 45 longitudinal studies, which were published between 1979 and 2000 and aimed to examine the demands–control–(support) model (Karasek & Theorell, 1990). They identified only 19 (42%) of the 45 longitudinal studies as having high methodological quality. Finally, Cigularov, Brusso, and Callan (2013) set out to extend the methodological review by Zapf et al. (1996) to the present day in order to provide an up-to-date assessment of the status of longitudinal research in occupational stress. They reviewed longitudinal occupational stress research published in the *Journal of Occupational Health Psychology* and *Work & Stress* between 1996 and 2012. Their findings indicated that only 7.2% of all articles published in these two major outlets for occupational stress research over that period reported longitudinal studies, which they loosely defined as involving two or more waves of data collection of variables related to occupational stress (excluding experimental and quasi-experimental studies). However, almost half (46%) of the longitudinal studies were published between 2007 and 2012, suggesting an increased activity in this kind of research. Furthermore, consistent with the previous reviews by Zapf et al. (1996) and de Lange et al. (2003), many of the longitudinal studies lacked methodological rigor. Please note that some of the same studies were included in more than one of the above-mentioned reviews due to overlap in time periods.

With this in mind, we approached the current chapter with the intent to provide a discussion of definitional issues related to longitudinal research in occupational stress, as well as a nontechnical review of a number of methodological concerns, which have been raised previously by Zapf et al. (1996) and others (Ployhart & Vandenberg, 2010; Taris & Kompier, 2003). We also offer an assessment of the gap between actual and best practices by gauging the extent to which researchers have heeded the calls for more rigorous longitudinal research as evidenced in methodological reviews of longitudinal research in occupational stress (e.g., Cigularov et al., 2013; de Lange et al., 2003; Zapf et al., 1996). Please note that this chapter is not intended to provide an in-depth treatment of theoretical (e.g., definition and models of change) and analytical issues (e.g., latent growth modeling) in longitudinal research, which have been extensively reviewed in general sources (see Chan, 1998; Hedeker & Gibbons, 2006; Menard, 2002; Ployhart & Vandenberg, 2010; Singer & Willett, 2003), as well as sources specific to occupational health psychology (see Kasl & Cooper, 1987; Kelloway & Francis, 2013; Frese & Zapf, 1988).

## What Constitutes (Good) Longitudinal Research?

Longitudinal research concerns the collection and analysis of data across time and can take on different forms depending on the variables, populations, and research questions of interest. Consequently, longitudinal research is a broad term, which has been subjected to different interpretations, definitions, and criteria, often varying across disciplines (Menard, 2002; Nessleroade & Baltes, 1979). For the purpose of this chapter, we focus our discussion on longitudinal research, which does not involve experimental manipulation of the causal variables as in experimental and quasi-experimental studies (i.e., passive longitudinal research, Zapf et al., 1996). In other words, we regard longitudinal research as observational in nature, that is, the researcher does not interfere with participants and instead participants are simply observed over time, such as cohort studies that monitor a group of people as they go through the process of finding and maintaining a career (e.g., Timms, 1996). Furthermore, we use the individual as the focal unit in our discussions below as it is most often the target of study in occupational stress research; however, we acknowledge that units of interest can also be groups or even whole organizations and that testing strongly theorized multilevel models of occupational stress with group- and organizational-level variables is much needed (Bliese & Jex, 2002).

## Longitudinal Research Defined Broadly

As a starting point of our discussion of definitional issues, let us consider Menard's (2002) broad definition, which qualifies research as longitudinal when: "(a) data are collected for each item or variable for two or more distinct time periods; (b) the subjects or cases analyzed are the same or at least comparable from one period to the next; and (c) the analysis involves some comparison of data between or among periods" (p. 2). Menard asserts that longitudinal research must allow at minimum the measurement of differences or change in the phenomenon of interest from one time period to another. He describes three types of research designs, which can be considered longitudinal according to the above broad definition: *prospective panel design, retrospective panel design*, and *repeated cross-sectional design*.

Prospective and retrospective panel designs are identical in all aspects except for the number of data collection times and the recall period. While the prospective panel design involves the collection of data at two or more distinct times, for those time periods, on the same set of individuals and variables at each time, the retrospective panel design requires data collection only at a single time for two or more time periods, again on the same set of individuals and variables of interest at each time. For example, the U.S. Longitudinal Studies of Aging (LSOA I & II), collaborative efforts between the National Center for Health Statistics and the National Institute on Aging, used prospective panel designs to follow two cohorts of nationally representative samples of 70+-year-old noninstitutionalized civilians over time. LSOA I used data from the 1984 National Health Interview Survey on 7,527 older persons as a baseline and conducted three follow-up interviews with these participants in 1986, 1988, and 1990. LSOA II followed a cohort of 9,447 older persons from the 1994 National Health Interview Survey through two follow-up interviews, which were conducted in 1997–1998 and 1999–2000. Alternatively, retrospective panel designs have been used effectively in life history studies to empirically assess social change, such as the Women and Employment Survey of 1980 in the United Kingdom, which used interviews to collect detailed work histories from a nationally representative sample of 4,788 working British women.

In the repeated cross-sectional design, data are collected "on the same set of variables for (and perhaps at) two or more periods but to include non-identical (but comparable) cases in each period" (Menard, 2002, p. 2). Although data for/at the different time periods are considered as distinct cross-sections, the researcher can still make comparisons across time periods if they used probability sampling to ensure that the individuals in the different cross-sections were drawn from the same population and hence were comparable. A good example is the National Health Interview Survey, which is the largest cross-sectional household interview survey in the United States and has been conducted annually since 1957 using probability sampling of the U.S. population.

## Longitudinal Research Defined Narrowly

Menard (2002) acknowledged that he purposely defined longitudinal research in broad terms to account for differences across disciplines and lack of overall consensus about what qualifies for longitudinal research, as well as to describe the variety of extant research methods and designs suited to collect data for different time periods. However, in practice, longitudinal research has been generally defined in narrower terms to include only studies which collect repeated measurements or observations of variables of interest on the same units (e.g., individuals, groups, organizations) at two or more time points (Nessleroade & Baltes, 1979). Furthermore, the utility of two-wave longitudinal studies has been increasingly contested over the years (Chan, 1998;

385

Rogosa, 1995), resulting in even stricter definitions, which recognized research as longitudinal only if it included at minimum three waves of data collection (Ployhart & Vandenberg, 2010; Singer & Willett, 2003).

Defining longitudinal research in the above narrow terms limits it to only prospective studies, while retrospective studies and studies using repeated cross-sectional designs may be considered "quasi-longitudinal" at best, because of the superiority of prospective studies in measuring change, establishing temporal order, and testing causal relationships (Ferrer & Grimm, 2012; Hakim, 1987; Menard, 2002; Nessleroade & Baltes, 1979). After all, the hallmark of longitudinal research is its emphasis on studying change and on illuminating the direction and magnitude of causal relationships, and prospective studies seem best suited to meet these objectives. Hereinafter, we limit our discussion to longitudinal research employing prospective panel designs. Below, we provide a more detailed discussion of the objectives of longitudinal research and their relevance to how longitudinal research is defined and designed.

## Objectives of Longitudinal Research

Longitudinal research can be used to study: (a) how each individual changes over time (i.e., intra-individual change); for example, how is burnout experienced by each employee over a 5-year period; (b) how individual changes differ across individuals (i.e., inter-individual differences in intra-individual change); for example, how do employees differ in experiencing burnout over a 5-year period; (c) how the relationships between two or more variables change over time (i.e., changes in interrelationships); for example, how does the relationship between burnout and turnover intentions change over the 5-year period; and (d) what are the "causes" of intra-individual change and inter-individual differences in such changes; for example, how does workload "cause" within-employee changes in burnout over a period of 5 years, as well as differences in such changes across employees (Nessleroade & Baltes, 1979). None of the above objectives can be accomplished effectively with cross-sectional research. Thus, longitudinal research is especially useful when researchers are concerned with understanding (a) dynamic phenomena or change, and (b) the direction and strength of causal relationships.

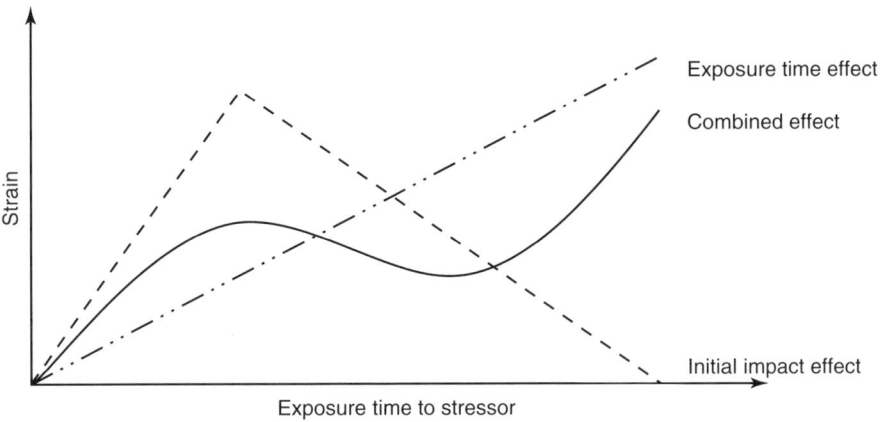

**Figure 18.1.** Different Stressor Effects as Illustrated by Zapf and Frese (1988).

## Longitudinal Research for Assessing Change

In order to examine intra-individual changes (i.e., growth trajectories) or inter-individual differences in such changes, repeated measures need to be collected over time on the same individuals (Singer & Willett, 2003). Moreover, it is argued that an adequate examination of change requires a minimum of three repeated measures; preferably more than three (Chan, 1998). Longitudinal studies which collect data at two times (i.e., two-wave studies) are thus considered deficient as they cannot adequately examine the form of change (especially if it is nonlinear or discontinuous, Ployhart & Vandenberg, 2010) or how change transpires over time, since any change from time 1 to time 2 can only be viewed as linear (i.e., a straight line) and little is known about the nature and form of change occurring between the two time points (Rogosa, 1995; Singer & Willett, 2003).

For example, dynamic models of occupational stress rarely take a linear form and thus cannot be adequately tested with two-wave studies. Frese and Zapf (1988) described models illustrating various stressor effects, including initial impact effect, exposure time effect, and combined effect (Figure 18.1). In the *initial impact effect* scenario, exposure to a new stressor (e.g., new work arrangements) produces an initial negative reaction (e.g., anxiety), which subsides over time with continuous exposure to the stressor due to adjustment and development of coping strategies. The *exposure time effect* occurs when prolonged exposure to a stressor (e.g., abusive supervisor) leads to higher incidence of health problems over time (e.g., high blood pressure). The *combined effect* is illustrated when exposure to a stressor (e.g., unemployment) initially produces a negative reaction (e.g., increase in illness), followed by some improvement (e.g., decrease in illness), which deteriorates again afterwards (e.g., increase in illness) (see Frese, 1985; Warr, 1987 for examples). In all three scenarios, the researcher ideally should collect data before exposure to the stressor (i.e., baseline) and at least on two subsequent (carefully determined) occasions during exposure to the stressor to be able to discern trends of changes in responses and to test alternative models, such as distinguishing between exposure time effect and combined effect or between initial impact effect and null effect.

Consider, for example, the decision of the Yahoo CEO Marissa Mayer in early 2013 to ban telecommuting or working from home with the goal of increasing productivity and innovation (Goudreau, 2013). Taking away flexible work arrangements is likely to act as a stressor for many employees, particularly parents, who rely on such arrangements to better juggle work and home responsibilities (Gajendran & Harrison, 2007). However, its exact effect on the wellbeing and productivity of Yahoo's employees over time is difficult to assess and ascertain vis-à-vis competitive effects with a two-wave prospective panel study; at minimum three waves of data collection are needed. For example, it is possible that the CEO's ban on telecommuting may have an initial impact effect, which can cause increased work–family conflict, job dissatisfaction, and turnover intentions, as well as lower job performance (Gajendran & Harrison, 2007). However, as employees adjust their work and home schedules (and mentality) to reflect the new reality, this initial effect may disappear over time. It is also plausible that the longer employees are restrained from telecommuting, the more they are likely to experience the above strains over time (i.e., exposure time effect). Or perhaps, the initial negative impact or "shock" of the CEO decision is followed by an adjustment period (i.e., decrease in strains), which, however, wears out as the employees, who have substantial home responsibilities, begin to exhaust their resources and to experience higher strains over time (i.e., a combined effect). As noted above, a two-wave panel study will have little utility in testing these alternative trajectories of change in the phenomenon of interest.

In addition, Frese and Zapf (1988) described five different exposure time models, in which stressors can have impacts of varying shapes on employee functioning and wellbeing lasting long after the removal of the stressor: (a) stress reaction model, (b) accumulation model, (c) dynamic accumulation model, (d) adjustment model, and (e) sleeper effect model. Taris and Kompier (2003) pointed out that a two-wave prospective study would make it impossible to appropriately model the hypothesized form of change in any of the above models and to distinguish them from their competing alternatives.

Further, true change may be confounded with measurement error in two-wave studies, as the observed change from time 1 to time 2 can be a measurement artifact if, for example, measurement error suppressed scores at time 1 and inflated scores at time 2 (Ployhart & Vandenberg, 2010; Singer & Willett, 2003). Thus, having three or more time points or data collection waves will increase reliability and statistical power (Willett, 1989).

Despite the popularity of the two-wave prospective panel design in longitudinal research, the increasing awareness of its limitations to assess change has led to the sobering conclusion that "Two waves of data are better than one, but maybe not much better" (Rogosa, 1995, p. 174). We share this skepticism about two-wave prospective studies and their ability to adequately assess change, which is reflected in recent definitions of longitudinal research emphasizing the use of three or more waves of data collection (Ployhart & Vandenberg, 2010; Singer & Willett, 2003). For example, Ployhart and Vandenberg (2010) define longitudinal research as "research emphasizing the study of change and containing at minimum three repeated observations (although more than three is better) on at least one of the substantive constructs of interest" (p. 97). Similarly, Taris and Kompier (2003) insist that "simple two-phase designs are insufficient to tell us much about the rate of change or about the shape of presumed causal relationships; thus multiphase designs should be preferred to these simple designs" (p. 4).

Unfortunately, reviews of longitudinal studies of occupational stress indicate that prospective panel designs with three or more waves of data collection remain underutilized in this field of research, which is still dominated by two-wave studies (Cigularov et al., 2013; de Lange et al., 2003; Zapf et al., 1996). For example, only 12% of the longitudinal studies reviewed by Zapf et al. (1996) included more than two waves, whereas Cigularov et al. (2013) and de Lange et al. (2003) found that near one-fifth of the longitudinal studies they reviewed used three or more data collection waves.

## Longitudinal Research for Assessing Causal Relationships

As stated by Cook and Campbell (1979), for causal relationships to be inferred, there must be (a) covariation between the antecedent (stressor) and outcome (strain) variables, (b) the antecedent (stressor) must precede the outcome (strain) temporally, and (c) alternative explanations for the covariation between the antecedent (stressor) and the outcome (strain) must be ruled out. Cross-sectional research can only be used to detect covariation between the stressor and the strain. In fact, voluminous cross-sectional research has documented the covariation between various occupational stressors and strains (Sonnentag & Frese, 2003). However, contributions of cross-sectional research can be limited by common method bias as a possible alternative explanation for the covariation (Lance, Dawson, Birkelbach, & Hoffman, 2010). Longitudinal studies, on the other hand, allow researchers to establish temporal order and more effectively test alternative explanations to the hypothesized causal relationship.

If it is hypothesized that stressor $x$ causes strain $y$, then there are two plausible alternative explanations to this causal relationship: strain $y$ causes stressor $x$ (i.e., reverse causation), and a third variable $z$ causes both $x$ and $y$, which results in an observed relationship between the stressor and the strain (Zapf et al., 1996). While longitudinal studies are generally regarded as capable of examining reverse (and reciprocal) causation hypotheses, they are considered still susceptible to the possibility of third variable influences, which may explain the covariation between the stressor and strain (Schooler, 1999; Spector, Chen, & O'Connell, 2000; Zapf et al., 1996).

## Methodological Considerations in Longitudinal Research

This section provides an overview of specific methodological issues related to longitudinal designs of occupational stress studies, which have been identified in the literature (e.g., Zapf et al., 1996) and can potentially hinder the adequate examination of change and causal stressor–strain relationships. We also summarize the findings from methodological reviews of the longitudinal occupational stress research pertaining to each issue (see Cigularov et al., 2013; de Lange et al., 2003; Zapf et al., 1996).

### Reverse Causation

The standard causal hypothesis, which is tested in most longitudinal studies of occupational stress, is that stressors cause strains. Researchers, however, rarely investigate alternative explanations of the stressor–strain relationship, such as reverse causation (Taris & Kompier, 2003; Zapf et al., 1996). A reverse causation hypothesis predicts that the stressor–strain relationship is due to the strain having a causal impact on the stressor (i.e., a strain–stressor relationship).

Zapf et al. (1996) illustrate two possible explanations for reverse causation: drift hypothesis and true strain–stressor hypothesis. The drift hypothesis states that those experiencing strains drift down to positions with more stressors, such as jobs with low job security or into unemployment. For example, individuals with poor health may drift over time to worse jobs, because of frequent absenteeism, which may lead to demotion or unemployment. Also, individuals with high absenteeism records may find it difficult to secure good jobs. Furthermore, Zapf et al. (1996) point out that because organizations tend to select employees who exhibit high social competence, confidence, and stress tolerance, people who are better adjusted and healthier will be more likely to get the better jobs. Some support for the drift hypothesis was found in a 30-year longitudinal study by Timms (1996), who observed that participants with mental illness were more likely to become unemployed over time.

In the true strain–stressor hypothesis, strains may lead to higher stressors. For example, just as job demands could cause illness in the traditional stressor–strain hypothesis, it is also plausible that illness can cause job demands because those who are ill are likely to be absent from work and fall behind on tasks or projects, which in turn may increase job demands for them upon their return. This issue is exemplified well in a study by Tucker et al. (2008), who investigated the relationships between task demands and job control and affective strains. The researchers collected data from 1,539 soldiers in various positions over six time points over the course of 2 years while the soldiers were deployed. At each time point, the participants were asked to rate work overload, job control, and affective strain. The researchers hypothesized lagged effects of work overload and job control on affective strain. However, their results suggested concurrent effects for the relationships of work overload and job control with affective strain, but no evidence for lagged effects was found. Most interestingly, tests for reverse causation found that when controlling for prior reported work overload, high affective strain reported in the previous time lag predicted increased task demands in the next time lag. Further, participants who reported less strain rated their job control as higher in the next time lag. Such results emphasize the need to examine reverse causation explanations as the anticipated stressor–strain relationship may actually run in the opposite direction (i.e., strain–stressor).

Unfortunately, Zapf et al. (1996) found that only 15 (35%) of the 43 longitudinal studies of occupational stress that they reviewed tested reverse causation. Furthermore, almost half of the 15 studies that examined reverse causation found some support for it. Not only was reverse causation not tested in the majority of the studies, but these articles rarely even discussed the possibility of this relationship between the stressors and strains. Of the studies that did examine reverse causation, many only investigated it for a few selected predictors. Even more troublesome were the findings by de Lange et al. (2003), who reported that only two of the 19 (11%) longitudinal studies of the demands–control–(support) models, which they categorized as high quality, actually examined reverse causation. The above results prompted these two research teams to explicitly recommend for researchers to routinely test for reverse causal effects in longitudinal studies of occupational stress in order to exclude them as an alternative explanation and to gain a better understanding of the dynamic relationship between work and worker health. Their recommendation, however, seems to have had little effect over time on actual practices, considering the similar recent findings by Cigularov et al. (2013), who revealed that about two thirds of the longitudinal studies they reviewed did not test reverse causation.

## Reciprocal Causation

In certain situations it is possible that a reciprocal causal relationship exists between the stressor and the strain. As in the job demands and illness example, it is plausible that both the traditional and the reverse causation hypotheses are true, such that job demands contribute to illness and illness in turn leads to higher job demands (a feedback loop). Consider another example in which de Lange, Taris, Kompier, Houtman, and Bongers (2004) found evidence of a reciprocal relationship between work characteristics and mental health. Data were collected from 668 Dutch employees across 10 organizations. At each of four time points over 3 years, employees responded to survey items assessing working conditions, changes in the workplace, psychosocial work characteristics, work satisfaction, physical workload, psychosocial and physical health, and background variables. Several structural models were tested, including a reciprocal causation model, which hypothesized that job demands, job control, and social support from supervisor had both direct and reverse causal relationships with employee wellbeing. For mental health, this reciprocal relationship was supported for all three working condition variables, although it was noted that the reverse relationships in the model were slightly weaker than the direct relationships. The authors argued for more research investigating reciprocal relationships between stressors and strains, echoing the concerns Zapf et al. (1996) had previously expressed.

Such concerns may be well justified given that Zapf et al. (1996) found only five (10%) of the 45 longitudinal studies they reviewed to explicitly test for reciprocal causal relationships. Of the five studies that examined reciprocal relationships, one study (20%) provided support for such relationship. Further, structural equation modeling was not used consistently to test a series of models in order to more fully investigate the possibility of reciprocal causation. Further, de Lange et al. (2003) reported that only two studies explicitly assessed reciprocal causation, representing only 11% of the high-quality longitudinal studies they reviewed.

However, Cigularov et al. found that close to one third of the studies they reviewed tested reciprocal causal effects. In fact, they observed that almost all studies that tested for reverse causation also tested for reciprocal causation. We consider this as a positive trend in current longitudinal occupational stress research and in contrast to Zapf and colleagues' earlier findings depicting a situation in which researchers rarely tested for reverse causation and almost never examined reciprocal causal relationships. In fact, any researcher who collects appropriate longitudinal data to test for reverse causation can and should test for reciprocal causation (Taris & Kompier, 2003), which is crucial in occupational stress research to disentangle the complexities of stressor–strain relationships. However, testing for reverse and reciprocal causal effects requires special methodological considerations, such as using appropriate longitudinal designs and statistical analyses.

## Third Variable Effects

Even selecting the appropriate longitudinal design and statistical analyses for testing both traditional and reverse/reciprocal causal relationships may not be enough to prove causality. Third variables, or extraneous variables, pose a potential threat to even well-designed longitudinal studies by influencing stressors, strains, or the stressor–strain relationship, either through the method used for the study (e.g., common method variance) or independently (e.g., age, sex, social status, caregiver status, etc.) (see Zapf et al., 1996). In other words, it is practically impossible to completely rule out the possibility that a variable or a set of variables not included in the longitudinal study may account for the observed relationship, unless the researcher measures all variables that are theoretically relevant to the relationship under study. For example, the methodology could influence the stressors and the strains through common method variance if participants first responded to items regarding negative experiences at work before responding to job satisfaction items. Participants may be more likely to report lower job satisfaction in this case because they were cued by the previous items, which could produce an inflated relationship between negative work experiences and job satisfaction. An example of a third variable not related to methodology could be caregiver status. Employees caring for a sick child or relative may report more strains than other employees following an intervention aimed at reducing strain. Unless this relationship is accounted for in statistical analyses, researchers could misinterpret the results and conclude that the intervention was unsuccessful due to this confounding relationship.

Further, third variables or confounds may create the appearance of a causal relationship that in reality does not exist (Spector, 2002). In non-experimental research, third variables are one of the most important threats to causal hypotheses (Dwyer, 1983). For this reason, it is crucial that researchers consider potential third variables and attempt to control for them either methodologically or statistically to support a causal hypothesis. However, no matter how hard we try to design the perfect longitudinal study, "we can never prove causal relationships; the best we can do is argue that it is plausible that certain statistical associations can be understood in causal terms" (Taris & Kompier, 2003, p. 1).

Zapf et al. (1996) differentiated three different types of third variables (*occasion factors, background variables*, and *nonconstant variables*) and their unique threats to internal validity in longitudinal occupational stress research. These are described in more detail below.

### Occasion factors.
Occasion factors are hypothetical and generally unmeasured third variables (e.g., weather, time of day, or mood) that influence the stressor and strain variables (Zapf et al., 1996). An example would be a study in which participants were administered a job satisfaction questionnaire on Monday versus Friday. Participants may report less satisfaction with their jobs on Monday because they are just coming back from the weekend. On the other hand, participants may report higher job satisfaction if asked on Friday because they are looking forward to the weekend and generally feel more optimistic.

Effects of occasion factors were found by Spector et al. (2000) in a longitudinal study examining stressors, strains, and negative affectivity. One occasion factor in particular, mood, was found to affect negative affectivity measures.

Zapf et al. (1996) noted that not controlling for occasion factors can attenuate or enhance an observed relationship in longitudinal studies. Specifically, not only are occasion factors a source of error variance (i.e., attenuating the observed effect), but they also may enhance the observed effect if the outcome or strain is stable over time. Such effects can be eliminated by partialling out the strain at time 1 from the effect of the stressor at time 1 on the strain at time 2.

*Background variables.*
Background variables are another type of third variables, which, unlike occasion factors, are stable over time. Zapf et al. (1996) operationalized background factors as generally demographical variables such as gender, age, education, etc., but also included personality traits such as negative affectivity. Including personality as a background variable may seem counterintuitive as research has shown that personality is not entirely stable across a person's lifetime (Haan, Millsap, & Hartka, 1986). However, the Big Five has been shown to be relatively stable (Hendriks, Hofstee, & De Raad, 1999). Spector et al. (2000) found that background variables, including negative affectivity, can influence stressor and strain measures but that stressor–strain relationship was not affected if the background variables were controlled for statistically. Similarly to occasion factors, the researcher can control the effects of background variables on the stressor (time 1)–strain (time 2) relationship when strain at time 1 is partialled out in the hierarchical multiple regression.

*Nonconstant variables.*
The final type of third variables that will be reviewed here are nonconstant variables, which are regarded as most problematic among the three types because they are stable over time and can influence both the stressors and the strains (Zapf et al., 1996). Nonconstant variables are often unmeasured and are most problematic because their semi-stable properties make them hard to predict and control for methodologically and statistically. An example of a nonconstant variable discussed by Zapf et al. (1996) is social desirability. They reasoned that social desirability is based on a sense of insecurity, which will vary across situations and therefore differentially influence stressors and strains over time.

Considering the above, including relevant third variables in models of longitudinal studies represents a critical step in eliminating possible alternative explanations for the observed causal relationships. Yet, this step was taken in less than half of the studies reviewed by Zapf et al. (1996). Further, de Lange et al. (2003) revealed that although more than 90% of the studies in their review controlled for some background variables (e.g., demographics), there was inconsistency and lack of rationale for choosing which background variables to be included. Similarly, Cigularov et al. (2013) observed that while background variables, such as age, sex, education, were most frequently included in the models tested, the effects of occasion factors and nonconstant variables were rarely examined.

## Time Lag

The length of the time period between data collection waves in a longitudinal study is extremely important when modeling change or testing causal relationships. Time lags that are ill-timed (e.g., too short, too long, or wrongly spaced) can make it difficult and even impossible to assess change and the true nature of causal relationships (Ployhart & Vandenberg, 2010; Zapf et al., 1996). Without an appropriate time lag, causal relationships between stressors and strains can be missed, misinterpreted, or underestimated. More specifically, a longer time lag may result in underestimation of the causal effect of the stressor on the strain, whereas a shorter time lag may prevent the researcher from detecting such an effect even if it exists (Zapf et al., 1996). Hence, a shorter (than needed) time lag may be more detrimental than a longer time lag: a conclusion also supported by simulation research (cf. Dwyer, 1983).

Unfortunately, researchers often lack a theoretical or empirical basis for hypothesizing the appropriate time lag when investigating causal relationships, which may explain some of the seemingly haphazard decisions made regarding this issue (Spector, 2002; Zapf et al., 1996). It is recommended that researchers should carefully consider the length of the exposure time to a stressor needed for strains to arise and develop a theoretical definition of time, before they determine how to incorporate time into their models (i.e., make decisions about the number and length of time lags in their studies) (Frese & Zapf, 1988; Kelloway & Francis, 2013; Ployhart & Vandenberg, 2010). The initial impact and exposure time models in Frese and Zapf (1988, see pp. 387–392), for example, can prove useful in that regard, although the authors caution that these models may oversimplify reality as stressor effects often do not have a distinct beginning and end and they may differ based on stressor intensity, type of stressor and strain, as well as individuals/populations studied.

In the literature review by Zapf et al. (1996), time lags utilized in longitudinal studies of occupational stress varied from one month to 15 years, with the majority of studies (58%) using time lags of up to one year. Also, the authors noticed that time lag selection was generally not discussed in detail by the researchers, although organizational reasons rather than theory seemed to be the dominant rationale for selecting a particular time lag. De Lange et al. (2003) found that the time lags used in the 45 longitudinal studies they reviewed varied from 28 days to 14 years, and 17 (38%) of the studies did not provide a theoretical or methodological rationale for choosing the time lags. Finally, Cigularov et al. (2013) found that more than two thirds of the reviewed studies had time lags of up to one year. Time lags ranged from 2 days to 11 years. They further observed that in the majority of the studies reasons for time lag selection were either arbitrary or not explicitly stated; less than a third of the studies provided theory-based reasons; and only a few justified their choice of time lag with organizational or administrative reasons.

## Longitudinal Research Designs

Not all prospective longitudinal designs are considered equal when it comes to ruling out reverse causation hypotheses and third variable effects. Zapf et al. identified three typical designs utilized to analyze causal relationships in longitudinal research of occupational stress: (1) stressor time 1 and strain time 2 design, (2) incomplete two-wave panel design, and (3) full two-wave panel design. Please note that these designs can be extended to three or more waves of data collection (e.g., Fay & Sonnentag, 2002), but we prefer to limit our discussion in this section to two-wave designs for illustrative purposes and because these are most commonly used in practice (Zapf et al., 1996).

### Stressor Time 1 and Strain Time 2 Design

Designs that measure the stressor (e.g., job demands) at time 1 and the strain (e.g., illness) at time 2 (Figure 18.2) are considered among the weakest to test causal relationships in longitudinal occupational stress research

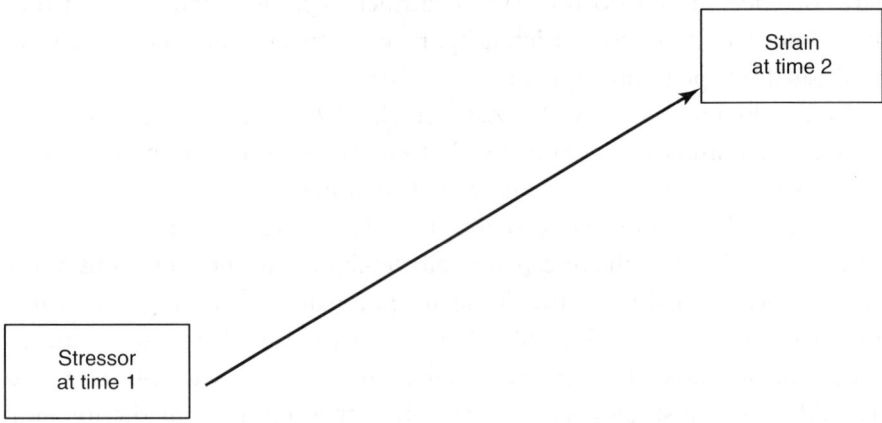

**Figure 18.2.**    Stressor Time 1 and Strain Time 2 Design.

(Kelloway & Francis, 2013; Zapf et al., 1996). In studies using such designs (e.g., Nielsen, Rugulies, Christensen, Smith-Hansen, Bjorner, & Kristensen, 2004), the researchers are unable to establish temporal order because it is possible that the illness, for example, which is measured at time 2 may also be present at time 1, but remains undetected because it is simply unmeasured. In this situation it is difficult to ascertain change in illness from time 1 to time 2. Likewise, measuring job demands at time 1 can be regarded as a proxy measurement for job demands at time 2, since they remain unmeasured at time 2 and might not have changed over the period of time.

The inability to account for changes in the stressor or strain over time is a serious shortcoming of this design. When stressors are only measured at the outset and strains only after some given period of time, researchers also have no way to test for alternative explanations such as reverse or reciprocal causation. Results could be falsely attributed to the theorized causal relationship when instead a reverse causal hypothesis may be a better explanation. As Spector (2002) cautions, researchers should not presume that when the strain is measured after the stressor, then the stressor must cause the strain. Although this design can be used to alleviate concerns for common method bias by temporally separating the data collection of the stressor and strain variables (Podsakoff, MacKenzie, Lee, & Podsakoff, 2003), its critical limitations as discussed above hardly qualify it as a longitudinal research design (Ployhart & Vandenberg, 2010).

A good illustration of the limitations of the stressor time 1 and strain time 2 design is provided in a study by Bauer and Truxillo (2000). The researchers

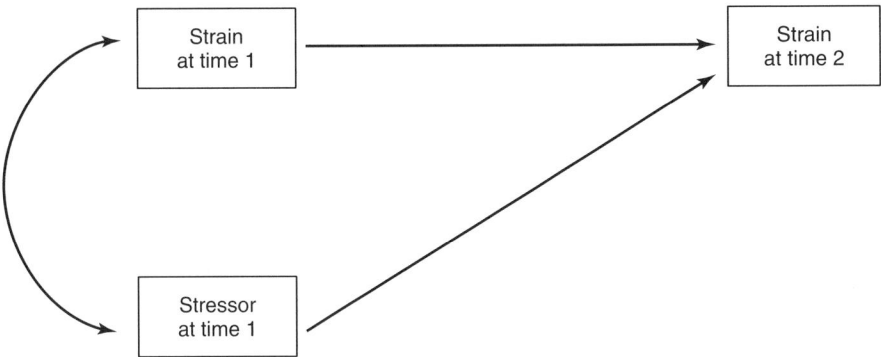

**Figure 18.3.** Incomplete Two-Wave Panel Design.

collected data from 136 temp-to-permanent employees (i.e., temporary workers who are on probation to become permanent employees) at four time points to examine the effects of individual differences, self-monitoring, tolerance for ambiguity, and role adjustment on their subsequent selection success. One of their key findings was that role adjustment (defined as low role ambiguity, high acceptance by coworkers, and high self-efficacy) predicted selection success over time. However, because role adjustment variables were only measured at time 2 and selection success was only measured at times 3 and 4, the researchers concluded (rightly so) that the causal direction of the significant relationship between their predictors and outcomes was unclear. They surmised that "early indications of performance may influence employee role adjustment . . . and vice versa" (Bauer & Truxillo, 2000, p. 345).

## Incomplete Two-Wave Panel Design

A better design for testing causal relationships is the incomplete two-wave panel design (Figure 18.3). In this design the stressor is measured at time 1, while the strain is measured at both time 1 and time 2, allowing the researcher to establish some temporal order. The advantage of this approach is that any changes in strain from time 1 to time 2 can be taken into account. In other words, when the effect of the stressor (at time 1) on the strain (at time 2) is estimated, the researcher can control for past strain (i.e., strain at time 1). However, Zapf et al. (1996) note that many researchers using this design fail to utilize it fully by excluding the time 1 measurement of the strain in their statistical analyses.

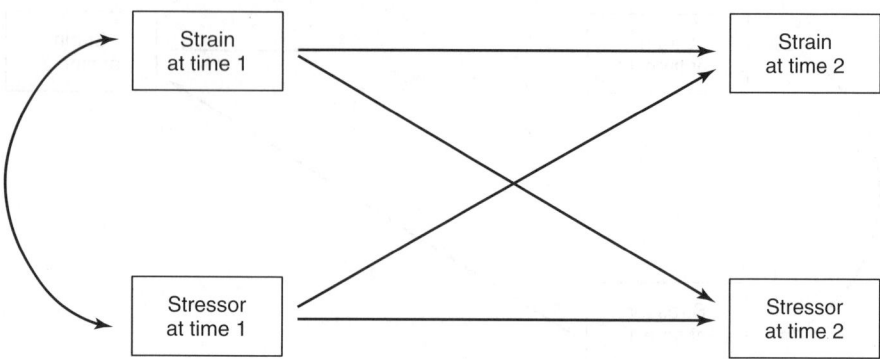

**Figure 18.4.** Full Two-Wave Panel Design.

A critical drawback of the incomplete two-wave panel design, which limits the ability of researchers to adequately test for reverse causation and third variable problems, is that change in the stressor over time is not measured and thus its stability remains unknown. Other limitations of this design include inability to control for unmeasured nonconstant third variables and assess synchronous stressor–strain effects, as well as issues with assumptions about uncorrelated measurement errors (Zapf et al., 1996). For these reasons, incomplete two-wave panel designs are not ideal for investigating alternative explanations (Zapf et al., 1996).

An example of a study using this design is Dikkers, Jansen, de Lange, Vinkenburg, and Kooij's (2010) two-wave investigation of the moderating effects of proactive personality on the relationship between job characteristics and engagement. The researchers assessed both job characteristics (i.e., demands and resources) and engagement (i.e., vigor, dedication, and absorption) at both waves, thus affording them the opportunity to examine reverse and causal relationships between the aforementioned endogenous and exogenous variables (although such an analysis was not conducted). Although the researchers found evidence for a moderating effect of proactive personality, in that proactive personality served as a tool leading to higher levels of expected vigor, dedication, and absorption in low demand environments, they could not test a causal relationship because personality was measured at just one time point, which the authors noted as a limitation. Specifically, it is possible that the engaged employee, feeling energized, could attempt to positively change their current working environment by acting more proactively.

## Full Two-Wave Panel Design

To overcome such limitations, researchers can dramatically improve the incomplete two-wave panel design by a relatively simple "move": make it complete by measuring both stressors and strains at each time point (Figure 18.4). This is referred to as the full (or complete) two-wave panel design, which is considered a superior method (compared to the other two) as it allows the researcher to test reverse and reciprocal causal relationships (Zapf et al., 1996). Thus, causal inferences drawn from this design can be much stronger than the previous two designs, indicating that the inclusion of the additional measurement of the stressor at time 2 can provide a substantial return for the researcher. For example, Hakanen, Perhoniemi, and Toppinen-Tanner (2008) investigated the effects of job resources, engagement, and personal initiative on innovation in the work unit. Because the authors utilized a full two-wave panel design, they were able to investigate not only the hypothesized causal relationships in their model but also reverse causation. Specifically for each hypothesized relationship (*job resources* to *work engagement, work engagement* to *personal initiative,* and *personal initiative* to *work-unit innovativeness*), the researchers were able to test and compare a (1) stability model (i.e., T1 factors predicting the same factor at T2 without cross-lagged effects), (2) causal model (i.e., autoregression paths from the stability model and the relationship between T1 exogenous and T2 endogenous variables), (3) reverse model (i.e., autoregression paths from the stability model and the relationship between T1 endogenous and T2 exogenous variables), and (4) reciprocal model (i.e., combination of the causal and reverse; all paths tested). This led the researchers to find support for both hypothesized and reverse causation hypotheses such that job resources had a reciprocal relationship with engagement, and engagement had a reciprocal relationship with personal initiative while personal initiative had a positive influence on innovation.

In their review, Zapf et al. (1996) indicated that the majority of the reviewed studies (58%) used a full two-wave panel design, followed by studies using incomplete panel designs. Similarly, full-panel designs were used by 53% of the longitudinal studies reviewed by de Lange et al. (2003), whereas in 42% of the studies an incomplete panel design was employed. More recently, Cigularov et al. (2013) reported that more than two thirds of the reviewed longitudinal occupational stress studies took advantage of full-panel designs.

## Statistical Procedures

Even the most rigorous design can fail to reveal an existing causal relationship, or conversely find a spurious result, if the appropriate statistical analysis is not conducted. Examples include not accounting for change in strains over time or not controlling for third variables correctly. To address this issue, Zapf et al. (1996) compared three types of analytical techniques, which can be used to examine causal relationships in data collected with a full two-wave panel design: *cross-lagged panel correlations, hierarchical multiple regression*, and *structural equation modeling*. In the *cross-lagged panel correlation* approach, the two cross-lagged correlations, $r$ (stressor time 1, strain time 2) and $r$(stressor time 2, strain time 1) are statistically compared to determine which one is dominant. This technique, although intuitive, has been generally discredited due to limitations in meeting statistical assumptions, providing effect size, and ability to test for certain third variable effects, such as occasion factors (see Williams & Podsakoff, 1989).

The use of *hierarchical multiple regression* allows for more rigorous comparisons between the hypothesized causal relationship (i.e., stressor–strain) and alternative explanations, such as third variable effects or reverse causal relationship (i.e., strain–stressor). Zapf et al. (1996) noted in their review that at times researchers may have overlooked alternative explanations at least in part due to using the incorrect statistical procedure, but also when they did not consider such explanations in the first place and consequently did not test them using appropriate hierarchical regressions (even though they used hierarchical regressions to test their hypothesized relationships).

Zapf et al. (1996) recommended that researchers should use *structural equation modeling* when analyzing data in studies using a full two-wave panel design. Not only can structural equation modeling achieve everything that can be accomplished with cross-lagged panel correlations and hierarchical regression analyses, but it also provides additional benefits, such as accounting for unreliability in observed variables, testing multivariate–multiwave models, and simultaneously modeling reverse/reciprocal relationships, as well as third variable and method effects (Williams & Podsakoff, 1989). Unfortunately, only seven (16%) of the longitudinal studies reviewed by Zapf et al. (1996) used measurement and structural models; three studies (7%) used only structural equations; 18 studies (42%) used hierarchical multiple regression; and seven studies (16%) relied on cross-lagged panel correlations. De Lange et al. (2003) reported that only two studies (4%)

used structural equation modeling, while the remaining 43 longitudinal studies in their review used multiple regression analysis. In contrast, about one third of the longitudinal studies most recently reviewed by Cigularov et al. (2013) used the structural equation modeling approach: the second most frequently used analytical procedure following hierarchical multiple regressions. It is interesting to note that their review identified only one study that exclusively used cross-lagged panel correlations. These findings indicate a desired shift toward the use of more rigorous and sophisticated analytical approaches to testing causal relationships in occupational stress.

## Concluding Comments

Given the dynamic view of occupational stress in current stress models, as well as the need to understand how occupational stressors and strains impact each other and how their causal relationships unfold over time, longitudinal research should be a natural choice for occupational stress researchers when planning their investigations (Frese & Zapf, 1988; Sonnentag & Frese, 2003). Yet, longitudinal research in the study of occupational stress is often underused, misunderstood, and misused, and plagued by methodological deficiencies, which limit the validity of inferences drawn from such research (Zapf et al., 1996).

In their concluding remarks, Zapf et al. presented a set of guidelines for researchers conducting longitudinal research, which included: (1) measuring all variables at all time points using the same measurement method, (2) considering and including third variables in their designs, (3) thoroughly planning the time lag, (4) making the necessary assumptions about the time course of the variables involved, (5) taking a structural equation modeling approach to analyzing the data, (6) assessing measurement models, and (7) testing multiple competing models. We believe that these "best practices," put forth more than 15 years ago, are still relevant, feasible, and have the potential to strengthen the causal inferences drawn from occupational stress research and further advance the field. Based on the evidence reviewed in this chapter, it seems that in recent years more occupational stress researchers are adhering to some of these "best practices," such as using full-panel designs and structural equation modeling, which has allowed them to better test hypothesized and alternative causal relationships. At the same time, there are indications that there is limited or no progress in other areas, revealing gaps between actual and recommended practices for conducting sound longitudinal research. For example, occupational stress researchers continue to over-rely on cross-sectional research methodologies and when they conduct longitudinal research, they tend to (a) give little theoretical or methodological consideration to including third variables in their models or about planning time lags, (b) rarely test reverse or reciprocal causal relationships, and (c) limit their studies to two-wave designs (Cigularov et al., 2013; de Lange et al., 2003). Although Zapf et al.'s review has certainly been influential in occupational health psychology since its publication in 1996, recent research still laments the lack of rigorous longitudinal designs in occupational stress studies (Nixon, Mazzola, Bauer, Krueger, & Spector, 2011). Therefore, we echo earlier calls for more and improved longitudinal research in occupational stress (Frese & Zapf, 1988; Kasl, 1987; Zapf et al., 1996).

# References

Amstad, F. T., Meier, L. L., Fasel, U., Elfering, A., & Semmer, N. K. (2011). A meta-analysis of work–family conflict and various outcomes with a special emphasis on cross-domain versus matching-domain relations. *Journal of Occupational Health Psychology, 16*, 151–169.

Bauer, T. N., & Truxillo, D. M. (2000). Temp-to-permanent employees: A longitudinal study of stress and selection success. *Journal of Occupational Health Psychology, 5*(3), 337–346.

Bliese, P. D., & Jex, S. M. (2002). Incorporating a mulitilevel perspective into occupational stress research: Theoretical, methodological, and practical implications. *Journal of Occupational Health Psychology, 7*, 265–276.

Chan, D. (1998). The conceptualization and analysis of change over time: An integrative approach incorporating longitudinal mean and covariance structures analysis (LMACS) and multiple indicator latent growth modeling (MLGM). *Organizational Research Methods, 1*, 421–483.

Chen, P. Y., Cigularov, K. P., & Menger, L. M. (2013). Experimental and quasi-experimental designs in occupational health psychology. In L. Tetrick, M. Wang, & B. Sinclair (Eds.), *Research methods in occupational health psychology: State of the art in measurement, design, and data analysis* (pp. 180–207). New York: Taylor & Francis.

Cigularov, K. P., Brusso, R. C., & Callan, R. C. (2013). *The state of longitudinal research in occupational stress: A 15-year follow-up review of methodological issues.* Unpublished manuscript, Department of Psychology, Old Dominion University, Norfolk, U.S.A.

Cook, T. D., & Campbell, D. T. (1979). *Quasi-experimentation: Design & analysis issues for field settings.* Boston: Houghton Mifflin.

Cooper, C. L. (1998). *Theories of organizational stress*. New York: Oxford University Press.

Crawford, E. R., LePine, J. A., & Rich, B. L. (2010). Linking job demands and resources to employee engagement and burnout: A theoretical extension and meta-analytical test. *Journal of Applied Psychology*, 95, 834–848.

de Lange, A. H., Taris, T. W., Kompier, M. A. J., Houtman, I. L. D., & Bongers, P. M. (2003). "The very best of the millennnium": Longitudinal research and the Demand-Control-(Support) model. *Journal of Occupational Health Psychology*, 8(4), 282–305.

de Lange, A. H., Taris, T. W., Kompier, M. A. J., Houtman, I. L. D., & Bongers, P. M. (2004). The relationships between work characteristics and mental health: Examining normal, reversed, and reciprocal relationships in a 4-wave study. *Work & Stress*, 18(2), 149–166.

Dikkers, J. S. E., Jansen, P. G. W., de Lange, A. H., Vinkenburg, C. J., & Kooij, D. (2010). Proactivity, job characteristics, and engagement: A longitudinal study. *The Career Development International*, 15, 59–77.

Dwyer, J. H. (1983). *Statistical models for the social and behavioral sciences*. New York: Oxford University Press.

Eatough, E. M., Chang, C., Miloslavic, S. A., & Johnson, R. E. (2011). Relationships of role stressors with organizational citizenship behavior: A meta-analysis. *Journal of Applied Psychology*, 96, 619–632.

Fay, D., & Sonnentag, S. (2002). Rethinking the effects of stressors: A longitudinal study on personal initiative. *Journal of Occupational Health Psychology*, 7, 221–234.

Ferrer, E., & Grimm, K. J. (2012). Issues in collecting longitudinal data. In H. Cooper (Ed.), *APA Handbook of research methods in psychology* (Vol. 2, pp. 275–290). Washington, DC: American Psychological Association.

Frese, M. (1985). Stress at work and psychosomatic complaints: A causal interpretation. *Journal of Applied Psychology*, 70(2), 314–328.

Frese, M., & Zapf, D. (1988). Methodological issues in the study of work stress: Objective vs. subjective measurement and the question of longitudinal studies. In C. L. Cooper & R. Payne (Eds.), *Causes, coping and consequences of stress at work* (pp. 375–411). New York: Wiley.

Gajendran, R. S., & Harrison, D. A. (2007). The good, the bad, and the unknown about telecommuting: Meta-analysis of psychological mediators and individual consequences. *Journal of Applied Psychology*, 92, 1524–1541.

Goudreau, J. (2013). *Back to the stone age? New Yahoo CEO Marissa Mayer bans working from home*. http://www.forbes.com/sites/jennagoudreau/2013/02/25/back-to-the-stone-age-new-yahoo-ceo-marissa-mayer-bans-working-from-home/.

Haan, N., Millsap, R., & Hartka, E. (1986). As time goes by: Change and stability in personality over fifty years. *Psychology and Aging*, 3, 220–232.

Hakanen, J. J., Perhoniemi, R., & Toppinen-Tanner, S. (2008). Positive gain spirals at work: From job resources to work engagement, personal initiative and work-unit innovativeness. *Journal of Vocational Behavior*, 73, 78–91.

Hakim, C. (1987). *Research design: Strategies and choices in the design of social research*. London: Allen and Unwin.

Hedeker, D., & Gibbons, R. D. (2006). *Longitudinal data analysis*. Hoboken, NJ: Wiley-Interscience.

Hendriks, A. A. J., Hofstee, W. K. B., & De Raad, B. (1999). The Five-Factor Personality Inventory (FFPI). *Personality and Individual Differences, 27*, 307–325.

Karasek, R., & Theorell, T. (1990). *Healthy work: Stress, productivity, and the reconstruction of working life*. New York: Basic Books.

Kasl, S. V. (1987). Methodologies in stress and health: Past difficulties, present dilemmas, future directions. In S. V. Kasl & C. L. Cooper (Eds.), *Stress and health: Issues in research methodologies* (pp. 307–318). Chichester: Wiley.

Kasl, S. V., & Cooper, C. L. (1987). *Stress and health: Issues in research methodologies*. Chichester: Wiley.

Kasl, S. V., & Jones, B. A. (2011). An epidemiological perspective on research design, measurement, and surveillance strategies. In J. C. Quick & L. E. Tetrick (Eds.), *Handbook of occupational health psychology* (2nd ed., pp. 375–398). Washington, DC: American Psychological Association.

Kelloway, E. K., & Francis, L. (2013). Longitudinal research and data analysis. In L. Tetrick, M. Wang, & B. Sinclair (Eds.), *Research methods in occupational health psychology: State of the art in measurement, design, and data analysis* (pp. 374–394). New York: Taylor & Francis.

Lance, C. E., Dawson, B., Birkelbach, B., & Hoffman, B. J. (2010). Method effects, measurement error, and substantive conclusions. *Organizational Research Methods, 13*, 435–455.

Macik-Frey, M., Quick, J. C., & Nelson, D. L. (2007). Advances in occupational health: From a stressful beginning to a positive future. *Journal of Management, 33*(6), 809–840.

Menard, S. (2002). *Longitudinal research* (2nd ed.). Thousand Oaks, CA: Sage.

Nessleroade, J. R., & Baltes, P. B. (1979). *Longitudinal research in the study of behavior and development*. New York: Academic Press.

Nielsen, M. L., Rugulies, R., Christensen, K. B., Smith-Hansen, L., Bjorner, J. B., & Kristensen, T. S. (2004). Impact of the psychosocial work environment on registered absence from work: A two-year longitudinal study using the IPAW cohort. *Work & Stress, 18*, 323–335.

Nixon, A. E., Mazzola, J. J., Bauer, J., Krueger, J. R., & Spector, P. E. (2011). Can work make you sick? A meta-analysis of the relationships between job stressors and physical symptoms. *Work & Stress, 25*(1), 1–22.

Ployhart, R. E., & Vandenberg, R. J. (2010). Longitudinal research: The theory, design, and analysis of change. *Journal of Management, 36*, 94–120.

Podsakoff, P. M., MacKenzie, S. B., Lee, J., & Podsakoff, N. P. (2003). Common method biases in behavioral research: A critical review of the literature and recommended remedies. *Journal of Applied Psychology, 88*, 879–903.

Rogosa, D. R. (1995). Myths and methods: "Myths about longitudinal research" plus supplemental questions. In J. M. Gottman (Ed.), *The analysis of change* (pp. 3–66). Mahwah, NJ: Lawrence Erlbaum.

Schooler, C. (1999). The workplace environment: Measurement, psychological effects, and basic issues. In S. L. Friedman & T. D. Wachs (Eds.), *Measuring environment across the life span: Emerging methods and concepts* (pp. 229–246). Washington, DC: American Psychological Association.

Singer, J. D., & Willett, J. B. (2003). *Applied longitudinal data analysis*. New York: Oxford University Press.

Sonnentag, S., & Frese, M. (2003). Stress in organizations. In J. C. Quick & L. E. Tetrick (Eds.), *Handbook of occupational health psychology* (2nd ed., pp. 453–491). Washington, DC: Wiley Online Library.

Spector, P. E. (2002). Research methods in industrial and organizational psychology: Data collection and data analysis with special consideration to professional issues. In N. Anderson, D. S. Ones, H. K. Sinangil, & C. Viswesvaran (Eds.), *Handbook of industrial, work and organizational psychology, Vol. 1: Personnel psychology* (pp. 10–26). Thousand Oaks, CA: Sage.

Spector, P. E., Chen, P. Y., & O'Connell, B. J. (2000). A longitudinal study of relations between job stressors and job strains while controlling for prior negative affectivity and strains. *Journal of Applied Psychology, 85*(2), 211–218.

Taris, T. W., & Kompier, M. (2003). Challenges in longitudinal designs in occupational health psychology. *Scandinavian Journal of Work Environment and Health, 29*, 1–4.

Tetrick, L. E., & Quick, J. C. (2011). Overview of occupational health psychology: Public health in occupational settings. In J. C. Quick & L. E. Tetrick (Eds.), *Handbook of occupational health psychology* (2nd ed., pp. 3–20). Washington, DC: American Psychological Association.

Timms, D. W. G. (1996). Social mobility and mental health in a Swedish cohort. *Social Psychiatry, 31*, 38–48.

Tucker, J. S., Sinclair, R. R., Mohr, C. D., Adler, A. B., Thomas, J. L., & Salvi, A. D. (2008). A temporal investigation of the direct, interactive, and reverse relations between demand and control and affective strain. *Work & Stress, 22*(2), 81–95.

Warr, P. B. (1987). *Work, unemployment, and mental health*. Oxford: Oxford University Press.

Willett, J. B. (1989). Some results on reliability for the longitudinal measurement of change: Implications for the design of studies of individual growth. *Educational and Psychological Measurement, 49*, 587–602.

Williams, L. J., & Podsakoff, P. M. (1989). Longitudinal field methods for studying reciprocal relationships in organizational behavior research: Toward improved causal analysis. In L. L. Cummings & B. M. Staw (Eds.), *Research in organizational behavior* (Vol. 11, pp. 247–292). Greenwich, CT: JAI Press.

Zapf, D., Dormann, C., & Frese, M. (1996). Longitudinal studies in organizational stress research: A review of the literature with reference to methodological issues. *Journal of Occupational Health Psychology, 1*, 145–169.

# 19

# Measuring Wellbeing in Modern Societies

## Paul Allin

Imperial College London, U.K.

## Introduction

> We hold these truths to be self-evident, that all men are created equal, that
> they are endowed by their Creator with certain unalienable rights, that among
> these are Life, Liberty and the pursuit of Happiness.
>
> United States Declaration of Independence, July 4, 1776

Governments have long been interested in the wellbeing and happiness of
citizens, as exemplified by one of the most famous and frequently cited
phrases from the United States Declaration of Independence. Of course
there has been debate over what Jefferson actually meant by "the pursuit
of happiness," but among the most interesting views is the one presented
by historian Garry Wills who, in his book, *Inventing America—Jefferson's
Declaration of Independence*, compared the original draft with the final
version and observed:

> When Jefferson spoke of pursuing happiness, he had nothing vague or private
> in mind. He meant a public happiness which is measurable; which is, indeed,
> the test and justification of any government.
>
> Wills (2002), p. 164

Jefferson may well have been influenced by the work of Scottish philoso-
pher Francis Hutcheson, who offered a test and justification for action, that

*Work and Wellbeing: Wellbeing: A Complete Reference Guide*, Volume III.
Edited by Peter Y. Chen and Cary L. Cooper.
© 2014 John Wiley & Sons, Ltd. Published 2014 by John Wiley & Sons, Inc.
DOI: 10.1002/9781118539415.wbwell19

it should achieve "the greatest happiness for the greatest number." This was, at its time in 1725, an early expression of utilitarianism, an ethical theory later developed by Jeremy Bentham and John Stuart Mill, but at least as old as the ancient Greek philosophers Aristotle and Plato. If Jefferson and, indeed, the early proponents of utilitarianism were alive today, it is tempting to think about what they would make of the resurgent interest in happiness by academics and economists from around the world. There is much that you would expect them to welcome, in particular the fact that governments of major economies are today exploring how the wellbeing of citizens can be measured, and how it can inform the decisions and actions they take. They might also welcome the increased engagement of citizens in national debates around what makes people happy. However, their positive reactions could well be tempered by an element of disappointment.

Much of the modern-day governmental and political interest in wellbeing is rooted less in utilitarianism and more in a growing appreciation by economists of the deficiencies of economic growth, especially measured by GDP (gross domestic product) as the sole objective of policy makers. To best understand this you can fast-forward from Jefferson, the third president, to the brother of the 35th, Robert F. Kennedy, whose well-quoted speech most eloquently expresses the issue:

> Yet the gross national product does not allow for the health of our children, the quality of their education or the joy of their play. It does not include the beauty of our poetry or the strength of our marriages, the intelligence of our public debate or the integrity of our public officials. It measures neither our wit nor our courage, neither our wisdom nor our learning, neither our compassion nor our devotion to our country, it measures everything in short, except that which makes life worthwhile. And it can tell us everything about America except why we are proud that we are Americans.
> Robert F. Kennedy, University of Kansas, March 18, 1968

Kennedy's key message in his speech, which is consistent with the much more recent findings of the 2009 Commission on the Measurement of Economic Performance and Social Progress (Stiglitz, Sen, & Fitoussi, 2009), is that GDP is a far from perfect indicator of societal progress and of the quality of life of a nation, including the state of the environment. Indeed it was not designed for this purpose. There are many deficiencies, not least that it does not capture whether people actually feel their own lives or those of others are improving. Objective measures of progress, such as GDP per capita, that describe the social and economic conditions of individuals, can

410

often be out of kilter with subjective assessments made by individuals and related to what they are actually experiencing in their lives; the difference between actual crime and fear of crime is a good example of this. The implications for policy makers can be significant, but this does not mean that governments are planning to drop GDP. Much of the effort and modern-day interest is focused on developing complementary measures of wellbeing to enable more rounded assessments of societal progress. This is backed by advances in science which mean that we can now more robustly measure subjective wellbeing, including life satisfaction and happiness.

Here again our utilitarian philosophers might well be disappointed to learn that happiness is only one of a number of subjective and objective measures that governments are considering; albeit an interesting one with historical roots and that understandably gains a lot of public attention. This broader perspective on wellbeing, with happiness only part of a dashboard of measures, might appear on the face of it to be slightly more prosaic, but the reality is quite the opposite. The wellbeing agenda represents a bold attempt to understand, beyond the economic, what really matters to people and what we value most in life. This stands to provide a much richer picture of societal progress than we currently have, and will as a consequence support better decision making not just by governments, but by individuals and civil society as well. By challenging the way we have measured progress for decades, and offering us new perspectives and insights around different challenges and courses of action, these developments arguably match the boldness of thought, if not the precise philosophy of Hutcheson, Bentham, and Mill. Furthermore, they are consistent with the ambition and vision of Jefferson; we clearly stand to learn much over the next few years.

In this chapter we focus on the specific experience of the United Kingdom. We start by exploring in more detail why governments are interested in wellbeing, outlining U.K. Government measurement policy, and highlighting some of the international context. We follow this by presenting the United Kingdom's national wellbeing measurement program, highlighting the results of a national debate on "What matters" in 2011 and some early measurement results from a population survey in the same year. The next section focuses on policy and explores what policy makers and practitioners can do practically to reflect wellbeing in the decisions they make. In the last section we explore one specific policy area—wellbeing at work—and highlight a few practical "wellbeing at work" policies and toolkits. The chapter ends with a few closing remarks.

It is important to highlight, up front, that this is a fast-developing area. In a sense we are presenting a snapshot of some of the progress made in the United Kingdom by early 2012 and as we write it is still very much "early days" for the wellbeing agenda.

# Wellbeing Policy in the United Kingdom

### Separating Wellbeing from Growth as a Policy Objective

Government policy is ultimately about improving the quality of life for citizens. Traditionally, policy makers have focused on and prioritized economic factors such as growth and income. Achieving economic growth, in particular, has often been viewed as being synonymous with improving the quality of life, and raising the living standards of all. Higher growth, the theory goes, leads to greater wealth, thus giving people more money to consume goods and services to which they attribute value, from which they gain utility, ultimately leading to their enhanced wellbeing. This traditional guiding theory for policy makers has, however, been challenged by the work of economists such as Richard Easterlin (1974). The "Easterlin Paradox" presents contrary evidence which highlights that despite getting wealthier, citizens are not reporting getting any happier. If you ask people to rate how satisfied they are with their lives, say on a scale of 0–10, one of a number of wellbeing questions that have been asked on international surveys over recent years, the survey results appear to show that average wellbeing scores have failed to rise in both the United States and United Kingdom even during periods when median incomes have risen. The argument from Easterlin, and other economists since, suggests that increasing economic prosperity does matter, but only to a point. Beyond this point the benefits to wellbeing slow down, further growth delivers decreasing marginal returns, and it can even potentially undermine wellbeing. In simple terms, and in line with earlier assessments of needs, the suggestion is that once our basic material needs for food, shelter, and clothing are met, then other factors rise to the surface as being intrinsically important to us. What we do in life, the knowledge we accumulate, our relationships, levels of autonomy, and the communities in which we live, all matter significantly to us and many of these factors are less material and much less dependent on income and economic growth.

There is, of course, debate around the relationship between growth and wellbeing. Some research, for example, indicates that even for industrialized

412

nations long-term growth is associated with increases in subjective wellbeing, with around two thirds of countries experiencing increases in life satisfaction between 1981 and 2007 over a period of global growth (Inglehart, Foa, Peterson, & Welzel, 2008). Furthermore, it is clear that incomes do matter to people and money does tend to contribute to our happiness, dispelling any idealistic notions that it does not. We also understand that the consequences of receding growth and recession can be particularly bad for people's wellbeing, for example, through increased unemployment. So where does this leave the policy maker?

The research and continued debate around the Easterlin Paradox has, at a minimum, challenged our traditional economic tenets. Whether you accept the paradox or not, it is clear that the relationship between economic growth and wellbeing, as measured from and experienced by citizens, is more complex than we have perhaps traditionally allowed for in policy. Growth still matters but it is also reasonable to conclude that other factors matter significantly as well. Many of these factors lie outside traditional market structures and beyond our national accounts but they can be at least as important to our wellbeing as our economic circumstances: our family, relationships, and the community in which we live. So measures of economic growth and consumption of goods and services can only ever provide a partial picture of societal progress and this might even be a diminishing picture if, as is suggested, other nonmarket factors become increasingly important as an economy matures.

The main implication for policy makers is that growth maximization policies can no longer be taken for granted as also improving the wellbeing of a nation. A shrewd policy maker, looking at the evidence, would separate the two objectives and expose the potential convergence and divergence between them in their decision making. In some cases the objectives will converge, with growth policies leading to improved wellbeing or vice versa. In others, however, there will be clear tensions between the objectives; for example, restrictions on promoting certain products (alcohol or tobacco) or advertising to vulnerable audiences such as young children might well have positive wellbeing benefits at the expense of short-term sales and growth. In some cases, especially during tough economic times, growth might still be the most important objective. Nevertheless, understanding the implications of policies on wellbeing enables us to decide where to draw the line and to ensure that economic policies do not inadvertently become "growth at any cost," at the expense of, for example, specific sections of society, future generations, the environment, or the cohesion of our communities.

Of course, one of the consequences of decoupling wellbeing from growth as a separate and distinct objective of policy making is that it becomes necessary to measure it. If, as is now widely recognized, GDP and GDP per capita are not the only measures of national progress and quality of life to focus on, and they are less reliable proxy indicators of citizen wellbeing than we previously thought, then we clearly need to develop other measures to support the decisions we make. This need is brought into even sharper relief when looking at the measurement deficiencies of GDP. Around this there is much broader agreement, much less debate, and a compelling case for moving beyond GDP.

## Seperating Wellbeing from GDP as a Measure

GDP is the value of the goods and services produced by defined sectors of the economy: agriculture, manufacturing, energy, construction, the service sector, and government. If the GDP measure is higher than the previous period, the economy is growing. If it is lower, the economy is contracting. GDP is measured to internationally agreed standards and therefore provides an idea of the relative performance of different countries' economies.

It has long been argued that the progress of a country or group of countries cannot be assessed by looking just at economic growth as measured by GDP. To be fair, economists and statisticians have always acknowledged this, and often emphasize that it was never designed to capture everything that determines society's wellbeing. Nevertheless, it has undoubtedly become the dominant measure of progress for policy makers. This is not surprising considering, in the postwar developed world, one of the principal concerns of governments has been to ensure continued economic growth. The problems and deficiencies with GDP are, however, becoming clearer, and it is not just the long-acknowledged issue that it provides an impartial picture of societal progress. It can provide a misleading one, which can impact the decisions we make. The criticisms leveled at GDP are numerous and we will only dwell on a few key ones here.

GDP does not account for important economic functions performed in the household and voluntary sectors. For example, when someone does their own laundry, it is not recorded in GDP, but paying someone else to do it is recorded. While this might, on the face of it, appear trivial, estimates by the U.K. Office for National Statistics (ONS) have shown that the total value of home production is around the same size as conventional GDP. This may change markedly our understanding of the size of total activity in the country and cause us to reassess whether changes in conventional GDP over time reflect, to some extent, shifts between the paid and unpaid components in a broadly stable volume of activity.

Some of the activities that are not included in GDP are significantly enhancing to our own wellbeing and that of others. Volunteering, for example, in the absence of any form of financial transaction, will not be fully reflected in national accounts. With two in five of the adult population of England volunteering on a regular basis, and two in three annually, this represents significant levels of unaccounted economic activity. If this had been routinely valued and reflected in published national wellbeing statistics, to be considered alongside or as part of GDP, then perhaps it would have exposed some important trade-offs in recent years. For example, employment is also important for our wellbeing, but if we work longer hours and give more time to our employers in either paid or unpaid overtime, this leaves us less time to participate in voluntary activities. At the extremes, GDP is boosted by the increased goods and services we produce, but this is at the expense of national wellbeing. Within the tension of these objectives there are real choices to make. With U.K. workers putting in some of the longest hours in Europe combined with declines in the rate of volunteering over the last decade, measuring wellbeing alongside GDP could help policy makers, and indeed individuals and businesses, to make more informed choices.

A further limitation of GDP is that it says nothing about the distribution of income between groups at a point in time or about the distribution of income over time. The headline national figures that attract most attention are silent on fairness and whether sections of society are missing out on the benefits. They are equally silent on whether underlying economic activities are sustainable (e.g., fueled by debt or the depletion of natural resources), or whether there are longer term societal risks associated with them that have to be managed (e.g., management and processing of other nations' nuclear waste).

Of particular concern, however, are activities which contribute positively toward GDP that are clearly associated with reductions in wellbeing. Divorce has a huge impact on wellbeing yet the associated legal fees contribute positively toward economic growth. High crime levels and fear of crime may drive growth through reparation costs, or via the sales of security products and services, yet few would claim that crime is good for our wellbeing. Other examples are associated with network effects: the more people travel, the more transport contributes toward growth but the greater the potential for congestion and delays. Finally, we also know that GDP can be boosted through reconstruction following natural disasters, in contrast to the human misery of the disaster itself.

So it is clear that for a full picture of "how we are doing" we need to look at wider measures of economic and social progress, including the impact of human activity on the environment. There has been much work on this at an international level to build on.

## The International Context

Recognizing the measurement deficiencies, there has been widespread cross-national interest not only in developing additional indicators of economic wellbeing, but in reporting these as part of an assessment of "the triple bottom line," covering the economy, society, and the environment. These arguments have been fundamental to several international initiatives set up to measure national wellbeing and progress, most notably the Organisation for Economic Co-operation and Development (OECD). Measuring the wellbeing and progress of societies is one of the key priorities of the OECD. As stated on their website: "The mission of the Organisation for Economic Co-operation and Development (OECD) is to promote policies that will improve the economic and social wellbeing of people around the world" (http://www.oecd.org). At the OECD World Forum on Statistics, Knowledge and Policy in Istanbul in 2007, a declaration was issued calling for the production of high-quality facts-based information that can be used by all of society to form a shared view of national wellbeing and its evolution over time. The Human Development Index (HDI), which was developed in 1990, continues to be an important part of this measurement landscape, providing internationally comparable indices of wellbeing covering health, knowledge, and income.

The agenda gained momentum from the report in 2009 to President Sarkozy of France from his Commission on the Measurement of Economic Performance and Social Progress, written by a team led by Joseph Stiglitz, Amartya Sen, and Jean-Paul Fitoussi (Stiglitz et al., 2009). It concluded that "the time is ripe for our measurement system to shift emphasis from measuring economic production to measuring people's wellbeing." There were 12 recommendations (see Box 19.1), including one that national statistical offices start measuring subjective wellbeing by incorporating "questions to capture people's life evaluations, hedonic experiences and priorities in their own survey."

**Box 19.1.** Stiglitz, Sen, Fitoussi Recommendations.

1. When evaluating material wellbeing, look at income and consumption rather than production.
2. Emphasize the household perspective.
3. Consider income and consumption jointly with wealth.
4. Give more prominence to the distribution of income, consumption, and wealth.
5. Broaden income measures to nonmarket activities.
6. Quality of life depends on people's objective conditions and capabilities. Steps should be taken to improve measures of people's health, education, personal activities, and environmental conditions. In particular, substantial effort should be devoted to developing and implementing robust, reliable measures of social connections, political voice, and insecurity that can be shown to predict life satisfaction.
7. Quality-of-life indicators in all the dimensions covered should assess inequalities in a comprehensive way.
8. Surveys should be designed to assess the links between various quality-of-life domains for each person, and this information should be used when designing policies in various fields.
9. Statistical offices should provide the information needed to aggregate across quality-of-life dimensions, allowing the construction of different indices.
10. Measures of both objective and subjective wellbeing provide key information about people's quality of life. Statistical offices should incorporate questions to capture people's life evaluations, hedonic experiences and priorities in their own survey.
11. Sustainability assessment requires a well-identified dashboard of indicators. The distinctive features of the components of this dashboard should be that they are interpretable as variations of some underlying "stocks." A monetary index of sustainability has its place in such a dashboard but, under the current state of the art, it should remain essentially focused on economic aspects of sustainability.

> 12. The environmental aspects of sustainability deserve a separate follow-up based on a well-chosen set of physical indicators. In particular there is a need for a clear indicator of our proximity to dangerous levels of environmental damage (such as associated with climate change or the depletion of fishing stocks).

Building on this momentum, international and national organizations have taken forward programs to develop their own measures. In May 2011 the OECD published an experimental set of measures comparing international evidence on wellbeing in developed countries and selected nonmember countries, as well as an online interactive instrument, the Better Life Index (http://www.oecdbetterlifeindex.org/). This allows users to measure wellbeing across countries and to create their own customized indices. The set of wellbeing indicators contained in the report represent an attempt to go beyond the conceptual stage, helping give a more accurate picture of the needs of citizens and policy makers. In October 2011, the OECD published a more in-depth analysis, "How's life," and also began, at this time, exploring potential comparable indicators for regions and other areas within countries (OECD, 2011).

The European Commission has also been progressing work on wellbeing. In response to the Stiglitz–Sen–Fitoussi Commission (Stiglitz et al., 2009) and the 2009 Communication of the European Commission on *GDP and beyond: Measuring progress in a changing world*, an EU Sponsorship Group on "Measuring progress, wellbeing and sustainable development" was convened, composed of 15 EU member states including the United Kingdom. This group began exploring wellbeing across the continent, working with Eurostat and each of the relevant National Statistics Institutes which together form the European statistical system.

Also, in July 2011, the United Nations (UN) General Assembly adopted a resolution calling on member states to undertake steps that give more importance to happiness and wellbeing in determining how to achieve and measure social and economic development (United Nations General Assembly, 2011). The resolution was proposed by Bhutan, which uses gross national happiness as well as GDP as markers of success.

## United Kingdom's Measurement Program: 2010–2012

It must be stressed that there has been government interest in wellbeing in the United Kingdom prior to 2010—for example, the Prime Minister's Strategy Unit published a report in 2002 (Donovan & Halpern, 2002)—but in this section we focus on policy at the time of writing this chapter around the period 2010–2012, key objectives, and the United Kingdom's experience implementing it. The international context presented in the preceding section, backed by a rigorous understanding of the limitations of our current international system of economic measurement for understanding societal progress, has provided a firm foundation for wellbeing policy in the United Kingdom. In 2010, the Prime Minister David Cameron committed to:

> start measuring our progress as a country, not just by how our economy is growing, but by how our lives are improving; not just by our standard of living, but by our quality of life.
>
> Prime Minister David Cameron (2010)

In response to national and international interest, the U.K. Office for National Statistics (ONS) established a program to develop and publish an accepted and trusted set of national statistics for wellbeing to complement traditional economic measures such as GDP (see ONS, 2011a for details of the program and for reports and outputs, including from the national debate on "what matters"). There were a number of goals associated with establishing this measurement program. The first of these was to focus government decisions on what really matters to people. The evidence is clear that we can no longer reliably conflate growth and wellbeing into a single policy objective. These are both, in themselves, distinct objectives of government. Of course they are interrelated, and interestingly, no sooner do you start to discuss separating them as objectives than policy makers instinctively bring them both together again; "Is wellbeing good for growth?" is a common question asked. The microeconomic equivalent is similarly asked by those working on individual policies, "can we monetize wellbeing benefits and add them into the economic case for a policy?" While these are worthy questions in many respects, and sometimes worth pursuing, they do miss the point of separating out wellbeing as a unique objective in the first place. It is by considering the implications of decisions on what really matters to people alongside, not in place of, economic impact that we can expose the trade-offs, tensions, and synergies between them.

Measuring wellbeing should lead to better policy decisions, and related to this it is useful to hypothesize whether we would have avoided the financial and debt crises in the first decade of this century if a broader dashboard of national measures had been available in the preceding years. There is more than a hint in the Stiglitz–Sen–Fitoussi Commission (Stiglitz et al., 2009) that different decisions might well have been taken by policy makers, business, and citizens if this had been the case. It is, of course, difficult to prove either way now, but this is perhaps one of a number of "success criteria" to consider: How fit for purpose are the final wellbeing measures as an "early warning system" for policy makers, businesses, and individuals?

Transparency is another goal of the wellbeing program. It is often said that "what gets measured gets done." Measuring and publishing data will clearly lead to an increase in the importance and consideration of wellbeing. If wellbeing reflects, as it should, what really matters to people, rather than what governments think matter or what they have traditionally measured, then this will provide a positive challenge to the public sector, and potentially a spur for innovation in policy and reform of public services. However, government is not solely responsible for the wellbeing of the nation; the human resource policies of businesses, the actions of a strong and vibrant civil society, and the life choices we all make as individuals matter tremendously. Transparent reporting will support the actions and choices of others as well as government.

A final point to consider is the benefit we derive as a nation from the process of measurement and the related consultation to define wellbeing. Asking people what makes them happy, and what matters most in their lives is relevant to a wider debate about the kind of society we want to live in. It is a debate that engages people and that they care about. There has been a clear appetite for consultation on wellbeing in the United Kingdom and a goal of the program has been to stimulate and nurture this. In addition to involving citizens and individuals there has also been a wider debate on measuring wellbeing in the media, and with think tanks and politicians participating. Box 19.2. highlights some of the debating points. It is fair to say that the most common focus is "happiness." This is engaging as a subject, people are able to relate to it personally, and, as such, it is a useful focal point for a consultation. However, "happiness" can tend to crowd out and obscure the breadth and importance of other wellbeing measures. As a result, some have questioned the case for developing a "happiness index," when in fact the program is neither developing an index nor defining wellbeing exclusively as happiness.

**Box 19.2.**  Wellbeing Measurement Debate in the U.K.

| Debating points made | Policy rationale |
|---|---|
| Easterlin Paradox false and growth/income is important to wellbeing | Still much debate, but Easterlin only part of the justification. There is much wider agreement on deficiencies of GDP, and issues with conflation of growth and wellbeing |
| It's a "Happiness Index"—out of touch with reality | No intention to create an index; happiness only one of a number of measures of wellbeing. Status quo arguably more out of touch because not capturing people's real life experiences |
| GDP is being replaced by happiness | No intention to replace GDP—wellbeing will complement it |
| Measuring happiness will lead to utilitarianism policies that have been largely discredited | Wellbeing much broader than happiness, to support more rounded decision making. No policy on utilitarianism |
| It is an attempt by government to "control" happiness | No attempt to control happiness. Recognizing government policy already impacts wellbeing in decision making and in public services; it can more proactively account for these |
| The implications of wellbeing will be more regulation and centralization | No, quite likely the opposite as wellbeing can be enhanced by these other stated aims of government including decentralization, localism, reducing regulation |

| Debating points made | Policy rationale |
|---|---|
| Cynical political timing to deflect attention from lower growth | A difficult time yes, cynical, no. Timing largely coinciding with maturing of academic literature and international work (e.g., Stiglitz) |
| Largely "middle class" agenda not rooted in the practical difficulties people are facing | Wellbeing should inform decisions and choices that affect all groups across society. There have been misery/deprivation indices for many years; wellbeing adds a new dimension |
| Subjective wellbeing (SWB) measures are weak and don't tell you anything you don't already know | The headline measures might give this impression, because for example the overall averages are relatively stable, but the underlying analytical power of SWB is unquestionable; also a potent analytical proxy for welfare/utility |
| It costs a lot to measure wellbeing and there are other priorities | It can't be measured robustly for free, but can be measured efficiently. Ultimately this is about measuring and better understanding what is important to people and their priorities. It is likely a very small investment to complement GDP, in relation to the costs of GDP measurement over the years |

It is also worth recognizing, at this point, that the United Kingdom enjoys a strong network of civil society organizations, universities, and think tanks with a real expertise in wellbeing and this has helped to enrich the political and policy debate considerably. Furthermore, there has been cross-political party support and interest in the agenda, as evidenced by a consistently well-attended and active All Party Parliamentary Group on Wellbeing Economics.

In this section we have covered, at a high level, the United Kingdom's policy of measuring wellbeing, some of the objectives of the program, and we have also touched upon aspects of the national debate. Later we outline how wellbeing can support policy making, but before that we will present more details on how the United Kingdom is actually measuring wellbeing.

## Approach to Wellbeing Measurement and Early Results

### Developing a Measurement Framework for Wellbeing

It is no small challenge to define and measure the wellbeing of a nation, for it to be robustly grounded in theory, yet practical enough for the policy maker, practitioner, citizen, business, and charity to use in supporting the varied decisions and choices they make. There are diverse sets of stakeholders with differing interests and perspectives, with some calling for clear definitions and conceptual frameworks, while others seek adoption of a more pragmatic and practical approach. In particular, there are differing views on what the focus should be, and the best approach to adopt.

There is a school of thought that says the wellbeing of the nation can be nothing other than the sum of the wellbeing of all its citizens. Individual wellbeing is certainly much better understood than community or national-level wellbeing. The World Health Organization's (WHO) definitions of health and of mental health both refer to wellbeing and there are several established approaches to the self-assessment of individual wellbeing grounded in psychological theory. Two examples are the Warwick–Edinburgh Mental Wellbeing Scale (http://wrap.warwick.ac.uk/543/) and the WHO quality-of-life measures developed at the WHO Field Centre at the University of Bath (http://www.bath.ac.uk/whoqol/). Under this school of thought, the task is to measure individual wellbeing, summarize how it is distributed, and analyze it against the various internal and external drivers and influences on individual wellbeing. Related to this is the capabilities approach, assessing how individuals are reaching their potential.

Others say there is more to national wellbeing than the sum of the individuals. The approach adopted in the Stiglitz–Sen–Fitoussi Commission (Stiglitz et al., 2009), drawing perhaps on the earlier social indicators movement, is essentially to present a statistical description of all aspects of the economy, society, and the state of the natural environment. In such descriptions, structure is provided by the three pillars: economic performance, quality of life/social progress, and the environment. These pillars, especially quality of life, can be further divided into a set of domains. There are also some cross-cutting issues that relate to each pillar that need to be reported against, especially equality and sustainability.

> At the national level, round-tables should be established, with the involvement of stakeholders, to identify and prioritise those indicators that carry to potential for a shared view of how social progress is happening and how it can be sustained over time.
>
> Commission on Measurement of Economic Performance and Social Progress, Stiglitz et al. (2009)

In order to take account of all of these various perspectives, the ONS established a number of panels and advisory groups at the beginning of the program. These were essential for informing the early measurement work and follow-on development. However, arguably more important than this was the citizen perspective. Success very much depends on establishing a set of measures that are accepted and trusted by citizens. From November 2010 to April 2011, the ONS undertook a national debate on "What matters to you?" holding hundreds of events around the country, involving thousands of people. Those interested could also express their opinions through online discussions, a survey and other social media activities, and this was further encouraged by considerable news media interest. There was an excellent overall response to this debate, demonstrating a clear appetite and interest; it generated tens of thousands of responses, some of which were from organizations and groups representing thousands more people.

The findings from the national debate were published in July 2011 and highlighted a wide range of opinions about what constitutes national wellbeing (ONS, 2011). Some common themes clearly emerged, however, such as health, good relationships with friends and family, job satisfaction, economic security, education, and the condition of the environment (present and future). It was also evident that to the public the wellbeing of the individual is central to an understanding of national wellbeing. This and other findings from the national debate have informed an overall measurement framework as presented in Figure 19.1.

The proposed measurement approach is balanced, comprising both objective and subjective measures for wellbeing. While some have argued that subjective assessments by individuals are the key indicators of wellbeing, the framework proposed emphasizes that objective measures are also important to get a fuller picture of progress. Furthermore, evidence of convergence and

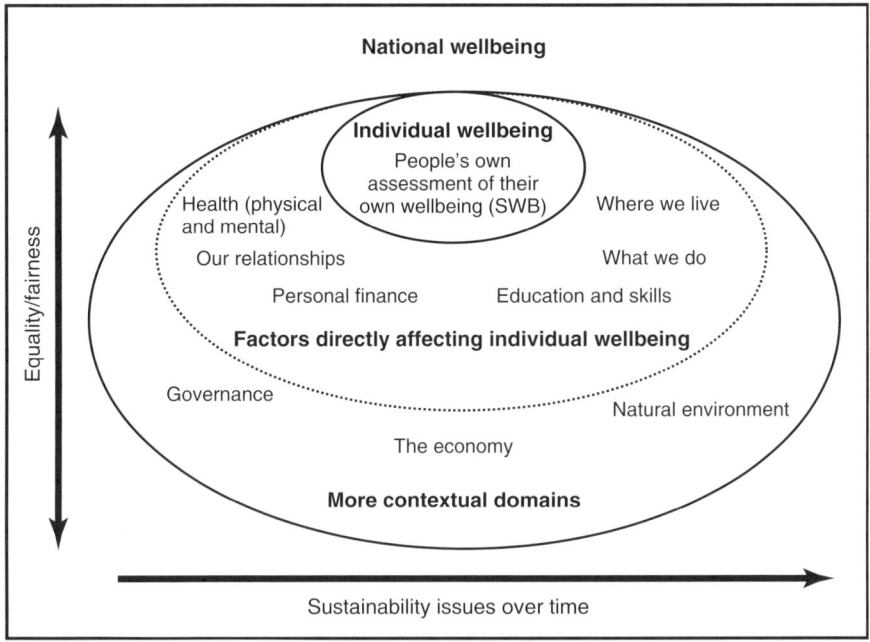

**Figure 19.1.** The Office of National Statistics Representation of National Well-being. Reproduced with permission from Beaumont (2011).

divergence of subjective and objective measures should be both interesting and valuable to the policy maker. That said, there are a number of real innovations in this national measurement framework and having individual subjective wellbeing at its core is undoubtedly one of them. For this reason we will dwell on it further.

## Subjective Wellbeing Measurement

Individual wellbeing is central to the proposed national measurement frame-work, and one of the most effective ways of capturing this is to ask people to make an assessment of their own wellbeing. Such subjective assessments have not traditionally attracted anywhere near the levels of attention from policy makers given to objective ones, so in many respects this is new and challeng-ing for the public sector. The United Kingdom is not alone in collecting subjective wellbeing information. The OECD and Eurostat, as well as other national statistical offices around the world, are increasingly recognizing its importance. Furthermore, there is a robust evidence base on which to build; questions have been asked for many years in United Kingdom and

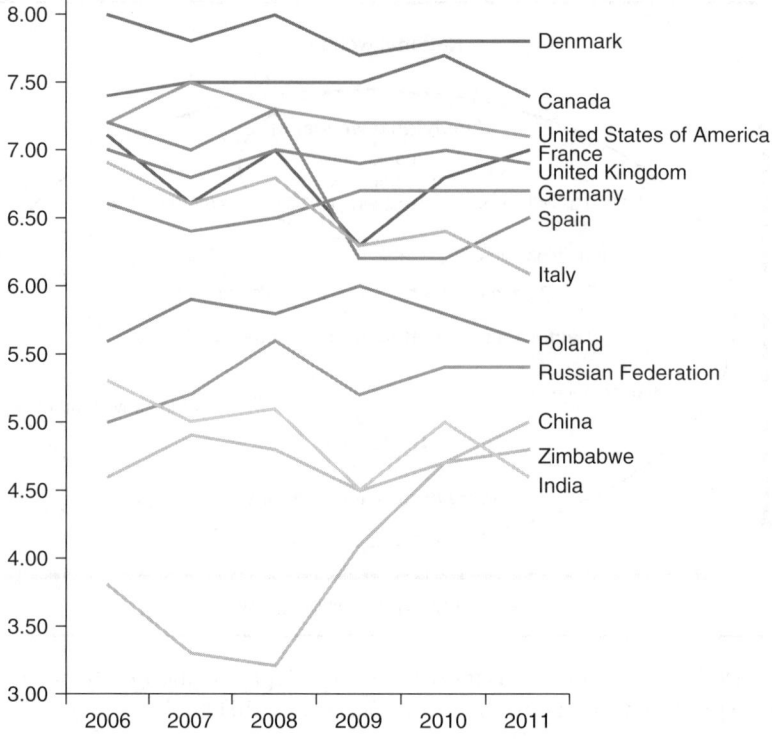

**Figure 19.2.** Life Satisfaction Scores for Selected Countries. The data are derived from a Cantril Scale ladder question. Gallup World View. Adapted from http://www.gallup.com/se/126848/WorldView.aspx.

international social surveys, such as Gallup World Poll, Eurobarometer, and the British Household Panel Survey, and there is a burgeoning academic literature around the results. All this means that it is now possible to collect reliable and meaningful data, albeit with a need for more research into collection, presentation, and analysis.

As an example of some of the international data available, Figure 19.2 presents subjective wellbeing scores for a selection of countries between 2006 and 2011. The data derives from the Gallup World View survey which asks respondents to rate their lives on a "Cantril Scale," an 11-step ladder with the top (10) representing the best possible life and the bottom step (0) the worst. Denmark has among the highest levels of life satisfaction of this set of countries. Canada, and other countries not shown, such as Holland, Australia, and Finland, also have relatively high levels of wellbeing. Zimbabwe has the lowest score in the group, although the trend is upwards with scores increasing significantly between 2006 and 2011, and it is also important to point out that there are other counties not presented that have lower scores still.

In April 2011, the ONS included subjective wellbeing questions for the first time in the United Kingdom's Integrated Household Survey (IHS) and the Opinions Survey (OPN). These questions were developed with expert academic advice and represent a balanced methodology, drawing from three different approaches:

- The *evaluative* approach asks individuals to step back and reflect on their life and make a cognitive assessment of how their life is going overall.
- The *eudemonic* approach is also sometimes referred to as the psychological or functioning/flourishing approach. This draws on self-determination theory and tends to measure such things as people's sense of meaning and purpose in life, connections with family and friends, a sense of control and whether they feel part of something bigger than themselves.
- The *experience* approach seeks to measure people's positive and negative emotions over a short time frame, to capture people's wellbeing on a day-to-day basis.

The four headline questions included in the ONS surveys are shown in Box 19.3.

---

**Box 19.3.** Experimental Subjective Wellbeing Questions Asked in the ONS Household Surveys.

Overall, how satisfied are you with your life nowadays? (evaluative approach)

Overall, to what extent do you feel the things you do in your life are worthwhile? (eudemonic approach)

Overall, how happy did you feel yesterday? (experience approach)

Overall, how anxious did you feel yesterday? (experience approach)

Respondents are asked to provide an answer from 0 to 10, where 0 is "not at all" and 10 is "completely."

---

An initial set of results against these questions was published in December 2011 (ONS, 2011b). Estimates for Great Britain, using data collected between April and August 2011, include:

- When asked, "Overall, how satisfied are you with your life nowadays?" the majority (76%) of adults (aged 16 and over) were estimated to have a rating of 7 out 10 or more. However, a minority (8%) were estimated to be below 5 out of 10. The mean score for this question was 7.4 out of 10.

- When asked, "Overall, to what extent do you think the things you do in your life are worthwhile?" a slightly larger proportion (78%) of adults rated this at 7 or more out of 10. A smaller proportion of adults gave lower ratings to this question, with 6% giving a rating below 5 out of 10. The mean score for the "worthwhile" question was higher than the "life satisfaction" question at 7.6 out of 10.

- When asked, "Overall, how happy did you feel yesterday?" again the majority (73%) of adults responded with 7 or more out of 10. However, the spread of ratings was wider than for the "life satisfaction" and "worthwhile" questions. For example, a higher proportion of people gave higher ratings (36% giving 9 or 10 out of 10) to the "happy yesterday" question as well as lower scores (12% below 5 out of 10). The mean score for the "happiness yesterday" question was 7.4 out of 10.

- When asked, "Overall, how anxious did you feel yesterday?" the ratings were even more spread out. Although over half (57%) had ratings of less than 4 out of 10, a sizable proportion (27%) of people had ratings above 5 out of 10 (that is, closer to 10, feeling "completely anxious" than 0, "not at all anxious"). The mean score for this question was 3.4 out of 10.

Table 19.1 presents pairwise correlations between the responses to the four subjective wellbeing questions from the 2011 Opinions Survey. The responses to all of the wellbeing questions are correlated, negatively or positively, as would be expected. However, the lower levels of correlation, particularly between anxiety and the three other questions, suggests that they are usefully picking up different responses. So the initial analysis appears to confirm that while the four questions are related and add to each other, they also pick up different concepts. There are interesting distinctions between them which emphasizes the multidimensionality of subjective wellbeing and

**Table 19.1.** Pairwise Correlations between Subjective Well-being Questions.

|  | Satisfied | Worthwhile | Happy | Anxious |
|---|---|---|---|---|
| Satisfied | 1 |  |  |  |
| Worthwhile | 0.66* | 1 |  |  |
| Happy | 0.55* | 0.51* | 1 |  |
| Anxious | −0.26* | −0.22* | −0.39* | 1 |

*Correlation is significant at the .01 level.
From ONS (2011b).

also suggests that subjective wellbeing is not easily reduced to a single response.

When the estimates were examined by age there appeared to be a "U-shape" relationship for the "life satisfaction," "worthwhile," and "happy yesterday" questions. That is, younger and older adults in Great Britain reported higher levels to these questions on average than people in their middle years. Highest levels were for those aged 16–19 and aged 65–74. For "anxious yesterday," this pattern did not appear in the data. Good health and having a partner also appear to be associated with higher levels of life satisfaction and happiness, while, in contrast, being unemployed is associated with lower levels. Results were also published on more detailed aspects of subjective wellbeing and on some methodological testing.

Getting below the headline descriptive statistics also begins to reveal some of the analytical power of wellbeing.

Table 19.2 presents the results of an ordinary least squares (OLS) linear regression with life satisfaction as the dependent variable against a range of independent variables. Interaction variables between income and employment have also been added to account for the relationship between employment status and income. The model uses early, part-year but nevertheless representative, data from the ONS measurement program in 2011 and is based on a relatively small sample size of 3,391 observations. Some points to note on the results:

- The model explains around 14% of the variation in life satisfaction. This fits with results in other studies and is typical of the amount of variation that can be explained by background characteristics and circumstances alone.
- Background characteristics and circumstances that are associated with higher levels of life satisfaction include:

**Table 19.2.** Linear Regression for Life Satisfaction, 2011 Opinions Survey.

| Numbers of observations | 3,391 |
| --- | --- |
| $F(36, 3354)$ | 10.42 |
| Prob $> F$ | 0.0000 |
| $R$-squared | 0.1444 |
| Root mean squared error | 1.8074 |

| Variable | Coef. | Std.err. | $t$ | $P > |t|$ | [95% Conf interval] | |
| --- | --- | --- | --- | --- | --- | --- |
| Female | 0.166* | 0.0747222 | 2.22 | 0.027 | 0.0192402 | 0.3122518 |
| Black, minority ethnic | −0.199 | 0.1590448 | −1.25 | 0.211 | −0.5105974 | 0.1130717 |
| Age | −0.137*** | 0.0176930 | −7.74 | 0.000 | −0.1717011 | −0.1023209 |
| Age squared | 0.002*** | 0.0001972 | 8.51 | 0.000 | 0.0012912 | 0.0020646 |
| Single (ref Married) | −0.561*** | 0.1186353 | −4.73 | 0.000 | −0.7937876 | −0.3285778 |
| Widowed | −0.833*** | 0.2137498 | −3.90 | 0.000 | −1.2521490 | −0.4139622 |
| Divorced separated | −1.024*** | 0.1315336 | −7.78 | 0.000 | −1.2817080 | −0.7659197 |
| 1 child (ref no children) | 0.090 | 0.1115662 | 0.81 | 0.420 | −0.1288403 | 0.3086489 |
| 2 or more children | 0.386*** | 0.1000087 | 3.86 | 0.000 | 0.1896694 | 0.5818376 |
| Long illness | −0.522*** | 0.0893707 | −5.85 | 0.000 | −0.6976732 | −0.3472200 |
| Mortgage(ref Own House) | −0.125 | 0.1037893 | −1.20 | 0.230 | −0.3280353 | 0.0789580 |
| Rent social | −0.609*** | 0.1486249 | −4.10 | 0.000 | −0.9006536 | −0.3178444 |
| Rent private | −0.281* | 0.1375316 | −2.04 | 0.41 | −0.5502075 | −0.0108989 |
| Other Quals (ref No Quals) | −0.001 | 0.1552240 | 0.00 | 0.997 | −0.3049472 | 0.3037393 |
| <Degree | 0.199 | 0.1286386 | 1.55 | 0.122 | −0.0530445 | 0.4513918 |
| Degree | 0.378** | 0.1434329 | 2.64 | 0.008 | 0.967754 | 0.6592249 |

| | | | | | |
|---|---|---|---|---|---|
| Low income | 0.218 | 0.1593124 | 1.37 | 0.171 | −0.0944415 | 0.5302772 |
| Unemployed (ref Inactive) | −0.693* | 0.3101891 | −2.24 | 0.025 | −1.3014880 | −0.0851297 |
| Employed | 0.447** | 0.1371528 | 3.26 | 0.001 | 0.1783819 | 0.7162050 |
| Unemployed low income | 0.161 | 0.4039684 | 0.40 | 0.690 | −0.6308982 | 0.9532005 |
| Employed low income | −0.712** | 0.2733276 | −2.60 | 0.009 | −1.2476990 | −0.1758874 |
| North East (ref London) | 0.629** | 0.2329004 | 2.70 | 0.007 | 0.1718988 | 1.0851810 |
| North West | 0.463** | 0.1782227 | 2.60 | 0.009 | 0.1132930 | 0.8121656 |
| Yorks and Humber | 0.432* | 0.1840641 | 2.35 | 0.019 | 0.0707502 | 0.7925288 |
| East Midlands | 0.293 | 0.1858166 | 1.58 | 0.115 | −0.0716492 | 0.6570013 |
| West Midlands | 0.222 | 0.1901088 | 1.17 | 0.242 | −0.1503726 | 0.5951094 |
| East of England | 0.286 | 0.1813418 | 1.58 | 0.115 | −0.0695160 | 0.6415872 |
| South East | 0.377* | 0.1701114 | 2.22 | 0.027 | 0.0438486 | 0.7109138 |
| South West | 0.435* | 0.1783501 | 2.44 | 0.015 | 0.0848582 | 0.7842302 |
| Wales | 0.385 | 0.2120216 | 1.82 | 0.069 | −0.0303454 | 0.8010640 |
| Scotland | 0.282 | 0.1915752 | 1.47 | 0.142 | −0.0939761 | 0.6572559 |
| Has a car | 0.028 | 0.1256900 | 0.22 | 0.825 | −0.2185625 | 0.2743113 |
| Survey self completion | −0.093 | 0.0726747 | −1.28 | 0.200 | −0.2355805 | 0.0494019 |
| Survey June (ref April) | −0.045 | 0.1000424 | −0.45 | 0.650 | −0.2414917 | 0.1508087 |
| Survey Jul | 0.099 | 0.0946419 | 1.04 | 0.297 | −0.0869062 | 0.2842171 |
| Survey Aug | −0.055 | 0.1008984 | −0.55 | 0.584 | −0.2530245 | 0.1426329 |
| Constant | 9.442*** | 0.4750136 | 19.88 | 0.000 | 8.5101630 | 10.3728500 |

From ONS (2011b).

- being female compared with being male;
- having two or more children compared with none;
- having a degree compared with having no qualifications;
- living in the Northern English regions compared with London.

- Background characteristics and circumstances that are associated with lower levels of life satisfaction include:

  - being single, widowed or divorced compared to being married, or cohabiting;
  - being in poor health;
  - renting or being in social housing compared to owning your own home.

- Examining the interaction between income and employment status, it appears:

  - unemployment and low income are both associated with lower life satisfaction.

- In this model the largest variations in life satisfaction appear to be around:

  - relationships (being divorced, separated or widowed);
  - employment and income;
  - where you live geographically (e.g., north-east England);
  - housing, particularly living in social housing;
  - health (having a long-term illness).

These high-level results are generally consistent with life satisfaction literature, although we have adopted slightly different approaches because of data restrictions (e.g., only a limited categorical income variable was available, which restricted our modeling options). That said, the results are useful and highlight the relative strength of association of different factors with life satisfaction. It is interesting, for example, to note how the model immediately draws attention to factors that are very important to people's wellbeing and that are not always prioritized or considered in policy decisions. Relationships is a good example, with divorce, separation, and widowhood appearing to be more associated with lower wellbeing than factors such as employment and income, which are the more traditional focus of policy makers. That is not to say relationships should become the number one goal of government. However, evidence like this might challenge the way we currently value and support voluntary sector counseling services, for example. It might also lead us to taking better account of relationships in the relevant decisions we make.

It is this type of analysis of the underlying drivers of wellbeing that stands to be particularly valuable to policy makers. The illustrative model in Table 19.2 highlights some of the known drivers of wellbeing, but the real analytical power comes from linking wellbeing data across policy surveys. So adding in data such as air pollution, crime, community activities, etc. can begin to build up a relative picture of the importance of different areas of policy to subgroups of the population. Furthermore, Table 19.2 is based on a small sample which is a fraction of the full annual sample of 200,000 observations that will be collected. Such a large sample size will enable detailed analysis of subgroups of the population and highlight variations across smaller areas of geography. It will undoubtedly push the boundaries of our knowledge, help to further "deshroud" the drivers of wellbeing, and be of greater value to policy makers as a result.

## Subjective Wellbeing Measurement: Conclusions and Future Work

Finally, it is also worth noting that the four overall subjective wellbeing questions have, at the outset, been considered experimental and there has been work to test their robustness. On the whole, the early evidence indicates that the questions seemed to have worked well and the vast majority of respondents were willing and able to provide answers to them. More cognitive testing would be useful in helping explore the way in which respondents answer the questions, and the extent to which these answers do provide a self-assessment of the respondent's wellbeing.

Different modes of completion of the wellbeing questions were tested in the 2011 Opinions Survey (ONS, 2011b). There is some evidence from research suggesting that respondents who self-complete wellbeing questions without an intermediary interviewer typically give lower scores than if responding to an interviewer. We tested for this effect in the model in Table 19.2 but found no significant difference for life satisfaction. However, there did appear to be statistically significant differences for the anxiety question when controlling for other factors in a similar model. Tests for variation in wellbeing by month of survey followed a similar pattern with no significant differences for the three positive wellbeing questions but some differences for anxiety over the 4-month period covered by these data. It is clear that care needs to be taken when comparing wellbeing across surveys using differing modes of administration and implemented across different time frames. Moreover, it is certainly important to control for these factors in analysis.

Further work is required on how best to present and interpret subjective wellbeing measures, and this should be explored with a wide range of potential users. Certainly the richness of the data appears more readily from distributions and from thresholds, rather than from the high-level mean scores that have been traditionally presented.

Further work is also required on children's subjective wellbeing. Most national wellbeing data collection in the United Kingdom has focused on people aged 16 and over, and while there are some nongovernmental organizations that do collect data on children, there are gaps in this area. In exploring what more can be done to address the gaps we also need to understand the ethical and practical issues involved in surveying children's wellbeing. There are also likely to be other gaps in the data for specific vulnerable groups, such as the homeless and people in care homes, for example, who are not routinely included in household surveys.

## Reflecting Wellbeing in Policy Decisions

So far in this chapter we have presented the case for moving beyond GDP, outlined the United Kingdom's policy of measuring wellbeing, set this within an international context and then recounted some of the national debate in the United Kingdom. We have also presented the early approach to measurement and some results and analysis from the 2011 Opinions Survey. At times we have hinted at how wellbeing could be used to support policy decisions and it is to this that we now specifically turn our attention.

It is fair to say that there is now a large body of evidence around wellbeing, and specifically subjective wellbeing. Much of this evidence is academic and it is, as a consequence, a significant challenge to bridge between this knowledge and real policy and practice. It is a challenge that is also compounded by the fact that there is no large existing body of practice and tools on which to build. To be successful, overburdened and time-poor policy makers will clearly need definitions, frameworks, and worked examples if they are going to start factoring wellbeing into their decision making. Presenting and communicating the wellbeing data effectively, and in an accessible way by integrating it into existing reporting structures that policy makers already use, will clearly help, though.

It is therefore very early days, but we will present some early thinking and highlight some of the tools that are already available. In the final section of this chapter we will look at one specific policy area—wellbeing and employment—as an example.

## National Account Extensions

A core part of the United Kingdom's national wellbeing program will be to publish data around the measurement framework, as presented in Figure 19.1. The headline measures will be reported on a consistent and regular basis, supplemented by regular reports on each of the wellbeing domains, including contextual and distributional analyses. Guidance and information, where possible, will be provided on replicating these headline measures and analyses for local areas. There will also be more in-depth analysis of the economy and the environment. This analysis has been labeled as national accounts extensions, because of the importance of maintaining links with the national economic accounts, and will explore:

- further development of U.K. environmental accounts;
- development of natural resource accounts;
- estimates of the human capital of the United Kingdom;
- alternative measures of economic wellbeing, taking a lead from the Stiglitz–Sen–Fitoussi Commission (Stiglitz et al., 2009) and considering all variations of gross and net, domestic, and national product, as well as focusing on the household sector and on distributions as well as aggregates.

With a robust development and publication program and by treating measures of economic wellbeing as extensions of national accounts, we expect this will enable better integration into future policy decisions. The U.K. program is ambitious and at an early stage. It may well take time to develop. We cannot possibly know now all of the uses that this will eventually be put to in future policy, although we expect it to provide a strong foundation for better decision making and to form the basis for sustainable economic policies.

But as we develop this measurement framework it begs the question, "Is there anything we can be doing in the meantime to reflect subjective wellbeing in policy?"

## Focusing on the Known Drivers of Subjective Wellbeing

One simple but potentially effective approach to reflecting wellbeing into policy is to focus on some of the known drivers of subjective wellbeing that emerge from academic literature. The illustrative model we presented in Table 19.2 highlighted a few such drivers, and ideally a policy maker would have additional data relevant to their specific area that could be reflected in such a model and linked to wellbeing to gain analytical insights. However, it is not always possible to do this. The data might not be available, a policy maker might not have the analytic skills and resources at his or her disposal, or there may be insufficient time to undertake the analysis.

Fortunately there is an excellent body of knowledge around the drivers of wellbeing for both adults and children. The breadth of these drivers confirms the great potential to support and enhance policy decisions. Some of the drivers are the kind of traditional areas that policy makers have always "systemically" focused on: income, employment, education, health, environment, culture, housing, and transport. These are typically the main business of an existing government department or public body. However, many of the drivers of wellbeing do not fall into this category. They are not always considered in policy decisions and can attract less attention: social interaction, family, community, participation, giving, religious activity, direct democracy, reciprocity, trust, fairness, sense of control, and meaningful activity. Over the years the importance of and focus on these factors has not been as consistent and has varied significantly with different administrations.

Table 19.3 presents a simple checklist of some of the known drivers of wellbeing, separating them illustratively into "systemic" and "nonsystemic." There is an argument that government and policy makers have no role, or less of a role to play in focusing on some of these nonsystemic factors (e.g., family, marriage, and religion). They are potentially quite politically sensitive and very challenging for how we develop policy. However, they are also very important and can, for example in the case of social interactions and relationships, matter hugely, even relative to "systemic" drivers such as health and education. The model in Table 19.2 hinted at this.

Setting aside whether it is government's role or not to intervene in these areas, it is evidently clear that government influences these drivers regardless, either intentionally or unintentionally. This influence is manifest in policy decisions and in the way in which these are implemented. Developing policies without due consideration of the drivers of wellbeing risks having a negative effect on people and communities. These risks are all the greater

**Table 19.3.** "Systemic" and "Nonsystemic" Wellbeing Drivers.

| Systemic wellbeing drivers (typically covered by policy) | Nonsystemic wellbeing drivers (not always covered by policy) |
| --- | --- |
| Mental health | Relationships |
| Physical health | Family, partnerships, and marriage |
| Employment | Friendships |
| Income/poverty/debt | Neighbors |
| Relative income/deprivation | Work relationships |
| Level of education | Personal security/stability |
| Leisure: participation in art, sport, and culture | Care giving |
| Safety/crime/terrorism | Work–life balance/leisure time |
| Housing and built environment | Continued learning |
| Climate change/variables | Faith/religious practice |
| Civil society | Power, control, autonomy |
| Local environment | Fairness/equality |
| Commuting/transport | Community/neighborhood/place |
| Natural disasters | Volunteering/giving time/money |
| | Civic participation and direct democracy |

given that many of the things that we know really matter to wellbeing are not systemically considered. As Prime Minister David Cameron points out, "the actions government takes can make people feel better as well as worse" (Cameron, 2010).

It is not just the policy decisions we make that can affect wellbeing. There is evidence that the way in which we implement a public service also matters. When you explore the relative importance of key drivers of customer satisfaction such as timeliness and fulfillment, the factors that can rise to the surface often relate to customer experience. People clearly care deeply about the "soft" experiences as well as "hard" outcomes of services, such as being treated with respect and dignity, fairness, and consistency; service providers doing what they said they would. So the way we design and run our public services has a clear role to play in supporting and improving the wellbeing of service users. We can actively design "wellbeing" drivers into our services, by focusing on what really matters to people: control, autonomy, fairness, process transparency, and active consideration of relationships and the social networks of service users. Consideration of wellbeing, therefore, challenges service providers to be innovative, to co-produce, co-design, personalize, and to adopt broader measures of success. It is possible that tracking subjective wellbeing and life satisfaction will become a useful complement to other customer satisfaction metrics in the future and help to improve customer journeys and relevant public services.

So the challenge for policy and service professionals is to actively build consideration of the drivers of wellbeing into their work, and strive, at a minimum, to lessen any negative or harmful impacts on them. Beyond this, though, there is the potential to open up new options to solving problems and improving services by looking at them through a "wellbeing lens." There is also the potential of achieving more effective outcomes while concurrently making an essential, positive, and complementary contribution to national quality of life. So, for example, using our checklist in Table 19.3:

- A childhood obesity program might factor in an element of peer sup-port/peer challenge rather than just a professional relationship between a health visitor and the child (relationships/ friendships).
- A community grant program might pass full responsibility to a neigh-borhood panel for deciding what to spend the money on and for actually spending it, rather than administering it centrally (power, control, civic participation, community, neighbors).
- An offending reduction program might add an element of restorative justice (fairness) and peer mentoring (learning, relationships) and take active steps to enhance victim wellbeing (personal security, safety, fear of crime).
- A public body might provide a personal budget to a service user and let them choose how to spend it themselves (control, autonomy) and it might arrange expert peer-advice in selecting the services (relationships, choice).

These are a few simple examples, but it is relatively straightforward to see how wellbeing drivers such as positive relationships, control, autonomy, volunteering, and learning can be built into decisions and services, and how they might lead to better outcomes (e.g., reduced obesity and reoffending) while concurrently improving wellbeing.

Another important question to ask from a policy perspective is "Whose wellbeing is being impacted?" In many cases policies are likely to impact the distribution of wellbeing rather than to raise the wellbeing of everyone involved. Furthermore, because people adapt to changes and their wellbeing can return to pre-change levels (e.g., following a divorce or bereavement), it is also important to consider the short- and long-term impacts. So, for example, a hypothetical policy to implement a smoking ban at work and in public buildings like pubs, combined with a tax increase, could:

- reduce smokers' sense of wellbeing in the short term (loss of control, power, fairness, possibly impact relationships, reduce social participation) but could increase wellbeing in the future if it reduces their smoking (health);
- improve the wellbeing of nonsmokers (increase control, sense of fairness, improved health through reduced exposure to passive smoke, increased social participation);
- have a mixed short-term effect on employees in pubs and hospitality sector—reducing job security but also improving health by reducing exposure to smoke;
- reduce the wellbeing of employees involved in tobacco production and retail, if consumer demand reduces significantly (employment, security);
- reduce the long-term wellbeing of smokers' families or co-residents if the ban displaces smoking from public places into cars and homes, and therefore increases their risks of exposure to passive smoke (health).

Obviously this is a quick and simplified wellbeing analysis of a hypothetical policy, but it highlights choices and trade-offs. Such consideration might also lead to mitigating actions to compensate for wellbeing reductions, for example, more support to help smokers quit, addressing the potential impact on employment in the tobacco industry through retraining or job support programs, and taking steps to mitigate risks of passive smoking due to displacement effects. There might also be opportunities to get local people involved in decision making (e.g., publish data on local traders selling cigarettes under-age), or build in positive relationships to the support services given to smokers (volunteer "quit smoking" mentors/text buddies).

So in practical terms an early assessment of a policy or a strategy against the drivers of wellbeing, accounting for the various stakeholders involved, and taking a view over the short and long term would seem like a valuable and relatively straightforward exercise that does not need significant data or analysis and can even be undertaken by a group through a short workshop. In practice, a table of drivers, such as those in Table 19.3, could be used to explore a policy change and to stimulate discussion around different interventions. It could also be used in decision making; different policy options could be scored against the wellbeing drivers, combined with other core goals of the policy, by a range of decision stakeholders in a deliberative and participatory process, such as multicriteria analysis (HM Treasury, 2003, p. 34).

There are also some simple and effective frameworks for designing wellbeing into policies and services. One of them is *Five ways to wellbeing* (Thompson & Aked, 2011), which was developed by the New Economics Foundation as part of the United Kingdom Government Office for Science Foresight project, Mental Capital and Wellbeing (Department for Business Innovation & Skills, 2008). The framework is the wellbeing equivalent of healthy eating, "five fruit and vegetables a day," and is strongly grounded in empirical research and what academic evidence suggests may lead to improvements in mental health and wellbeing:

- *Connect*—with the people around them, with family, friends, colleagues and neighbours.
- *Be active*—walk, run, cycle, exercise, and play.
- *Take notice*—take time to be aware of the world around, appreciate the natural environment, art, culture, and wildlife.
- *Keep learning*—try something new, take a course, fix something, cook or learn an instrument.
- *Give*—help a friend, peer, or a stranger, volunteer time or join a community group.

Clearly this framework can be used by individuals to improve their own wellbeing. However, it can also be applied by organizations to policies and services, or by employers to improving their working environment for staff wellbeing. So, for example, a director of housing for an elderly sheltered housing scheme could look to build all of these elements into service provision through social events (*connect*), walking clubs (*active*), attention to the built environment (*notice*), classes (*learning*), and peer support or buddy schemes (*give*).

## Policy Screening

Policy screening is a more formal process for assessing the impact on key drivers of wellbeing. At its simplest we ask the question: "Will this policy have a positive, negative, or neutral impact on national wellbeing or the drivers of wellbeing?" This can be backed by a governance structure empowered to make decisions on the results of the policy screening analysis. This is, in fact, an approach that the government of Bhutan has used. Policies are scored by stakeholders against questions relating to a list of factors such as stress, equality, health, learning, family, and leisure. The distribution of relevant scores across the questions can then be assessed or even combined to develop a total score on which to base a decision.

There are a few important considerations with policy screening. Clearly, screening can accomplish what it is designed to do, and divide policies into those that are either acceptable or unacceptable, resulting in a "stop" or "go" decision. But there is a third potential category, of "improve." If screening exposes a particular deficiency there is also the potential to adapt the policy to meet wellbeing objectives along with the core aim. Policy makers might be much more willing to engage in such a process on a voluntary basis if they see it less as a hurdle and more as a positive process for improving policy.

Another consideration is whether a policy that is acceptable from a wellbeing perspective is also consistent with the other stated aims of a government or whether there are tensions and trade-offs. In the United Kingdom some commentators have suggested that a focus on wellbeing will inevitably lead to more burdens on businesses and a swing toward great centralization and government control. This is unlikely for a number of reasons, not least that there are other stated aims of government around "red tape reduction" and "localism," and the natural machinery of government would ultimately expose and resolve any conflict of objectives. However, reviewing any wellbeing policies, or adaptations to policies, alongside other stated aims of government at the earliest stages of development, would seem to make sense, both to head off later issues and also to improve the strategic fit of policies from the outset.

Table 19.4 presents a simple, illustrative tool to review the impact of a policy or strategy against wellbeing and other government priorities. It has deliberately focused on a few example priorities that are of a cross-cutting nature rather than owned by one specific area of government such as health or education. The tool enables a policy maker to make a quick initial impact assessment and also to develop new ideas to "stretch or adapt a policy" to achieve greater consistency across all government priorities including wellbeing. By rating the current and potential impact it becomes clear where improvements can be made, and also exposes trade-offs.

In the United Kingdom, the Children's Society has developed a tool for policy makers to help to understand the potential impact of decisions on children's wellbeing (Children's Society, 2012). Table 19.5 presents the checklist. It consists of six priority areas which are empirically derived from research into children's subjective wellbeing. Policy makers can assess

**Table 19.4.** Illustrative Tool to Assess Policy Impact Against Example Government Priorities Including Wellbeing.

| No. | Example government priorities | Key questions: Does your policy or action: | Current impact | Assessment of your current policy or strategy | Potential ideas to improve/stretch policy or strategy | Potential impact? |
|---|---|---|---|---|---|---|
| 1 | Wellbeing and family | enhance or diminish wellbeing? | Neutral | | | Positive |
| | | support family and social interaction? | Negative | | | Positive |
| 2 | Open public services | extend competition, diversity, choice and control? | Negative | | | Neutral |
| 3 | Localism | devolve power? | | | | |
| 4 | Better regulation | reduce bureaucracy and red tape? | | | | |
| 5 | Reduce costs. Support growth | cut the deficit? grow the economy? | | | | |
| 6 | Increase transparency | promote openness and transparency? | | | | |

**Table 19.4.** (*Continued*)

| No. | Example government priorities | Key questions: Does your policy or action: | Current impact | Assessment of your current policy or strategy | Potential ideas to improve/stretch policy or strategy | Potential impact? |
|-----|-------------------------------|--------------------------------------------|----------------|-----------------------------------------------|--------------------------------------------------------|-------------------|
| 7   | Incorporate behavioral research | build on evidence about how people behave? | | | | |
| 8   | Increase social mobility | improve social mobility? | | | | |
|     | | support the neediest? (Is it fair?) | | | | |
| 9   | Sustainable development | sustainable for future generations? | | | | |
| 10  | Strengthen civil society | encourage responsibility? | | | | |
|     | | promote freedom? enhance participation? | | | | |

**Table 19.5.** Checklist for Understanding the Impact of Decisions on Children's Wellbeing.

| What do children need? | How can they get it? | Policy effect (positive/ neutral/negative) |
|---|---|---|
| 1. The conditions to learn and develop | • Have opportunities for free play<br>• Get high-quality and appropriate education and care<br>• Have positive relationships with teachers | |
| 2. A positive view of themselves and an identity that is respected | • Be comfortable with their appearance<br>• By physically and mentally healthy<br>• Are respected and valued for who they are | |
| 3. Enough of what matters | • Have the items and experiences that matter<br>• Have some financial autonomy through pocket money<br>• Live in a household which is economically stable | |
| 4. Positive relationships with their family and friends | • Be active participants in decisions that affect them<br>• Have caring, loving relationships<br>• Spend time with their family and with friends | |
| 5. A safe and suitable home environment and local area | • Be, and feel, safe at home and in their local area<br>• Live in good quality housing<br>• Have space at home that is theirs for privacy | |
| 6. Opportunity to take part in positive activities to thrive | • Have a say in how they use their time<br>• Have affordable activities in their local area<br>• Have access to outdoor spaces for play | |

From the Children's Society (2012), p. 9.

whether their policy has a positive, negative, or neutral impact on each of these priority areas. The results can potentially lead to some practical steps to improve children's wellbeing.

It must be emphasized that all these tools and approaches are presented for illustration only, and they are not routinely used in policy in the United Kingdom. However, they are relatively simple and straightforward approaches to embedding wellbeing into policy which lend themselves to participatory and deliberative decision making. Furthermore, they do not need specialist expertise or scarce analytic resources to implement.

## Modeling and Valuing Social Impacts using Subjective Wellbeing

If data are available and it is possible to model responses to questions in your policy area of interest against wellbeing, then subjective wellbeing can be particularly powerful to investigate the potential impact of interventions on the welfare of different groups, or to inform cost–benefit analysis.

Effective policies typically lead to desirable social impacts in one form or another; for example, an increase in a target group taking weekly exercise or more positive contact between neighbors in a particular community. The valuation of these social impacts is very difficult and cannot easily be inferred from market prices. It is, nonetheless, advantageous to be able to value them in monetary terms in order to construct the business case for action. Valuation is central to cost–benefit analysis and appraisal, but valuations are inherently subjective in nature. The traditional approach is to assess the decisions people make through revealed or stated preference techniques. However, these techniques assume rational behavior, which has been challenged over recent years by behavioral economics. An alternative approach to stated and revealed preference is to look at changes in wellbeing. The technique estimates the increase in wellbeing associated with a particular good or service and then calculates the equivalent money, say in the form of income from employment, to give the same boost to wellbeing. The U.K. Treasury and Department for Work and Pensions have published a discussion paper on this approach (Fujiwara & Campbell, 2011). Using this technique, for example, frequent volunteering has been valued at £13,500 p.a. and societal trust at £15,900 p.a. for British households (Fujiwara, Oroyemi, & McKinnon, 2012). These are figures that could inform business cases for interventions that promote volunteering or community cohesion respectively. There are many examples of social impact valuations using

445

subjective wellbeing, and it is clearly a useful emerging tool for policy makers and analysts to build wellbeing into decision making.

## Geographical and Geodemographic Tools

So far we have looked at approaches predominantly for central and local government policy makers and practitioners to embed wellbeing into their decisions. However, we know it is not just governments that influence wellbeing, but businesses and civil society and of course individuals themselves. So it is important to communicate the wellbeing data in a meaningful and accessible way so that other organizations and individuals can act on it themselves.

We have already seen in Table 19.2 that wellbeing can vary significantly by location, so maps or geographical tools could prove to be useful. Figure 19.3 presents estimates of wellbeing by small geographical areas in England. This map was produced by estimating mean wellbeing levels for 52 area-based classifications in the England, using data from the British Household Panel Survey (University of Essex, Institute for Social and Economic Research, 2010), and then plotting these mean values for each area classification. The results indicate some correlation between deprivation and wellbeing, and also between rurality and wellbeing—when compared to the relevant maps. However, this map really does only provide indicative and illustrative estimates; in future we will be able to develop much more robust estimates on larger survey samples which should help to inform local decisions. Larger samples will for example allow for differences in the age structure of areas to be taken into account, recognizing that reported wellbeing varies over the life course. There are also some presentational challenges to address, for example that large rural areas with high wellbeing scores tend to stand out.

There are already some tools and techniques for assessing wellbeing at a local area level. The Young Foundation has developed a Wellbeing and Resilience Measure (WARM) (Mguni & Bacon, 2010) and the Greater London Authority has developed an interactive tool that calculates wellbeing scores for every London borough between 2005 and 2009 (Greater London Authority Intelligence Unit, 2012). There are also opportunities to embed wellbeing into geo-demographic classifications that are commonly used (e.g., OAC, ACORN, MOSIAC). This will ensure that a wellbeing perspective can be added into the many pieces of analysis that these classifications support.

**Figure 19.3.** Estimates of Wellbeing in England by Small Geographic Areas. Data from British Household Panel Survey, used with permission from the University of Essex Institute for Social and Economic Research.

## Wellbeing and Policy Development: A Framework

Finally, it is worth considering at what stage of policy development and appraisal it is best to consider wellbeing. Successful policy depends on the development and use of a sound evidence base, understanding and managing the political context, and focusing on delivery from the outset. The policy maker must bring together these three elements to deliver a successful

447

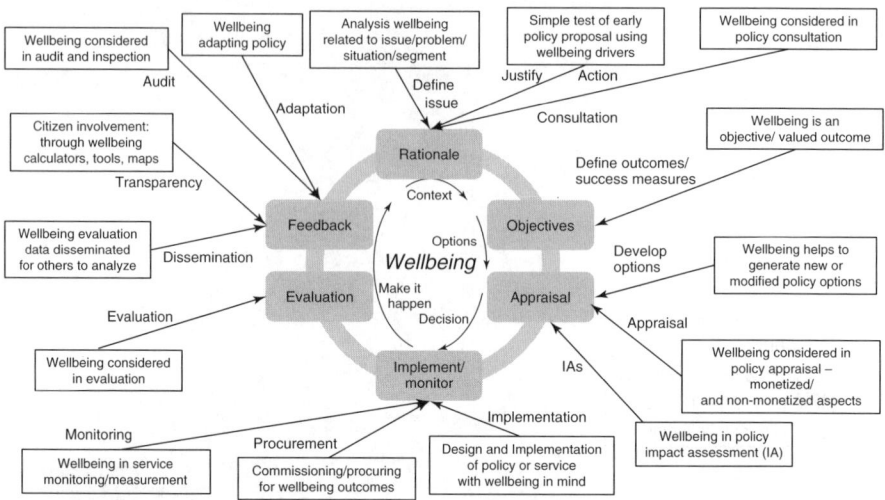

**Figure 19.4.** Wellbeing and the Policy Appraisal Cycle.

outcome. There are four areas of activity where these three elements of successful policy apply, although they do not necessarily happen in a specific order:

- understanding the context;
- developing the options;
- getting to a decision;
- making it happen.

Exploring this in more detail Figure 19.4 presents the stages of a broad policy appraisal cycle commonly referred to in U.K. Central Government as ROAMEF (Rationale, Objectives, Appraisal, Monitoring, Evaluation, and Feedback) (HM Treasury, 2003). We have added to this cycle the four areas of activity above. A wellbeing perspective can enhance each element of this policy appraisal cycle.

At the earliest stages of policy development it might be possible to analyze existing wellbeing data and relate it to the specific policy challenge or population segment of interest. This might involve using historic data sets or analyzing wellbeing questions that have been purposely added into a policy survey to support the decision. It might also involve commissioning specific qualitative or longitudinal analysis. Viewing the policy challenge through a wellbeing lens should provide a new perspective and lead to a better definition of the problem to be solved, and a more robust justification for action. At this stage in the cycle there are often some early ideas and solutions. These can be assessed against wellbeing drivers or by adopting some of the approaches that we have already highlighted.

At the second stage of the policy appraisal cycle it might be possible to explicitly set wellbeing as a target, goal, or outcome of the policy being developed. Setting it as an objective up front to complement core policy objectives (e.g., health, crime, and education) will help to embed consideration at all subsequent stages of the cycle. At the appraisal stage it is possible to consider the drivers of wellbeing to help to develop a broader set of options and adaptations of existing options. At this stage it might be possible to use the wellbeing valuation methodology, presented earlier to calculate monetary values for the intended social impacts of the policy. It might also be possible to complement this with nonmonetary techniques such as multicriteria analysis (HM Treasury, 2003, p. 34), to undertake an inclusive and participatory appraisal of the options involving a diverse set of relevant stakeholders; the drivers of wellbeing could clearly be used to form the criteria in such a process. Ultimately wellbeing could open up new options, help choose between them, and help value the intended impact of the preferred approach.

At the implementation stage, tools like *Five ways to wellbeing* could be used to enhance the service design or policy implementation. If there is a service contract to award then wellbeing could be accounted for in the commissioning framework; we could contract for, or incentivize these outcomes. The impact on wellbeing could also be used as a tender evaluation criterion. This is also a good stage to consider measuring baseline data through customer surveys so that wellbeing can be monitored throughout implementation. For example, if the policy is for a job support program that intends to help people into work, and to remain in work for at least a year, then it should be possible to measure subjective wellbeing before, during, and after the intervention. Such information could help to improve service operations as the learning is formed, or support an independent evaluation to inform follow-on decisions if the implementation is a small-scale pilot.

Finally, after a policy evaluation which has included a wellbeing assessment there are opportunities to release the raw, anonymized data to enable third-party organizations to undertake further analysis, and to present the data in engaging formats for civil society organizations, customer advocates, or service users to access themselves. All this can support feedback mechanisms, highlighting new issues or challenges to address, and thus starting the cycle again, leading to more effective policies. At this point there is also the potential for inspection and audit organizations to consider wellbeing, and highlight if there are shortcomings to be addressed.

In this way a wellbeing perspective can be thoroughly embedded into policy and add value to the whole process. It adds to the robustness and roundness of the evidence base with wellbeing research and data providing a better understanding of the context for policy work. As we have seen, the drivers for wellbeing can also provide a solid set of criteria for developing options and decision making as well as practical tools to make change happen in the real world.

Wellbeing is relevant to almost all areas of policy in some way or another, and we cannot present on each of these in this chapter, so for the final section we will just look at one specific area, wellbeing at work.

## Policy Focus: Wellbeing at Work (Contributed by Laura Austin Croft)

Employment clearly impacts our wellbeing, with research indicating it can explain between a fifth and a quarter of the variation in life satisfaction (Harter, Schmidt, & Keyes, 2002). We spend much of our adult lives at work and there are aspects of the workplace that intuitively influence our wellbeing, such as relationships with colleagues, levels of autonomy, and fairness associated with performance, pay, and promotion.

There has been much focus in recent years on measuring employee engagement and on human resources (HR) policies that boost staff commitment and discretionary effort. This raises many questions, not least:

- What is the relationship between wellbeing and engagement?
- Do the HR policies of an organization which focuses on engagement look different from those that also have employee wellbeing as an explicit objective?
- Is staff wellbeing good for business performance?

With around 29 million people in employment in the United Kingdom, it would seem that businesses and employers are already making an important contribution to the wellbeing of the nation through the workplace environments and cultures they create and sustain. But perhaps more can be done

450

for them to contribute to national wellbeing through, for example, sharing good practice and learning from high-wellbeing workplaces.

Government should be interested in this for a number of reasons. If improving the wellbeing of employees is good for business performance then perhaps there is the potential to enhance growth and competitiveness through more widespread adoption of good practice. Conversely, if poor workplaces are negatively impacting wellbeing and increasing sickness absence, this is bad for the economy and also public services can end up picking up the costs of any resulting mental or physical ill-health. Government should also be interested in improving wellbeing at work as a major employer of people itself.

In this final section we start by presenting some of the literature on wellbeing, work, and employee engagement. We then explore what this might mean in terms of employment practice, particularly around light-touch, low-cost, nonregulatory initiatives. In the case of practical tools we only really begin to touch on the subject, but we hopefully provide some suitable inspiration for others to build on.

## Review of Literature and Recent Policy Papers

No other technique for the conduct of life attaches the individual so firmly to reality as laying emphasis on work: for work at least gives one a secure place in a portion of reality, in the human community.

Sigmund Freud

It is well recognized that work not only provides for us in material ways but also gives people a sense of purpose, opportunity to learn, build relationships with others, and participate in society. Systematic reviews conclude that work in general is good for health and wellbeing, recognizing the fundamental characteristics of employment that correlate with better rates of good physical and mental health (Waddell & Burton, 2006). What is more challenging is identifying the components that distinguish a job that promotes wellbeing from one that does not, partly due to the multifactorial nature of wellbeing and work characteristics (Wadsworth, Chaplin, Allen, & Smith, 2010). However, the evidence suggests that there are common processes that help create a positive working environment.

Contemporary understanding of workplace wellbeing builds on theorists such as Maslow (1943), Herzberg (1966/1997), and McGregor (1960), believing that employees are motivated and affected by the ability of work to support a person's "self-actualizing needs" as much or to a greater extent than its external conditions. Herzberg's study of the cross-section of Pittsburgh industry in 1959 concluded that "A positive 'happiness' seems to require some attainment of psychological growth" (Herzberg, 1966/1997, p. 375) that can be provided at work. The Pittsburgh participants reported high rates of job satisfaction connected to work itself, in addition to feelings of recognition, achievement, responsibility, and advancement, while dissatisfaction was directed to factors outside of their individual environment such as working conditions and organizational processes. Further research has since shown that it is not easy to separate the "intrinsic" factors of work (such as job satisfaction, learning, and development) from the "extrinsic factors" (such as working conditions and pay). However, extrinsic factors such as pay, once a certain level is attained, seem to work best when they inform an employee about their accomplishments, for example a bonus can promote wellbeing if it recognizes personal achievement (Arnold, Cooper, & Robertson, 1998).

Among the evidence base of what supports wellbeing at work is the importance of job design, for example where role structure gives clarity of purpose and responsibility, and the balance between demand and control (Payne, 1987). The Whitehall Studies were established in 1967 to track the health outcomes of 18,000 British civil servants over a number of decades. This longitudinal research has highlighted the danger of jobs that have a high level of demand but low level of control, creating a psychological imbalance and strain on the individual. Its recommendations to mitigate this harm include greater involvement of employees at all levels in the decision making of the organization and improvements in social support at work from managers and between colleagues (Council of Civil Service Unions/Cabinet Office, 2004). Another model supported by this research that helps understand achievement of wellbeing at work is the balance between effort and reward, with the Whitehall Studies showing that praise and support for individual development helps promote positive wellbeing compared to a job role that requires a significant amount of effort but receives little recognition.

The United Kingdom has recently published a number of reviews and reports on health and work, building the government's momentum to promote the workplace as an environment to support wellbeing. In particular, the U.K. Government commissioned three high-profile reports. Professor Dame Carol Black, an eminent physician appointed as the U.K. National Director for Health and Work from 2005 to 2011, was commissioned to review the health of Britain's working-age population. The review, *Working for a healthier tomorrow*, identified that over £100 billion is lost to the economy because of working-age ill health and associated sickness absence, and worklessness (Black, 2008). It also highlighted the importance of job characteristics that enhance feelings of satisfaction, reward, and control, and consequently health and wellbeing, with particular reference to the role played by the line manager. *Engaging for success: Enhancing performance through employee engagement* (MacLeod & Clarke, 2009), commissioned by the Department for Business, Innovation and Skills, put forward the case that employers should focus effort on increasing levels of employee engagement, which will in turn improve business performance and innovation. This report linked employee wellbeing to engagement, citing research from Gallup that 86% of engaged employees report to "very often feel very happy at work" against 11% of the disengaged (MacLeod & Clarke, 2009). Michael Marmot reiterated the important role of the work environment in *Fair society, healthy lives*, a review commissioned by the government to propose evidence-based effective strategies for reducing health inequalities in the United Kingdom. An objective included creating fair employment and good work for all, promoting jobs that offer in-work development, flexibility to balance work and family life, and protection from harmful working conditions (Marmot, 2010).

A number of evidence reports have been published to demonstrate the economic benefits to organizations of improved wellbeing among employees, such as higher levels of employee engagement, reduced turnover, and improved productivity and performance. A specific return on investment for employer-funded wellbeing initiatives is hard to identify, depending on what is being measured and the organizational context. For employee engagement, research suggests that if organizations increased investment in a range of good workplace practices related to engagement by 10%, profits would increase by £1,500 per employee per year (MacLeod & Clarke, 2009). A report by the London School of Economics predicts that a return on investment for a mental wellbeing program run for a year for 500 employees is more than nine to one (Knapp, McDaid, & Parsonage, 2011). All FTSE 100 companies have been found to include wellness and engagement in public reporting, but with gaps in certain metrics such as measuring the impact of support programs provided for staff (Business in the Community, 2009). Better measurement might lead to greater understanding of interventions that support employee wellbeing.

**Table 19.6.** Summary of Factors Associated with the "Optimum" Employee Experience.

| Higher than average wellbeing | Higher than average employee engagement | Higher than average retention | Lower than average absence[a] |
|---|---|---|---|
| • Supportive colleagues | • Fun place to work | • Good relations between managers and employees | • Good relations between managers and employees |
| • Fewer than 5 sick days in last 12 months | • Senior managers delivering on promises | • Employee engagement scores of 95+ | • Senior managers delivering on promises and seeking staff views |
| • Employee engagement scores of 80+ | • No sick days in last 12 months | • Flexible working | • Employee engagement scores of 70+ |
| • Information on managing staff stress | • Wellbeing scores of >28 • Working as a manager/ senior official • Information on managing staff stress | • Older workers (aged 55+) | • No sick pay • Working <1 year • Private sector |

[a]Lower than average in terms of any absence or average number sick days.
From Young and Bhaumik (2011).

Despite difficulties in comparing measurements of employee wellbeing across different organization environments, there is a growing consensus about the characteristics associated with a good work environment. Table 19.6 sets out a framework from research on health and wellbeing of U.K. employees (Young & Bhaumik, 2011). It summarizes demographic, attitudinal, and behavioral characteristics associated with an "optimal" employee experience. It is useful in understanding different factors that might underpin a specific health and work business indicator, for example higher than average employee engagement is associated with the information on managing staff stress and the environment being considered a fun place to work as well as high wellbeing scores. These characteristics do not present causality, but that they are commonly associated with positive workplace environments.

## Approaches to Improving Wellbeing at Work

Wellbeing and engagement, while related, are essentially different concepts, and measuring both in the workplace should provide valuable insights to reflect into HR practices. HR policies developed with the objective of maximizing staff engagement might not, therefore, be the same as HR policies which focus on both wellbeing and engagement. Wellbeing adds an important new dimension that is actionable. Measuring wellbeing can draw attention to different groups of staff who might welcome and benefit from additional support—carers, those in poor health, staff with dependent children, mid-career staff, or those in specific job functions. Further consultation with these staff members, afresh, in light of the results, could well lead to practical ideas to improve workplace wellbeing. It is also notable that both wellbeing and engagement can vary by organization, after controlling for other factors. So this opens up the potential, in the future, of good practice sharing between organizations incorporating wellbeing practices with those that do not.

That said, there is no magic formula to promoting wellbeing at work. An organization needs to consider its own culture, needs of its staff (through internal communications), and then develop a plan that suits and supports their needs. Best practice examples can help provide inspiration, but wellbeing policies and programs need to develop from the individual business culture, including its overall aims and demographic.

Where evidence exists, there is strong association between a positive workplace and flexible working (Young & Bhaumik, 2011). This follows career development trends that show that balancing work and outside commitments is an increasingly important consideration for women and men. Flexible working also increases an individual's control over their work environment, helping employees make decisions on work patterns that best suit good job performance. Flexible working comes in many forms, including part-time, home-working, job sharing, and flexi hours. As well as being an option for an individual, it can be considered as something that is built into job design at the HR strategy stage. For example, creation of 3-day and 4-day jobs across the organization.

Another important association with a positive workplace environment is line management training, particularly with regards to managing stress at work. A line manager plays an important role in supporting other factors already discussed that promote wellbeing at work, such as recognition of work undertaken, support for skill development, and clarity of job design. Business literature promotes the view that it is the manager that supports people work at their best, which is generally when people feel good about themselves. This should be the role of individuals who enjoy (and show ability in) the management role rather than people who become managers through promotion as a result of being good at their own job.

In the United Kingdom, there are currently many frameworks and tools for supporting individual and organization wellbeing. For example, these include *10 Keys to happier living* by Action for Happiness, Business in the Community's Workwell Model, and a Workplace Wellbeing Charter developed by NHS Liverpool and now being rolled out to different English regions. To illustrate some ideas on promoting wellbeing at work, this section uses the *Five ways to wellbeing* (Thompson & Aked, 2011) introduced earlier in this chapter (Table 19.7).

In summary, wellbeing in the work environment needs to be considered according to the specific organizational context. Recent research in this area supports the view that promoting wellbeing at work is not associated with introducing new procedures for business to follow, but links to characteristics already associated with successful organization environments. For example, supporting staff involvement, presence of visible and senior leadership, alignment of wellbeing initiatives with business overall aims and goals, and monitoring of informatics through staff surveys, focus groups, or company indicators on turnover and attendance. This is not to ignore the fundamental aspects that "good" work brings to wellbeing, such as secure employment, a "living" income, and being treated with fairness and respect. The focus on the psychological work environment, however, shows processes that can take place to promote wellbeing at work across society and for a broad range of professions.

## Closing Remarks

In this chapter we have focused on the experience of the United Kingdom, outlining government policy and the rationale underpinning it. We have presented the United Kingdom's national measurement program, including some wellbeing measurement results from a population survey in 2011. We have provided some thinking on what policy makers and practitioners can

**Table 19.7.** Five Ways to Wellbeing versus Workplace Practices.

| Way to wellbeing | | Wellbeing practice in the workplace |
|---|---|---|
| Connect. . . | "With the people around you. With family, friends, colleagues and neighbours. At home, work, school or in your local community. Think of these as the cornerstones of your life and invest time in developing them. Building these connections will support and enrich you every day" | Strong evidence exists on the benefit of social support in an organization. A good social environment can modify the impact of jobs that fit the "high demand and low control" formula; for example, working in a customer- or client-focused role. Ways to promote positive interaction between colleagues include away-days involving teamwork or identifying a charity to support through collective activities. Importantly, it is also about instilling a culture of support and respect in the organization, often established by senior leaders in an organization. So encourage "hellos" and "thank yous" and a leadership style that recognizes all areas of work |
| Give. . . | "Do something nice for a friend, or a stranger. Thank someone. Smile. Volunteer your time. Join a community group. Look out, as well as in. Seeing yourself, and your happiness, linked to the wider community can be incredibly rewarding and creates connections with the people around you" | Mentoring schemes are often provided for employees joining organizations, or in early stages of their career. However, a mentor can offer support to people across an organization and at any stage of their career, providing space to discuss issues in a neutral environment and strengthen self-confidence. Employees might be interested in offering mentor skills to other organizations, for example to small charities. Action learning sets are also popular ways for employees to give their time in supporting constructive development of other employees (as well as themselves) |

*(Continued overleaf)*

**Table 19.7.** (*Continued*)

| Way to wellbeing | | Wellbeing practice in the workplace |
|---|---|---|
| Keep learning... | "Try something new. Rediscover an old interest. Sign up for that course. Take on a different responsibility at work. Fix a bike. Learn to play an instrument or how to cook your favourite food. Set a challenge you will enjoy achieving. Learning new things will make you more confident as well as being fun" | Skill development and utilization is important for all jobs in an organization and has been shown to be an important factor in job retention. It is therefore good to monitor who is taking up training opportunities, and if this is not representing all areas of the organization, finding out why and how this can be addressed. An organization learning and development program can include informal learning, such as language classes or subsidizing courses provided by local colleges. However, there is likely to be benefit in promoting learning that supports employees in delivering their own work (e.g., email management and stress management training), particularly in a high-pressured environment |
| Be active... | "Go for a walk or run. Step outside. Cycle. Play a game. Garden. Dance. Exercising makes you feel good. Most importantly, discover a physical activity you enjoy and that suits your level of mobility and fitness" | Ways to promote walking and cycling at work have become popular, building fitness into the commute or travel to meetings. A more unusual example is a project led by the English National Ballet (ENB) called Dance to Work. ENB worked with over 150 employees in 10 employers in the commercial, local authority, charity, and health sectors across London to run dance activities in the workplace. Project evaluation showed improvements in the physical, mental, and emotional health of participants and team working. Organizations like ENB are likely to be willing to set up lunchtime or afterwork classes in workspaces, and employees are often happy to pay for activities that are easy to access |

*(Continued overleaf)*

Table 19.7. (*Continued*)

| Way to wellbeing | Wellbeing practice in the workplace |
| --- | --- |
| Take notice. . . | "Be curious. Catch sight of the beautiful. Remark on the unusual. Notice the changing seasons. Savour the moment, whether you are walking to work, eating lunch, or talking to friends. Be aware of the world around you and what you are feeling. Reflecting on your experiences will help you appreciate what matters to you" | Mindfulness is an approach to help people "take notice" by building awareness of thoughts and feelings and how to manage them. Its philosophy is being applied to workplaces with very promising results. For example, Transport for London offers a 6-week stress reduction workshop using mindfulness techniques to any of its 20,000 employees. It has seen the number of days taken off due to stress or depression fall by 71% for course participants, and 53% citing improvements in happiness at work (Mental Health Foundation, 2010) |

practically do today to reflect wellbeing in the decisions they make. We have finished up by focusing on one specific area of policy and highlighted that wellbeing at work presents particularly fertile ground for raising both national wellbeing and business performance. We close this chapter by returning to where we started.

GDP, developed in the early 1930s, is well over three quarters of a century old. Throughout this time it has served us well as an internationally comparable measure of defined economic activity. However, its limitations, and those of other economic measures that policy makers rely on, are stark in light of international failures to recognize the unsustainability of growth and levels of debt that preceded the financial crisis of the first decade of this century. Just as a modern-day manufacturing business would perhaps baulk at the idea of using 80-year-old plant and equipment, developed before even the first computer, so economists and policy makers are right to question the tools and data they use for modern decision making, and even more so given that the world's financial and economic systems have grown and changed beyond recognition since the 1930s. Because things wear out, a business must periodically invest in new plant and machinery to remain "a going concern." It is similarly right for governments to invest in the statistical systems which both guide the economy and provide ways for others to assess the nation's progress. It is now widely recognized that such an investment is long overdue.

The nostalgic or traditionalist, who worries that governments are going to immanently drop GDP in favor of new social measures of progress, need not have cause for concern. GDP will likely serve us well for many years to come but we evidently need other measures if we are going to develop a more rounded view of progress on which to base our future decisions. In particular, we need better measures of welfare and living standards. The U.K.'s Measuring National Wellbeing program that we have focused on in this chapter represents a proportionate and timely response to develop a balanced picture of economic, societal, and environmental progress. Combined with the work of other nations and international bodies, this collective effort represents an ambitious plan to reflect what really matters to citizens and communities back into policy. The second decade of this century has begun with much debate across developed economies about the kind of societies that we want to live in. This debate has spilled out on the streets of major international cities, and with much soul searching, has raised many questions over unsettling aspects of capitalism, consumerism, debt, and growth. Measuring national wellbeing is, in part, a

460

response to these questions. It is intended to reconnect citizens and their life experiences directly back into policy, and by doing so, will give us better answers in the future than we currently have today.

## Disclaimer

The authors have benefited greatly from the comments and work of others, for which they are grateful. This chapter does not represent the official view of HM Government, nor does it represent HM Government or Greater London Authority policy.

## References

Arnold, J., Cooper, C., & Robertson, I. (1998). *Work psychology—Understanding human behaviour in the workplace* (3rd ed.). Harlow, Essex: Pearson Education.

Beaumont, J. (2011). *Measuring national wellbeing. Discussion paper on domains and measures.* Office for National Statistics, October 31, 2011. http://www.ons.gov.uk/ons/dcp171766_240726.pdf.

Black, Dame Carol (2008). *Dame Carol Black's Review of the health of Britain's working age population: Working for a healthier tomorrow.* London: The Stationery Office.

Business in the Community (2009). *Emotional Resilience Toolkit, Healthy people = healthy profits.* http://www.bitc.org.uk/our-resources/report/emotional-resilience.

Cameron, D. (2010). PM speech on wellbeing on 25 November 2010. https://www.gov.uk/government/speeches/pm-speech-on-wellbeing.

Children's Society (2012). *Promoting positive well-being for children.* http://www.childrenssociety.org.uk/sites/default/files/tcs/promoting_positive_well-being_for_children_final.pdf.

Commission of the European Communities (2009). *GDP and beyond: Measuring progress in a changing world.* COM(2009) 433 final. http://eur-lex.europa.eu/LexUriServ/LexUriServ.do?uri=com:2009:0433:FIN:EN:PDF.

Council of Civil Service Unions/Cabinet Office (2004). *Work stress and health: the Whitehall II study.* http://www.ucl.ac.uk/whitehallII/pdf/Whitehallbooklet_1_.pdf.

Department for Business Innovation & Skills (2008). *Mental capital and wellbeing: Making the most of ourselves in the 21st century. Final project report.* http://bis.ecgroup.net/Publications/Foresight/MentalCapitalandWellbeing/113-08-FOB.aspx.

Donovan, N., & Halpern, D. (2002). *Life satisfaction: The state of knowledge and implications for government.* London: Prime Minister's Strategy Unit.

Easterlin, R. (1974). Does economic growth improve the human lot? Some empirical evidence. In P. A. David & M. W. Reder (Eds.), *Nations and households in economic growth: Essays in honour of Moses Abramovitz* (pp. 89–125). New York: Academic Press.

Fujiwara, D., & Campbell, R. (2011). *Valuation techniques for social cost-benefit analysis: Stated preference, revealed preference and subjective well-being approaches.* London: HM Treasury and Department for Work and Pensions.

Fujiwara, D., Oroyemi, P., & McKinnon, E. (2012). *Wellbeing and civil society: Estimating the value of volunteering to British households using subjective wellbeing.* London: Cabinet Office and Department for Work and Pensions.

Greater London Authority Intelligence Unit (2012). *London wellbeing scores at ward level.* http://data.london.gov.uk/datastore/package/london-ward-well-being-scores.

Harter, J. K., Schmidt, F. L., & Keyes, C. L. (2002). Well-being in the workplace and its relationship to business outcomes: A review of the Gallup Studies. In C. L. M. Keyes & J. Haidt (Eds.), *Flourishing: Positive psychology and the life well-lived* (pp. 205–224). Washington, DC: American Psychological Association.

Herzberg, F. (1966/1997). Work and the nature of man. In D. Pugh (Ed.), *Organisational theory—Selected readings* (4th 1997 ed.). London: Penguin Books.

HM Treasury (2003). *Green Book: Appraisal and evaluation in central government.* London: The Stationery Office.

Hutcheson, F. (1725). *Inquiry into the original of our ideas of beauty and virtue.* Treatise II, Section 3. Dublin.

Inglehart, R., Foa, R., Peterson, C., & Welzel, C. (2008). Development, freedom, and rising happiness: A global perspective (1981–2007). *Perspectives on Psychological Science, 3*(4), 264–285.

Knapp, M., McDaid, D., & Parsonage, M. (2011). *Mental health promotion and mental illness prevention: The economic case.* London: Department of Health.

MacLeod, D., & Clarke, N. (2009). *Engaging for success: Enhancing performance through employee engagement.* A report to government. http://www.mbsportal.bl.uk/secure/subjareas/hrmemplyrelat/bis/11152909-1075engaging09.pdf.

Marmot, M. (2010). *Fair society, healthy lives, The Marmot review. Strategic Review of Health Inequalities in England post-2010.* UCL Institute of Health Equity. http://www.instituteofhealthequity.org/Content/FileManager/pdf/fairsocietyhealthylives.pdf.

Maslow, A. (1943). A theory of human motivation. *Psychological Review, 50,* 370–396.

McGregor, D. (1960). *The human side of enterprise.* New York: McGraw-Hill.

Mental Health Foundation (2010). *Be mindful report.* London: The Mental Health Foundation.

Mguni, N., & Bacon, N. (2010). *Taking the temperature of local communities: The Wellbeing and Resilience Measure (WARM).* London: Young Foundation.

OECD (Organisation for Economic Co-operation and Development) (2011). *How's life? Measuring wellbeing.* http://www.oecd.org/statistics/ howslife.htm.

ONS (Office for National Statistics) (2011). *Measuring what matters: National statistician's reflections on the national debate on measuring national well-being.* http://www.ons.gov.uk/ons/guide-method/user-guidance/well-being/ index.html.

ONS (2011b). *Initial investigation into subjective wellbeing from the opinions survey.* http://www.ons.gov.uk/ons/dcp171776_244488.pdf.

Payne, R. (1987). Organisations as psychological environments. In Peter Warr (Ed.), *Psychology at work* (pp. 291–313). London: Penguin Books.

Stiglitz, J. E., Sen, A., & Fitoussi, J.-P. (2009). *Report of the Commission on the Measurement of Economic Performance and Social Progress.* http://www.stiglitz-sen-fitoussi.fr/documents/rapport_anglais.pdf.

Thompson, S., & Aked, J. (2011). *Five ways to wellbeing.* London: New Economics Foundation.

United Nations General Assembly (2011). *Resolution: Happiness: Towards a holistic approach to development.* http://www.earth.columbia.edu/bhutan-conference-2011/sitefiles/UN%20Resolution%20on%20Happiness.pdf.

University of Essex, Institute for Social and Economic Research (2010). *British Household Panel Survey, Waves 1–18, 1991–2009: Secure Access, National Grid Reference (Easting, Northing, OSGRDIND)* [computer file] (2nd ed.). Colchester, Essex: U.K. Data Archive, SN: 6340.

Waddell, G., & Burton, A. K. (2006) *Is work good for your health and well-being?* London: The Stationery Office.

Wadsworth, E., Chaplin, K., Allen, P., & Smith, A. (2010). What is a good job? Current perspectives on work and improved health and well-being. *The Open Occupational Health & Safety Journal, 2,* 9–15.

Wills, G. (2002). *Inventing America — Jefferson's Declaration of Independence.* New York: Houghton Mifflin.

Young, V., & Bhaumik, C. (2011). *Health and well-being at work: A survey of employees.* Department for Work and Pensions Research Report No 751. http://research.dwp.gov.uk/asd/asd5/rports2011-2012/rrep751.pdf.

# Index

Notes: Page numbers in *italics* denote Figures. Page numbers in **bold** denote Tables.

6 Essentials (Robertson Cooper), 254–255, *254*

*10 Keys to happier living* tool, 456

A
absenteeism, 44, 47, 207, **454**
  *see also* return to work
abusive supervision, 237, 238–240, 246, 265, 267
academic focus, leadership, 236
academic stress, 357–377
accidents at work, 346
accommodation, 209–210, 225–226
  cancer and, 215–233
  defining, 224
Accommodation Adaptation Intervention Paradigm, 208–210, 213–214, 224, 226
accountability, 362
achievement needs, leadership, 182
active happiness, 147, 149
active learning hypothesis, 40
activity element, *Five ways to wellbeing*, 440, **458**
ADA (Americans with Disabilities Act), 215–216
adaptation, 209–210

cancer and, 220–224
coping as, 67–68, 83
definition, 220, 224–225
research, 225–226
return to work, 339–340
self-awareness, 181
  *see also* Accommodation Adaptation Intervention Paradigm
Adelaide university study, 360–361
adolescents, 179–180
  *see also* children
adult learning theory, 323
advice provision, cancer, 223–224, 227
aesthetics of injuries, 344
affect
  eudaimonic wellbeing, 12
  hedonic wellbeing, 10–11
  job demands–resources (JD–R) theory, 51
  productivity–happiness thesis, 115, 118–119, 120–122, 126
  scales, 16
  subjective wellbeing, 15–16
  training outcomes, 322, 330–331

affect (*cont.*)
  work overview, 16–17
  *see also* affective wellbeing; emotions
affective commitment, 16, 143–144
affective wellbeing, 113–114,
    117–118, 128, 131, 244–245
  *see also* affect
affiliation, 153
Affleck, G., 83
aggression at work, 265–266
alcohol use, 238
Allin, Paul, overview, 6
altruism, 182, 183–184
Amabile, Teresa, 150–153
ambiguous gestures, 265
Americans with Disabilities Act (ADA),
    215–216
analysis debate
  coping research, 68
  longitudinal research, 383
Ancient Greece, 410
Anderson, D., 309
Anderson, V. V., 160
Andersson, I. M., 264–266, 268–271,
    278–279
anticipatory coping, 75
antisocial behaviors, 265
  *see also* incivility
anxiety, 428–429
apology-making, 246–247
appraisals
  coping and, 66, 71–72, 81, 83
  policy appraisal cycle, *448*, 449
Archer, W. R., 197–198
Aristotle, 410
Armour, R. A., 359
arousal feelings, 11, 12
Ashforth, B., 19
Aspinwall, L. G., 77–79
assessments
  change, 386–389
  needs, sexual harassment awareness
    training, 327, 330

policy tools, **442–443**
  stress/health interventions, 193
  sustainability, 417–418
attitudes
  cancer and work, 220–221
  job characteristics model, 40
  organizational happiness, 149
  satisfaction-related, 15–16
  sexual harassment awareness training,
    331
  subjective wellbeing, 15
attitudinal judgments, 15
attributed idealized leadership
    influence, 245–246
Austin Croft, Laura, 450–456
Australian academic stress study,
    357–377
authentic happiness model, 13–14
authoritarian leadership style, 286
authoritative parenting style, 275
authority, 285
  *see also* leadership; management
    practices; supervisors
autonomy
  control and, 93, 95–96, 98, 104
  DCM model, 42
  job characteristics model, 39
  moral, 164–165
  power balance, 185
  redesigning jobs, 54
awareness
  self-awareness, 177, 180–181
  sexual harassment, 319–338
  social, 180

B
Bakker, Arnold B.
  hedonic wellbeing, 17
  job demands–resources (JD–R)
    theory, 46, 47, 48–49, 50–52,
    55–56
  overview, 4
balance
  concept/definition, 300–301

workload balancing, 255
*see also* positive/negative...; work–life
    balance
banking crisis, 1980s, 179
Barling, J.
    leadership, 237
    overview, 5
Bass, B. M., 242
Baumeister, R. F., 13
behavioral factors
    character, 159
    incivility, 264–294
    leadership, 236, 238–239, 241,
        242–243, 245–247
    organizational happiness, 140–141,
        149
    research, 9
    self-reports, 368
    social wellbeing, 20–21
    training effectiveness models, 322
    values connection, 180
behaviorism, 20–21
beliefs *see* perceptions
belonging, sense of, 21, 124
benefit concept, 72, 83
benefit-reminding coping, 83
Bennett, Joel, overview, 5
Bentham, Jeremy, 410
best practice
    health promotion, 193, 194,
        197–198
    longitudinal research, 383
biases
    injured workers' return, 347
    productivity–happiness thesis, 121,
        126–127
    surveys, 272
"Big Five" personality factors, 257
bipolar view, positive/negative affect,
    10–11
Black, Carol, 452
Blau, G., 271–272
blood pressure problems, 163

boards of directors, 186–187
de Boer, A. G. E. M., 211–212
Bonett, D. G., 162
bosses *see* leadership; management
    practices; supervisors
Bouknight, R. R., 215
Bowes-Sperry, L., 326
Bradley, C. J., 212
"brain drain", academics, 363–364
breadth issues, measuring wellbeing,
    23–24, 26
    *see also* broad...
breast cancer, 215, 220
British Household Panel Survey, *446,*
    447
broad coping strategies, 253–256
broad-mindedness, 73–74
buffering effects, workplace control, 91,
    94
bullying, 267–268
Burnham, D. H., 182
burnout
    abusive supervision, 239–240
    causes, 37–38
    ERI model, 41, 42
    job demands–resources (JD–R)
        theory, 46–47, 50
    organizational happiness, 142
    transformational leadership,
        245–246
    university academics, 359–360,
        362–363
Burns, J. M., 242
business performance, 128, 450
    *see also* organizational performance

C
calling at work, 20
Cameron, David, 419, 436
cancer, 207–233
cancer survivors, 210–212
    definition, 211
    quality of survival, 208
    review of literature, 214

cancer survivors (*cont.*)
  unemployment, 212
Cantril Scale, 426
cardiovascular health, 41, 91, 94,
    162–163
cardiovascular heart disease (CHD),
    163
career breaks, 311
careers, 9
  control and, 96–98, 101–103
  sustainable workforce, **305**,
    309–313, 314–315
  VIA-Inventory of Strengths,
    165–166
  *see also* calling at work
caregivers, work–life balance, 302
Carnegie Foundation for the
    Advancement of Teaching survey,
    359
case–control studies, cancer, 217–218
catalysts, inner work life system, 152
causal engagement indicators, 145
causal models, 37–38, 50–51, 401
causal pathways, coping, 66
causal relationships
  assessing, 389–397
  change, 386
  stressors/strains, 382
Caza, B. B., 281–282
challenge stressors, 176–177, 258, 362
Chan, F., 215–216
change
  6 Essentials model, 255
  assessing, 386–389
  job crafting, 51–52
  leadership and, 146, 186, 192–193
  organizational, 255, 328, 332
character and wellbeing, 157–204
  defining character, 164–167
  future research directions, 167–169
  positive stress, 175–204
  primary objectives, 159
  strength of character, 177, 178–180

  *see also* personality characteristics
Charney, Dennis, 257
CHD (cardiovascular heart disease),
    163
checklist approach
  children's wellbeing, 441, **444**, 445
  coping research, 68
children, 187, 434, 441, **444**, 445
  *see also* adolescents
Children's Society policy checklist, 441,
    **444**
Cigularov, K. P.
  national policy, 382–383, 393
  overview, 6
citizen perspective, measuring
    wellbeing, 424
citizenship behavior, 149, 243
civic responsibility, 189
Civility, Respect, and Engagement in
    the Workplace (CREW), 287–289,
    *288*
civility training, 285–289, 322–323
clinical research, 177
cognitive changes, job crafting, 52
cognitive demands, job
    demands–resources (JD–R)
    theory, 45
cognitive outcomes, training, 322, 330
cognitive process, incivility, 280
cognitive revolution, 20–21
cognitive work, 43
colleague education, cancer, 216–217
combined effect, longitudinal research,
    387–388
commitment, 16
  happiness and, 143–145, 149
  job demands–resources (JD–R)
    theory, 46–49
  organizational happiness, 149
  overcommitment, 41
  proactive coping, 75–76
  stress research, 362
commonsense ideas, 113, 119–120

communication
  computer-based, 274
  ill-health accommodation, 219
  inner work life system, 152
  stress/health interventions, 193, 197
community participation decrease, 273–274
compassion satisfaction, 49
compensation systems, injured workers, 341
competitiveness, 139, 146
computer-based technology, 130, 274, 313–314
conceptualization issues
  happiness, 114–115, 140
  incivility, 270
  support at work, 222
  sustainable workforces, 297–303, **304**
  wellbeing at work, 9–33
  work–life balance, 297–303, **304**
conclusion–resolution, coping, 80
conflicts
  incivility and, 267–268
  leadership, 181–182
  work–life, 300, 308
Confucianism, 164
connect element, *Five ways to wellbeing*, 440, **457**
conservation of resources theory, 363
consideration, inner work life system, 152
construct definitions, leadership, 236–237
contact strategies, stigma/return to work, 350–351
contemporary "happy–productive worker" thesis, 127–129
content-general/-specific social support, 312
contextual factors
  coping effectiveness, 81

measuring wellbeing, 416–418, 426–427
  training effectiveness models, 321, 328–329, 332
contractual flexibility, 217
control, 35–109
  cancer and work, 217–218
  career management, 310–311
  illusion of, 121
  job demands–resources (JD–R) theory, 37–64
  lack of, 93–94
  nature of, 92–93
  positive health/wellbeing role, 91–109
  positive outcome relationships, 94–100, 101–103
  self-reliance and, 185, 188
  stress research, 362
  sustainable workforce, **306**, 307–309
  *see also* coping; resources
coordination, inner work life system, 152
coping, 35–109
  with bad bosses, 235
  benefits/limitations of, 259, **260**, 261
  components of, 69
  defining, 67–68
  effectiveness, 66, 80–82
  with incivility, 279
  job demands–resources (JD–R) theory, 37–64
  measurement, 67–68, 71
  positive psychology and, 65–90
  strategies, 74–80, 253–262, **260**, 261, 279
  trends in research, 66
  *see also* control; resources
core job characteristics, defining, 39–40
core qualities, stress pathways, 189–191

Cortina, L. M., 268, 271, 279, 280–282

costs *see* economic costs; health-care costs

cost–benefit analyses, 445

coworker relations
   incivility, 277–278, 283
   injured workers, 340, 342–343, 345–351

coworker satisfaction, 280–283

coworker support, 340, 351

Cox, Tom, overview, 5

CPSs (critical psychological states), 39–40

crafting jobs, 51–53, 55–56

CREW *see* Civility, Respect, and Engagement in the Workplace

criteria autonomy, 93

critical psychological states (CPSs), 39–40

Croft, Laura Austin, 450–456

Cropanzano, R., 120–122, 161

cross-lagged panel correlations, 402–403

cross-sectional studies
   academic stress, 367–368, 371
   occupational stress, 381–382, 385–386

Csikszentmihalyi, M., 65–66

cultural norms, 273

culture
   civility, 288
   incivility, 273, 285, 290
   injured workers' return to work, 340
   inner work life system, 152
   socialization training, 323
   stress/health interventions, 197
   sustainable workforces, **305**, 312, 314

curse words, 275

customers
   incivility effects, 279–280, 283

satisfaction drivers, 437

cynicism, 323–325, 327–328, 422

D

daily progress/happiness/performance, 150–153

Daniels, K., 16–17

data sources
   academic stress, 368, 371
   measuring wellbeing, 448
   *see also* interviews; surveys

DBP (diastolic blood pressure), 163

DCM *see* demand–control model

de Boer, A. G. E. M., 211–212

decision making, 97, 121–122

Declaration of Independence, U.S., 409

definitional issues
   accommodation, 224
   adaptation, 220, 224–225
   balance concept, 300–301
   cancer survivors, 211
   character, 164–167
   coping, 67–68
   core job characteristics, 39–40
   engagement, 144
   flourishing, 14
   happiness, 10, 120, 140–141
   health, 4, 423
   incivility, 263, 264–269, 270
   job crafting, 51
   job design, 37
   leadership, 185, 236–237, 241
   longitudinal research, 383–386
   mental health, 423
   mistreatment at work, 269
   occupational stress, 383
   organizational socialization, 323
   performance at work, 120
   proactivity, 77
   satisfaction, 120
   stigma, 341
   strain/strains, 362, 381
   stress/stressors, 70–71, 381
   sustainable careers, 309–310

sustainable workforce, 299
work–life balance, 299–302
de Lange, A. H., 382, 392–393
demand–control model (DCM), 40, 42–43, 94, 96, 103–104, 362–363
*see also* Job Demand–Control (JDC) model
demands *see* family demands; job demands; job demands–resources (JD–R) theory
Demerouti, Evangelia
job demands–resources (JD–R) theory, 48–49, 55
overview, 4
demographic measurement tools, 446–447
depression, 120–122, 244
Depressive–Realism vs. Enthusiasm–Naivety hypothesis, 120–122
Derks, D., 52
design *see* job design; research, design; training, design; work design
deviant behaviors, 265
Dewe, Philip, overview, 4–5
diastolic blood pressure (DBP), 163
Diener, E., 24–25, **24**
Dik, B. J., 19–20
directors' boards, 186–187
Disability Discrimination Act 1995, U.K., 215
disabled workers, 345, 349
*see also* injured workers
discretion at work, 307–308
*see also* control
discriminatory practices
gender/racial, 268
injured workers, 342
diseases, 94
*see also* ill-health
dispositional affect, 120–122
disruptive injuries, 346–347

dissatisfaction, 38–39, 118, 361
*see also* satisfaction
distal training outcomes, 321–322, 331
distress, 239, 241, 281
active/relaxed balance, 149
eustress contrast, 147
university academics, 361, 366
distribution of income measures, 415, 417
diversity, support networks, 177, 186–189
diversity training, 325–326
drift hypothesis, reverse causation, 391
drinking problems, 238
drivers of wellbeing, 432–433, 435–440, 448–450
Duffy, R. D., 19–20
duration of absence, job demands–resources (JD–R) theory, 47
Dutton, J. E., 21, 52
dynamic longitudinal research, 386–387

E
Eakin, J. M., 346–347
EAPs *see* employee assistance programs
early retirement packages, 364
early-stage broad coping strategies, 253–256
Easterlin Paradox, 412–413, 421
Easterlin, Richard, 412
Eatough, Erin, overview, 5
economic benefits *see* economic wellbeing
economic costs
incivility, 284
injured workers, 339
measuring wellbeing, 422
economic growth objective, 412–414, 419
economic uncertainty, 255
economic wellbeing
leave control, 311

economic wellbeing (*cont.*)
  measuring, 416, 435
  productivity–happiness thesis, 122
  *see also* gross domestic product;
    material wellbeing
education
  employers/managers/colleagues,
    216–217
  health/social care professionals, 226
  mental illness stigma reduction,
    349–350
effect indicators, engagement, 144–145
effectiveness
  coping effectiveness, 66, 80–82
  training, sexual harassment
    awareness, 319–338
effort, coping and, 67
effort–reward imbalance (ERI) model,
  40–43, 362–363
Eldrige, B. M., 20
ElRakhawy, Nada, overview, 5
emotional exhaustion, 142, 240, 241,
  245, 280
  *see also* exhaustion
emotional support, 153
emotional wellbeing, 160
emotion-focused coping, 75
emotions
  character and, 160–161
  coping and, 66, 70–75, 82–83, 256
  happiness dimensions, 115, 142
  inner work life system, 150
  measuring, 17
  performance relationship, 121
  research, 9
  *see also* affect; moods
empirical research
  character, 161–162
  control, 98
  happiness at work, 145
  leadership, 177, 188–189, 241, 246
  productivity–happiness thesis, 114
  stigma/injured workers, 342

employee assistance programs (EAPs),
  259, 367
employee character *see* character and
  wellbeing; personality
  characteristics
employee–customer incivility, 279–280
employee engagement *see* engagement
employee job negotiations, 43–44
employee retention, 162
employee wellbeing
  academic focus on, 236
  leadership influence, 235–251
  "Optimum" Employee Experience,
    **454**
  physical, 238–239, 240–241,
    243–244
  psychological, 239–240, 241–242,
    244–246
  return to work, 339–356
  sustainable workforces, 295–318
  *see also* job...; worker...; workforce
    sustainability; workgroup
    interactions
employers
  costs of health care, 297–298
  education, cancer, 216–217
  employee engagement, 303
  worker relationships, 297
  work–life balance, 301–302
empowerment *see* control
enabled work intensification, 309
encouragement, 153
engagement, 18–19, 303
  coping strategies, 256
  happiness as, 143–145
  job demands–resources (JD–R)
    theory, 38, 46, 49, 51
  leadership, 146
  policy focus, 450–455
  work–life balance, 308
  *see also* work engagement

*Engaging for success: Enhancing performance through employee engagement* report, 452–453

England
  academic stress, 360
  geographic measuring tools, *446*, 447
  *see also* United Kingdom

Enthusiasm–Naivety vs. Depressive–Realism hypothesis, 120–122

entrepreneurial character, 166

environmental factors
  control concept, 92, 95
  happiness dimensions, 115
  incivility, 282–283
  measuring wellbeing, 418
  person × environment interaction, 208
  person–environment theory, 168–169
  pro-environmental initiatives, 247
  sustainable workforce, 298
  *see also* working conditions

ERI model *see* effort–reward imbalance model

ethics, 178, 180, 326

ethnicity, 268

eudaimonic wellbeing, 10–12, 17–20, 23, 26, 256, 427

Europe
  cancer survival, 211–212
  measuring wellbeing, 222–223, 418
  occupational health services, 222–223

European Commission measures, 418

Eurostat measures, 425

eustress, 147, 176, 189

evaluative measurement approach, 427

"events", inner work life system, 151–153

evidence-based guidance, organizations, 140, 142

evidence-based programs, stress, 193–194, **195–196**, 197

evidence sources, control–positive outcomes, 99–100

exchange, work intensification, 309

exclusionary behavior subscale, UWBQ, 272

executive team, 186
  *see also* leadership

exhaustion
  abusive supervision and, 240
  incivility and, 280
  job demands–resources (JD–R) theory, 50
  laissez-faire leadership and, 241
  organizational happiness, 142
  transformational leadership and, 245
  *see also* burnout

experience measurement approach, 427

experience-sampling research, 17, 22

experimental research, leadership, 246

experimental surveys, 427

exposure time effect, longitudinal research, 387–388

extraneous research variables, 393–396

extra-role job performance, 47

extrinsic work factors, 452

F
faces scales, satisfaction, 16

face-to-face interactions, 274, 326–327

facet satisfaction scales, 16

Factual Autonomy Scale (FAS), 98

faculty stress, 358–359

*Fair society, healthy lives* review, 453

family demands, 299–300, 302, 309

family facilitation, control, 97

FAS (Factual Autonomy Scale), 98

feedback
  measuring wellbeing, 448–449
  redesigning jobs, 55
  strengths-based interventions, 58

Filter, R. O., 164

Finland, 211, 221, 222

Fisher, Cynthia D.
    "happy–productive worker" thesis,
        119–120
    measuring wellbeing, 23
    overview, 4
Fisher, Shirley, 358, 365
fit
    coping effectiveness and, 80–81
    person–environment, 208, 363, 367
    work–life, 300
Fitoussi, Jean-Paul *see* Stiglitz, Sen and
        Fitoussi Commission
*Five ways to wellbeing* framework, 440,
        449, 456, **457–459**
flexibility
    cancer accommodation, 217–218
    career management, 309–310
    intensification of work, 309
    job demands–resources (JD–R)
        model, 45
    positive workplace association, 455
flourishing, 11
    defining, 14
    models of, 13–14
    positive psychology role, 66, 73, 82
    scales, 24–25, **24**
    sustainable workforce, 298
flow construct, 19
focus group research, 167, 369
Folkman, S., 68, 74–75, 80, 82–83
follow-up research, academic stress,
        371–372
Ford Motor Company study, 177
formal training, 322–323
Francis, Lori, overview, 6
Fredrickson, B., 73–74, 258
Frese, M., *387*, 388
full two-wave panel research design,
        400–401, *400*
funding academic work, 365

G
Gallagher, M. W., 13
Gallup Q-12 survey, 303

Gallup Workplace Audit (GWA),
        18–19, 145
Gallup World View survey, 426
GDP *see* gross domestic product
gender differences
    power motivation, 183
    sexual harassment awareness training,
        327
    support at work, 221
gender discrimination, 268
"general incivility", definition, 268
general practitioner role, 222–223
"general" social support, 312
general wellbeing *see* overall wellbeing
genetics, happiness and, 141
geodemographic/geographical
        measurement tools, 446–447
giving element, *Five ways to wellbeing*,
        440, **457**
globalization effects, 130, 308, 313
goal accomplishment, 57
goal-related components, 6 Essentials
        model, 256
goal-related sensitivity to stigma,
        344
goal self-concordance, 49
"goodness of fit", coping effectiveness,
        80–81
Goolsby, John, 183, 186–187
gossiping subscale, UWBQ, 272
government measures, 303,
        409–463
    *see also* policy making/actions
Grant, Joseph M., 179
gratitude, 123
Greater London Authority measures,
        447
Greek history, 410
gross domestic product (GDP),
        410–411, 414–416, 419, 421,
        456, 460
group activities, 312
    *see also* workgroup interactions

group coping strategies, 256–259
growth
    economic policy, 412–414, 419
    stress-related, 83
GWA *see* Gallup Workplace Audit

H
Hackman, J. R., 39
Hakanen, J., 46–48
halo effect, 126, 139
Hanrahan, Michael, overview, 5–6
happiness, 3–7
    as commitment/engagement,
        143–145
    conceptualizing, 9–11, 13–14, 17,
        114–115
    control relationship, 99, 100, 102
    daily progress/performance,
        150–153
    defining, 10, 120, 140–141
    enhancing, 145–146
    historical perspectives, 409–411
    as job satisfaction, 118, 143–145
    micro-/macro-level variables, 139
    objective/subjective dimensions,
        114–115
    ONS survey questions, 428–429
    organizational characteristics,
        111–156
    performance link, 113–114
    policy objectives, 420–421
    of stress/stress of, 146–150
    subjective wellbeing and, 17
    terminology, 160
    unhappiness interdependence, 147
    of wellbeing, 142–143
    workers, 111–156
"happy–productive worker" thesis,
    113–138
    becoming a "happy worker",
        123–124
    facilitating factors, 124–125
    inhibiting factors, 124–125
    measurement evaluation, 143

outcome measures, 125–129
    significance, 118–122
harassment *see* sexual harassment
    awareness
hardiness and stress, 362
hard skills, 322
Hargie, O., 274
Hargrove, M. Blake, overview, 5
Harter, J., 21, 117
Hawthorne studies, 115
Hay Group research, 180
HDI (Human Development Index),
    416
health
    control and, 91–109
    defining, 4, 423
    impairment process, 45–47
    job demands–resources (JD–R)
        theory, 45–47, 50
    longitudinal research, 381–382
    organizational strategies, 296
    outcomes
        control, 96
        job demands–resources (JD–R)
            theory, 45–47, 50
    positive pathways to, 177–178
    "precarious work", 297
    promotion interventions, 191–198
    psychological wellbeing and,
        162–163
    quality of working life, 207–233
    stress and, 175–204
    WHO's definitions, 423
    work relationship, 207–233
    *see also* cardiovascular health;
        ill-health; mental health;
        occupational health; physical
        wellbeing
health-care costs, U.S., 297–298
health-care professionals' role,
    226–227
health and safety practices, 259, 261
heart health *see* cardiovascular health

hedonic wellbeing, 10–11, 12, 17, 256
Hersey, R. B., 115–116, 160
Hershcovis, M. S., 266–268
Herzberg, F., 38–39, 116, 451–452
hierarchical linear modeling, 49–50
hierarchical multiple regression, 402
high performance work systems
    (HPWS), 149
"high-strain jobs", 40, 178
hindrance-related stress, 176, 258–259
Hine, D. W., 272
historical perspectives, 4, 409–411
Holistic Stress model, 147, *148*
hormones, stress-related, 96, 307
Hosie, Peter, overview, 5
hostility subscale, UWBQ, 272
household surveys, 427, *446*, 447
Howard Hughes Corporation case,
    183, 186–187
HPWS (high performance work
    systems), 149
Hsieh, Tony, 139
Human Behaviour School, 116
Human Development Index (HDI),
    416
Human Relations Movement, 116
human resource practices
    coping strategies, 259, 261
    high performance work systems, 149
    improvement approaches, 454–455
    policy focus, 450
    productivity–happiness thesis,
        127–129
    sustainable workforce, 298
Hutcheson, Francis, 409–410
Hyett, M. P., 25
hygiene factors, two-factor theory,
    38–39

I
IARC (International Agency for
    Research on Cancer), 210
idealized leadership influence, 242,
    245–246

identification with role, stigma
    prediction, 344
IHS (Integrated Household Survey),
    427
ill-health
    control and, 91, 93–94
    job demands effect on, 47
    return to work after, 207–233
    *see also* health; mental illness
Illingworth, N., 216–217
imperial power motivation, 182–183
imposed work intensification, 309
incivility
    at work, 263–294
    conceptualizing, 270
    consequences, 280–284
    defining, 266, 268
    measuring, 270–273
    solving the problem, 284–289
"incivility spiral", 278–279, 281
income distribution measures, 415, 417
incomplete two-wave panel research
    design, 399–400, *399*
inconsistent leadership, definition, 241
Indian social support study, 188
individual factors/differences
    cancer and, 220–224
    change and, 192
    coping, 81–82, 256–259
    measurement framework, 423
    self-reliance, 185
    stress, 71, 192
    training effectiveness models, 321,
        327–328
    *see also* adaptation; character and
        wellbeing; personality
        characteristics
individualized consideration, leadership,
    242, 245
individual-level interventions, 55,
    57–58
    *see also* job crafting
indulgent parenting style, 275

industrial psychology, 4
industry-specific stress, 361–362
Indvik, J., 283–284
influence spheres, 66
informational influence, 329
information provision, cancer,
    223–224, 227
inhibitors, inner work life system, 152
initial impact research effect, 387–388
injured workers
    course of injury factor, 345
    designation effects, 341
    origin of injury factor, 345–346
    return to work, 339–356
inner work life system, 150–153
in-role job performance, 47
integrated approaches
    accommodation–adaptation,
        209–210, 225–226
    stress, 189–192
Integrated Household Survey (IHS),
    427
intellectual stimulation, leadership, 242,
    245–246
intensification of work, **306**, 307–309
interactional injustice, 278–279
interaction hypothesis, job demands ×
    resources, 47–48
inter-individual differences, research,
    386
internal locus of control, 185
International Agency for Research on
    Cancer (IARC), 210
international context, measuring
    wellbeing, 416–418, 426–427
interpersonal conflict *see* conflicts
interpersonal leadership influence, 182
interpretation debate, coping research,
    68
interrelationship changes, research, 386
intervention-level job
    demands–resources interventions,
    54, *54*

intervention levels, stress, 366–367
intervention targets, job
    demands–resources, 54, *54*
interviews
    academic stress study, 369
    incivility information, 272–273
    jobs, locus of control, 102–103
intraindividual change, research, 386
intraindividual-level stress measures, 71
intrinsic job satisfaction, 113–114,
    117–118, 131
intrinsic motivation, 19, 39
intrinsic work factors, 452
involvement-in-job construct, 18
i-resilience model (Robertson Cooper),
    257–258, *257*
irritable bowel disorder, 218, 219

J
James, William, 164
Jarrett, R. J., 360–361, 366
JDC model *see* Job Demand–Control
    (JDC) model
JDS (Job Diagnostic Survey), 98
JD–R theory *see* job
    demands–resources (JD–R) theory
Jefferson, Thomas, 409
job characteristics model, 39–40, 43,
    95, 103
job control *see* control
job crafting, 51–53, 55–56
job demands
    control relationship, 103–104, 307
    crafting jobs, 52–53
    examples of, 45
    ill-health effects, 47
    resource interactions x, 47–48
    *see also* demand–control model
job demands–resources (JD–R) theory,
    37–64, *46*
    crafting jobs, 51–53
    flexibility, 45
    interaction hypothesis, 47–48
    interventions, 53–58, *54*

job demands–resources (JD–R)
  theory (*cont.*)
  personal resources, 48–50
  processes in, 45–47
  university academics study,
    362–363
Job Demand–Control (JDC) model,
  307
  *see also* demand–control model
job design
  crafting jobs, 51
  definition, 37
  redesigning jobs, 54–55
  theory, 37–38
  *see also* work design
Job Diagnostic Survey (JDS), 98
job engagement, measuring/defining,
  144
  *see also* engagement
job interviews, 102–103
job involvement, 18
job performance
  control and, 98
  happiness link, 114
  injured workers' return, 344–345
  interaction hypothesis, 47
  predicting, 44–45, 47, 162
  two-factor theory, 39
  *see also* performance at work
job redesign interventions, 54–55
job-related affect, 118–119
job resources
  crafting jobs, 52–53
  demand interactions x, 47–48
  examples of, 45
  motivating potential, 38
  organizational commitment effects,
    47
  as predictors, 45–46
  using, 53
  *see also* job demands–resources
    (JD–R) theory; resources
job satisfaction, 9, 15–16, 39

control and, 95, 99–100
happiness as, 118, 143–145
incivility and, 280–281, 282–283
intrinsic, 113–114, 117–118,
  131
performance link, 116–118
psychological wellbeing and, 161,
  162
support link, 221
two-factor theory, 39
  *see also* satisfaction
jobs, changing nature of, 43–44
job security, 255
job-skills training, 322–323
job strain *see* strain/strains
job stress/stressors, 3, 4
  causes, 37
  effort–reward imbalance model,
    40–41
  focus of studies, 6
  one-sidedness of models, 41–42
  theory, 38
  university academics, 357–377
  *see also* occupational stress/stressors;
    strain/strains; stress/stressors
Johnson, P. R., 283–284
*Journal of Occupational Health
  Psychology*, 383
journal research, 314
Judge, T. A., 23
"just in time" working, 127
"just world" bias, 347

K
Kalleberg, A. L., 297
Kammeyer-Mueller, J. D., 23
Karasek, R. A., 40, 94, 96,
  103–104
Kath, Lisa M., overview, 6
Kelliher, C., 309
Kelloway, E. K., 237, 240–241
Kennedy, Robert F., 410
Kirkpatrick, D. L., 321–322
Kluger, A. N., 119–120

Kompier, M., 388–389, 392–393

Kossek, Ellen, overview, 6

Kramer, Steven, 150–153

L

Laird, D., 177

laissez-faire leadership, 237, 240–242, 246

de Lange, A. H., 382, 392–393

language, incivility and, 275–276

Laschinger, H. K. S., 281

late-stage narrow coping strategies, 259

Lauer, Tyler, overview, 5

Lawler, E. E., 39

Lazarus, R. S., 65–66, 68, 71–72, 74–75, 81

leadership
  academic focus on, 236
  civility training, 286
  construct definitions, 236–237
  defining, 185, 236–237
  employee wellbeing and, 235–251
  future research, 246–247
  organizational happiness, 146, 151–152
  positive stress, 175–204
  social support activities, 312
  wellbeing of leaders, 246–247
  *see also* management practices; supervisors

lean production methods, 298

learning element, *Five ways to wellbeing*, 440, **458**

learning outcomes, training, 322, 330–331

Leary, M. R., 13

leave control, 311

Lee, A., 282–283

legal aspects, 319–320, 330–331, 339, 349

leisure time, 310

Leiter, Michael
  incivility, 276–278, 279, 288, 290

overview, 5–6

Levinson, H., 184

liability claims, sexual harassment, 324–325

life satisfaction (LS), 11
  abusive supervision and, 239
  character and, 167
  control and, 95, 99, 100
  incivility study, 283
  measuring wellbeing, 412–413, *426*, 428–429, **430–431**, 432
  modeling, 14
  organizational happiness, 142

life wellbeing, 10–14, *13*

life–work balance, 97, 295–318

Lim, S., 282–283

linear modeling, 49–50

linear regression, OLS method, 429, **430–431**, 432

line management training, 455

Lippel, K., 342

Littman-Ovadia, H., 168

Llorens, S., 50–51

locus of control, 92–93, 97, 101–103, 185, 188

London borough measures, 447

longitudinal research/studies
  academic stress, 368, 371
  cancer and work, 218
  change assessment, 386–389
  constituents of, 383–386
  definitional issues, 383–386
  design, 397–403
  leadership/employee wellbeing, 246
  methodological considerations, 390–397
  objectives of, 386–390
  occupational stress, 381–407
  statistical procedures, 401–403
  third variable effects, 393–396
  variable types, 393–396
  work–life balance, 314

Lopez, S. J., 13
low-wage workers, U.S., 298
LS *see* life satisfaction
Luthans, F., 56
Lyubomirsky, S., 125

M
McClelland, D. C., 182
McGregor, D., 451
MacLennan, Sara, overview, 5
Macmillan cancer charity, 223, 227
macro-level happiness variables, 139
Magley, V. J.
   incivility, 279, 282
   overview, 6
malingering, charges of, 343
management practices
   cancer accommodation, 216–217,
      219, 226
   health/productivity, 194, 197
   human resources, 127–129
   incivility, 285
   intensification of work, 308–309
   line management training, 455
   safety climate, 348–349
   stigma in return to work, 349–351
   support, 329
   sustainable workforces, 302–303
   *see also* leadership
Marmot, Michael, 453
Martin, R. J., 272
Maslow, A., 451
material wellbeing, 417
   *see also* economic wellbeing
Mausner, B., 116
Mayer, Marissa, 388
meaning
   in life, 168
   in work, 19–20, 245
meaning-centred coping, 82–83
mean scores, coping, 69
measurement issues
   approaches/early results, 423–434
   coping research, 67–68, 71

framework development, 423–425
government measures, 303
happiness at work, 141–145
incivility, 270–273
international context, 416–418,
      426–427
job demands–resources (JD–R)
      theory, 37–64
modern societies, 409–463
perceived control, 100
stress measurement, 71
work–life balance, 300
work wellbeing, 9–33
*see also* outcome measures
men
   cancer and, 221
   sexual harassment awareness training,
      327
   *see also* gender...
Menard, S., 385
mental health
   cancer and, 212
   conceptualizing, 9
   job stress determining, 364–365
   "precarious work", 297
   return to work, 347–348, 349–350
   sexual harassment effects, 319
   transformational leadership
      indicators, 244
   WHO's definitions, 423
   *see also* psychological...; psychology;
      stress
mental illness, 347–348, 349–350
Messervey, D., 49–50
meta-analyses
   control, 100–103
   engagement, 145
   job satisfaction, 144
   leadership/employee wellbeing, 237
   satisfaction–performance, 117
   social support, 187
method autonomy, 93
method variance problem, 368

METIS Collaboration, 208, 210

microeconomic wellbeing effects, 419

micro-level happiness variables, 139

mid-stage coping strategies, 256–259

Miller, S. M., 92

   *see also* minimax hypothesis

Mill, John Stuart, 410

mindfulness, 181

minimax hypothesis, 92, 99

mismatches, person–environment fit,
   367

mistreatment at work, 263–294

modeling

   early models, 38–44

   JDC model, 307

   job demands–resources (JD–R)
      theory, 37, 46–52

   multidimensional models, 13–14

   one-sidedness of models, 41–42

   overall life wellbeing, *13*

   sexual harassment awareness training,
      319–338, *320*

   simplicity of models, 41–42

   social impacts, 445

   static character of models, 41, 42–43

   subjective wellbeing, 445

   training effectiveness, 319–338, *320*

   two-wave panel designs, 401

   work–life balance, 301

   work overview, 22

modern society measurements,
   409–463

momentary task
   satisfaction/performance, 117, 119

Monash university study, 361

monetary rewards, 125

   *see also* economic wellbeing

moods

   measuring, 17

   research, 9

   *see also* emotions

"moonlighters", 243

moral discipline/attachment/
   autonomy, 164–165

motivation

   control relationship, 100–101

   cynicism as predictor of, 323–325

   intrinsic, 19, 39

   job demands–resources (JD–R)
      theory, 38, 45–47, 51

   one-sidedness of models, 41–42

   organizational happiness, 150–151

   power, 177, 182–184

   proactive coping, 75, 77–78

   process, 45–47

   training, 321, 322–323, 325

   two-factor theory, 38–39

multidimensional models, 13–14

multiple regression methods, 402

M"A nsterberg, Hugo, 4

myth endorsement, sexual harassment,
   330–331

N

narrative review methods, 214

narrow coping strategies, 259

Nash, L., 22

national account extensions, U.K.
   policy, 435

National Institute of Occupational
   Safety and Health (NIOSH), 194,
   364

national policy

   measuring wellbeing, 409–463

   research and, 379–463

   U.K., 412–423

   *see also* policy making/actions

National University Stress Study,
   Australia, 369–372

national wellbeing measurement, 424,
   *425*

N'Dow, James, overview, 5

needs assessment, sexual harassment
   awareness training, 327, 330

needs of leadership, 182

negative, absence of, 143

negative affect, 10–11, 15, 16, 121–122, 126
  *see also* negative emotions
negative effects
  poor leadership, 235–237, 240, 242, 244
  sexual harassment awareness training, 320
  stigmatized workers, 342
negative emotions, 66, 73, 115, 142
  *see also* negative affect
negatively-toned appraisals, 72
negative/positive debate
  coping effectiveness, 80
  psychology, 66
negative stress, 147, 176–177, 361–362
negative work pressures, coping strategies, 255
negotiation, 43–44, 121
Nelson, D., 146–147, 184
New England university study, 361
NIOSH *see* National Institute of Occupational Safety and Health
NOCWO (Nordic Study Group of Cancer and Work Life), 221–222
nonconstant research variables, 395–396
"nonsystemic" wellbeing drivers, 436, **437**
nontraditional work, 178
nonwork roles, work–life balance, 299, 301, 303, 308, 310–311, 314
Noor, N. M., 102
Nordic Study Group of Cancer and Work Life (NOCWO), 221–222
normative commitment, 16
normative influence
  incivility, 265–266, 270, 276
  sexual harassment awareness training, 329
  *see also* cultural norms; social norms
Norway, 221, 222

noticing element, *Five ways to wellbeing*, 440, **459**
nourishers, inner work life system, 152–153
nurse studies, 49–50, 241, 245, 281

O
obesity, 175–176, 193, 197–198
objective control, 98–99
objective data, 368
objective dimensions
  happiness, 114–115, 411
  incivility, 289
objective success, careers, 310
objective wellbeing measurement, 417
OCB (organizational citizenship behavior), 149
occasion factors, longitudinal research, 394–395
occupational health, 4, 207
  academic focus on, 236
  professionals' role, 226
  research, 381–382
  services, 222–223, 225
  *see also* health
occupational stress/stressors
  defining, 383
  longitudinal research, 381–407
  overview, 3
  *see also* job stress/stressors; stress/stressors
occupation-specific stress, 361–362
O'Connell, B. J., 102
OECD *see* Organisation for Economic Co-operation and Development
Oerlemans, W., 17
Office for National Statistics (ONS), U.K., 414, 419, 424, *425*, 427–429
  *see also* Opinions Survey
O'Kane, P., 274
O'Leary-Kelly, A. M., 326
OLS method *see* ordinary least squares method

one-sidedness of models, 41–42
online sexual harassment awareness
    training, 326–327
ONS *see* Office for National Statistics
on-the-job injuries, 346
Opinions Survey (OPN), 427–428,
    **430–431**, 433, 434
optimism bias, 121
optimistic leadership, 186
"Optimum" Employee Experience
    study, **454**
ordinary least squares (OLS) method,
    429, **430–431**, 432
Organisation for Economic
    Co-operation and Development
    (OECD), 416, 418, 425
    *see also individual countries*
organizational accommodation *see*
    accommodation
organizational behavior
    citizenship, 149
    leadership, 236
organizational change, 255, 328, 332
organizational characteristics,
    happiness, 111–156
organizational citizenship behavior
    (OCB), 149
organizational commitment, 16,
    46–49, 143–145, 149
    *see also* commitment
organizational communication,
    ill-health, 219
organizational coping strategies,
    253–262
    *see also* coping
organizational culture *see* culture
organizational happiness, 111–156
organizational-level actions
    Accommodation Adaptation
        Intervention Paradigm,
        208–210, 224, 226
    job demands–resources (JD–R)
        theory, 56–57

organizational norms, incivility,
    265–266, 270
organizational performance, 129
    *see also* business performance
organizational psychology, 4, 9
organizational research
    character and wellbeing, 159–163
    promoting wellbeing, 456
organizational restructuring, 255, 360
Organizational Scholarship, 122–124
organizational socialization, 323
    *see also* socialization training
organizational strategies
    coping, 253–262
    overview, 5–6
    promoting wellbeing, 205–377
    return to work, 339–356
    sexual harassment awareness training,
        319–338
    sustainable workforce, 295–318,
        **305–306**
    university academic stress,
        357–377
    work–life balance, 295–318
organizational support perceptions,
    327–328
orientation to stress, 189–191
Osatuke, K., 287–290
outcome differentiation, coping
    effectiveness, 80
outcome measures
    "happy–productive worker" thesis,
        125–129
    job demands–resources (JD–R)
        theory, 45–47, 50
    sexual harassment awareness training,
        329–331
    social support, 312–313
    sustainable careers, 311
    training effectiveness models,
        321–322, **324**, 332
    VIA-Inventory of Strengths,
        165–166

outcome measures (*cont.*)

work intensification reduction, 309

workplace control, 94–100, 101–103

outcome variables, workplace incivility, 268

overall wellbeing

components of, 14, *15*

measuring, 23

modeling, *13*

overcommitment, 41

overload *see* work overload

P

pairwise correlations, subjective wellbeing, **429**

PANAS (Positive and Negative Affect Scales), 16

panel correlations, cross-lagged, 402–403

panel research designs, 384–385, 388–389, 399–403

parenting styles, 274–275

Parker, G. B., 25

Parker, S. L., 308–309

Park, N., 168

participation

in communities, 273–274

decision making, 97

passive leadership *see* laissez-faire leadership

patients' advice *see* advice provision

PCPs (personal crafting plans), 55

Pearson, C. M., 264–266, 268–271, 273–275, 278–279, 284–286

Peeters, M., 55

perceptions

of control, 92–93, 98–100, 104

inner work life system, 150

organizational support, 327–328

of success, 301

performance at work

affect relationship, 120–122

biases, 127

character and, 161–162

daily progress/happiness, 150–153

definitions, 120

dispositional affect link, 120–122

emotions relationship, 121

engagement and, 145

happiness link, 113–114

human resource practices, 128

injured workers' return, 344–345

inner work life system, 150–151

satisfaction relationship, 116–118, 119–120

*see also* business performance; job performance; organizational performance

peril/threats, injured workers' return, 347–349

personal crafting plans (PCPs), 55

personality characteristics

control, 92–93, 97, 101–103

effort–reward imbalance model, 41

leadership, 146

productivity–happiness thesis, 124

*see also* character and wellbeing

personal resilience, 256–258

personal resources, job demands–resources (JD–R) theory, 48–50, 53, 55, 56

personal success, control and, 96–98

person × environment interaction, 208

person–environment fit, 208, 363, 367

person–environment (P–E) theory, 168–169

pessimistic leadership, 186

Peterson, C., 165

P–E theory (person–environment) theory, 168–169

Petrou, P., 53

philosophy, 410

physical changes, job crafting, 51–52

physical demands, job demands–resources (JD–R) theory, 45

physical health *see* health
physical ill-health *see* ill-health
physical injuries, returning to work,
     339–356
physical wellbeing
     abusive supervision and, 238–239
     injured workers' return to work,
          339–356
     laissez-faire leadership and, 240–241
     transformational leadership and,
          243–244
     *see also* health
physical work space control, 95
     *see also* environmental factors
Pittsburgh study, 451–452
Plato, 410
POB *see* positive organizational
     behavior
Pocock, B., 308
policy appraisal cycle, *448*, 449
policy making/actions
     development framework, 447–450
     literature review, 451–454
     measuring wellbeing, 409–463
     recent papers, 451–454
     reflecting wellbeing in, 434–450
     research and, 379–463
     tools to assess, **442–443**
     U.K., 412–423
     work focus, 450–456
policy screening, 440–445
politics and measurements, 410
poor leadership effects, 235–237, 240,
     242, 244
Porath, C. L., 271, 273–275, 284–286
positional power, leadership, 182
positive affect/emotions
     6 Essentials model, 256
     coping research, 66, 73–74, 82–83
     eudaimonic wellbeing, 12
     happiness dimensions, 115
     hedonic wellbeing, 10–11
     inner work life system, 150

job demands–resources (JD–R)
     theory, 51
     productivity–happiness thesis,
          121–122, 126
     scales of, 16
     subjective wellbeing, 15, 17
     transformational leadership, 244
positive health *see* positive wellbeing
positive leadership
     defining, 236–237
     effects of, 240, 242, 246–247
     transformational leaders, 242–246
positively-toned appraisals, 72
Positive and Negative Affect Scales
     (PANAS), 16
positive/negative debate
     coping effectiveness, 80
     psychology, 66
positive organizational behavior (POB),
     9, 140–141, 159
positive organizational scholarship, 9,
     122–124
positive outcomes
     control and, 94–100, 101–103
     of stress, 175–204
positive psychology, 4–5, 302
     character and, 159
     coping and, 65–90, 258
     description of, 65
     goal of, 66
     interest in, 9
     movement, 65–66, 73, 82
     organizational happiness, 140
positive self-evaluations, 48–50
positive stress, 147, 175–204
     diverse support application, 189
     five pathways summary, 189–191
     power motivation application,
          183–184
     requisite self-reliance application,
          185–186
     self-awareness application, 181
     strength of character application, 180

positive stress (*cont.*)
   university academics, 361
   *see also* positive work pressures
positive training effects, sexual
   harassment awareness training, 320
positive wellbeing
   character and, 160
   control role, 91–109
   flexible working, 455
positive work attitude effects, 220–221
positive work pressures, 254–255
   *see also* positive stress
posttraumatic stress disorders (PTSDs),
   187–188
power
   autonomy balance, 185
   as motivation, 177, 182–184
practical applications of stress research,
   175–204
Pratt, M., 19
Preacher, K. J., 13
"precarious work", 297
predictive power
   character research, 162
   cynicism/motivation, 323–325
   job demands–resources (JD–R)
     theory, 44–46, 47
   stigma/injured workers, 343–348
pressure rationale, incivility, 276–278
pressures *see* strain/strains;
   stress/stressors; work pressures
pre-training conditions, sexual
   harassment awareness training,
   **324**, 325–329
prevention measures
   intensification of work, **306**,
     307–309
   obesity, 197–198
preventive coping, 75, 78, 253
primary appraisals, 71–72
primary control, 92
primary stress interventions, 366–367
privacy invasion subscale, UWBQ, 272

proactive coping, 66, 75–80, 82
proactivity, defining, 77
problem drinking, 238
problem-focused coping, 74–75
process approach, stress definitions,
   70–71
productivity
   incivility consequences, 283–284
   intensification of work and, 309
   stress/health interventions, 194, 197
   support link, 221
productivity–happiness thesis,
   113–138, 143
pro-environmental initiatives, 247
profane language, 275–276
professional support
   cancer, 226–227
   diversity of, 177, 186–189
progress principle, 150–153, 411, 414
project work, 54
promoting wellbeing
   organizational strategies, 205–377
   policy approaches, 455–456
   research, 302
   stress/health, 191–198
   work–life balance, 295–318
promotion-focused coping, 78
prospective panel research design,
   384–385, 388–389
prostate cancer, 210, 213
protective factors, stress, 176
protest strategies, stigma in return to
   work, 350
proximal training outcomes, 321–322,
   **324**, 329–331
psychological distress, 239, 241, 281,
   361, 366
   *see also* anxiety; depression; distress
psychological engagement, 144
psychological outcomes, control, 94, 96
psychological states, job characteristics
   model, 39–40
psychological wellbeing (PWB)

6 Essentials model, 256
    abusive supervision and, 239–240
    character and, 160–163
    defining characteristics, 161
    dimensions of, 12
    as happiness dimension, 142
    injured workers' return to work, 340
    laissez-faire leadership and, 241–242
    transformational leadership, 244–246
psychology, 302
    character and, 159
    coping and, 65–90, 258
    "happy–productive worker" thesis,
        123
    industrial, 4
    interest in, 9
    occupational health, 207, 236,
        381–382
    organizational, 4, 9, 140
    overview, 4–5
PTSDs (post traumatic stress disorders),
    187–188
pulse product, blood pressure study,
    163
Purcell, J., 128
purposeful work, 256, 258
PWB *see* psychological wellbeing

Q
QoL *see* quality of life
quality connections, social wellbeing, 21
quality of life (QoL)
    cancer and work, 207–233
    drivers of wellbeing, 438
    Stiglitz, Sen and Fitoussi
        Commission, 417, 424
    Warwick–Edinburgh Mental
        Wellbeing Scale, 423
quality of survival, cancer, 208
"quasi-longitudinal" research *see*
    cross-sectional studies
questionnaires, incivility, 271–272
Quick, James Campbell

overview, 5
    requisite self-reliance, 184
Quick, J. D., 184
quitting work, incivility consequences,
    281, 284

R
racial discrimination, 268
Ragins, B. R., 21
Rath, T., 21
Rationale, Objectives, Appraisal,
    Monitoring, Evaluation, and
    Feedback (ROAMEF), U.K., 448
reaction outcomes, sexual harassment
    awareness training, 329–330
reactive coping, 66, 75
reciprocal causation, longitudinal
    research, 392–393
reciprocal models, two-wave designs,
    401
reciprocity
    civility training, 286
    incivility, 278–279
    social support, 188–189
recognition, importance of, 124
redesigning jobs, 54–55
reduced-load working, 309, 310
redundancies, 364
regression methods, 402
rehabilitation strategies, 223
    *see also* return to work
Reiter, N., 301
relationships *see* social relationships
relaxed happiness, 147, 149
remote working, 309
repeated cross-sectional research design,
    385–386
requisite self-reliance, 177, 184–186,
    198
research, 9–33
    academic stress, 361–362, 369–372
    accommodation–adaptation,
        225–226
    character, 159–163, 167–169

research (*cont.*)
  control, 98
  coping, 65–90, 256
  designing, 388–389, 397–403
  happiness at work, 114–118, 129,
      145
  incivility effects, 273–280, 289–290
  job demands–resources (JD–R)
      theory, 53
  leadership/employee wellbeing,
      243–244, 246–247
  measuring wellbeing, 409–463
  national policy and, 379–463
  positive psychology, 65–90
  productivity–happiness thesis,
      114–118, 129
  return to work, 340
  stigma/injured workers, 342
  stress, 175–204
  sustainable workforce, 296, 302,
      313–315
  training effectiveness, 321, 323,
      332–333
  university activities, 364
resilience, 256–258
resolution–conclusion, coping, 80
resources, 35–109
  accumulation of, 82
  conservation of, 363
  *see also* control; coping; job
      demands–resources (JD–R)
      theory; job resources
respect, 152
restructuring organizations, 255, 360
retention of employees, 162
retirement packages, 364
retrospective panel research design,
      384–385
return to work
  disruption stemming from, 346–347
  after illness, 207–233
  injured workers, 339–356
  stigma and, 339–356

reverse causation, 38, 50–51, 390–392
reverse models, two-wave designs, 401
rewards, 40–41, 125, 362–363
risk factors, stress, 176
ROAMEF (Rationale, Objectives,
      Appraisal, Monitoring, Evaluation,
      and Feedback), U.K., 448
Robertson Cooper
  6 Essentials, 254–255, *254*
  i-resilience model, 257–258, *257*
Robertson, Jennifer, overview, 5
Robertson, N., 359–360
roles approach, social psychology, 123
rudeness, 265, 277
  *see also* incivility
Ryff, C. D., 12

S
safety behaviors, 238–239, 241, 243
  *see also* health and safety practices
safety climate, 348–349
safety hazards, 347
safety-specific leadership, 241, 243
Salanova, M., 50–51
sampling for research, 17, 22
Santayana, G., 159
Sarbanes–Oxley Act (SOX), 187
Sarkozy, President *see* Stiglitz, Sen and
      Fitoussi Commission
satisfaction
  compassion satisfaction, 49
  conceptualizing, 9, 11, 15–16, 21
  control and, 94–95, 99–100
  customer satisfaction, 437
  definitions, 120
  happiness as, 143–145
  incivility and, 280–281, 282–283
  organizational happiness, 149
  performance relationship, 116–118,
      119–120
  two-factor theory, 38–39
  work–life balance, 301
  *see also* job satisfaction
SBP (systolic blood pressure), 163

scales
  affect, 16
  flourishing, 24–25, **24**
  satisfaction, 16
  stress, 361–362
  work engagement, 18
scenario planning, 255
schedule autonomy, 93
science of wellbeing, 139
scoring coping components, 69
screening of policies, 440–445
search terms, cancer literature, 214
secondary appraisals, 71–72
secondary control, 92
secondary stress interventions, 366–367
security in jobs, 255
selective incivility, definition, 268
self-awareness, 177, 180–181
self-efficacy, 93, 97, 101–103, 239,
    256
self-evaluations, 48–50
  *see also* self-reports
self-leadership, definition, 185
self-regulation, 181
self-reliance, 177, 184–186, 188, 198
self-reports, 52, 368
  *see also* self-evaluations
self-support, 186
Seligman, Martin, 13–14, 65, 122,
    165, 258
SEM *see* structural equation modeling
Sen, Amartya *see* Stiglitz, Sen and
    Fitoussi Commission
senior leadership team, 186
sensitive rationale, incivility, 277–278
sensitivity to stigma, 344
service sector customers, 437
setbacks, inner work life system, 151
sex differences
  power motivation, 183
  sexual harassment awareness training,
    327
  support at work, 221

*see also* gender discrimination; women
sexual harassment awareness (SHA)
  future research, 332–333
  general model, *320*, 321–322
  outcome possibilities, 329–331
  training effectiveness, 319–338, *320*
SHA *see* sexual harassment awareness
Sheldon, K. M., 125
Shirom, A., 17
Short, P. F., 216–217
sickness absenteeism, 44, 207, **454**
  *see also* absenteeism
Simmons, Bret, overview, 5
simplicity of models, 41–42
Singapore, 282–283
situational factors, training, 328–329
skill-based outcomes, training,
    322–323, 330
skill clusters, human resources, 128
Skinner, N., 308
sleep behavior, 238
Smeed, Matthew, overview, 5
smoking ban policies, 438–439
social awareness, 180
social benefits *see* social wellbeing
social care professionals' role, 226–227
social comparison, control perceptions,
    104
social exchange theory, 324–325,
    327–328
social impact valuation, subjective
    wellbeing, 445
social interaction
  drivers of wellbeing, 436
  incivility and, 270–271, 274, 276,
    287–289
  sexual harassment awareness training,
    326–327
  *see also* social networks; social
    relationships
socialization training, 322–323
socialized power motivation, 177,
    182–184

social media, 314
social networks, 274
social norms, incivility, 273, 278–280
social psychology, 123
social relationships
    importance, 12–13, 20–22
    injured workers, 342–343, 345–351
    measuring wellbeing, 432
    productivity–happiness thesis,
        123–125, 126
    sustainable workforce, 298
    *see also* social interaction; social
        networks
social roles, work–life balance,
    299–300
social support, 21, 187–189, 221–222,
    **305**, 312–314, 351
social values
    productivity–happiness thesis, 126
    subjective wellbeing, 445
social wellbeing, 12–13
    leave control, 311
    measuring, 23
    productivity–happiness thesis, 122
    work overview, 17, 20–22, 26
soft skills, 322
Solomon, R. C., 178
somatic complaints, 239
SOX (Sarbanes–Oxley Act), 187
SPANE measure, 25
spatial flexibility, 217
"specific" social support, 312
Spector, Paul
    control, 100–102
    overview, 5
    satisfaction–performance, 117
spells of absence, job
    demands–resources (JD–R)
    theory, 47
spheres of influence, 66
Spiegelman, D., 217–218
Spreitzer, G. M., 19, 21
stability models, 401

staff survey, National University Stress
    Study, 369–370
static character of models, 41, 42–43
statistical procedures, 401–403
status at work, injured workers,
    344–345
Steger, M., 19–20, 168
Steiner, J. F., 213
Stevenson, H., 22
Stiglitz, Sen and Fitoussi Commission,
    416–418, 420, 423–424
stigma
    defining, 341
    predicting, 343–348
    return to work and, 339–356
strain/strains
    causal relationships, 382, 389–397
    definitions, 362, 381
    demand–control model, 40
    job demands–resources (JD–R)
        theory, 50
    leadership/employee wellbeing, 245
    mid-stage coping strategies, 256, 258
    stressor time 1/strain time 2 research
        design, 397–399, 402
    stressor–strain framework, 253, *254*
    *see also* job stress/stressors;
        stress/stressors
strength of character, 177, 178–180
strengths approach
    coping strategies, 258–259
    eudaimonic wellbeing, 12
strengths-based interventions, 57–58
stress/stressors, 3–7
    academics, 357–377
    cancer and, 216, 218, 225
    causal relationships, 382, 389–397
    control and, 91, 93–94, 96
    coping research, 66–67, 70–72, 81,
        83–84
    definition, 70–71, 381
    double-edged nature, 176–177
    early-stage coping strategies, 255

effect differences, *387*

five pathways summary, 189–191

of happiness/happiness of, 146–150

hormones, 307

intensification of work, 307

longitudinal research, 381–407

measuring, 71

mid-stage coping strategies, 256, 258–259

orientation pathways, 189–191

positive outcomes, 175–204

"precarious work", 297

promotion interventions, 191–198

scales of, 361–362

stressor time 1/strain time 2 research design, 397–399, 402

terminology, 70

*see also* job stress/stressors

stress hormones, 96

stressor time 1/strain time 2 research design, 397–399, *398*, 402

stressor time 2/strain time 1 research design, 402

stressor–strain framework, 253, *254*

stress-related growth, 83

structural approach, stress, 70

structural equation modeling (SEM), 46–47, 49, 52, 402

subjective data, 368

subjective dimensions

happiness, 114–115

incivility, 289

subjective success, careers, 310

subjective wellbeing (SWB), 10–11

aspects of, 12

character and, 160

components of, 14

future research, 433–434

happiness dimensions, 115, 140, 142–143

measuring, 23, 411, 417, 422, 425–433, **429**, 433–434, 445

pairwise correlations, **429**

social impact valuation, 445

work overview, 15–17, 26

success outcomes

control and, 96–98, 102–103

productivity–happiness thesis, 125–126

success perceptions, work–life balance, 301

supervisors

abusive supervision, 237, 238–240, 246, 265, 267

incivility, 277–278

safety climate, 348–349

satisfaction, 280–281, 282

support, 247, 340, 351

training, sexual harassment awareness, 330

*see also* leadership; management practices

support at work

academic stress, 357

benefits/limitations, **260**

cancer accommodation, 221–222, 226–227

diversity of networks, 177, 186–189

injured workers' return, 340

late-stage coping strategies, 259

policy programs, 453

sexual harassment awareness training, 327–329

sustainable workforce, **305**

*see also* social support

surveys

academic stress, 359, 369–372

employers' use, 303

incivility information, 272, 280–282

measuring wellbeing, 426–427, *446*, 447

sustainability assessments, 417–418

sustainable careers, 309–310, 311

*see also* careers

sustainable workforce, 295–318
 conceptualization/linkages,
  297–303, **304**
 defining, 299
 future research, 313–315
 organizational strategies for,
  303–313, **305–306**
SWB *see* subjective wellbeing
Synderman, B., 116
systematic reviews, cancer literature,
 213–214
systemic stress interventions, 191–193
systemic wellbeing drivers, 436, **437**
systolic blood pressure (SBP), 163

T
Taris, T. W., 388–389, 392–393
task enjoyment, job demands–resources
 (JD–R) theory, 48
Taskila-Abrandt, T., 211–212
task satisfaction/performance, 117, 119
teaching activities, academics, 364
technology *see* computer-based
 technology
temporal flexibility, 217
Tennen, H., 83
tensions
 leadership, 181–182
 policy screening, 441
tenure, academic, 365–366
tertiary stress interventions, 366–367
theorization issues
 academic stress, 361, 362–364
 coping, 75, 80
 incivility effects, 276–278
 job demands–resources (JD–R)
  theory, 37–64
 longitudinal research, 383
 sexual harassment awareness training,
  319–338
 *see also* research
therapeutic interventions, 161
third variable research effects, 393–396
Thompson, A. D., 178–179

Thompson, S. C., 92
threats/peril, injured workers' return,
 347–349
thriving at work, 19
Tikochinsky, J., 119–120
time diary research, 314
time frame, measuring wellbeing, 22
time lag, longitudinal research,
 396–397
timing
 cancer advice/information, 223–224
 coping strategies, 75, 77–78
Tims, M., 52
Tinline, Gordon, overview, 5
toilet facilities/access, 218, 219–220,
 225
toughness rationale, incivility, 277–278
trade-offs, policy screening, 441
training
 civility training, 285–289
 design
  components, 321
  future research, 332
  sexual harassment awareness
   training, 325–327
 effectiveness, 319–338, *320,*
  321–322
 generalization, 328
 general model, *320,* 321–322
 interventions, job
  demands–resources (JD–R)
  theory, 56–57
 line management, 455
 motivation, 321–323, 325
 sexual harassment awareness,
  319–338, *320*
 transfer, 328–329
transactional theory, stress, 71
transcendence strengths, 179–180
transformational leadership, 237,
 242–246
transparency of policies, 420
treatment evaluations, cancer, 212, 224

Tremblay, M. A., 49–50
true strain–stressor hypothesis, 391
trust, 243–244
Tugade, M. M., 74
turnover of staff, 162, 359
two-factor theory, 38–39
two-wave panel research design
    full, 400–401, *400*
    incomplete, 399–400, *399*
two-wave prospective studies,
    388–389

U
U.K. *see* United Kingdom
UN (United Nations) measures, 418
uncertainty, economic, 255
uncivil behavior *see* incivility
Uncivil Workplace Behavior
    Questionnaire (UWBQ), 272
unemployment, 212
unhappiness, 118, 147
    *see also* happiness
unidimensional transformational
    leadership, 245
unipolar view, positive/negative affect,
    10–11
United Kingdom (U.K.)
    2010–2012 measurement program,
        419–423
    academic stress, 359–360
    Accommodation Adaptation
        Intervention Paradigm,
        208–210
    cancer survival, 211
    geographic measuring tools,
        *446*, 447
    human resource practices, 128
    information/advice at work, 223
    measuring wellbeing, 411–463
    occupational health services,
        222–223, 225
    organizational accommodation, 215
    sustainable workforce, 298
United Nations (UN) measures, 418

United States (U.S.)
    academic stress, 358–361, 364, 367
    cancer survival, 211–212
    Declaration of Independence, 409
    measuring wellbeing, 412
    organizational accommodation,
        215–216, 218
    sexual harassment cases, 319–320
    sustainable workforces, 297–298
university academics, 357–377
university student study, 281–282
urological cancers, 210, 214, 219, 225
U.S. *see* United States
utilitarianism, 410–411, 421
Utrecht Work Enthusiasm Scale, 18
UWBQ (Uncivil Workplace Behavior
    Questionnaire), 272

V
Vaillant, G. E., 182
valor–wellbeing relationship, 167
valuation of social impacts, 445
values
    behavior connection, 180
    power motivation, 183
    productivity–happiness thesis, 126
    stress pathways and, 191
    subjective wellbeing, 445
Van den Heuvel, M., 55
variable types, longitudinal research,
    393–396
Verdecchia, A., 211
VIA-Inventory of Strengths (VIA-IS),
    165–166
vigor concept, 17, 18
violence, 265–266
virtue ethics tradition, 178
visibility of injuries, 343
visualizing happiness, 125
vocational choice control, 102–103
vocational rehabilitation, 223
voluntary redundancies, 364
volunteering, 415

W
Wall, T. D., 129
WAMI (Work and Meaning Inventory),
    19–20
Wanous, J. P., 328
WARM *see* Wellbeing and Resilience
    Measure
Warr, P., 16, 114, 125, 147, 149
Warwick–Edinburgh Mental Wellbeing
    Scale, 423
Waterman, A. S., 12
Watts, J., 359–360
Wegman, D. H., 217–218
Weiss, H. M., 120–122
wellbeing
    constructs, 14
    defining, 10, 237, 302–303, **304**,
        420
    drivers of, 432–433, 435–440,
        448–450
    happiness of, 142–143
    Seligman's theory of, 14
    separating from
        GDP as measure, 414–416
        growth as policy objective,
            412–414
    terminology, 160
    *see also* conceptualization issues
Wellbeing and Resilience Measure
    (WARM), 447
whistleblowing research, 168
Whitehall Studies, 452
WHO *see* World Health Organization
Winefield, A. H.
    academic stress, 360–361, 364, 366
    overview, 6
WIS (Workplace Incivility Scale),
    271–272, 277
within-person analyses, 117
women
    cancer and, 215, 220, 221
    sexual harassment awareness training,
        327
    *see also* gender...

Wood, S. J., 129
*Work & Stress* journal, 383
work design, 216, 219, 226
    *see also* job design
work engagement, 18–19, 49, 51, 145
    *see also* engagement
work environment *see* environmental
    factors; working conditions
worker–employer relationships, 297
worker happiness, 111–156
    *see also* employee wellbeing
work–family facilitation, 97
    *see also* work–life balance
workforce sustainability, 295–318
workgroup interactions, 276, 287–289
    *see also* group activities
work–health relationship, 207–233
work hours
    intensification of work, 307
    measuring wellbeing, 415
    sustainable workforce, 313
working conditions, 43–44, 50, 51
    *see also* environmental factors
*Working for a healthier tomorrow*
    review, 452
"working wounded" construct,
    339–356
work intensification, **306**, 307–309
work–life balance, 97, 295–318, **304**
workloads
    balancing, 255
    intensification of, 308, 309
    sustainable careers, 310
Work and Meaning Inventory (WAMI),
    19–20
work motivation *see* motivation
work outcomes, control, 94–100,
    101–103
work overload, 308, 310–311
work performance *see* job performance;
    performance at work
workplace control *see* control
workplace culture *see* culture

workplace incivility, 263–294
  consequences, 280–284
  defining, 263, 264–269, 270
  future research, 289–290
  measuring, 270–273
  research origins, 273–280
  solving the problem, 284–289
Workplace Incivility Scale (WIS),
  271–272, 277
workplace leadership *see* leadership
workplace-level changes, stress,
  192–193
workplace mistreatment, definition, 269
  *see also* mistreatment at work;
    workplace incivility
workplace norms *see* organizational
  norms
workplace social support *see* social
  support
work pressures, 253–262
  *see also* strain/strains; stress/stressors
work-related stress *see* stress/stressors
work satisfaction measures, **25**
  *see also* job satisfaction; satisfaction
Work Well-Being Questionnaire, 25, **25**

World Health Organization (WHO),
  210, 423
"worthwhile" measurement indicators,
  428–429
Wright, P. M., 129
Wright, T. A.
  character, 161–163, 165–166, 167
  overview, 5
Wrzesniewski, A., 52
Wynn, P., 222–223

X
Xanthopoulou, D., 49, 51

Y
Yahoo case, 388
Young Foundation, 447

Z
Zapf, D., 382–383, *387*, 388,
  391–394, 402
Zappos company, 139
Zauderer, D. G., 268–269
Zohar, D., 348